THE OXFORD HANDBOOK OF

FOOD HISTORY

THE OXFORD HANDBOOK OF

FOOD HISTORY

Edited by

JEFFREY M. PILCHER

OXFORD
UNIVERSITY PRESS

OXFORD
UNIVERSITY PRESS

Oxford University Press is a department of the University of Oxford.
It furthers the University's objective of excellence in research, scholarship,
and education by publishing worldwide.

Oxford New York
Auckland Cape Town Dar es Salaam Hong Kong Karachi
Kuala Lumpur Madrid Melbourne Mexico City Nairobi
New Delhi Shanghai Taipei Toronto

With offices in
Argentina Austria Brazil Chile Czech Republic France Greece
Guatemala Hungary Italy Japan Poland Portugal Singapore
South Korea Switzerland Thailand Turkey Ukraine Vietnam

Published in the United States of America by
Oxford University Press
198 Madison Avenue, New York, NY 10016

Library of Congress Cataloging-in-Publication Data
The Oxford handbook of food history / edited by Jeffrey M. Pilcher.
p. cm.—
(Oxford handbooks)
Includes bibliographical references and index.
ISBN 978-0-19-972993-7 (hardcover : alk. paper)
1. Food—History. 2. Food—Social aspects—History.
I. Pilcher, Jeffrey M.
TX353.O94 2012
641.309—dc23
2012011582

ISBN 978-0-19-972993-7

Acknowledgments

I thank Nancy Toff for suggesting the volume and for providing encouragement along the way. Sonia Tycko stepped in at a critical moment with sound guidance that helped bring the work to completion. Thanks also to my copy editor Suzanne Copenhagen and to the production staff at OUP and Newgen for their diligent work. Of my contributors, I can only say that they have been amazing, simply amazing. Their deep knowledge and enthusiasm have made the project. I am especially grateful to a pair of former "hippies," Warren Belasco and Carole Counihan, whose wisdom, scholarship, warmth, and generosity have left a lasting impression on the field. I dedicate this volume to Tim and Liss.

Contents

Part III. The Means of Production

Part IV. The Circulation of Food

Contributors

Ken Albala is professor of history at the University of the Pacific in Stockton, California. He is the author of many books on topics ranging from Renaissance nutrition and fine dining to beans, as well as a cookbook. He has edited three food series with twenty-nine volumes in print and is co-editor of the journal *Food, Culture and Society*.

Rachel A. Ankeny is program coordinator for the new food studies graduate program (and formerly was program manager for the graduate program in gastronomy) and associate professor of history at the University of Adelaide, Australia. Her research interests include food ethics, food habits of women and children, and the relationship of science to cuisine. She also has expertise and ongoing research on health and science policy, particularly regarding public engagement and bioethics.

Warren Belasco teaches American studies at the University of Maryland, Baltimore County, United States. He is the author of *Americans on the Road* (1979), *Appetite for Change: How the Counterculture Took on the Food Industry* (1990), *Meals to Come: A History of the Future of Food* (2006), and *Food: The Key Concepts* (2009). He edited *Food, Culture and Society: An International Journal of Multidisciplinary Research* (2003–2009). He lives and gardens in Washington, D.C.

Charlotte Biltekoff is an assistant professor in American studies and food science and technology at the University of California, Davis. Her research focuses on the cultural politics of dietary health in the United States from the late nineteenth century to the present. Her book, *Eating Right in America: Food, Health and Citizenship from Domestic Science to Obesity*, is forthcoming from Duke University Press.

Sierra Clark Burnett is a doctoral candidate in food studies and instructor at New York University. Her research examines the politics of heritage and craft in the modern food system through the study of American whiskey. She holds a B.A. in International Relations from Brown University and a Grande Diplôme in Culinary Arts from the French Culinary Institute.

Yong Chen is associate professor of history at the University of California, Irvine, where he also served as associate dean of graduate studies. He is author of *Chinese San Francisco, 1850–1943* (2000), co-editor of *New Perspectives on American History* (2010), and co-curator of "'Have You Eaten Yet?': The Chinese Restaurant in America" (New York and Philadelphia). His research on diverse topics such as Chinese American history, food, and higher education has been published in various leading academic journals and has received extensive media coverage in the United States and beyond.

Carole Counihan is emerita professor of anthropology at Millersville University in Pennsylvania. For thirty years she has been studying ethnographically food, culture, gender, and identity in Italy and the United States. She is the author of *The Anthropology of Food and Body: Gender, Meaning and Power* (1999), *Around the Tuscan Table: Food, Family and Gender in Twentieth Century Florence* (2004), and *A Tortilla Is Like Life: Food and Culture in the San Luis Valley of Colorado* (2009). She is co-editor with Penny Van Esterik of *Food and Culture: A Reader* (1997, 2008) and is editor-in-chief of the scholarly journal *Food and Foodways*.

Jonathan Deutsch is a classically trained chef and associate professor of culinary arts at Kingsborough Community College, City University of New York and public health at the CUNY Graduate Center. He is the author or editor of six books including (with Annie Hauck-Lawson) *Gastropolis: Food and New York City*, and (with Jeff Miller) *Food Studies*. When not in the kitchen he can be found playing tuba in community bands around New York City.

Tracey Deutsch is associate professor of history at the University of Minnesota. She is the author of *Building a Housewife's Paradise: Gender, Government and American Grocery Stores in the Twentieth Century* (2010) and teaches, researches, and writes on food politics, gender systems, and capitalism.

Rebecca Earle is professor of history at the University of Warwick. Her research concerns the cultural and intellectual history of colonial and independent Spanish America. Her most recent book, *The Body of the Conquistador: Food, Race and the Colonial Experience* (2012), investigates the centrality of food to the construction of the colonial body in the early modern Hispanic world. Previous work examined nineteenth-century elite nationalism's engagement with the preconquest past (*The Return of the Native: Indians and Mythmaking in Spanish America, 1810–1930*, 2008) and the Spanish American wars of independence (*Spain and the Independence of Colombia, 1810–1825*, 2000).

Sterling Evans holds the Louise Welsh Chair in Borderlands History at the University of Oklahoma. Previously he taught at Brandon University (Manitoba), Humboldt State University (California), and the University of Alberta after having completed graduate school at the University of Kansas. His research and teaching interests include environmental, agricultural, and transnational history.

Paul Freedman is a professor in the history department at Yale University. A medieval historian, he has specialized in the history of the Catalan peasants, church, and nobility in the period 1000 to 1500. His work on food history has been developed over the last ten years. He is the author of *Out of the East: Spices and the Medieval Imagination* (2008) and editor of *Food: The History of Taste* (2007), which was translated into ten languages. He is working on dining in the United States in the nineteenth century.

Donna R. Gabaccia is the Rudolph J. Vecoli Professor of History and director of the Immigration History Research Center at the University of Minnesota. She is the author of many books and articles on international migration, immigrant life in the United States, and Italian life around the world. Among her books are *We Are What We Eat: Ethnic Food and the Making of Americans* (1998), *Italy's Many Diasporas* (2000), and *Foreign Relations: Global Perspectives on American Immigration* (2012).

Rayna Green has served as curator at the Smithsonian Institution's National Museum of American History since 1984, following fifteen years in university as a professor of Native studies and American studies. She is known for her exhibitions, monographs, essays, and documentary productions on American Indian representations, performance, and American identity. To her customary repertoire, she has added exhibitions (e.g., "Bon Appétit: Julia Child's Kitchen at the Smithsonian"), films (e.g., *Corn Is Who We Are: The Story of Pueblo Indian Food*), and writings (e.g., "Mother Corn Meets the Dixie Pig: Native Food in the Native South") on American and American Indian food and foodways.

Lucy M. Long (Ph.D., Folklore, University of Pennsylvania) runs a nonprofit Center for Food and Culture and teaches food studies at Bowling Green State University in the tourism and American culture studies programs. She is the author of *Culinary Tourism: Eating and Otherness* (2003) and *Regional American Food Culture* (2009) and has published on a wide range of topics connected to food, ranging from Appalachian food and music to Irish soda bread to Korean restaurants.

André Magnan is assistant professor of sociology and social studies at the University of Regina, Canada. His principle research interest is the historical political economy of local and global food systems, especially as it applies to the Canadian prairies. He has published research on political conflicts over genetically modified crops, the politics of collective grain marketing, and the historical evolution of the Canada-U.K. commodity chain for wheat.

Elias Mandala received his B.A. and M.A. from the University of Malawi and Ph.D. from the University of Minnesota, and now is professor of African history at the University of Rochester. He is a student of African peasants, with particular interest in agriculture, food systems, gender, intergenerational conflict, and rural differentiation. His major publications include *Work and Control in a Peasant Economy: A History of the Lower Tchiri Valley in Malawi, 1859–1960* and *The End of Chidyerano: A History of Food and Everyday Life in Malawi, 1860–2004*.

Bertie Mandelblatt is a historical geographer, teaching in the departments of historical studies and geography at the University of Toronto (Mississauga). Her research concerns commodity exchanges in the French Atlantic, focusing on the production, provision, and consumption of food and drink in the French Antilles in the seventeenth and eighteenth centuries, with particular emphasis on the economic effects of slave consumption in the Caribbean and the wider Atlantic world.

Jeffrey Miller is an associate professor and acts as program coordinator for the Hospitality Management program at Colorado State University. In addition to teaching various hospitality courses, including culinary arts, he teaches the Food and Society class at CSU. Prior to becoming a teacher, he was a chef in various white tablecloth hospitality operations for twenty years.

Corrie E. Norman holds the Doctor of Theology degree from Harvard University. She has authored several articles on food and religion, along with books and articles on religion and culture in the United States and Italy. She is at work on a book on spirituality and food in contemporary America.

Enrique C. Ochoa is professor of Latin American studies and history at California State University, Los Angeles. His publications include *Feeding Mexico: The Political Uses of Food Since 1910* (2000) and *Latina/o Los Angeles: Migrations, Communities, and Political Activism* (co-editor, 2005). His current book project is entitled "Sin Maíz, No Hay País: Mexico's Struggle for Food Sovereignty."

Emiko Ohnuki-Tierney, William F. Vilas Research Professor at the University of Wisconsin, is a native of Japan. Her research foci have been on various symbols of identities of the Japanese, such as rice, the monkey, and cherry blossoms, in socio-political contexts and in historical perspective. She penned fourteen single-authored books in English and five in Japanese. She was the Distinguished Chair for Modern Culture at the Library of Congress in 2009.

Steve Penfold is an associate professor in the department of history at the University of Toronto. His research focuses on the political, social, and cultural history of North American capitalism, especially mass consumption in Canada. His last book was *The Donut: A Canadian History* (2008).

Gabriella M. Petrick is an associate professor in the department of nutrition and food studies and the department of history and art history at George Mason University. Her research focuses on the development of industrial foods and dietary change in twentieth-century America. In addition to her work on food science and technology, she is currently writing a sensory history of taste.

Jeffrey M. Pilcher, a professor of history at the University of Minnesota, teaches classes on food and drink in world history. His books include the award-winning *¡Que vivan los tamales! Food and the Making of Mexican Identity* (1998), as well as *Food in World History* (2006), *The Sausage Rebellion: Public Health, Private Enterprise, and Meat in Mexico City* (2006), and *Planet Taco: A Global History of Mexican Food* (2012).

Krishnendu Ray is an associate professor of food studies at New York University. Earlier he taught for a decade at the Culinary Institute of America. He is the author of *The Migrant's Table: Meals and Memories in Bengali-American Households* (2004) and co-editor of *Curried Cultures: Globalization, Indian Cuisine, and the South Asian Middle Classes* (2012).

Jayeeta Sharma is an assistant professor of history at the University of Toronto, teaching courses on the history and cultures of South Asia and the British Empire. Her research and teaching interests include migration, food, race, labor, childhood, and diasporic and post-colonial cultures. Her book, *Empire's Garden: Assam and the Making of India* (2011), examines the intersections of colonial tea capitalism with identity making in modern and contemporary India.

Alison K. Smith, Associate Professor of history, University of Toronto, is the author of several articles on imperial Russian foodways, and the book, *Recipe for Russia: Food and Nationhood Under the Tsars* (2008). She is now working on a monograph on social categories and social mobility in eighteenth and nineteenth-century Russia.

R. Kenji Tierney received his Ph.D. in anthropology from the University of California, Berkeley, and he is now an assistant professor at Skidmore College. He has published articles on the anthropology of food and sumo wrestling, and he co-edited *Multiculturalism in the New Japan: Crossing the Boundaries Within* (2007).

Sydney Watts received her Ph.D. in French history from Cornell University, and is now Associate Professor of early modern European history at the University of Richmond. She has published *Meat Matters: Butchers, Politics and Market Culture in Eighteenth-Century Paris* (2006) and articles on the history of the butcher guild and public hygiene. Her current research on Lent and secular society focuses on changing food habits and religious norms in early modern urban France.

INTRODUCTION

JEFFREY M. PILCHER

THE history of food, long derided as an amateur's avocation, has finally won professional respectability based on a generation of high-quality scholarship. The defensive justifications for studying food often given by the field's pioneers, many of whom labored in obscurity at provincial colleges and universities, has given way to a new self-confidence and recognition.[1] Food matters, not only as a proper subject of study in its own right, but also as a captivating medium for conveying critical messages about capitalism, the environment, and social inequality to audiences beyond the ivy tower. This handbook seeks to recognize the contributions of early scholars, consolidate our understanding of the field, and point out new challenges for future researchers.

Although professional historians were slow to perceive the importance of food, the evidence was always there waiting in the primary sources. Ancient Chinese social philosophers acknowledged cooks as state ministers and butchers as role models of enlightened behavior, demonstrating the critical importance of feeding the people to political legitimacy and of decorum at the table to a well-ordered society. By contrast, the Greek intellectual tradition disdained the practical labor of the scullery as inferior to the theoretical musings of the philosopher king, although that did not stop early Greek historians and geographers from taking careful note of eating and drinking habits as markers of cultural difference. Renaissance humanists' textual criticism, a methodological foundation of the historical profession, was directed toward culinary works by Athenaeus and Apicius along with other classical writings. Enlightenment philosophes produced the first national histories of food, including Le Grand d'Aussy's *Histoire de la vie privée des françois* (History of the Private Life of the French, 1782) and Richard Warner's *Antiquitates Culinariae, or Curious Tracts on Culinary Affairs of the Old English* (1791).[2]

The professionalization of history, initiated in nineteenth-century German universities, marked a step backward for the study of food. Leopold von Ranke and his colleagues considered nation building to be the proper subject of history, and they privileged state archives as the appropriate sources for such a project. Eager to claim scientific objectivity, professors carefully policed the boundaries of their masculine, nation-centered discipline and derided any deviations or attempts to write history as literature. Lucy Maynard Salmon, author of the path-breaking social history *Domestic Service* (1897), incurred the ridicule of colleagues when her Vassar College seminar analyzed historical recipes and kitchen appliances alongside more traditional documents.[3]

Scholars who dared to study food history generally did so outside of national and disciplinary boundaries. Early immigration historian Theodore Blegen examined food in works such as *Grass Roots History* (1947). The French Annales school likewise included food in their broad geographical and interdisciplinary vision of "total history"; but although Fernand Braudel focused on demography and nutrition by counting the calories in historical diets, he gave less attention to the social and cultural contexts of eating. The recent burst of historical scholarship on food was inspired largely by anthropologists. Kwang-Chih Chang organized perhaps the first major English-language collection, *Food and Chinese Culture* (1977); as an archaeologist, he perceived the importance of establishing a basic chronology of the historical development of Chinese cuisine. Sidney Mintz's landmark history of sugar, *Sweetness and Power* (1985), set a model for commodity studies by linking the production of Caribbean slaves with European consumption and the rise of modern industry.[4]

Meanwhile, professional scorn had not prevented a dedicated clan of culinary historians from pursuing valuable research on historical cookery. Profoundly knowledgeable of their subject, although often lacking in professional credentials, they combined careful textual analysis of old cookbooks with archival research and the historic recreation of old recipes using period technology. Through such historical reenacting, at times in museums and other public history settings, they acquired a detailed acquaintance with the materiality of food, which professional historians would do well to emulate. Some of these nonprofessionals, most notably Mark Kurlansky, have won enormous popular audiences, which seemed all the more evidence that they were not serious scholars. More appropriate criticisms of culinary historians would be that they have frequently failed to ask difficult social questions, ignored previous historical works, both by culinary and academic historians, and as a consequence, often reinvented the wheel, even while insisting that they were correcting myths and errors perpetuated by unnamed rivals. I should add that I intend these remarks not in the spirit of academic gatekeeping—culinary historians were, after all, among the pioneers of the field—but rather as an encouragement to engage more fully with a historiography that is growing rapidly in scope and quality.[5]

This handbook is intended for a number of audiences: graduate students preparing for comprehensive exams and dissertation research, established scholars interested in food as a research or teaching field, and culinary historians who want to kick it up a notch. The essays take stock of the field, review literatures, evaluate methodologies, and compile historiographies. Some authors focus in depth on illustrative topics, for example, the medieval spice trade or modern culinary tourism. Others survey the entire sweep of world history by way of fundamental thematic categories such as human mobility, labor, and the environment. Together they illustrate the wide range of approaches taken by contemporary historians of food and society.

Historical debates around food—in contrast to highly polarized contemporary food politics—remain relatively diffuse. In part, this openness reflects the wide range of topics that involve food; as a "total social phenomenon," it influences virtually every aspect of human life. The potential for research in the history of food is therefore limited only by our own imaginations. Yet too often scholarship responds to the particular concerns of national historiographies, precisely because the profession is still institutionally constrained by national boundaries, particularly in training graduate students and hiring faculty. This volume is purposely organized along thematic and comparative lines in the hopes that national concerns will not become blinders to larger historical processes. Scholars who read narrowly in their own period and area miss valuable insights and often reinvent wheels of their own. Broad interdisciplinary reading is particularly important to avoid perpetuating what Richard Wilk has evocatively called "zombie theories," pernicious concepts such as modernization that have been buried in the fields that spawned them, only to rise from the dead and wreck havoc in neighboring departments.

Until at least the 1950s, food tended to appear in historical works haphazardly as it related to other topics. For example, early historians of agriculture investigated the production of staple crops, while showing little interest in consumption.[6] Likewise, political historians at times examined the institutions for urban provisioning and food distribution.[7] Richard O. Cummings's *The American and His Food* (1940) was basically a study in the historical development of nutritional science.[8] Meanwhile, the Cambridge orientalist Arthur J. Arberry translated a medieval Baghdad cookbook as a linguistic curiosity alongside the Quran and works of Sufi poets.[9]

The rise of social history in the 1960s and 1970s first embroiled food in controversies at the center of the historical profession, particularly debates about standards of living. The question, whether industrialization led to an improvement in the livelihood of European workers in the eighteenth and nineteenth centuries, was approached via the interdisciplinary, quantitative methods that had been pioneered by Fernand Braudel and his Annales colleagues in their sweeping histories of agricultural production and demographic change in the medieval and early modern Mediterranean.[10] In the United States, polemics erupted most fiercely over contested claims by economic historians Stanley Engerman and Robert Fogel that slaves on antebellum plantations were well fed.[11] Although such arguments helped push economic and demographic history to the margins of the profession by the 1990s, scholars have continued to refine our understanding of the quality of historic diets and health, most notably through the examination of skeletal remains.[12]

Already in the early 1970s, scholars had begun to question the deterministic assumptions behind economic studies, thus setting the stage for a culturally attuned political history of food. One starting point was E. P. Thompson's essay on the "moral economy" of the crowd and food riots in England during the transition to capitalism. Rather than chart the rise of food riots as a "spasmodic" response of hungry people to rising prices, Thompson sought to understand the cultural logic used to justify rioting at a time when a new commercial economy began to violate the long-standing rules of an older moral economy that were intended to protect the most vulnerable members of society.[13] This anthropological approach to the politics of hunger was reinforced by Amartya Sen's economic theory of entitlement, which demonstrated more generally that hunger has resulted not from food shortages alone but primarily from failures of distribution.[14] Inspired by these works, scholars have examined the links between food distribution and political legitimacy in a wide range of societies. Peter Garnsey, for example, located the origins of Western ambivalence toward food welfare programs in classical Greek and Roman notions of self-reliant citizenship and the belief that food assistance should come in the form of private charity rather than as a government entitlement. Lars Lih demonstrated the importance of food politics in the Russian Revolution, both in the collapse of the Tsarist regime due to its failure to ensure urban food supplies and in the Civil War between the Bolshevik power base in grain-consuming regions and loyalist agricultural centers in the Caucuses and Siberia.[15]

The political history of food has also reached beyond struggles over distribution to examine other ways that food has contributed to hegemonic rule, which allowed elites to cultivate legitimacy through consent rather than naked force. Warren Belasco wrote his classic book, *Appetite for Change* (1989), as a case study in hegemony by the food industry, which co-opted the 1960s counterculture by marketing various forms of "yuppie chow."[16] In a similar fashion, Natalia Milanesio has noted that the government of Juan Domingo Perón sought to gain populist support by creating an entitlement to beef, an iconic food in Argentina; the policy backfired, however, when drought and mismanagement crippled the livestock industry. In ancient Athens, as James Davidson has observed, fish were considered to be a luxury food whose allure could tempt citizens into profligate spending, which posed a threat to the egalitarian, democratic order.[17] Scholars have also examined hegemonic contests fought out over food by marginalized peoples, including women, the working classes, and racial and ethnic minorities. For example, Amy Bentley has discussed the ways that women in the United States used domestic labor as a means for claiming patriotic citizenship during World War II.[18]

A second important focus of historical research on food has sought to explain cultural and culinary change over time. Alfred W. Crosby Jr.'s foundational study of globalization, *The Columbian Exchange* (1972), examined a crucial moment of culinary transformation at the dawn of the early modern era, giving particular attention to agents of change and to environmental contexts. Trained as a Latin American historian, Crosby interpreted the spread of foods from the Old World to the New as a case of cultural conquest based on the Spaniards' insistence on having access to familiar foods and their rejection of indigenous staples. In narrating the return voyages of American foods, however, Crosby made an essentially Malthusian argument based on the productivity of crops within broadly defined ecologies.[19] Sucheta Mazumdar, James McCann, and others have revised Crosby's argument by giving closer attention to local social and environmental conditions. Moreover, scholars such as Judith Carney have challenged Crosby's focus on conquistadors and merchants as agents of cultural transfer by showing that plebeian and even enslaved farmers and cooks largely determined the acceptance of new foods.[20]

Marcy Norton has argued for consideration of taste as an autonomous force in shaping cultural change, thereby moving historical causation beyond either biological determinism or cultural functionalism. Using the case of chocolate, she observed that traditional explanations for European adoption point either to the addictive biological properties of theobromine, a chemical relative of caffeine that is found in cacao, or to the adaptation of chocolate into European cultural systems by adding sugar and spices to a bitter indigenous drink. Neither approach can fully explain the European taste for chocolate; she argued instead for a close examination of complex social relationships linking Natives and Spaniards in the early era of the conquest.[21] Paul Freedman has likewise shown the potential for historicizing taste in a book on spices and the medieval imagination. He examined the uses of spices not only to flavor food but also as perfume, medicine, and even a source of spiritual power. By revealing the ways that medieval Europeans imagined the unknown origins and seductive allure of spices, Freedman conveyed a sense of the mystery in their mental world.[22] In addition to the Columbian exchange and the spice trade, another perennial topic of research in food history has been the early modern transformation in French cooking from what Alberto Capatti and Massimo Montanari have described as a "taste of artifice," exemplified by spice-laden medieval banquets, to a supposedly more naturalistic and modern "analytical taste" in which flavors were kept distinct, for example, sour was the predominant flavor of the salad course while sweet was reserved for dessert. The meticulous work of Jean-Louis Flandrin, a successor to Braudel in the French Annales school, served to formulate the terms of this debate.[23]

A third basic area of historical research has been the connections between food and identity. One of the earliest and finest such works was Caroline Walker Bynum's *Holy Feast and Holy Fast* (1987), which examined the importance of food as an expression of religiosity for medieval women. Food imagery was particularly prominent in the lives of female saints, who performed charity and miracles to feed the community, in imitation of Christ.[24] In the modern era, secular versions of commensality, shared meals taken at restaurants or clubs, have become important site for building class identities, whether elite distinction claimed in exclusive temples of haute cuisine, as expressions of middle-class ideals of democracy, or working-class solidarities forged over fish and chips.[25] Food has also helped preserve ethnic identities through rituals that maintain family and community traditions. Such practices of cooking and eating together were particularly important among marginalized groups, whose foods were often derided as unhealthful or immoral by dominant social groups.[26] Nevertheless, even as foods contributed to social differentiation, they also provided a nonthreatening bridge for crossing ethnic and racial boundaries. Scholars have found interethnic sharing of meals to be particularly common among the lower classes and other marginalized groups.[27] Eating across ethnic boundaries has also been the basis for a sense of national identity, as Arjun Appadurai discovered in a formative article on middle-class cookbooks in postcolonial India. Yet domestic attempts to define a nation have frequently served as tools for particular social groups to deny others from citizenship.[28] Moreover, Eric Rath has warned against fetishizing a nation; his study of culinary culture in early modern Japan found fantasies of beauty, morality, and emotion at the dinner table, but found little evidence of the "imagined community" that would later constitute the Japanese nation, nor even of such iconic dishes as sushi or tempura.[29]

A fourth point of contention, and one that extends far beyond the historical profession, has concerned the rise of the modern industrial food system. Activists within the "good food movement" have blamed agrifood corporations for a host of evils, including contamination, obesity, social anomie, and environmental devastation.[30] Supporters of industrial food have argued to the contrary that technological advances of the past two centuries have created unprecedented abundance, whereas in premodern eras the vast majority of the population labored on the brink of famine.[31] Historians should have something to contribute to these polemics, but far from offering a clear chronology of the process of food industrialization, recent scholarship has done more to unsettle accepted narratives than to offer a comprehensive new interpretation. Although some scholars date the modern industrial farm to twentieth-century improvements in mechanization, irrigation, and the like, economic historians Alan Olmstead and Paul Rhode have argued that biological innovations in plant breeding and fertilizers dating back to the nineteenth century have had far greater effects on agricultural productivity.[32] In a similar fashion, Nick Cullather has challenged the traditional chronology of the Green Revolution, which supposedly prevented massive starvation during the Cold War era by diffusing highly efficient capitalist agricultural systems. In fact, the productivity gains of the Green Revolution were not as dramatic as they have been portrayed and in any event grew out of earlier farm improvement programs, often carried out by experts from Third World countries.[33]

There is also no clear understanding of the effects of industrialization on consumption habits. Although some have argued that consumers have been duped by food processors into eating inferior products by intensive advertising campaigns and the availability of subsidized commodities, a revealing study by Martin Bruegel demonstrated the slow acceptance of canned foods by the French, who began to eat them on a large scale only after a century of efforts by the food processing industry and government educational efforts. One might attribute this resistance to French culinary exceptionalism, but the chapter by Gabriella Petrick in this handbook shows a similar delay in accepting industrial processed food in the United States.[34] Of course, it is hard to deny the growing industrial concentration of the global food system under the control of transnational corporations, from the seed (Monsanto) to the grocery store (Walmart) and the fast food restaurant (McDonald's).[35] Nevertheless, we still have much to learn about the historical nature of commodity chains, as well as of consumer reactions to new products and technologies.[36]

Changing beliefs about dietary health have been a final important focus of the recent boom in food history. The history of medicine was long concerned with documenting the progressive advance of knowledge in understanding the cause of disease; for example, Daphne Roe's *A Plague of Corn* (1973) examined medical descriptions of the nutritional disease pellagra from outbreaks in eighteenth-century Europe to the adoption of vitamin B fortification in the decades around World War II.[37] Although valuable, such works have tended to naturalize scientific description as objective accounts of reality. More recently scholars have sought to understand nutritional beliefs instead as expressions of particular cultural systems rather than as approximations of ultimate truth, which turns out to be another way of saying modern Western nutritional science. For example, E. H. Collingham, Rebecca Earle, and Trudy Eden have examined the fears of early modern European colonizers in South Asia and the Americas that eating indigenous foods would cause them to degenerate to the level of their colonial subjects.[38] As these examples reveal, nutritional knowledge is deeply embedded in moral systems and cultural beliefs. Modern campaigns that stigmatize obesity in the United States reflect the same desire to control the lower classes as did the middle-class social workers trying to transform the dietary behavior of immigrants a century earlier. Moreover, Western nutritional science has become an international regime of power that has been widely accepted by medical experts in the Global South.[39] Charlotte Biltekoff has called for a "critical nutrition studies" that will examine the ways that dietary knowledge reproduces social relations of power, as well as a "critical dietary literacy" that will empower citizens to understand the vested interests behind nutritional claims made by industry and the medical professions and thereby forge healthier lives for themselves.[40]

These five themes—political history, cultural change over time, food and identity, industrial transformation, and nutritional health—by no means exhaust the rich potential of food history. Yet another, more implicit, debate in food history concerns the proper narrative form for the field. Perhaps because food has been peripheral to the wider profession, scholars have felt free to experiment with novel ways of framing their studies. The biography, a staple of traditional history, has been turned to nonhuman subjects, including sugar, codfish, bananas, and pineapples, although there have also been numerous biographies of people such as Julia Child.[41] Chronological and civilizational narratives, another traditional historical approach, have also been common.[42] My own attempt to write a brief survey of food in world history used thematic, comparative case studies.[43] Felipe Fernández-Armesto wrote of historic "revolutions" in production, distribution, and consumption, while Kenneth Kiple organized his history around successive waves of globalization.[44] Indeed, the crucial role of food in the two most fundamental transformations in human history—the Neolithic revolution and the industrial revolution—has encouraged such sweeping narratives.

One final, existential question has long persisted among food studies scholars: can we even speak of ourselves as a distinctive field, one with its own methodologies and literatures, one that will not just rely on innovative work borrowed from others but also repay old intellectual debts by contributing new ideas and approaches to the broader pursuit of knowledge? Without trying to impose any one vision or agenda, the essays in this volume provide a resounding affirmative answer.

Notes

1. Jennifer K. Ruark, "A Place at the Table: More Scholars Focus on Historical, Social, and Cultural Meanings of Food, but Some Critics Say It's Scholarship-Lite," *The Chronicle of Higher Education*, July 9, 1999, A17. As an example of this recognition, the *American Historical Review*, the flagship journal of the American Historical Association, has published at least half a dozen articles on food history since 2004. These titles illustrate the wide range of scholarly literatures to which research on food has contributed. Roger Horowitz, Jeffrey M. Pilcher, and Sydney Watts, "Meat for the Multitudes: Market Culture in Paris, New York City, and Mexico City over the Long Nineteenth Century," *AHR* 109, no. 4 (October 2004): 1055–83; James Vernon, "The Ethics of Hunger and the Assembly of Society: The Techno-Politics of the School Meal in Modern Britain," *AHR* 110, no. 3 (June 2005): 693–725; Marcie Norton, "Tasting Empire: Chocolate and the European Internalization of Mesoamerican Aesthetics," *AHR* 111, no. 3 (Jun 2006): 660–91; Nick Cullather, "The Foreign Policy of the Calorie," *AHR* 112, no. 2 (April 2007): 337–64 Michael A. LaCombe, "'A continuall and dayly Table for Gentlemen of fashion': Humanism, Food, and Authority at Jamestown," *AHR* 115, no. 3 (June 2010): 669–87; Rebecca Earle, "'If You Eat Their Food …': Diets and Bodies in Early Colonial Spanish America," *AHR* 115, no. 3 (June 2010): 688–713.

2. David Knechtges, "A Literary Feast: Food in Early Chinese Literature," *Journal of the American Oriental Society* 106, no. 1 (1986): 49–63; Deane W. Curtin, "Food/Body/Person," in *Cooking, Eating, Thinking: Transformative Philosophies of Food*, ed. Deane W. Curtin and Lisa M. Heldke (Bloomington: Indiana University Press, 1992), 5; Ken Albala, "Cooking as Research Methodology: Experiments in Renaissance Cuisine," in *Renaissance Food from Rabelais to Shakespeare: Culinary Readings and Culinary Histories*, ed. Joan Fitzpatrick (Farnham: Ashgate, 2010), 73–74; Jean-Baptiste-Donaventure de Roquefort Le Grand, *Histoire de la vie privée des françois: depuis l'origine de la nation jusqu'a nos jours* (1782; repr., Paris: Laurent-Beaupré, 1815); Richard Warner, *Antiquitates Culinariae, or, Curious Tracts on Culinary Affairs of the Old English* (London: R. Blamire, 1791).

3. Bonnie Smith, *The Gender of History: Men, Women, and Historical Practice* (Cambridge, MA: Harvard University Press, 1998), 115; Lucy Maynard Salmon, *Domestic Service* (New York: Macmillan, 1897).

4. Theodore Blegen, *Grass Roots History* (Minneapolis: University of Minnesota Press, 1947); Fernand Braudel, *The Structures of Everyday Life: The Limits of the Possible*, vol. 1 of *Civilization and Capitalism, 15th-18th Century*, trans. Siân Reynolds (New York: Harper and Row, 1979); K. C. Chang, ed., *Food in Chinese Culture: Anthropological and Historical Perspectives* (New Haven: Yale University Press, 1977); Sidney W. Mintz, *Sweetness and Power: The Place of Sugar in Modern History* (New York: Viking, 1985).

5. Among the best of these culinary histories are Mark Kurlansky, *Cod: A Biography of the Fish that Changed World* (New York: Walker and Company, 1997); Anne Mendelson, *Stand Facing the Stove: The Story of the Women Who Gave America* The Joy of Cooking (New York: Henry Holt and Company, 1996); D. Eleanor Scully and Terence Scully, *Early French Cookery: Sources, History, Original Recipes and Modern Adaptations* (Ann Arbor: University of Michigan Press, 1995); Laura Shapiro, *Perfection Salad: Women and Cooking at the Turn of the Century* (New York: Farrar, Straus, and Giroux, 1986); Andrew F. Smith, *Eating History: Thirty Turning Points in the Making of American Cuisine* (New York: Columbia University Press, 2009); Barbara Ketcham Wheaton,

Savoring the Past: The French Kitchen and Table from 1300 to 1789 (Philadelphia: University of Pennsylvania Press, 1983).

6. Naum Jasny, *The Wheats of Classical Antiquity* (Baltimore, MD: Johns Hopkins University Press, 1944); Redcliffe N. Salaman, *The History and Social Influence of the Potato* (Cambridge: Cambridge University Press, 1949).

7. Raymond L. Lee, "Grain Legislation in Colonial Mexico, 1575–1585," *Hispanic American Historical Review* 27, no. 4 (November 1947): 647–70; Murray Benedict, *Farm Policies in the United States: A Study of their Origins and Development* (New York: Twentieth Century Fund, 1955).

8. Richard O. Cummings, *The American and His Food: A History of Food Habits in the United States* (Chicago: University of Chicago Press, 1940).

9. A. J. Arberry, "A Baghdad Cookery-Book," *Islamic Culture* 13 (1939): 21–47, 189–214.

10. Braudel, *The Structures of Everyday Life*; Robert Forster and Orest Ranum, eds., *Food and Drink in History: Selections from the Annales Economies, Sociétés, Civilisations*, trans. Elborg Forster and Patricia Ranum (Baltimore, MD: Johns Hopkins University Press, 1979); Louis Stouff, *Alimentation et ravitaillement en Provence aux XIVe et XVe siècles* (Paris: Mouton, 1970).

11. Robert William Fogel and Stanley L. Engerman, *Time on the Cross* (Boston: Little, Brown, 1974); Herbert Gutman, *Slavery and the Numbers Game: A Critique of Time on the Cross* (Urbana: University of Illinois Press, 1975).

12. Richard H. Steckel and Jerome C. Rose, ed., *The Backbone of History: Health and Nutrition in the Western Hemisphere* (Cambridge: Cambridge University Press, 2002).

13. E. P. Thompson, "The Moral Economy of the English Crowd in the Eighteenth Century," *Past and Present* 50 (February 1971): 76–136. See also Cynthia Bouton, *The Flour War: Gender, Class, and Community in Late Ancien Régime French Society* (University Park: Penn State University Press, 1993); Judith A. Miller, *Mastering the Market: The State and the Grain Trade in Northern France, 1700–1860* (Cambridge: Cambridge University Press, 1999).

14. Amartya Sen, *Poverty and Famines: An Essay on Entitlement and Deprivation* (Oxford: Clarendon Press, 1984).

15. Peter Garnsey, *Food and Society in Classical Antiquity* (Cambridge: Cambridge University Press, 1999); Lars T. Lih, *Bread and Authority in Russia, 1914–1921* (Berkeley: University of California Press, 1990). See also Pierre-Étienne Will and R. Bin Wong, *Nourish the People: The State Civilian Granary System in China, 1650–1850* (Ann Arbor: University of Michigan, Center for Chinese Studies, 1991); LaCombe, "'A continuall and dayly Table."

16. Warren J. Belasco, *Appetite for Change: How the Counterculture Took on the Food Industry, 1966–1988* (New York: Pantheon Books, 1989).

17. Natalia Milanesio, "Food Politics and Consumption in Peronist Argentina," *Hispanic American Historical Review* 90, no. 1 (February 2010): 75–108; James Davidson, "Fish, Sex and Revolution in Athens," *Classical Quarterly* 43, no. 1 (1993): 53–66.

18. Amy Bentley, *Eating for Victory: Food Rationing and the Politics of Domesticity* (Urbana: University of Illinois Press, 1998).

19. Alfred W. Crosby, Jr., *The Columbian Exchange: Biological and Cultural Consequences of 1492* (Westport, CT: Greenwood Press, 1972). Crosby built on the work of Ping-Ti Ho, *Studies on the Population of China, 1368–1953* (Cambridge, MA: Harvard University Press, 1959); and William Langer, "Europe's Initial Population Explosion," *American Historical Review* 69, no. 1 (October 1963): 1–17.

20. Sucheta Mazumdar, "The Impact of New World Food Crops on the Diet and Economy of China and India, 1600–1900," in *Food in Global History*, ed. Raymond Grew (Boulder, CO: Westview Press, 1999), 58–78; James McCann, *Maize and Grace: Africa's Encounter with a New World Crop, 1500–2000* (Cambridge, MA: Harvard University Press, 2005); Judith Carney, *Black Rice: The African Origins of Rice Cultivation in the Americas* (Cambridge, MA: Harvard University Press, 2001); Arturo Warman, *Corn and Capitalism: How a Botanical Bastard Grew to Global Dominance*, trans. Nancy L. Westrate (Chapel Hill: University of North Carolina Press, 2003).

21. Norton, "Tasting Empire," 660–69, 691.

22. Paul Freedman, *From Out of the East: Spices and the Medieval Imagination* (New Haven: Yale University Press, 2008).

23. Alberto Capatti and Massimo Montanari, *Italian Cuisine: A Cultural History*, trans. Aine O'Healy (New York: Columbia University Press, 2003), 86; Stephen Mennell, *All Manners of Food: Eating and Taste in England and France from the Middle Ages to the Present* (Oxford: Basil Blackwell, 1985); Jean-Louis Flandrin, *Arranging the Meal: A History of Table Service in France*, trans. Julie E. Johnson, Antonio Roder, and Sylvia Roder (Berkeley: University of California Press, 2007); T. Sarah Peterson, *Acquired Taste: The French Origins of Modern Cooking* (Ithaca, NY: Cornell University Press, 1994); Susan Pinkard, *A Revolution in Taste: The Rise of French Cuisine, 1650–1800* (New York: Cambridge University Press, 2009).

24. Caroline Walker Bynum, *Holy Feast and Holy Fast: The Religious Significance of Food to Medieval Women* (Berkeley: University of California Press, 1987). See also Nathan MacDonald, *Not Bread Alone: The Uses of Food in the Old Testament* (Oxford: Oxford University Press, 2008).

25. Rebecca Spang, *The Invention of the Restaurant: Paris and Paris and Modern Gastronomic Culture* (Cambridge, MA: Harvard University Press, 2000); Priscilla Parkhurst Ferguson, *Accounting for Taste: The Triumph of French Cuisine* (Chicago: University of Chicago Press, 2004); Andrew P. Haley, *Turning the Tables: Restaurants and the Rise of the American Middle Class, 1880–1920* (Chapel Hill: University of North Carolina Press, 2011); John K. Walton, *Fish and Chips and the British Working Class, 1870–1940* (Leicester: Leicester University Press, 1992).

26. Harvey A. Levenstein, "The American Response to Italian Food, 1880–1930," *Food and Foodways* 1, no. 1 (1985): 1–23; Hasia Diner, *Hungering for America: Italian, Irish, and Jewish Foodways in the Age of Migration* (Cambridge, MA: Harvard University Press, 2001); Tracy N. Poe, "The Labour and Lesiure of Food Production as a Mode of Ethnic Identity Building Among Italians in Chicago, 1890–1940," *Rethinking History* (2001): 131–48; Franca Iacovetta and Valerie J. Korinek, "Jell-O Salads, One-Stop Shopping, and Maria the Homemaker: The Gender Politics of Food," in *Sisters or Strangers: Immigrant, Ethnic, and Racialized Women in Canadian History*, ed. Marlene Epp, Franca Iacovetta, and Frances Swyripa (Toronto: University of Toronto Press, 2004), 190–230; Psyche Williams-Forson, *Building Houses Out of Chicken Legs: Black Women, Food, and Power* (Chapel Hill: University of North Carolina Press, 2006).

27. Donna R. Gabaccia, *We Are What We Eat: Ethnic Food and the Making of Americans* (Cambridge, MA: Harvard University Press, 1998); Marcie Cohen Ferris, *Matzoh Ball Gumbo: Culinary Tales of the Jewish South* (Chapel Hill: University of North Carolina Press, 2006); Frederick Douglass Opie, *Hogs and Hominy: Soul Food from Africa to America* (New York: Columbia University Press, 2008).

28. Arjun Appadurai, "How to Make a National Cuisine: Cookbooks in Contemporary India," *Comparative Studies in Society and History* 30, no. 1 (January 1988):

3–24; Emiko Ohnuki-Tierney, *Rice as Self: Japanese Identities Through Time* (Princeton, NJ: Princeton University Press, 1993); Jeffrey M. Pilcher, *¡Que vivan los tamales! Food and the Making of Mexican Identity* (Albuquerque: University of New Mexico Press, 1998); Warren Belasco and Philip Scranton, eds., *Food Nations: Selling Taste in Consumer Societies* (New York: Routledge, 2002).

29. Eric C. Rath, *Food and Fantasy in Early Modern Japan* (Berkeley: University of California Press, 2010).

30. Marion Nestle, *Food Politics: How the Food Industry Influences Nutrition and Health* (Berkeley: University of California Press, 2002); Eric Schlosser, *Fast Food Nation: The Dark Side of the All-American Meal* (New York: Harper Collins, 2002); Michael Pollan, *The Omnivore's Dilemma: A Natural History of Four Meals* (New York: Penguin, 2006).

31. Rachel Laudan, "A Plea for Culinary Modernism: Why We Should Love New, Fast, Processed Food," *Gastronomica* 1, no. 1 (February 2001): 36–44; Robert Paarlberg, *Food Politics: What Everyone Needs to Know* (New York: Oxford University Press, 2010).

32. Alan L. Olmstead and Paul W. Rhode, *Creating Abundance: Biological Innovation and American Agricultural Development* (New York: Cambridge University Press, 2008); Vaclav Smil, *Enriching the Earth: Fritz Haber, Carl Bosch, and the Transformation of World Food Production* (Cambridge, MA: MIT Press, 2001); Deborah K. Fitzgerald, *Every Farm a Factory: The Industrial Ideal in American Agriculture* (New Haven: Yale University Press, 2003); J. L. Anderson, *Industrializing the Corn Belt: Agriculture, Technology and Environment, 1945–1972* (DeKalb: Northern Illinois University Press, 2008).

33. Nick Cullather, *The Hungry World: America's Cold War Battle Against Poverty in Asia* (Cambridge, MA: Harvard University Press, 2010). See also Joseph Cotter, *Troubled Harvest: Agronomy and Revolution in Mexico, 1880–2002* (New York: Praeger, 2003).

34. Martin Bruegel, "How the French Learned to Eat Canned Food, 1809–1930s," in Belasco and Scranton, *Food Nations*, 113–30; Gabriella M. Petrick, "Industrial Food," *Oxford Handbook of Food History*, ed. Jeffrey M. Pilcher (New York: Oxford University Press, 2012). On the meatpacking industry, see Roger Horowitz, *Putting Meat on the American Table: Taste, Technology, Transformation* (Baltimore: Johns Hopkins University Press, 2006); Jeffrey M. Pilcher, *The Sausage Rebellion: Public Health, Private Enterprise, and Meat in Mexico City, 1890–1917* (Albuquerque: University of New Mexico Press, 2006).

35. For exemplary works, see Jack Kloppenburg, *First the Seed: The Political Economy of Plant Biotechnology* (Madison: University of Wisconsin Press, 2004); Steve Penfold, *The Donut: A Canadian History* (Toronto: University of Toronto Press, 2008).

36. William Cronon, *Nature's Metropolis: Chicago and the Great West* (New York: Norton, 1991); John Soluri, *Banana Cultures: Agriculture, Consumption, and Environmental Change in Honduras and the United States* (Austin: University of Texas Press, 2005); Warren Belasco and Roger Horowitz, eds., *Food Chains: From Farmyard to Shopping Cart* (Philadelphia: University of Pennsylvania Press, 2009).

37. Daphne Roe, *A Plague of Corn: A Social History of Pellagra* (Ithaca: Cornell University Press, 1973).

38. E. M. Collingham, *Imperial Bodies: The Physical Experience of the Raj, c. 1800–1947* (Cambridge: Polity Press, 2001); Earle, "'If You Eat Their Food …'"; Trudy Eden, *The Early American Table: Food and Society in the New World* (DeKalb: Northern Illinois University Press, 2008).

39. Cullather, "The Foreign Policy of the Calorie"; James Vernon, *Hunger: A Modern History* (Cambridge, MA: Harvard University Press, 2007); Mark Swislocki, "Nutritional

Governmentality: Food and the Politics of Health in Late Imperial and Republican China," *Radical History Review* 110 (Spring 2011): 9–35; Sandra Aguilar-Rodríguez, "Nutrition and Modernity: Milk Consumption in 1940s and 1950s Mexico," *Radical History Review* 110 (Spring 2011): 36–58.

40. Charlotte Biltekoff, *Eating Right in America: Food, Health and Citizenship from Domestic Science to Obesity* (Durham: Duke University Press, forthcoming).

41. Notable examples include Kurlansky, *Cod*; Mintz, *Sweetness and Power*; Warman, *Corn and Capitalism*; Pierre Boisard, *Camembert: A National Myth*, trans. Richard Miller (Berkeley: University of California Press, 2003); Gary Y. Okihiro, *Pineapple Culture: A History of the Tropical and Temperate Zones* (Berkeley: University of California Press, 2009). See also Noël Riley Fitch, *Appetite for Life: The Biography of Julia Child* (New York: Doubleday, 1997).

42. Reay Tannahill, *Food in History* (New York: Stein and Day, 1973); Chang, *Food in Chinese Culture*; Jean-Louis Flandrin, Massimo Montanari, and Albert Sonnenfeld, eds., *Food: A Culinary History from Antiquity to the Present*, trans. Clarissa Botsford, et al. (New York: Columbia University Press, 1999); Paul Freedman, ed., *Food: The History of Taste* (Berkeley: University of California Press, 2007).

43. Jeffrey M. Pilcher, *Food in World History* (New York: Routledge, 2006).

44. Felipe Fernández-Armesto, *Near a Thousand Tables: A History of Food* (New York: Free Press, 2002); Kenneth F. Kiple, *A Movable Feast: Ten Millennia of Food Globalization* (Cambridge: Cambridge University Press, 2007).

Bibliography

Belasco, Warren. *Food: The Key Concepts*. Oxford: Berg, 2009.

Bynum, Caroline Walker. *Holy Feast and Holy Fast: The Religious Significance of Food to Medieval Women*. Berkeley: University of California Press, 1987.

Chang, K. C., ed. *Food in Chinese Culture: Anthropological and Historical Perspectives*. New Haven: Yale University Press, 1977.

Counihan, Carole M. *The Anthropology of Food and Body: Gender, Meaning, and Power*. New York: Routledge, 1999.

Flandrin, Jean-Louis, Massimo Montanari, and Albert Sonnenfeld, eds. *Food: A Culinary History from Antiquity to the Present*. Translated by Clarissa Botsford, et al. New York: Columbia University Press, 1999.

Freedman, Paul, ed. *Food: The History of Taste*. Berkeley: University of California Press, 2007.

Kiple, Kenneth F., and Kriemhild Coneè Ornelas, eds. *The Cambridge World History of Food*. 2 vols. Cambridge: Cambridge University Press, 2000.

Mintz, Sidney. *Sweetness and Power: The Place of Sugar in Modern History*. New York: Viking Books, 1985.

Scholliers, Peter. "Twenty-five Years of Studying *un Phénomène Social Total*: Food History Writing on Europe in the Nineteenth and Twentieth Centuries." *Food, Culture, and Society* 10, no. 3 (Fall 2007): 449–71.

Teuteberg, Hans J., ed. *European Food History: A Research Overview*. Leicester: Leicester University Press, 1992.

PART I

FOOD HISTORIES

CHAPTER 1

FOOD AND THE ANNALES SCHOOL

SYDNEY WATTS

THE emergence of food history as a serious academic pursuit followed a major reorientation in the field of history led by French scholars of the Annales school. This change began prior to World War II and eventually took shape several decades later when a generation of social historians acquired posts with institutional authority. In a disciplinary shift that occurred throughout academia—both within and beyond France's borders—historians turned away from the history of great men and began to address the history of society through new sources and approaches. Although the rise of social history cannot be solely accredited to the Annales school, its founders undertook ambitious studies of historical standards of living, demographic trends, material lives, and mentalities of premodern peoples, a research interest that frequently focused on the history of agriculture and problems of subsistence. At the same time, their research openly acknowledged the relationship of history to contemporary issues, thus breaking free of the positivist notion of an early generation of historians who sought to study the past for its own sake. This chapter charts the role of the Annales school in shaping the field of food history through a discussion of three significant "moments": the first drawing attention to agricultural patterns and cognitive frameworks of premodern societies; the second giving greater weight and purpose to food production and consumption as a foundation of social and economic life; and the third lending interpretive depth to the history of cuisine through a cultural approach to taste and identity. A final section examines the influence of the Annales school on the history of food outside of France.[1]

The moment that gave birth to the Annales school occurred in the interwar years with the shift away from national political narratives toward topical studies that were sociological in nature. French historians Marc Bloch and Lucien Febvre established the *Annales* in 1929 as a ground-breaking journal open to historical and contemporary research in economics and sociology, and in two decades, the publication developed an international standing. With a strong commitment to innovative methods that made history more of a social science than a humanist endeavor, Bloch and Febvre followed the intellectual inspiration of sociologist Emile Durkheim. The energy, talent, and commitment of these founders soon brought them to the center of French academic life, and they held prestigious posts at the Collège de France. More than their collective enterprise, however, the journal's influence as a "school" came from the examples of its founders who set high standards for archival research and broad historical inquiry that would characterize the Annales school for future generations. Bloch and Febvre did not espouse a single method or paradigm. Rather it was their own work that emphasized the psychological and cultural underpinnings of social and economic history, an approach that would later appear as the history of mentalities and led to the cultural turn in historical scholarship beginning in the 1980s.

The second defining moment of the Annales school took place under the direction of Fernand Braudel, who as successor to Febvre led its institutionalization at the University of Paris. Through the 1950s and 1960s, Braudel oversaw hundreds of historical projects on geohistory and historical demography. Most historiographies represent Braudel as the central, defining figure of the Annales school. Numerous historians in France and throughout the world have adopted his explanatory model that emphasizes the material foundations of civilization, conceptualized around geographic units and geological measures of time. He, along with economic historian Ernest Labrousse, engaged in the quantification of serial sources, particularly sequences of commodity prices over centuries. Both historians focused on the economic history of primary goods such as grain. Under Braudel the study of food became a significant part of the study of economic growth and stagnation, something best exemplified through food crises and consumer revolutions.

In the third moment, the history of cuisine emerged in response to the quantitative hegemony of Braudel. Historian Jean-Louis Flandrin, along with Françoise Sabban and Maurice Aymard, perceived the intellectual value of symbolic and social analyses of food as a system of culture. Focusing on the history of sexuality and the family, Flandrin's early work was far more attentive to social practices within the household, and his methodology more closely aligned with social anthropology than with economic models. Flandrin, his students, and collaborators sought to explain the history of culinary practices, eating habits, and food regimes of various eras and civilizations through the close reading of cookbooks, literary sources, and medical texts. By the end of the twentieth century, scholars had widened their view of food as part of historical experience. These Annalistes brought greater academic rigor to the study of food and expanded the sources of information on eating, cooking, and shopping. The history of food and cuisine, too often relegated by the historical profession as an anecdotal amusement, had established itself—through the expansive scholarship of the Annales School—as a serious field of study.

FOUNDATIONS: BLOCH AND FEBVRE

In the period after World War I, historians were disillusioned with romantic, national narratives and sought to understand the whole of society. In France, the most ambitious thinking came from the fringes of the French university system in Strasbourg, the original home of the *Annales* journal and its founders Marc Bloch and Lucien Febvre. Recognizing the narrowness of historical research on political leaders and events, they embraced a multidisciplinary and international focus with a strong emphasis on economic history. Although influenced by Emile Durkheim's unifying vision of "a science of human society," they rejected the heavily theoretical and deterministic models of sociology in favor of a more practical notion of history as "that of life itself."[2] They drew together a maverick group of researchers who had what they liked to call an "insatiable appetite" for interpretation, innovation, experimentation, and confrontation.[3]

As an historian of medieval society, Marc Bloch sought to explain feudalism through various social institutions by examining the distribution of property, social groups, and the form and functions of the state. In *Feudal Society*, Bloch portrayed the "rhythm" of society through a description of its customs and habits. In the opening lines of "Man's Attitude to Nature and Time," he wrote:

> The men of the two feudal ages were close to nature—much closer than we are; and nature as they knew it was much less tamed and softened than we see it today. The rural landscape, of which the past formed so large a part, bore fewer traces of human influence. The wild animals that now only haunt our nursery tales—bears and, above all, wolves—prowled in every wilderness, and even amongst the cultivated fields. So much was this the case that the sport of hunting was indispensable for ordinary security, and almost equally so as a method of supplementing the food supply.[4]

Bloch's ethnographic approach tended toward a rich description of the psychological and the material, as well as the social ritual and symbolic meanings of work and worship. Febvre, by contrast, pursued the relationship between the individual and the community with an eye to popular belief. He was interested in uncovering past ways of thinking and the mental tools that historical actors used to make sense of the impossible without falling prey to anachronism. His deepest convictions about historical method come forth in his approach to the history of sixteenth-century thought.

> We instinctively bring to bear on these [sixteenth-century] texts our own ideas, our feelings, the fruit of our scientific inquiries, our political experiences, and our

> social achievements. But those who leafed through them when they were brand-new, under a bookseller's awning on Rue Mercière in Lyon or Rue Saint-Jacques in Paris—what did they read between the carefully printed lines? Just because the sequence of ideas in these texts confers on them a kind of eternal verity, to our eyes at least, can we conclude that all intellectual attitudes are possible in all periods? Equally possible? This is a great problem for the history of the human mind. It compounds the methodological problem and gives it extraordinary scope.[5]

This passage, taken from one of Febvre's later works, made the strategic process of historical thinking and research transparent to its readers. Bloch's work emphasized the necessary engagement of the historical imagination for readers. Such was the didactic enterprise of these two Annalistes.

While seemingly opposed to past historical traditions, many of their calls to research across disciplines (known as *enquêtes collectives*) were inspired by the writings of earlier, nationalist historians. One such call for the pursuit of food history, published in 1944, simultaneously applauded the early work of Fernand Braudel on the "food revolutions" of the potato and maize, while beckoning the journal's followers to reconsider the great Romantic writer and "Father of French history," Jules Michelet and his reflections on coffee and the revolutionary history of France. Febvre claimed that "we of the *Annales* have devoted attention to the problem of food supply from the beginning," the problem being as much historical as current.[6] To phrase the pursuit of food in history as a problem was in keeping with the focus of the Annales school on interrogation and analysis, questioning what is assumed about the past. In another vein, the call pointed to the need for scientific approaches (history being one of them) to address problems of subsistence. With a growing awareness of poverty and famine in Africa and Asia, Febvre pointed to the need for historians to respond to the world crisis of hunger and malnutrition with a longer perspective that "recalled human reality."[7]

The call for a collective research of alimentary habits, in the characteristic spirit of the *Annales,* solicited attention to a central historical problem that had to be explored in multiple ways. By raising the very question about the revolutionary history of foods, Febvre inspired a downtrodden nation in the midst of World War II. His originality lay in the "scientific volunteerism" inviting French scholars of all related disciplines, then under the German Occupation, to pursue a vital area of scholarship despite, or because of, the difficult conditions of the era.[8] Febvre's commitment to "cross-research" in food history would finally see fruition in 1954; while holding the Chair of Modern History and Civilization, he undertook the publication of a French encyclopedia "not of entries but of problems."[9] This unorthodox compendium of knowledge is neither alphabetical nor chronological; its conceptual structure embodies the spirit of the Annales school of history as social science. Its first volume, devoted to "mental tools," offered a comprehensive assessment of the rise of popular beef consumption and the decline of nobleman's game in early modern history as an illustration of the evolving definitions of standards of living. The fourteenth volume of the *Encyclopédie française*, dedicated to *la civilisation quotidienne* (everyday life), contains an eighty-page section devoted entirely to food consumption, with contributions from food scientists, demographers, geographers, and historians. The present became a template to ask questions of the past. In one instance, Febvre used prewar surveys to show how the western region of Poitou-Charente remained committed to lard, even though by the mid-1950s it had become the chief center for dairy production. In other regions, past preferences for butter over olive oil, for example, belied geographical boundaries of current agricultural production.[10]

The Annales school's characteristic presentism, much more apparent in the early, polemical period of the journal, distinguished it from other history reviews. This attitude would also elevate the significance of food as an extranational concern of humankind, not simply to eat, but to subsist. Questions of food security, nutritional needs, and undernourishment would direct the *Annales* into its next era with the establishment and expansion of a leading school of history. In this period, the journal's editors and its followers directed their interest in food history explicitly to the economic structures of food production and consumption and its conjunctures in moments of famine, agricultural crises, and food riots.

Institutionalization: Febvre and Braudel

The *Annales* gained institutional backing and research support beginning in 1947, after Marc Bloch's tragic war death, when Lucien Febvre was elected president of the newly founded École Pratique des Hautes Études (EPHE), the VIe section of the University of Paris. In this powerful position, Febvre was able to reform the academic system in ways that clearly unified history with the social sciences through the powerful Centre Nationales des Recherches Historiques (a research center that Febvre directed for several years). Soon after, the VIe section gained the title École des Hautes Études en Sciences Sociales (EHESS). Febvre also served as the French representative on the UNESCO commission for the creation of a Center for the Science of Mankind (*Maison de science de l'homme* or MSH), further assisting the institutionalization of the Annales School. Together with Braudel, Febvre built a network of researchers, teachers, and editors throughout postwar France, elevating the status of history as part of an ambitious federalist enterprise that built institutional structures emanating from Paris through the provinces of France.

Fernand Braudel supported Febvre in the administration of the Historical Research Center, sharing similar goals of historical innovation and an international if not global perspective of civilization. Even before Febvre's death in 1956, Braudel became the key person in the *Annales*, revising the journal's name with a new subtitle: *Economies, Sociétés, Civilisations*, which gave it a quasi-Marxist, structuralist stamp. Having succeeded Febvre as director of the EHESS and chief editor on the journal, Braudel became the undisputed representative of the *Annales* for more than a decade. Under his patronage, the EHESS and its close cousin, the MSH, grew in international stature—the MSH through Ford Foundation support that established grants to fellows from abroad and helped organize international conferences, research projects, and publications. Under Braudel's leadership, the pages of the *Annales* were filled with calls to further study in outlying regions of France—both urban and rural—that had been overlooked, if not ignored, by previous generations of historians. With a burgeoning post-World War II population, greater numbers of students entering university, and the rise of history as a leading discipline in the French academy, the prodigious work of Annales historians was ensured not only institutional hegemony, but also worldwide recognition.

By the early 1960s, the articles published and books reviewed in the *Annales* had returned to "the problem of alimentation" as first defined by Lucien Febvre, but with a more systematic, regional focus on agriculture as a window into patterns of work and issues of food security, especially among peasants. A number of monographs emerged from different areas of France, the most renown being Emmanuel Le Roy Ladurie's study of Languedoc, first published in France in 1966.[11] Annales historians, who had long been focused on the historical problems of food supply in pre-industrial Europe, looked to the most recent research at world organizations that focused on meeting the demands for undernourished populations in developing nations of Africa and Asia. Ideas of human geography and rural sociology emerged as key influences in the history of food, which gave rise to numerous Annaliste monographs in later decades that focused on food security, most particularly in Russia and China, where famine was eradicated over the course of the twentieth century, and in Africa where famine continues to plague emerging nations.[12]

As an historian, Fernand Braudel made perhaps the most important contribution to the geohistorical vision of the Annales school by laying out a unique conceptual framework that would become emblematic of the Annales method of historical analysis. He first established this historical model in his monumental work, *The Mediterranean and the Mediterranean World in the Age of Philip II* (1949).[13] This thirteen-hundred-page tome described in rich detail the development of a world region through its economic, social, and political life. More significant for historians outside this area of specialty was the concept that would later be commonly identified with the Annales: the *longue durée* ("long term"). In his introduction, Braudel described the three historic levels of time, each moving in different expanses, which he compared to the depths of the sea, the tides, and the crest of waves. These levels corresponded to three interpretive fields: structure, conjuncture, and event. While Braudel did eventually mention the political events of Philip II's reign at the end of the second volume, far more attention was given to the ways in which Mediterranean civilization was shaped by slower moving economic forces, such as the spread of technology and the development of trade routes. Later in his career, Braudel described the structural characteristics of dietary regimes that evolved over decades if not centuries with limited flexibility.

These structural changes, like the ebb and flow of tides, could not be traced to single events; they reflected different rhythms of historical time. Braudel's work demonstrated the value of studies of historical structures that moved at a glacial pace. In 1967, Emmanuel Le Roy Ladurie made this metaphor concrete by publishing a history of climate in Europe during the past millennium that utilized records of crop yields to reveal a "mini ice age" in the seventeenth century.[14]

Braudel's study of the Mediterranean world also offered a regional framework that became the focus for many histories of the Mediterranean diet. The basis of this diet, the trinity of wine, bread, and fish, defined the civilizations of Greeks and Romans through the early modern period. Massimo Montanari later traced the clash of civilizations and dietary regimes that occurred under the barbarian invasions of the Roman Empire. The confrontations between the game-hunting, nomadic, barbarian tribes and the fish-centered, reclining banquets of Classical civilization were finally synthesized in the stylized court dining rituals of the Renaissance, where meat and game took center stage.[15] Regional food cultures also became the focus of much of China's food history written in the past fifty years, not necessarily due to the direct influence of Braudel, although the *Annales* frequently published comparative studies, in some cases using Chinese foodstuffs and rice culture as a counterpoint to Western foodways. China's long written history embedded in geographical administrative units and bureaucratic record-keeping also helped form the basis for many institutional studies of provisioning and food policy.[16]

Braudel extended his interpretive framework in the magisterial three-volume study of early modern Europe, which appeared in English as *Civilization and Capitalism, 15th–18th Century*. The first volume, *The Structures of Everyday Life*, focused on what Braudel defined as the "parahistoric," a conceptual category under which he placed such material needs as food, housing, and clothing, along with the structural categories of demography, technology, and towns or urban life. Complete with maps of trans-Atlantic trade, graphs of price fluctuations for grain and bread, and illustrations of farmers and plantations, his richly detailed history of material life privileged the rule of things over the rule of people, further reorienting Braudel's vision of human action and thought. For Braudel these material aspects of the past were central to the history of civilization; "only until now," he stated, "had they been in the margin of traditional history."[17]

Stated as such, Braudel may have overlooked the many accomplishments his predecessors brought to the center of academic debate. For in many ways, Braudel's work was a continuation of the work of Febvre, who had identified if not pursued to the same degree the ways in which the material culture of food served as a window into the history of everyday life. But Braudel was less interested in mental structures of dietary preferences and more interested in economic structures of food regimes. In his detailed discussion of capitalist world exchange, Braudel included the labor input and the nutritional yields of primary foods such as maize, rice, and wheat, as well as the social and economic implications of new-found luxuries-turned-necessities such as spices and sugar, but little of the cultural meaning or symbolic importance of these foods. To be sure, Braudel spawned a new stage in the development of food history as a historical topic with greater diachronic variants than the synchronic studies of earlier food histories. Through his own work and the collective enterprise of the *Annales*, he sought to explain the broader repercussions that New World foods had over the *longue durée*, putting the numerous (and often redundant) histories of coffee, tea, and chocolate into a larger historical narrative.[18]

By 1975, the study of food had come into its own. Fourteen years after Braudel had issued a second call for an *enquête collective* (collaborative research project) to pursue a comprehensive study of food and nutrition, historian Maurice Aymard acknowledged that the call "had been widely heard." Aymard pointed in particular to the studies on food consumption by Jean-Claude Toutain and Jean-Jacques Hemardinquer. Their exhaustive research established the primacy of grains in the early modern period as much as the historical tallies of the intake of calories, proteins, vitamins, and minerals.[19] Yet even as Aymard's review of the current field of food studies reiterated what had been proven about the minimal standards of nutrition in peasant societies of the past, he did not hesitate to undercut the findings of his colleagues by showing the great variation in the sources where the "available supply" could differ greatly from the actual calories consumed.[20]

Aymard recognized the need to classify data effectively and make "interpretive hypotheses" about the history of nutrition based upon minimum standards established by the UN's Food and Agriculture Organization and the World Health Organization. His call echoed the goals of several other governmental and nongovernmental world organizations that were proliferating at this time, many of which invested themselves in solving temporary and endemic food crises. The FAO and World Bank compiled aggregate analyses of macro-economic performance and agricultural policies, generating mountains of data for Asia and Latin America as part of the post-World War II push into development economics. Yet the study of food history both within and outside of Europe had encountered shortcomings in its method; in premodern Europe, as much as in Africa, statistics on agricultural production are the least reliable of aggregate economic indicators. Annales scholars pointed to the frailties of serial analyses of prestatistical sources and raised new questions to further refine the historical problem of subsistence in light of international focus on famine and the world food supply. The world food crisis spurred studies of food security in developing nations throughout the 1980s, often incorporating Marxist theories to examine the political economy of famine as a failure of western capitalism. Geographers and economic historians of Africa and China drew on the Annales concepts of "structure" and "conjuncture" to give coherence and logic to their analysis of food crises.[21]

Most food studies in the 1960s and 1970s, including the serial studies generated by Annalistes during this period, gave greater emphasis to quantitative findings about such things as average caloric intake rather than qualitative analysis of subsistence issues such as food policy, work organization, and symbolic value of certain food staples. This tendency to see food history as a series of statistical investigations had incurred (and would continue to incur) the opposition of other Annales historians. Even as far back as 1942, Lucien Febvre criticized this mechanistic view of subsistence, pointing to "the great tendency to consider material civilization like a group of objects and the gestures of man as like the natural acts." According to Aymard, this "human machine" must not be limited to a balance sheet.[22] What was needed, as Febvre, Aymard, and many other Annalistes would concur, was a greater understanding of the social institutions that shaped food consumption and distribution.

At this time, few studies joined the temporal politics of food with its long-term economic and social realities; even the Annales paradigm claimed the primacy of structures and conjunctures. Little was written about the rule of monarchies and local lords that dictated the lives of the vast majority of people living in Europe between the sixteenth and the nineteenth centuries, who were subject to the "tyranny of grain."[23] Not until the 1980s and early 1990s did historians outside France, such as Steven Kaplan, pose questions about policy and policing, changing the focus of food history from a geographic, macro-economic view of early modern rural society to a political, micro-economic study of eighteenth-century Paris. Kaplan's research drew on the state offices of the Paris Parlement, Royal Procurator, and the monarchy's Lieutenant General of Police, as well as the work institutions of guild bakers and flour merchants, all of whom were imbricated in urban provisioning. Subsequent agricultural studies in other areas of the world centered on subsistence issues as the raison d'être of paternal governments, employing Kaplan's juxtaposition of the actual marketplace as a site of regulation against abstract the market principal as the emerging economic concept, foreign to the literal-minded premodern thinker.[24]

Beyond this critique of serial studies, Aymard also saw the need for new approaches that consider "the study of cooking in the widest sense, that is, the entire areas of food preparation." To be sure, the journal had published a series of articles on the diet and nutrition of Dutch, Swedish, Russian, English, and French soldiers and sailors in the 1960s. Published in 1973, Jean-Paul Aron's book on the diner (*le mangeur*) of the nineteenth century gave credence to culinary history as a "new historical object" in the revisionist movement of the Annales under Jacques LeGoff and his three-volume *Faire de l'histoire*.[25] But Aron's anecdotal survey of bourgeois manners and cuisine, as well as Jean-Claude Bonnet's literary deconstruction of "the broad and multiform verbalization of food habits" in Diderot's *l'Encyclopédie*, seemed to gain few followers.[26] One monograph that did more to give attention to the history of diet than previous work came forth by Louis Stouff in 1970. His study of household food consumption in Provence in the late Middle Ages brought in new types of sources and offered a more rigorous methodology in keeping with the Annales school's inclination for serial analysis. The regional study of market records and household accounts, in direct response to Braudel's call, gave a clear indication of the importance of meat in the fourteenth and fifteenth centuries, and with it offered a close analysis of the quality of food consumption through descriptions of kitchens, the spacing of meals, and the order of menus.[27] No doubt, the scholarship of Braudel and the Annales school had elevated food, no longer too banal for historical inquiry, as a discernable object of material culture and the focus of world systems of trade. Through Braudel's work and his academic position, the careers of a third and fourth generation of Annales historians came into the fore, some of whom delved further into probate records and other sources to recover the consumption history of household objects such as cooking and eating utensils.[28] Still others adopted a Braudelian world-system approach toward emerging markets and agricultural development, thus giving greater empirical weight to the social and economic life of New World foods.

Aymard's call for greater rigor follows the critical spirit of the *Annales* that acknowledged the work that had been done while offering pointed criticism of method in order to gain a more complete understanding of the problem to pursue. His review also expanded the terrain for food historians and their interdisciplinary work with cultural anthropology by underscoring the importance of symbolic analysis of the meal itself. From the outset, Aymard recognized the cultural meanings embedded in diet, something he termed the "psychosociology of diet." As he stated, "human beings do not live on nutrients but on food items." This method, seen as a totally different approach than the macroeconomic that governed so much of nutritional studies, recognized the values, symbols, and rules that followed a certain alimentary "code." It signaled an alternative avenue of research that was informed by the structural theories of culture (exemplified by anthropologist Claude Lévi-Strauss); this new approach aligned the components of human nutrition within a cultural system that followed a "dietary regime." While Braudel had used the term "dietary regime" to describe food habits, it was clear that the Annalistes were reclaiming the "mental tools" (*utilles mentaux*) with which to pursue questions through the semiotics of culinary vocabulary and sociopsychology of consumption. Lévi-Strauss's famous dictum, that food is not only good to eat but to think, would spur others to study food consumption as "a system of communication, a body of images, a protocol of usages, situations, and behaviors" in the present and in the past. Apart from Stouff's early and limited forays into dietary preferences, few historians responded to the call for such interpretive studies of the meaning and practice of food habits without giving primacy to quantitative analysis of macroeconomic issues. Even as the journal cried for an cultural-anthropological approach to food studies, it would be another ten years before Jean-Louis Flandrin and others would employ these methods to break new ground in the history of food.

Under Braudel's leadership in the 1950s and 1960s, the scholarship on food studies was instilled with a sense of legitimacy in the academic world, particularly in the areas of economic history of food systems and consumer society, and in comparative approaches of social geography. Yet while food—regarded almost always as an agricultural commodity—became one of the primary elements of material life, it was situated most often within larger questions of historical change over long periods. The importance of meals was clearly a part of a history of nutrition, but little attention was paid to history of cuisine as a cultural practice or "taste" as an aesthetic principle. Little was understood about the social organization of food preparation, food markets, and cooks or about the significance of ingredients that composed a meal. There remained many areas of food history to explore; the cultural analysis of the culinary arts had not emerged a topic in its own right.

Flandrin's History of Taste and Cuisine

Clearly, much of the training and direction of food history under the Annales school focused on eclecticism and aimed to capture the environmental, demographic, and material forces that governed men and women through the ages. But how do we explain the lack of studies on consumerism and food markets, not to mention questions of food preparation that Maurice Aymard and others had identified? Apart from psychosociological approaches to contemporary food preferences by Roland Barthes,[29] little work had been devoted to the history of taste or food preferences.[30] One explanation for this oversight, suggested by Robert Forster in his introduction to the 1979 *Annales* anthology of food-related articles translated for an English-speaking audience, was that the topic was elitist. To ask about food choice was condescending to those who lived in a world with few choices, "especially considering that at least three-fourths of Europe's population was close to the subsistence level from the sixteenth to the late nineteenth century."[31] The privilege of choice would not appear until well into the nineteenth century, and then as a bourgeois attribute. Yet even in Braudel's work, the historical problem of food habits and dietary choices persisted. The most notable example was Michel Mornieau's examination of the question of the historical resistance to the potato, a New World food introduced to Europe in the early sixteenth century but not adapted into the popular diet until well into the eighteenth century.[32]

With the journal's self-proclaimed "critical turn" in the March-April 1988 issue, the economic and social structures that preoccupied many of the Annalistes would soon after give way to a retitled review, *Annales: Histoire et sciences sociales*, and a new wave of cultural historians. At the time, a fourth generation of Annalistes, led by Roger Chartier and Jacques Revel, reclaimed *mentalités* as a primary determinant of historical reality.[33] Much of the new cultural history followed the literary turn in the humanities and its focus on language and metaphor. It also delved further into the study of culture as the interpretation of traditions, value systems, ideas, and institutional forms of human interaction. Suddenly the questions about the value and customs of private life became the entry point to the study of cultural practices and the formation of social identity. Jean-Louis Flandrin, as part of this later generation of Annalistes, would bring his anthropological expertise to this field, along with the semiotics of cuisine of Françoise Sabban.[34] Philip and Mary

Hyman's mastery of early French culinary literature opened up the study of cuisine through a close reading of cultural artifacts: the cookbook.[35] Historians were delving further into the meaning and practice of culinary history.

Flandrin first established himself as an historian of sexuality and the family and spent the last twenty years of his life pursuing new questions of human behavior through taste and food choices. He defined "taste" first as a bodily sense from which a person judges as well as perceives flavors that are both agreeable and disagreeable. But he also saw taste as a "tributary of culture, of social milieu, of space and time"[36] that made it intrinsically historical. Drawing his conclusions from exhaustive research of culinary texts, historical dictionaries, and medical treatises, Flandrin charted the variables of food habits and culinary innovations from the Middle Ages through the eighteenth century. One of his earliest articles on taste, which appeared in the *Annales* in 1983, posited the taste for butter not as preference but as necessity. As a basic ingredient in classical French cooking, butter's increasing importance in cooking led many French people to transgress its Lenten prohibitions.[37] Elsewhere Flandrin argued that the newly discovered taste for "bourgeois beef" became the criterion of social distinction in the early modern period, demonstrating how the gulf between the bourgeois penchant for "gross meats" (especially beef) and noble taste for game and wildfowl had narrowed. Using culinary techniques to show the how the two groups came together, he demonstrated how taste became "an object of fashion and a creator of social distinctions, a pole around which new social groups were formed."[38] Through his continued pursuit of the reasons for particular tastes, Flandrin had proved that there was nothing arbitrary about food choices and taste preferences as they often expressed the values and inclinations of social groups if not entire populations of a certain period.

Flandrin's writings built upon the Annales models laid out by Braudel and others, yet he was openly critical of the school's propensity to quantify and its focus on aggregate consumption patterns.[39] In the 1980s and 1990s, when historians were readily embracing the field of cultural anthropology, colloquia and seminars on the subject of food were proliferating. Scholars recognized how food history as a thematic topic opened up new ways to examine a range of crucial variables on identity and culture in a manageable way. They also broadened the field of food history, returning to the cookbook as a primary source for the analysis of food habits and culinary practices. In 1987, a conference at the University of Nancy on cuisines, alimentary regimes, and regions, featuring Flandrin as a keynote speaker, drew over thirty ethnographers, geographers, and historians. According to the conference chair, this interdisciplinary endeavor sought "to revive the area of alimentary geography" that had proliferated in the 1960s and 1970s under Braudel. But in this instance, the historical problem of taste and the cultural meaning of food choice appeared as the keystone to a varied and changing expression of food habits.[40] In 1989, Annales historian Maurice Aymard, along with sociologist Claude Grignon and anthropologist Françoise Sabban (then the editors of the newly formed journal *Food and Foodways*), led a conference on food habits and the temporality of social life (*le temps social*), which brought together over two dozen scholars from various fields. In true Annales school fashion, cross-research among social scientists continued to interrogate the problem of how (in the present and the past) food habits structure and consume specific times of day, at work, at rest, and how people devote time in the shopping, cooking, and eating of food. Seen from multiple, disciplinary vantage points, the questions posed allowed nutritionists, sociologists, and time-study experts to further detail and complicate the study of everyday life that Braudel had sketched out over two decades earlier.[41]

During this period in the late 1980s and 1990s, after the death of Braudel, the *Annales* journal became less dominant among the French academy and other food journals were established.[42] Flandrin served as one of the founding editors of *Food & Foodways*, conceived as an interdisciplinary, international publication on the history of human nourishment. The refereed journal continues to support the scholarly pursuit of food-related topics to elevate the stature of food studies in very much the same tradition of the early *Annales*. In collaboration with Massimo Montanari, Flandrin drew together a number of historians, geographers, archeologists, and sociologists from across Western Europe to create an impressive anthology of culinary history, first published in 1996, that extends from pre-historical periods to the twentieth century.[43] The collection demonstrates the encounter of different dietary regimes whose cultural identity were shaped by religious, geographical, social, and national meanings. It also shows the consolidation of numerous fields of research devoted to culinary topics: archeological evidence from cave drawings, tomb paintings, and human remains, semiotic studies of ancient texts, the history of New World foods within the context of rising market economies, the infusion of slave labor in the mass production of cash crops, the expansion of food trades and the industrialization of food, and the cultural meanings that surround the economic and social triumph of such important consumables as sugar, chocolate, coffee, and tea, the rise of the restaurant and the history of the inn, as well as the McDonaldization of culture.

Throughout his career, Flandrin took an active role in shaping the field of food history. He developed a following in his weekly seminar at the EHESS, where students pursued food-related topics that focused on the history of comportment and gesture, and identified decisive shifts in culinary traditions and food habits. While acknowledging the more sedentary structures of alimentary regimes, Flandrin also broke free of the synchronic description in favor of more diachronic explanations, forwarding the thesis on the modernization of French cuisine, a significant turn that had allowed France (and most of Europe) to sever the ties of medieval recipes (called "receipts" and written by health experts) from their medicinal lineage.[44] Flandrin's thesis had given a new periodization to the history of food: the birth of the gastronome in the late eighteenth century. His own findings have been followed by studies of gastronomy as an historical phenomenon tied to the professionalization of the chef, the rise of the restaurant, and the elevation of cooking from royal servitude to an independent profession with claims to high art.[45]

The *Annales* Tradition Beyond the Hexagon

The Annales school has left an imprint on many historians who continue to advance food history through means that further institutionalize this area of study in European-wide associations and research centers. In addition to the examination of cuisine and manners as part of food history across Europe, the field has expanded with increasing attention to the processes of diffusion and to cultural reactions of Europeans to "other" foods. The four generations that have contributed to the journal and built the school have published a number of monographs and edited collections on food history, inspiring others to do the same in their region of the world.

Food historians across Europe increasingly have collaborated in teams, following a tradition of the Annales school that gives greater shared purpose and methodological rigor to any field of historical study. These collaborative efforts, which draw participants to conferences on food history of particular conceptual themes, have encouraged the participation of scholars across national boundaries.

In 2001, a group of food scholars led by Maurice Aymard held the first meeting of the Institut Européen d' Histoire et des Cultures de l'Alimentation (IEHCA) in Strasbourg, France. The theme of the founding conference centered on the historical identity of food in Europe, drawing on a range of disciplines in the social sciences to study cultural food practices as "alimentary ways of being" (*manières d'être alimentaires*) to identify "particularities and differences among groups" across Europe, and "to reconstitute the discourse on food that expresses sentiments of belonging."[46] This European perspective deliberately avoided national identities in favor of alimentary ones such as "a carnivorous Europe," a concept drawn from Braudel himself. It also broke through barriers of historical periodization in favor of the Braudelian *longue durée*. This francophone organization, now instituted in Tours, continues to support and encourage European research in the areas of food history through fellowships for young scholars who use its research center and library, as well as through ongoing seminars and annual conferences in food history.

A parallel to this collaborative work in food history that is produced for the Anglophone community is the biannual colloquium of the International Commission for Research into European Food History (founded in 1989). Peter Scholliers has edited several of these conference proceedings, one on European cooking, eating, and drinking since the Middle Ages. This edited volume includes essays on topics from Norway to Spain and, taken together, provide deeply researched examples that engage in the latest historical methods of identity formation as negotiated practice. Scholliers's introduction draws on recent social theories to describe identity as an analytical tool that points to "the precise role of food in peoples' identity making." In his own assessment of the field of food history, Scholliers (a Belgian) engages with Flandrin and others with aims to further the methodological rigor of food and identity. Scholliers's collection offers a number of examples that give a theoretical reworking of identification from within historical sources and from without, even as the object of these studies remain bound by Europe's own national boundaries.[47]

Much of the scholarship outside of Europe has followed Braudel's global perspective that links the commoditization of food and the worldwide problems of food supply with the development of capitalism. As Braudel demonstrated in his three-volume study of civilization from 1500 to 1800, "the wheels of commerce" advance the market specialization of food trades and the shifts in popular and elite cuisine in an expanding market of acquisitive consumers. Braudel's seminal work inspired the convergence of social geography and economic history. Immanuel Wallerstein, an American follower of the Annales school, established a Braudelian Center at SUNY Binghampton in September 1976 dedicated to the study of "world-systems" over long periods. Braudelian geohistory can be seen as an antecedent of transnational studies of food systems. Africanists in the last two decades have given evidentiary rigor to Braudel's broad frameworks, providing detailed local studies of agricultural development and climatic studies of food cultures.[48] Flandrin and Massimo Montanari have led other researchers into studies of food diffusion from the Americas to Europe, and the migration of spices and aromatics that link Europe, the Middle East, and Asia. These studies often look to broader patterns of social and economic change to chart the effect of these new culinary regimes.[49] Others have concentrated on the history of a single food to chart its culinary diffusion and the commercial and cultural linkages between distant areas of the world.[50]

Historians from other regions of the world also fell under the influence of the Annales school. Enrique Florescano carried the French tradition of total history to El Colegio de México, one of the leading postgraduate institutions in Latin America. He received a Ph.D. degree from the EPHE studying with Braudel, Pierre Vilar, and Ruggiero Romano. Florescano's dissertation examined the conjunctures of eighteenth-century maize prices, linking agrarian crises with social disruptions and ultimately the coming of Mexican independence. Meanwhile in South Asia, K. N. Chaudhuri sought to do for the Indian Ocean world the sort of sweeping regional history that Braudel wrote for the Mediterranean.[51] Such works follow the *Annales* tradition in that they employ the same intensive archival research, the rigorous methods of quantitative and qualitative analysis, and the focus on historical problems to sharpen our vision of the past.

A Longue Durée of Food History

For nearly a century, the Annales school has addressed the question, "Why study food?" with a number of resounding arguments: (1) Because food is a part of the history of everyday life and therefore must be approached as an integral part of economic and social structures, as well as a key indicator of broad cultural practices; (2) because the security and safety of food has been the preoccupation of state leaders and household heads since the earliest civilizations; and (3) because the study of food and cuisine tells us a great deal about who we are and what we value as a civilization. Furthermore, Annales historians took great pains to find evidence that would allow them to answer such fundamental historical questions as the following: What did people eat and how did they survive on it? What role did the environment play in shaping diet from season to season, as well as from periods of dearth to abundance? How did technology, human capital, social networks, and taste influence dietary regimes? By focusing on large economic and social structures, by revealing the symbolic meanings and material realities, by problematizing the mentalities that encouraged innovation and preserved traditions, the Annalistes cast aside the singular pursuit of food history through its popularized "mythic origins." Just as Flandrin reminds us, the history of food cannot be limited to the story of inventors of notable dishes and elixirs.[52] But as the latest generation of food historians contends, the fact that food myths predominate among civilized peoples of the past and present must force scholars to examine them as the basis of identification.[53]

Over the past eighty years, monographs, theses, and conference proceedings published by MSH and EHESS and, more recently, by the IEHCA demonstrate the propensity for cross-disciplinary research investigations that have filled the pages of the *Annales* from its beginnings. These studies detail how agricultural products and regional and national cuisines were produced, distributed, and consumed, and make larger claims about how food shaped and was shaped by market forces, political policy, social hierarchy, and cultural identity. Such comprehensive approaches that present food as an integral part of the past could not have occurred without historians first posing questions as far-reaching as regarding the fluctuations of dietary subsistence among the peasantry or the rise of bourgeois taste. And such questions about the lived experience of the past could not be discerned without a broader vision of society and the forces that shaped it, as well as the written and physical evidence to recover the lives of people absent from the historical record. For these contributions to the study of history that made way for the establishment of food studies throughout academe, we must credit the Annales school.

Notes

1. An enormous literature exists on the historiography of the Annales school. Most authors credit Braudel as leader of the school, but recent work by André Burguière gives greater attention to Bloch and Febvre. A. Burguière, *The Annales School: An Intellectual History*, trans. Jane Marie Todd (Ithaca, NY: Cornell University Press, 2009); Peter Burke, *The French Historical Revolution: The Annales School, 1929–89* (Stanford: Stanford University Press, 1990); Robert Forster, "Achievements of the Annales School,"

The Journal of Economic History 38, no. 1 (March 1978): 58–76; Samuel Kinser, "Annalist Paradigm? The Geohistorical Structuralism of Fernand Braudel," *The American Historical Review* 86, no. 1 (February 1981): 63–105; Troian Stoianovich, *French Historical Method: The Annales Paradigm* (Ithaca, NY: Cornell University Press, 1972). A recent collection of essays on the Annales includes the reflections of the school's leaders, as well as critical assessments of the journal by leading historians and the *Annales* editors over the course of eighty years. Stuart Clark, ed., *The Annales School: Critical Assessments*, 4 vols. (London: Routledge, 1999).

2. Jacques Revel, "Introduction," in *Histories: French Constructions of the Past*, ed. Jacques Revel and Lynn Hunt (New York: The New Press, 1995), 11–12.

3. Ibid, 12.

4. Marc Bloch, *Feudal Society*, trans. L. A. Manyon, 2 vols. (Chicago: Phoenix Books, 1967), 1:72.

5. Lucien Febvre, *The Problem of Unbelief in the Sixteenth Century*, trans. Beatrice Gottlieb (Cambridge, MA: Harvard University Press, 1982), 5–6.

6. Lucien Febvre, "Alimentation," *Mélanges d'histoire sociale* 6 (1944): 38.

7. "Depuis l'origine, nos Annales n'ont cessé, avec des collaborations comme celles du R. Gidon, d'André Varangnac, d'Haudricourt, d'autres encore, d'accorder une attention suivie aux problèmes alimentaires. A l'heure où on se constitue, dans les laboratories, une physiologie de alimentation toute nouvelle: à l'heure où, dans un domaine que l'on vit longtemps et paradoxalement occupé par la seule chimie des chimistes purs, et peuplée des illusions de Berthelot [...], les physiologists reprennent leurs droits et nous rappellent à la realité humaine." *Mélanges d'histoire sociale* 6 (1944): 39.8. Burguière, *The Annales School*, 92–93.

9. Lucien Febvre, ed., *Encyclopédie française*, 21 vols. (Paris: Librairie Larousse, 1935–40).

10. Ibid, 14:85–87.

11. Emmanuel Le Roy Ladurie, *The Peasants of Languedoc*, trans. John Day (Urbana: University of Illinois Press, 1974). For a complete list of these monographs see Bartolomé Bennassar and Joseph Goy, "Contribution à l'histoire de la consommation alimentaire du XVe au XIXe siècle," *Annales: Histoire, Sciences Sociales*, 30, no. 2/3 (March-June 1975): 402–30.

12. See a review article by Jean-Jacques Hémardinquer, "Problèmes et techniques alimentaires: Un panorama mondial," *Annales: Histoires Sciences Sociales*, no. 6 (November-December 1969): 1468.

13. Fernand Braudel, *The Mediterranean and the Mediterranean World in the Age of Philip II*, trans. Siân Reynolds, 2 vols. (New York: Harper & Row, 1972–1973 [1949]).

14. Emmanuel Le Roy Ladurie, *Times of Feast, Times of Famine: The History of Climate since the Year 1000*, trans. Barbara Bray (New York: Doubleday, 1971).

15. Massimo Montanari study of "nutritional regimes" synthesized much of his research of diet among the early civilizations of the Greco-Roman periods. See also his *The Culture of Food*, trans. Carl Ipsen (Oxford: Blackwell Publishers, 1994).

16. See Kung-chuan Hsiao, *Rural China: Imperial Control in the Nineteenth Century* (Seattle: University of Washington Press, 1967); Pierre-Etienne Will and R. Bin Wong, with James Lee, *Nourish the People: The State Civilian Granary System in China, 1650–1850* (Ann Arbor: University of Michigan Press, 1991).

17. Fernand Braudel, *The Structures of Everyday Life: The Limits of the Possible*, vol. 1 of *Civilization and Capitalism 15th–18th Century*, trans. Siân Reynolds (New York: Harper & Row, 1981), 27.

18. Jean Leclant provides an excellent literature review of the early works in "Le café et les cafés à Paris (1644–1693)," *Annales E.S.C.* 6 (January-March 1951): 1–12, which appears in translation in *Food and Drink in History: Selections from the Annales: Economies, Sociétés, Civilisations*, ed. Robert Forster and Orest Ranum, trans. Elborg Forster and Patricia Ranum (Baltimore, MD: Johns Hopkins University Press, 1979), 86–97.

19. J.-C. Toutain, *La Consommation alimentaire en France de 1789 à 1964* (Geneva: Droz, 1971); J.-J. Hémardinquer, *Pour une histoire de l'alimentation* (Paris: A. Colin, 1970).

20. Aymard suggests as much as 10 to 12 percent in losses due to spoilage, food preparation, and waste, as well as the uneven distribution relative to a hierarchical social structure that would skew any classification of data. See Maurice Aymard, "Pour l'histoire de l'alimentation. Quelques remarques de méthode," *Annales, E.S.C.* 30 (March-June 1975): 431–44.

21. Michael Watts, *Silent Violence: Food, Famine & Peasantry in Northern Nigeria* (Berkeley: University of California Press, 1983); Pierre-Etienne Will, *Bureaucratie et famine en Chine au 18e siècle* (Paris: EHESS, 1980).

22. Lucien Febvre, "Enquêtes et suggestions," *Mélanges d'historie sociales* 2 (1942): 56.

23. One important exception is Jacques Revel, "A Capital City's Privileges: Food Supplies in Early Modern Rome," in Forster and Ranum, *Food and Drink in History*, 37–49.

24. Steven Laurence Kaplan, *Bread, Politics, and Political Economy in the Reign of Louis XV*, 2 vols. (The Hague: Nijhof Press, 1976); idem, *Provisioning Paris: Merchants and Millers in the Grain and Flour Trade in the Eighteenth Century* (Ithaca, NY: Cornell University Press, 1984); R. E. F. Smith and David Christian, *Bread and Salt: A social and economic history of food and drink in Russia* (Cambridge: Cambridge University Press, 1984); Jane I. Guyer, ed., *Feeding African Cities: Studies in Regional Social History* (Bloomington: Indiana University Press, 1987); Francesca Bray, *The Rice Economies: Technology and Development in Asian Societies* (Oxford: Blackwell, 1986).

25. Jacques LeGoff, ed., *Constructing the Past: Essays in Historical Methodology* (Cambridge: Cambridge University Press, 1985).

26. Jean-Paul Aron, *The Art of Eating in France: Manners and Menus in the Nineteenth Century*, trans. Nina Rootes (New York: Harper & Row, 1975); Jean-Claude Bonnet, "Le réseau culinaire dans l'Encyclopédie," *Annales E. S. C.* 31 (Sept.-Oct. 1976): 891–914.

27. Louis Stouff, *Ravitaillement et alimentation en Provence au XIV-XV siecles* (Paris: Mouton, 1970).

28. Annik Paradailhé-Galabrun, *The Birth of Intimacy: Private and Domestic Life in Early Modern Paris*, trans. Joselyn Phelps (Cambridge: Polity Press, 1991); Daniel Roche, *The People of Paris: An Essay in Popular Culture in the 18th Century*, trans. Marie Evans (Berkeley: University of California Press, 1987).

29. Roland Barthes, "Toward a Psychosociology of Contemporary Food Consumption," in Forster and Ranum, *Food and Drink in History*, 166–73; Jean Soler, "The Semiotics of Food in the Bible," in ibid, 126–38.

30. To be sure, Braudel and other Annalistes acknowledged the great shift in taste from the Middle Ages when heavily spiced food dominated prepared dishes and the seventeenth-century rejection of this cuisine. But taste as a conceptual tool for understanding consumer preferences and social identity was not the focus of these discussions. For early works on consumer taste, see P. H. Chombart de Lauve, *La Vie quotidienne des familles ouvrieres* (Paris: CNRS, 1956); Marguerite Perrot, *Le Mode de vie des familles bourgeoisies, 1873–1953* (Paris: A. Colin, 1961) Stephen Mennell, *All Manners*

of Food: Eating and Taste in England and France from the Middle Ages to the Present (Oxford: Blackwell, 1985).

31. Robert Forster, "Introduction," in Forster and Ranum, *Food and Drink in History*, vii–xiii.

32. Michel Morineau, "The Potato in the Eighteenth Century," in Forster and Ranum, *Food and Drink in History*, 17–36.

33. Lynn Hunt, "Introduction: History Culture, Text," in *The New Cultural History*, ed. Lynn Hunt (Berkeley, CA: University of California Press, 1989), 6–7.

34. Françoise Sabban, "Le système des cuissons dans la tradition culinaire chinoise," *Annales: E.S.C.* 38 (March-April 1983): 341–68.

35. They collaborated with Flandrin in a scholarly edition of the seventeenth-century cookbook by La Varenne, *Le cuisinier françois* (Paris: Mantalba, 1983).

36. Jean-Louis Flandrin, "Histoire du goût," OCHA Textes Exclusifs en Sciences Humaines [Online]. Available: http://www.lemangeur-ocha.com/uploads/tx_smilecontenusocha/09_Histoire_du_gout_int.pdf. [April 3, 2010].

37. J-L Flandrin, "Le goût et al nécessité: Sur l'usage des graisses dans les cuisines d'Europe occidentales (XVIe-XVIIIe siècles)," *Annales: E. S. C.* 38, no. 2 (1983): 369–401.

38. J-L Flandrin, "Distinction through Taste," in *History of Private Life*, ed. Philippe Ariès and Georges Duby, trans. Arthur Goldhammer, 5 vols. (Cambridge, MA: Belknap Press, 1981–1991), 3:265–307.

39. J-L Flandrin, "Préface," in *Tables d'hier, tables d'ailleurs. Histoire et ethnologie du repas*, ed. J.-L. Flandrin and L. Cobbi (Paris: O. Jacob, 1999), 17–36.

40. Jean Peltre and Claude Thouvenot, eds., *Alimentations et régions: Actes du colloques* (Nancy: Presses Universitaires de Nancy, 1989).

41. Maurice Aymard, Claude Grignon, and Françoise Sabban, eds., *Le temps de manger: Alimentation, emploi du temps et rythmes sociaux* (Paris: Editions de la Maison des sciences de l'homme, 1993).

42. *Food and Foodways* (1989); *Gastronomica* (2000); *Food & History* (2003); *Food, Culture and Society* (2004).

43. J.-L. Flandrin and Massimo Montanari, eds., *Histoire de l'alimentation* (Paris: Fayard, 1996).

44. J-L Flandrin, "Dietary Choices and Culinary Technique, 1500–1800," in *Food: A Culinary History from Antiquity to the Present*, ed. Jean Louis Flandrin, Massimo Montanari, and Albert Sonnenfeld, trans. Clarissa Botsford, et al. (New York: Columbia University Press, 1999), 403–17 and "From Dietetics to Gastronomy: The Liberation of the Gourmet" in ibid, 418–32.

45. These include Jean-Robert Pitte, *French Gastronomy: The History and Geography of a Passion*, trans. Jody Gladding (New York: Columbia University Press, 2002); Priscilla Parkhurst Ferguson, *Accounting for Taste: The Triumph of French Cuisine* (Chicago: University of Chicago Press, 2004); Susan Pinkard, *A Revolution in Taste: The Rise of French Cuisine* (Cambridge: Cambridge University Press, 2009); Rebecca L. Spang, *The Invention of the Restaurant: Paris and Modern Gastronomic Culture* (Cambridge, MA: Harvard University Press, 2000).

46. Martin Bruegel and Bruno Laurioux, eds., *Histoire et identités alimentaires en Europe* (Paris: Hachette, 2002), 12.

47. Peter Scholliers, ed., *Food, Drink and Identity: Cooking, Eating and Drinking in Europe since the Middle Ages* (Oxford: Berg, 2001).

48. For an excellent review of the African literature, see Sara S. Berry, "The Food Crisis and Agrarian Change in Africa: A Review Essay," *African Studies Review* 27, no. 2 (June 1984): 59–112.

49. Kenneth F. Kiple and Kriemhild Coneè Ornelas, eds., *The Cambridge World History of Food*, 2 vols. (Cambridge: Cambridge University Press, 2000); Raymond Grew, ed., *Food in Global History* (Boulder, CO: Westview, 1999).

50. See, for example, Redcliff Salaman, *The History and Social Influence of the Potato* (1949, reprint: Cambridge: Cambridge University Press, 1987); Marcy Norton, *Sacred Gifts, Profane Pleasures: A History of Tobacco and Chocolate in the Atlantic World* (Ithaca, NY: Cornell University Press, 2008); Nikita Harwich, *Histoire du Chocolat* (Paris:Desjonquères, 1992).

51. Enrique Florescano, *Precios del maíz y crisis agrícolas en México (1708–1810)* (Mexico City: El Colegio de México, 1969); K. N. Chaudhuri, *Asia Before Europe: Economy and Civilisation of the Indian Ocean from the Rise of Islam to 1750* (Cambridge: Cambridge University Press, 1990).

52. Flandrin, *Food: A Culinary History*, 1.

53. Bruegel and Laurioux, "Introduction," in Bruegel and Laurioux, *Histoire et identités alimentaires en Europe*, 18.

Bibliography

Aron, Jean-Paul. *The Art of Eating in France: Manners and Menus in the Nineteenth Century.* Translated by Nina Rootes. London: Peter Owen, 1975.

Braudel, Fernand. *The Structures of Everyday Life: The Limits of the Possible.* Vol. 1 of *Civilization and Capitalism, 15th–18th Century.* Translated by Siân Reynolds. New York: Harper & Row, 1979.

Flandrin, Jean-Louis. *Arranging the Meal: A History of Table Service in France.* Translated by Julie E. Johnson. Berkeley: University of California Press, 2007.

Flandrin, Jean-Louis, Massimo Montanari, and Albert Sonnenfeld, eds. *Food: A Culinary History from Antiquity to the Present.* Translated by Clarissa Botsford, et al. New York: Columbia University Press, 1999.

Forster, Robert, and Orest Ranum, eds. *Food and Drink in History: Selections from the Annales Economies, Sociétés, Civilisations.* Translated by Elborg Forster and Patricia Ranum. Baltimore, MD: Johns Hopkins University Press, 1979.

Le Roy Ladurie, Emmanuel. *The Peasants of Languedoc.* Translated by John Day. Urbana: University of Illinois Press, 1974.

Scholliers, Peter, ed. *Food, Drink and Identity: Cooking, Eating and Drinking in Europe Since the Middle Ages.* Oxford: Berg, 2001.

CHAPTER 2

POLITICAL HISTORIES OF FOOD

ENRIQUE C. OCHOA

DESPITE decades of policies ostensibly intended to eradicate hunger, basic access to food remains highly unequal in the new millennium. Skyrocketing food prices between 2006 and 2008 increased the number of undernourished people in the world by 75 million people and drove an estimated 125 million people into extreme poverty, leading to widespread food riots.[1] In the most extreme cases, such as in Haiti, where 80 percent of the population subsist on less than two dollars a day, price increases led to a hunger so torturous that people reportedly called it Clorox hunger since they "felt like their stomachs were being eaten away by bleach or battery acid."[2]

Scholars and policy analysts differ sharply on the extent of hunger and malnutrition and on its causes and solutions. While a billion people remain malnourished, some scholars maintain that increased food production has alleviated bouts of famine over the past few centuries and that there has been a decline in the overall share of the population without access to sufficient food. Others argue that although production has increased, market policies and structural inequalities have hampered efforts to eradicate hunger and have even increased the absolute numbers of the chronically undernourished. Indeed, many analysts contend that homogeneous development policies foster a global food economy dominated by corporate interests that erase traditional ways of knowing and ways of life. Nevertheless, recent scholarly analysis has shown foodways to be an important vehicle for resisting these homogenizing trends and creating alternative and more egalitarian systems for producing and distributing food.

This essay seeks to disentangle these debates and examine the assumptions and ideologies behind the politics of food over the past few centuries. Central to this discussion is an analysis of power relations shaped by shifting capitalist developmental policies and by various state and international institutions. Food policies, based on particular assumptions and worldviews, have sought to create hegemonic visions for societies that shape what food is grown and who grows it, what is exported or imported, who has access to foods. By examining how these factors change over time and drawing from the large bodies of scholarly research on the topic, this chapter hopes to show how producers, consumers, activists, and scholars are challenging the dominant narratives of food and society and articulating a range of alternatives.

Food, Capitalism, and Colonialism

Since the late fifteenth century, European colonial expansion and the development of capitalism sought to reshape world diets and the relationship of humans to the land. Imperial powers introduced sweeping ecological changes in their efforts to capture the wealth of overseas colonies, while at the same time seeking to transform these societies into replicas of Europe. To obtain plantation labor, empires carried out vast population movements, most notably through the Atlantic slave trade. Europeans ultimately created elaborate commodity chains to feed themselves on the agricultural wealth of the entire world. These new systems of provisioning also entailed fundamental changes in the nature of foods, forcing consumers to adapt their tastes as well. Yet despite the efforts of colonial and capitalist powers to shape global diet, workers proved ingenious at adapting their foodways to changing conditions.

In his path-breaking book *The Columbian Exchange* (1972), Alfred Crosby demonstrated the vast plant and animal exchange that occurred as a result of European colonization of the Americas beginning in 1492. The genocidal death of indigenous peoples, approximately 85 percent within the first hundred years of contact, initiated the process of European domination of land, labor, and culture of the Americas. Europeans began to appropriate and export many food items from the Americas at the same time they introduced foods to the Americas for their own comfort and commerce.[3] The spread of highly productive "new world" maize and potatoes spurred demographic growth and trade around the world. Maize became a staple food for the millions of Africans enslaved between the sixteenth and nineteenth centuries, while in southern Europe and wide stretches of Asia it provided subsistence for the lower classes working marginal land. The Columbian exchange of plants and animals had variable effects on existing social relations. Some scholars argue that new crops such as potatoes in Ireland or maize in the Balkans allowed colonial landlords to monopolize the best fields for commercial production, while others emphasize the revolutionary potential of new rotations for subjugated peasants, who could use subsistence production to break free from oppressive demands, for example, in the mountains of Greece and the floodplains of Venice. Nevertheless, when maize was consumed globally without the local knowledge of Mesoamerican alkaline processing, it became closely associated with the vitamin-deficiency disease pellagra.[4]

The movement of peoples, as well as plants and animals, were essential for the development of colonial and capitalist food systems. Sidney Mintz's classic analysis of the development of the world sugar market illustrates the ways that more than ten million Africans were forcibly incorporated into a global capitalist economy dedicated to the production of food for European consumers. Mintz challenges views of slavery as a premodern labor system antithetical to capitalism by noting that the tight organization of slave tasks anticipated European factory systems and also set patterns for the control of contemporary migrant farm labor.[5] Yet even under the dehumanizing oppression of the Atlantic plantation system, slaves maintained a measure of autonomy and control over their own foodways. The notable work of Judith Carney has emphasized how African traditional knowledge and plants traveled with women and men during the slave trade and have had significant impact in preserving and transforming African foodways in the Americas.[6]

Over time, global commodity chains institutionalized the inequalities of a capitalist, colonial food system, in the process transforming what constitutes food. Mintz was one of the first to examine how a particular food, sugar, was tied into networks of production, consumption, and power, and his methodological approach utilized the emerging world systems analysis as a way to explore the macroscopic impact of Western imperialist expansion on communities and cultures across the globe.[7] Recent scholarship has expanded on this theme, showing how local societies have increasingly been absorbed into a world economy dominated by larger capitalist powers and global corporate interests that have had the power to transform and define food. During the nineteenth century, for example, large milling and transporting firms such as Archer Daniels Midland and Cargill used horizontal and vertical integration strategies to achieve oligopolistic domination of grain markets around the world.[8] Moreover, Harriet Friedmann and Philip McMichael argue that growing power of capital in Europe and the United States created a close relationship between the agricultural and industrial sectors.[9] Steven Topik and Allen Wells have called this process the "second conquest of Latin America."[10]

The resulting transformation of traditional agrarian regimes often violently disturbed local communities and ecologies. Independently, Mike Davis and Richard Tucker have demonstrated the ecological impact on capitalist expansion during this period.[11] Davis boldly argues that the growth of capitalist markets can be linked to massive famines beginning in the late nineteenth century in colonial societies ranging from India to Brazil. Transnational companies worked with imperial powers and local elites to enclose community lands, topple nationalist governments that opposed them, wage war against indigenous populations, and drive massive outmigration, all for their own profits and to supply cheap food to consumers in Europe and North America.

The boom in world markets also required the transformation of consumer tastes in the global north. The United Fruit Company created consumer demand in the United States for bananas, which had only been introduced in the late nineteenth century as an exotic fruit. By the early 1920s, through intensive marketing aimed at housewives, tropical fruits became a staple of many households. Images of backward yet exotic lands were constructed for the imperial imaginary. As Gary Okihiro has argued, Dole and other pineapple producers created an advertising campaign "capitalizing upon Hawai'i's carefully crafted image of a lush, tropical paradise," while at the same time obscuring the working and laboring conditions on the plantations.[12] The difficult struggles of life on these plantations, called a "green prison" by one novelist, have been amply documented.[13] Nevertheless, scholars have begun to demonstrate how workers also transformed the social and cultural landscape. For example, according to Patricia Vega Jiménez, UFCO imported rice and beans for its West Indian workers, thereby transplanting Jamaican rice and beans as a Costa Rican national dish, *gallo pinto* ("spotted rooster").[14]

The rise of industrial food processing in the late nineteenth and early twentieth centuries sparked battles between reformers, workers, capitalists, and government modernizers, particularly in the case of meatpacking. Scholars have examined these struggles from a number of perspectives; business histories have tended to focus on the rise of oligopolies in the industry, while labor historians have emphasized the struggle over the transformation of labor conditions from artisanal to industrial labor.[15] Recent studies have addressed issues of public health and consumer taste to provide a more integrated understanding of the process of culinary modernization.[16] These scholars, influenced by cultural approaches to history, have entered into the discussion and in the process have demonstrated "how market culture is grounded in social processes that shape and are shaped by particular claims of healthfulness, necessity, and what is just, if not democratic. Market culture highlights how consumer expectations vary depending on particular goods and services."[17]

Recent scholarship has underscored the role of scientific approaches to food and nutrition. Scholars of gender have demonstrated the ways that the rise of nutritional science and advertising has played an important role in transforming diets and mechanizing food production. Wilbur Atwater's 1896 discovery of a process for measuring food intake and labor output in units of thermal energy (calories) set in motion a new way for thinking about food and the body.[18] Nutritional sciences was often used in the Global South as a reason to eliminate traditional diets, as Jeffrey Pilcher has shown in the case of Mexico.[19] Along with this conceptual revolution of nutrition came new economic understandings of food markets that sought to rationalize distribution but at the expense of food security.

Food Shortages, Famines, and Political Legitimacy

Since the rise of the archaic state, political legitimacy has depended in large measure on the ability of rulers to ensure that their subjects were fed. This belief underlay the "Mandate of Heaven" in China and the massive imports of grain from Egypt to Imperial Rome. In Medieval Europe, merchants had a religious obligation to sell food for a "just price" during times of shortage. As E. P. Thompson famously showed, with the rise of capitalism in the eighteenth century, this "moral economy" was replaced by a "political economy" in which prices were believed to move according to natural laws and government interference was condemned as counterproductive.[20] Only recently have economists begun to put the politics back into political economy by shifting their focus from production to distribution and showing how access to food is inherently political.

In an important new synthesis, economic historian Cormac Ó Gráda describes the magnitude of major documented famines ranging from 1.5 million deaths during a French famine of 1693–1694 to a series of droughts in China in 1877, 1927, and 1959 that left millions dead, and several more recent and smaller-scale famines in various parts of Africa during the twentieth century. He observes that major famines entail "rising prices, food riots, an increase in crimes against property, a significant number of actual or imminent deaths from starvation, a rise in temporary migration, and frequently the fear and emergence of famine-induced infectious diseases."[21]

Among the first major treatises on famine and by far the most influential was Thomas Malthus's 1798 treatise *An Essay on the Principle of Population*. Malthus's study built on several earlier attempts to chronicle major famines in the context of population growth.[22] However, he alerted people to the importance of demography and argued that population grew in geometrical proportions whereas food production grew at a much slower rate. For Malthus, famines and mass hunger were deemed to be ultimate checks on population growth and were part of a natural cycle. While Malthus had many critics, his analysis dominated discussion of famines for centuries and is still often accepted as conventional wisdom. As a result, the British government failed to act decisively during the Great Famine in Ireland, allowing food exports from the island to continue even as half a million starved to death. The narrative of inevitable hunger has continued to be influential among neo-Malthusians.[23]

A major shift in the scholarly analysis of famines and policy came with the work of the Nobel laureate economist Amartya Sen. In his now classic *Poverty and Famines: An Essay on Entitlement Deprivation* (1981), Sen used the cases of the Bengal famine of 1942–1944, Ethiopian famines of 1973–1975, famines in the Sahel region of African in the 1970s, and the Bangladesh famine of 1974 to substantially revise our understanding of the causes and consequences of famine.

For Sen, starvation "is not the characteristic of there being not enough food to eat," but instead has more to do with access to resources that can provide food. Thus, Sen works to decouple population and food supply because "the mesmerizing simplicity of focusing on the ratio of food to population has persistently played an obscuring role over centuries, and continues to plague policy discussions today much as it has deranged anti-famine policies in the past."[24] Instead, Sen proposes an entitlements approach to understanding the relationship between food distribution and the legal structures of a society, including access to land, social security, and job opportunities. By exploring these larger relationships, Sen demonstrates how democratic nations such as post-Independence India succeeded in ending starvation even without dramatic rises in food supply.

Sen's analysis has been corroborated and bolstered by subsequent interdisciplinary studies that take seriously the role of the peasantry within the larger political economy.[25] Recently, Thomas Bassett and Alex Winter-Nelson have demonstrated that traditional measures of food availability are misleading, since in many countries malnutrition and food abundance exist side by side. To better understand the inequalities of food distribution within societies, they have constructed a Hunger Vulnerability Index using measures of food supply, household income, and individual nutrition indicators. This index allows more precise measurement of the vulnerability to hunger within countries.[26]

Food and Nation-States, 1930–1970s

The Great Depression of the 1930s brought the capitalist system and free markets to their knees and redirected the role of the state in capitalist countries. Many governments sought to control the vagaries of the market by actively intervening in the marketplace. Whether under capitalism, communism, or fascism, market regulations attempted to balance the interests of diverse sectors of the population. James Scott's concept of high modernism is useful for understanding the ways that states seek to create order and manage natural resources efficiently, regardless of political ideology. Scott sees high modernism as "a muscle bound version of the self-confidence about scientific and technical progress, the expansion of production, the growing satisfaction of human needs, the mastery of nature, and above all the rational design of social order commensurate with the scientific understanding of natural laws."[27] Such an approach influenced a range of governments in their efforts to consolidate their power in the state-building process.

In capitalist countries, the growth of state intervention and cooperation with business often bolstered the capitalist state and specific sectors of the capitalist classes. In the United States, New Deal agricultural price supports and production controls became key elements of food supply management policies beginning in the 1930s. According to Bill Winders, regional farm coalitions secured such favorable policies despite the lobbying of other sectors that pointed out that they contradicted free market rhetoric.[28] In addition, as the work of Tracey Deutsch shows, grassroots consumer activism began to be undermined as "officials grew skeptical of democratic controls on consumption and moved toward tighter alliances with large, centrally controlled stores that could better administer government policy."[29] Thus, government support for emerging supermarket chains came at the expense of smaller stores and consumer cooperatives, partly owing to a distrust of women's organizations.

Similar efforts to manage supply in other nations led to aggressive marketing policies using many of the same tools as the United States, with twists depending on different historical contexts. For example, the fascist regime of Benito Mussolini sought to achieve self-sufficiency in food supplies, although its campaign to increase basic grain production actually undermined the quality and diversity of the Italian diet.[30] The Mexican government maintained a rhetoric of land reform, but gave priority to urbanization and industrialization, a contradictory attitude that led to policies favoring large producers and subsidized urban supplies at the expense of the incomes and subsistence of small farmers.[31] In Argentina, beef supplies to urban workers provided an important bulwark of the populist government of Juan Perón. Playing on the masculine associations of beef in Argentine popular culture, the regime created an entitlement to beef for working-class constituents, known as *descamisados* (shirtless ones), although the populist policies backfired when droughts devastated the livestock industry around 1950.[32] Many African governments held a similar urban bias in the post-Independence era, thereby benefiting powerful political interests at the expense of the agricultural sector and producers.[33] Yet in Tanzania, rural communities found ways of taking advantage of these policies, at least for a time.[34]

Socialist economies asserted even harsher controls over the countryside in order to speed the transition from the market production to socialist collectivization. The Soviet Union shared with capitalist countries a push to industrialization and discourses of rationality that denigrated peasant agriculture and ways of life as backward. Rapid collectivization of rural lands under Stalin, beginning in 1929, led to the expulsion of hundreds of thousands of better-off peasants and an effort to create large-scale state farms to take advantage of economies of scale and support Soviet industrialization. Millions died in the famines that accompanied collectivization, particularly in the Ukraine and other rich farming regions.[35] Unlike Lenin and Stalin, the Chinese Revolution led by Mao Zedong embraced the peasant as a revolutionary force within society. Nevertheless, the utopian idealism of the Great Leap Forward and the distrust of technical experts produced widespread ecological devastation and famines that surpassed those of Russia.[36] The revolutionary governments of Cuba and Nicaragua learned from these previous mistakes and sought to ensure adequate nutrition while struggling to strike a balance between the countryside and the city.[37]

The so-called Green Revolution marks a high-water point in the high modernist project whereby capitalist powers and multilateral agencies, working under the guise of modernization theory, encouraged developing nations to boost agricultural output by adopting modern technology and capitalist investment. Developed in the early 1940s by scientists from the Rockefeller Foundation, the U.S. Department of Agriculture, and the Mexican government, this project sought to boost yields of basic crops through plant breeding, chemical fertilizers, and pesticides. Crop yields in large private agriculture increased, at the expense of smaller peasant farmers, and the project was quickly exported to crucial Cold War allies around the world, including Turkey, India, and the Philippines. Nevertheless, as Nick Cullather has recently shown, the supposed productivity gains of the Green Revolution were largely a myth, built on earlier plant breeding programs and intended more to change peasant mentalities than to increase agricultural yields.[38]

Corporate Globalization and Food Politics, 1970s–2000s

With the rise of neoliberal policies, beginning in the late 1960s and early 1970s, there has been a sharp transformation of the global food system. While many economists and pundits argued that the liberalization of agricultural markets offered a rational, scientific approach toward economic development, the political ramifications of radical market-oriented policies have clear winners and losers, dropping all pretenses of social welfare in food policy. Liberal markets have increased production in some areas but at the expense of exacerbated inequality. In this social transformation, producers and consumers in many areas have struggled to find spaces to articulate alternative and more inclusive production models.

Neoliberal economic policies, advocated for radical deregulation of markets and deep cuts in social spending, accelerated the transformation of the countryside and relations of production. Such policies were pursued by governments in a number of countries, ranging from General Augusto Pinochet in Chile to Ronald Reagan in the United States, Margaret Thatcher in the United Kingdom and Deng Xiaopeng in China. Debt crises and oil shocks in the early 1980s spread these policies through much of the Third World as the International Monetary Fund (IMF) conditioned loans on neoliberal "structural adjustment policies." The World Trade Organization meanwhile implemented a system of trade liberalization, spurring a radical restructuring and demise of national regulatory systems in the latter half of the twentieth century.[39] For example, in Japan and South Korea, where postwar democratic governments sought to protect small farmers, a liberalization of rice prices has undermined the social bases of the countryside.[40] In general, there has been decline in basic food production in many areas of the world as staple grains were increasingly produced in a few countries in the Global North. At the same time, food crops in the Global South have often been substituted by animal feed, thereby shifting production away from human subsistence to meat and dairy production for consumers in affluent regions.[41]

The recent transformation in food economies has led to further concentration of agricultural markets by a few large companies on a global scale. University of Missouri rural sociologists William Heffernan and Mary Hendrickson have analyzed the rapidity with which oligopolistic firms have gained control of agricultural markets in the United States since the 1970s.[42] Meanwhile, Selma Tonzalini has demonstrated the growing market power of the world's largest multinational food processing firms.[43] Supermarkets have likewise been part of the multinational consolidation process, as Thomas Reardon and Peter Timmer have documented. Such chains achieved very high densities in relatively affluent parts of South America and East Asia in the 1990s, moved on to the middle-class regions of countries such as Mexico, Bulgaria, and Indonesia, and achieved slight penetration in a few areas of Africa, as well as Nicaragua and Peru. Much of Africa, however, has yet to see the growth of supermarkets.[44] The rise of global supermarkets has been dominated by just a few firms based in the Global North, most notably Wal-Mart, which has nearly four times the sales of its nearest rival, the French giant Carrefour.[45] Wal-Mart led the discounting revolution, spurring globalization and demanding low-cost labor at all stages of production.[46] The vertical integration and global reach of multinational supermarkets has thus transformed the global food chain and restructured relationships with producers.[47]

Consumers have also been drawn into the global food chain through the development of sophisticated marketing techniques. Marion Nestle has demonstrated how the political power of the U.S. food industry has been used to subvert scientific nutritional research and advice, thus weakening government oversight.[48] Other research has demonstrated how this occurs in the current global food industry, since "the products most frequently promoted tend to be the highly processed food introduced through FDI [foreign direct investment]. The evidence shows that such advertising influences dietary habits among children."[49]

The neoliberal transformation of global food systems has resulted not only from the market power of large firms but also from the political governance of new technologies. For decades, international property law has ensured that seed companies can profit from the germplasm of commercial varieties but has treated peasant landraces as a natural resource with no economic value, although patentable varieties depend on access to the biodiversity created by the knowledge and labor of peasant farmers and indigenous peoples. Together with the Bayh-Dole Act of 1980, which helped extend U.S. patent protection to living organisms, these legal regimes became the basis for the industrial production of genetically modified organisms (GMOs). By the 1990s, research foundations and scientists heralded a Second Green Revolution of biotechnological innovations and genetic engineering in the name of solving world hunger and malnutrition.[50]

The use of GM foods has met with widespread suspicion and often vociferous opposition by large numbers of both consumers and producers. Particularly in Europe, consumers have successfully organized to block the sale of GMO foods, arguing that the potential risks to health and the environment have not been adequately studied.[51] Meanwhile, many rural analysts and advocates argue that the problem of world hunger is not about supply but is primarily about distribution and land and income inequality, therefore emphasis on increasing output is misplaced and not really about the eradication of hunger and malnutrition.[52] Others point to how a handful of companies have come to control the food supply and in the process have further disadvantaged small-scale producers by allowing Monsanto, Aventis, and a few other seed companies and other middlemen to reap the benefit. Although farmers are supposedly the beneficiaries of new technologies, they must purchase new seeds each year because of restrictions on replanting, including both contractual obligations and so-called "terminator technologies" that prevent seeds from germinating. In a recent volume on the impact of the biotechnology revolution in Latin American, the contributors demonstrate how the biotechnology transformations coincide with the sharp neoliberal restructuring to increase the power of a handful of powerful corporations while doing little to address the unequal distribution and malnutrition.[53] In fact, several scholars underscore the ethnocentric attitudes in assuming U.S. and European approaches are "not only superior but also universally applicable," essentially ignoring the social, cultural, economic, and political contexts of individual societies.[54]

Debates about the value of agricultural modernization cut across the contemporary North-South political divide. Many intellectuals and policymakers denounce critiques of biotechnology as a luxury of wealthy consumers in the North. For example Professor Jennifer Thomson of the University of Cape Town, South Africa, argues: "From the perspectives of many developing and newly industrialized countries, agriculture biotechology's benefits are very real and urgently needed today and indispensible tomorrow. The developing world cannot afford to let Europe's homemade problems negatively impact the future growth in our countries."[55] Proponents of neoliberal and biotechnology revolution argue that such policies are aimed to expand markets, circumvent bureaucratic and cultural obstacles to production, and improve the lot of small farmers and poor consumers. Critics counter that agrarian transformation has undermined traditional producers and national food sovereignty, squeezing some of the poorest populations on earth, transforming communities, spurring migration, and leaving once-productive lands fallow or cultivated by export crops. Miguel Teubal has suggested that Argentina in the course of a few years has gone from "breadbasket of the world to the soybeans republic."[56] Nobel Peace Prize winner Wangari Maathai argues that "biotechnology and patenting of life forms is now the new frontier for conquest, and Africa ought to be wary because a history of colonialism and exploitation is repeating itself."[57]

Low-paid migrant farm workers and service employees have also become essential for transnational commodity chains. Globalized production divides workers in border-crossing industries and leads to a general deskilling of agricultural and agro-industrial jobs. Displaced rural populations in the Global South have been actively recruited to work as low-wage seasonal hands on large-scale farms and in agro-industrial enterprises such as meatpacking and cannery plants. Employers have fomented divisions of race, class, gender, and region to divide workers and to alienate producers from consumers.[58] For example, Deborah Barndt and her colleagues have studied women, work, and globalization in the North American "tomato trail," a commodity chain linking women who work as migratory field hands in Mexico and as supermarket and fast food restaurant clerks in Canada. They have found that although "flexible" labor systems have impoverished both groups of women, there are limits on the ability to organize workers across national, cultural, and class lines.[59]

Just as the "enlightened" market reforms of the eighteenth century led to a wave of food riots, contemporary neoliberal policies have inspired food riots and austerity protests throughout the world. For the years 1976 to 1992 alone, John Walton and David Seddon have documented at least 146 austerity protests, large-scale collective actions against structural adjustment policies imposed by the IMF. These authors observe that "the food riot as a means of popular protest is a common, perhaps even universal, feature of market societies—less a vestige of political-industrial evolution than a strategy of empowerment in which poor and dispossessed groups assert their claims to social justice."[60] Indeed, the orderly nature and theatrical quality of many contemporary food riots illustrates a widespread popular understanding of Amartya Sen's dictum that hunger results not from food shortages but rather from unequal distribution policies that leave particular social groups vulnerable.

Struggles for Food Sovereignty: Alternatives to Corporate Food Politics

While rural producers and communities have been struggling for survival for centuries, in the last few decades growing movements valorizing local production, local ways of production, and local control over decision making have emerged. Given that many of these global movements started from local struggles and have evolved with local conditions on principles of sovereignty and sometimes autonomy, this is a varied movement that shares some basic principles but has numerous permutations and organizing strategies. In general, these strategies have sought to create food sovereignty for communities by using available resources to produce food for local consumption while respecting nature and community values and traditions. The common struggle against the top-down globalization of corporations, neoliberal governments, and multilateral organizations such as the WTO and IMF has united diverse groups of farmers, peasants, consumers, and activists to forge a bottom-up globalization of resistance.

One of the opening salvos in this war came on January 1, 1994, when an uprising of indigenous peoples under the banner of the Zapatista Army of National Liberation (EZLN) brought into public view the long-hidden struggles of rural populations marginalized by the world economic system. Timed to coincide with the implementation of the North American Free Trade Agreement, the EZLN's cry of *Basta!* (Enough!) was directly aimed at the juggernaut of global capital and its march to destroy what was left of indigenous communities.[61] Scholars have subsequently confirmed the EZLN prediction that NAFTA would be a death blow to small maize farmers unable to compete against subsidized maize from the United States. The Zapatista uprising directly challenged the view that food crops are just another interchangeable commodity and instead made the case that maize was a way of life and central to the identity of millions of people.[62] They called for an end to the totalizing worldview of globalization from above and demanded a "world where all worlds fit." Their aggressive use of the Internet to publicize their struggle and to forge solidarity with peoples in resistance throughout the globe gained global attention.

Another rural movement that challenged traditional agrarian relations and confronted neoliberal visions for the countryside has been Brazil's Landless Workers Movement (Movemento Sem Terra, MST). Established in 1984, the MST uses direct action to challenge Brazil's highly unequal land holding patterns and blistering social inequality. Workers organize collectively and plan their own strategy for occupying lands and building communities. Under the banner of "occupy, resist, and produce," participants democratically construct their own lives to grow their own food, establish their own schools, and govern their own communities.[63] During the first twenty years of its existence, the MST has occupied and settled 350,000 families on 10 million hectares of land throughout Brazil.[64]

In 1993, diverse nation-based rural social movements united to form an international organization, Vía Campesina, to resist neoliberal policies against the peasantry and to advance global justice and democracy. A decade after its founding, Vía Campesina comprised 149 organizations from 56 countries.[65] Central to its organizing principles is the articulation of food sovereignty: "the right of the peoples to define their own food and agriculture; to protect and regulate domestic agricultural production and trade in order to achieve sustainable development objectives; to determine the extent to which they want to be self-reliant."[66] While not inherently opposed to trade, this approach allows producers to determine their methods of farming and ways of life, explicitly democratizing daily life and putting trade and technology at the service of communities.

The growing agroecology movement seeks to achieve a sustainable agriculture by using indigenous knowledge of farmers such as those in the Vía Campesina network together with scientific advances of ecology. Drawing from thousands of years of agricultural history,[67] the science of agroecology takes a holistic and thus more environmentally and socially sensitive approach to ensure the health of food, land, and community. As one of its leading proponents has argued, "new agro-ecological approaches and technologies spearheaded by farmers, NGOs, and some local governments around the world are already making a sufficient contribution to food security at the household, national, and regional levels."[68] Indian physicist Vandana Shiva has called for viewing "the planet as a commons," instead of seeing it as "private property." In contrast to short-sighted globalization, she argues, "communities are resolutely defending and evolving living communities that protect life on earth and promote creativity." [69]

In seeking to create humane and inclusive societies without hierarchies, food sovereignty or earth democracy approaches have sought to directly place women at the heart of the food sovereignty movement. Women in Vía Campesina have demanded from its inception, "the right to produce our own food in our own territory."[70]

While food sovereignty movements have emerged in the Global South, they also have firm roots in Europe and the United States. French famer and activist José Bové burst onto the international scene through his high-profile destruction of a McDonald's restaurant in southwest France in 1999 to protest U.S. trade barriers on Roquefort cheese.[71] European consumers have been in the forefront of the anti-GMO movement and have led boycotts that have pressured European governments to ban GMO products. Guerrilla gardening efforts have taken off in European and North American cities as local food begins to gain ground. The Fair Trade Movement is meanwhile struggling to break down the walls between consumers and producers that have been carefully erected by years of capitalist policies. These various movements are fostering a greater awareness on the true costs of inexpensive foodstuffs and their economic and cultural impacts.[72]

Conclusion

Foodways have been historically and continue to be a hotly contested subject today. Although the development of capitalist relations of production in the food and agriculture sectors increased production, it also sharply transformed what food is and who has access to it. Moreover, the use of statecraft to rationalize food systems, often a product of class and regional struggles, has tended to yield unequal benefits to urban populations, often consciously at the expense of rural producers and traditional ways of life. Currently famine seems to have been significantly reduced in most areas of the world, but chronic hunger and malnutrition still abound. Nevertheless, resistance and popular movements have succeeded at forging spaces to adapt to changing situations in ways that have led traditional foodways to persist in new forms. Globalization from below and the formation of transnational networks of producers and consumers, such as Vía Campesina and the anti-GMO movement, have heightened awareness of the social and cultural impact of development policies driven by corporate interests and multilateral institutions of the global north. This struggle has underscored the wide range of alternative forms of production and foodways that have survived and thrive even in the face of daunting political and economic constraints.

NOTES

1. United Nations, *World Economic Situation and Prospects 2009* (New York: United Nations, 2008), 8; Walden Bello, *The Food Wars* (London: Verso Books, 2009), 1–3.

2. Bello, *The Food Wars*, 3.

3. Alfred W. Crosby, Jr., *The Columbian Exchange: Biological and Cultural Consequences of 1492* (Westport, CT: Greenwood Press, 1972).

4. Arturo Warman, *Corn and Capitalism: How A Botanical Bastard Grew to Global Dominance*, trans. Nancy L. Westrate (Chapel Hill: University of North Carolina Press, 2003); James C. McCann, *Maize and Grace: Africa's Encounter with a New World Crop, 1500–2000* (Cambridge, MA: Harvard University Press, 2005); William H. McNeill, "American Food Crops in the Old World," in *Seeds of Change: A Quincentennial Commemoration*, ed. Herman J. Viola and Carolyn Margolis (Washington, DC: Smithsonian Institution Press, 1991), 43–59; Alfred Jay Bollett, "Politics and Pellagra: The Epidemic of Pellagra in the U.S. in the Early Twentieth Century," *The Yale Journal of Biology and Medicine* 26 (1992): 211–21.

5. Sidney W. Mintz, *Sweetness and Power: The Place of Sugar in Modern World History* (New York: Viking Books, 1985).

6. Judith Carney, *Black Rice: The African Origins of Rice Cultivation in the Americas* (Cambridge, MA: Harvard University Press, 2010); idem, "'With Grains in Her Hair': Rice History and Memory in Colonial Brazil," *Slavery and Abolition* 25, no. 1 (2004): 1–27; idem, with Richard Nicholas Rosomoff, *In the Shadow of Slavery: Africa's Botanical Legacy in the Atlantic World* (Berkeley: University of California Press, 2009).

7. Mintz, *Sweetness and Power.*

8. Dan Morgan, *Merchants of Grain* (New York: Viking Press, 1979).

9. Harriet Friedmann and Philip McMichael, "Agriculture and the State System: The Rise and Decline of National Agricultures, 1870 to the Present," *Sociologia Ruralis* 29, no. 2 (1989): 93–117. See also Steven Topik, Carlos Marichal and Zephyr Frank, eds., *From Silver to Cocaine: Latin American Commodity Chains and the Building of the World Economy, 1500–2000* (Durham: Duke University Press, 2006).

10. Steven C. Topik and Allen Wells, eds., *The Second Conquest of Latin America: Coffee, Henequen, and Oil during the Export Boom, 1850–1930* (Austin: University of Texas Press, 1998).

11. Mike Davis, *Late Victorian Holocausts: El Niño Famines and the Making of the Third World* (London: Verso Books, 2002); Richard P. Tucker, *Insatiable Appetites: The United States and the Ecological Degradation of the Tropical World*, rev. ed. (Lanham, MD: Rowman and Littlefield, 2007).

12. Gary Y. Okihiro, *Pineapple Culture: A History of the Tropical and Temperate Zones* (Berkeley: University of California Press, 2009), 143–44. See also Virginia Scott Jenkins, *Bananas: An American History* (Washington, DC: The Smithsonian Institute Press, 2000).

13. See Ramón Amaya Amador's 1950 novel *Prisión Verde* (El Progreso: Editorial Ramón Amaya Amador, 2003); John Soluri, *Banana Cultures: Agriculture, Consumption, and Environmental Change in Honduras and the United States* (Austin: University of Texas Press, 2005), chapter 5. See also Aviva Chomsky, *West Indian Workers and the United Fruit Company in Costa Rica, 1870–1940* (Baton Rouge: Louisiana State University Press, 1996).

14. Patricia Vega Jiménez, "*El Gallo Pinto*: Afro-Caribbean Rice and Beans Conquer the Costa Rican National Cuisine," *Food, Culture & Society* 15, no. 2 (June 2012): 223–40.

15. See, for example, Mary Yeager *Competition and Regulation: The Development of Oligopoly in the Meatpaking Industry* (Greenwich, CT: Jai Press, 1981).

16. Jeffrey M. Pilcher, *The Sausage Rebellion: Public Health, Private Enterprise, and Meat in Mexico City, 1890–1917* (Albuquerque: University of New Mexico Press, 2006); Sydney Watts, *Meat Matters: Butchers, Politics and Market Culture in Eighteenth-Century Paris* (Rochester, NY: University of Rochester Press, 2006).

17. Roger Horowitz, Jeffrey M. Pilcher and Sidney Watts, "Meat for the Multitudes: Market Culture in Paris, New York City, and Mexico City over the Long Nineteenth Century," *American Historical Review* 109, no. 4 (October 2004): 1062.

18. Nick Cullather, "The Foreign Policy of the Calorie," *American Historical Review* 112, no. 2 (April 2007): 337–64.

19. Jeffrey M. Pilcher, *¡Qué vivan los tamales! Food and the Making of Mexican Identity* (Albuquerque: University of New Mexico Press, 1998).

20. E. P. Thompson, "The Moral Economy of the English Crowd in the Eighteenth Century," *Past and Present* 50 (February 1971): 76–136.

21. Cormac Ó Gráda, *Famine: A Short History* (Princeton, NJ: Princeton University Press, 2009), 23–24.

22. Geoffrey Gilbert, introduction to Thomas Malthus, *An Essay on the Principle of Population* (Oxford: Oxford University Press, 2004), vii–xxv; Gráda, *Famine*, 8.

23. Warren Belasco, *Meals to Come: A History of the Future of Food* (Berkeley: University of California Press, 2006).

24. Amartya Sen, *Poverty and Famines: An Essay on Entitlement Deprivation* (Oxford: Oxford University Press, 1981), 1, 8.

25. Timothy M. Shaw, "Towards a Political Economy of the African Crisis: Diplomacy, Debates, and Dialectics," in *Drought and Hunger in Africa: Denying Famine a Future*, ed. Michael Glantz (Cambridge: Cambridge University Press, 1987), 127–47; Michael Watts, "Drought, Environment and Food Security: Some Reflections on Peasants, Pastoralists and Commoditization in Dryland West Africa," in ibid, 181–211.

26. Thomas J. Bassett and Alex Winter-Nelson, *The Atlas of World Hunger* (Chicago: University of Chicago Press, 2010), chapter 8.

27. James C. Scott, *Seeing Like a State: How Certain Schemes to Improve the Human Condition Have Failed* (New Haven: Yale University Press, 1998), 4.

28. Bill Winders, *The Politics of Food Supply: U.S. Agricultural Policy and the World Economy* (New Haven: Yale University Press, 2009).

29. Tracey Deutsch, *Building a Housewife's Paradise: Gender, Politics, and American Grocery Stores in the Twentieth Century* (Chapel Hill: University of North Carolina Press, 2010), 156.

30. Carol Helstosky, *Garlic and Oil: Food and Politics in Italy* (Oxford: Berg, 2004).

31. Enrique C. Ochoa, *Feeding Mexico: The Political Uses of Food Since 1910* (Wilmington, DE: Scholarly Resources, 2000).

32. Natalia Milanesio, "Food Politics and Consumption in Peronist Argentina," *Hispanic American Historical Review* 90, no. 1 (February 2010): 75–108.

33. Robert H. Bates, *Markets and States in Tropical Africa: The Political Basis of Agricultural Policies* (Berkeley: University of California Press, 1981).

34. Deborah Bryceson, *Food Insecurity and Social Division of Labor in Tanzania, 1919–1985* (New York: St. Martin's Press, 1990); idem, *Liberalizing Tanzania's Food Trade: Public and Private Faces of Urban Marketing Policy* (Geneva: United Nations Research Institute, 1993).

35. Elena Osokina, *Our Daily Bread: Socialist Distribution and the Art of Survival in Stalin's Russia, 1927–1941* (Armonk, NY: M.E. Sharpe, 1999); Scott, *Seeing Like a State*, chapter 6.

36. Judith Shapiro, *Mao's War against Nature: Politics and the Environment in Revolutionary China* (Cambridge: Cambridge University Press, 2001).

37. Medea Benjamin, Joseph Collins, and Michal Scott, *No Free Lunch: Food and Revolution in Cuba Today* (New York: Grover Press, 1984); Joseph Collins, et al, *Nicaragua: What Difference Could a Revolution Make* (San Francisco: Food First Books, 1985).

38. Nick Cullather, *The Hungry World: America's Cold War Battle Against Poverty in Asia* (Cambridge, MA: Harvard University Press, 2010).

39. Peter M. Rosset, *Food Is Different: Why We Must Get the WTO Out of Agriculture* (London: Zed Books, 2006), 20.

40. Philip McMichael and Chul-Kyoo Kim, "Japanese and South Korean Agricultural Restructuring in Comparative and Global Perspective," in *The Global Restructuring of Agro-Food Systems*, ed. Philip McMichael (Ithaca, NY: Cornell University Press, 1994), 46.

41. David Barkin, Rosemary L. Batt, and Billie R. DeWalt, *Food Crops vs. Feed Crops: Global Substitution of Grains in Production* (Boulder, CO: Lynne Reinner Publishers, 1990), 4.

42. Mary Hendrickson and William Heffernan, "Concentration of Agricultural Markets," Department of Rural Sociology, University of Missouri. [Online]. April 2007. Available: http://www.foodcircles.missouri.edu/07contable.pdf [September 8, 2010].

43. Selma Tozanli, "The Rise of Global Enterprises in the World's Food Chain," in *Multinational Agribusiness*, ed. Ruth Rama (New York: Food Products Press, 2005), 22.

44. Thomas Reardon and C. Peter Timmer, "The Rise of Supermarkets in the Global Food System," in *Globalization of Food and Agriculture and the Poor*, ed. Joachim von Braun and Eugenio Díaz-Bonilla (New Delhi: Oxford University Press, 2008), 184–213.

45. "Global Powers of Retailing 2010: Emerging from the Downturn," a report by Deloitte Touche and Tohmatsu and STORES Media. [Online]. February 2010. Available: http://www.deloitte.com/view/en_GX/global/industries/consumer-business-transportation/retail/6b79c2cd67b06210VgnVCM200000bb42f00aRCRD.htm. [September 9, 2010].

46. See Nelson Lichtenstein, *The Retail Revolution: How WAL-MART Created a Brave New World of Business* (New York: Metropolitan Books, 2009); idem, *WAL-MART: The Face of Twenty-First Century Capitalism* (New York: The New Press, 2006).

47. Reardon and Timmer, "The Rise of Supermarkets in the Global Food System," 201.

48. Marion Nestle, *Food Politics: How the Food Industry Influences Nutrition and Health* (Berkeley: University of California Press, 2002).

49. Corinna Hawkes, "Globalization of Agrifood Systems and the Nutrition Transition," in von Braun and Díaz-Bonilla, *Globalization of Food and Agriculture*, 230.

50. Per Pinstrup-Andersen and Ebbe Schiøler, *Seeds of Contention: World Hunger and the Global Controversy over GM Crops* (Baltimore, MD: The Johns Hopkins University Press, 2000); Jack Kloppenburg, *First the Seed: The Political Economy of Plant Biotechnology, 1492–2000*, 2nd ed. (Madison: University of Wisconsin Press, 2004).

51. Rachel Schurman and William A. Munro, *Fighting for the Future of Food: Activists vs. Agribusiness in the Struggle Over Biotechnology* (Minneapolis: University of Minnesota Press, 2010).

52. This position is best articulated in the work of Frances Moore Lappé, Joseph Collins, and Peter Rosset, *World Hunger: Twelve Myths*, 2nd ed. (New York: Grove Press, 1998).

53. Gerardo Otero, ed., *Food for the Few: Neoliberal Globalism and Biotechnology in Latin America* (Austin: University of Texas Press, 2008).

54. Kathy McAfee, "Exporting Crop Biotechnology: The Myth of Molecular Miracles," in ibid, 61–62.

55. Cited in Pinstrup-Andersen and Schiøler, *Seeds of Contention*, 108.

56. Miguel Teubal, "Genetically Modified Soybeans and the Crisis of Argentina's agricultural Model," in Otero, *Food for the Few*, 189–216.

57. Wangari Maathai, "The Link Between Patenting of Life Forms, Genetic Engineering and Food Insecurity," *Review of African Political Economy* 25, no. 77 (September 1998): 529–31.

58. For example of these recent transformations in the food processing industry, see Deborah Fink, *Cutting into the Meatpacking Line: Workers and Change in the Rural Midwest* (Chapel Hill: University of North Carolina Press, 1998); Steve Striffler, *Chicken: The Dangerous Transformation of America's Favorite Food* (New Haven: Yale University Press, 2005); Carolina Bank Muñoz, *Transnational Tortillas: Race, Gender, and Shop-Floor Politics in Mexico and the United States* (Ithaca, NY: Cornell University Press, 2008).

59. Deborah Barndt, *Tangled Routes: Women, Work, and Globalization on the Tomato Trail* (Lanham, MD: Rowman and Littlefield, 2002); idem, ed., *Women Working the NAFTA Food Chain: Women, Food and Globalization* (Toronto: SUMACH Press, 1999).

60. John Walton and David Seddon, *Free Markets and Food Riots: The Politics of Global Adjustment* (Oxford: Blackwell Publishers, 1994), 54.

61. "Declaración de la Selva Lacandona," January 1, 1994, reproduced in *Rebellion in Chiapas: A Historical Reader*, ed. John Womack, Jr. (New York: The New Press, 1999), 247–49.

62. Ochoa, *Feeding Mexico*; Tom Barry, *Zapata's Revenge: Free Trade and the Farm Crisis in Mexico* (Boston: South End Press, 1995).

63. Monica Dias Martins, "Learning to Participate: The MST Experience in Brazil," in *Promised Land: Competing Visions of Agrarian Reform*, ed. Peter Rosset, Raj Patel, and Michael Courville (Oakland, CA: Food First Books, 2006), 265–76; Angus Wright and Wendy Wolford, *To Inherit the Earth: The Landless Movement and the Struggle for a New Brazil* (Oakland, CA: Food First Books, 2003).

64. Bassett and Winter-Nelson, *The Atlas of World Hunger*, 80.

65. Annette Aurélie Desmarais, *La Vía Campesina: Globalization and the Power of Peasants* (London: Pluto Press, 2007), 6–7.

66. Cited in Rosset, *Food is Different*, 125–26.

67. Susan B. Hecht, "The Evolution of Agroecological Thought," in *Agroecology: The Science of Sustainable Agriculture*, ed. Miguel A. Altieri, 2nd ed. (Boulder: Westview Press, 1995), 1.

68. Miguel A. Altieri, "Agroecology, Small Farms, and Food Sovereignty," *Monthly Review* (July-August 2009): 109.

69. Vandana Shiva, *Earth Democracy: Justice, Sustainability, and Peace* (Cambridge, MA: South End Press, 2005), 2.

70. Cited in Sofia Monsalve Suárez, "Gender and Land," in Rosset, Patel, and Courville, *Promised Land*, 194; Desmarais, *La Vía Campesina*, 161–81.

71. José Bové and François Dufor, *The World is Not for Sale: Farmers Against Junk Food*, trans. Anna de Casparis (London: Verso Books, 2001).

72. Daniel Jaffee, *Brewing Justice: Fair Trade Coffee, Sustainability, and Survival* (Berkeley: University of California Press, 2007); Henry J. Frundt, *Fair Bananas: Farmers, Workers, and Consumers Strive to Change an Industry* (Tucson: University of Arizona Press, 2009).

Bibliography

Bassett, Thomas J., and Alex Winter-Nelson. *The Atlas of World Hunger.* Chicago: University of Chicago Press, 2010.

Bello, Walden. *The Food Wars.* London: Verso Books, 2009.

Cullather, Nick. *The Hungry World: America's Cold War Battle Against Poverty in Asia.* Cambridge, MA: Harvard University Press, 2010.

Deutsch, Tracey. *Building a Housewife's Paradise: Gender, Politics, and American Grocery Stores in the Twentieth Century.* Chapel Hill: University of North Carolina Press, 2010.

Friedmann, Harriet, and Philip McMichael. "Agriculture and the State System: The Rise and Decline of National Agricultures, 1870 to the Present." *Sociologia Ruralis* 29, no. 2 (1989): 93–117.

Nestle, Marion. *Food Politics: How the Food Industry Influences Nutrition and Health.* Berkeley: University of California Press, 2002.

Ochoa, Enrique C. *Feeding Mexico: The Political Uses of Food Since 1910.* Wilmington, DE: S.R. Books, 2000.

Ó Gráda, Cormac. *Famine: A Short History.* Princeton: Princeton University Press, 2009.

Schurman, Rachel, and William A. Munro. *Fighting for the Future of Food: Activists Vs. Agribusiness in the Struggle Over Biotechnology.* Minneapolis: University of Minnesota Press, 2010.

Sen, Amartya. *Poverty and Famines: An Essay on Entitlement Deprivation.* Oxford: Oxford University Press, 1981.

von Braun, Joachim, and Eugenio Díaz-Bonilla, eds. *Globalization of Food and Agriculture and the Poor.* New Delhi: Oxford University Press, 2008.

Walton, John, and David Seddon. *Free Markets and Food Riots: The Politics of Global Adjustment.* Oxford: Blackwell Publishers, 1994.

Winders, Bill. *The Politics of Food Supply: U.S. Agricultural Policy and the World Economy.* New Haven: Yale University Press, 2009.

CHAPTER 3

CULTURAL HISTORIES OF FOOD

JEFFREY M. PILCHER

THE cultural history of food might seem to be a redundant phrase, at least when defined by recent disciplinary practice. As an essential part of human life, food has appeared in historical narratives since antiquity, but as the proper subject of professional inquiry, it gained recognition only in the 1990s with the ascendancy of the "new cultural history." Nevertheless, the field of food history has continued to grow with vigor, even as the disciplinary hegemony of culture has begun to fragment and decline. Therefore, it seems an appropriate moment to reflect on the historical study of food as a cultural expression, as distinct from cultural approaches to the history of food politics, nutrition, and the like.[1] Cultural history is at the most basic level a search for meaning in the past, an attempt to understand how people have made sense of their world. In this chapter I survey the ways that historians have interpreted cuisines and explained their change over time.

Changing scholarly notions of culture have influenced the understanding of cuisine. Jack Goody harkened back to a nineteenth-century idea of cuisine as high culture—produced by male chefs, consumed in public ceremonies, and recorded in writing—to argue a comparative sociological thesis attributing culinary distinction to literate, hierarchical societies, in contrast to the simpler, more egalitarian practices of everyday foods—prepared by female cooks, eaten at home, and largely absent from the historical record.[2] Sidney Mintz, by contrast, employed a useful anthropological definition of cuisine as the culture of food within a society, encompassing material ingredients and cooking technologies, as well as shared attitudes and beliefs about what constitutes a proper, healthy, and tasty meal.[3] Priscilla Parkhurst Ferguson, following the linguistic turn, emphasized the discursive nature of cuisines as cultural codes that formalize everyday practices into stable patterns, thereby creating the basis for collective identities.[4] Informed by these approaches, I examine historical change at three connected levels: the circulation of texts, the tastes of dining, and the practices of cooking.

In researching these processes, food historians have shown distinct preferences from among the wide range of theories that inspired the new cultural history.[5] Structuralist anthropologists of the 1960s, who used semiotic analysis to search for universal mental codes, offered less direct guidance, notwithstanding their attention to culinary systems. Claude Lévi-Strauss famously observed that foods were "good to think," but ahistorical assumptions limited the usefulness of his opposition between the raw and the cooked. Mary Douglas's work on purity and pollution may also have been more of an indirect influence, by way of her anthropology of the body, than directly through her interpretation of dietary rules. Meanwhile, the materialist, historical approach of Sidney Mintz in *Sweetness and Power* (1985) gained recognition as a landmark of food history.[6]

Equally formative were the works of historical sociologists, particularly Norbert Elias, who used the history of table manners to illustrate what he called the "civilizing process" of early modern European state formation. Stephen Mennell, a student of Elias, applied this theory to explain the development of French and English cooking in *All Manners of Food* (1985).[7] Another important influence was the practice theory elaborated by Pierre Bourdieu, Michel de Certeau, and others, who explored the improvisations employed by ordinary people to manipulate power structures and achieve a measure of autonomy. By contrast, Michel Foucault, the French theorist perhaps most revered by new cultural historians, offered scant fare for food historians. Still other emerging fields, including performance studies, literacy studies, and sensory studies, deserve greater attention than they have received so far.

To give focus to this essay, I limit it primarily to works on early modern history, a period of dramatic culinary change resulting from the Columbian exchange, rising agricultural productivity and commercialization, and, in many places, increased social mobility. The transformation of taste in Europe has been well documented, both on the tables of the wealthy and with the advent of mass consumerism. Starting in France around the mid-seventeenth century, an elaborate cuisine fragrant with spices began to give way to a simplified approach that sought to highlight the flavors of individual ingredients. This nouvelle cuisine, associated with naturalist Enlightenment ideals, spread across Europe and, by way of colonialism, to elites around the world. The seemingly inexorable advance of French cuisine led some scholars to associate it with a unlinear modernity, although the dean of French food historians, Jean-Louis Flandrin, gave a more measured interpretation, emphasizing the diversity of national cuisines, even in Europe.[8] Meanwhile, a growing trade in foreign stimulants—chocolate, coffee, tea, and sugar—afforded brief moments of luxury to a wider cross section of society and created new spaces for sociability such as the "bourgeois" coffeehouse.

We know far less about global developments, but there can be little doubt that early modern societies around the world responded creatively to the opportunities and challenges of new forms of agriculture, trade, and colonialism. Fortunately, a growing number of historical works have begun to fill the gaps in our knowledge of Asia, Africa, the Americas, and the Islamic world. As a result, we can gain comparative perspective on patterns of culinary change, as well as the diversity of cultural meanings attached to food.

The Circulation of Texts

I begin with cookbooks and other culinary texts not from any assumption that they determine practices but simply out of a pragmatic consideration that they offer the most accessible source of historical evidence about change over time. The study of early modern culinary texts may well help us understand the significance of literacy, as well as the ongoing conversations between print and oral cultures. Published cookbooks and gastronomic literature derived from multiple genres, practical and artistic, and they simultaneously documented and encouraged transformations in the kitchen. While individual authors might claim distinction from their works, they also sought to build communities, both the immediate gatherings of family and neighbors and the imagined communities of nations, markets, and social movements.

The British social anthropologist Jack Goody came to his landmark study *Cooking, Cuisine, and Class* (1982) by way of an earlier interest in the "grand dichotomy" between literate and nonliterate societies. His previous book, *The Domestication of the Savage Mind* (1977), had considered writing as a technology of the intellect that enabled the development of civilized life. Prominent among the tables, lists, and formula that Goody identified as prerequisites for abstract thought were the ironically concrete genres of menus, shopping lists, and recipes. Banquet menus imposed social hierarchies, not only through the selection of dishes, but also through seating arrangements that placed high-ranking people at the head of the table. Cookbooks, in turn, allowed their owners to break free from a limited routine of local dishes to develop a wider repertoire of offerings, which ensured social distinction for the elite or mobility for the ambitious.[9]

Yet already by the 1980s, an emerging field of literacy studies had begun to question such sweeping generalizations about the supposed divide between print and oral cultures. Scholars called instead for close attention to the social contexts in which reading and writing took place, particularly within genres of functional literature that existed on the margins of formal schooling and high literature. Studies of culinary texts offer great potential contributions to this field by revealing points of communication between the seemingly separate realms of print and orality.[10]

Culinary historians, inspired largely by Flandrin, initiated this research for early modern Europe by developing a benchmark chronology of dietary change through textual analysis of cookbooks. Briefly, this periodization indicated three significant moments of publishing activity: the first around the turn of the sixteenth century, when printed volumes began to replace medieval manuscripts; a second in the mid-seventeenth century, as a set of influential texts established new culinary ideals; and a third with the mid-eighteenth-century consolidation of a specialized market in cookbooks, which prompted each new volume to assert claims of novelty. The methodologies of this culinary historical analysis included genealogies of recipes, which revealed, for example, the shift away from medieval standards already in the first published cookbooks. Culinary historians also conducted intense biographical research on prominent authors such as François Pierre, known as La Varenne, whose *Le cuisinier françois* (1651) canonized the shift from medieval artifice to modern simplicity in French cooking.[11]

Scholars have meanwhile considered the significance of print on the professionalization of cooking. Alain Girard observed in a brief but suggestive essay that printed cookbooks gradually began to undermine ties of apprenticeship and the oral transmission of knowledge. This change led not to the decline of the authority of masters but rather to their increasing recognition as artists and to greater experimentation and innovation in elite kitchens.[12] Stephen Mennell has extended this argument through his connected comparison of French and English publishing traditions. Whereas French volumes were produced by and for male professionals, English cookbooks were often written by women for country housewives, who resisted many of the innovations of French cuisine.[13]

The emergence of modern European cuisines and of a distinctive genre of cookbooks depended on a growing separation between cuisine and medicine. Galenic humoral medicine inherited from the ancient world considered foods, especially spices, essential to the humoral balance needed to maintain health. Indeed, Flandrin has argued that the decline of humoral medicine allowed a more aesthetic approach to cookery, unhindered by conservative notions of health.[14] Elizabeth Spiller has meanwhile examined traditions of knowledge within early modern print culture to understand the migration of recipes from "books of secrets" associated with mechanical arts into specialized works dedicated to cookery. She concludes that the resurgence of English cookbooks in the mid-seventeenth century depended not on borrowings from La Varenne but rather on the breakdown of royal control over medical treatment enshrined by the *Pharmacopoea Londoninses*, a regulatory manual that, when translated into English in 1649, encouraged the proliferation of all manner of instrumental texts.[15]

Another important literary context for early English cookbooks was the domestic manuscript, a common possession of well-to-do families that was passed from one generation to the next. Each successive owner added to the text with new recipes and annotations reflecting their experiences with existing recipes. As Sandra Sherman has shown, these open-ended documents formed extensions of oral communities, carrying on conversations across generations. By contrast, published cookbooks operated in the imagined community of the literary marketplace, and authors tried at first to break radically with oral traditions. Yet even as they claimed authority based on professional experience as chefs, they often unconsciously retained the assumptions of an apprenticeship model. Thus, Robert May's 1660 recipe "To roast a hen" provided detailed instructions for garnishing the finished bird but neglected to explain how to roast it in the first place. As the print market grew more competitive in the eighteenth century, such oversights were quickly denounced by rival volumes. Authors learned to mimic the immediacy of oral communities to gain a loyal readership. By analyzing these textual strategies and literary contexts, Sherman offers historical insights on the genre's development in England.[16]

By the early nineteenth century, gastronomic literature had emerged in France as yet another literary market, offering guides not only to production but also to the consumption of foods in a culinary field defined by a nascent social institution, the restaurant. Priscilla Ferguson has explored the growth of this literature using Bourdieu's theory of the cultural field, showing how chefs, food critics, novelists, and essayists sought to indoctrinate a rising middle class into the dictates of a formerly aristocratic cuisine. This literature served not only to bolster the professional standing of its authors but also to consolidate a French national identity, defining the nation around Parisian standards and incorporating the rest of the world according to its hegemonic dictates.[17]

Yet culinary literature could inspire not only the imagined communities of nations and markets but also very different forms of fantasy. Eric Rath has demonstrated in his work on early modern Japan that food could embody beauty, morality, and emotion, even when it was not intended for human consumption. Elite banquets of the Tokugawa era often began with "knife ceremonies," elaborate, inedible food sculptures of carved fish and fowl, which set the tone for the meal and aroused the diners' curiosity more than their appetites. Cookbooks, formerly "secret" manuscripts passed between chefs, gained a wider audience with the seventeenth-century growth of popular publishing in Japan. These works conveyed model banquets, recipes, and advice on table manners, and although most consumers could not hope to actually eat these elaborate feasts, their descriptions became a medium for aesthetic contemplation.[18]

Chinese gastronomic literature also inspired the imagination, although in very different ways, helping to situate local cultures within an imperial geography of taste. Mark Swislocki has emphasized the importance of culinary nostalgia in shaping attitudes about the local and the universal in Chinese culture. As in Japan, notable foods such as the honey nectar peach of Shanghai offered a focus for aesthetic appreciation. But these foods also functioned as points of pride for boosters within a hierarchy of gazetteers and other print culture, which began at the local level and could gain recognition and wider circulation by authors writing for regional and even imperial audiences. These works sought to affirm the distinctiveness of Chinese agriculture and taste.[19]

Scholars have also paid attention to societies where gastronomic and culinary literature did not develop, despite deep cultural interest in food. Arjun Appadurai has puzzled over the neglect of such writings in India; he concluded that food carried too much moral and religious freight for a culture of pleasure to develop before the emergence of an Anglicized, postcolonial, middle-class culture. Colonial Latin American writers likewise published little on food and cooking, perhaps because of the ambivalence of social hierarchies between Spaniards and Indians. Native foods and culture were frowned upon by the Hispanic elite, and yet they nevertheless intruded into elite culture, at least on the margins of everyday life, for example, through the indulgence of street foods. Culinary literature clearly passes through periods of growth and decline; for example, medieval Arabic societies produced lavish cookbooks, yet such literary production declined during the early modern Ottoman Empire. Özge Samanci has attributed the nineteenth-century resurgence of Ottoman cookbooks to a form of cultural competition with European imperial powers.[20]

Notwithstanding such national and imperial aspirations, most cookbook authors and users were likely concerned with more immediate and mundane objectives and communities, for example, making dinner for family and friends. Yet these texts and communities were nevertheless significant in the lives of women, as literary scholars have ably demonstrated. Susan Leonardi conceived of recipes as embedded discourses that served to reproduce social networks within gendered communities. By examining the framing around recipes and the intertextual conversations between them, she was able to interpret the cultural values that bonded women. Barbara Kirschenblatt-Gimblett has discussed the politics of food within Jewish charitable community cookbooks, which varied greatly between reform and conservative congregations. Anne Bower and the contributors to her edited volume on community cookbooks further elaborated this point, showing how such seemingly formulaic works could develop the basic elements of literature: setting, character, plot, and theme. Finally, Janet Theophano explored the cookbook as female autobiography, and the ways these volumes served as archives of domesticity.[21]

The process of archiving also held out the potential for excluding individuals and groups from the historical memory of a community. The work of African American cooks, in particular, has been rendered invisible in the construction of Southern cuisine. White cookbook authors often gave lip service to the labor of their cooks, but in the fashion of Aunt Jemima, they depicted it not as a form of artistry but rather as the product of a primitive oral culture, thus heightening the contrast with the sophisticated elite. In a similar fashion, Judith Carney has described how historians have written skilled black labor out of accounts of South Carolina rice production.[22]

Historical memory also lay at the heart of an innovative recent investigation by Donna Gabaccia and Jane Aldrich to reveal the unknown female author of *The Carolina Receipt Book* (1832), the first cookbook published in the Carolinas. The toolkit of the culinary historian allowed them to discount the usual suspects among the local elite, including the family of Sarah Rutledge, author of a better known work, *The Carolina Housewife* (1847). Gabaccia and Aldrich therefore explored more broadly the hidden world of gastronomic literary production in the antebellum South, considering not only the traditional female networks of domestic literature and charitable works, but also the decidedly masculine politics of Nullification, which led ultimately to the Civil War. Having discovered the outsider author of the work, they conclude by discussing how, in a city dedicated to memorializing historical firsts, elite families marginalized her position within historical memory, thereby forgetting one of Charleston's culinary pioneers.[23]

As this brief survey has shown, cookbooks can perform labors far beyond their primary role of assisting cooks to get dinner on the table. As prescriptive literature, they serve to construct and reinforce a canon of proper dishes. This role entails considerable power to exclude particular recipes, individuals, and groups. These works can also serve as aspirational literature, a means of social climbing, and a way of exploring fantasy. In part, this role comes about through their ability to translate foreign ideas into local practices. For their authors, cookbooks offer a literary medium for constructing communities, asserting status, archiving the past and preserving historical memory, and achieving artistic fulfillment—no small accomplishment for a humble genre long neglected by professional scholars.

The Tastes of Dining

Historicizing taste is the basic goal of a cultural history of food written from the perspective of the dinner table. The dilemma in such a project, as many scholars have observed, is not only the ephemeral nature of flavors but also the fundamental difference between sensory perceptions and the language with which we seek to convey them. Faced with such a daunting prospect, some scholars have focused not on individual experiences but rather on the preferences of social groups. Such an approach can be particularly useful for identifying the hierarchies that pervade food consumption. Yet others, inspired by the potential of the new "sensory history," have begun to explore the subjectivities and social meanings of taste. The interpretation of flavors may ultimately tell us as much about the "spirit" of a particular time and place as do the supposedly higher arts of the eye and the ear.[24]

Historians of taste and consumption draw on a rich literature in sociology dating back to Thorstein Veblen, whose original insights on conspicuous consumption and the prestige associated with rare goods still go far to explaining the social status attached to foods. Pierre Bourdieu elaborated this notion into a theory of distinction that describes how economic capital is converted into symbolic or cultural capital, and how elite taste, acquired through formal education and everyday life within a particular milieu, serves to reproduce social inequality.[25] Stephen Mennell placed these social tastes in historical perspective with his work on the "civilizing appetite," connecting the development of food preferences to larger processes of class competition and state formation, particularly the divergent trajectory of absolutism in France and England. Finally, in his work on the bourgeois "public sphere," Jürgen Habermas called attention to the significance of taste as a criterion for inclusion as a member of the "public."[26]

Moreover, the social construction of taste depends on the spaces of consumption as much as on the foods that are actually consumed. Norbert Elias pointed to the courts of Renaissance Europe as the formative environment for new sensibilities and manners, which spurred the rise of a more refined cuisine. Food historians, with their tendency to focus on the elite, have shown less interest in the work of another influential theorist, the Russian linguist Mikhail Bakhtin, who explored the popular culture of the early modern marketplace. The feasts of carnival, with overstuffed sausages and seas of blancmange, represented the disorder against which courtly culture sought to define its sophistication.[27] Yet another culinary space, the restaurant, emerged in eighteenth-century France from between these two poles as a source of nourishment for the bourgeois public sphere.

The jockeying between these three positions raises questions of cultural hegemony, defined by Antonio Gramsci as the ability of rulers to control subordinate classes by consensus rather than force.[28] Does taste always move down from the elite, demonstrating a natural aristocracy? Does the appearance of popular dishes on elite tables indicate cultural appropriation, subverting resistance? In considering these questions, Bahktin's reminder of the interpenetration of popular and elite cultures remains relevant.

A sensory history of food would integrate these social and spatial positions with perceptions of flavor. Flandrin and his colleagues have begun this project with their attempts to periodize taste in early modern Europe. Alberto Capatti and Massimo Montanari nicely summarize the distinctions between a taste of "artifice," or the "mixture of flavors" characteristic of the Renaissance as well as of many non-Western cuisines, and the "analytical" taste of modern Europe, which "tends to *distinguish between* flavors (sweet, salty, tart, sour, or spicy), reserving a separate place for each."[29] Sarah Peterson described the sensory dimensions of this shift in European cooking from sweet and spicy to salty, herbal flavors. Marcy Norton called for a consideration of taste as an alternative to the pervasive reliance on biological determinism and cultural functionalism in the historical literature on food.[30] Meanwhile, Gerard Fitzgerald and Gabriella Petrick have developed narrative and analytical strategies for overcoming the linguistic difficulties of writing sensory history. They conclude: "Rather than arguing for some universal or ahistorical sense of taste, we are suggesting that reading and writing with a sense of taste, one that is both sensitive to context and experience and also infused with historical imagination, can help historians think through the contingent nature of taste and its historical meanings."[31]

Studies of European courtly feasting—and its religious counterpart fasting—draw on the interpretive tools of cultural anthropology, while remaining aware of the physicality of food. Caroline Walker Bynum's *Holy Feast and Holy Fast* (1987) analyzed the meanings of food for medieval women, who often abstained from eating as a way of gaining control over their lives and religiosity. Female saints held a particular devotion to the Eucharist, and although they could not be ordained as priests, by feeding others they were united with Christ, who also fed the Christian community. Moving from fast to feast, Ken Albala, a student of Bynum, reconstructed the microhistory of an Italian Renaissance banquet to show how it functioned as political propaganda. Drawing on a caterer's manual by Giovanni Battista Rossetti, *Dello Scalco* (1584), Albala interpreted the classical allegories of menu and table decorations in the geopolitical context of Italian city states negotiating between rival great powers. He noted that the French and German variations given for recipes not only demonstrated the cosmopolitanism of Italian courts, crucial for impressing foreign ambassadors, but also facilitated the labor migrations of skilled chefs.[32]

Within the Ottoman Empire, the courtly banquets at Topkapi palace conveyed both religious and secular meanings, asserting the emperor's claim as protector of the Faithful, while serving as a model for the empire. In the semi-public meals of the imperial council of state, officials feasted on multiple courses of rice, chicken soup, roast mutton, and sweets, while vast quantities of "leftovers," rice sweetened with butter and raisins, remained for slaves and commoners of Istanbul. Such meals offered a form of conspicuous consumption that was quite different from the intensive approach of early modern French haute cuisine, which focused on delicacies reserved for a tiny elite, although imperial viziers did have more choice than lowly clerks. Instead, it was extensive, measured in the ranks of courtiers and commoners fed by the imposing ovens of Topkapi. Nevertheless, such an institutional approach to banqueting did not preclude experimentation and historical change. Historians Tülay Artan and Christoph Neumann have discovered eighteenth-century shifts in the consumption of fats, from butter to olive oil, and in spices, from the heat of pepper and ginger toward the savory flavors of cinnamon and cloves. Although they can offer only tentative explanations for these changes in political trends and the social history of trade and urban consumption, Ottoman tastes, like those of Europeans, were clearly subject to fashion.[33]

Comparative scholarship has not only highlighted the diverse expressions of taste and fashion, it also revealed the limitations of focusing strictly on courtly banquets. In 1977, Michael Freeman suggested that the elements of Chinese gastronomy took shape already during the Song dynasty (960–1279) not in the ritual-bound environment of the imperial court but rather among restaurants, teahouses, and street vendors of the capital, Hangzhou. Joanna Waley-Cohen has since extended this argument, pointing to multiple periods of consumerism in the subsequent late-Ming and Qing dynasties. Unlike Europe, a Chinese gastronomic culture of refinement and pleasure emerged not with the waning of medical beliefs but rather as a complement to them, supporting the ideal that good eating could reinforce good health. Early modern Japan likewise had a flourishing public culture of dining and drinking centered on the "floating world" of courtesans, where samurai mingled with a rising merchant class.[34]

European historians have lately begun to look beyond the court for the origins of modern French cuisine. Susan Pinkard recently argued for the centrality of the Parisian dinner party. The rise of absolutism in the mid-seventeenth century afforded social mobility through the purchase of noble rank, but these servants of the crown still had to prove their status to peers. The dinner party, along with the salon, became a space for those with questionable lineage to display their refinement in intimate gatherings. As the profusion of banquets gave way to a few well-chosen dishes, detail and technique became more important. Chefs sautéed smaller cuts of choice meats and prepared sauces from pan drippings, emulsified with butter and garnished with seasonal ingredients and herbs. Flandrin, in his final, unfinished work, sought to impose rigor on this trend toward simpler table arrangements by laying out the changing rules and variations of table service in France over the *longue durée* from medieval to modern eras.[35]

Meanwhile, the growth of consumerism in early modern Europe was associated with new imperial commodities: chocolate, coffee, tea, and the sugar used to sweeten them. Scholars have long recognized the social transformations that accompanied these new goods, the rise of a critical bourgeois public sphere of male, rational discussion and its feminine counterpart in the private sphere of domesticity. Sobriety thus provided the basis for a rising middle class to assert a voice in government based on talent rather than birth. Less well known have been the ways that non-Western cultural practices shaped their consumption, but recent studies by Marcy Norton and Ross Jamieson have documented the European borrowing of indigenous technologies and tastes, Native American cacao prepared on a *metate* (grinding stone) and frothed with a *molinillo* (wooden "whisk"). In a similar fashion, tea was steeped and served with Chinese porcelain.[36]

Trends in European elite and bourgeois consumption converged with the rise of the restaurant in eighteenth-century Paris. In a recent book, Rebecca Spang has replaced the creation myth of French restaurants—revolutionary guillotines leaving unemployed chefs to serve the public—with the far more interesting tale of an evolving social institution. The original *restaurants* were restorative broths, specifically prepared for the individual sensibilities of enlightenment philosophes. By expanding to serve a complete meal, restaurateurs soon replaced the common offerings of the innkeeper's *table d'hote* (communal meal) and allowed diners a choice based on personal taste rather than health. Spang draws on Habermas's notion of the public sphere to argue that revolutionaries imbued restaurants with radical meanings, which were lost with the subsequent de-politicization of gastronomy as an aesthetic realm, a shift she dates perhaps too precisely to Napoleonic censorship. In any event, she insightfully maps the shifting boundaries between public and private as the restaurant took shape. Moreover, her insistence on viewing the restaurant as historically contingent rather than the inevitable product of French gastronomic exceptionalism is supported by Beat Kümin's recent observation of a broader shift toward individualized consumption in early modern inns throughout Europe.[37]

The focus on elite and middle-class consumption has often carried a more or less implicit assumption that taste, in all of its manifestations, is a luxury of reserved for the affluent. Fernand Braudel clearly distinguished between luxury and necessity, while conceding that "feasts undoubtedly kept alive the popular tradition of cookery."[38] Flandrin has noted, moreover, that although people may grow accustomed to a particular diet, it does not necessarily indicate choice. But even without romanticizing peasant cuisines, it is possible to discern a sense of taste in the food cultures of even the most impoverished societies. Doing so requires pushing against Norbert Elias's "threshold of shame and repugnance," to take seriously, for example, the Mexican connoisseur of toasted grasshopper or the Chinese epicure of durian fruit. It is perhaps more difficult still to discern the subtleties in a smear of *fufu* paste on the hand or a corn tortilla flavored only with salt. For those accustomed to the refinements of the "civilizing process," such an undifferentiated mass of complex carbohydrates may indeed have no taste. But as Richard Wilk has observed, the peasant can find a world of distinction within these foods.[39] The historian Piero Camporesi has explored most thoroughly the fantasy world of food in early modern subsistence societies. The anxieties of an uncertain harvest were expressed most memorably in the grotesque overflowing bodies of Bakhtin's carnival.

Camporesi described the elaborate dreams of abundance that pervaded Italian peasant folklore, which he attributed controversially to the presence of hallucinogens in herbs, mushrooms, and other substances commonly used to extend grains. Religious feasts, perhaps once a year, also provided intensely emotional moments, relieving hunger through gorging. By giving attention to unconventional sides of material and emotional life, Camporesi illustrated the great distances separating us from peasants of the past.[40]

Sidney Mintz has also examined the meanings of taste among the oppressed. He observed that although sugar diffused historically through British society from a luxury of the elite in the Renaissance to an item of everyday consumption by modern factory workers, the latter did not emulate the conspicuous consumption of aristocratic spun sugar sculptures or bourgeois tea time. Instead, they endowed sugar with their own meanings as a pick-me-up during factory breaks. Among slave societies of the Caribbean, who labored to produce sugar for European consumers, taste had still other meanings, as Mintz has shown. He concluded that the ability to choose their own culturally meaningful foods afforded slaves a measure of human dignity and a taste of freedom.[41]

The history of food in Mexico has been defined since the Conquest by a tension "between gluttony and moderation," in the words of Sonia Corcuera de Mancera, between a Spanish, urban cuisine of luxury featuring abundant wheat bread and meat on the one hand, and an indigenous, rural, poverty diet founded corn tortillas and chiles, on the other. Yet despite their material poverty, indigenous cooks overcame the conquistadors' scorn and conquered their palates, in part through the remarkable versatility of their peasant cuisine, the infinite malleability of corn dough, and the addictive flavors of chiles. Even Spanish elites consumed enchiladas and tamales, as street foods if not in domestic settings, thereby subverting hierarchies of taste and class.[42] Understanding such culinary worlds-turned-upside-down requires probing further into the actual labor of the kitchen.

The Practices of Cooking

Just as the food historian must bridge the divide between written menus and the fleeting tastes of the table, there is an equally wide gap between cookbooks and the labor of the kitchen. Although authors of the eighteenth century had already become quite adept making their works useful and appealing to cooks, written texts can never explain all the steps required to prepare a dish, nor anticipate all the contingencies that may arise in the process. Cooking, in short, requires improvisation, and a history of kitchen labor must foreground this inventiveness, even if based largely on the primary sources of fixed texts. Reconstructing the practices of cooking in nonliterate societies is all the more difficult. Nevertheless, by combining textual documents with material culture and culinary performances, we can hope to perceive the meanings of cooking, the rewards and frustrations, the dreary repetition and artistic satisfaction that women derived from their labor.

That cooking was considered women's work has contributed to its long-standing neglect in Western society. Philosopher Lisa Heldke traced this disdain to the ancient Greeks and to Plato's dichotomy between theory and practice, mind and body, the eternal and the ephemeral. Heldke was not the first to question these arbitrary divisions; the seventeenth-century Mexican savant Sor Juana Inés de la Cruz suggested that Aristotle would have understood nature better if he had worked in a kitchen. Heldke called for a reconsideration of cooking as a "thoughtful practice," drawing on both abstract and bodily knowledge. Meredith Abarca extended this argument to invert artistic hierarchies that discount flavor as an inferior aesthetic experience. Her ethnographies of working-class Mexican women revealed the self-conscious artistry that can be present in everyday cooking.[43]

While cookbook authors have often asserted professional authority, their claims have been historically contingent. Ferguson neatly summarized the conflict: "Insofar as cookbooks legislate rather than document, they necessarily construct cuisine *against* practice, which it aims to constrain and contain."[44] Mennell added historical perspective, citing Elizabeth David, who suggested that written recipes appeared in early modern English cookbooks only several decades after they became common in kitchens, whereas cookbooks had become a source of innovation in eighteenth-century France, driving new techniques and practices. Amy Trubek's history of the French culinary profession described in greater detail the ways chefs created associations, schools, and standards as a means to gain status and improve working conditions. Nevertheless, Michel de Certeau and Luce Giard emphasized the continued improvisation and inventiveness of French domestic cooks, who employ a repertoire of basic skills, not always congruent with professional standards, in their everyday practices of cooking.[45]

We still have much to learn about the modes through which cooks as readers interact with culinary texts, and performance studies offers great potential insights on this process. Defining performance broadly as "embodied practice," scholars in the field face many of the same challenges as do food historians. Particular meals, like physical performances, are ephemeral experiences, captured only to a limited degree by scripts, stage directions, menus, and cookbooks. Repertoires, often unwritten codes or skill sets, may be more valuable for appreciating the improvisations and meanings that emerge during a particular instance of a play or a dinner. Performance studies also offers useful analogues for approaching the indeterminacy of culinary texts; the script of a Shakespearean play, for example, may exist in multiple, distinct, yet equally authoritative versions, which are, in turn, merely signifiers of the play as it was performed. By shifting the focus of inquiry from texts to the cooking performances and audience responses they elicited, we can gain a fuller understanding of the embodied and emotional experiences of a meal. Diana Taylor has ambitiously called for a broader epistemological research agenda: "By taking performance seriously as a system of learning, storing, and transmitting knowledge, performance studies allows us to expand what we understand by 'knowledge.'"[46]

Such an approach to embodied knowledge can be particularly useful when combined with a careful study of material culture. Archaeologists, for example, have shown how Stone Age cooks periodically redesigned kitchen utensils to utilize resources most efficiently. Through experiments processing various nuts and seeds, such research has shown the skilled design and construction of mortars, pestles, and other ground stone technology. Culinary historians have likewise illustrated the value of using period equipment to understand the practices of kitchen labor. Ken Albala applied these techniques to seemingly outlandish Renaissance recipes to refute frequent claims of their impracticality made by modern readers who had failed to reconstruct the cooking process accurately. In one heroic research procedure he roasted an entire beef spine complete with ribs for hours on a spit beside a backyard fire pit, rather than following the more expedient options of tossing a roast in an oven or grilling it directly over coals. In the process he found that a thick crust formed on the meat, sealing in the liquids of the roast without burning the spice-rubbed surface. This experiment in cooking technology also helped explain the historical basis for changing French tastes from well-done to rare meat, which would have dried out if sautéed to a similar degree in smaller cuts in a skillet.[47]

Daniel Roche, in his monumental studies of the "history of everyday things," has reminded us of the importance of improvisation and practice in the use of material culture. Combining material and symbolic analysis, he showed how people used goods to fashion their identities, not only among the privileged elite, but also for those whose choices were constrained by poverty. Early modern France had a thriving trade in second-hand food of retailers redistributing leftovers from wealthy tables. Moreover, the probate records of eighteenth-century Parisian artisans and domestics reveal a growing ownership of frying pans. While they could afford only offal meats rather than filet mignon, they could nevertheless cook the meat to a rosy pink and serve it in an emulsified sauce of reduced drippings. The working classes not only prepared this nouvelle cuisine for their employers but could also reproduce it at home for their own families.[48]

The early modern French culinary revolution depended not solely on the skills of domestic cooks but also the labor of master butchers, as Sydney Watts has shown in her recent history of the Parisian meat guild. She described the elaborate hierarchy of cuts developed in the eighteenth century to utilize the entire animal to greatest advantage. Craftsmen reserved select cuts of beef and veal for wealthy families, while selling variety meats at lower prices to workers, thereby helping to determine status identity in a society of privilege. Aristocratic households contracted with butchers on a seasonal basis for entire sides of lamb and veal and quarters of beef and mutton, retaining skilled chefs to break down these primal cuts for individual meals. Servants for less exalted families purchased their meat daily, and were often forced to argue over the quality of cuts they received. Such negotiations involved not just price and freshness, but also social status, judged by peers in the exacting world of the dinner party. Drawing on performance theory, Watts showed how market haggling devolved into public contests of authority and status in which guild masters asserted their honor and reputation while consumers sought to position themselves within a culinary taxonomy of prestige.[49]

James McCann has meanwhile coupled performance studies with oral history methodologies in his recent survey of African food history. Rejecting Goody's notion of undifferentiated cooking, based on timeless and tasteless pots of porridge, he reconstructed the development of African regional cuisines by first establishing a "historical baseline of cookery" and then following the accumulation over time of ingredients and techniques by way of multiple networks: the Indian Ocean trade, the Columbian exchange, internal migrations, and colonialism. McCann relied less on colonial records than on oral history—"the living transcripts of daily cooking"—which he viewed broadly as sensory experiences and exchanges over bubbling, aromatic, and flavorful stews. He concluded: "Africans have maintained the oral form more thoroughly than other world areas. Yet, like jazz, what appears to be a free form was actually a deeper structure understood by the performer and by the informed within the audience. Its essential orality was carefully preserved and passed on via performance, practice, and the response of those who appreciated the final result and encouraged the cook to repeat the performance."[50]

Working along similar lines, anthropologist Steffan Igor Ayora-Diaz proposed a theory of the "naturalization of taste" to explain the historical development of flavor principles within regional cuisines. Using the Yucatán as a case study, he explained this process of naturalization as the product of encounters between vernacular cooking practices and successive waves of globalization. Ayora-Diaz, like McCann, recognized the creativity and cosmopolitanism of domestic cookery. It was through the repetition, exchange, and standardization of particular constellations of sensory experiences that combinations of *recado* (spice rub) or *escabeche* (pickle) became inscribed within regional identities, while still allowing for varying preferences of individuals, families, communities, and social groups.[51]

Just as good taste is not the exclusive prerogative of elite consumers, inventive and artistic cooking has emerged from even impoverished communities. Although outsiders have often perceived peasant cuisines as static products of ethnography, insiders recognized the subtle distinctions of taste and talent between individual cooks in any community. The task for cultural historians of food is to comprehend those practices and meanings from the archive and the repertoire surviving from the past.

Cultural historians will find great potential in the study of food, whose rich symbolic, material, and embodied meanings offer valuable points of entry for interpreting societies of the past. The sources for such histories are varied but diffuse, affording both challenges and opportunities for the researcher. Archives, travel accounts, and culinary literature—the meat and potatoes of cultural history—are widely available and, thanks to digital catalogs and search engines, no longer require such tedious digging to unearth the precious truffle. Nevertheless, the real promise of cultural history lies in the innovative use of new types of sources, not only in the documentary record but also in material culture, oral histories, sensory perceptions, and kitchen repertoires. Without overlooking the discourses that give meaning to foods, we must always reconnect these symbolic systems to the embodied materiality of our subject.

Equally important is keeping the history in culture by remaining aware of chronology, change, and continuity. Since the eighteenth century at least, the French have repeatedly invented *nouvelles cuisines* that simultaneously embraced nature and modernity. It is therefore ironic that the latest version of Western haute cuisine, self-consciously "modernist" in outlook, should advocate not an "analytical cuisine" but rather a "cuisine of artifice," deconstructed dishes awash in savory foams, juxtaposing unexpected flavors and textures by way of industrial food processing technologies such as dry ice and vacuum sealers.[52] At the same time, chefs have been turning away from European "naturalism" and seeking inspiration from supposedly premodern, plebeian "cuisines of mixture" from lands such as India, Ethiopia, and Mexico. Thus, the history of food, like other cultural realms, can unsettle unilinear narratives of Western progress and modernity, surprising us with the diversity of tastes from the past.

Notes

1. For examples, see in this volume Enrique C. Ochoa, "Political Histories of Food," and Charlotte Biltekoff, "Critical Nutrition Studies," in *The Oxford Handbook of Food History*, ed. Jeffrey M. Pilcher (New York: Oxford University Press, 2012), 23–40, 172–90.
2. Jack Goody, *Cooking, Cuisine, and Class: A Study in Comparative Sociology* (Cambridge: Cambridge University Press, 1982), vii, 97–99.
3. Sidney Mintz, *Tasting Food, Tasting Freedom: Excursions into Eating, Culture, and the Past* (Boston: Beacon Press, 1996), 96.
4. Priscilla Parkhurst Ferguson, *Accounting for Taste: The Triumph of French Cuisine* (Chicago: University of Chicago Press, 2004), 3.
5. See Peter Burke, *What is Cultural History?* (Cambridge: Polity, 2004).

6. Claude Lévi-Strauss, *The Raw and the Cooked,* trans. John and Dorren Weightman (New York: Harper & Row, 1969); Mary Douglas, *Purity and Danger: An Analysis of Concepts of Pollution and Taboo* (London: Routledge, 1966); Sidney W. Mintz, *Sweetness and Power: The Place of Sugar in Modern History* (New York: Viking Books, 1985).

7. Norbert Elias, *The Civilizing Process: The History of Manners and state Formation and Civilization*, trans. Edmund Jephcott (Oxford: Blackwell, 1994); Stephen Mennell, *All Manners of Food: Eating and Taste in England and France from the Middle Ages to the Present* (Oxford: Basil Blackwell, 1985).

8. Jean-Louis Flandrin, "Introduction: The Early Modern Period," in *Food: A Culinary History from Antiquity to the Present*, ed. Jean-Louis Flandrin, Massimo Montanari, and Albert Sonnenfeld, trans. Clarissa Botsford, et al. (New York: Columbia University Press, 1999), 372–73; c.f., Jean-François Revel, *Culture and Cuisine: A Journey Through the History of Food*, trans. Helen R. Lane (Garden City, NY: Doubleday, 1982).

9. Jack Goody, *The Domestication of the Savage Mind* (Cambridge: Cambridge University Press, 1977), 129–35, 140–43.

10. See, for example, Harvey J. Graff, ed., *Literacy and Historical Development: A Reader* (Carbondale: Southern Illinois University Press, 2007).

11. Barbara Ketcham Wheaton, *Savoring the Past: The French Kitchen and Table from 1300 to 1789* (Philadelphia: University of Pennsylvania Press, 1983); D. Eleanor Scully and Terence Scully, *Early French Cookery: Sources, History, Original Recipes and Modern Adaptations* (Ann Arbor: University of Michigan Press, 1995); Philip Hyman and Mary Hyman, "Printing the Kitchen: French Cookbooks, 1480–1800," in *Food: A Culinary History*, 394–402; François Pierre de La Varenne, *Le cuisinier françois*, ed. Jean-Louis Flandrin, Philip Human, and Mary Hyman (1651; repr., Paris: Montalba, 1983).

12. Alain R. Girard, "Du manuscrit à l'imprimé: le livre de cuisine en Europe aux 15e et 16e siècles," in *Pratiques et discours alimentaires à la Renaissance*, ed. Jean-Claude Margolin and Robert Sauzet (Paris: G.-P. Maisonneuve et Larose, 1982), 107–17.

13. Mennell, *All Manners of Food*, 64–101.

14. Flandrin, "Introduction: The Early Modern Period," 364.

15. Elizabeth Spiller, "Recipes for Knowledge: Maker's Knowledge Traditions, Paracelsian Recipes, and the Invention of the Cookbook, 1600–1660," in *Renaissance Food from Rabelais to Shakespeare: Culinary Readings and Culinary Histories*, ed. Joan Fitzpatrick (Farnham: Ashgate, 2010), 65.

16. Sandra Sherman, *Invention of the Modern Cookbook* (Santa Barbara, CA: Greenwood, 2010), 42.

17. Ferguson, *Accounting for Taste*, 83–109.

18. Eric C. Rath, *Food and Fantasy in Early Modern Japan* (Berkeley: University of California Press, 2010).

19. Mark Swislocki, *Culinary Nostalgia: Regional Food Culture and the Urban Experience in Shanghai* (Stanford: Stanford University Press, 2009).

20. Arjun Appadurai, "How to Make a National Cuisine: Cookbooks in Contemporary India," *Comparative Studies in Society and History* 30, no. 1 (January 1988): 3–24; John C. Super, "Libros de cocina y cultura en la América Latina temprana," in *Conquista y comida: Consecuencias del encuentro de dos mundos*, ed. Janet Long (Mexico City: UNAM, 1996), 451–68; Özge Samanci, "Culinary Consumption Patterns of the Ottoman Elite During the First Half of the Nineteenth Century," in *The Illuminated Table, the Prosperous House: Food and Shelter in Ottoman Material*

Culture, ed. Suraiya Faroqhi and Christoph K. Neumann (Würzburg: Ergon Verlag, 2003), 161–64.

21. Susan J. Leonardi, "Recipes for Reading: Summer Pasta, Lobster à la Riseholme, and Key Lime Pie," *PMLA* 104, no. 3 (May 1989): 340–47; Barbara Kirschenblatt-Gimblett, "Recipes for Creating Community: The Jewish Charity Cookbook in America," *Jewish Folklore and Ethnology Review* 9, no. 1 (1987): 8–12; Anne L. Bower, "Cooking Up Stories: Narrative Elements in Community Cookbooks," in *Recipes for Reading: Community Cookbooks, Stories, Histories*, ed. Anne L. Bower (Amherst: University of Massachusetts Press, 1997), 29–50; Janet Theophano, *Eat My Words: Reading Women's Lives through the Cookbooks They Wrote* (New York: Palgrave, 2002).

22. Doris Witt, *Black Hunger: Food and the Politics of U.S. Identity* (New York: Oxford University Press, 1999), 26–39, 54–61; Andrew Warnes, "'Talking' Recipes: *What Mrs Fisher Knows* and the African-American Cookbook Tradition," in *The Recipe Reader: Narratives—Contexts—Traditions*, ed. Janet Floyd and Laurel Forster (Aldershot: Ashgate, 2003), 52–71; Judith Carney, *Black Rice: The African Origins of Rice Cultivation in the Americas* (Cambridge, MA: Harvard University Press, 2001).

23. Donna R. Gabaccia and Jane Aldrich, "Recipes in Context: Solving a Small Mystery in Charleston's Culinary History," *Food, Culture & Society* 15, no. 2 (June 2012): 197–221; [Caroline Howard Gilman], *The Carolina Receipt Book* (Charleston: James S. Burges, 1832); Sarah Rutledge, *The Carolina Housewife* (1847; repr., Columbia: University of South Carolina Press, 1979).

24. Paul Freedman, "Introduction: A New History of Cuisine," in *Food: A History of Taste*, ed. Paul Freedman (Berkeley: University of California Press, 2007), 22.

25. Thorstein Veblen, *The Theory of the Leisure Class* (1899, repr., New York: Penguin Books, 1994); Pierre Bourdieu, *Distinction: A Social Critique of the Judgment of Taste*, trans. Richard Nice (Cambridge, MA: Harvard University Press, 1984).

26. Mennell, *All Manners of Food*, 20–39; Jürgen Habermas, *The Structural Transformation of the Public Sphere*, trans. Thomas Burger (Cambridge, MA: The MIT Press, 1989).

27. Mikhail Bakhtin, *Rabelais and His World*, trans. Helene Iswolsky (Cambridge, MA: The MIT Press, 1968).

28. Antonio Gramsci, *The Prison Notebooks*, trans. Joseph A. Buttigieg and Antonio Callari (New York: Columbia University Press, 1992).

29. Alberto Capatti and Massimo Montanari, *Italian Cuisine: A Cultural History*, trans. Aine O'Healy (New York: Columbia University Press, 2003), 86.

30. Marcy Norton, "Tasting Empire: Chocolate and the European Internalization of Mesoamerican Aesthetics," *American Historical Review* 111, no. 3 (June 2006): 660–91; T. Sarah Peterson, *Acquired Taste: The French Origins of Modern Cooking* (Ithaca: Cornell University Press, 1994).

31. Gerard J. Fitzgerald and Gabrielle M. Petrick, "In Good Taste: Rethinking American History with Our Palates," *Journal of American History* 95, no. 2 (September 2008): 392–93, 395.

32. Caroline Walker Bynum, *Holy Feast and Holy Fast: The Religious Significance of Food to Medieval Women* (Berkeley: University of California Press, 1987); Ken Albala, "Food and Feast as Propaganda in Late Renaissance Italy," in *Dining on Turtles: Food Feasts and Drinking in History*, ed. Diane Kirkby and Tanja Luckins (New York: Palgrave Macmillan, 2007), 33–45; Giovanni Battista Rossetti, *Dello scalco* (Ferrara, Italy: D. Mammarello, 1584).

33. Tülay Artan, "Aspects of the Ottoman Elite's Food Consumption: Looking for 'Staples,' 'Luxuries,' and 'Delicacies,' in a Changing Century," in *Consumption Studies and the History of the Ottoman Empire, 1550–1922: An Introduction*, ed. Donald Quataert (Albany: SUNY Press, 2000), 107–200; Hedda Reindl-Kiel, "The Chickens of Paradise: Official Meals in the Mid-Seventeenth Century Ottoman Palace," in Faroqhi and Neumann, *The Illuminated Table*, 59–88; Christoph K. Neumann, "Spices in the Ottoman Palace: Courtly Cookery in the Eighteenth Century," in ibid, 127–60.

34. Michael Freeman, "Sung," in *Food in Chinese Culture: Anthropological and Historical Perspectives*, ed. K. C. Chang (New Haven: Yale University Press, 1977), 143–45; Joanna Waley-Cohen, "The Quest for Perfect Balance: Taste and Gastronomy in Imperial China," in *Food: The History of Taste*, 99–132; Nishiyama Matsunosuke, *Edo Culture: Daily Life and Diversions in Urban Japan, 1600–1868*, trans. Gerald Groemer (Honolulu: University of Hawai'i Press, 1997).

35. Susan Pinkard, *A Revolution in Taste: The Rise of French Cuisine, 1650–1800* (New York: Cambridge University Press, 2009), 83–94; Jean-Louis Flandrin, *Arranging the Meal: A History of Table Service in France*, trans. Julie E. Johnson (Berkeley: University of California Press, 2007).

36. Brian Cowan, *The Social Life of Coffee: The Emergence of the British Coffeehouse* (New Haven: Yale University Press, 2005); Marcy Norton, *Sacred Gifts, Profane Pleasures: A History of Tobacco and Chocolate in the Atlantic World* (Ithaca, NY: Cornell University Press, 2008); Ross W. Jamieson, "The Essence of Commodification: Caffeine Dependencies in the Early Modern World," *Journal of Social History* 35, no. 2 (Winter 2001): 269–94.

37. Rebecca L. Spang, *The Invention of the Restaurant: Paris and Modern Gastronomic Culture* (Cambridge, MA: Harvard University Press, 2000); Beat Kümin, "Eating Out Before the Restaurant: Dining Cultures in Early-modern Inns," in *Eating Out in Europe: Picnics, Gourmet Dining and Snacks Since the Late Eighteenth Century*, ed. Marc Jacobs and Peter Scholliers (Oxford: Berg, 2003), 71–87.

38. Fernand Braudel, *The Structures of Everyday Life: The Limits of the Possible*, vol. 1 of *Civilization and Capitalism, 15th-18th Century*, trans. Siân Reynolds (New York: Harper & Row, 1979), 187.

39. Richard Wilk, *Home Cooking in the Global Village: Caribbean Food from Buccaneers to Ecotourists* (Oxford: Berg, 2006), 43 and personal communication; Elias, *The Civilizing Process*, 492.

40. Piero Camporesi, *Bread of Dreams: Food and Fantasy in Early Modern Europe*, trans. David Gentilcore (Chicago: University of Chicago Press, 1989).

41. Mintz, *Sweetness and Power*, 151–86; idem, *Tasting Food, Tasting Freedom: Excursions into Eating, Culture, and the Past* (Boston: Beacon Press, 1996), 33–49.

42. Jeffrey M. Pilcher, *¡Que vivan los tamales! Food and the Making of Mexican Identity* (Albuquerque: University of New Mexico Press, 1998), 19–22, 55–57; Sonia Corcuera de Mancera, *Entre gula y templanza: Un aspecto de la historia mexicana*, 3rd ed. (Mexico City: Fondo de Cultura Económica, 1991).

43. Lisa M. Heldke, "Foodmaking as a Thoughtful Practice," in *Cooking, Eating, Thinking: Transformative Philosophies of Food*, ed. Deane W. Curtin and Lisa M. Heldke (Bloomington: Indiana University Press, 1992), 203–29; Meredith E. Abarca, *Voices in the Kitchen: Views of Food and the World from Working-Class Mexican and Mexican American Women* (College Station: Texas A & M University Press, 2006), 54–68.

44. Ferguson, *Accounting for Taste*, 44.

45. Mennell, *All Manners of Food*, 65; Amy B. Trubek, *Haute Cuisine: How the French Invented the Culinary Profession* (Philadelphia: University of Pennsylvania Press, 2000); Luce Giard, "The Nourishing Arts," in *Living and Cooking*, vol. 2 of *The Practice of Everyday Life*, ed. Michel de Certeau, Luce Giard, and Pierre Mayol, trans. Timothy J. Tomasik (Minneapolis: University of Minnesota Press, 1998), 151–69.

46. Diana Taylor, *The Archive and the Repertoire: Performing Cultural Memory in the Americas* (Durham: Duke University Press, 2003), 16; W. B. Worthen, "Disciplines of the Text: Sites of Performance," in *The Performance Studies Reader*, ed. Henry Bial (New York: Routledge, 2004), 10–25.

47. Ken Albala, "Cooking as Research Methodology: Experiments in Renaissance Cuisine," in *Renaissance Food from Rabelais to Shakespeare*, 73–88. See also Jenny L. Adams, *Ground Stone Analysis: A Technological Approach* (Salt Lake City: University of Utah Press, 2002).

48. Daniel Roche, *A History of Everyday Things: The Birth of Consumption in France, 1600–1800*, trans. Brian Pearce (Cambridge: Cambridge University Press, 2000), 5–8, 234; idem, "Cuisine et alimentation populair à Paris," *Dix-Huitième Siècle* 15 (1983): 7–18. I thank Sidney Watts for this reference.

49. Sydney Watts, *Meat Matters: Butchers, Politics, and Market Culture in Eighteenth-Century Paris* (Rochester: University of Rochester Press, 2006), 27–41.

50. James C. McCann, *Stirring the Pot: A History of African Cuisine* (Athens: Ohio University Press, 2009), 12, 85, 110, 135.

51. Steffan Igor Ayora-Diaz, *Foodscapes, Foodfields, and Identities in Yucatán* (Oxford: Berghahn, 2012), 114–52.

52. Nathan Myhrvold, "The Art in Gastronomy: A Modernist Perspective," *Gastronomica* 11, no. 1 (Spring 2011): 18–19.

Bibliography

Bynum, Caroline Walker. *Holy Feast and Holy Fast: The Religious Significance of Food to Medieval Women*. Berkeley: University of California Press, 1987.

Capatti, Alberto, and Massimo Montanari. *Italian Cuisine: A Cultural History*. Translated by Aine O'Healy. New York: Columbia University Press, 2003.

Faroqhi, Suraiya, and Christoph K. Neumann, eds. *The Illuminated Table, the Prosperous House: Food and Shelter in Ottoman Material Culture*. Würzburg: Ergon Verlag, 2003.

Fitzpatrick, Joan, ed. *Renaissance Food from Rabelais to Shakespeare: Culinary Readings and Culinary Histories*. Farnham: Ashgate, 2010.

Flandrin, Jean-Louis. *Arranging the Meal: A History of Table Service in France*. Translated by Julie E. Johnson. Berkeley: University of California Press, 2007.

Flandrin, Jean-Louis, Massimo Montanari, and Albert Sonnenfeld, eds. *Food: A Culinary History from Antiquity to the Present*. Translated by Clarissa Botsford, et al. New York: Columbia University Press, 1999.

Freedman, Paul, ed. *Food: The History of Taste*. Berkeley: University of California Press, 2007.

McCann, James C. *Stirring the Pot: A History of African Cuisine*. Athens: Ohio University Press, 2009.

Pilcher, Jeffrey M. *¡Que vivan los tamales! Food and the Making of Mexican Identity.* Albuquerque: University of New Mexico Press, 1998.

Rath, Eric C. *Food and Fantasy in Early Modern Japan.* Berkeley: University of California Press, 2010.

Spang, Rebecca L. *The Invention of the Restaurant: Paris and Modern Gastronomic Culture.* Cambridge, MA: Harvard University Press, 2000.

Swislocki, Mark. *Culinary Nostalgia: Regional Food Culture and the Urban Experience in Shanghai.* Stanford: Stanford University Press, 2009.

CHAPTER 4

LABOR HISTORIES OF FOOD

TRACEY DEUTSCH

WHAT does the lens of labor help us perceive about food and its history? This essay argues that the answer is just about everything. Work transforms the raw materials of nature into food. Work makes otherwise indigestible collections of organic material into an indispensible source of physical energy and nutrients. Work imbues these materials with social meanings. In brief, food and work are inextricably linked. Labor is central to food and, indeed, the need for food has motivated much of the labor humans have expended. Using the lens of labor sharpens our vision of the social processes, technological frameworks, and material needs that lay behind food in particular times and places. The kinds of labor systems in place dramatically shaped the kinds of food that were available and, conversely, changes to food often changed labor systems.

And yet the relationship between food and work has never been straightforward. People have used an enormous range of strategies to transform raw materials into food, and these strategies reflect the myriad social contexts and systems in which food has been eaten. The gendered division of labor, the way in which food is provisioned, ideas about what and how to cook, and the strategies of extraction, processing, or hunting that produce ingredients for food—all can vary profoundly even within the same era.

This question is particularly vexing in our own historical moment, when so much of the labor of food production is hidden from its ultimate consumers. Much of the work around food is now done by people who will not eat the food (agricultural workers on farms, truck drivers, line workers in canning factories, restaurant cooks). Migrant and guest workers epitomize this invisibility, their labor crucial to much agricultural harvest but their presence temporary and contingent on state policy. When these people are identified by consumers, it is often by demands that they be expelled from the borders of the nations in which they labor.

This essay, then, sheds light on the enormous amount of labor that has been required to produce food and establishes the centrality of labor to studies of food history. It does so by being mindful of changes to the basic tasks that surround food: gathering, production, and consumption over time. Following an overview of the early history of food work and the "commercial turn" that marked global food production and consumption beginning in the late middle ages, a discussion of three sites of food-related labor—(1) the commercial world of food processing (especially manufacturing and retail), (2) farms, and (3) domestic spaces—structures the subsequent relatively loose chronological structure. This organization reflects the historical shift of the modern era toward elaborate specialization and pronounced spatial separation of food tasks. It does not, however, represent stark disconnection; indeed, the cultural and physical links among these different spaces are crucial to the culture and physical needs surrounding food. The final section reflects upon the implications of these histories for food, work, and their connections, concluding that food problematizes typical ways of categorizing work and labor.

Throughout, the essay emphasizes the enormous amount of work required to create food, a quality that exists even under modern systems of production. Furthermore, this essay emphasizes the social embeddedness of that labor. That is, it points to the way that food labor is often structured by local systems of power and identity—and especially gender. These two themes hold true across time. But food labor has of course also undergone enormous changes. In tracing these, two other themes emerge: first, that commercial revolutions and industrialization dramatically altered older forms of food work and, second, that industrialization, in particular, had differing and uneven effects globally, often resulting in increasing divergence in food work between wealthy and poor people.

The continuities among the different historical eras and linkages between systems of producing food is as important as their divergence; a central point of the essay is that the spaces and methods of food production have always necessarily overlapped, and often articulated in symbiotic ways, with each other. For instance, even the most industrialized of spaces has relied on agriculture for its food. Similar connections emerge across time (e.g., the ongoing importance of foraging and hunting even in the "modern" world). This emphasis on the overlap and connections among systems of labor reflects the complications of food production, as well as the emphasis in much recent scholarly literature on the limits of capital and economies to standardize, homogenize, and remake daily practices.[1] Finally, my analysis also reflects the particular importance to food of unpaid, household work that family members undertake to sustain themselves and each other. Domestic labor reveals important facts about the work necessary for food, and about the cultural footings of economies more generally. Thus the essay narrates a complicated and holistic view of the work of food production that emphasizes the ongoing significance of older systems and domestic spaces alongside more recent modifications and reshapings.

The First Tasks: Origins of Human Food Production

The emerging narrative of the work patterns required by ancient foodways usefully frames the relationship between food and work in several ways. First and foremost, it suggests the centrality of labor to studies of food. For most of human history, food's production and distribution, stood at the center of social and political structures—and of most peoples' daily work. It also suggests, as many scholars have pointed out, that taste and culture guided people. There has never been a time when food, and work around food, proceeded solely based on efficiency. Finally, understanding ancient food technologies and systems allows scholars to appreciate what has remained, and hence both the historical specificity and long roots of techniques such as hunting, foraging, herding, and communal farming.

Evidence of the significant labor required for food goes back to the prehistoric period. The earliest flint blades for killing and butchering animals are over 1.5 million years old; 30,000 years ago people wove baskets and crafted clay pots for the purposes of storing food. And these are just the activities that left material remains. We have no record at all of the detailed knowledge of seasonal migration paths, edible plants, and animal habits, food preservation methods, and countless other proficiencies that allowed people to survive.[2] Even the so-called "original affluent" foraging societies described by Marshall Sahlins exerted coordinated effort to get food, for instance, smoking out bees from their hives and collecting honey, gathering berries and leading organized expeditions into oceans and seas in search of fish and sea mammals (such as whales).[3] Although, as Sahlins rightly observed, these peoples could often obtain subsistence with only a few hours of daily work, that work was highly skilled and depended on generations of collected knowledge and experience.

Food was not only hunted; it was also cooked. For at least 200,000 years, and possibly much longer, the hominid ancestors of modern humans gathered fuel for, built, and maintained fires to cook food. Records of firepits and cracked rocks suggest their efforts to boil and remove fat even from the marrow of animals they hunted; and we know that berries were not only gathered, but also preserved and dried.[4] Scholars speculate that even in the most ancient times, taste mattered to what people ate.[5] This observation suggests the long-standing importance of even rudimentary techniques such as roasting or stewing to social, cultural, and physical survival.

Settled agriculture emerged about 10,000 years ago and dramatically changed both food production and the societies that adopted it. As a central transformation in the way food is produced, it was also a transformation in labor systems and in the politics and society in which labor is embedded. Indeed, the appearance of permanent agrarian settlements has long been taken by anthropologists and historians as a crucial turning point in human history, allowing for the construction of more towns and cities, the growth of elaborate cultural and political systems around labor, access to land, and the invention of writing.[6] We can see this in the rise of archaic states, which began around 4,000 years ago in fertile river valleys of Asia, from the Tigris and Euphrates in the west, to the Indus and Ganges in the south, and the Huang He and Yangtze in the east. Urbanization followed shortly thereafter across Africa, Europe, and the Americas, as newer irrigation methods, improved crops, and food processing and preserving technologies could support larger populations. The first centralized states emerged as a result of, and also to sustain, large-scale agriculture.

Early farming developed dramatically new ways of wresting food from the landscape, even as it also drew from some long-standing techniques. The skills of planting and harvesting, already known to gatherers, were supplemented by new methods of preparing fields through slash and burn. As grains and legumes became central to human diets, bodies changed also: skeletal evidence suggests the backbreaking and joint-damaging nature of agriculture, as well as the deficiencies of the diet it produced. The ways that people cooked also shifted to accommodate new foods. Cooks used spices to create sauces that would flavor the otherwise monotonous diet. In all of these ways, food continued to require enormous amounts of work. Early agriculturalists also relied on, and eventually domesticated, sheep and goats (in Eurasia and the Middle East) and pigs (in Asia). The milk and meat produced by animals became crucial to nomadic pastoral societies, whose members herded, bred, and traded livestock—and whose food supply was heavily based on daily milking chores.

Both agricultural and pastoral ways of producing food relied on intricate social systems and relations. For instance, in Mesoamerica, the invention of alkaline processing called *nixtamalization* magnified the nutritional content of maize. This permitted the growth of large cities such as Teotihuacan, but required hours of intensive female labor every day. Arnold Bauer has suggested that patriarchy intensified in situations such as this, when men took control of farming and women's labor focused solely on cooking and processing within the household. The work of agriculture was often conditioned on changes in gender systems.[7]

As in agricultural settlements, pastoralism emerged from very particular social arrangements. Transhumanance, or regular patterns of seasonal migration between pastures, became a way of life for many herders. Cooks in these societies learned to ferment and culture dairy products (for instance, buttermilk, cheese, yogurt, and the alcoholic beverage *koumiss*) both to preserve them and to make dairy products digestible to adults (who typically lack the enzymes needed to digest lactose).[8] And, while gender remained an important force in these societies, lines of authority were often more fluid than in settled agrarian places.

Agriculture in particular was structured around increasingly centralized, hierarchical, and expansive systems of labor-intensive food production. Central authorities, operating on larger scales than ever before, coordinated irrigation systems, grain production, and storage. For instance, ancient Egyptians typically spent much of the "dry" season (when the Nile was not flooding) working for elites and rulers on the infrastructure that controlled water flow. In many agricultural societies, food was produced for, and often distributed by, a central governing authority.

No single system fully described the many ways people got food. Even in the most agrarian of societies, people continued to hunt and forage. Indeed these alternate methods of getting food allowed laborers to resist the demands of elites, at times through violent uprisings and rebellions, but at other times through everyday forms of resistance that James Scott dubbed "weapons of the weak."[9] Agriculturalists, foragers, and pastoralists interacted and occasionally sought refuge with each other when crops failed, when the most important wild foods were scarce, or when herds were lost. They traded foodstuffs with each other in better times. All of this is to say that agriculture changed the way people worked for food, but that humans employed a variety of ways of wresting nutrition from the world around them, relying on new innovations and older methods as environment, politics, and culture allowed.

The Transformations of Commercialization: Plantations, Imperialism, and Global Food Exchange

Even more than agriculture, the advent of commercialized, global European empires transformed the way that food was produced and how it was accessed. Diets changed, both in response to new foods (sugar, tea, and coffee in Europe for instance) and to poverty (dislocation of rural populations in the face of conquest, enslavement, or systems of enclosure and industrialization). New social systems and politics, in particular new ways of extracting work, catalyzed the commercialization of food and also came to depend on it; for instance, the enormous amount of labor that lay behind new systems of food production was made particularly visible and particularly ugly in the global enslavement that centered on plantation production. Plantation agriculture, embedded as it was in far-off industries and global economies, open a window onto the role of coerced labor in the commercialization of basic foods.

In Europe, commercialization of food grew out of new coercive systems of labor. One of most infamous, serfdom, emerged in the late Roman Empire and spread across much of Europe over subsequent centuries. Although there was enormous variation in serfdom, serfs—like subjects of other empires—produced their own food on land they farmed. However, they also typically provided food to the noble family from their plots and provided labor on larger tracts of farmland that nobility operated directly. The surplus that serf families produced on lords' lands were traded or shipped abroad.[10]

Middling farmers and peasants, as well as powerful elites throughout Europe and Eurasia, increasingly produced for exchange and the market, rather than simply for subsistence. Current research suggests that over time it was these colonizing or otherwise advantaged agriculturists who expanded their farming and produced foodstuffs for export to cities and abroad (especially vegetables, grains, and dairy).[11]

Foods of the Americas became commodified through other forms of unfree labor. Sugar and coffee plantations in the Americas, tea plantations in Asia, and cocoa bean plantations in Africa all powered European commercial empires—and expanded systems of coerced labor and enslavement to a global scale. The labor techniques to produce foods such as coffee, tea, sugar, and chocolate were extreme. In Central and South America, infamous sites of exploitative colonial labor relations around food production and other tasks, indigenous peoples were often forced to forego work on their own plots to labor on Spanish mining projects and to produce food for elites through the *repartimiento*—a forced labor draft of indigenous subjects. Denied the chance to produce enough food for themselves, native people were particularly vulnerable to the diseases and abuse of colonizers, and populations declined precipitously. Owners of sugar plantations soon began enslaving African people, transporting them to the "new world." Over time, the European demand for sugar led many overseers to employ gang labor systems adapted from contemporary military discipline, beating slaves who lagged in their tasks of planting, weeding, fertilizing, and harvesting cane. Meanwhile, work in the mills and boiling houses was regimented and dangerous but also relied on enslaved workers' considerable skills to maximize productivity. It is important to note that this sort of forced work around food depended on skill as well as simple force. Judith Carney's work on rice agriculture in the Americas shows that West African slaves supplied both the labor and the technology of levies and milling that made rice production possible.[12]

Enslavement and forced plantation labor proved crucial to far-flung food supplies—and especially to European workers. Sugar, once a rarity, eventually became a staple on the tables of much of Western Europe.[13] Rum, coffee, and tea also all became common features of even working-class Europeans' diets, depending on the unfree labor of workers in the Americas, the Caribbean, the Pacific, Africa, and Asia. Meanwhile, other foods traveled the opposite direction, feeding settler colonies formed by Europeans' enormous Atlantic empires In all of these cases, new kinds of political power transformed agricultural food production.[14]

The Transformations of Commercialization: Selling Labor, Buying Food

The emergence of European empires in the Americas and their networks of trade transformed the relationship between work and food. Slowly, eating came to require, not farming or gathering or hunting, but rather engaging in commerce and industrial production. In the increasingly commercialized landscapes of the fifteenth, sixteenth, and seventeenth centuries, more and more impoverished European peasants became migratory populations that roamed rural areas and cities in search of wage work. The enclosure movement of Europe nearly obliterated the possibilities of hunting, foraging, or pasturing animals for most rural people—practices that had been crucial for supplementing household food supplies. In the Western hemisphere more and more indigenous peoples were brought into relations of trade for everyday cooking implements such as metal pots or forced to work for Europeans on plantations that exported commodities. Exchange, or labor that created exchangeable goods, became the conduit to food. When the market first entered families' lives, it was often through food. Medieval traders had sustained global trading networks through which spices and preserved foods flowed.[15] In some places, like European cities, alcoholic drinks, bread, and many baked goods had long been purchased. Jams, butter, and other heavily processed foods were often traded between neighbors, sometimes (although rarely) purchased for cash. Certainly the increasingly prevalent imported foods such as sugar were almost always purchased, rather than produced by the ultimate consumer. Finally, in all commercialized and industrialized places, food was increasingly purchased rather than grown and processed within a household.

Although would-be sellers obtained different levels of wealth as a result of market endeavors, work in and around food sales remained crucial to almost every region of the world. This was particularly true in the wake of the migrations and urbanization from the sixteenth to the nineteenth centuries, when new occupations around food opened up. Market stalls and stands offered vital work to otherwise itinerant or marginally employed urbanites, and sometimes also to unfree workers who lived in cities. The financial possibilities of small-scale food distribution were felt globally; one of the most common entrepreneurial occupations for women in nineteenth-century Mexico was selling tortillas and tamales from house to house. Similarly, oysters seem to have been commonly sold by both free and enslaved African Americans in eighteenth- and nineteenth-century coastal U.S. cities.[16] African markets have long been home to women food sellers; in some markets women have been the exclusive purveyors of foodstuffs.[17] The low entry costs and relative availability of some food allowed people with little or no capital to add to their income by selling both raw and cooked provisions in these spaces. Peddling prepared foods into densely settled residential areas often provided one of the few opportunities for people of limited means to supplement family income and occasionally amass the capital for more lucrative commercial endeavors.[18] Their work, in turn, became crucial to the variety, quality, and sheer availability of food.

It was not only sellers whose labor provided food in crowded urban settings. To their efforts we should add that of fishermen, sailors, porters, barrel-makers, and countless others whose work formed new links in the food chain. These far-flung networks of people, many of whom did not (and still are not) understood as doing food work, were nonetheless crucial to luxuries and necessities in urban diets.

Industrialization: Making Food Outside of Homes and Creating Domesticity

These changes were, as it turned out, only the beginnings of the ways that industrialization would transform the work done around food. New foods were consumed in industrialized societies, created by industrialized processors, and grown on farms that were increasingly embedded in industrial supply chains. Industrialization accentuated the differences between regions and nations that were heavily based on manufacturing and mechanization, and those that were not. It raised new possibilities for, and enormous anxieties about, some of the oldest forms of food work—cooking and consuming in family groups. In all these ways, a focus on industrial production and industrial labor point especially to historical change. The industrial era, however, continued to reflect social systems through which work is accomplished and cultural beliefs about the relative significance of that work; lines of classed, raced, and gendered authority run through and help structure these spaces.

The foods at the center of European commercial empires were of particular importance in the diets of industrial workers. Sugar, rice, tea, and coffee were eaten in greater amounts than ever before by both rich and poor, but high-calorie foods and stimulating drinks occupied places of enormous importance in the diets of workers in industrialized countries. Their consumption helped their eaters to survive the requirements of wage labor, since these items offered the calories, energy, and, in the case of alcoholic beverages, the emotional release that facilitated long and sustained periods of monotonous work.[19]

The emergence of modern industrial manufacturing methods applied to food goes back at least to the mid-nineteenth century, when systems for canning meat cheaply and quickly were developed in Europe. Flour milling, too, became increasingly mechanized (and efficient) over the course of the nineteenth century. The techniques of vacuum sealing, glass jarring, and the slow invention of safe tin cans all became part of entrepreneurs' desire to meet large orders—first from governments (for soldiers) and then from civilian distributors. The result was that more and more people in industrialized areas worked at food to get wages, rather than to produce food for themselves. This also entailed a loss of control over the production process, transforming independent craftspeople such as bakers or jam makers into factory workers and shop clerks.[20]

The transformation of the work of food processing into wage labor is illustrated especially clearly by looking at meat. Originally meat had been butchered in relatively small quantities, and smoked, dried, processed into sausage, or simply cooked by individual households or small artisanal shops. In early modern and modern cities, butchers were well organized, and maintained licensing requirements to regulate the trade and restrict entry. Nonetheless, wage labor and industrialization took hold early in commercial meat processing—and with dramatic effects.

Beginning in the mid-nineteenth century, a large-scale meatpacking industry emerged in the midwestern United States, first in Cincinnati and then in Chicago.

The industrial division of labor utilized the famous "disassembly line," in which teams of workers systematically killed and dismembered animals at rapid speeds, sending the various parts off for a nausea-inducing number of products. Salted, canned, and eventually refrigerated meats and other products were then shipped across the United States and, increasingly, the world. Indeed, workers in many of the extractive and transportation industries that supported large businesses and mass production, such as sailors, railway workers, and miners, were important consumers of processed, canned meats.[21]

Employees in these sectors have worked in notoriously unsafe conditions. Upton Sinclair's famous 1906 account of the hazards of meatpacking (and meat eating) epitomized the disastrous working conditions of meatpacking; it is worth noting that the story has been retold in slightly different forms in recent exposés of chicken and beef production. Beginning in the late nineteenth century, a pattern in meatpacking emerged in which immigrant workers performed highly repetitive and difficult tasks, often under circumstances that led to meat contamination and their own injuries. Indeed, late twentieth-century centralization of poultry processing has made it one of the most dangerous industries in the United States. As numerous scholars have documented, divisions of language, class, and ethnicity complicate efforts at unionization—and these have been compounded by sporadic policing of workers' immigration status and the disruption of families and communities.[22] Unlike independent butchers, these processors have little control over the conditions of their work and less hope of achieving economic independence or exercising political influence.

However, industrial food work cultures are also sites of resistance. Food processing plant workers of different ethnicities sometimes find common ground and coordinate ways to control the work process. Vicki Ruiz points to Chicanas who worked in early twentieth century canneries as important mediators of U.S. culture for children, people who formed some of the most effective unions in any part of the food processing industry and instilled ethnically distinctive identities in the midst of the pleasures of mass culture and consumption.[23] And as historians have documented, meatpackers overcame barriers of race and ethnicity to mount powerful organizing campaigns in the 1930s and to operate powerful unions for decades afterwards.[24] Even among the lowest-paid workers, social networks can reshape work.

In this new landscape of food work, restaurants and restaurant labor emerge as especially important. These sites became common options for urbanites in the nineteenth century. Taverns, saloons, restaurants, peddlers, and delicatessens populated working-class neighborhoods, while restaurants in business districts and the increasing number of hotels catered to upper-class men.[25] Urban residents, in other words, purchased whole meals as well as ingredients to make them.

Kitchen workers in such establishments have experienced a transition similar to that of other wage workers. As in other businesses, restaurants became more likely to be parts of centrally controlled chains, rather than small stalls, taverns, or peddlers' carts. As with other food workers, kitchen workers in wealthier parts of the world came from less wealthy rural areas. And although high-end serving and cooking remained an important route to professionalization and living wages, such jobs were also often routinized, subject to tayloristic notions of efficiency, and given to workers who had few other options.[26] Still, in restaurants, as elsewhere, kitchen labor provided workers with moments to perform and create identities, form important cultures of support and solidarity, and push back against guidelines from above. As the historian Robin D.G. Kelley recalls of his and his high school shiftmates' refusal to wear hairnets, insistence on commanding the restaurant's radio, and attempts to impose their own work rhythms on pre-set routines, "the employees at the Central Pasadena McDonald's were constantly finding new ways to rebel." In the midst of profound change in where and how people got food, the work remained embedded in socialities and solidarities that both facilitated and disrupted food's production.[27]

Commercialization and industrialization moved the site of food production outside of homes, even as it also created the conditions under which "home" emerged as a separate category of space from "work." Over time, a gendered discourse of the separation of public and private spaces obscured the actual work that went into such domestic tasks as cooking, tending fires, and washing dishes for one's own family. Of course, household food production and processing was the crucial step in survival for most people—but it was precisely this sort of activity that, under industrialization, became a category of work that seemed curiously untouched by the technologies and the power relations of modern economies.[28] Home, one 1830s pastor explained, was "where... a man seeks a refuge from the vexations and embarrassments of business, an enchanting repose from exertion... "[29]

Industrialization and Provisioning: Making Work Visible

As the preceding discussion suggests, and in spite of the pastor's words, it is profoundly misleading to identify "domestic" labor, including cooking or preparing food, as restful activities contained in the home. These tasks have always required effort and exertion, and between 1500 and 1900, this work became embedded in outside wages, large-scale economic systems, and far-flung labors. Indeed, one of the most visible and important marks of the effects of industrialization is the way that most intimate and small-scale food work—preparing and serving food within homes—came to rely on economics and exchange.

Commercialized food became the mainstay of diets not only in industrialized places and among the well to do, but also in places far removed from industrialization and among the far less wealthy. Canned meats and milk were integrated into cuisines in India and Britain, albeit in ways that reflected differences in preference and resources of local eaters. From India to Asia to Mexico, colonized peoples also found ways to process and preserve foods that then were distributed locally and also globally, often via diasporas and migration. Adopted and adapted by its users, such food has reshaped menus even when, as in the modern Caribbean, it has contributed to distinctive ethnic and nationalist identities.[30]

As some families purchased food outside of their homes, others kept workers in their homes to prepare food. Domestic service was another way that wage work seeped into food production—in this case by modifying older patterns of service and social order. Modern domestic service took on different functions across time, space, and population, but cooking was long at the center of the work servants performed—and was also an important route to paid labor for impoverished or displaced women. Those female servants changed what their employers ate, resulting in hybrid cuisines that, although claimed and often promoted by elites, reflected the labor and ingenuity of paid employees.[31]

In all cases, paid domestic work had complicated meanings—serving as vital jobs for people in need of them, sometimes as stepping stones to authority within their employers' households, and also as sources of autonomy for women involved, who often chose this work over more dangerous industrial occupations or as a way out of impoverished families of origin. Immigrant, racialized, rural migrant, and colonized women took these positions—in places from Europe to the Americas to Asia—as they entered a world that increasingly rewarded wages rather than labor itself. Although family or household cooks have become less common in industrialized nations, in much of the world, hiring someone to cook or clean is a predictable life course event for middle-class families. Many women continue to turn to domestic service in areas that are undergoing rapid economic dislocation.[32]

The actual tasks required to prepare and serve food remained remarkably stable in spite of who did the work. Although nineteenth-century urbanites might procure food differently than rural inhabitants, they still cooked food. And although the accoutrements and styles changed, the work of serving still had to get done. Cooking techniques themselves changed relatively little over the modern period; women were still expected to perform the lion's share of domestic food preparation using cookstoves, fires, and enormous amounts of their own labor in the process (for instance, grinding corn for tortillas in Mexico and Central America or pounding tubers into fufu in West Africa).

This changed somewhat in the early twentieth century as part of a new prescriptive discourse that reframed kitchens as modern spaces where methods of efficiency and science could and should be applied by women doing their own cooking. Beginning in the mid-nineteenth and through the twentieth century, professional nutritionists, cookbook authors, and home economists claimed new authority over home food preparations. Rooted in western and industrialized nations, this new media had global ambitions and reach. Many experts sought to Americanize female immigrants by teaching them to replace traditional foods with food deemed healthier and also by imparting new techniques for cooking;

other texts and teachers traveled along with missionaries and western educators to colonies.[33] The prescriptions forwarded were contradictory. On the one hand, women were consistently urged to adopt labor-saving devices so as to make their food labor more efficient and less demanding. On the other, they were encouraged to plan cooking and meals as if they were operating businesses—introducing taylorist conceptions of time-management and efficiency into kitchen design and meal planning.

This advice did not always transform how women worked but it did have an impact on food preparation.[34] In industrialized parts of the world, many home cooks used the discourse and the material possibilities of industrial systems to ease the work of cooking and overseeing a household's food. The invention and distribution of coal or kerosene stoves promised a dramatic improvement over open hearth cooking, which was often dangerous and required constant tending of the fire; later gas and electric ovens offered equally important changes—eliminating the need to mind the stove to be sure coal didn't run out, for instance. Similarly, refrigerators and freezers limited the need to spend days canning and preserving food so that it would last the winter. Dishwashers simplified another time-consuming task that followed eating. Finally, in a continuation of the much older trend of purchasing foods commercially, more and more families began purchasing food in its final, consumable form and also having it served and cleaned up—by going to restaurants. Increased use of restaurants and fast-food establishments have further reduced the work families expend preparing their own food. By the 1950s, when even middle-class families began to frequent restaurants and diners, U.S. women spent an average of less than twenty hours a week in meal preparation and clean-up; by 1998, 47 cents of every dollar spent on food was, on average, spent away from home.[35]

Nevertheless, these changes have certainly not eliminated the work of cooking. Poorer households and poorer regions of the world have seen less use of commercially prepared food and cutting-edge appliances. Indeed, one mark of the difference between wealthy and non-wealthy households (and regions) is the degree to which cooks use appliances and modern technology and prepare food indoors. Even in industrialized societies famous for their use of new technologies, the tasks involved in cooking food and procuring changed, but were hardly eliminated. As time spent cooking or preparing food decreased, far more time was spent provisioning (shopping), planning meals, and procuring food. Marjorie DeVault studied women in late 1980s Chicago who sometimes spent whole days planning meals and procuring food for households, even if they sometimes purchased much of it. Joanne Vanek argued that, although families in the mid-1960s did spend less time cooking than in earlier times, time spent shopping for food and carrying it home had dramatically increased. Even this shopping, celebrated as a pleasure under mass retailing, remained effortful. Elsewhere I have argued that post World War II supermarkets were premised on women's traveling, planning, buying food, and carrying it home again; even "streamlined" mass retailers required significant labor from women.[36] Finally in much of the world (including western industrialized nations such as Italy and France), shopping and cooking were, and were expected to be, central elements of women's days.[37] Domestic production, then, offers a sense of the limits as well as effects of industrial systems on food work.

Agriculture: Ancient Food Production Meets Industrial Logic

Farming tells an even more dramatic tale of transformation. Arguably to a larger degree than was true in household cooking and food work, the nature of agricultural labor was remade in the nineteenth and twentieth centuries. It has been particularly marked by what many have called the "industrialization" of agriculture over the course of the twentieth century. Briefly, this can be described as an expansion of the trend of specialization of farms around particular crops (from sugar, coffee, rice, and tea to almost all grains and vegetables) and the widespread use of chemical fertilizers, pesticides, and carefully bred (and corporately controlled) types of plants and animals to increase yields. The industrialization of agriculture has both effected and reflected most farmers' decreased leverage over the food system and often over their own farms; in this way, agriculture remained central to food production even as nonagriculturalists increasingly offered the logic and resources with which work was accomplished. The tasks required to cultivate food remained strikingly similar to earlier periods (planting, fertilizing, irrigating, and harvesting plants; feeding, rearing, and slaughtering animals for meat; rearing and milking cows). And in much of the world, farming techniques continued as they long had—as did the importance of domesticated animals and agriculture to their proprietors' own diet and the local food supply.

Over time, however, both the logic and techniques of farming changed. For most of human history, farmers increased the size of their harvests by increasing the size of land they farmed, relying on more workers (both paid and unpaid), or both. Industrialization and the "green revolution" changed this. Yields were no longer limited by the size of land operated or the number of workers in a farmers' household, but by their investments in equipment, chemical fertilizers and pesticides, and, more recently, bio-engineered seeds.

Changes proceeded slowly at first. For example, plows gradually changed into heavier, more expensive, and more effective iterations that eased the back-breaking working of tilling fields. Farmers also increased, and began importing, fertilizers as a way to stabilize and predict yields. Many Western hemisphere farmers had imported guano and nitrates from Peru and Chile since the early nineteenth century. By the late nineteenth and early twentieth centuries, even small agriculturists in industrialized places began to use phosphate fertilizer and the fertilizers offered by reprocessers of industrial waste products. In the post World War II period, the use of these fertilizers exploded and farmers all over the world had access to the products of agribusiness, and often strong encouragement to use them.

Farmers' adoption of new techniques, and their focus on markets and the technologies of capitalism, was encouraged by prescriptive literature and, over time, by policies like those adopted during the green revolution. Indeed, "buying into" a particular technology often led to ancillary mechanization and a greater focus on market production for commercial processors and equipment. For instance, dairy farmers who purchased expensive milking equipment also often acquired significant debt. They then increased the size of their herds in part to pay off these debts.[38] New and popular seed varieties often must be purchased every season rather than, as had been the practice, growing from seed saved from previous years.[39]

Some agricultural work continued to require enormous amounts of hand labor (harvesting for instance). Even here, however, the transformative effects of a new labor model were felt. While small-scale agriculturalists continued to work in household and communal groups on these tasks, only occasionally supplemented with paid workers, large farmers, particularly in industrialized settings, increasingly hired displaced rural people as wageworkers. Paid agricultural workers, long an important supplement to family labor, have now become the mainstay of the global agricultural labor force. The result is that people who will not eat it, and cannot afford to purchase it, under conditions of very limited political and social power, harvest much of the world's food supply. Even recent sustainable and organic movements, designed to encourage smaller scale production, have come to rely on large-scale, wage-labor forces.[40]

Changes in production often did quickly increase yields, particularly in the wake of the green revolution in Asia and mechanization in the Americas. There is no question that farmers' work and planning, including their investments in fertilizers and machinery, have increased the amount of food in the world. However, the proceeds from farming (and in Africa, also of animal husbandry) did not, in general, proportionately increase. In many places farmers chose to or were forced to produce for export markets, and foods for home markets consequently became relatively expensive and in short supply. Indeed, in some areas of the world, this has resulted in more production but also dramatic inequality in wealth and ongoing poverty and malnutrition and enormously difficult work lives for many farmers, farm workers, and pastoralists.[41]

Rethinking the Work of Food

The tasks with which human food work began—procuring food from the environment—remain central to people's ability to eat. However, unlike the first peoples, in the new food regime many, many people who do this work most directly (farmers, commercial foragers, people who hunt, gather, or scavenge their own food) also rely on the work of far-away people growing and processing foods under industrial methods. This reliance has come with inequality; the people doing much of the labor for the world's food supply often, themselves, work in unhealthy conditions with very limited food to eat. These sorts of productive tasks epitomize the ongoing centrality of labor to food supplies—and the sometimes problematic and inadequate routes by which food travels to those who do food-related work.

But straightforward production-oriented tasks are only the beginning of the dissonance created by contemporary food work. For instance, home cooking is often not done in the home, and certainly not using ingredients that have been sourced from household members' labors. Often, the *lack* of food labor informs current discourse. Contemporary efforts to encourage people to eat locally grown foods and improve their diet often focus on the need for families—and especially mothers—to cook at home and from scratch.[42] By the late twentieth century, popular texts featured celebrations of labor-intensive cooking and lamented its demise.[43] Home-prepared family dinners have been credited with everything from reducing obesity rates to limiting drug use and premarital sexuality among teenagers.[44] Both the amount of labor (by paid workers) and its lack (by unpaid family members) are, in the current moment, cause for concern for many observers in wealthy countries. Eating food one has not labored to cook or to grow has always come with complex baggage, and never more so than in the contemporary world.

Amidst the injustices of the present, it is easy to forget that some things about food work have not been transformed by systems of commercialization or industrialization. The scale of agricultural production has increased, but agricultural labor also continues to exist, as it always has, in unpredictable and small-scale but enormously important ways. For instance, some historians have drawn our attention to farmers' resistance to exhortations that they produce for an export market and the limited efficacy to undo collective land ownership.[45] Nor is agriculture a self-contained sector in an industrialized era. All over the world, agriculture was carried with rural populations into cities and keeping livestock for food, gardening, and small-scale farming remained part of urban landscapes through much of the nineteenth century and in many cases into the twentieth and twenty-first. Examples include the wartime gardens, neighborhood plots, and other informal and private gardens tilled by individuals of many different classes. These have provided, and continue to provide, food to households. Finally, renewed interest in organic food and food-justice has resulted in a surge in small-scale farms. Even when these farms make use of migrant labor, they do so on a limited scale, sometimes in concert with community supported agriculture programs, in which consumers of produce help with harvests.[46] As these examples demonstrate, the work of growing and finding food remains part of many peoples' lives, even as the amounts produced by individuals and its proportion of peoples' diets varies widely.

Other things, too, disrupt the narratives of modernization that we so often use. For instance, public food markets remain important sources of income for impoverished peoples; recent research on Africa, Latin America, and parts of Eastern

Europe points to the ongoing importance of public markets and food sales, particularly for women's incomes.[47] And regardless of the particular tasks and the distribution of labor, gender orders often stand, as they have long done, at the center of food work.

Just as we might use labor to rethink food, I would argue that food can also be used to rethink typical (and problematic) categories of work. Food bridges neat divisions of chronology, space, scale, and organization that are often used to talk about workers. Despite the ostensibly progressive advance of civilization from foraging to farming to industry, older methods of food preparation have persisted, often using technologies (mortar and pestle; grilling on an open fire) that have changed only slightly since the Neolithic era. Even more modern arenas see the interconnectedness of industrial and farming practices. Nor, as Siegfried Giedion first observed, have discourses of rationality and efficiency transformed food processing that, by its organic nature, is inevitably inefficient and unpredictable.[48]

Perhaps most striking, the modern separation of "home" from "work" disintegrates when the discussion turns to family or household meals. Certainly, "food labor" in homes is a task without neat boundaries, encompassing much more than simply cooking food and washing the dishes. This has broad implications. While Marxist thought holds that industrial work is by definition waged work, unwaged home cooking is no less embedded in capitalism. However, it and other tasks done for one's own family (provisioning, shopping, dishwashing) are often omitted from the category of work and from labor history as a whole. This obscures the alienation of domestic labor and the centrality of unpaid work to economies and exchange. Placing food work at the center of our attention reveals new truths about economic systems as a whole.

In short, thinking about the histories of food and labor usefully disrupts the constraints on whose work and what work scholars examine, and the spaces where they look for labor. Analysts of food and how it is obtained, from modernization theorists of the green revolution to Karl Marx, seek neat separations between historical epochs and labor systems. But empirical studies of food do not allow for that. Rather, these point to the way that work happens everywhere, and that theories of work need to account for paid and unpaid labor, for affect as well as hard-nosed self interest. Thinking through food and labor allows us to integrate into scholarly analyses what people have long enacted in daily life; integration of public and private, thinking always of the many different kinds of work required to keep ourselves going.

Notes

1. On the ongoing importance of foraging, see Marla R. Emery and Alan R. Pierce, "Interrupting the Telos: Locating Subsistence in Contemporary US forests," *Environment and Planning* 37 (2005.): 981–993; Jane Kramer, "The Food at Our Feet," *New Yorker*, November 21, 2011, 80–91; Anna Tsing for the Matsutake Research Group, "Beyond

Economic and Ecological Standardisation," *The Austrailian Journal of Anthropology* 20 (December 2009): 347–68. On the limits of globalization, see J. K. Gibson-Graham, *The End of Capitalism (As We Knew It): A Feminist Critique of Political Economy* (Cambridge, MA: Blackwell, 1996). Anna Tsing, *Friction: An Ethnography of Global Connection* (Princeton, NJ: Princeton University Press, 2005).

2. Martin Jones, *Feast: Why Humans Share Food* (Oxford: Oxford University Press, 2007), 48–58, 77–79, 107–8; Richard Wrangham, *Catching Fire: How Cooking Made Us Human* (New York: Basic Books, 2009).

3. Marshall Sahlins, "The Original Affluent Society," in *Stone Age Economics* (Chicago: Aldine Publishing Co, 1974), 1–39.

4. Alan Outram, "Hunter-Gatherers and the First Farmers: The Evolution of Taste in Prehistory," in *Food: The History of Taste*, ed. Paul Freedman (Berkeley: University of California Press, 2007), 41, 48.

5. Ibid, 35–61.

6. Ibid; Marcel Mazoyer and Laurence Roudart, *A History of World Agriculture from the Neolithic Age to the Current Crisis*, trans. James H. Membrez (New York: Monthly Review Press, 2006), 82–83.

7. Arnold J. Bauer, *Goods, Power, History: Latin America's Material Culture* (Cambridge: Cambridge University Press, 2001), 27–33.

8. Sterling Evans, "Agricultural Production and Environmental History," in *The Oxford Handbook of Food History*, ed. Jeffrey M. Pilcher (New York: Oxford University Press, 2012); Peter B. Golden, "Nomads and Sedentary Societies in Medieval Eurasia," in *Agricultural and Pastoral Societies in Ancient and Classical History*, ed. Michael Adas (Philadelphia: Temple University Press, 2001), 71–115.

9. James Scott, *Weapons of the Weak: Everyday Forms of Peasant Resistance* (New Haven: Yale University Press, 1985).

10. John Mears, "Agricultural Origins in Global Perspective," in Adas, *Agricultural and Pastoral Societies*, 37; Richard Abels, "The Historiography of a Construct: 'Feudalism' and the Medieval Historian," *History Compass* 7 (2009): 1008–31.

11. Aldo Lauria-Santiago, *An Agrarian Republic: Commercial Agriculture and the Politics of Peasant Communities in El Salvador, 1823–1914* (Pittsburgh: University of Pittsburgh Press, 1999); Mazoyer and Roudart, *A History of World Agriculture*, 345.

12. Sidney Mintz, *Sweetness and Power: The Place of Sugar in Modern History* (New York: Viking Press, 1985); Judith Ann Carney, *Black Rice: The African Origins of Rice Cultivation in the Americas* (Cambridge, MA: Harvard University Press, 2001); Frederic Knight, *Working the Diaspora: The Impact of African Labor on the Anglo-American World, 1650–1850* (New York: New York University Press, 2010).

13. Mintz, *Sweetness and Power*, 146–50.

14. For more on the relationship between Atlantic slavery and the emergence of capitalism, see Walter Johnson, "The Pedestal and the Veil." *Journal of the Early Republic* 24 (Summer 2004): 299–308; Stephanie Smallwood, *Saltwater Slavery: A Middle Passage from Africa to American Diaspora* (Cambridge, MA: Harvard University Press, 2007). See also Eric Williams, *Capitalism and Slavery* (Chapel Hill: University of North Carolina Press, 1994).

15. On the everyday work of medieval merchants, see Kathryn Reyerson, *The Art of the Deal: Intermediaries of Trade in Medieval Montpelier* (Boston: Brill, 2002).

16. Helen Tangires, *Public Markets and Civic Culture in Nineteenth-Century America*. (Baltimore, MD: Johns Hopkins University Press, 2003).

17. For an overview of this work, see Bessie House-Soremekun, "Revisiting the Micro and Small Enterprise Sector in Kenya," *History Compass* 7 (2009): 1444–58.

18. Tracey Deutsch, *Building a Housewife's Paradise: Gender, Politics and American Grocery Stores in the Twentieth Century* (Chapel Hill: University of North Carolina Press, 2010), 28–32.

19. Mintz, *Sweetness and Power*, 186.

20. Jack Goody, *Cooking, Cuisine, and Class: A Study in Comparative Sociology* (Cambridge: Cambridge University Press, 1982).

21. Roger Horowitz, *Putting Meat on the American Table: Taste, Technology, Transformation* (Baltimore, MD: Johns Hopkins University Press, 2006); Richard With, "The Extractive Economy: An Early Phase of the Globalization of Diet," *Review: A Journal of the Fernand Braudel Center* 27 (2004): 285–306.

22. See, for instance, Steven Striffler, *Chicken: The Dangerous Transformation of America's Favorite Food* (New Haven: Yale University Press, 2005).

23. Vicki Ruiz, *Cannery Women, Cannery Lives: Mexican Women, Unionization and the California Food Processing Industry, 1930–1950* (Albuquerque: University of New Mexico Press, 1987).

24. For accounts of the coherence and divisions among meatpacking workers, see James Barrett, *Work and Community in the Jungle: Chicago's Packinghouse Workers, 1894–1922* (Urbana: University of Illinois Press, 1990); Roger Horowitz, *"Negro and White, Unite and Fight!": A Social History of Industrial Unionism in Meatpacking, 1930–1990* (Urbana: University of Illinois Press, 1997).

25. W. Scott Haine, "The Priest of the Proletarians: Parisian Café Owners and the Working Class, 1820–1914," *International Labor and Working Class History* 45 (Spring 1994): 16–28; Peter Scholliers, "The Diffusion of the Restaurant Culture in Europe in the Nineteenth Century: The Brussels Connection," *Food and History* 7 (2009): 45–68; Alison K. Smith, "Eating Out in Imperial Russia: Class, Nationality and Dining before the Great Reforms," *Slavic Review* 65 (Winter 2006): 747–768; Katherine Leonard Turner, "Buying, Not Cooking," *Food, Culture, and Society* 9 (Spring 2006): 13–39.

26. Tracie McMillan, *Foodless: On (Not) Eating Well in America* (New York: Scribners, 2012); Hans-Dieter Ganter, "Changes in Work Organization in French Top-Quality Restaurants," *Business History* 46 (July 2004): 439–460.

27. Robin Kelley, *Race Rebels: Culture, Politics, and the Black Working Class* (New York: The Free Press, 1994), 3. See also Dorothy Sue Cobble, *Dishing It Out: Waitresses and Their Unions in the Twentieth Century* (Urbana: University of Illinois Press, 1991).

28. Jeanne Boydston, *Home and Work: Housework, Wages, and the Ideology of Labor in the Early Republic* (New York: Oxford University Press, 1990); Michelle Dowd, *Women's Work in Early Modern English Literature and Culture* (New York: Palgrave Macmillan 2009).

29. Quoted in Nancy Cott, *The Bonds of Womanhood: Women's Sphere in New England, 1780–1835*, 2nd ed. (New Haven: Yale University Press, 1997), 64.

30. Richard Wilk, *Home Cooking in the Global Village: Caribbean Food from Buccaneers to Ecotourists* (Oxford: Berg, 2006).

31. Rebecca Sharpless, *Cooking in Other Women's Kitchens: Domestic Workers in the South, 1865–1960* (Chapel Hill: University of North Carolina, 2010); Cecilia Leong-Salabir, *Food Culture in Colonia Asia: A Taste of Empire* (New York: Routledge, 2011).

32. See, for instance, Hairong Yan, *New Masters, New Servants: Migration, Development, and Women Workers in China* (Durham: Duke University Press, 2008);

Raka Ray and Seemin Qayum, *Cultures of Servitude: Modernity, Domesticity, and Class in India*. (Stanford: Stanford University Press, 2009).

33. On these points see Megan Elias, *Stir it Up: Home Economics in American Culture* (Philadelphia: University of Pennsylvania Press, 2010); Priya Lal, "Mothers, Families, and the Nation: Home Economics and Rural Development in Tanzania, 1964–1975," paper presented at the Berkshire Conference of Women Historians, University of Massachusetts, Amherst, June 2011; Amelia Lyons, "The Civilizing Mission in the Metropole: Algerian Immigrants in France and the Politics of Adaptation during Decolonization," *Geschichte und Gesellschaft* 32 (October 2004): 489–516.

34. Susan Strasser, *Never Done: A History of American Housework* (New York: Pantheon Books, 1982); Ruth Schwartz Cowan, *More Work for Mother: The Ironies of Household Technology from the Open Hearth to the Microwave* (New York: Basic Books, 1983).

35. Douglas E. Bowers, "Cooking Trends Echo Changing Roles of Women" (January-April 2000), 23–29 [Online]. Available: www.ers.usda.gov/publications/foodreview/jan2000/frjan2000d.pdf [December 15, 2011]; Andrew Hurly, "From Hash House to Family Restaurant: The Transformation of the Diner and Post-World War II Consumer Culture," *Journal of American History* 83, no. 4 (March 1997): 1282–08.

36. Deutsch, *Building a Housewife's Paradise*; Joanne Vanek, "Time Spent in Housework," *Scientific American* 231 (November 1974): 116–20; Marjorie DeVault, *Feeding the Family: The Social Organization of Caring as Gendered Work* (Chicago: University of Chicago Press, 1991).

37. Emanuela Scarpellini, "Shopping American Style: The Arrival of the Supermarket in Postwar Italy," *Enterprise and Society* 5 (December 2004): 625–68; Peter Scholliers, "Worker's Time for Cooking and Eating in 19th and 20th Century Western Europe," *Food and Foodways* 6 (April 1996): 243–60.

38. On the efforts to persuade Asian peasant agriculturalists to adopt new technologies and "industrialize" agriculture, see Nick Cullather, *The Hungry World: America's Cold War Battle against Poverty in Asia* (Cambridge, MA: Harvard University Press, 2010). For a classic statement of this "treadmill" effect of mechanization in the United States, see Willard Wesley Cochrane, *The Development of American Agriculture: A Historical Analysis*, 2nd ed. (Minneapolis: University of Minnesota Press, 1993). On the industrialization of American agriculture in the first half of the twentieth century, see Deborah Fitzgerald, *Every Farm a Factory: The Industrial Ideal in American Agriculture* (New Haven: Yale University Press, 2003).

39. On the politics of twentieth-century seeds and agribusiness, see Jack Kloppenburg, *First the Seed: The Political Economy of Biotechnology, 1492–2000*, 2nd ed. (Madison: University of Wisconsin Press, 2004).

40. For similar labor conditions in agriculture, see Richard Walker, *The Conquest of Bread: 150 Years of Agribusiness in California* (New York: The New Press, 2004); Julie Guthman, *Agrarian Dreams? The Paradox of Organic Farming in California*, (Berkeley: University of California Press, 2004).

41. Cullather, *The Hungry World*; Michael Lipton with Richard Longhurst, *New Seeds and Poor People* (Baltimore: Johns Hopkins University Press, 1989).

42. Rachel Slocum, et al, "'Properly, with Love, from Scratch': Jamie Oliver's Food Revolution," *Radical History Review* 110 (Spring 2011): 178–191; Josée Johnston and Shyon Baumann *Foodies: Democracy and Distinction in the Foodie Landscape* (New York: Routledge, 2010).

43. For celebration of this see Michael Pollan, "Out of the Kitchen, Onto the Couch," July 29, 2009 [Online]. Available: http://www.nytimes.com/2009/08/02/

magazine/02cooking-t.html. [December 15, 2011]; Barbara Kingsolver with Steven Hopp and Camille Kingsolver, *Animal, Vegetable, Miracle: A Year of Food Life* (New York: Harper Perennial, 2008).

44. J. E. Fitzpatrick, L. S. Edmunds, and B.A. Dennison, "Positive Effects of Family Dinner Are Undone by Television Viewing," *Journal of the American Dietetic Association* 107, no. 4 (April 2007): 666–71; J. A. Fulkerson, et al, "Family Dinner Meal Frequency and Adolescent Development: Relationships with Developmental Assets and High-Risk Behaviors," *Journal of Adolescent Health* 39 (September 2006): 337–45. For a popularized version of this discourse, see Miriam Weinstein, *The Surprising Power of Family Meals: How Eating Together Makes Us Smarter, Stronger Healthier and Happier* (Hanover, NH: Steerforth, 2006).

45. David Vaught, *Cultivating California: Growers, Specialty Crops, and Labor, 1875–1920* (Baltimore, MD: Johns Hopkins University Press, 1999); Lauria-Santiago, *An Agrarian Republic.*

46. Laura Lawson, *City Bountiful: A Century of Community Gardens in America* (Berkeley: University of California Press, 2005).

47. On Eastern Europe, see Julie Hessler, *A Social History of Soviet Trade: Trade Policy, Retail Practices, and Consumption, 1917–1953* (Princeton, NJ: Princeton University Press, 2004).

48. Siegfried Giedion, *Mechanization Takes Command: A Contribution to Anonymous History* (New York: Oxford University Press, 1948).

Bibliography

Adas, Michael, ed. *Agricultural and Pastoral Societies in Ancient and Classical History.* Philadelphia: Temple University Press, 2001.

Boydston, Jeanne. *Home and Work: Housework, Wages, and the Ideology of Free Labor in the Early Republic.* New York: Oxford University Press, 1990.

Deutsch, Tracey. *Building a Housewife's Paradise: Gender, Politics and American Grocery Stores in the Twentieth Century.* Chapel Hill: University of North Carolina Press, 2010.

Lauria-Santiago, Aldo. *An Agrarian Republic: Commercial Agriculture and the Politics of Peasant Communities in El Salvador, 1823–1914.* Pittsburgh: University of Pittsburgh Press, 1999.

Leong-Salabi, Cecilia. *Food Culture in Colonia Asia: A Taste of Empire.* New York: Routledge, 2011.

Mapes, Kathryn. *Sweet Tyranny: Migrant Labor, Industrial Agriculture, and Imperial Politics.* Urbana: University of Illinois Press, 2009.

Mintz, Sidney. *Sweetness and Power: The Place of Sugar in Modern History.* New York: Penguin, 1985.

Robertson, Claire. *Trouble Showed the Way: Women, Men, and Trade in the Nairobi Area, 1890–1990.* Bloomington: Indiana University Press, 1997.

Striffler, Steven. *Chicken: The Dangerous Transformation of America's Favorite Food.* New Haven: Yale University Press, 2005.

Tsing, Anna, for the Matsutake Research Group. "Beyond Economic and Ecological Standardisation." *The Australian Journal of Anthropology* 20 (December 2009): 347–68.

CHAPTER 5

PUBLIC HISTORIES OF FOOD

RAYNA GREEN

WITHIN the arena of what is customarily called "public history," archivists, cultural resource and historical interpreters, museum professionals, and government and academic scholars (primarily archaeologists, scientists, and historians) engage a broad audience with food history. While no comprehensive list of public history practitioners or institutions follows this introduction to food history in the context of public history, what does follow is a description of the types and styles of food history found in public institutions and some discussion of notable examples of that history in practice in the United States. This essay also offers some examples of what is missing, and why, in the institutional (or public) recollection of major stories in food history.

In sites as diverse as museums, historic houses and communities, national parks, and food production facilities, these public historians collect, document, preserve, and present knowledge and practices, known as foodways, in the historical production, preservation, service, distribution, and consumption of food. Though ordinarily in service of presenting a larger social, cultural, and environmental or natural history, some food histories have more limited (and often, more commercial) goals. In most places, the histories can be presented in a highly accessible, often theatrical form of public education (e.g.: "living history"); in others, the presentation is more conventionally didactic and academic. Indeed, some sites produce a more complex activist or advocacy food history, directed toward, for example, gaining public understanding of and support for biological and cultural diversity, sustainability, improvements in community health, and recognition of the contributions of indigenous knowledge to the general health and nutrition of all.

In the United States and Canada, public museums, national parks, and historic homes and sites regularly feature exhibits and programs on food history, amidst all the other histories collated by any site. Historians specializing in food and agricultural history, together with archaeologists, biologists, and historians of the period, undertake the necessary research and planning for the "living history" or performance aspects of some museum programs. They write labels, handbooks, and guides to the objects and practices associated with food history. Commonly, they make certain of the authenticity of narratives or life histories of the plants, animals, specific foods, and food practices presented, largely in the context of a period or community history. Through food history, they often debunk common and popular myths about history. They demonstrate the connections of food and foodways to the economies treated, and describe the social and political relationships prescribed and conscribed by foods and foodways in the areas they present. Some of them, along with reenactors or living history interpreters, actually participate in the growing, harvesting, and preserving of crops and food, and advise and participate in the re-creation of tools and utensils of food storage and in cooking, from bake ovens to pots. In this respect, those who do food history as public history need to be, and generally are, experts in the material culture as well as in the period or community history of the food and foodways they research. But what is the food history they choose to reveal?

Some of the most vibrant forms of food history are found at those sites of early history that deal with the daily lives of the inhabitants of a site or region. Indeed, one may always find information in each of the ancient and historic sites about the gathering, preserving, storage and preparation of food, about the tools used for hunting, gathering, farming, and fishing, and about early methods of food preparation, storage, cooking, and preserving. The national parks that contain most of the ancient sites rarely engage (except for presentations by theatrically inclined park rangers) in a living history approach. More often, the accessible presentation of research (mostly archaeological) takes place in print and expert oral presentation. There is, quite often, considerable information in print form, or on labels at specific sites, about the plants and animals exploited by the peoples who occupied the site at different times. In most parks, it is the natural history of the site and its inhabitants that counts, and the food history is found largely in descriptions of the biodiverse universe and the relationships between the humans, plants, and animals living there. In such places, it is primarily through food history that environmental and social change is discussed.

At both archaeological and living history sites, the former residents' manner of getting, preserving, and cooking food (e.g., grinding and drying corn) attracts the most interest from the public. While eighteenth and nineteenth-century hearth cooking is the most commonly represented form of cooking in historic house and park sites, other forms of cooking demonstrations or methodologies also attract an audience. Excavated or restored pit ovens (*imu*) in Hawaii, adobe ovens or *hornos* in Arizona and New Mexico, various spaces, that is, pits or caves given over to the storage of food (such as corn, dried meat, or fish), and the garbage heaps or middens provide sites from which scholars have learned much about the foods and foodways of ancient peoples. The restorations and histories of the structures devoted to ceremonial gatherings in the Pacific Northwest, a Hawaiian men's eating house, and the several restored royal fishponds (*loko*) in Hawaii, where huge numbers of fish were "cultivated" for the consumption of the hundreds who lived around the sites, are essential to any understanding of the complex socio-political and environmental management systems which governed the lives of indigenous people.[1] In these, the histories and cultures of the eaters and the eaten generally receive equal time.

One of the most interesting of all the ways in which food history is used to educate the public is in the application of food history to advocacy, often and most successfully in the context of natural history, in places much like those mentioned above. Where the natural and cultural histories are told—about specific foods, plants, and animals, and humans—they are often told in order to convince the public of the need to support the survival of the species for their uses (to humans, animals, and the environment). An example of this kind of food-based public history can be found at botanical gardens throughout the country, for example, at the Desert Botanical Garden or the Arizona-Sonora Desert Museum. There, teams of historians, botanists, and anthropologists explore the relationships of indigenous peoples, birds, and animals to the land and its wild, edible, and functional plants from agaves and amaranths to beans and squashes.[2]

Such places track the histories of plant and animal uses and exploitation by native peoples, as well as those environmental and human factors that caused change, sometimes dangerous changes, in their environments. Their teams demonstrate how native knowledge can be used to care for the environment, and how using that knowledge can help save water, prevent erosion, shade the desert floor, reflect urban heat, and provide food and shelter for wildlife. The histories of these plants, animals, and humans, reflected in the public presentation and interpretation of them, have been used in the extensive efforts by historians, scientists, and native knowledge bearers to preserve biodiversity, improve health, build sustainable environments, and facilitate cultural revitalization.

Under the rubrics of groups such as the Renewing America's Food Tradition Consortium, plant biologists, ethnobotanists, historians, foresters, fishermen, political activists, and native knowledge bearers operate in specific regions to document, restore, and preserve traditional foodways. From the Seed Saver's Exchange to Native Seeds/SEARCH to the Northwest Indian Fisheries Commission to the Chef's Collaborative to Slow Food, USA (and International), from the American Livestock Breeds Conservancy to the Center for Sustainable Environments at Northern Arizona University to the White Earth Land Recovery Project in Minnesota, they use the natural histories of native foods to document endangered species and routes for biological recovery and cultural revitalization. The public histories presented are, in fact, well organized public relations campaigns in which scholars and community activists have joined forces to "save" and reinvigorate the cultivation of these important heritage plants and animals for the better cultural and biological health of people, animals, plants, land, and water.[3]

At early American living history museums such as Plimoth Plantation, for example, historians have documented both seventeenth-century English and Native American coastal Algonkian/Wampanoag foodways. They have given particular attention to those dynamics that changed both groups as a result of their early interactions. At Plimoth Plantation, food historians have also deconstructed and dismissed the mythologies central to a nationalist ideology and have reinterpreted an early meeting, commonly and mistakenly referred to as "the First Thanksgiving," between Wampanoags and Pilgrims. The resultant recasting successfully offered through food history a new context for the interpretation of Native American history, settler history, and environmental history. That recasting has enabled an interested public to know what was and what was not served (deer and eel, not turkey; baked pumpkin and squash, but not pumpkin pie), the social and political nature of the occasion (perhaps including a thanksgiving, practiced by both peoples), what foodstuffs and cooking practices were available to both the English and the Wampanoags (corn, of course, fresh and dried, but not much sugar, dairy, or wheat flour), and which group was likely responsible for what at the "feast" (ducks and geese from the English, dried fruits such as blueberries, cranberries, some nuts from the Wampanoags, some fresh vegetables, such as cabbages and carrots, from the settlers) in each instance, all quite different from the story recounted in the standard popular narrative.[4]

The new story rebalances the relationships between Pilgrims and Indians, making a more realistic and less self-serving, less "colonial" history of the English settlers on native lands. The new story is as much about interdependencies and native agency as about the satisfactions of a successful "conquest." Newer programs offered at Plimoth do not gloss over the differences between the settlers and the native people, nor do they minimize the discussions about the losses suffered and survival strategies of natives as a result of the "conquest." Both the stories of the contact-era and present-day people are told by living descendants of those people, often most profoundly through the demythologizing of "the First Thanksgiving." Even better, the story of "Thanksgiving" foods, as reimagined in Plimoth, is embedded in a significant tale of environmental history and change in New England.

Like Plimoth, the Jamestown Settlement presents the history of the first interactions between native peoples and the would-be settlers of this "New World." Jamestown begins slightly earlier than Plimoth, in seventeenth-century Virginia (1610), when the first British colonists were dependent on native foods and Native American peoples, then moves to "the starving time," when colonists tried and failed to be independent of natives and native foods, then to a later period (1624) in which they learned to support their own community. The colonists ultimately sought to separate themselves, replace Indians (and plants and animals) in their eco-niche, and begin to transform the local environment with their imported crops, foods, and foodways. In the parts of the Settlement that deal with the earliest period, in the Powhatan (Paspahegh) village, historical interpreters grow corn, forage and hunt, prepare fish and game, and process animal hides. After the "starving," inside the James Fort, "colonist" interpreters cultivate food and tobacco crops, prepare meals, and demonstrate colonial baking techniques using imported wheat flour. At Jamestown, as at Plimoth, they raise and present authentic animal breeds (chickens, sheep, and cattle) common to the seventeenth and eighteenth centuries.[5] The emphasis is neither on the native foods the colonists once treasured, nor on the environmental changes wrought by the new crops, animals, and human interventions in the ecosystem, but on the new life carved out of the first encounters by the settlers. The triumph of the new foods over the old native foods and provisions speaks to the triumph of the new cultures as they survive and prosper, but the consequences of those triumphs, to humans and to the landscape, remain obscured.[5]

At Colonial Williamsburg, the Department of Historic Foodways conducts and presents their ongoing dynamic research, and Williamsburg is the richest of all the living history sites in presenting a coherent food history. Like Jamestown, it is a triumphalist history, but nevertheless, more accurate, detailed, and complete. Here, the content providers understand the degree to which the public is interested in food, and the programs reflect that interest into the food and foodways of the period. The site has restored and interpreted kitchens and pantries and related outbuildings such as dairy barns and smokehouses, formal and kitchen gardens, bake houses, and wine cellars in the historic renovation of the village. Inns and taverns, open to the public, along with bake shops and butchers, are among the most commonly restored and interpreted structures along with the food and drink served in them. Williamsburg (and other historic sites) rely on the taverns and food sites to provide an income, but they also explore the history of the many treats enjoyed by the colonists from their trade with the Caribbean, Europe, Africa, and Asia, including, in particular, drink (tea, chocolate, coffee, rum, and wine) and locally produced whiskey, cider, and beer.[6]

The role of these foods in the local and global economies and in social, political, and diplomatic relations are the sources of presentation to visitors by the craftsmen and food producers who populate the village. In more recent interpretations of the site, often through the histories of the foods and foodways that became central to the daily lives of the eighteenth-century residents of Williamsburg, one can increasingly examine the more complete histories of the presence and contributions of slaves and free blacks to the cultural and economic complexities of a slave-holding society.

At Monticello, Jefferson's influence on and compelling interest in the development of American agriculture, viticulture, and horticulture, native and imported, reveals itself. His notes from his many experiments (on apples and grapes for example) in agronomy, viticulture, and domestic agriculture constitute the first American textbooks on the subject. In many ways, Jefferson was the first American food historian. His own documentation of his passions for plants, wine, and for food are extraordinary in their detail, as revealed in his papers and in his plans for Monticello (and the White House). He was, in fact, both a plant naturalist and plant nationalist, finding equal interest in the native repertoire and the imported (mostly French) store of good things. We should not find it curious then that he, most enamored of good French wine, would express hope for the production of American wines that would be "doubtless as good" as those of the Continent, although he would have had to live many lifetimes over before he would have seen that native expression grown and bottled at Monticello and in the rest of the country. Jefferson's notes on what to grow, eat, and drink—where, when, and how—are now realized in the faithfully renovated fields, gardens, and kitchens at Monticello.[7]

If an American natural history is furthered by the presentation of a Jeffersonian food and wine history at Monticello, it is in that same history that we find some of the seeds of a peculiarly American social history. In recent works we find much new evidence for Jefferson's passions for his slave Sally Hemings, but if we examine the known history of his life, we may find equal passions for food and wine more evident in his relationship with Hemings's brother James. In Jefferson's treatment of James, the only slave whom he eventually freed, we may find the compelling complexities and ironies in the eighteenth-century process of "becoming American" and of race, identity, and struggle. The obvious struggle for control takes place, indeed, in the bedrooms of the slaveholder, but also in the kitchens where slaves could and did begin to assert a culturally compelling command over a domain for men like Jefferson—equally politicized as the bedroom. Jefferson sent James to France to learn French and to learn the French command of the kitchen. Later, when James returned voluntarily to Philadelphia, instead of remaining in antislavery France where he could have remained free, Jefferson actually paid his slave a salary for his achievements in the kitchen. James's command of the kitchen was so revered by Jefferson that he set, as the price of Hemings's requested freedom, the servitude of James's brother, Peter Fossett, who was forced into kitchen service when Jefferson let his beloved chef free. Jefferson's sentiments then, were not toward a generically offered freedom for all, but only for the one who had served him, quite literally, so well. These subtleties in his attitudes and practices toward slavery and servitude are handled very carefully at Monticello alongside Jefferson's well-documented and unstinting passion for agriculture, for wine, for food, and for fine service.[8]

At Monticello, as at Williamsburg and other reconstructions of plantation era America, the physical structures associated with the daily lives and work of slaves, particularly the cultivation of food and cash crops and the preparation and service of food by slaves, have been increasingly interpreted along with the lives of the masters. In the documented histories of the "big houses," particularly in Jefferson's and a few other early plantation owners' extensive notes on what was grown in their gardens, prepared in their kitchens, and served at their tables, we can begin to see the rejection and modification of Native American foods, the introduction of African foods, foodways, and cooking techniques into the European repertoire, and the increase in European and American made fine foods as the house developed in wealth and stature. Regarding slave-holding houses, research has begun at last to reveal the extent to which slaves cultivated their own gardens and were allowed to hunt and manage their own food supplies and distribution, Since the histories of sugar and rice, rum and molasses can be found on all the old plantations-turned-historic-houses, we find that we can also examine environmental degradation and decline and regional economic history in the plantation stories in tandem with the essential histories of slavery and race. So a good food history, one that begins to address some of the more complex issues of class, race, and gender, for example, is completely tied to the excellence of its historic archaeology and archival research programs, along with an institutional commitment to the interpretation and presentation of such material in the program.[9]

In the less grand communal kitchens, gardens, and foodways of intentional communities, such as the Amana Colonies or any one of the Shaker restorations, a specialized kind of food history appears. In the case of the Shakers, where much is made of their philosophies and practices regarding religion and work, the sites also explore the Shakers' unique and successful ways with gardening, farming, animals, seed saving, food storage, and cooking, as well as in their innovative and lucrative seed business. Shaker sites, for example, specialize in the serving of Shaker meals and in the development of cookbooks based on Shaker recipes, along with the generally reverential treatment accorded their furniture making. One assumes that although the general audience may not at all relate to the restrictive pietism of the Amana faithful or the self-defeating Shaker demand for celibacy, they can relate to the revelations of the joys of collective life and the setting of a fine table, as well as to the utterly admirable business instincts of the faithful. The same surprises, one suspects, apply to the marvelous history of the American monastic orders connected to the post-Prohibition restoration of the American wine industry, told at such sites as the several restored monastery wineries in Napa, California. In the histories of wine and seeds might rest an American religious and communitarian history unrevealed in textbook treatments of religious history.[10]

A more conventional food history also appears in a few museums associated with religious history, for example, at the Jewish Museum in New York. The museum has both a collection and a history of exhibitions in which they explore the connection of food and drink to worship, ritual, and culture. The collection includes objects ranging from Passover seder sets from Germany to a modern sculptural rendering of a kiddush cup to photographs from Russia of the baking of matzoth for Passover. The exhibition narratives comment on the ceremonial functions of food and drink in Judaism, as part of ritual meals in the Sabbath and festivals, or in fulfilling Jewish dietary laws (kashrut). In explaining the material culture of Passover—for example, the wine cups, the seder plate on which rest six elements symbolic of the Jews' delivery from slavery in Egypt, the matzo plate, its covers, the special dishes only used during Passover seder—essentially the entire religious ritual is discussed along with a considerable lesson in the histories of Jewish diasporic communities. The food histories, told through the objects, often highlight more information about the diversity of communities from the Jewish Diaspora, from Mexico to Brazil to the United Kingdom to Argentina to Sweden to Iraq. This approach yields a much more compelling, less universalized notion of Judaic cultures than the narrative presented in most museums and archives, which is confined to that of an Ashkenazic majority with an East European dominance.

Farm and ranch history dominates most of the historic sites, and those sites present a thin food history. Most of the interpretations offer a familiar and repetitive story, a variant on business history connected with a particular venue. At most, a mild modern fixation on reenacted ranch and cowboy cooking of the nineteenth century, buried under the story of industrial cattle production, surfaces in the very popular cowboy cooking competitions held across the western states. Rarely, however, do attendees at either the competitions or the historic sites learn of the consequences—to humans, land, and water—of industrial cattle ranching (or dairy farming or poultry production) and marketing. As in other venues for business or corporate history, the stories told here about the food itself (e.g., how to cook biscuits in a cast iron pot), the cooks (ranch cooks provisioning their chuckwagons), and the daily lives of cowboys and ranchers are generally celebratory, romanticized, and uncritical.

An increasing number of public institutions are devoted to things maritime, in sites such as Mystic Seaport (in Connecticut), and in these venues the food history is a bit deeper and more thoughtful than in the farm and ranching museums. The larger maritime museums have consulted food historians in the process of seeking authenticity and detail in their presentation and demonstration of various maritime food practices. They examine food as it was prepared and served from the galleys to the decks of water-going vessels (schooners, whaling ships, fishing and lobster boats, oyster sloops, crab boats) or as it was experienced in daily life in a maritime community. Many of these have paid attention to the history of specific food and drink productions from the early sea trade—for example, the sugar, rum, molasses, and spice trades—the food connections of the whaling industry, and local fishing industries, as well as to the provisioning and preserving of food and drink in the daily lives of seamen.

These institutions have paid a great deal of attention to the foods that derive from the particular and demanding conditions of life at sea, such as the preparation of durable hardtack (instead of fresh bread that will mold), the provision of several forms of citrus (to provide Vitamin C and prevent scurvy) over long months at voyage, and the trades (barrel making, for example) needed for the successful storage of foods that must survive dry in a wet environment. As a result, contemporary audiences show almost as much interest in the foods of watermen as in the foods developed for astronauts (a big hit in the National Air and Space Museum in Washington, D.C.). A few maritime sites have taken seriously the decline of ocean and waterway food resources to help visitors understand the need for sustainable resource behaviors, the preservation of biodiversity, and the ravages of climate change and global warming in maritime environments.

Industrial museums also depend on food history to tell their stories, even if the food or foodstuff essential to the industry is only mentioned incidentally in the stories the museum tells. Although these museums focus primarily on the corporate businesses that produce food, occasionally they also teach a social history of the people who worked for the corporate entity. For instance, built on the site of what was once the world's largest flour mill, the Mill City Museum is located on the Mississippi River. Here visitors may learn about "the intertwined histories of the flour industry, the river, and the city of Minneapolis." The site had a major role in the production of a food substance (in this case, flour from wheat) but primarily interprets and presents a history of an industrial mill, along the way saying something about wheat agriculture and labor in the Great Plains, the technologies of milling, the industrialization of flour, and, of course, the influential presence of flour products in American kitchens. In this museum, however, baking actually takes place alongside the industrial flour mill exhibitions, and the kitchens there introduce audiences to the most popular products (i.e., baked goods) of flour milling.

There are hundreds of old mill sites around the country, and even an association of mill enthusiasts, but their enthusiasm is generally reserved for the old, scenic grist mills rather than for the grain ground in them, the history of the grain that came to be milled, or the social, cultural, or economic histories implicit in the utilization of the grains and the mills. The focus here is almost always on grist mills rather than on the less widespread but economically important rice, syrup, sorghum, or cane mills and the disastrous consequences of the labor and environmental practices associated with them.[11] Rarely do the historic mill sites in North America ever treat the history and economics of grain milling in their region, much less the traditions of milling practiced in Europe. They most assuredly do not treat the unhealthful germ-removing milling techniques of nineteenth-century Anglo American industrial mills, techniques responsible for the nutritional deficiencies in early twentieth-century flours.

Throughout Europe, museums related to specific foods treat important cultural and economic focuses within their region. In these, the history of that particular food and drink—most often wine, beer, cheese, bread, or chocolate—accompanies the exegesis of the work traditions and the environmental and cultural attachments of that region or country to the particular food. There are substantially fewer of these in the United States and Canada than in Europe. Most of the museums in the United States that deal with a specific food are corporate or brand-driven museums (the SPAM® Museum, the Jell-O Gallery Museum, the Tabasco Factory and Country Store, the World of Coca-Cola) or part of a culinary business. These collect, display, and research only items associated with their brand and product. Everything displayed is essentially part of their corporate history. Some of these corporate museums have available to them excellent technological and cultural histories of the cultivation or production of the main ingredients in the branded products, and the development, marketing, merchandising, and consumer histories of these products. For example, the SPAM Museum used to feature wonderful narratives about the importance of SPAM to U.S. military rations in the Pacific during World War II and the consequent cross-cultural influence and importance of SPAM in Hawaiian cultural practices and foodways after the war. It no longer does so, either at the museum or on its website. Instead, it offers recipes for SPAM.[12] At the Tabasco Factory and Store, one may take tours of the factory and watch the product being made, but along with that process the factory museum now offers only tiny bits of the local, economic, environmental, cultural, and family history that it used to feature, which is now reduced unfortunately to a branded hype of the product and associated goods (Tabasco hats, shirts, and servingware).

The main effect of these museums is an often-entertaining education in the connections of American popular culture to American food culture and thus to a capitalist enterprise, but these connections rest in a kind of branded and politicized food history peculiar to the United States. Most offer substantial histories of their advertising, often associated with long-used beloved and often notorious and controversial food figures—Betty Crocker (flour), Uncle Ben (rice), Aunt Jemima (pancake mix), the Land O'Lakes Indian maiden (butter), Miss Mazola (corn oil) and the Frito Bandito (corn chips). Critiqued in scholarly literature and in public discourse for their racialized and gendered stereotypes, such ad campaigns cover up the connections of these products to the appropriation of Native American lands and foods and the enslavement and servile labor of Latinos and African-Americans.

Most of these sites and the large history museums in the United States are as remarkable for the food histories they do not tell as for the ones they do tell. At the National Museum of the American Indian (NMAI) in Washington, D.C., the gardens and grounds surrounding the museum begin to demonstrate the significant contributions of native peoples of the Americas to foods of the world. Yet these plants remain relatively uninterpreted; an occasional tour or program based on the plantings helps bring the complex history into play. That focus on Native American influences on America's natural history and on the American food repertoire continues inside the museum with Mitsitam, a café that serves native foods of the Americas—though, as in the gardens, the foods are served without interpretation to the public. Only the occasional special program (on chocolate or corn, for example) fills in the historical blanks. A huge percentage of NMAI's collections, as with every other culturally focused museum in the country, can be related to food, but the collections are rarely seen and presented in that way. The objects presented are about hunting or fishing, about women's work and men's work, about art and craft, about social and political relationships, but almost never about how the history of the serving vessel, the weapon, the basket, or the obverse side of the Peace Medals (with Indian hands at the plow) can be used to illumine those other human conditions and relationships.

No site examines the history of corn agriculture in the Americas, the technologies and observational science deployed by the Native American women who developed corn agriculture, or the methods employed by them to treat corn that released B-vitamins and magnified nitrogen-based proteins (the process of nixtamalization). Nowhere, at NMAI or in the grain museums, does anyone treat the genius of Native American women in securing the diversity in prehybridized native corns, with their complex adaptations to climate and place. Nor does any site treat those women's development of companion planting or intercropping (with beans, squash, and other plants) for nutritional gain, predator plant suppression, and other environmental efficiencies of Native American site management. That is a food history left only to scholars, regrettably untranslated for a public audience. But the capabilities to tell that story exist in the museums that have the intellectual and material wherewithal to tell all these stories and more. These are revolutionary tales that can transform the general public's image of indigenous people, and have meaning for the current nutritional and cultural health. Certainly, any attempt to rise above the usual "contributions" arguments (e. g,. Native American people gave corn to the world) would be, as in the Plimoth model, an incredibly important public history.

Other museums, as part of new initiatives, have begun to collect in food history and to present that history to their publics. Libraries and archives, ever repositories for early cookbooks and guides to housekeeping (which included recipes for food preservation, preparation, and service), have increased their holdings and made them more available to a wider audience. Huge collections of cookbooks and other books on wine and food published and in manuscript form, from every part of the world, are now available to the public at the Library of Congress, the University of Michigan, the Schlesinger Library at Radcliffe College (Harvard University), Cornell University, the New York Public Library, New York University, and the University of California at San Diego. Most of these places now feature archival and library collections of famed culinary collectors such as Eleanor Lowenstein, writers such as M.F.K. Fisher, and public figures such as Julia Child. Websites make them accessible to a wider public, and materials from the collections are beginning to see the light in electronic and print publications and in exhibitions that feature them. These institutions have made available materials such as cookbooks, to scholars—in gender and class studies for example—who have begun to treat them as the culturally significant documents they are.

Like most large museums, the National Museum of American History at the Smithsonian has many old food-related collections that were not assembled because of their connections with food but under some other rubric. Museum archival collections, for example relating to food and drink, have as their center of interest mid-twentieth century advertising (e.g., Pepsi Cola), business history (e.g., Hills Bros. Coffee, Krispy Kreme Doughnut Corp.), and the history of individual inventors and innovators (Earl Tupper and Tupperware). Material collections focus on industrial and technological production of food, from whaling to cotton farming, brewing to milling, canning to candy making, and chicken farming to dairying. Many examples of food preservation, production, and packaging, mostly mass produced and infinitely pop cultural (SPAM, the first frozen TV dinner tray, the Krispy Kreme Ring King) fill the storage shelves. From ovens to kettles, cookie cutters to aprons, from ice cream to coffee making, textiles, earthen and ceramic wares, glass and metal tools, utensils, and serveware related to home food preparation, service, and consumption, mostly represent nineteenth and early twentieth century domestic life. There are, of course, rare eighteenth-century pieces and even rarer objects from the late twentieth and early twenty-first centuries. Most older objects are from middle and upper class worlds, largely from east of the Mississippi, and might have been used to illuminate, in research and exhibition, American business, corporate, industrial, or upper class history and, in many cases, the history of "founding fathers" and "captains of industry" or, more rarely, the lives of middle and upper class women.

Late twentieth century's historians, folklorists, and anthropologists, with their emphasis on the material culture of daily life and hitherto unrepresented communities, began to repair the substantial gaps in the collections, exhibit the new, and reinterpret the old. Food historians, folklorists, and cultural historians have discovered these collections and are now using them in popular and academic books, some directly understood as food history. Public historians have begun to use many of these items in films and in electronic media. At the National Museum of American History at the Smithsonian Institution, newer collections on American modern winegrowing, Julia Child's Kitchen, and foodways in Mexican-American communities are used to explore the intersections of race, class, and identity, as well as changing gender roles and global economies. They gravitate away from an older agricultural history that focused on crops of economic significance in the Midwest and South (tobacco, cotton, corn, wheat) to a social and cultural history that considers the consequences of agrarian growth and decline.

In collecting and exhibiting the material culture of the daily lives of people under imprisonment, relocation, migration, distress, and war, a different sort of history is achieved by juxtaposing the tools (short hoes, for example), utensils, and clothing of *braceros* (Mexican agricultural contract workers) and those of farm owners, of sweatshop laborers and those of their "bosses," of slaves and those of masters, of sharecroppers and those of landholders, of Japanese internment camp residents and those of their military "supervisors." Taken as food history, rather than as the history of technology or business history, a more complex analysis yields a better public education, one that is global, transnational, and transcultural, as well as technological and national.

These new material collections will be understood in new ways when they are collected with the widest interdisciplinary methods and presented with the widest audiences in mind. No longer are they understood only as research collections, these objects are collected with the larger public in mind, especially the new audiences of communities identified with these objects within a globalized America. The new collections come complete with oral histories (in photography, film, video, and audio) of the makers, inventors, and users and the cultural and social relations of these things, a set of relationships that can produce serious food history in the context of public history. As an example of what new objects collected and exhibited in this new manner can offer, we might look at the recent collections in

Mexican American food history at NMAH. In a 2009 temporary exhibition, followed by a longer-term exhibit in 2012, NMAH has begun to show and interpret things that reveal the intersections between ethnicity, identity, immigration, gender, culture, and labor. Collections, complete with oral histories and photo documentation, come from a California family who labored in ranching, fruit growing, and owning a grocery store before they operated a neighborhood tortilleria (tortilla and tamale bakery). The exhibition of the family's collected material features the history of their *molino*, or corn mill, and its companion pieces, a *tortilladora* (tortilla press) and *comal* (griddle), and grandmother's baking apron. Such display goes beyond the customary technological history of hand mills, griddles, and bread making machines to examine the tortilla and its centrality to women's work. It projects questions about identity in the Latino world, to immigration history from Mexico to California, and to an economic history of how immigrants may move from migrant labor to entrepreneurial success in the mainstream economy.[13] A simple food history of tortillas and tamales—now common in every grocery store across the country—can be used to comment upon relationships, through public history, in a world where noisy daily conflict over Latino immigration and labor abounds.

Such a public discourse might be complex and prove controversial, however. As with public art, the funds for furthering such public discourse are public. Officials often think that they, who collect and dispense public funds, should control the content of public discourse. Any complaint over institutional departures from received history (e.g., Plimoth Plantation and myth-busting reinterpretations of "the First Thanksgiving") often elicits demands from officials for a return to the older interpretations as well as threatened and actual budget cuts for the offending programs and institutions. Even privately funded programs and exhibitions in public institutions offer the double-edged sword of possible donor interference in content alongside threats of critique by public officials, in spite of private funding. Rather than face public and private donor-driven wrath over the dismantling of publically and politically beloved "sacred" mythologies, institutions often struggle for years to alter exhibitions and collections, often making less significant and often intellectually indefensible changes over time. A thoughtful food history offers a remarkable opportunity for challenging these "sacred" mythologies, but often, as in the story of American Thanksgiving, the food history itself is centered in the mainstream interpretation.

This chapter speaks only briefly to the problems and promise of food history as public history, just as it refers to only a limited number of American public food histories. The popularity of food and food history, with a public clearly hungry for more, suggests the extraordinary possibilities for history that can be explored in the public domain. Food histories, large and small, offer not only a unique way of getting to "big" issues in conventional areas of historical research, but also an interesting route for deconstructing arguments about contemporary debates on topics such as nutrition and class to further an informed public discourse.

Notes

1. "Puuhonua of Honaunau National Historical Park." [Online]. Available: http://www.nps.gov/puho. [December 20, 2011]. "Canyon de Chelly National Monument." [Online]: Available: http://www.nps.gov/cach/historyculture/index.htm. [December 20, 2011].

2. "Desert Botanical Garden." [Online]. Available: http://www.dbg.org. [January 31, 2011]. "Arizona Sonora Desert Museum." [Online]. Available: http://www.desertmuseum.org. [December 20, 2011].

3. Gary Paul Nabhan and Annette Rood, comp. and ed., *Renewing America's Food Traditions (RAFT): Bringing Cultural and Culinary Mainstays of the Past into the New Millennium* (Flagstaff: Center for Sustainable Environments at Northern Arizona University, 2007). Many of these individual projects are described in this comprehensive source.

4. "Plimoth Plantation." [Online]. Available:http://www.plimoth.org/learn/thanksgiving-history/partakers-our-plenty. [January 31, 2011].

5. "Jamestown National Historic Site" (part of Colonial National Historical Park). [Online]. Available: www.historyisfun.org/jamestown-settlement.htm. [December 20, 2011].

6. "Colonial Williamsburg." [Online]. Available: http://www.history.org/foundation/journal. [January 31, 2011].

7. Damon Lee Fowler, *Dining at Monticello: In Good Taste and Abundance* (Charlottesville, VA: Thomas Jefferson Foundation, 2005); Dave Dewitt, *The Founding Foodies: How Washington, Jefferson, and Franklin Revolutionized American Cuisine* (Naperville, IL: Sourcebooks, 2010); James M. Gabler, *Passions: The Wines and Travels of Thomas Jefferson* (Baltimore: Bacchus Press, 1995), 205; from Jefferson's letter to C.P. de Lasteyrie, July 15, 1808, Library of Congress, Papers of Thomas Jefferson. "We could in the United States make as great a variety of wines as are made in Europe, not exactly of the same kinds, but doubtless as good. Yet I have ever observed to my countrymen, who think its introduction important, that a laborer cultivating wheat, rice, tobacco, or cotton here, will be able with the proceeds, to purchase double the quantity of the wine he could make . . . In general, it is a truth that if every nation will employ itself in what it is fittest to produce, a greater quantity will be raised of the things contributing to human happiness, than if every nation attempts to raise everything it wants within itself."

8. Annette Gordon-Reed, *The Hemingses of Monticello: An American Family* (New York: W.W. Norton & Company, 2008).

9. Sidney W. Mintz, *Sweetness and Power: The Place of Sugar in Modern History* (New York: Viking Books, 1985); Jessica Harris, *The Welcome Table: African-American Foodways* (New York: Simon and Schuster, 1995).

10. There is not much scholarly material on food and religious history. See Daniel Sack, *Whitebread Protestants: Food and Religion in American Culture* (New York: St. Martin's, 2000), for a general reference on the topic. See also any material on the transformation of the Christian Brother's Winery, known as Greystone Abbey, in St. Helena, California, into a commercial winery and then to the Culinary Institute of America. While monastic prodders everywhere in the United States and in Europe are producers of foodstuffs (breads, wines, liqueurs, cheeses, and condiments), they are not particularly much interested in the exhibition or public examination of their work.

11. See Mintz, *Sweetness and Power*, for extensive commentary on labor, power relations, and slavery in his treatment of sugar production in the Americas.

12. See George H. Lewis, "From Minnesota Fat to Seoul Food: SPAM in America and the Pacific Rim," *Journal of Popular Culture* 34, no. 2 (2000): 83–105, for his decent treatment of the cultural and political meanings of SPAM in the South Pacific.

13. See Jeffrey M. Pilcher, *¡Que vivan los tamales! Food and the Making of Mexican Identity* (Albuquerque: University of New Mexico Press, 1998), for extensive comment on the role of corn, tortillas, and tamales in Mexican women's identity along with a general Mexican identity.

Bibliography

"Colonial Williamsburg." [Online]. Available: http://www.history.org/foundation/journal. [January 31, 2011].

"Desert Botanical Garden." [Online]. Available: http://www.dbg.org. [January 31, 2011].

Dubin, Steven C. *Displays of Power, Memory, and Amnesia in the American Museum.* New York: New York University Press, 1999.

Dusselier, Jane. "Does Food Make Place? Food Protests in Japanese American Concentration Camps." *Food and Foodways* 10, no. 3 (2002): 137–165.

"The Food Museum." [Online]. Available: http://www.foodmuseum.com. [January 31, 2011].

"Jamestown National Historic Site" (part of Colonial National Historical Park). [Online]. Available: www.historyisfun.org/jamestown-settlement.htm. [December 20, 2011].

Kirshenblatt-Gimblett, Barbara. *Destination Culture: Tourism, Museums, and Heritage.* Berkeley: University of California Press, 1998.

Long, Lucy, ed. *Culinary Tourism.* Lexington: University Press of Kentucky, 2003.

Nabhan, Gary Paul and Annette Rood, comp. and ed., *Renewing America's Food Traditions (RAFT): Bringing Cultural and Culinary Mainstays of the Past into the New Millenium.* Flagstaff: Center for Sustainable Environments at Northern Arizona University, 2007.

Ory, Pascal. "Gastronomy." In *Traditions*, vol. 2 of *Realms of Memory: The Construction of the French Past.* Edited by Pierre Nora, translated by Arthur Goldhammer, 442–67. New York: Columbia University Press, 1997.

"Plimoth Plantation." [Online]. Available:http://www.plimoth.org/learn/thanksgiving-history/partakers-our-plenty. [January 31, 2011].

PART II

FOOD STUDIES

CHAPTER 6

GENDERING FOOD

CAROLE COUNIHAN

WITH great anticipation on the morning of March 21, 2009, I entered the conference hall in Fiumicino, Italy, which was buzzing with the excitement of approximately 500 delegates to the Slow Food Italy National Assembly of chapter leaders. Slow Food (SF) is an international membership organization devoted to "good, clean, and fair food" that had its origins in Italy in 1986 and had grown to over 100,000 members in 130 countries by 2010.[1] All members belong to a local chapter, of which there are 1,300 in the world and approximately 300 in Italy. The Fiumicino meeting brought together chapter leaders and members from all over Italy for two days of brainstorming about Slow Food's national and local efforts to make food more tasty, healthy, sustainable, and democratic.

The 2009 chapter assembly was the biggest and most diverse to date—with greater age ranges and more women than ever before. At the same time, however, the front stage on opening day was striking—it consisted of seven men and one woman and symbolically depicted the dominance of men in the Slow Food power structure. The men consisted of SF International president and founder Carlo Petrini, SF Italy president Roberto Burdese, SF Italy vice president and national secretary Silvio Barbero, and others; the lone woman was Valeria Commeti, director of the SF Education office and member of the SF National Council. Throughout the morning, in their five-minute speeches, several delegates spoke—jokingly and seriously—about the composition of the head table. On the second morning a new panel greeted us—consisting of two men—Burdese and Barbero—and six women, several of whom were on the SF National Council or worked for SF, but none of whom was a major leader of the organization as the two men were.[2] Again that day there were more gender jokes and comments about tokenism, and it did not escape notice that few of the women at the head table had any official role on the program.

These observations led me to pose the question: does gender matter in food activism? Whether gender matters is a central question in feminism. In the case of food activism, where does a focus on gender lead us? I define food activism as the conscious effort to promote social and economic justice through food practices. How do foodways—the beliefs and behaviors surrounding food production, distribution, and consumption—constrain and empower men and women to become political actors? How are gender power and identity enacted in food activism? Gender is part of a bigger story of human relationships, alliances, divisions, hierarchies, and power; studying gender is fundamentally an interrogation of equality in the food system.

In this essay, I survey the literature on food and gender while using my own current research as a methodological model of how to examine a particular problem—in this case, how gender can enlighten the study of food activism. I take a feminist anthropological approach to this question but tap into works from a range of social sciences. I refer to my own ethnographic research on food, culture, and gender in Sardinia and Florence, Italy, and Pennsylvania and Colorado, USA, where I have used a food-centered life history methodology to explore people's depictions of the role of food in their lives. I have found that food provides a rich voice especially for women to talk about their experiences, their cultures, and their beliefs—making available to the public lives that would otherwise go unnoticed—the lives of ordinary women. In my new research I am joining scholars who are increasingly turning their attention to women taking food public—to the ways that women use food in the public sphere, particularly as voice and practice of activism.[3]

Gender, Feminism, and Food Activism

Gender is the social construction of sex differences—the ways that different cultures define male, female, and—in some cultures—third genders separate from male and female, the Zuni "two-spirit" for example.[4] Whereas biology determines men's and women's reproductive and physiological differences, culture defines their meaning and value through gender codes and distinctions. Across cultures and epochs, gender has played a key role in foodways.[5]

Feminism is the approach to social life and social theory whose central question is: does gender matter? Henrietta Moore's definition of feminist anthropology has four components that can frame an approach to foodways research.[6] First, it focuses on women—not at the exclusion of men, but as the center of analysis and starting point of research. Second, feminism affirms and addresses women's diversity and challenges universalizing generalizations about "woman." It pays attention to what sociologists have called "intersectionality," which refers to the ways that gender and other social categories—such as race, ethnicity, religion, class, and age—intersect, compounding and confounding what it means to be female.[7]

Third, feminism identifies and challenges not only gender inequality, but all forms of inequality. Fourth, through the generation of new data on women's roles, perspectives, and contributions, feminist social science reconstructs theories about human behavior. To Moore's definition I would add a fifth component of feminist research—the critical construction of methodologies that privilege women's ways of knowing. One such way comes through food, which is an important domain for women. Capturing women's food voices has been an incisive methodology for several feminist scholars.

The concept of food democracy provides a useful lens to train on the question of gender and food activism. For Tim Lang, food democracy is the ability for all citizens to have secure access to culturally appropriate, sustainable, and healthy food.[8] For Patricia Allen and her collaborators it is a food system that is "environmentally sustainable, economically viable, and socially just."[9] For Neva Hassanein food democracy is when "all the voices of the food system" are represented and "have equal and effective opportunities for participation in shaping that system."[10] This is an important issue in regards to gender because, as Melanie DuPuis and David Goodman note, an uncritical food politics can reproduce already entrenched gender, class, and race hierarchies; the incorporation of traditionally muted voices such as those of women can challenged those hierarchies.[11]

In the rest of this essay I will apply insights generated from studying gender and food to interrogate food activism in Italy. Home of the International Slow Food Movement, Italy has a rich and diverse culinary tradition and a widespread appreciation for food and recognition of its economic potential, which have rendered foodways a potent channel for diverse political actions and initiatives.[12] I began studying Slow Food in 2009 by interviewing thirty-eight leaders and members of Slow Food local chapters from diverse regions of Italy. I was interested in what these local food activists did, how they conceptualized their work, what they accomplished, and what role gender played. I plan to continue this study in future research and want to lay out some of the approaches to food activism generated from using a gender lens.

Food Voice and Gender

Focusing on food as voice has been a powerful methodology for studying gender and particularly women's experiences. In many cultures, women have not had a public voice and have had to find creative ways to be heard. In her study of the history of anorexia nervosa, Joan Brumberg found that Western women overcame their public silencing by using "appetite as voice." By manipulating their food consumption through fasting, picky eating, and binging, they expressed their strivings, frustrations, powerlessness, and power. Similarly, historians Rudolph Bell and Caroline Walker Bynum found much evidence of women using food to attain social influence and piety through extreme fasting, donating food to the poor, exuding holy oils or milk from their bodies, and identifying with Christ's suffering through their own painful food self-deprivation.[13]

Contemporary social scientists have pushed deeper and looked not only at how women used food consumption or denial to "speak," but also at how talking about and through food can be a powerful form of self-expression. Several scholars have used this method: Annie Hauck-Lawson examined what insights into women's lives are generated when "food is the voice"; Meredith Abarca explored how "culinary chats"—unstructured interviews centered on foodways—revealed not only the experiences but also the philosophy of Mexican and Mexican-American working-class women; and Ramona Lee Perez has used "kitchen table ethnography"—loosely structured interviews conducted with women in their kitchens as they prepared food, ate with family and friends, or planned meals—to gain insights into the transnational and cross-border experiences of Mexican and Mexican-American women.[14] In my own research in Italy and the United States, I have used food-centered life history methodology—digitally recorded semistructured interviews with willing participants on everything to do with food in their lives—to investigate the subjective and objective realities of men and women.[15]

While scholars focusing on women's food voices have found rich terrain, those looking at men's have had mixed results. For example, I did research on U.S. college students' food journals and found that most male students wrote much less richly about food than many females did.[16] Jonathan Deutsch uncovered fruitful material when he interviewed New York City firemen about their firehouse cooking. He found that the firemen's food speech self-consciously reinforced hyper-masculinity while they were performing roles culturally scripted as feminine (shopping, cooking, clean-up), thus reinforcing ideologically the gender dichotomies that they were in practice reducing.[17] Men's and women's food voices can reveal how gender definitions, identities, roles, and relationships help or hinder progress toward food democracy.

Food and Body: Eating, Comfort, Body Image, Sensoriality

Food mediates people's relationships to their bodies in ways that vary across cultures, ethnicities, and genders. Public expressions of food activism are therefore likely to be influenced by men's and women's corporeal relation to food, gendered meanings of eating, body image expectations, and sensorial relationship to eating. In Western cultures, ideas about appropriate consumption and the body reproduce gender and race or ethnic hierarchy, but they can also promote healthier eating in women.[18] In Italy and the United States, for example, women's consumption is regulated by cultural values linking self-control and thinness with femininity, and hearty eating and body size and strength with masculinity. Furthermore, there is evidence that there are cultural associations of certain foods such as meat and alcohol with men, and vegetables, fruit, and sweets with women; in fact, "meat appears to function as a marker of masculinity in a transcultural manner."[19] The association of men with meat, Carol Adams argues, goes hand in hand with patriarchal power, which links the dominance of humans over animals with that of men over women.[20]

Across cultures there are varying standards of body beauty for men and women.[21] In cultures where surfeit is rare, fatness is often valued, for example for men in Cameroon or for women in Niger.[22] In Western cultures, K. O'Doherty Jensen and L. Holm write, "Women consume significantly fewer calories on average than men" and are perceived as more feminine the less they eat; "overweight among women is subject to social sanctions to a strikingly greater extent than overweight among men."[23] Paradoxically, men are more often overweight yet women more often diet and are more knowledgeable about and concerned with nutrition, eat less fat, and have healthier diets. What are the implications of these consumption patterns for men's and women's interest and participation in food activism? Are women more likely than men to participate in food activism because they are more concerned about eating light and healthy? Or are men more likely to participate because of their hearty approach to food consumption? Are men and women likely to be involved in different aspects of food activism, with men concerned about safeguarding and improving animal products and alcohol while women focus on fruits and vegetables? Certainly in Italy, for example, wine has traditionally been the near exclusive realm of men, and Slow Food wine experts, writers, and tasters are usually male.

Across cultures and time, women appear to be more involved with food emotionally than men, speaking of food as a comfort, crutch, and psychological support.[24] Women have much more commonly than men practiced private self-directed food behaviors—extreme fasting, compulsive eating, and purging—to communicate unspoken longings, to define the self, to create meaningful relationships, to express control, and to fight oppression. Eating disorders have traditionally been much more common, even nine times more common by some estimates, among women than among men.[25] Some women deny themselves food while cooking frenetically for others in an effort to balance conflicting cultural expectations: cook but stay thin, nurture others but self-abnegate. Are women's emotional ties to and through food significant in food activism? An interesting hint is provided by Fernando Bosco's research on the Mothers of the Plaza de Mayo in Argentina, who developed a long-term activist network out of spontaneous protests against the "disappearances" of their children. Bosco suggests that, "the emotional dimensions of social networks... are crucial for the emergence, sustainability, and cohesion of activists in social movements."[26] Does the heightened emotional relationship of many women with food provide an important gendered basis for establishing networks crucial to the success of food activist efforts?

Another question surrounding food and body concerns the role of the senses in food activism. Slow Food, for example, makes taste education a central pillar of its efforts to change the food system. The SF Master of Food classes involve a sequence of lessons on key foods such as cheese, cured meats, honey, coffee, wine, grains, spices, and so on. Learning how to taste, developing sensory acuity, and discerning tasty from tasteless foods are all key parts of many Slow Food efforts. The premise is that people will change their food choices and seek "good, clean, and fair food" once they learn that it is not only better for the environment and for social justice but also for the taste buds.[27] Does gender figure in the sensory appreciation of food? Although some studies have been inconclusive on this point, a recent study of taste perception undertaken by researchers at University College Cork concluded, "females outperformed males by far in all perceptions tested except chewing ability," including "taste, odor, texture."[28] Does this mean that women will have a more passionate and appreciative commitment to tasty food, which will animate their food activism?

Division of Labor, Public-Private, Production-Reproduction, Value, and Power

Not only do men and women have different corporeal and emotional relationships to eating, but they also have distinct roles surrounding food, and they enact their social relationships in food-centered productive and reproductive roles. Many cultures assign women reproductive roles inside the home and men productive roles outside the home, although everywhere there is much permeability and fluidity of these boundaries. However, the production-reproduction, male-female dichotomy has had major implications for gender power.[29] I found in Italy that even as social roles change and women are increasingly working outside the home for wages and men are increasingly involved with food preparation inside the home, culturally women are identified with cooking and feeding and expected to manage if not carry out these tasks; women's food work is taken for granted whereas men's is celebrated.[30] So how do cultural expectations about men's and women's food roles inside the home affect their power and agency outside the home and in particular their roles in food activism?

Women are almost universally in charge of reproduction: cooking, feeding, teaching table manners and gender roles, and of course breastfeeding.[31] This gendering of feeding and caring work defines women in ways that confine them and restrain their choices, but also give them a channel for creating important ties that bind. The obligations to cook and feed others have been ambiguous sources of oppression, violence, drudgery, power, and creativity for women.[32] Men, on the other hand, have been able to take or leave cooking. Although sometimes constrained to prepare meals in all-male spaces such as the Colorado mountain sheep camps Mexicanos inhabit in summer or in the boy scouts, fire hall, or other all-male sites, they are not expected to put their cooking expertise at the service of their families.[33] This nonreciprocity of feeding and caring upholds gender hierarchy inside and outside the home.[34] Women must resolve conflicts between carrying out unpaid and devalued reproductive roles, such as feeding, and doing socially valued, economically remunerated work.[35]

One way women have resolved this conflict is by using food skills developed at home to make money outside the home, often in the underground economy. For example, Psyche Williams-Forson has shown how African American women sold home-fried chicken to travelers at train stations in the South.[36] Jeffrey Pilcher wrote about the "chili queens" who sold food in the main plaza of San Antonio in the late nineteenth and early twentieth century until they were put out of business by health codes.[37] Abarca has coined the term "public kitchens" to refer to the small taco stands and similar street food sites established by women to earn a living.[38] Women's long-standing use of food skills to earn a meager and marginal yet sustainable living has been a significant reflection of gender roles in foodways. Today there are other dimensions of this division of labor. Women increasingly prevail in the lowest status, lowest paying, and most servile roles in agribusiness and the food industry as fieldworkers, waitresses, kitchen help, fast food servers, and cannery and meat-packing workers, whereas men, although also exploited, have a slight advantage over women in getting the more permanent, better paying jobs.[39]

Yet at the other end of the employment spectrum, some women have joined noted male counterparts such as Craig Claiborne, Michael Pollan, Anthony Bourdain, Eric Schlosser, and others and made successful high-end careers out of food as critics, memoirists, magazine editors, chefs, and food scholars—women such as former *Gourmet* editor and *New York Times* food critic and wildly successful author Ruth Reichl, chef Ann Ross, writer M.F.K. Fisher, restaurateur and Slow Food activist Alice Waters, scholar Marion Nestle, and many others.[40] Food has been a double edged sword—tying women to the home yet also enabling them to cross the production-reproduction boundary and use domestic food knowledge to achieve social and economic power outside the home and to influence the public political arena.

Meanings Surrounding Food: Inside and Outside Meanings

The assignation of private roles in the home to women and public roles in the workplace to men brings to mind Sidney Mintz's delineation of inside and outside meanings. Inside meanings are emotional, personal, and generated by individuals in concert with cultural logic; outside meanings are structured and generated by powerful institutions such as corporations, government, and the mass media to promote profit and power.[41] Mintz does not address directly the question of whether these meanings are gendered, but his work implies the importance of this question.

Mintz writes, "Power and meaning are always connected. . . . The power resting within outside meaning sets terms for the creation of inside, or symbolic, meaning."[42] This would imply that if outside meanings are more controlled by men and inside by women, then men's imposed meaning structures will dominate women's. Is this really so one-way? I believe that inside and outside meanings are constantly in flux, interpenetrating and influencing each other. For example, in Slow Food, mothers' desire for less toxic and more healthy foods for their children has fueled the school garden movement in both Italy and the United States, which has conjoined with First Lady Michelle Obama's political program to reform school lunches and challenge childhood obesity. In Antonito, Colorado, Mexicanas challenged the local priest who wanted to impose outside meanings and values on the food bank by requiring all recipients to apply and qualify for the Federal Food Stamp Program (now the Supplemental Nutrition Assistance Program or SNAP). The women refused to change their long-standing practice of giving food to anyone who showed up at the door; they imposed "inside" meanings of sharing food typical of the family onto the wider community.[43]

Mintz underscores an important point when he cites anthropologist Eric Wolf, who said: "The ability to bestow meanings—to 'name' things, acts, and ideas—is a source of power."[44] Food activism can be conceptualized as seizing the power to give meaning and in some cases to impose inside meanings generated from women's cooking, feeding, and sharing food onto the outside world. This approach coheres with recent scholars' claims that contemporary food activism fits into "new social movements." These aim for change by "transforming values, lifestyles, and symbols"[45] rather than by direct action strategies such as organizing labor unions, protests, strikes, and boycotts.

Food, Gender, Political Power, and Food Activism

The question of who controls political action in the food sector is important and fascinating, for it pits two trends against each other—the trend that men have dominated politics and continue to do so, and the trend that women have dominated feeding and continue to do so. There is much evidence of women's participation in grassroots food activism, but what about their role in the increasing number of formal institutions concerned with food change, such as the Slow Food organizational power structure, whose obvious male dominance sparked this essay?[46]

In their ground-breaking study of women and work after the North American Free Trade Agreement (NAFTA), Deborah Barndt and her collaborators show that women play major roles in many diverse local forms of food activism. They do so because they are the principal food preparers all over the world, they are more often poor and vulnerable to hunger than men, they often have children whose needs propel them, and they are often allied with other women in similar circumstances. They have led efforts for legislative changes to make food more accessible, and they have been main players in child feeding programs, "community kitchens, community gardens, and bulk-buying clubs."[47] Deborah Moffett and Mary Lou Morgan focus on women involved in Toronto's Good Food Box and Focus on Food training programs, which they call "vehicles of small-scale resistance" and "examples of how women use food as a catalyst for personal and political change" and empowerment.[48]

Maria Dolores Villagomez describes the urban women in Irapuato, Mexico who set up a community kitchen where they pooled resources and labor so that a rotating group of women cooked for all each day. This furnished a balanced diet and saved time and money for middle class women, but it did not help poor women, who lacked time and resources to participate.[49] Schroeder studied community kitchens in Peru and Bolivia and wrote, "Community kitchens tap into women's unpaid kitchen labor and have become a vital part of many families' strategies for surviving economic crisis."[50] However, she also pointed out that they serve as kind a safety valve, keeping hunger at bay but not fundamentally transforming the political structure. Clearly, food activism must work on the local level to change the food system in the here and now, but it also must transform political institutions to bring about major structural change. What role does gender play in both local and structural change? Is the gendering of food activism significant in Italy? Are men and women playing different roles with different aims at different sociopolitical levels or are they working together on similar goals?

Gender and Food Activism Research in Italy

My new research project on gender and food activism in Italy uses food-centered life history interviews to explore how men's and women's definitions, identities, roles, and relationships help and hinder the principal goal of food activism—the promotion of food democracy. Following Hassanein, I pay particular attention to gender and food democracy by asking whether men's and women's voices are equally heard in food activism, where, and how. Do men and women have equal access to good, clean, and fair food? What are the gender dynamics in the food activism and do they reproduce or challenge gender hierarchy? Julie Guthman points out how sometimes the language and ideology of groups working in the U.S. alternative food movement alienate people of color; a similar effect could obtain across gender and class. as well as race lines.[51] How do age, class, and race interact with gender to affect the success of food activist efforts? Are they bringing about real democratic change in the food system, particularly as regards gender, or are they only producing benefits and "cultural capital" for a relatively small number of participants, and if so, who? This is a major question for scholars of alternative food movements.

At this point in my research and review of the literature, the gender considerations are inconclusive, suggesting the need for further fieldwork. I will continue to use food-centered life histories to explore gender and food activism in three main areas suggested by preliminary research. The first focus is *gender, networks, and participatory action*. I will ask: How does gender figure in the networks, relationships, and coalitions of food activists? What part does gender play in the activities, target groups, participants, and endurance over time? With which institutions and individuals do food activists construct relationships, and do these transcend or reproduce race, class, gender, and age boundaries?

Preliminary evidence suggests that Slow Food activists construct networks beginning with people they know, and that men and women draw more heavily from friends of their own gender and work together to construct projects that fit their shared inclinations. Historically, Slow Food has roots in Arcigola, born out of ARCI, the Recreation Association of Italian Communists, embodied in the after-work clubs frequented almost exclusively by men, a fact that may in part explain the enduring male cast to some Slow Food chapters.[52] However, there do not appear to be huge differences in the activities of chapters headed by men and women, for all chapters participate in at least some of the centrally organized Slow Food projects, for example the Master of Food classes and school garden initiatives. One of the youngest chapter leaders I interviewed, Giulia Annis, the head of the Cagliari (Sardinia) *condotta*, told me that her collaborators were mostly female; she called them "an army of young women" *(un esercito di ragazze)*. They organized all kinds of projects that appealed to men as well as women: chocolate, cheese, and wine tastings; visits to artisanal beer producers and traditional net fishermen; and the revitalization of horticulture in a nearby village and the formation of a buying group to provide a market for the produce.

Mauro Bagni, the leader of the very successful Scandicci chapter, told me that they have about eight women and twelve men in the organizing group called the "small table" *(piccola tavola)*, but in spite of this relative gender parity, he said, "when it comes to controlling things, the men prevail" *(quando c'è da da comandare gli uomini prevalgono)*. However, the work of the Scandicci chapter was inclusive and focused on expanding the network between producers and consumers that is a main goal of Slow Food.[53] For Bagni, creating the network on the local level was of paramount importance: "the network is to construct all the ties—for example between the group that works on local history, the cheese producer, the local restaurants, the town hall, the group working with the Hungary chapter, the children from the school gardens, and so on."[54] Interestingly, in 2009, Bagni defined the "connecting thread" *(filo conduttore)* of the chapter to be their study of "daily shopping" *(la spesa quotidiana)*—not a typical male domain.

Bagni, however, did not mince words when he spoke about gender relations in the Slow Food central office in Bra: "Slow Food is male chauvinist . . . The directors are all male, there are very few women." *(Slow Food è maschilista . . . il gruppo dirigente è tutto maschile, c'è pochissime donne.)* However, most of the women I interviewed said that they encountered few problems of gender discrimination within

Slow Food and were generally positive about women's place in the organization, but a few did mention occasional silencing of women or dominating of discourse by men. More and more women are becoming chapter leaders and active members of the national organization, though they are still far fewer than their male counterparts, and this gender imbalance surely affects the formation of networks and choice of projects, although perhaps in subtle and muted ways.

The second focus of my research on food activism is on *gender and education.* In food and taste education projects, what role does gender play in who is teaching, what is taught, who is learning, what are the pedagogies, what are the underlying ideologies, and what are the results? To what extent are education projects gender-biased or inclusive and diverse? Do they reflect "inside" or "outside" meanings?

My preliminary research revealed the major importance of education in all Slow Food chapter initiatives, regardless of the gender of the chapter leader. I have classified SF education projects by their focus on taste/sensoriality, food culture/history, and quality production/biodiversity. I need to do more research to determine whether there are any gender trends in the type or focus of education. One hint is that women appeared to be particularly involved in education projects with children, for example, the Ravenna school garden project, which SF activist and retired teacher Angela Ceccarelli described to me as initiated and organized by a female chapter member working with a female elementary school teacher and a female garden docent trained by Slow Food. Another project aimed at children was the Modena chapter's book project *The Adventure of Magalasso and the Magic Vinegar (L'Avventura del Magalasso e del Magico Aceto)* by Giuseppe Pederiali (Slow Food Editore), recounted to me by SF member and elementary school teacher Mirella Ferrari. Pederiali is a Modenese writer who narrates a tale about the renowned local monster, the Magalasso, who is "super gluttonous" *(golosissimo)* of balsamic vinegar—the culturally and economically most important Modenese food. Women from the Slow Food Modena chapter ran a contest for elementary school children to design the cover of the book, and they simultaneously educated the children about the centuries-old local tradition of making balsamic vinegar by taking them to visit producers.

In contrast to the prevalence of women in child education projects, preliminary evidence suggests that more of the Slow Food tasting "experts" are men than women, particularly those concerned with wine, beer, coffee, cheese, honey, and cured meats. This fact is not surprising, since in Italian culture men have been the primary producers of these foods, but it may also reflect the cultural bias according men the status of food professionals and women that of unpaid domestic food preparers. Slow Food member Noemi Franchi said she found the hegemonic older male claim to expertise off-putting and suggested that Slow Food engage more young people and women to lead taste education workshops—showing how gender can indeed matter in activist efforts conducted through teaching.[55]

The third focus of my research on food activism is on *gender and food consumption/taste/gastronomy:* How do men and women use eating and tasting to conduct food activism? How do they relate through food to their bodies? How does their comfort or discomfort with food affect their work? What are the meanings of food, eating, and taste to them? How do meanings and practices surrounding eating express agency and power for men and women?

As I suggested earlier, men seem to have attained a strong position as tasting "experts" and eclipse women in this professionalization of taste, but I need to gather more data not only on men's and women's sensory relationship to the art of tasting but also to the practice of eating. When I asked people what drew them to Slow Food, both men and women answered with words like those of Noemi Franchi, "an infinite gluttony" *(una golosità infinita).* Noemi went on to emphasize the role of the senses in learning and the importance of sensory education to Slow Food. She said, "I think the things I remember most from school are those that I lived with my body... and that the physical way of approaching food is the best way to convey things to young people."[56] Similarly, Marco Bechi, head of the Siena SF chapter, said, "I love to cook, I also love to eat.... I have important memories tied to food.... I always say, remember your senses because if... you pay attention you can absolutely remember pleasant moments of your life, but also unfortunately unpleasant ones, linked to smells and tastes."[57] Bechi and Franchi confirmed what I found in my past research in Florence, that both men and women loved eating and had strong memories associated with sensory experiences. Women, however, had a more ambivalent and emotionally fraught relationship to food because they felt social pressure to be thin in order to be attractive to men, whereas men enjoyed food with little concern about their body size and attractiveness to women. However, in Italy, enjoyment of food is culturally sanctioned for all, so most men and women eat with gusto and can use their pleasure in food as a path to activist efforts to improve food's quality and taste.

Conclusion

In this essay, I have explored how a gender focus can guide research into food activism. Using food-centered life histories is a productive methodology that gathers the diverse voices of food activists and promotes food democracy, fulfilling feminism's goals of including women's experiences and perspectives alongside men's and acknowledging men's and women's diversity by class, religion, race or ethnicity, and culture. Insights gathered from feminist food studies guide three areas of inquiry in this research: (1) the ways gendered definitions of body image, body use, proper eating, comfort, and sensoriality affect food activism; (2) the ways the gendered division of labor around food affects men's and women's value, power, and effectiveness as food activists; (3) the ways gender shapes inside and outside meanings surrounding food and their execution in food activism. The act of asking "does gender matter?" stimulates a number of interesting lines of inquiry into food activism, which Raj Patel has called "the world's largest social movement."[58] Studying the role of gender in food activism will illuminate the workings of this important grassroots political movement and offer insights into its effectiveness.

NOTES

1. "Slow Food." [Online]. Available: http:www.slowfood.com. [January 20, 2011].

2. There were seven placards for women at the head table but only six were present. The names were Raffaela Ponzio, Silvia De Paulis, Cristina Cavallo, Rita Abagnale, Gaia Gianotti, Giovanna Licheri, and Maura Biancotto.

3. Some studies of women in the public sphere are Meredith Abarca, "*Charlas Culinarias*: Mexican Women Speak from the Public Kitchens," *Food and Foodways* 15, no. 3–4 (2007): 183–212; Joan Wardrop, "Private Cooking, Public Eating: Women Street Vendors in South Durban," *Gender, Place and Culture* 13, no. 6 (2006): 677–83.

4. Will Roscoe, *The Zuni Man-Woman* (Boston: Beacon 1991).

5. Some studies of gender, food, and culture are Josephine Beoku-Betts, "'We Got Our Way of Cooking Things': Women, Food, and Preservation of Cultural Identity among the Gullah," in *Food in the USA: A Reader*, ed. Carole Counihan (New York: Routledge, 2002), 277–94; Christopher Carrington, *No Place Like Home: Relationships and Family Life among Lesbians and Gay Men* (Chicago: University of Chicago Press, 1999); Alice Julier, "Hiding Gender and Race in the Discourse of Commercial Food Consumption," in *From Betty Crocker to Feminist Food Studies*, ed. Arlene V. Avakian and Barbara Haber (Amherst: University of Massachusetts Press, 2005), 163–84; Alice Julier and Laura Lindenfeld, "Mapping Men onto the Menu: Masculinities and Food," *Food and Foodways* 13, no. 1–2 (2005): 1–16; Anna S. Meigs, *Food, Sex, and Pollution: A New Guinea Religion* (New Brunswick, NJ: Rutgers University Press, 1984); Bridget O'Laughlin, "Mediation of Contradiction: Why Mbum Women Do Not Eat Chicken," in *Women, Culture and Society*, ed. Michelle Rosaldo and Louise Lamphere (Stanford: Stanford University Press, 1974), 301–18; Fabio Parasecoli, "Feeding Hard Bodies: Food and Masculinities in Men's Fitness Magazines," *Food and Foodways* 13, no. 1–2 (2005): 17–38; Elspeth Probyn, *Carnal Appetites: FoodSexIdentities* (New York: Routledge, 2000); Mary J. Weismantel, *Food, Gender and Poverty in the Ecuadorian Andes* (Philadelphia: University of Pennsylvania Press, 1988); Jeffrey Sobal, "Men, Meat and Marriage: Models of Masculinity," *Food and Foodways* 13, no. 1–2 (2005): 135–58.

6. Henrietta L. Moore, *Feminism and Anthropology* (Cambridge: Cambridge University Press, 1988).

7. On the concept of "intersectionality" and its application in diverse feminist approaches, see Maxine Baca Zinn and Bonnie Thornton Dill, "Theorizing Difference from Multiracial Feminism," *Feminist Studies* 22, no. 2 (1996): 321–331; H. Y. Choo and M. M. Ferree, "Practising Intersectionality in Sociological Research: A Critical Analysis of Inclusion, Interaction and Institutions in the Study of Inequalities," *Sociological Theory* 28, no. 2 (2010): 129–149; Kimberlé Williams Crenshaw, "Mapping the Margins: Intersectionality, Identity Politics & Violence Against Women of Color," *Stanford Law Review* 43, no. 6. (1991): 1241–99; Kathy Davis, "Intersectionality as a Buzzword: A Sociology of Science Perspective on What Makes a Feminist Theory Successful," *Feminist Theory* 9 (2008): 67–85; Ann Denis, "Review Essay: Intersectional Analysis: A Contribution of Feminism to Sociology," *International Sociology* 23 (2008): 677–93.

8. Tim Lang, "Food Policy for the 21st Century: Can It Be Both Radical and Reasonable?" in *For Hunger-Proof Cities: Sustainable Urban Food Systems*, ed. M. Koc, et al. (Ottawa: International Development Research Centre, 1999), 216–24.

9. Patricia Allen, et al, "Shifting Plates in the Agrifood Landscape: The Tectonics of Alternative Agrifood Initiatives in California," *Journal of Rural Studies* 19 (2003): 63.

10. Neva Hassanein, "Practicing Food Democracy: A Pragmatic Politics of Transformation," *Journal of Rural Studies* 19 (2003): 84.

11. E. Melanie DuPuis and David Goodman, "Should We Go 'Home' To Eat?: Toward a Reflexive Politics of Localism," *Journal of Rural Studies* 21 (2005): 359–71.

12. Fabio Parasecoli, "Postrevolutionary Chowhounds: Food, Globalization, and the Italian Left," *Gastronomica* 3, no. 3 (2003): 29–39.

13. Joan Jacobs Brumberg, *Fasting Girls: the Emergence of Anorexia Nervosa as a Modern Disease* (Cambridge: Harvard University Press, 1988); Rudolph M. Bell, *Holy Anorexia* (Chicago: University of Chicago, 1985); Caroline Walker Bynum, *Holy Feast and Holy Fast: The Religious Significance of Food to Medieval Women* (Berkeley: University of California Press, 1987).

14. Annie Hauck-Lawson, "Hearing the Food Voice: An Epiphany for a Researcher," *The Digest: An Interdisciplinary Study of Food and Foodways* 12, no. 1–2 (1992): 6–7; idem, "When Food Is the Voice: A Case Study of a Polish-American Woman," *Journal for the Study of Food and Society* 2, no. 1 (1998): 21–28; Meredith Abarca, "Los Chilaquiles de mi 'ama: the Language of Everyday Cooking," in *Pilaf, Pozole and Pad Thai: American Women and Ethnic Food*, ed. Sherrie A. Inness (Amherst: University of Massachusetts Press, 2001), 119–44; idem, *Voices in the Kitchen: Views of Food and the World from Working-Class Mexican and Mexican American Women* (College Station: Texas A & M University Press, 2006); Ramona Lee Pérez, "Tasting Culture: Food, Family and Flavor in Greater Mexico" (Ph.D. diss., New York University, 2009).

15. Carole Counihan, "Food, Culture and Political Economy: Changing Lifestyles in the Sardinian Town of Bosa" (Ph.D. diss., University of Massachusetts, Amherst, 1981); idem, "The Border as Barrier and Bridge: Food, Gender, and Ethnicity in the San Luis Valley of Colorado," in *From Betty Crocker to Feminist Food Studies: Critical Perspectives on Women and Food*, ed. Arlene Avakian and Barbara Haber (Amherst: University of Massachusetts Press, 2005), 200–17; idem, "*Mexicanas'* Food Voice and Differential Consciousness in the San Luis Valley of Colorado," *Food and Culture: A Reader*, ed. Carole Counihan and Penny Van Esterik, rev. ed. (New York: Routledge, 2007), 354–68.

16. Carole Counihan, "Food Rules in the U.S.: Individualism, Control, and Hierarchy," *Anthropological Quarterly* 65, no. 2 (1992): 55–66.

17. Jonathan Deutsch, "'Please Pass the Chicken Tits': Rethinking Men and Cooking at an Urban Firehouse," *Food and Foodways* 13, no. 1–2 (2005): 91–114.

18. Mimi Nichter, *Fat Talk: What Girls and Their Parents Say about Dieting* (Cambridge, MA: Harvard University Press, 2001).

19. K. O'Doherty Jensen and L. Holm, "Review: Preferences, Quantities and Concerns: Socio-Cultural Perspectives on the Gendered Consumption of Foods," *European Journal of Clinical Nutrition* 53, no. 5 (1999): 352.

20. Carol J. Adams, *The Sexual Politics of Meat: A Feminist-Vegetarian Critical Theory* (New York: Continuum, 1990).

21. Don Kulick and Anne Meneley, eds., *The Anthropology of Fat: An Obsession* (New York: Penguin, 2005); Hortense Powdermaker, "An Anthropological Approach to the Problem of Obesity," *Bulletin of the New York Academy of Medicine* 36 (1960): 286–95.

22. Igor de Garine and Nancy J. Pollock, *Social Aspects of Obesity* (Amsterdam: Gordon and Breach, 1995); Rebecca Popenoe, *Feeding Desire: Fatness, Beauty, and Sexuality among a Saharan People* (London; New York: Routledge, 2003).

23. Jenson and Holm, "Review: Preferences, Qualities, and Concerns," 353–54.

24. Laurette Dubé, Jordan L. LeBel, and Ji Lu, "Affect Asymmetry and Comfort Food consumption," *Physiology & Behavior* 86, no. 4 (2005): 559–67; Julie L. Locher,

William C. Yoels, Donna Maurer, and Jillian Van Ells, "Comfort Foods: An Exploratory Journey into the Social and Emotional Significance of Food," *Food and Foodways* 13, no. 4 (2005): 273–97.

25. On eating disorders and gender, see Kim Chernin, *The Hungry Self: Women, Eating and Identity* (New York: Times Books, 1985); Bell, *Holy Anorexia*; Brumberg, *Fasting Girls*; Bynum, *Holy Feast, Holy Fast*; Counihan, *The Anthropology of Food and Body* (New York: Routledge, 1999).

26. Fernando J. Bosco, "The Madres de Plaza de Mayo and Three Decades of Human Rights' Activism: Embeddedness, Emotions, and Social Movements," *Annals of the Association of American Geographers* 96, no. 2 (2006): 343.

27. Allison Hayes-Conroy and Jessica Hayes-Conroy, "Visceral Difference: Variations in Feeling (Slow) Food," *Environment and Planning A* 42 (2010): 2956–71.

28. C. Michon, M. G. O'Sullivan, C. M. Delahunty, and J. P. Kerry, "The Investigation of Gender-Related Sensitivity Differences in Food Perception," *Journal of Sensory Studies* 24 (2009): 934.

29. Frederick Engels, *The Origin of the Family, Private Property and the State* (New York: International, 1972); Eleanor Burke Leacock, "Introduction," in *The Origin of the Family, Private Property and the State*, Frederick Engels (New York: International, 1972), 7–67; Louise Lamphere, "The Domestic Sphere of Women and the Public World of Men: the Strengths and Limitations of an Anthropological Dichotomy," in *Gender in Cross-Cultural Perspective*, ed. Caroline B. Brettell and Carolyn F. Sargent (Upper Saddle River, NJ: Prentice Hall, 2000), 100–9; Karen Sacks, "Engels Revisited: Women, the Organization of Production, and Private Property," in *Women, Culture and Society*, ed. Michelle Z. Rosaldo and Louise Lamphere (Stanford: Stanford University Press, 1974), 207–22.

30. Carole Counihan, *Around the Tuscan Table: Food, Family and Gender in Twentieth Century Florence* (New York: Routledge, 2004).

31. Penny Van Esterik, *Beyond the Breast-Bottle Controversy* (New Brunswick, NJ: Rutgers University Press, 1984); Linda Blum, *At the Breast: Ideologies of Breastfeeding and Motherhood in the Contemporary United States* (Boston: Beacon Press, 1999); Elizabeth Dixon Whitaker, *Measuring Mamma's Milk: Fascism and the Medicalization of Maternity in Italy* (Anne Arbor: University of Michigan Press, 2000).

32. Carole Counihan, "Food as Women's Voice in the San Luis Valley of Colorado," in Counihan, *Food in the USA*, 295–304; Marjorie L. DeVault, *Feeding the Family: The Social Organization of Caring as Gendered Work* (Chicago: University of Chicago Press, 1991); Rhian Ellis, "The Way to a Man's Heart: Food in the Violent Home," in *The Sociology of Food and Eating*, ed. Anne Murcott (Aldershot: Gower Publishing, 1983), 164–71; Sherrie Inness, *Cooking Lessons: The Politics of Gender and Food* (Lanham, MD: Rowman & Littlefield, 2001); idem, *Kitchen Culture in America: Popular Representations of Food, Gender and Race* (Philadelphia: University of Pennsylvania Press, 2001).

33. Carole Counihan, "Food as Mediating Voice and Oppositional Consciousness for Chicanas in Colorado's San Luis Valley," in *Mediating Chicana/o Culture: Multicultural American Vernacular*, ed. Scott Baugh (Cambridge: Cambridge Scholars Press, 2006), 72–84; James M. Taggart, "Food, Masculinity and Place in the Hispanic Southwest," in Counihan, *Food in the USA*, 305–13; Jay Mechling, "Boy Scouts and the Manly Art of Cooking," *Food and Foodways* 13, no. 1–2 (2005): 67–90; Deutsch, "'Please Pass the Chicken Tits,'" 91–114; Richard Wilk and Persephone Hintlian, "Cooking on Their Own: Cuisines of Manly Men," *Food and Foodways* 13, no. 1–2 (2005): 159–68; T. M. J. Holden, "The Overcooked and Underdone: Masculinities in Japanese Food Programming," *Food and Foodways* 13, no. 1–2 (2005): 39–65.

34. Anne Allison, "Japanese Mothers and Obentōs: The Lunch Box as Ideological State Apparatus," in *Food and Culture: A Reader*, ed. Carole Counihan and Penny Van Esterik, 2d ed. (New York: Routledge, 2008), 221–239; Nickie Charles and Marion Kerr, *Women, Food and Families* (Manchester: Manchester University Press, 1987).

35. Carole Counihan, *The Anthropology of Food and Body: Gender, Meaning and Power* (New York: Routledge, 1999).

36. Psyche A. Williams-Forson, *Building Houses out of Chicken Legs: Black Women, Food, and Power* (Chapel Hill: University of North Carolina Press, 2006).

37. Jeffrey M. Pilcher, "Who Chased Out the Chili Queens? Gender, Race and Urban Reform in San Antonio, Texas, 1880–1943," *Food and Foodways* 16, no. 3 (2008): 173–200.

38. Abarca, "*Charlas Culinarias*." See also Sidney Perutz, "A Tale of Two Fondas: Scrambling Gender in Tepoztlán in the Decade of the New Economy," *Food and Foodways* 15, no. 3–4 (2007): 237–59; Irene Tinker, *Street Foods: Urban Food and Employment in Developing Countries* (Oxford: Oxford University Press, 1997); Gisèle Yasmeen, "'Plastic-bag Housewives' and Postmodern Restaurants? Public and Private in Bangkok's Foodscape," in Counihan and Van Esterik, *Food and Culture*, 523–38.

39. On gender in the agriculture, food, and restaurant industry, see Deborah Barndt, ed., *Women Working the NAFTA Food Chain: Women, Food and Globalization* (Toronto: Sumach Press, 1999); Deborah Barndt, "On the Move for Food: Three Women Behind the Tomato's Journey," *Women's Studies Quarterly* 1&2 (2001):131–43; idem, "Fruits of Injustice: Women in the Post NAFTA Food System," *Canadian Women's Studies* 21, no. 4 (2002): 82–88; idem, *Tangled Routes: Women, Work, and Globalization on the Tomato Trail*, 2nd ed. (Lantham, MD: Rowman and Littlefield, 2010); David Beriss and David Sutton, eds., *The Restaurants Book: Ethnographies of Where We Eat* (Oxford: Berg, 2007); Deborah Fink, *Cutting into the Meatpacking Line: Workers and Change in the Rural Midwest* (Chapel Hill: University of North Carolina Press, 1998); Meika Loe, "Working for Men—At the Intersection of Power, Gender, and Sexuality," *Sociological Inquiry* 66, no. 4 (1996): 399–421; Katherine Newman, *No Shame in My Game: The Working Poor in the Inner City* (New York: Penguin, 2000); Greta Foff Paules, *Power and Resistance among Waitresses in a New Jersey Restaurant* (Philadelphia: Temple University Press, 1991); Ester Reiter, *Making Fast Food: From the Frying Pan into the Fryer* (Montreal: McGill-Queen's University Press, 1996); Penny Van Esterik, "Gender and Sustainable Food Systems: A Feminist Critique," in *For Hunger-Proof Cities: Sustainable Urban Food Systems*, ed. M. Koc, et al. (Ottawa: IDRC Books, 1999); Patricia Zavella, *Women's Work and Chicano Families: Cannery Workers of the Santa Clara Valley* (Ithaca, NY: Cornell University Press, 1987); idem, "Engendering Transnationalism in Food Processing: Peripheral Vision on Both Sides of the U.S.-Mexican Border," in *Transnational Latina/o Communities: Politics, Processes, and Cultures*, ed. Carlos G. Vélez-Ibañez and Anna Sampaio (Lanham, MD: Rowman and Littlefield, 2002), 225–45.

40. Ruth Reichl, *Tender at the Bone: Growing Up at the Table* (New York: Random House, 2010); M. F. K. Fisher, *The Art of Eating* (New York: Morrow, 1954); Alice L. Waters, *The Art of Simple Food: Notes, Lessons, and Recipes from a Delicious Revolution* (New York: Clarkson Potter, 2007); Marion Nestle, *Food Politics: How the Food Industry Influences Nutrition and Health* (Berkeley: University of California Press, 2002); idem, *What to Eat* (San Francisco: North Point Press, 2007); idem, *Safe Food: The Politics of Food Safety* (Berkeley: University of California Press, 2010).

41. Sidney W. Mintz, *Sweetness and Power: The Place of Sugar in Modern History* (New York: Viking Press, 1985), 151–52.

42. Sidney W. Mintz, *Tasting Food, Tasting Freedom: Excursions into Eating, Culture and the Past* (Boston: Beacon, 1996), 30.

43. Carole Counihan, *"A Tortilla Is Like Life": Food and Culture in the San Luis Valley of Colorado* (Austin: University of Texas Press, 2009).

44. Eric R. Wolf, *Europe and the People Without History* (Berkeley: University of California Press, 1982), 388.

45. Hassanein, "Practicing Food Democracy," 80; see also Stephen Schneider, "Good, Clean and Fair: The Rhetoric of the Slow Food Movement," *College English* 70, no. 4 (2008): 384–402.

46. On gender and food activism, see Patricia Allen and Carolyn Sachs, "Women and Food Chains: The Gendered Politics of Food," *International Journal of Sociology of Food and Agriculture* 15, no. 1 (2007): 1–23; Barndt, *Women Working the NAFTA Food Chain*; Allison Hayes-Conroy and Jessica Hayes-Conroy, "Taking Back Taste: Feminism, Food, and Visceral Politics," *Gender, Place and Culture: A Journal of Feminist Geography* 15, no. 5 (2008): 461–73; Hayes-Conroy and Hayes-Conroy, "Visceral Difference," 2956–71.

47. Debbie Field, "Putting Food First: Women's Role in Creating a Grassroots Food System Outside the Marketplace" in Barndt, *Women Working the NAFTA Food Chain*, 203.

48. Deborah Moffett and Mary Lou Morgan, "Women as Organizers: Building Confidence and Community through Food," in Barndt, *Women Working the NAFTA Food Chain*, 222, 223.

49. Maria Dolores Villagomez, "Grassroots Responses to Globalization: Mexican Rural and Urban Women's Collective Alternatives" in Barndt, *Women Working the NAFTA Food Chain*, 209–19.

50. K. Schroeder, "A Feminist Examination of Community Kitchens in Peru and Bolivia." *Gender, Place & Culture* 13, no. 6 (2006): 663.

51. Julie Guthman, "Bringing Good Food to Others: Investigating the Subjects of Alternative Food Practice," *Cultural Geographies* 15 (2008): 431–47; idem, "'If They Only Knew': Color Blindness and Universalism in California Alternative Food Institutions," *The Professional Geographer* 60 (2008): 387–97.

52. Parasecoli, "Postrevolutionary Chowhounds."

53. Slow Food is working to expand global networks between producers and consumers through its Terra Madre effort: "Terra Madre brings together those players in the food chain who together support sustainable agriculture, fishing, and breeding with the goal of preserving taste and biodiversity." "Terra Madre." [Online]. Available: http:www.terramadre.org. [January 14, 2011].

54. Mauro Bagni's words were, *"La rete è costruire cioè tutti i legami legati alla—ci può essere il circolo che si occupa di storia locale, il produttore di formaggi, l'osteria, la trattoria, il comune, il gruppo appunto di Italia Ungheria, i bambini dell'orto dello schoolgarden . . . "*

55. Noemi Franchi said that a taste education lesson "should be conducted by young people so that we all feel equal because what most intimidates me during the tastings is to see an expert man—man because they are almost always men—expert, adult, who asks me about my sensations and I feel that he is already judging me as an incompetent *(deve essere condotta sempre secondo me da personale giovane per farci sentire tutti alla pari perché quello che intimorisce di più me durante le degustazioni è vedere un uomo esperto, uomo perché sono quasi sempre uomini, esperto, adulto che mi chiede le mie sensazioni e io mi sento come se mi stesse già giudicando come un'incapace).*"

56. Noemi Franchi's words were, *"Credo le cose che io ricordo di più della scuola sono quelle che io ho vissuto con il mio corpo . . . e il modo anche fisico di accostarsi al cibo sia il modo migliore per trasmettere qualcosa ai giovani."*

57. Marco Bechi's words were, "*io amo cucinare, amo anche mangiare . . . ho ricordi legati al cibo importanti . . . dico sempre ricordatevi dei vostri sensi perché . . . se fate attenzione potete assolutamente ricordare alcuni momenti della vostra vita piacevoli, purtroppo anche spiacevoli, legati a degli odori, a dei sapori.*"

58. Raj Patel, *Stuffed and Starved: The Hidden Battle for the World Food System* (Brooklyn, NY: Melville House, 2007), 2.

Bibliography

Abarca, Meredith. *Voices in the Kitchen: Views of Food and the World from Working-Class Mexican and Mexican American Women.* College Station: Texas A & M University Press, 2006.

Avakian, Arlene Voski, ed. *Through the Kitchen Window: Women Explore the Intimate Meanings of Food and Cooking.* Boston: Beacon Press, 1997.

———, and Barbara Haber, eds. *From Betty Crocker to Feminist Food Studies: Critical Perspectives on Women and Food.* Amherst: University of Massachusetts Press, 2005.

Barndt, Deborah, ed. *Women Working the NAFTA Food Chain: Women, Food and Globalization.* Toronto: Sumach Press, 1999.

Bynum, Caroline Walker. *Holy Feast and Holy Fast: The Religious Significance of Food to Medieval Women.* Berkeley: University of California Press, 1987.

Counihan, Carole. *The Anthropology of Food and Body: Gender, Meaning and Power.* New York: Routledge, 1999.

———. *Around the Tuscan Table: Food, Family and Gender in Twentieth Century Florence.* New York: Routledge, 2004.

DeVault, Marjorie L. *Feeding the Family: The Social Organization of Caring as Gendered Work.* Chicago: University of Chicago Press, 1991.

Inness, Sherrie A., ed. *Pilaf, Pozole, and Pad Thai: American Women and Ethnic Food.* Amherst: University of Massachusetts Press, 2001.

Kahn, Miriam. *Always Hungry, Never Greedy: Food and the Expression of Gender in a Melanesian Society.* New York: Cambridge University Press, 1986.

Probyn, Elspeth. *Carnal Appetites: FoodSexIdentities.* New York: Routledge, 2000.

Williams-Forson, Psyche A. *Building Houses out of Chicken Legs: Black Women, Food, and Power.* Chapel Hill: University of North Carolina Press, 2006.

———, and Carole Counihan, eds. *Taking Food Public: Redefining Foodways in a Changing World.* New York: Routledge, 2011.

CHAPTER 7

ANTHROPOLOGY OF FOOD

R. KENJI TIERNEY AND
EMIKO OHNUKI-TIERNEY

For anthropologists, food and foodways offer uniquely powerful windows to understand individual cultures and societies, especially when they are situated in the context of global and historical flows and connections. There are many ways to study food: the media is flooded with books, articles, television shows, blogs, and websites on food—from recipe books to restaurant reviews to histories of particular cuisines or food items. Anthropologists in the main are interested in understanding culture and society through objects, words, and behavior. They consider how individuals are "localized" in their culture and society, which nonetheless are always subject to global influences. As a member of a particular society (social group), a person's thoughts, feelings, and behavior to a large extent are learned from others within that society, although culture is never a straightjacket in this respect. Another premise of many anthropologists is that not only meaning but also the physical characteristics of an object are culturally construed. Many things are edible, but each culture determines what is considered food. Something may "stink" in one culture but be fragrant in another. Given these two premises, anthropologists study food, its production, and consumption in order to understand the culture and society of a people.

Ethnography, the methodology used by anthropologists as well as by some other social scientists, takes a holistic and embodied approach that derives from lived experience among the people who are being studied. The methods for acquiring data include interviews, the analysis of written materials, and observation, particularly "participant observation," which means that an anthropologist shares in the lives, and of course foods, of a people. Enjoying a feast, working in a restaurant, or helping to harvest a cornfield are examples of how one can engage in participant observation. Observation need not entail direct participation; walking around a city to survey different types of restaurants, open markets, food vendors, and food stores are all valid methods. In so doing, an anthropologist seeks to respect the thoughts and practices of the people, even in cases where this proves to be problematic. For example, many religious rituals, which often include commensality, prohibit women. Likewise, there is a common taboo in fishing communities prohibiting women from boarding fishing boats.[1]

Historical perspective on change over time is also crucial for understanding a society's food culture. Anthropological fashions tend to shift back and forth between cultural analyses focused on a fixed point in time and historical studies that emphasize the processes that construct and transform cultures. Nevertheless, for the past century, since Franz Boas, most anthropologists have rejected evolutionary models of cultural change that posit "progress" toward a particular, usually Western, ideal. It is inaccurate even to presume that the history of humanity from hunter-gatherer to agriculturalist to factory worker follows a linear development from food scarcity to abundance. As Marshall Sahlins pointed out, small-scale societies were the "original affluent societies"—rich in leisure time if not material goods—because they could gather sufficient food with a few hours of daily work. The Ainu, a hunting-gathering-fishing people of southern Sakhalin, illustrate how small numbers could survive drastic reductions in food supply, for example, when snowfall reduced the local deer population.[2] Although the modern, industrial diet seems to exemplify, indeed be plagued by, abundance, there are still profound inequalities in access to food and regular food shortages.

Another important premise is that the nature of food and foodways—even the most basic category of what foods are "edible"—are culturally defined and given local meanings, particularly as staple foods are placed at the center of a culture and by taboos forbidding other items. People in many societies express dissatisfaction and hunger after a meal without their customary staple, whether rice, wheat, maize, potatoes, or cassava, regardless of how many calories they may have ingested. Moreover, these staples play a role beyond the function of filling the stomach; by sustaining life, they also sustain the self. Grains often symbolize deities: rice in Japanese culture, maize in many indigenous American cultures, and wheat in the Christian Eucharist. Not all objectively "edible" items are regarded as food for a people, even in times of severe food shortages. For example, frogs are abhorred by the Ainu, while the French consider them a great delicacy. Some Japanese men relish blowfish, whose poison can kill instantly, not necessarily for its taste but in order to demonstrate masculinity. Food taboos can offer important insights on the values and thoughts of people, for example, the Jewish taboo against pork or the Buddhist prohibition against eating meat.[3]

As a basic element of material culture and social life, food has been central to the discipline of anthropology from its earliest days. In the 1890s, one of the founders of modern anthropology, William Robertson Smith, focused on the rituals of commensality, the shared sacrificial meal.[4] British social anthropologist Audrey Richards placed food at the heart of functionalist analysis by examining how food exchange contributed to social cohesion in her pioneering study, *Land, Labour and Diet in Northern Rhodesia* (1939). In the postwar era, French structuralist anthropologist Claude Lévi-Strauss used linguistic analysis of myths to argue for common conceptual structures across cultures, and employed binary oppositions, most famously "the raw and the cooked," to classify cultural practices such as Tupinamba cuisine. Structuralism, in turn, was challenged by the cultural ecology school, which sought material explanations for food habits.[5] Sidney Mintz, who began his career doing fieldwork in Caribbean sugar plantations, combined a material focus on production with a cultural analysis of British sugar consumption in his influential work, *Sweetness and Power* (1985). Contemporary approaches include the gendered analysis of feminist anthropology, poststructuralist attempts to destabilize cultural boundaries, multi-sited transnational studies, and economic anthropology's examination of the cultural foundations of markets.[6]

This essay adopts a thematic organization to survey the anthropological study of food with a focus on social and cultural approaches. Commensality has been a perennial interest among anthropologists as both source and expression of group identities. Analysis of gifts and manners provides another important means for studying sociality. Hierarchies inevitably structure access to food, and state control over its distribution is also important. Finally, attention to relationships between the global and the local is essential, not only for contemporary societies, but also for the past. Whatever the focus of study, cultural or symbolic value is extremely important in both "defining" what is food and what meanings it has. Yet we should not think of food only in terms of cultural and symbolic meanings, but also understand how the daily need to fill one's stomach makes access to food a powerful political tool.

Taste: Embodied, Emotive, and Aesthetic Dimensions of Food

Food is perceived with sense and enjoyed with feelings, demanding an embodied approach to its study. Mary Douglas pioneered an "anthropology of the body" in her book *Purity and Danger* (1966), which sought to explain the physical experience of pollution as a form of disorder, a violation of cultural rules. Thus, she attributed Jewish dietary restrictions against pork to the differences between pigs and proper ruminants such as sheep and cattle, which chewed the cud and did not eat carrion. Psychologist Paul Rozin has demonstrated the intense physical disgust felt by humans when given foods that violate notions of purity,[7] but these emotional reactions are culturally ingrained rather than innate. Mintz has noted that although newborn infants express a preference for sweetness, the nature of the consumption of sugar varies widely between societies.[8] An anthropology of food must therefore take into account both body and culture.

If the emotive dimensions of our dietary practices are important to study, so is the aesthetic dimension of food. This aesthetic emphasis is not meant to imply the high culture of elite taste, but rather the quotidian appreciation by ordinary people in day-to-day objects such as foods and eating utensils. For example, the Japanese have considered rice, both in raw and cooked forms, as innately beautiful, especially in the past. Ripe ears of rice stalks are described as having a golden luster. Since the character *kin* (or *kane*) refers both to gold and money, the association derives both from color and the usage of rice as currency. Expressed in poems, essays, and visual arts, the aesthetic of rice is further propagated as a symbol of beauty.

The senses also interact with memory in the creation of foodways, as Marcel Proust showed by reconstructing an entire social world through the taste and smell of a madeleine. Anthropologist David Sutton has followed up on this insight and examined the social construction of food memories on the Greek island of Kalymnos. He found not only a powerful sense of nostalgia for past meals, but also that future memories of commensality are imagined before the fact.[9] Efrat Ben-Ze'ev has likewise described the significance of food memories in the lives of Palestinian refugees displaced after the creation of Israel in 1948. Fruits and herbs serve as mnemonic devices allowing exiles to recreate their homeland, and temporary returnees traveling on European or North American passports eagerly gather olives, figs, hyssop, and sage to share with relatives who cannot make the journey.[10]

Within these deeply affective cultural values lurk potential snares for the fieldworker undertaking participant observation. Anthropologists, like diplomats, are supposed to share politely the foods of their informants, however distasteful they may be at home, but what happens when the native offerings are purposely intended to disgust? Paul Stoller related the story of a young Songhay cook who served "the worst damn sauce I've ever eaten"—not only in the anthropologist's opinion but also to family members who declared: "Let the goats eat this crap."[11] The intentionally repulsive meal responded to a complex but not uncommon set of relationships between the young woman, her family, and their guest. Personal convictions may also pose obstacles in cross-cultural encounters; David Sutton has described the experience of maintaining a vegetarian diet while doing fieldwork on Kalymnos. Colleagues had warned that he risked disdain in a society that associated meat with masculinity, but in fact the locals accorded him great respect, interpreting his self-restraint in light of Lenten fasting, which they understood intimately. That his refusal of meat was self-imposed rather than a religious injunction made it all the more praiseworthy.[12] Other complications result from the mutual and reflexive nature of anthropological research and the ways that subjects "study" their researchers. In an article on French grand cru chocolate, Susan Terrio confessed her fears that she would be revealed by master *chocolatiers* to be lacking in "good taste."[13]

Commensality: Food as Metaphor of the Collective Self

Food is unique as a metaphor for the self and for social groups through two interlocking mechanisms that assign symbolic power. First, food is *embodied* in each individual and therefore operates as a *metonym* by being incorporated as part of the self. Second, food has historically been consumed collectively by a social group—the rise of solitary dining being very much a modern phenomenon. This communal consumption therefore renders food a *metaphor* of "we"—the social group and often of people as a whole. This double linkage—metaphor underscored by metonym—gives foods a powerful symbol for the collective self not only conceptually but also *at the gut level.* This visceral experience of eating together provided the foundations for a range of communities, from families and school groups to the "imagined communities" of modern nations, to use Benedict Anderson's term.[14]

Commensality is institutionalized in many cultures, starting with family meals eaten together. In Japan a common expression for commensality is "to eat from the same rice-cooking pan" *(onaji kama no meshi wo kuu).* By contrast, expressions such as "to eat cold rice" (since rice is preferably served hot) and "to eat someone else's rice" refer to the opposite situation—the hardship in life, whether eating alone or away from one's kin group. Drinks are equally important, and *sake* (rice wine) is a vital point of commensality in Japan, especially among men. Following the basic rule that one never pours sake for oneself, people take turns pouring sake into another's cup in a never-ending series. The phrase "drinking alone" *(hitorizake)* indicates an individual on the verge of becoming a social nonentity. In a similar fashion, anthropologist Jack Goody cites the Prophet Muhammad: "Eat together and do not eat separately, for the blessing is with the company." Goody further contrasts eating with excretion, observing: "Public input, private output. Eating alone is the equivalent of shitting publicly."[15]

Nevertheless, commensality can take many different forms. In Western societies, the carving of a turkey may represent the pinnacle of a festive occasion, yet even in ordinary meals, bread is shared when other dishes are distributed individually. To "break bread together" is to become one. Students eating together at prestigious universities—the High Table at Oxford and Cambridge or the eating co-ops of Ivy League schools—provide the basis for life-long friendships, helping to cement class solidarities. The inverse of commensality, fasting, or commensality without food, is important to every institutional religion, including Muslim Ramadan, Christian Lent, and Jewish Yom Kippur.[16] But lest commensality seem to have a straight line to comradeship, consider the case of *chanko*, a hearty stew eaten by Japanese sumo wrestlers. Its consumption is commensality par excellence, but a closer look reveals hierarchy among the wrestlers, who eat in order of rank. The training house master and the top wrestlers (or important guests) eat first, and as one wrestler finishes, another takes his place around the pot. Lower-ranked wrestlers stand behind those eating in order to serve them and refill their bowls and glasses. By the time the lower-ranked wrestlers' turn comes, the broth has ironically gotten richer, although the meat, fish, and vegetables may have been consumed.[17]

The symbolic power of food as metaphor for the collective self also derives from its close linkage to space cum time. The connections between food and earth, reinforced by human efforts to transform nature into culture in the form of farm land, make agriculture a potent symbol of the primordial self in urban, industrial societies. Examples of this bond can be seen in the nineteenth-century haystack paintings of French artist Claude Monet and in the rice paddy woodblock prints of Hokusai and Hiroshige in burgeoning Edo (Tokyo).[18] During the Cultural Revolution, Mao Zedong attempted to recapture the Chinese self by returning to the rural, to agriculture and peasants, renouncing the urban life and intellectuals while attempting to "conquer nature."[19] With agriculture as a symbol of both communal space and pristine nature, seemingly uncontaminated by urbanization and industrialization, advertisements for "natural," "fresh," and "organic" foods have become increasingly common. These deep emotional attachments have also made agricultural subsidies an intractable problem for international trade negotiations in the World Trade Organization and the European Union.[20]

In the construction of communal identities, staple grains often play a powerful role, both in unifying and differentiating groups. Thus, the Eucharist served as a common symbol throughout Christian Europe, even as white bread distinguished aristocrats from the dark breads eaten by peasants in past centuries. Similar examples abound: the wheat-eating people of northern India opposed the rice-eating south, while the Pende of Central Africa identified with sorghum in contrast to the neighboring Mbuun, who grew maize in the nineteenth century.[21] Contemporary Japanese attempts to restrict imported California rice appear less extreme, given the careful distinctions made between French, German, and Italian bread, each representing a collective identity.

The importance of staple grains in the social imagination points to a long-standing bias in the history of anthropology, a Western emphasis on meat, especially big game meat, as the defining characteristic of commensality. Robertson Smith insisted that animal sacrifice alone constitutes *communion* between gods and humans, and that cereal oblation is only a *tribute* to the gods: "Those who sit at *meat* together are united for all social effects; those who do not eat together are aliens to one another, without fellowship in religion and without reciprocal social duties."[22] He relegated to a footnote the information from James Frazer that a sacrificial feast can be made from grain as well, thus failing to recognize the lack of an "objective" difference between animal and plant foods in regard to commensality. Ferdinand Braudel, the eminent French historian, expressed a similar prejudice: "Now fields were cultivated *at the expense* of hunting-ground and extensive stock-raising. As centuries passed a larger and larger number of people were *reduced to* eating vegetable foods... *often insipid and always monotonous.*"[23]

An early anthropological emphasis on hunters of "big game" is often attributed to the size and perishable nature of meat, which lends itself to common feasting after a sacrificial ritual. When Ainu males hunt bears or !Kung San kill a giraffe, they call it *the* food, whereas tubers and *mongongo* nuts gathered by women, which constitute the largest part of the diet, are never elevated to the same level of prestige. Gender inequalities among informants contribute to the anthropology's high valuation of meat. Yet the scholarly literature also reflects an attribution of western cultural biases to indigenous peoples. In Greek mythology Hercules was the prototype of "Man the Hunter," whereas Deianira was "Woman the Tiller." Likewise in the book of Genesis, the Lord had no regard for the offering of the fruit of the ground by Cain, the tiller, and preferred instead the animal offering by Abel, the herdsmen. Although Biblical scholarship offers various explanations for the story of Cain and Abel, the lower status given to plant food seems deeply embedded in Western culture.

Moreover, although commensality is by definition the act of shared eating, cooking is an equally important communal experience that reinforces both social ties and hierarchies. In rural Mexico, for example, households often maintain two separate kitchen spaces, an indoor *cocina de diario* (everyday kitchen) for family meals, which are generally cooked on modern appliances, and an outdoor *cocina de humo* (kitchen of smoke) for preparing festival dishes in giant earthenware pots over open fires. In a recent ethnographic study, Marie Elisa Christie has found that while a single individual will often make ordinary meals, festival cooking is by definition a collective task undertaken by circles of women, whose labor helps bind together communities. The work for festival labor is highly gendered, with men often involved in the preparation of meat but never the *mole* (chile sauces) at the heart of the dish. These tasks are also hierarchical, and the female head of the household takes responsibility for the feast. Work parties serve to pass culinary traditions between generations, although younger women often complain that elders withhold crucial steps in recipes as a way of preserving their own position.[24]

Sociality: Food, Gifts, and Manners

Food is crucial in constituting every social relationship. A person's first social act is nursing, taking what was part of the mother's body and thereby reuniting with her through the sharing of body substance. In almost every society, food is a major item of "gift exchange," reinforcing bonds of social solidarity, although gifts can also be a medium for rivalry and status competition. An understanding of these culturally defined rules allows one to see how gifts of food often serve to reflect, define, and express the nature of social relationships. Equally important for establishing the social persona is observance of table manners. Failing to behave in prescribed manner while eating can incur strong reactions from others, leading to possible loss of status or even exclusion from the social group. Yet as the sociologist Norbert Elias has observed, the often visceral physical reactions to eating behaviors are not only learned socially, they also change historically over time.[25]

Gift giving, particularly the reciprocal exchange of food, is charged with highly symbolic associations that reveal much about the values of a society. Food is a source of life, and the gift of food to a hospital patient can transmit the energy of healthy visitors to ensure a speedy recovery. Yet an inappropriate gift can have a powerful negative effect on a relationship. Offering a simple bottle of wine can backfire if given either to a superior who is a wine connoisseur or to a companion who prefers beers and considers wine to be snobbish.[26] In most societies, food and drinks—both perishable—are among the most preferred gift items. In the United States, it is inappropriate to give a material object to the host in most circumstances, but the perishable nature of food or wine, along with flowers, makes them acceptable gift items. As the Japanese would say: "it does not stay," which facilitates easy acceptance. A highly expensive bottle of wine would therefore be accepted when a material object of the same value would be considered a faux pas.

Table manners, like gift giving, are laden with social implications that can communicate social identity and status hierarchies. Norbert Elias considered western manners in a historical fashion, showing their changing nature from medieval to modern times. In particular, he pointed to the growing individualization of eating, through the rise of personal table settings, silverware, and cups, which distanced diners from one another. Eventually, table manners developed into a subtle language communicating fine gradations of formality, status, and progress through the meal, for example, indicating when a particular dish was finished by the placement of utensils. The observance and violations of these rules immediately indicate rank—as a country bumpkin or a sophisticated cosmopolitan—with consequences for the social treatment of the diner. Non-Western cultures have equally rigid prescriptions for eating with fingers; the Hindus, for example, use the right hand for eating and the left hand for defiling activities. Chopsticks are considered to be clean, by definition, although when reaching into a common dish, the Japanese reverse their chopsticks to take a portion, while the Chinese use the same end for serving and eating.

The historical development of manners can also be observed in the westernization of Japan. The introduction of chairs eliminated the most basic of traditional manners, the practice of sitting on one's legs *(seiza)*, leading to the abandonment of cushions and straw mat *(tatami)* floors in everyday life. These changes have been reinforced by the introduction and spread of American-style fast food, eaten with fingers while standing, which violated a basic distinction between human and animal behavior. Indeed, the first Japanese McDonald's restaurant, which opened in the exclusive Ginza shopping district of Tokyo in 1971, had neither tables and nor chairs. The emergence of a global youth culture facilitated these changes by making it fashionable to eat McDonald's hamburgers while standing and wearing blue jeans.[27]

Curiously, while youth around the world have embraced the manners of mass consumption, the counterculture in the United States rejected modern conformist lifestyles and industrially processed foods. Warren Belasco has described the hippie approach to eating of the 1960s and 1970s, which favored natural and ethnic foods and a communal lifestyle of producing it themselves. The original movement fragmented, as many young people pursued a more comfortable, convenient lifestyle, but a hard core took the anti-capitalist lifestyle even further in the 1980s. Dylan Clark has examined the eating habits of the punk subculture in an essay extending Lévi-Strauss's dichotomy: "The Raw and the Rotten: Punk Cuisine." Based on ethnography in a Seattle punk café, Clark illustrated the subversion of market systems by offering free food in exchange for gifts of raw ingredients or labor washing dishes, the rejection of animal exploitation through veganism, and a radical feminist refusal of dominant views of female beauty through punk body culture. The logic of punk cuisine culminated in the practice of dumpster diving, salvaging discarded refuse from American consumer society.[28]

Hierarchy: Food and Social Differentiation

Food is an important marker of social differentiation, defining both the boundaries between social groups and a closely related notion of social hierarchy that entails class, status, and power inequality. Here we focus on the cultural constructions of status and groups within particular societies. The French sociologist Pierre Bourdieu has been particularly influential in his emphasis on how *distinction* in taste serves to mediate between class and gender, on the one hand, and the body, on the other: "Taste, class culture turned into nature, that is, *embodied*, helps to shape the class today... the body is the most indisputable materialization of class taste."[29] In examining these forms of distinction, we can clearly see the historically changing nature of tastes as markers of status and the ways in which they are culturally encoded.

The status of particular foods reflects a complex mixture of both rarity as social distinction and the workings of power among the dominant classes. The court cuisines of medieval Europe relied on spices, imported at great cost from Asia, and on large quantities of meat, particularly game animals, which were restricted to the aristocracy by poaching laws. A cultural watershed of changing tastes in the early modern era resulted from the growing influence of European colonialism. The establishment of seaborne empires, first by Portugal and then Holland, brought a great influx of spices, dramatically lowering their cost. Having lost the aura of exclusivity, spices were banished from elite cookery, to be replaced by more "natural" sauces derived from the cooking juices of meat, reduced in saucepans and flavored with subtle herbs. Meanwhile, population growth and increased cereal production at the expense of livestock raising—a trend lamented by the historian Braudel—gave new cachet to butcher's meat, particularly prime cuts of beef.[30]

These changes draw a relatively straightforward line between supply and status, but the connections are not always so obvious, as Mintz has demonstrated in the case of sugar—another commodity that transformed cuisine by European imperialism. At first sugar was simply another spice, although it came to be used with great elaboration in Renaissance banquets. The creation of American plantations, worked by slave labor, greatly increased the supply, making sugar accessible in vast quantities at all levels of society. Yet as Mintz observes, sugar became a staple food among the working classes not in emulation of elite practices, but rather on distinctive occasions, consumed with coffee and tea on factory breaks. Thus, sugar provided a "stimulus to greater effort without providing nutrition." Mintz concludes: "There was no conspiracy at work to wreck the nutrition of the British working class, to turn them into addicts, or to ruin their teeth. But the ever-rising consumption of sugar was an artifact of intraclass struggles for profit—struggles that eventuated in a world-market solution for drug foods."[31]

Foods not only served to distinguish social classes, but also worked within particular social groups to construct hierarchies of gender and generation. "Man the hunter" survives in modern, urban societies most notably through the preferential access by men to steak, barbecued meat, or the prerogative of carving the holiday turkey, ham, or roast beef.[32] While there are many gendered dimensions to the production and distribution of food, often overlooked are the generational differences, particularly in the United States. They may not always involve overt inequality, but baby and children's foods are often separated from adult food in supermarket shelves and children's menus in restaurants. Foods are often seen as more appropriate for particular age groups, such as milk for children and coffee for adults, although these distinctions are seemingly decreasing with the spread of Starbucks.

The postmodern refutation of culinary social boundaries in the United States has led to a culture of "omnivorism" in which hamburgers, tacos, and street noodles have begun to rival truffles and sushi as gourmet foods, the latter having originated as a street food in early-nineteenth-century Edo. Yet this trend marks not so much a democratization of taste as new vehicles for asserting distinction. The stratification of food symbolism appears not just through different food items, caviar as opposed to tomatoes, but even within the same food item—organic, heirloom tomatoes and tasteless, industrial hothouse varieties. In their study of "foodies," Josée Johnston and Shyon Baumann describe the ways in which omnivorous tastes are used to assert social distinction and cultural capital. The pursuit of authenticity and simplicity in artisanal bakeries or distinctive regional cuisines allows foodies to demonstrate their knowledge and good taste.[33] Yet the ability of modern consumers to choose is tightly constrained by market structures. In a study of "yuppie coffee," William Roseberry has observed: "As I visit the gourmet shop, it might be a bit disconcerting to know that I have been so clearly targeted as a member of a class and generation, that the burlap bags or minibarrels, the styles and flavors of coffee, the offer of a 'gourmet coffee of the day,' have been designed to appeal to me and others in my market niche. But such are the circumstances surrounding my freedom of choice."[34] The structures of power and inequality in the distribution of food make it particularly important to study the role of the state in mediating access.

State Control of Food

Food preferences are assumed to derive "naturally" from human choices, yet the state often exercises control over production and distribution, thereby historically creating and shaping the cultural tastes of citizens. Of course, rulers have long gained legitimacy by ensuring adequate food supplies to subjects, such as the Chinese "mandate of heaven" from the millet god. Conversely, rulers have claimed the power to mobilize labor to guarantee production, for example, through irrigation works, public granaries, and other state projects. The ancient Inca state relocated entire communities from highland potato fields to lower Andean valleys in order to grow corn for making *chicha*, a fermented beverage used for state religious rituals.[35] Modern authoritarian regimes have made similar explicit attempts to control the diets of their subjects in order to increase their power. Even democratic governments have used foods as a crucial part of what Louis Althusser called the ideological state apparatus, consisting of hegemonic attempts to gain the acquiescence of subjects as distinct from the explicitly repressive powers of the state.

In Mussolini's Italy, the Roman ideal of the citizen-soldier-farmer placed food at the heart of the state's symbolic and economic structure. Spaghetti, polenta, and other Italian regional dishes had no place in the modern cuisine imagined by Fascist ideologue Filippo Marinetti in the *Futurist Cookbook* (1932). Already in 1925, the regime had declared a "Battle of Wheat" to achieve self-sufficiency and break the country's dependence on imported grain. Mussolini exhorted his followers to increase production, posing bare-chested as a heroic thresher for propaganda posters. This campaign came at the expense of profitable export crops, including fresh produce, citrus fruits, and olives, while also decreasing the diversity of the Italian diet. Yet the dictator showed little concern for declining standards of living, even before the ravages of World War II reduced Italians to the brink of starvation. As Carol Helstosky has shown, the Duce's failure to ensure the well-being of the masses was met by intransigence among the popular classes to alter their dietary preferences.[36]

State control over food in Japan had historically focused on the production and distribution of rice, and in deference to Buddhist doctrines, a prohibition on eating the meat of livestock, although not wild game. The "reopening" in the mid nineteenth century, after 250 years of isolation, along with the threat of western colonial incursions prompted a national debate on diet. The high incidence of beriberi, caused by vitamin B deficiency in polished rice, made traditional foodways a threat to Japan's military strength and independence. In 1871, the Emperor Meiji officially removed the prohibition on eating meat, adding beef, mutton, pork, venison, and rabbit to the menu at the Imperial Palace. As a further encouragement, on January 24, 1872, he publicly ate meat. The embrace of dietary reform was part of a wider adoption of western modernity—eating meat symbolically brought Japan closer to the West, and the emperor even introduced French cuisine to state banquets. Moreover, improved nutrition was considered vital to building strong "soldiers' bodies" and thereby avoiding the fate of other Asian countries that had fallen under the control of European imperial powers.[37]

Food remains a powerful mechanism for state control of the population, even in democratic postwar Japan. Anne Allison has described the cultural significance of children's school lunchboxes, called *obentō*. Although they are designed in the whimsical shape of animals, flowers, or landscapes, these lunchboxes impose responsibilities on both the mother, to prepare a suitable and tasty box, as well as on the child, who is required to eat the entire meal in the public setting of the school lunchroom. The labor of preparing an artistic box typically requires about half an hour a day, without counting the time and money spent looking for new ideas in the many specialized cookbooks and magazines. Nursery school teachers, bolstered by the authority of the Ministry of Education, thus maintain an intrusive form of surveillance over family life, shaming mothers and children who fail to meet standards and setting patterns for future school performance. The state benefits from the gendered labor supporting this system directly in educational terms and indirectly by ensuring that male employees can be exploited through long hours at work confident of a well-managed domestic sphere. Allison concludes: "Motherhood *is* state ideology, working through children at home and at school and through such mother-imprinted labor that a child carries from home to school as the *obentō*."[38] Whether in Italy, Japan, or elsewhere, the state is always an active agent in the foodways of a people.

The Global and the Local

Close attention to the texture and detail of a particular culture has been one of the traditional strengths of anthropology, and this local perspective can also provide valuable insight into the nature of global processes. Indeed, the anthropologist's focus on the processes of "localization" whereby new goods and ideas become incorporated into a culture is crucial to understanding the history of global flows. Still, the methodologies of participant observation, originally designed for the study of traditional societies, must be adapted to a changing world, just as Oscar Lewis pioneered urban anthropology in the 1950s, when, upon returning to the village of Tepoztlán, he found that his peasant informants had all moved to the slums of Mexico City in search of work.[39] George Marcus has called for a "multi-sited ethnography" to capture more complex and mobile societies of diasporic communities or media by shifting to new objects of study, for example, following the people, the thing, the metaphor, or the conflict.[40] Such an approach holds dangers, tempting anthropologists to abandon in-depth ethnography and instead conduct their "participant" observation in the first-class lounges of international airports. However, if grounded in a deep familiarity with a particular culture, an anthropology connecting that local to global networks holds great potential for understanding the movements of commodities, corporations, or migrant workers.

Although commodity chain analysis is often associated with the work of rural sociologists, anthropologists have also provided important insights on the historical movement of goods. Virtually all staple foods have traveled widely, with important consequences for the societies that they reach. Sidney Mintz's account of sugar ably connects the trans-Atlantic slave trade with the origins of British industrialization. Arturo Warman's global history of maize has shown how the New World crop gained acceptance throughout large parts of the world, but because of the localization of cooking practices, and the failure to adopt Native American forms of alkaline processing to boost its vitamin content, Mediterranean societies dependent on corn suffered plagues of pellagra.[41] Wet-rice agriculture was introduced into Japan around 400 B.C.E., and gradually supplanted the previous hunting-gathering subsistence economy, providing the basis for an incipient state. Japan's myth-histories are replete with references to rice as deities; in one version, the legendary Emperor Jinmu, the grandson of the Sun Goddess, received the original rice grains grown in heavenly fields and transformed the wilderness into a civilized land of rice paddies. This myth establishes a symbolic equation not only between rice and deities, but also between rice paddies and the Japanese soil. The history of rice in Japan demonstrates how the "global" became thoroughly "local," and the food of the other became the taste of the self.

Corporate fast food also illustrates the distinctive connections between globalization and localization. McDonald's has become an icon of the ways that these foods have attained such a rapid, visible, and dramatic presence. Thus, the French are well-known for their resistance against American "cultural hegemony" and the Millan sheep farmer José Bové, who dismantled a local outlet of the chain, has became a prominent anti-globalization protestor. Nevertheless, McDonald's has made inroads in part through its localization, supplying wine to customers in Paris. The metamorphosis of McDonald's in non-Western societies is more extensive. Since its introduction in Japan, the menu has undergone enormous changes, including Chinese fried rice (Mc-Chao), chicken-tatsuta (a soy-sauce flavored chicken sandwich), and the teriyaki burger, ironically called the "samurai burger" in Hong Kong. McDonald's has also inspired local competitors, such as MOS Burger chain, famous for bun-shaped rice patties and carry-out *obentō* boxes. MOS Burgers have even latched onto the "local food" trend and prominently displays photographs and information about farms where the vegetables come from. Customers originally flocked to McDonald's as an inexpensive way for Japanese to experience American life, but within a generation, it had lost its exotic appeal, having been indigenized and domesticated. Den Fujita, the founder of McDonald's in Japan, tells of Japanese boy scouts visiting the United States who were relieved to find a taste of home at a McDonald's in Chicago.[42]

The highly visible presence of "globalization from above" in the form of McDonald's restaurants often serves to obscure the equally vital flows of "globalization from below" taking place through the migration of working peoples. Mintz shows how the forced relocation of millions of Africans into plantation slavery was essential for the creation of the modern European diet. Farm labor in the modern United States likewise depends overwhelmingly on cheap migrant workers, although their presence is widely condemned by the very people who benefit from their labor. Susanne Freidberg reveals how contemporary supply chains can carry out their exploitative nature long distance, by growing green beans in West Africa for air shipment to European consumers.[43] Yet migratory peoples bring not only their labor but also their customary foodways to new lands. The ubiquitous Chinese global presence offers a testament to the entrepreneurial abilities of working-class migrants, which began with early modern migrations in Southeast Asia.[44] In the United States, Chinese food acquired its characteristic image of chop suey and chow mein because of the predominance of Cantonese migrants, whose regional cuisine was localized to fit western tastes. With the influx of new migrants from all over China after 1965, these acculturated ethnic dishes were quickly replaced by diverse regional specialties from Sichuan, Hunan, Shanghai, and Teochew, at least in communities with sizeable Chinese populations.[45]

While we witness the globalization of "ethnic foods" and their localization in multiple directions, the process is far from a simple transformation of the global by the local. Jeffrey Pilcher poses an important question: "While observers of globalization have devoted increasing attention to the international relations of power that determine whose culture is packaged and marketed around the world, an equally relevant question is: Who does the globalizing?"[46] Mexican food in the United States has emerged through a series of encounters between the ethnic community and the Anglo mainstream; in nineteenth-century San Antonio, Texas, a group of vendors known as "chili queens" introduced their flavorful stews to tourists, but outsiders quickly developed industrial simulacra such as chili powder and canned chili. Mass-produced chili and taco shells were carried around the world, not by Mexicans but by Americans, particularly military personnel and members of the counterculture. The so-called Mexican food we find from New York to Berlin to Ulan Bator is a product of the food-processing industry, which manufactures its own authenticity through advertising. In constructing a multisited ethnography of global Mexican, Pilcher trailed the taco, visiting restaurants and examining cookbooks on six continents to see how diverse local societies interpreted the image of Mexican culture.

In a similar fashion, Theodore Bestor explains the "magic logic of global sushi" in terms of the place of Japan in the popular North American imagination. The Tsukiji fish market is steeped in Japanese food culture, Japanese distribution channels, Japanese social and cultural rules, and yet it is most intimately integrated into the world economy. It has become, in fact, hegemonic in the world blue fin tuna market, which is regulated, at least officially, by the International Commission for the Conservation of Atlantic Tunas.[47] Thus, the picture is far from an "authentic" Mexican food or Japanese sushi traveling from the local across the globe, naturally changing the global palate. Instead, these changing food practices result from a complex system of capital, production, distribution, and advertising, all of which play upon the "idea" of Mexico or Japan.

Conclusion

Anthropology was one of the first of the social sciences to take food seriously as a subject of inquiry, and it has remained at the cutting edge of research in food studies. The ethnographic methods of participant observation are ideally suited to grasping the material processes and the symbolic meanings surrounding the production, distribution, and consumption of foods. Only by paying attention to the localization of universal practices can we understand the particular meanings of foods within a given society. These meanings are always culturally construed and changing over time. Anthropology has likewise revised its approach over time through critical self examination of methods and concepts. The recent proliferation of anthropological studies of food demonstrates the vitality of the discipline in posing—and answering—important questions about society and culture.

Notes

1. For a useful guide to the methodologies of food anthropology, see Helen Macbeth and Jeremy MacClancy, eds., *Researching Food Habits: Methods and Problems* (New York: Berghahn, 2004).
2. Marshall Sahlins, *Stone Age Economics* (Chicago: Aldine Publishing Co, 1974), 1–39. See also Emiko Ohnuki-Tierney, *The Ainu of the Northwest Coast of Southern Sakhalin* (New York: Holt, Rinehart & Winston, 1974).
3. Edmund Leach, "Animal Categories and Verbal Abuse," in *The Essential Edmund Leach*, vol. 1, *Anthropology and Society*, ed. S. Hugh-Jones and J. Laidlaw (1964; repr., New Haven: Yale University Press, 2000), 322–43; Francis Zimmermann, *The Jungle and the Aroma of Meats: An Ecological Theme in Hindu Medicine* (Berkeley: University of California Press, 1987).
4. William Robertson Smith, *Religion of the Semites* (1894; repr., New Brunswick, NJ: Transaction Publishers, 2002).
5. See, for example, Marvin Harris, *Good to Eat: Riddles of Food and Culture* (New York: Simon and Schuster, 1985).
6. For reviews of the literature, see, Ellen Messer, "Anthropological Perspectives on Diet," *Annual Review of Anthropology* 13 (1984): 205–49; Sidney W. Mintz and Christine M. Du Bois, "The Anthropology of Food and Eating," *Annual Review of Anthropology* 31 (2002): 99–119.

7. Paul Rozin, "Food and Eating," in *Handbook of Cultural Psychology*, ed. Shinobu Kitayama and Dov Cohen (New York: Guilford Press, 2007), 391–416.

8. Sidney W. Mintz, *Sweetness and Power: The Place of Sugar in Modern History* (New York: Viking Press, 1985), 14–16.

9. David E. Sutton, *Remembrance of Repasts: An Anthropology of Food and Memory* (Oxford: Berg, 2001).

10. Efrat Ben-Ze'ev, "The Politics of Taste and Smell: Palestinian Rites of Return," in *The Politics of Food*, ed. Marianne Elisabeth Lien and Brigitte Nerlich (Oxford: Berg, 2004), 141–60.

11. Paul Stoller, *The Taste of Ethnographic Things: The Senses in Anthropology* (Philadelphia: University of Pennsylvania Press, 1989), 19.

12. David E. Sutton, "The Vegetarian Anthropologist," *Anthropology Today* 13, no. 1 (February 1997): 5–8.

13. Susan J. Terrio, "Crafting Grand Cru Chocolates in Contemporary France," *American Anthropologist* 98, no. 1 (March 1996): 67–79.

14. Benedict Anderson, *Imagined Communities: Reflections on the Origin and Spread of Nationalism*, rev. ed. (London: Verso, 1982).

15. Jack Goody, *Cooking, Cuisine and Class: A Study in Comparative Sociology* (Cambridge: Cambridge University Press, 1982), 206.

16. Pat Caplan, *Feasts, Fasts, Famine: Food for Thought* (New York: Berg, 1994); Gillian Feeley-Harnik, *The Lord's Table: The Meaning of Food in Early Judaism and Christianity* (1981; repr., Washington, DC: Smithsonian Institution Press, 1994).

17. R. Kenji Tieney, "Drinking like a Whale, Eating like a Horse: The Place of Food in the Sumo World," in *Cuisine, Consumption, and Culture: Food in Contemporary Japan*, ed. Theodore Bestor and Victoria Bestor (Berkeley: University of California Press, forthcoming).

18. Emiko Ohnuki-Tierney, *Rice as Self: Japanese Identities through Time* (Princeton, NJ: Princeton University Press, 1993), 89–90.

19. Judith Shapiro *Mao's War against Nature* (Cambridge: Cambridge University Press, 2001).

20. John Feffer, "Korean Food, Korean Identity: The Impact of Globalization on Korean Agriculture" (Stanford: APARC Working Paper, Stanford University, 2005); Raj Patel, *Stuffed and Starved* (New York: Random House, 2008).

21. Jan Vansina, *The Children of Woot: A History of the Kuba Peoples* (Madison: University of Wisconsin Press, 1978), 177.

22. Robertson Smith, *Religion of the Semites*, 269; italics added.

23. Fernand Braudel, *Capitalism and Material Life, 1400–1800*, trans. Miriam Kochan (London: Weidenfeld and Nicolson, 1973), 68; italics added.

24. Marie Elisa Christie, *Kitchenspace: Women, Fiestas, and Everyday Life in Central Mexico* (Austin: University of Texas Press, 2008).

25. Elias, Norbert, *The Civilizing Process: Sociogenetic and Psychogenetic Investigations*, trans. Edmund Jephcott (New York: Wiley-Blackwell, 2000).

26. See, for example, Josephine Smart, "Cognac, Beer, Red Wine or Soft Drinks? Hong Kong Identity and Wedding Banquets," in *Drinking Cultures: Alcohol and Identity*, ed. Thomas M. Wilson (Oxford: Berg, 2005), 107–28.

27. Isao Kumakura, "Zen-Kindai no Shokuji Sahō to Ishiki (Table Manners and their Concepts during the Early Modern Period)," in *Shokuji Sahō no Shisō* (Conceptual Structure of Eating Manners), ed. T. Inoue and N. Ishige (Tokyo: Domesu Shuppan, 1990), 108; Motoko Murakami, "Gendaijin no Shokuji Manâ-kan (Eating Manners of Contemporary Japanese)," in ibid, 133.

28. Warren Belasco, *Appetite for Change: How the Counterculture Took on the Food Industry* (Ithaca, NY: Cornell University Press, 1993); Dylan Clark, "The Raw and the Rotten: Punk Cuisine," in *Food and Culture: A Reader*, ed. Carole Counihan and Penny Van Esterik, 2nd ed. (New York: Routledge, 2008), 411–22.

29. Pierre Bourdieu, *Distinction: A Social Critique of the Judgment of Taste*, trans. Richard Nice (Cambridge, MA: Harvard University Press, 1984), 190. See also Claude Fischler, *L'homnivore: Le gout, la cuisine et le corps* (Paris: Odie Jacob, 1990).

30. Stephen Mennell, *All Manners of Food: Eating and Taste in England and France from the Middle Ages to the Present* (Oxford: Basil Blackwell, 1985), 72–73.

31. Mintz, *Sweetness and Power*, 186.

32. Richard Shweder, *Why Do Men Barbecue?* (Chicago: University of Chicago Press, 2002).

33. Josée Johnston and Shyon Baumann, *Foodies: Democracy and Distinction in the Gourmet Foodscape* (New York: Routledge, 2010).

34. William Roseberry, "The Rise of Yuppie Coffees and the Reimagination of Class in the United States," *American Anthropologist* 98, no. 4 (December 1996): 771.

35. Paul S. Goldstein, "From Stew-Eaters to Maize-Drinkers: The Chicha Economy and the Tiwanaku Expansion," in *The Archaeology and Politics of Food and Feasting in Early States and Empires*, ed. Tamara L. Bray (New York: Kluwer, 2003), 143–72.

36. Carol Helstosky, *Garlic and Oil: Politics and Food in Italy* (Oxford: Berg, 2004); Simonetta Falasca-Zamponi, *Fascist Spectacle* (Berkeley: University of California Press, 1997); Filippo Tommaso Marinetti, *The Futurist Cookbook*, ed. Lesley Chamberlain, trans. Suzanne Brill (London: Trefoil, 1989 [1932]).

37. Nobuo Harada, *Rekishi no Naka no Kome to Niku—Shokumotsu to Tennō Sabetsu* (Rice and Meat in History—Food, Emperor and Discrimination) (Tokyo: Heibonsha, 1993), 17, 19, 70–76; Yanesaburō Gushima, *Bunmei eno Dappi—Meiji Shoki Nihon no Sunbyō* (Exodus Toward Civilization—A Sketch of Early Meiji) (Kyūshū: Kyūshū Daigaku Shuppankyoku, 1983), 194.

38. Anne Allison, "Japanese Mothers and *Obentōs*: The Lunch-Box as Ideological State Apparatus," in Counihan and Van Esterik, *Food and Culture*, 236.

39. Oscar Lewis, *The Children of Sánchez: Autobiography of a Mexican Family* (New York: Random House, 1961).

40. George E. Marcus, "Ethnography in/of the World System: The Emergence of Multi-Sited Ethnography," *Annual Review of Anthropology* 24 (1995): 95–117.

41. Arturo Warman, *Corn and Capitalism: How a Botanical Bastard Grew to Global Dominance*, trans. Nancy L. Westrate (Chapel Hill: University of North Carolina Press, 2003).

42. Emiko Ohnuki-Tierney, "We Eat Each Other's Food to Nourish Our Body: The Global and the Local as Mutually Constituent Forces," in *Food in Global History*, ed. Raymond Grew (Boulder, CO: Westview Press, 1999), 255–60.

43. Susan Freidberg, *French Beans and Food Scares: Culture and Commerce in an Anxious Age* (New York: Oxford University Press, 2004).

44. David Y. H. Wu and Sidney C. H. Cheung, eds., *The Globalization of Chinese Food* (Honolulu: University of Hawai'i Press, 2002).

45. Haiming Liu and Lianlian Lin, "Food, Culinary Identity, and Transnational Culture: Chinese Restaurant Business in Southern California," *Journal of Asian American Studies* 12, no. 2 (June 2009): 135–62.

46. Jeffrey M. Pilcher, "Eating Mexican in a Global Age: The Politics and Production of Ethnic Food," in *Food Chains: From Farmyard to Shopping Cart*, ed. Warren Belasco and Roger Horowitz (Philadelphia: University of Pennsylvania Press, 2009), 158.

47. Theodore C. Bestor, *Tsukiji: The Fish Market at the Center of the World* (Berkeley: University of California Press, 2004); idem, "How Sushi Went Global," *Foreign Policy* (November-December 2000): 54–63.

Bibliography

Bestor, Theodore C. *Tsukiji: The Fish Market at the Center of the World*. Berkeley: University of California Press, 2004.

Caplan, Pat. *Feasts, Fasts, Famine: Food for Thought*. Oxford: Berg, 1994.

Counihan, Carole, and Penny Van Esterik, eds. *Food and Culture: A Reader*. 2nd ed. New York: Routledge, 2008.

Douglas, Mary. *Purity and Danger: An Analysis of Concepts of Pollution and Taboo*. London: Routledge, 1966.

Elias, Norbert. *The Civilizing Process: Sociogenetic and Psychogenetic Investigations*. Translated by Edmund Jephcott. New York: Wiley-Blackwell, 2000.

Goody, Jack. *Cooking, Cuisine and Class: A Study in Comparative Sociology*. Cambridge: Cambridge University Press, 1982.

Lévi-Strauss, Claude. *The Raw and the Cooked*. Translated by John and Dorren Weightman. New York: Harper & Row, 1969.

Mintz, Sidney W. *Sweetness and Power: The Place of Sugar in Modern History*. New York: Viking Books, 1985.

Ohnuki-Tierney, Emiko. *Rice as Self: Japanese Identities through Time*. Princeton, NJ: Princeton University Press, 1993.

Plotnicov, Leonard, and Richard Scaglion, eds. *The Globalization of Food*. Prospect Heights, IL: Waveland Press, 2003.

Richards, Audrey I. *Land, Labour and Diet in Northern Rhodesia*. Oxford: Oxford University Press, 1939.

Sahlins, Marshall. *Stone Age Economics*. Chicago: Aldine Publishing Co., 1974.

Smith, William Robertson. *Religion of the Semites*. 1894. Reprint: New Brunswick, NJ: Transaction Publishers, 2002.

Sutton, David E. *Remembrance of Repasts: An Anthropology of Food and Memory*. Oxford: Berg, 2001.

Wilk, Richard. *Home Cooking in the Global Village: Caribbean Food from Buccaneers to Ecotourists*. Oxford: Berg, 2006.

CHAPTER 8

SOCIOLOGY OF FOOD

SIERRA CLARK BURNETT AND
KRISHNENDU RAY

NOTWITHSTANDING the clarion call to critical thinking, everyday practice in the academy tends to naturalize disciplinary boundaries and consecrate only a few sites and forms of knowing. Today's assumptions about methods, modes of inquiry, and styles of explication are understood as the frontiers of knowledge, with little reflection on how temporal and spatial locations mold these assumptions. American academics are often blinded by the global reach of the American university, which obfuscates their own national location and its site-specific epistemologies. They take national traditions for granted—unaware that what is considered anthropology in the United States may legitimately be called sociology in India—and disciplinary labels tend to preclude fertile conversations across academic departments and state lines. Furthermore, scholars share the presumption that disciplinary modes of knowing are superior to other nondisciplinary and nonacademic ways of comprehending the world. This is partially a product of unfamiliarity with what others are doing, which in turn is related to the demands of specialization, boundary-work, and community building (for the practical quest of job-getting) with its attendant parochialisms. But it is equally the result of a self-serving ideology of the academy. University-based American disciplines appear to have reached a consensus that research universities are where new knowledge is produced—a claim that unites the historian, the sociologist, and the anthropologist, no matter how acutely aware they are of each other's faults. If they are critical of other disciplines' epistemologies, they are eminently more dismissive of nonacademic work.

But new knowledge is in fact produced across a spectrum of locations, ranging from the individual to households to craft guild to gendered groups to social networks to coffee klatches to neighborhoods to for-profit companies, not-for-profits, governments, and universities. Universities (and governments) are merely best positioned to consecrate their own knowledge-producing capacity as the disinterested pursuit of truth. Much of this would be self-evident if we looked outside the academy and into our everyday lives, and if we heeded lessons from academics elsewhere. In India, for instance, there is a robust discussion about knowledge produced on the streets and within movements, which is posing a serious challenge to university-based knowledge.[1] The strength of food studies *could* precisely be that it acknowledges other sites of knowledge production and considers the university discipline to be only one of those sites, taking it seriously but not as the last word. In doing that, food studies might remind cloistered social scientists of their origins on the street, and help them hear the voices emanating from immigrant ghettos, settlement houses, and back alleys that abound in their genealogies. In this essay we show how awareness of the contingent production of knowledge at particular places, at specific times, and in peculiar institutions not normally valorized by sociology (or really any academic discipline) allows us a glimpse into an alternate reality. We also argue that research on food provides a particularly productive nexus at this moment in the academy. It challenges some of the disciplinary walls that originally provided a home, but in so doing it opens windows that allow us to set our sights on a much broader notion of the social world and more nuanced ways of knowing it.

The study of food, an area associated with domesticity and women's work, suffered from sociological neglect for decades. Folklorists and anthropologists long ago saw the importance of food in the development of cultures, religions, group dynamics, symbolism, communication, and other sources of meaning in human life. But sociologists have been reluctant to adopt food as a central focus. Even today, when food makes a stronger appearance in studies of class and stratification, consumption, and labor, rich sociological work on food is limited to a few areas. This neglect has resulted in two polar tendencies. Some scholars put in a great effort to justify the study of food by upholding the strictest of disciplinary rules and operating with only highly consecrated methodologies. For others, however, the lack of a canon has allowed greater flexibility and permitted creative and productive syntheses of different theoretical bodies of work. While the former group should be credited for much of the field's initial acceptance, it is with the latter that we believe the study of food will offer the most significant contributions. In order to explain our ambitious conclusions about the merits of food studies in general and its lessons for sociology in particular, we must begin with a few words about the discipline of sociology, its theories and methods, strengths and limitations that have been adapted to the study of food.

Sociology is a large, sprawling discipline with various subspecializations that focus on what are considered problems of modernity such as underdevelopment, agricultural modernization, urbanization, migration, race and gender, consumption, communication, science and religion, group formation and disintegration, elites and subcultures, identity, and community. Since its inception as an academic discipline, sociology has been shaped by a number of questions that continue to influence the direction of sociological work today, thereby legitimizing certain fields of research and relegating others to different disciplines or delegitimizing them altogether.

The first is a tension between policy change and knowledge building, closely related to the questions about the relationship between theory and empirical research. Early American sociologists positioned themselves in the public sphere and sought to provide evidence and ethics for shaping reform agendas. Sociologists at the University of Chicago, home of one of the earliest American sociology departments, at first followed the Baptist vision of its financier John D. Rockefeller and a moral imperative for social work. But as the discipline grew and strengthened in university settings in the 1920s and 1930s, the Chicago School of Sociology congealed around the work of Robert Park, Ernest Burgess, Lous Wirth, and Herbert Blumer, who distanced themselves from the activism of the school's founders and became less explicitly politically and morally engaged.[2] They celebrated empirical research and characterized their work as social *science*, distinct from moralizing social philosophy, focusing on their own urban setting. American pragmatism, with its emphasis on human interpretation and reaction, influenced Chicago sociologists' ideas about the attitudes, values, and experiences of marginal social actors. Immigrants, hobos, children, slum dwellers, Negros, ghetto residents, and the jack-roller responded to situations based on the meanings they ascribed, and understanding these was seen as empirically necessary for the study of broader social processes. Sociologists examined the forms of practical reasoning and meaning-making within their subject's own "worlds," an approach that was eventually crystallized into the sociological dictum, "If men define situations as real, they are real in their consequences."[3]

The second question influencing the evolution of sociology over the years relates to methodology. As American sociology spread through the eastern universities, and eventually to the West coast, the urban empirical approach was sustained, augmented by the growing field of statistics and other quantitative tools of analysis. After World War II the pace of professionalization hastened, and applied research acquired new visibility at universities. It was at Columbia University, more than in any other department, that "quantitative methods were" increasingly "linked to professionalizing projects," an association that continues today.[4] By the 1960s, formal analyses of survey data and the growing use of multivariate analysis had become standard for the field. Ethnographic, microsociology characterized by deep interpretation and thick description, pursued by scholars such as Gary Alan Fine and some areas of historical sociology such as the works of Stephen Mennell and Priscilla Parkhurst Ferguson, survive, but they often rely on epistemological claims of other disciplines (for example anthropology and history) in order to assert their validity in the face of an otherwise quantitatively oriented discipline.

As scholars approach food surrounded by these ongoing tensions in sociology, their work has clustered in a few areas. As is true in many disciplines, methodologies and topics of study have typically correlated. Identifying changing *patterns* in consumption attracts researchers to large numbers of surveys or purchase records, while understanding the *meaning* that people attribute to their own consumption and to the habits of others has been pursued through more interactional, ethnographic, or interview-driven approaches. What results are clustering across multiple factors (policy versus knowledge building, theory versus empiricism, diachronic versus synchronic analyses, and qualitative versus quantitative studies). A brief overview of these groupings will help illustrate this point.

Today's policy-focused sociology generally addresses the entrenched inequalities in food production and consumption, focusing on discrepancies in health, well-being, and opportunity. Sociology of health, for example, rests on theoretical foundations pertaining to power and class, and generally steers toward empiricism through statistical analysis. Scholars working in this field typically rely on large-population studies, which are very good at providing a broad overview of clusters and corelationships but often cannot address questions involving more intimate and intensive interactions with food. In contrast to large quantitative studies that seek knowledge through numbers, qualitative methodologies have guided scholars into areas where nuance, variety, and intimate human interaction are more compelling than aggregations and generalizations. To study how culinary cultures evolve, the links between food and identity, and the ways that food preferences influence and reflect social relations, scholars have engaged with methodologies ranging from historical sociology and ethnography to discourse and textual analysis. Finally, a large body of rural sociology focuses on agrarian life and its cultural and environmental consequences. Understanding agrarianism is critical to the study of any food system, not only because farmland remains the initial point of most food production but also because ideologies and policies relating to agriculture greatly impact the abundance and price of foods available for purchase and consumption. Much recent rural sociology related to food production has engaged with questions of localism and environmental sustainability.[5]

While acknowledging the importance of these approaches, we believe that the lessons food studies can teach sociologists are perhaps best illustrated in sites of cooking and eating, as it is here that sensory experience and intense human interactions are most explicit. This allows us to move beyond theories of labor and technology applicable to multiple sites of production and into a realm that at once is universal to human life and has long been dismissed by sociologists as too quotidian and corporeal. But things are changing. Here feminist sociologists' attention to the family meal and the gender dynamics of doing and distribution of resources, including the making and gifting of food, provided the earliest openings, which has become its own specialized subfield.[6] We bracket that discussion here to focus on taste and point to other lines of development.

Recent developments in sociological thought have opened up some promising new opportunities for the study of food, taking qualitative analysis in rich new directions. As we will explain, the cultural and practice "turns" in sociology in the last few decades (that developed out of theorizations on gender and sexuality) heightened attention to daily life and the intimate space of bodies, dreams, and routines. Moving away from the discipline's past emphasis on structure (a legacy of Talcott Parsons in American sociology) and conflict (a legacy of Karl Marx in Euro-American sociology) has allowed scholars to reconsider the human mind and body within the everyday social, suspended between outright conflict or consensus. It is here where the tension between abstract theory and empirical research, material conditions and mental and bodily practices, becomes the most interesting from our perspective within food studies. Moreover, it is here that scholars are increasingly reflective of their own presence and the contingent nature of interpretation, which is in turn beginning to make room for new forms of knowledge not previously accepted as legitimate sociology.

Much of the material we discuss in the following pages has been categorized under the title "sociology of consumption," as it employs theories pertaining to taste and food habits. However, we hope to show that the term "consumption" is not always accurate and pigeonholes important scholarship that would benefit broader academic circles. In fact, the study of food offers a compelling case for challenging the distinction between production and consumption. Not only are producers also consumers, and vice versa, but the line between moments of production and those of consumption are blurry if not illusory. The restaurant, for example, is both a site of cooking and of eating, one where meals are made while tastes are determined, performed, negotiated, and upheld or rejected. As we will see, chefs or critics operate in both spheres simultaneously. Workers in food businesses may be studied through a lens of labor relations, as craftsmen or artisans, or as bodies and social groups, often shaped by migration, but they can also be seen as taste-makers, consumers, and integral to evolving culinary standards and trends. Thus, we would describe our focus in this chapter not as the "sociology of consumption" but as the nexus between consumption and production, as we emphasize the ways in which the two irrevocably intertwine.

In the following pages, we discuss the academic scholarship that we believe has contributed most significantly to the current form and trajectory for the study of food. We discuss historical sociology and its relevance to contemporary theories of culinary and other cultural norms. We then move to scholarship on the social aspects of taste preferences, largely explored through interview and ethnographic methods and, more recently, discourse analysis. Next, we examine new developments in sociology and related disciplines that may, or should, be highly productive for the study of food and its contribution more broadly. By illuminating the practice of research, theory-building, data collection, and analysis, we identify the specificity and advantages of different forms of sociological research. We hope to explain why the limitations of disciplinary boundaries and the restricted conceptions of knowledge that characterize the academy today may unnecessarily restrict our ability to understand food, cooking, and eating in daily life. We finally turn to our hopes for the future of food studies and propose ways in which we may be able to move beyond these entrenched limitations.

Food in Sociology

When food has appeared in sociology it has often played a minor role, a backdrop for the study of other social issues such as the transition from feudalism to capitalism, rural development or the lack thereof, malnutrition, gender relations, and so forth. Agricultural production has its own vast subfield that scrupulously stays away from any discussion of the final, sensorial, culinary product. Scholars have also considered food processes as a point of entry into questions about factory labor and safety, immigrant assimilation and its barriers, or gender relations and household labor.[7] In much of this work, the food that is cooked and consumed is at most a lens. It is our intention to identify instead instances when food, or the act of cooking and eating it, is the intended focal point, as well as exemplary works that have fundamentally changed the way we think about food. We begin with what many consider the founders of modern consumption theory, Thorstein Veblen and Norbert Elias, not because we position food studies as a direct descendent of their work, although we remain deeply indebted, but rather because they were among the first to treat patterns of behavior and norms of consumption and display as worthy of academic inquiry.

Thorstein Veblen, in *The Theory of the Leisure Class* (1899), offers a critique of modern consumerism. He sees the division of labor and the resulting surplus accumulation to have reached a pinnacle in American society in the late 1800s, and he identifies the coercive role of the upper class's "conspicuous" consumption and waste and the pressure of emulation in the propagation of class inequality. His work is both historical and contemporary in that he identifies the forces that contributed to specific forms of consumption, waste, and class relations over time while painting a dire picture of his present based on his own observations. He not only provided a foundation on which others continued the study of consumerism, but he also exemplified the historical and synchronic approaches that would be taken up by sociologists for decades to come.

Forty years after Veblen, German sociologist Norbert Elias published *The Civilizing Process* (1939), an analysis of the history of manners in Early Modern Europe and the function of etiquette and repugnance in differentiating social groups. A student of Karl Mannheim, Elias produced a distinctive sociology that sought to resolve the central contradictions between structure and agency, conflict and consensus, and the individual and society. His work on manners anticipated by decades the fascination of sociology for etiquette, emotions, and habits. Although long ignored in the Anglophone world, Elias was one of the first to observe that individuals and societies are co-produced, contrary to Liberal Social Contract assumptions that preexisting individuals come together to form society. Individuals develop a socially constructed "habitus" or second nature. And he proposed an astonishing theoretical link between the production of the individualized but socialized body and state formation (preceding Michel Foucault by three decades). Furthermore, Elias, like Foucault, insisted on diachronic analysis, studying change over time to understand large social formations. His temporal schema is less "catastrophic" than Foucault's archaeology of knowledge, but it also focuses on the development of sweeping social norms.

Elias was also one of the earliest sociologists to employ textual analysis, which drew from early modern guides to etiquette in order to trace the standardization of behavior and, by interpolation, the psyche (an innovation that would be taken up much later by social historians and feminist scholars in the United States). He argued that as individuals we traverse in quick succession the stages of social development from the barbarian child to the civilized modern subject, with greater repressive self-controls, which is a function of increasing interdependence and social differentiation (contra Foucault). His work has been criticized for unilinear notions of social evolution (stages of development) and excessive dependence on Freud, in the sense that he accepted the argument that civilization is a product of repression of instincts and affects (emotional expression including outbursts). Nevertheless, Christopher Lasch noted: "Long before American scholars had discovered the idea of historical sociology Elias understood the possibilities of this new genre and worked them out with an imaginative boldness that still surpasses later studies in this vein."[8] Zygmunt Bauman considered Elias to be one of the last representatives of classical sociology, someone striving after the great synthesis, rather than working under the self-conception of a narrow technician of knowledge.[9]

Stephen Mennell, a student of Elias, adopts the notion of the "civilizing process" to show how tastes are culturally constructed and justified after the fact. He remains a useful proponent of materiality against the tide of discourse analysis and emphases on revolving social pressures. He uses historical texts as an archival record of events past, much as a historian would, rather than as an evolving discourse to be examined internally. Based on a close reading of a wide range of archival material—early modern cookbooks, the trade press, and cookery columns in women's magazines—Mennell seeks to answer the question of why the French developed haute cuisine and the English did not.

He explains national difference through class dynamics and state formation, contrasting absolutist France, where relatively powerless nobles engaged in social competition in the kitchen and at the table, with parliamentary England, where a landed gentry retained political influence and avoided the temptations of London. His book, *All Manners of Food* (1985), begins in the late Middle Ages, when courtly culture provided sites of symbolic social competition. By the fifteenth century elites displayed and consumed vast quantities of valuable meat and spices in feasts that served as theaters of power. But as the rising middle classes gained access to such comestibles by the seventeenth century, aristocratic competition shifted toward a new sense of refinement, eschewing spices in favor of delicate sauces and more natural flavors, which became codified in cookbooks via the printing revolution. Print and the professional culture of elite cooks now drove the self-conscious dynamic of haute French cuisine between 1650 and 1750, when a courtly cuisine became hegemonic, driven equally by recipes and rhetorics. In contrast, regionalized country cookery remained dominant within the English imagination as the failure of absolutism denied the English court the symbolic power of Versailles. Cookbooks for and by women continued to dominate the print record, and slowly the domesticity of the English country gentlemen was redefined as a source of English virtue and power, against French dandyism. Mennell's use of remarkable archival resources and deft comparative-theoretical conceptualization makes *All Manners of Food* a profoundly important work in the historical sociology of taste.

Meanwhile, Jack Goody, a British social anthropologist concerned with the origins and evolution of culture, explains a connection between agricultural technologies, surplus, writing, and the rise of class differentiation. In *Cooking, Cuisine, and Class* (1982), he argues that stratified cuisines are the result of productive societies where surplus accumulates in the hands of a few and systemic inequality prevails. With a comparative and historical lens, he argues that such cuisines did not develop in precolonial Africa as they did in Eurasia largely because of a lack of advanced agricultural techniques and literacy. Much of his story involves preliterate societies, and even in the case of modern ones written words and texts are shown to only partially determine or reveal social systems. This tension between the study of texts and of material conditions, or the intellectual world of man versus the physical one, remains both critical and challenging for scholars today.

While Mennell and Goody encourage us to think beyond the written record for the roots of our social processes and structures, others look explicitly at the connection between discourses and practices, highlighting the power of words particularly in modern Europe. In fact, many would argue that the study of food requires particularly close engagement with words, given the ephemerality and corporeality of food and its consumption. Priscilla Parkhurst Ferguson's *Accounting for Taste* (2004) is a strong recent example of scholarship in the field of historical sociology that prioritizes words not only as source of evidence but as a potent social force. Ferguson sets out to answer the question, why have the French dominated Western conceptions of "cuisine," which she defines in discursive terms as a "cultural construct that systematizes culinary practices and transmutes the spontaneous culinary gesture into a stable cultural code."[10] She stands with a long line of writers such as Albert Sonnenfeld, Massimo Montanari, Pascal Ory, and Jean-Louis Flandrin, who assert that cuisine is a product of double orality, taste and talk.[11] Cuisine happened, they say, when cooking left the domestic kitchen to enter the Court in Early Modern Europe and the restaurant in Paris, at about the time of the French Revolution. But of course orality is as ephemeral as a dish. Thus cooking and the talk about it had to be written down, replicated by way of print, and enter the field of cultural production through the work of journalists, novelists, and philosophers to become a cuisine. Through its textualization in this particular moment in history, cuisine entered what Jürgen Habermas called "the new domain of a public sphere whose decisive mark was the published word."[12] The crucial player here was Antonin Carême, who rationalized French restaurant practices and created a stable technical repertoire. He also helped aestheticize culinary discourse and nationalize both talk and taste.[13] Carême and his followers would eventually write their way out of the kitchen and into an autonomous cultural field of gastronomy. Cuisine was thus consecrated and valorized in the written form, or at least that is the story for Europe.[14]

In this narrative, both restaurants and cuisine are presumed to be French inventions. Ferguson suggests it is misleading to seek the reason for this in the variety and freshness of French produce, the profusion of its regional cuisines, or *terroir*. As Sonnenfeld put it long ago, "The glorious diversity of French soil and produce, the cliché of France as 'the garden of Europe,' does not adequately distinguish France from Italy or, for that matter, from California."[15] Ferguson tells us that it was only in the early nineteenth century with the invention of gastronomy that the reputation of French food was fully established, not the other way around. Talk and text solidified France's supremacy, through the parallel appearance of cookbooks and culinary treatises by prominent chefs and the rise of the reader-diner "whose consumption of texts rivals their ingestion of food."[16] These reader-diners not only ate but discussed, compared, evaluated, and ultimately aesthetized food. As writing and reading on culinary subjects flourished, the gastronomic superiority of France was iterated and reiterated, eventually convincing not only the French but the world of its supremacy. Amy Trubek clarifies and contains that claim by suggesting that "the French invented the cuisine of culinary professionals" not just a national cuisine.[17]

Arjun Appadurai prefigured some of this discussion on nation, cooking, and textualization in his seminal article on cookbooks in India. Appadurai's trajectory also draws attention to the arbitrariness of disciplinary boundaries with which we opened this essay. He is typically considered an anthropologist and began his academic career as one, yet as early as his cookbook article he was already locating his work as a comparative sociological exercise, substantively engaging with Goody's construction of social hierarchy and taste. Appadurai's problem is the opposite of the French problem: why we do not see the kind of textualization of taste and recipes in Indian sources—something that has come to define haute cuisine in the French model—in spite of all the social ingredients identified by Goody. Appadurai's ultimate answer is that India never developed a centralized haute cuisine because food may have been too important morally and medicinally in the Indic imagination to develop an aesthetic approach essential to gastronomy. In looking for explanations of India's culinary universe, Appadurai moves fluidly between historical and contemporary materials, highlighting cultural persistence and moments of critical change. For him, the key to unlock this universe is to trace its origins in material conditions and moral codes.

The connection between food, social stratification, consumption, and class has intrigued more than the historically minded sociologists. In fact, some of the best work in this area comes from sociologists looking through synchronic and comparative lenses. These scholars focus less on origins and more on how inequalities are sustained, reproduced, and naturalized in daily practice. Likely the most prominent scholar to influence the sociology of consumption and the study of food in particular in the last half century, and a preeminent force in the study of food, is French sociologist Pierre Bourdieu. The fluidity with which Bourdieu weaves together voluminous empirical data of daily practices with deep theorization about the body and preconscious dispositions, rendered largely from his own ethnography, set the gold standard for sociological work on taste and consumption.

Reflecting his training at the pinnacle of the French university system (although he was also its most trenchant critic), Bourdieu represents a philosophically informed sociologist, who sets his task in *Distinction* (1979) to transform understandings of "culture" as aesthetics (in philosophy) into culture as everyday life (as in anthropology). He exposes how judgments of taste reveal not intrinsic value but socialized, and measurable, negotiations over power and class. His science of taste effectuates, he contends, a "barbarous reintegration of aesthetic consumption into the world of ordinary consumption," and "abolishes the opposition which has been the basis of high aesthetics since [Immanuel] Kant, between the 'taste of sense' and the 'taste of reflection,' and between facile pleasure, pleasure reduced to a pleasure of the senses, and pure pleasure, pleasure purified of pleasure, which is predisposed to become a symbol of moral excellence and a measure of the capacity of sublimation which defines the truly human man."[18] The question he is interested in is: how do social systems reproduce themselves by means of culture?

Culture is understood as an asset to the formation of class relationships. Bourdieu's sustained argument is that all symbolic systems—language, arts, science, religion—are both the mechanisms of knowledge creation and the source of systems of domination. At home and in school, agents are invested with bodily dispositions—habits—that support the hierarchical structure, which he, like Elias, calls *habitus*. He sets his task as unpeeling the social unconscious by paying attention to everyday practice. His analysis in *Distinction* is based on a national French sample of 1,217 people with data on income, occupation, and consumption patterns conducted between 1963 and 1968. He is the rare sociologist who combines the mastery of a philosophical argument with the quantitative skills to make a statistical judgment about the superiority of multiple correspondence analysis over regression analysis, and yet is still attuned to the depth of subjective and intersubjective judgments on taste that he elucidates through long open-ended interviews. Hence it is not a surprise that Bourdieu has come to dominate the work on taste over the last generation, and *Distinction* has become a standard within and outside of sociology.

Recent years have seen an explosion in sociological work on consumption, most of which are positioned in direct dialogue with Bourdieu. Scholars question his relevance in different geographies and test whether his model still works today, while others employ and build on his theories to explain a range of group and intersubjective interactions and social processes.[19] In this context, many scholars have turned to food as a lens for studying taste and class in contemporary society. British sociologist Alan Warde, along with his colleagues, has dedicated much academic attention to changing food habits and the widening of consumers' food repertoires. Utilizing broad surveys and rigorous statistical methods, these scholars explore questions of residual class hierarchy, social competition, and the significance of a shift from models of snobbery and connoisseurship to those that celebrate knowledge of a wide variety of consumable goods. They, like others, conclude that such omnivorous tastes do not eliminate status competition and social exclusion. Rather, they perpetuate inequality, but in an increasingly fragmented social hierarchy that is marked by subgroups and fights for distinction internal to them.[20]

Warde, in collaboration with six other sociologists, published an ambitious study of consumption in England. In probing into the social organization of British tastes, they mimic and update Bourdieu in a remarkable work titled *Culture, Class, Distinction* (2009). It is based on a survey administered to 1,564 individuals between 2003 and 2004 by the National Center for Social Research as a cross-sectional sample—stratified, clustered, randomized—designed to be representative of all adults living in private households in England, Scotland, and Northern Ireland. Qualitative elements were added through focus groups, ethnic samples, and elite interviews. The authors also recursively redesigned the research method by seeking out leaders in the corporate sector, political life, or the civil service. Notwithstanding what standard textbooks tell us, no research follows the design outlined at the initial moment. Good research depends on improvising while doing it.[21]

In developing their methods the British researchers sought to overcome three major criticisms of Bourdieu's *Distinction*. First, they rejected the presumption that nation-states, such as France or Great Britain, are closed containers of culture, where class is produced in each national pot separately. Recognizing recent work on globalization and transnationalism, they sought to account for national boundary crossing by people, things, and cultural forms in the production of cultural distinction. Second, their current research answers a related criticism that Bourdieu's *Distinction* was based on a survey conducted in the 1960s. Third, *Distinction* was based on a survey that could not, by constraints of French law, ask questions about subnational or transnational identities such as race and ethnicity, which makes it impossible to address other important dimensions of group identity beyond class and occupation. Predictably, *Culture, Class, Distinction* shows that class matters in cultural division in Great Britain today, but it does not necessarily count for more than gender or ethnicity on all issues of taste.

Interestingly, their multiple correspondence analysis of the survey data showed that ethnicity does *not* play as significant a role in the organization of the social space of lifestyles in contemporary Britain as do measures of class, education, age, and gender. Yet from their lived experience the researchers knew that ethnicity does play an important role. So they eventually hypothesized that "because we constructed this space through questions on tastes and preferences for genres (but not named works) in the literary, art, music, sports and media fields, we are not readily able to pick up on the more nuanced, though powerful, ways that ethnicity is related to cultural tastes." In part the disjuncture between their lived experience and the survey data may have been a product of the interviewee's assumptions about the survey and the consideration of the "interview" as a "public show." In addition, the researchers came to the conclusion that a number of Muslim men were responding to the standard questions "from a position outside many of" the cultural referents of the interviewers. "Majid seems to understand few of our questions, and the vignette where we ask him to imagine himself in an embarrassing situation in a pub completely passes him by—it is doubtful he had ever been to a pub in his life."[22]

These reflections hit at the heart of the limitations of the often quantitative work of researchers that, by relying on numbers and patterns, presume to know better what drives their subjects' perceptions and actions than the subjects themselves. Surveys do not include contextual questions, and people's attitudes toward things cannot be understood without an understanding of the context of the interview, thus making it essential for the researchers to engage more thoroughly with their qualitative data and make their own subjective position within the field explicit. This is of course what pragmatists, phenomenologists, ethnomethodologists, and symbolic interactionists have been saying all along—that if we are interested in peoples' notions of their world, then the knowledge we produce and the process of producing it has to be much more nuanced and dialogic than positivist, synchronic, monologues will ever reveal. Meaning emerges in the interaction, and values are never fully constituted before the transaction with the other, even if the other is the researcher with his questionnaire. As the National Science Foundation's "Workshop on Interdisciplinary Standards for Systematic Qualitative Research" noted, one of the particular strengths of qualitative work is the "flexibility and recursivity it affords researchers that are made possible by a closer engagement to people and groups being studied," especially when issues of power and prestige are involved. Furthermore, systematic qualitative techniques of archival research, interviews, and ethnographies are better suited to studying changes over time, experience, and interactions, and in positing causal relationships.[23] Unfortunately, many of these lessons continue to be ignored, much to the chagrin of those intent on developing theories of taste that take interaction and subjectivity seriously.[24]

The latest major iteration in North America of the study of food as a means for achieving distinction and building cultural capital is Josée Johnston and Shyon Baumann's *Foodies: Democracy and Distinction in the Gourmet Foodscape* (2010). Johnston and Baumann argue that in spite of broadening palates, the gastronomic discussion that has caught fire in bicoastal American cities (specifically in their representative newspapers and food magazines) is burdened with the quest for class distinctions. This, they contend, is happening despite the decline of old-fashioned snobbery and the dethroning of French and Continental cuisines. Their book confirms the detailed empirical work on the United Kingdom in arguing that taste hierarchies exist, culture irrevocably marks class, and omnivorousness is a rarefied (but not rare) phenomenon in which the rich and the better educated devour even working class subcultures, whereas the working classes (especially men) do not consume highbrow genres such as avant-garde art, classical music, art cinema, or exotic cuisines in restaurants.

Despite similar questions, Johnston and Baumann adopt a very different methodology from that of Warde and his colleagues. Instead of large-population studies and advanced statistical analyses, Johnson and Baumann turn to discourse and textual analysis for their empirical evidence. They rely on the rhetoric offered in gourmet food magazines and interviews of "foodies" to explore a tension between democracy, defined by an ideology of meritocracy, and distinction, marked by struggles for cultural capital and status. Like most work of discourse analysis, Johnston and Baumann analyze consumption and taste from a position far removed from actual sites of cooking and eating and apart from the vast majority of conversations that are not captured in textualized form or reproduced in interviews. Yet these spatial and temporal dimensions of food consumption and production are absolutely central to the social importance of food. So let us now consider the situated nature of taste, the sites and moments in which it is produced, contested, and negotiated.

The sites of food consumption, from coffee houses and boarding houses to the modern restaurant, have long intrigued sociologists studying public spaces and interactions within them. Jürgen Habermas, in his groundbreaking and widely influential work *The Structural Transformation of the Public Sphere* (1962), identifies the emergence of a bourgeois public sphere with the coffee-house of eighteenth-century Europe. These coffee-houses and similar establishments served as prominent nondomestic sites for face-to-face meetings and conversations, which led to a rising public consciousness. It was through this intimate communication, what he calls "rational-critical debate," that individuals became self-reflexive of their position in society, as a member of the public, and shaped public opinion as a force distinct from the sphere of state authority. The significance of eating establishments in the public realm has been explored by historians.[25] Very few sociologists have followed Habermas and made public eating establishments central to their work, as spaces to observe and theorize interaction and conversation. A notable exception is Gary Alan Fine, whose book *Kitchens: The Culture of Restaurant Work* (1996) offers an ethnographic study of the organization of kitchen labor and of negotiations over taste and aesthetics. While not explicitly influenced by Habermas or interested in the same question, Fine prioritizes face-to-face interaction and dialogue in both the structuring of labor and site and network specific negotiation over judgments of taste.

As mentioned above, developments in philosophy and anthropology, under the labels of pragmatism and phenomenology, have encouraged sociologists both to consider how subjects interact and create their own understandings of the world and to reflect on their own processes of knowledge production. Fine does both. Regarding the first point, adopting the insights of Erving Goffman, he focuses on how actors understand their situations and how they manage the impressions they give to others. He searches for how knowledge (in his case culinary and aesthetic) is constituted through interaction within communities of practitioners (in his case restaurant cooks and waiters). For him, culture is conjoined evaluation of everyday practices. These are habits not easily understood from an academic distance or ones that easily offer themselves to positivism, but rather habits that require physical intimacy over time to understand and interpret. Fine reminds us that meaning, the object of sociology, may not be imagined only as getting to the real truth out there, but revealing processes and protocols through which practitioners reach judgments about truth, verification, and validation.

It is in ethnographic works like Fine's that we most explicitly see moments of validation of forms of knowledge not traditionally consecrated in the academy. A consequence of taking such knowledge seriously and prioritizing both body and communication is the need for researcher self-reflection. Here Fine, acutely aware of his own position and physical presence in the field, illustrates the point. Sharing Maurice Merleau-Ponty's insight that our sense and conception of the world is tied to our perceptions of our own bodies within it, he positions himself in contrast to the quantitative studies that attempt objectivity through distance and large numbers. Fine echoes Michel de Certeau and Luce Giard's call to insert the author's body into a body of doctrine, and to develop an epistemology that allows for the intrusion of the everyday into theory and history.[26] Fine's work is engaged primarily with epistemological questions, especially the gap between representations and practices, and the relationship between "strategic" social and intellectual programs and "tactical" political or poetic activity.

Fine suggests no systematic relationship to abstract academic theory and provides no encouragement to advance such theorization. He dips into symbolic interactionism, neo-Marxism, and New Institutionalism and other theories to help frame his observations, but does not select or build on a single theoretical orientation throughout. He shares with Goffman the cool, ironic style and the vision that the self resides on the surface, in performance as a complex dance of interactive rituals, and is visible in small groups. Hence he emphasizes qualitative studies in intimate spheres and his own self-reflection. This critical view points to much postmodern theory on gender, race, and sexual identity which asserts that we are what we do.[27]

Unfortunately most sociology of food production has not proceeded ethnographically, presumably due to the reality of the restaurant labor and space and the challenges they pose. Whether in the dining room or in the kitchen, this space is often cramped and every inch and minute is integral to a fast-paced system. It is difficult to gain access to such spaces, particularly during service. So instead, many sociologists of restaurants have studied them from afar. Such approaches often result in an attempt to systematize and classify either restaurants or diners through interviews and visual observations. What results are some curious typologies (such as Finkelstein's *fête spéciale*, bistro or parodic, and *café mundane*, ethnic or fast-food establishments) that remain poorly substantiated and likely would fall apart with more ethnographic fieldwork.[28]

Recent agendas in sociology have initiated fruitful discussions on urban geography, the social construction of space and place, and the role of human experience in both.[29] Theories of practice, encompassing the imagination, embodied knowledge and habits, and the senses, have further enriched this literature.[30] While work specifically on food in this area has been basically absent, possibilities abound. With its relationship to practice, both theoretically and literally through ties with chefs, cooks, and food journalists, and its appearance at a time when sociology, anthropology, media, and cultural studies share promising conceptualizations of both scales, from global networks to bodily experience, food studies sits at an important nexus in contemporary sociology. Its unique position allows it to retain critical distance from the boundary-work of other more established disciplines. It can draw from the epistemological strengths of multiple disciplines and identify the weaknesses of some of the more-celebrated approaches, such as big number crunching and arm-chair speculation. Moreover, because of its historical association with home economics and its strong ties to popular and activist work on food, food studies is well suited for self-reflection and genuine engagement with practices and forms of knowledge outside the academy. And it is to these opportunities that we now move.

An Agenda for the Study of Food

Because of its low investment in disciplinary boundary work, food studies offers a number of directions that draw on sociological theorization and methods and push them further in productive directions. To start, food studies can push sociology toward a practical, sensory understanding of space, one that incorporates work of bodies molding to their surroundings. People walk the streets with needs and desires that the built environment must accommodate. We pass through cafes, restaurants, coffee houses, grocery stores, and farmers markets, sensing, judging, and negotiating our presence. Bodies both respond to their environment and shape it, through practices that are at once individual and highly socialized. It is in this realm, on the streets and in restaurants, hovering over cooking pots or dishes, day in and day out, that cooks and diners negotiate space and time in the city and create room for their own dreams and ambitions. Their ways of living in the world, and of knowing it, should not be dismissed as uninteresting or invalid forms of knowledge, but should shape our academic theories and research practices.

Many of the public spaces we reference here are sites of exchange, and in this capacity they are sites of economic processes of valuation and trade. They simultaneously reveal a dense mixture of cultural norms and human interaction that are far removed from textbook economics. Much of the research on food has worked through a lens of capital—economic capital, cultural capital, and to a certain extent social capital (although this remains less developed). While sociologists rarely describe decisions about food as stemming purely from economic calculi, they nonetheless offer theories of rational equations based primarily on money and social status, contained of course by context and individual *habitus*. In such work, agency is challenged and the material, tasting body remains all but invisible. This is a tendency easily attributable to simplistic readings of Bourdieu, and it is one that obscures what could be revealed by revisiting daily life and lived experience. Here, we would like to suggest that the apparent contradictions between the rational actor and the sensorial body can perhaps be identified and resolved through food. After all, food is a point in which these disparate theoretical perspectives collide. How we cook and eat is a combination of embodied knowledge and preferences, on-the-tongue tastes, socialized tastes, rational calculations, manifested dreams, habits, and so forth. To study food in this way is to discard disciplinary boundaries in favor of a far deeper comprehension.

Food complicates the relationship between production and consumption. Daily experiences of cooking and eating, creation and ingestion, force a reexamination of the boundaries that sociologists have previously drawn between these two activities. The act of cooking, whether in the commercial or the home kitchen, is profoundly shaped by sensorial memories of taste, color, and texture. To treat the restaurant cook as a producer, as much sociology of labor has done, and thus a noneating body and a nontasting subject, ignores some of the most vital influences of the perceptions and experiences of millions of workers in food industries around the world. And to view diners as agents facing fully developed options from which they must choose, a choice that is seen to be determined by habitus and social position, denies their own productive and creative capacity. Not only are they critical players in the construction of any dining experience, but also they have likely cooked in a literal sense at some point in their lives. Food studies, following the work of Fine, can promote fluid conversations between the literatures on production and labor and on consumption and taste, conversations that track-bound sociologists would benefit from overhearing.

The study of food not only serves to augment existent knowledge. The kind of research we are proposing would in fact have great real-world, policy implications for those working on health, immigration, entrepreneurship, and class inequalities. The body has been climbing into analytical view in sharper focus with modern medicine. Its care, its cures, its governance, both by the self (diet, exercise, excess, temperance, desire, pleasure, and pain) and as an object of public policy (obesity, epidemics, vaccination, medical research) are in full play in popular culture and policy initiatives. It is thus imperative that sociologists consider new forms of knowledge, embodied and un-"disciplined," if they hope to influence policy in productive, critical ways.

It should by now be clear that the agenda we are proposing for food studies requires a reworking of the relationship among methodology, epistemology, and theory. In all research, questions about method—how to identify, isolate, interpret, and explicate data—inevitably lead to theoretical-philosophical questions about what is knowledge, where and how it is produced, and what kinds of relationships to other places, peoples, and ways of understanding and acting in the world are assumed. Awareness of these questions has become particularly necessary over the last generation, when issues about representation, representativeness, ideology, and authority, have been critically interrogated, most notably through postmodernist, feminist, and critical race theory that resists and rearticulates dominant theories of knowledge. Feeding entails transactions across various kinds of presumed boundaries—mind-body, dreams-reality, self-other, citizen-alien, life-death, animal-vegetable-thing, health-disease–at the heart of modern western epistemologies that are crumbling under the assault from philosophy and science. New knowledge could be produced at those intersections, and the study of food can play a central role in reconceiving our world.

Notes

1. Veena Das, ed., *Handbook of Indian Sociology* (Delhi: Oxford University Press, 2004); Arjun Appadurai, "The Right to Research," *Globalisation, Societies and Education* 4, no. 2 (2006): 167–77.

2. See, Craig Calhoun, *Sociology in America: A History* (Chicago: University of Chicago Press, 2007), 26.

3. William I. Thomas and Florian Znaniecki, *The Polish Peasant in Europe and America*, 3 vols. (Boston: The Gorham Press, 1918–21), 572.

4. Calhoun, *Sociology in America*, 34.

5. Sarah Bowen, "Embedding Local Places in Global Spaces: Geographical Indications as a Territorial Development Strategy," *Rural Sociology* 75, no. 2 (2010): 209–43; Angela Tregear, "From Stilton to Vimto: Using Food History to Re-think Typical Products in Rural Development," *Sociologia Ruralis* 43, no. 2 (2003): 91–107.

6. See Marjorie L. DeVault, *Feeding the Family. The Social Organization of Caring as Gendered Work* (Chicago: University of Chicago Press, 1991); Alan Beardsworth and Teresa Keil, *Sociology on the Menu* (London: Routledge, 1997).

7. Judith G. Goode, Karen Curtis and Janet Theophano, "A Framework for the Analysis of Continuity and Change in Shared Sociocultural Rules for Food Use," in *Ethnic and Regional Foodways in the United States: The Performance of Group Identity*, ed. Linda Keller Brown and Kay Mussell (Knoxville: University of Tennessee Press, 1984), 66–88; Alex McIntosh and Mary Zey, "Women as Gatekeepers of Food Consumption: A Sociological Critique," *Food & Foodways* 3, no. 4 (1989): 317–32.

8. Christopher Lasch, "Historical Sociology and the Myth of Maturity: Norbert Elias' 'very simple formula,'" *Theory & Society* 14 (1985): 705; Anthony Giddens, review of *The Society of Individuals*, by Norbert Elias, *American Journal of Sociology* 98, no. 2 (September 1992): 388–89.

9. Zygmunt Bauman, "The Phenomenon of Norbert Elias," *Sociology* 13 (1979): 117–25.

10. Priscilla Parkhurst Ferguson, *Accounting for Taste: The Triumph of French Cuisine* (Chicago: Chicago University Press, 2004), 3.

11. Albert Sonnenfeld, "The Chef as Hero: Microwaves in the Sea of Culinary History," *The Journal of Gastronomy* (1987): 27–37; Massimo Montanari, *The Culture of Food*, trans. Carl Opsen (Oxford: Blackwell, 1994); Pascual Ory, "Gastronomy," in *Realms of Memory. The Construction of the French Past*, ed. Pierre Nora, trans. Arthur Goldhammer (New York: Columbia University Press, 1997), 442–67; Jean-Louis Flandrin, Massimo Montanari, and Albert Sonnenfeld, eds., *Food: A Culinary History from Antiquity to the Present*, trans. Clarissa Botsford, et al. (New York: Columbia University Press, 1999).

12. Jürgen Habermas, *The Structural Transformation of the Public Sphere*, trans. Thomas Burger (Cambridge: MIT Press, 1989 [1962]), 16.

13. The unexplained paradox is how French haute cuisine became canonical in the rest of Europe in the age of nationalism. There is an interesting story yet to be told about the tension between the national and the professional in the modern world and how that has shaped the fortunes of the culinary profession in different parts of the world.

14. We know relatively little about China, where the evidence is tantalizingly subversive of French claims of singularity, but that is a tale that cannot be addressed here.

15. Sonnenfeld, "The Chef as Hero," 33.

16. Ferguson, *Accounting for Taste*, 17.

17. Amy Trubek, *Haute Cuisine. How the French Invented the Culinary Profession* (Philadelphia: University of Pennsylvania Press, 2000), 3.

18. Pierre Bourdieu, *Distinction: A Social Critique of the Judgment of Taste*, trans. Richard Nice (Cambridge, MA: Harvard University Press, 1984 [1979]), 6.

19. Douglas B. Holt, "Distinction in America? Recovering Bourdieu's Theory of Tastes from Its Critics," *Poetics* 15 (1997): 93–120; Richard Peterson and Roger Kern, "Changing Highbrow Taste: From Snob to Omnivore," *American Sociological Review* 61, no. 5 (1996): 900–7.

20. Alan Warde, Lydia Martens, and Wendy Olsen, "Consumption and the Problem of Variety: Cultural Omnivorousness, Social Distinction and Dining Out." *Sociology* 33, no. 1 (1999): 105–27; Alan Warde and Lydia Martens, *Eating Out: Social Differentiation, Consumption and Pleasure* (Cambridge: Cambridge University Press, 2000).

21. Tony Bennett, et al, *Culture, Class, Distinction* (London: Routledge, 2009).

22. Ibid, 237.

23. Michèle Lamont and Patricia White, eds., *Workshop on Interdisciplinary Standards for Systematic Qualitative Research* (Washington, DC: National Science Foundation, 2005), 10. [Online]. Available: http://www.nsf.gov/sbe/ses/soc/ISSQR_workshop_rpt.pdf. [February 1, 2011]. That NSF report is worth perusing for a number of succinct and useful tips to doing research: (a) Have a clear research question framed in the relevant theoretical and methodological literature (qualitative researchers typically attempt to answer a question rather than test a hypothesis); (b) Define and operationalize key constructs; (c) Provide a clear description and explanation of case selection—why particular sites, people, events will be studied; (d) Systematic sampling is important even if it is not random and representative of the whole universe; (e) Systematic and thorough data collection, and triangulating with multiple data sources and types; try to balance experience-near and experience-distant data; (f) Explicate connections between data and theory; (g) Show how you engaged with negative or disconfirming evidence in the analysis; (h) Be open to unanticipated but empirically significant discoveries when in the field.

24. Geneviève Teil and Antoine Hennion, "Discovering Quality of Performing Taste? A Sociology of the Amateur," in *Qualities of Food*, ed. Mark Harvey, Andrew McMeekin, and Alan Warde (Manchester: Manchester University Press, 2005), 19–37.

25. Most notably, Rebecca L. Spang, *The Invention of the Restaurant: Paris and the Modern Gastronomic Culture* (Cambridge, MA: Harvard University Press, 2000).

26. Michel de Certeau and Luce Giard, *The Practice of Everyday Life*, trans. Steven Rendall (Berkley: University of California Press, 1984).

27. Judith Butler, "Performative Acts and Gender Constitution: An Essay in Phenomenology and Feminist Theory," *Theatre Journal* 40, no. 4 (December 1988): 519–31.

28. Joanne Finkelstein, *Dining Out: A Sociology of Modern Manners* (Cambridge: Polity Press, 1989). See also, Shun Lu and Gary Alan Fine, "The Presentation of Ethnic Authenticity: Chinese Food as a Social Accomplishment," *Sociological Quarterly* 36, no. 3

(1995): 535–53; Zachary Paul Neal, "Culinary Deserts, Gastronomic Oases: A Classification of US Cities," *Urban Studies* 43, no. 1 (2006): 1–21; Kenneth R. Lord, Sanjay Putrevu, and H. G. Parsa, "The Cross-Border Consumer: Investigation of Motivators and Inhibitors in Dining Experiences," *Journal of Hospitality & Tourism Research* 28, no. 2 (2004): 209–29.

29. See Sharon Zukin, *The Cultures of Cities* (Malden: Blackwell Publishing, 1995).

30. Theodore R. Schatzki, Karin Knorr Cetina, and Eike von Savigny, eds., *The Practice Turn in Contemporary Theory* (London: Routledge, 2001).

Bibliography

Appadurai, Arjun. "How to Make a National Cuisine: Cookbooks in Contemporary India." *Comparative Studies in Society and History* 30, no. 1 (January 1988): 3–24.

Bennett, Tony, et al. *Culture, Class, Distinction*. London: Routledge, 2009.

Bourdieu, Pierre. *Distinction: A Social Critique of the Judgment of Taste*. Translated by Richard Nice. Cambridge, MA: Harvard University Press, 1984. First published 1979.

DeVault, Marjorie L. *Feeding the Family: The Social Organization of Caring as Gendered Work*. Chicago: University of Chicago Press, 1991.

Elias, Norbert. *The Civilizing Process*. Vol. 1. *The History of Manners*. Translated by Edmund Jephcott. Oxford: Blackwell, 1969. First published 1939.

Ferguson, Priscilla Parkhurst. *Accounting for Taste: The Triumph of French Cuisine*. Chicago: Chicago University Press, 2004.

Fine, Gary Alan. *Kitchens: The Culture of Restaurant Work*. Berkeley: University of California Press, 1996.

Goody, Jack. *Cooking, Cuisine and Class: A Study in Comparative Sociology*. Cambridge: Cambridge University Press, 1982.

Habermas, Jürgen. *The Structural Transformation of the Public Sphere*. Translated by Thomas Burger. Cambridge, MA: MIT Press, 1989. First published 1962.

Johnston, Josée, and Shyon Baumann. *Foodies: Democracy and Distinction in the Gourmet Foodscape*. New York: Routledge, 2010.

Mennell, Stephen. *All Manners of Food: Eating and Taste in England and France from the Middle Ages to the Present*. 2nd ed. Urbana: University of Illinois Press, 1996. First published 1985.

Veblen, Thorstein. *The Theory of the Leisure Class*. 1899. Reprint: New York: Penguin Books, 1994.

Warde, Alan, and Lydia Martens. *Eating Out: Social Differentiation, Consumption and Pleasure*. Cambridge: Cambridge University Press, 2000.

Zukin, Sharon. *The Cultures of Cities*. Malden: Blackwell Publishing, 1995.

CHAPTER 9

GEOGRAPHY OF FOOD

BERTIE MANDELBLATT

At its most basic and at its most powerful, the study of food explores the connections between the social and cultural worlds of humans and the zoological and physical worlds of ecology and climate, connections constituted across millennia by such food-related practices as hunting and gathering; agriculture and livestock-raising; the preparation and preservation of foodstuffs; their exchange, provision and distribution locally and across long distances; and the consumption and disposal of food in wide varieties of milieux. The interdisciplinarity of geography as a field of study, and particularly of human geography as a large and sprawling subfield, permits geographers to draw on and contribute to debates across a wide spectrum within the humanities and social sciences in which this vast array of practices occupies the central stage. These domains include history, anthropology, ethnology, sociology, agriculture, ecology, development studies, political economy, nutrition, folklore, and cultural studies.

However, and perhaps as a function of this complex interdisciplinarity, the attention paid to food studies within academia at large and more specifically within geography has remained relatively haphazard and scattered, as geographers (and others) continue to observe.[1] Nevertheless, several distinct and recognizable arenas of study have evolved, as geographers continue to insist on the rightful place of the study of food within their discipline and, conversely, the relevance of geography to the study of food.[2] Taking these arguments as a point of departure, the goal of this chapter is to trace the lines of the debates over food as they have developed within geography in both Anglophone and Francophone worlds, particularly in light of the explosion of recent interest in food studies both within academia and in the public sphere more broadly.[3] Largely because of this proliferation in interest and in publishing, separating the geographers from the rest of the scholars who work in the field of food studies is somewhat awkward and indeed artificial. Nevertheless, while making reference to the broader context of food studies, this chapter concentrates on the contributions to this broader context made by human geographers from a range of subfields, while not, however, making claims for any natural coherence between them.

To begin, given their disciplinary focus on the spatial element of human life, geographers typically conceptualize foodways in fluid relation to place.[4] Specific debates within various subfields of geography—historical, cultural, economic, agricultural, urban and medical geography, for instance—have developed around the nature of these relations: how physical, territorial, and cultural boundaries succeed or do not succeed at defining, dividing, and keeping separate the food practices of particular places or regions; the cultural histories and political economies of the movement of food across and within places or regions which are more or less bounded; and the practices of food production, exchange, and consumption that characterize certain places. Indeed, while one category of tasks that geographers take on is the study of food practices as they are connected to place—or conversely, the study of the locality of certain food practices (i.e., the mapping of food cultures)—another is questioning how food practices disrupt, confuse, challenge, and otherwise contribute to ongoing redefinitions of place.

Central to these lines of questioning regarding the definitions of places and their boundaries is the issue of scale. The vast (or extremely limited) range of activities associated with the production, exchange, and consumption of food, as well as the production of the value and meanings that accompany these activities, take place within and across a wide variety of scales, stretching from the global scale to that of the individual body. Although geographers who study food can address the subject of scale directly,[5] many do not, and its role as a structuring device within their work remains implicit. This chapter is constructed around overlapping notions of scale, examining how debates over food-related activities taking place at diverse scales have emerged within geography (or variously how geographers have contributed to debates that have developed in other fields). These categories are hardly neatly bounded; indeed, the expressed intention of many of the works under examination is to challenge conventionally separated scales of activity, and consequently, this chapter makes constant reference back and forth across these divides in order to draw out and clarify the patterns under examination.

Global and Transnational Food Scales

One of the most vibrant areas of food research to which geographers continue to make extensive contributions is the study of commodity chains, examining the transnational connections created through the production, exchange, and consumption of a given commodity or range of commodities. Historian Shane

Hamilton has defined the analysis of these connections as one that "seeks to identify and illuminate the individuals, institutions, technologies, forms of knowledge, and forms of capital involved in transforming raw agricultural products into consumable goods."[6] In a recent overview of geographers' mobilization of the methodology of commodity chain analysis, Alex Hughes and Suzanne Reimer point to two broad sets of debates that have influenced this work, and describe critical reactions to them.[7] The first set of debates serves to underline the transformation of largely economic value at each sequence of the chain linking producers and consumers of commodities, conceptualized as a strict vertical, linear progression, and this set of debates in turn draws on several older areas of research: that of global commodity chains based on a center (consumption)–periphery (production) model; that of the political economy of agriculture; that emanating from the field of the sociology of agriculture, especially the work of William Friedland; and, lastly, that of the research into *filières agro-alimentaires* ("food chains") that emerged in France in the 1980s.[8] Often, although not always, geographers concentrate on the spatiality of commodity chains, examining how the relations of actors across and within territorial boundaries challenge existing frameworks and both explicitly and implicitly lead to the creation of new ones.[9]

In regards to the influence of the *filières* literature, it is notable that the concept of *filières agro-alimentaires* was not used with great frequency by French geographers working on food in this period, but rather by researchers attached to France's national institute devoted to agri-food research, the *Institut national de la recherche agronomique* (INRA) and to the *École supérieure d'agriculture* (ESA). French geographers' foci were somewhat different from these agronomic researchers. For example, the collection of articles assembled by Claude Thouvenot and published as a special issue of the *Annales de géographie* in 1980 under the collective title "Géographie de l'alimentation" offers considerably more focus on the biological and nutritional aspects of food than on either the creation and transformation of economic value in the production and exchange of food commodities, or the challenges posed by the transnational scales of reference generated through these processes.[10] Insofar as food was considered on the global or transnational scale within French geography in this period, the model remained "international"—i.e., accords on food policy established between nations—hearkening back to Maximilien Sorre's foundational postwar geography texts on food in which he called for geography research to be undertaken and assembled in support of multilateral international cooperation to combat worldwide crises of malnutrition and famine.[11] Several generations later, the international framework has been dropped in much French geographical writing on food, in favor of a consciously geopolitical and global vision of food production and consumption, in which the *agro-alimentaire* is fully present although without reference to the earlier *filieres* literature.[12] In Hughes and Reimer's discussion of global commodity chain analysis, referred to earlier, they identify a second approach toward conceptualizing producer-consumer relations, which they name the network approach. This approach shares a common concern with the transformation of value that is central to the political economic concerns of the first approach, although with substantial differences. As the name suggests, the network approach offers an alternative vision to, and indeed a critique of, the vertical, linear, and hierarchical nature of relations between actors involved in the movement of commodities between places of production and consumption implicit in the notion of commodity chains. That is, the interdependence of actors and flows of information, and the multi-directionality of the nodes themselves, are brought to the fore in this type of analysis. Geographer Peter Jackson in his own survey of the commodity chain literature presents a slightly different genealogy of these conceptual metaphors in which the concept of the circuit is contrasted to that of the chain. He argues that recent human geographers have found that the concept of the chain "too linear, too mechanistic and too focused on the simple metric of length as opposed to other issues such as complexity, transparency or regulation. Circuits have no beginning and no end... and analysis should recognise that origins are always constructed."[13] The 1990s and 2000s saw a host of cultural geographers in the United Kingdom especially—Philip Crang, Ian Cook, Mark Thorpe, Michelle Harrison, and others—seizing on the concept of circuit to explore the complex spatialities brought into being through the transnational movement of commodities between actors involved in moments of production, distribution, and consumption. Using the example of Japanese fish paste, Becky Mansfield has argued, for example, that the globalization of industrial food production has significant implications for definitions of food "quality."[14]

More particularly, while these geographers were acutely aware of the power of the economic value of food commodities to generate, sustain, or force mutations in circuits and relations between actors, their focus was more on the qualitative transformation in the *meanings* of commodities, places, and the identity of actors at each step and throughout the progression of foodstuffs through the commodity circuit, with a special emphasis on moments of consumption.[15] In their attentiveness to such questions, these geographers were at least in part responding to the Marxist call made by David Harvey in an influential article in which he called on the analysis of food commodities to lead to a renewed politics of consumption.[16] Capitalist commodity chains (or circuits) hide the conditions of commodity production (labor), Harvey argued, a process through which the commodity necessarily becomes fetishized. By revealing the truths of the labor processes, commodity analysis defetishizes the commodity, he maintained, and enlightened consumers, armed with this knowledge, can consume more equitably. In their response to this appeal, many cultural geographers interrogated this logic, in particular questioning the notion of permanent and unchanging geographic "knowledges" associated with commodities. They focused on both the impossibility of fixing firm origins and on the intense ambiguities involved in their very naming.[17]

Global scales of analysis are also present in the works of geographers (and others) in which they follow individual food commodities along and through global trajectories from production to consumption, whether their focus is predominantly quantitative or qualitative. This methodology has proved exceedingly popular in recent years, paralleling the rise in scholarly interest in global and world history, in the everyday, and in histories of consumption. Restricting this discussion to only recent work by geographers, we find studies on the papaya, imitation crab, Irish salt beef in the early modern French Atlantic, rice in the African diaspora in the eighteenth and nineteenth centuries, and African green beans in France in the nineteenth and twentieth.[18] In the Francophone world, in a special issue on food geographies published in the *Bulletin de l'association des géographes français*, there are articles on "the milk planet" *(la planète laitière)* and Quebec maple syrup.[19] The focus on a single commodity has an extensive history in France, where the study of wine and spirits within the discipline of geography has long been represented by such scholars as Henri Enjalbert, Roger Dion, Alain Huetz de Lemps, and, later, Jean-Robert Pitte.[20] Pitte's more recent work on wine adds to his first, monumental work on trans-European chestnut culture from the Middle Ages to the twentieth century.[21] The methodology of focusing on a single commodity and its movement from production to consumption permits these geographers to highlight a wide variety of issues related to the definitions and boundaries separating (or failing to separate) locations on transnational commodity scales (i.e., the concept of *terroir* or "taste of place"),[22] as well as those related to the identity and agency of actors involved in each commodity network.[23] For instance, by placing historicized power relations at the fore of the analysis, studies of commodity trades that took and take place in the context of imperial expansion, colonial development, or the trans-Atlantic slave trade, scholars contest simplified global and national commodity scales and insist on the role of slaves and colonial subjects as consumers within metropolitan political economies and as knowledge transmitters critical to the functioning of empire.[24]

National and Regional Food Scales

Specifically national scales of reference for the study of food have inspired relatively less recent interest than have global scales. Human geographers who study food as cultural and economic phenomena typically propose challenges to clear-cut national frames of reference defined by national territorial borders. One notable exception within cultural geography is Jean-Robert Pitte, whose focus on a specifically French gastronomic tradition includes his long-standing campaign to have the gastronomic French meal inscribed on UNESCO's list of intangible cultural heritage in need of safeguarding, a bid that in 2010 was successful.[25] National scales have most often remained valuable frames when they are themselves the object of study, as for example in the realm of food policy analysis that is defined at the national level.[26]

Conversely, historical and cultural geographers commonly focus on the porous nature of national boundaries and the difficulty in deriving meaning from borders that are historically vulnerable and changeable.[27] Two options to which they often turn in order to counter the idea of the fixed and unified nation-state in the realm of food production, distribution, and consumption are the regional frame of reference and the concept of multiculturalism. Both, for instance, are clearly represented in geographer Barbara Shortridge's extensive work on American regional foodways and her presentation of sources of geographic data for this study.[28] Wilbur Zelinsky, a student of the great American cultural geographer Carl Sauer, pioneered the geographic study of American food multiculturalism in his classic study on ethnic restaurants.[29]

Outside the United States, the regional and the multicultural have also been invoked in order to interrogate other national frames of reference. In the United Kingdom, they were reprised by Ian Cook, Philip Crang, and Mark Thorpe in work in which they question the notion of culinary authenticity, whether applied to British food or any of the many other "national" foods marketed and sold in Britain, and in which they examine the social imaginaries associated with multicultural foods in Britain.[30] Similarly Jean Duruz has studied the fault lines of culinary nationalism and multiculturalism in Australia.[31] In France, as has been the case with wine, the nature and history of regional culinary cultures have long been subjects of study, certainly more so than the study of multiculturalism. These studies have, in the main, been undertaken by historians not by geographers.[32] This point notwithstanding, geographer Gilles Fumey has discussed both American and European culinary multiculturalism in *Géographie et Cultures*, the latter in a special issue devoted to the *Géographie des Saveurs*, in which also appear articles about the regional "tastes" of Nice and Aubrac.[33] Another notable exception is the collection of papers presented at the conference "Cuisines, Régimes alimentaires, Espaces régionaux" held at Nancy in 1987.[34] In this volume, geographers interrogate the meaning of region in relation to culinary practice in France and elsewhere, as well as display early signs of concern at the possibility of the erasure of culinary specificity in the face of fast food. This conference was initiated by the *Commission de Géographie historique*, the third in a series of food conferences organized specifically by geographers around the theme of the *géographie de l'alimentation* ("geography of food").[35]

Urban Scales

When the scale of investigation of food issues shifts from the nation or region to the city, there is a notable transformation in the nature and volume of research carried out by geographers. Although there is relatively less work done on multiculturalism and food specifically within cities (by geographers), related questions such as race, class, and ethnicity are still being addressed in food research.[36] At this scale, research questions have shifted to reflect a focus on access to food within the urban environment, broadly understood.[37] Through a variety of conceptual lenses, geographers examine the modalities of urban residents' access to food in a range of Canadian, American, and European cities: food availability via markets, gardens, and supermarkets;[38] food security and food deserts in the urban landscape;[39] urban residents' food citizenship;[40] and urban food sustainability.[41] In their engagement with these contemporary issues, geographers are actively contributing to interdisciplinary urban public health and policy initiatives also being carried out by architects, town planners, and health professionals, on the one hand, and other scholars such as anthropologists, urbanists, and nutritionists, on the other.[42] Although the large share of this work is on the contemporary city, historical geographer Peter Atkins' recently coedited collective work, *Food and the City in Europe since 1800*, contains contributions investigating similar themes over the last 200 years: the effect of urbanization on diet and concomitant changes to access to food; urban food quality and food adulteration; restaurants, food shops, and other food retail outlets; and the effect of immigration on urban diets.[43]

A corollary of the urban scale in food issues can be identified as the local scale, although the meaning of the line that divides the two categories depends greatly on how the subject under scrutiny is defined. While some geographers writing about food do focus explicitly on "the local" and are careful to address these questions directly,[44] the boundaries are slippery. That is, "the local" can be understood either to be integral to the fabric of urban or, conversely, to be utterly unique and existing in distinction from it, or indeed from other scales as well. Indeed, the local is invoked most commonly in contemporary popular food discourse as the antithesis of global.[45] As scholars writing about food and localism argue, some of the key ways that the local takes on meaning is through the embodiment and institutionalization of associated practices connected to food production and consumption in a given neighborhood, including, for example, retail food shops, markets and restaurants.[46] In her bibliography of the cultural geography of American foodways, Barbara Shortridge includes many references to studies of restaurants and other eating places that characterize locales and regions, noting that they tend to attract the attention of geographers in particular.[47]

Rural and Agricultural Food Scales

The countryside is a more traditional comparison to cities, a comparison in which the rural is contrasted to the urban, and in which, in relation to food production and consumption, the local can appear either as binding the two together or as defining one against the other.[48] With its obvious and long-standing engagement with agriculture, animal husbandry, and rural food production and distribution networks, geography has a lengthy history of producing studies of both the historical development and contemporary transformations of these phenomena. In this realm, geographers' investigations can be seen to fall into three broad categories: (1)

those which study the interrelations between political economy and agrarianism, on scales ranging from and connecting the global to the extremely local; (2) those which focus on the industrialization of food production and manufacture; and (3) those which, through their active concern with rural food producers, concentrate on fair and ethical trade and the related class issues that have emerged in parallel to these trades. Although these categories are useful lenses through which to examine the ways geographers have grappled with aspects of rurality in the realms of food production, distribution, and consumption, it is crucial to understand them as simply that—one set of lenses that could easily be substituted for another or others. That is, in these subject areas, even more than in others, it seems clear that the geographers in question often do not identify as scholars of rurality, specifically.

In the first category—political economy and agrarianism—this principle is somewhat less true. Michael Watts, for instance, is a geographer who has spent decades working on the global interrelations among political economy, agrarianism, and evolving industrial capitalism within the energy and agro-food sectors, and rural producers stand at the forefront of his analysis.[49] Similarly, although with relatively less focus on the central and evolving role of industrial capitalism, the relations between global agro-food systems and rural food producers and networks form core sections of three recent and influential collective volumes by geographers: *The Sustainability of Rural Systems: Geographical Interpretations* (2002); *Worlds of Food: Place, Power, and Provenance in the Food Chain* (2006); and *Agri-Food Commodity Chains and Globalising Networks* (2008).[50] Other work within geography has provided broader historical contexts for the mobilization of these concepts.[51]

The study of the industrialization of food production and manufacture in a given milieu has proved an effective method for understanding how the larger questions related to agro-food and global capital can be seen to operate on a more local and clearly delimited scale. There have been a number of studies examining the industrialization of agriculture, and how it and food production mediate the relations between cities and the countryside,[52] but as often the focus is on a particular industrial practice or food sector. For instance, Susanne Freidberg's book, *Fresh: A Perishable History* (2009), examines the nineteenth and twentieth century drive for the effective conservation of foodstuffs, as well as the concept of "freshness" itself, which she historicizes as it relates to a series of specific foodstuffs (beef, fish, vegetables, milk, fruit, eggs), and the emergence of locavorism.[53] Food sectors that have received sustained analysis from geographers include the dairy industry in particular,[54] but also the salmon canning industry, the frozen meat industry, and the apple industry.[55]

Rurality equally occupies a central place in the geography literature that has emerged in relation to fair and ethical trade and organic farming, as well as in relation to the more diffuse issues of class that characterize both public and scholarly debates over the socioeconomics of the retail and consumption aspects of these practices. Julie Guthman has engaged with these issues: organic farming and the emergence of what she has called "yuppie chow."[56] Susanne Freidberg has also investigated the paradoxes implicit in U.K. supermarkets' embrace of ethical trade, specifically in connection to the long-haul provision of African horticultural goods.[57] A heightened concern for the ethical aspects of food distribution, exchange, and, above all, consumption is both central and critical to these debates. It harkens back to David Harvey's call for a renewed politics of consumption, and it signals the appearance of a growing body of work on what has been called the "alternative" geographies of food. This term has been applied as the title of a collective volume published in 2007, and indeed appears in the title of almost every one of its contributions, evoking alternative food networks; alternative food economies; and alternative food producers and retailers.[58] Similarly, other studies in geography examine alternative food provision and alternative food politics.[59] The editors of the 2007 volume explain the use of "alternative" in these contexts most simply as characterizing "a perceived trend towards the emergence of food production-consumption relationships which offer an 'alternative' set of possibilities to those provided by the 'conventional' industrialized agro-food complex."[60] Interestingly, in this body of work, the actions of the scholar, as much as those of the food producers, distributors, and consumers being studied, take on a moral or ethical cast. That is, undertaking and designing research (i.e., establishing a standardized division between conventional and alternative) and disseminating research results are seen as interventions capable of bringing about desired change. And, indeed, these actions are envisioned as necessary to the continued expansion of the realm of the "alternative."

Domestic Scales of Food Consumption and the Individual as Consumer

The final categories of food activities under examination in this chapter are those associated with the studies by geographers of domestic and individual scales of action. In the first instance, food buying and consuming by families and households is receiving increased attention in the United Kingdom and in North America. These activities are seen as having a great impact on food-related health issues pertaining to children, and on connecting families to their surrounding communities.[61] A multiyear Leverhume Trust-funded research program in the United Kingdom entitled "Changing Families, Changing Food" was undertaken with geographer Peter Jackson as the principal investigator at the University of Sheffield between 2005 and 2008 to explore just these issues. In equal measure, the study of domestic food consumption has also been the optic through which to explore individual, gendered, and collective identities.[62]

At the most bounded scale of analysis, the way the individual has interacted with food can be seen to fall into two categories that have developed within different fields of geography: those of the moral purchaser and consumer and of the physical consuming body. First, drawing on and extending the recent evocations of morality within the geography of food described above, as well as on much older traditions of moral economy, Peter Jackson in particular has developed the notion of the morality of consumption.[63] In this work, he explores the enormous influence of individuals' moral and ethical choices in the realm of food consumption on specific outcomes in food economies, nevertheless articulating a vision of collective responsibility. In a related vein, individual consumer self-consciousness about the weightiness attached to the food consumption decisions is one aspect of another multiyear research program currently being led by Jackson at the University of Sheffield, under the name of "Consumer Culture in an Age of Anxiety."[64]

This focus on consumers' moral consciousness provides a strong contrast to a final subdiscipline within geography that relates to individuals and food consumption: that of physical health and nutrition. While the majority of scholars who study the complex relations between food and health are nutritionists or dieticians, geographers' contributions to these fields concentrate on spatial factors influencing food-related health risks and other phenomena. For instance, the interdisciplinary U.K. research program entitled "Eating, Food, and Health," which concluded in 2005, included geography research and outputs that focused on food deserts in British cities.[65] Geographer Corinna Hawkes, on the other hand, employs the global scale for research on obesity and diet-related chronic diseases, on the global regulation of nutrition labels, and on the effects of trade liberalization on global diets.[66] Both in the moral and the physical spheres, then, individuals' food consumption has engaged geographers who examine the economic and health implications at a range of scales (from household to global) of the activities associated with these consuming practices.

Conclusion

The impression produced from an examination of the range of questions posed by geographers in the study of food is of a disconcerting although rich multiplicity. While the attention geographers bring to bear upon food studies may be summarized by reference to spatiality, or ideas of place, as the introduction to this chapter argues, the very enormity and amorphousness of these expressions render them difficult to apply with precision and certitude to a given topic or subfield within the study of food. This assertion, however, might arguably be forwarded for many other disciplines as well, with their own broad foci substituted for spatiality (history and anthropology included). Certain themes and arenas within food studies are particularly well researched by geographers: wine and spirits by Francophone geographers and global commodity chains or circuits by Anglophone geographers constitute two examples, although there certainly are many more. These subjects benefit from geographical analysis in which the spatial frame of food practices is considered a constitutive element, both dynamic and multidimensional. Although the pluralism and interdisciplinarity of geography as a field can appear to reduce the coherence between geographical debates over food, it also results in geographers' capacity to approach food on a range of spatial scales and registers. More important, because of the breadth of the field, geographers are uniquely placed to approach the disciplinary and conceptual challenges posed by the inherent complexities of food research itself, complexities arising from food's intricate uniting of the material, the textual, and the intellectual and of worlds concurrently social, cultural, environmental, and physical.

Notes

1. Gilles Fumey, *Manger local, manger global: l'alimentation géographique* (Paris: CNRS Éditions, 2010), 9–26, examines the tentative and relatively recent emergence of food studies within French cultural geography; Warren Belasco, "Food Matters: Perspectives on an Emerging Field," in *Food Nations: Selling Taste in Consumer Societies*, ed. Warren Belasco and Philip Scranton (New York: Routledge, 2002), 4–10.

2. Peter Atkins, "Mapping Foodscapes," *Food & History*, 3, no. 1 (2005): 267–80; Barbara Shortridge, "Geographical Data Sources for the Study of Regional Foods in the United States," *Journal for the Study of Food and Society* 4, no. 1 (2000): 11–18; Jean-Robert Pitte, "La Géographie du goût: entre mondialisation et enracinement local," *Annales de géographie* 621 (September-October 2001), reprinted in his *Géographie culturelle* (Paris: Librairie Arthème Fayard, 2006), 823–51.

3. While the focus here will be on the contributions to the study of food made by geographers, for a very useful outline of the place of food history in the French *Annales* between the 1960s and the 1980s, see Eva Barlösius, "The History of Diet as a Part of the *Vie materielle* in France," in *European Food History: A Research Review*, ed. Hans J. Teuteberg (London: Leicester University Press, 1992), 90–108.

4. For a discussion of the (false) distinctions between concepts of "space" and "place," see Doreen Massey, "Geographies of Responsibility," *Geografiska Annaler* 86B (2004): 7–9.

5. For a work structured explicitly around the scales of food-related activities, see David Bell and Gill Valentine, eds., *Consuming Geographies: We Are Where We Eat* (London: Routledge, 1997).

6. Shane Hamilton, "Analyzing Commodity Chains: Linkages or Restraints," in *Food Chains: From Farmyard to Shopping Cart*, ed. Warren Belasco and Roger Horowitz (Philadelphia: University of Pennsylania Press, 2009), 17.

7. Alex Hughes and Suzanne Reimer, "Introduction," in *Geographies of Commodity Chains*, ed. Alex Hughes and Suzanne Reimer (London: Routledge, 2004), 1–16.

8. On commodity chain analysis, see William Friedland, "Reprise on Commodity Systems Methodology," *International Journal of Sociology of Agriculture and Food* 9, no. 1 (2001): 82–103. On the filières, see the special issue of *Économies et Sociétés: cahiers de l'ISMEA*, Série AG, no. 17 (May 1983), especially, F. Lauret, "Sur les études des filières agro-alimentaires," 721–40; Groupe de recherche économique and sociologique sur la consommation alimentaire, "Consommation et système agro-alimentaire: quelques

approches et quelques résultats," 877–909; and the special issue entitled "Dossiers: les filières agro-alimentaires," *Agriscope*, no. 3 (Spring 1984): 6–96.

9. This process is addressed directly in Deborah Leslie and Suzanne Reimer, "Spatializing Commodity Chains," *Progress in Human Geography* 23, no. 3 (1999): 401–20.

10. Claude Thouvenot, ed., "Géographie de l'alimentation," a special issue of *Annales de géographie* 89, no. 493 (May-June 1980): 258–398.

11. Maximilien Sorre, "Géographie de l'alimentation," *Annales de géographie* 61, no. 325 (1952): 184–99; translated as "The Geography of Diet," in *Readings in Cultural Geography*, ed. and trans. Philip Wagner and Marvin Mikesell (Chicago: University of Chicago Press, 1962), 445–56.

12. See much of Gilles Fumey's current work including: *Manger local, manger global . . .* ; *Géopolitique de l'alimentation* (Auxerre: Sciences Humaines Éditions, 2008); idem, with Olivier Etcherverria, *Atlas mondial des cuisines et gastronomies: une géographie gourmande* (Paris: Éditions Autrement, 2009). See also Éric Bordessoule, "Produire et échanger des biens alimentaires," in *Nourrir les hommes: questions de géographie*, ed. Jean-Paul Charvet (Nantes: Éditions du temps, 2008), 5–26. For a similar focus on geopolitics, political economy and global food scales, see Peter Atkins and Ian Bowler, *Food in Society: Economy, Culture and Geography* (London: Arnold, 2001).

13. Peter Jackson, Neil Ward, and Polly Russell, "Mobilising the commodity chain concept in the politics of food and farming," *Journal of Rural Studies* 22 (2006): 132.

14. Becky Mansfield, "Spatializing Globalization: A 'Geography of Quality' in the Seafood Industry," *Economic Geography* 79, no. 1 (January 2003): 1–16.

15. The idea of the social life of the commodity has proved particularly influential in this regard: see Arjun Appadurai, "Introduction: Commodities and the Politics of Value," in *The Social Life of Things: Commodities in Cultural Perspective*, ed. Arjun Appadurai (Cambridge: Cambridge University Press, 1986), 3–63; Igor Kopytoff, "The Cultural Biography of Things: Commoditization as Process," in ibid, 64–91.

16. David Harvey, "Between Space and Time: Reflections on the Geographical Imagination," *Annals of the Association of American Geographers* 80 (1990): 418–34.

17. Philip Crang invoked the concept of "displacement" to describe the undefinable spatialities associated with the movement of commodities in his "Displacement, Consumption and Identity," *Environment and Planning A* 28, no. 1 (1996): 47–67. See also Ian Cook, Philip Crang, and Mark Thorpe, "Tropics of Consumption: 'Getting with the Fetish' of 'Exotic' Fruit?" in *Geographies of Commodity Chains*, ed. Alex Hughes and Suzanne Reimer (London: Routledge, 2004), 173–92; Ian Cook and Philip Crang, "The World on a Plate: Culinary Cultures, Displacement and Geographical Knowledges," *The Journal of Material Culture* 1, no. 2 (1996): 131–53.

18. Ian Cook, "Follow the Thing: Papaya," *Antipode* 36 (2004): 642–64; Becky Mansfield, "'Imitation Crab' and the Material Culture of Commodity Production," *Cultural Geographies* 10, no. 2 (2003): 176–95; Bertie Mandelblatt, "A Transatlantic Commodity: Irish Salt Beef in the French Atlantic," *History Workshop Journal* 63 (Spring 2007): 18–47; Susanne Freidberg, *French Beans and Food Scares: Culture and Commerce in an Anxious Age* (New York: Oxford University Press, 2004); Judith Carney, *Black Rice: The African Origins of Rice Cultivation in the Americas* (Cambridge, MA: Harvard University Press, 2001); idem and Richard Nicholas Rosomoff, *In the Shadow of Slavery: Africa's Botanical Legacy in the Atlantic World* (Berkeley: University of California Press, 2009).

19. Eugène Calvez, "La planète laitière: quelques aspects de la production dans le Monde," *BAGF* 84 (March 2007): 45–63; Vincent Moriniaux, "Un sirop au goût amer: le

sirop d'érable québécois, produit industriel standardisé ou produit de terroir," *BAGF* 84 (March 2007): 81–96.

20. Henri Enjalbert, *Histoire de la vigne et du vin: l'avènement de la qualité* (Paris: Bordas, 1975); Roger Dion, *Histoire de la vigne et du vin en France des origines au XIXe siècle* (1959, reprint: Paris, Flammarion, 1977); idem, *Le Paysage et la vigne: Essais de géographie historique* (Paris: Payor, 1990); Alain Huetz de Lemps, *Vignoble et vins d'Espagne* (Bordeaux: Presses Universitaires de Bordeaux, 1993). For a review of the French wine historiography within the discipline of geography, see Raphaël Schirmer, "Le Regard des géographes français sur la vigne et le vin," *Annales de géographie*, no. 614–615 (July-October 2000): 345–63. For a recent contribution that places the French wine and brandy literature in an Atlantic context, see Bertie Mandelblatt, "L'Alambic dans l'Atlantique: production, commercialisation, et concurrence d'eau-de-vie de vin et de rhum dans l'Atlantique français au XVIIe et au début du XVIIIe siècle," *Histoire, Économie, Société* 2 (2011): 63–78.

21. Jean-Robert Pitte, *Les Terres de Castanide: Hommes et paysages du châtaignier de l'antiquité à nos jours* (Paris: Fayard, 1986). See also idem, ed., "La Nouvelle planète des vins," a special issue of *Annales de géographie*, no. 614–615 (July-October 2000); idem, *Bordeaux, Burgundy: A Vintage Rivalry*, trans. M. B. DeBevois (Berkeley: University of California Press, 2008).

22. On the concept of *terroir*, see: Jean-Robert Pitte, "Pour en finir avec le pseudo-terroir: les vrai facteurs de la qualité du vin," in *Pratiques anciennes et genèse des paysages: Mélanges de géographie historique à la mémoire du Professeur Jean Peltre*, ed. André Humbert (Nancy: CERP, 1997), 195–212. Works by non-geographers include, Laurence Bérard and Philippe Marchenay, *Les produits de terroirs entre cultures et reglements* (Paris: CNRS Éditions, 2004); Olivier Assouly, *Les Nourritures nostalgiques: essai sur le mythe du terroir* (Paris: Actes Sud, 2004).

23. For a interconnected series of articles on this methodology within the cultural geography of food, see: Ian Cook, et al., "Geographies of Food: Following," *Progress in Human Geography* 30, no. 5 (2006): 655–66; Ian Cook, et al., "Geographies of Food: Mixing," *Progress in Human Geography* 32, no. 6 (2008): 821–33; Ian Cook, et al., "Geographies of Food: 'Afters,'" *Progress in Human Geography* 35, no. 1 (2011): 104–20.

24. See also in this regard: Bertie Mandelblatt, "'Beans from *Rochel* and Manioc from *Prince's Island*': West Africa, French Atlantic Commodity Circuits, and the Provisioning of the French Middle Passage," *History of European Ideas* 34, no. 4 (December, 2008): 411–23; Susanne Freidberg, "Postcolonial Paradoxes: the Cultural Economy of African Export Horticulture," in *Food and Globalization: Consumption, Markets and Politics in the Modern World*, ed. Alexander Nützenadel and Frank Trentman (Oxford: Berg International, 2008), 215–34. For a discussion of how the study of food (and material culture more generally) actively contributes to theories of postcolonialism too tightly focussed on texts and representation, see Ian Cook and Michelle Harrison, "Cross over Food: Re-Materializing Postcolonial Geographies," *Transactions of the Institute of British Geographers*, no. 28 (2003): 296–317.

25. Jean-Robert Pitte, *Gastronomie française: histoire et géographie d'une passion* (Paris: Fayard, 1991). For the UNESCO petition, undertaken with the support of the French state under Nicolas Sarkozy and with the participation of the *Institut Européen d'Histoire et des Cultures de l'Alimentation* (IEHCA), see "The Gastronomic Meal of the French" [Online]. Available: http://www.unesco.org/culture/ich/index.php?RL=00437. [March 26, 2011]. For critiques, see Roger Célestin et al, "Editors Introduction," *Contemporary French and Francophone Studies* 14, no. 2 (March 2010): 129–33.

26. Examples include Terry Marsden, Andrew Flynn, and Michelle Harrison, *Consuming Interests: The Social Provision of Foods* (London: University College London Press, 2000); Jackson, Ward, and Russell, "Mobilising the commodity chain," which examines the British institutional use of the commodity chain concept, and Carol Morris and Craig Young, "New Geographies of Agro-Food Chains: An Analysis of UK Quality Assurance Schemes," Hughes and Reimer, in *Geographies of Commodity Chains*, 83–101.

27. Interestingly, Pitte has himself actively contributed to the questioning of national frames via a collection he edited with Massimo Montanari, *Les Frontières alimentaires* (Paris: CNRS Éditions, 2009), which takes as its point of departure the questioning of all manner of food borders.

28. Amongst her many publications, see Barbara Shortridge and James Shortridge, "Cultural Geography of American Foodways: An Annotated Bibliography," *Journal of Cultural Geography* 15 (1995): 79–108; Barbara Shortridge, "Apple Stack Cake for Dessert: Appalachian Regional Foods," *Journal of Geography*, 104, no. 4 (2005): 65–73; idem, "A Food Geography of the Great Plains," *Geographical Review* 93, no. 4 (2003): 507–29; idem, "Geographic Data Sources for the Study of Regional Foods in the United States," *Journal for the Study of Food & Society*, 4, no. 1 (Spring 2000): 11–18.

29. Wilbur Zelinksy, "The Roving Palate: North America's Ethnic Restaurant Cuisines," *Geoforum* 15 (1985): 51–72.

30. Ian Cook, Philip Crang and Mark Thorpe, "Eating into Britishness: Multicultural Imaginaries and the Identity Politics of Food," in *Practising Identities: Power and Resistance*, ed. Sasha Roseneil and Julie Seymour (Basingstoke: Palgrave Macmillan, 1999), 223–47; idem, "Regions to be Cheerful: Culinary Authenticity and its Geographies," in *Cultural Turns/Geographical Turns: Perspectives on Cultural Geography*, ed. Simon Naylor, et al (Harlow: Prentice Hall, 2000), 109–38.

31. Jean Duruz, "Eating at the Borders: Culinary Journeys," *Environment and Planning D: Society and Space* 23, no. 1 (2005): 51–69.

32. On the Annales food history, see Barlösius, "The History of Diet." For two examples of contemporary studies of colonial influences on metropolitan French cooking practices written by non-geographers, see Kolleen M. Guy, "Imperial Feedback: Food and the French Culinary Legacy of Empire," *Contemporary French and Francophone Studies* 14, no. 2 (March 2010): 149–57; David Burton, "Curries and Couscous: Contrasting Colonial Legacies in French and British Cooking," in *Gastronomic Encounters*, ed. A. Lynn Martin and Barbara Santich (Adelaide: East Street Publications, 2004), 49–61.

33. Gilles Fumey, "La Question culinaire aux États-Unis: peut-on parler de multiculturalisme alimentaire," *Géographie et cultures*, no. 58 (2006): 33–49; idem, "Brassages et métissages de l'Europe culinaire," *Géographie et cultures*, no. 50 (2004): 7–27.

34. Jean Peltre et Claude Thouvenot, eds., *Alimentation et Régions: actes du colloque «Cuisines, Régimes alimentaires, Espaces régionaux»* (Nancy: Presses Universitaires de Nancy, 1989).

35. The proceedings from the first conference, held at Bordeaux in 1982, were published as Alain Huetz de Lemps, et al, eds., *Eaux-de-vie et spiritueux* (Paris: CNRS, 1985); the second, at Caen in 1985, Pierre Brunet, ed., *Histoire et Géographie des fromages* (Caen: Université de Caen, 1987).

36. For studies by non-geographers, see Jason Block, Richard Scribner, and Karen DeSalvo, "Fast food, race/ethnicity, and income: A geographic analysis," *American Journal of Preventative Medicine* 27, no. 3 (2004): 211–17; LaVonna Blair, et al, "African Americans' Access to Healthy Food Options in South Los Angeles Restaurants,"

American Journal of Public Health 95, no. 4 (2005): 668–73. Geography research includes, Betsy Donald and Alison Blay-Palmer, "The urban creative-food economy: producing food for the urban elite or social inclusion opportunity?" *Environment and Planning A* 38, no. 10 (2006): 1901–20.

37. For a broader reflection on food in the city, see David Bell, "Fragments for a New Urban Culinary Geography," *Journal for the Study of Food and Society* 6, no. 1 (Winter 2002): 10–21.

38. Benjamin Coles and Philip Crang, "Placing Alternative Consumption: Commodity Fetishism in Borough Fine Foods Market, London," in *Ethical Consumption: A Critical Introduction*, ed. Tania Lewis and Emily Potter (London: Routledge, 2010); Sarah Wakefield, et al, "Growing Urban Health: Community Gardening in Southeast Toronto," *Health Promotion International* 22, no. 2 (2007): 92–101; Robin Kortright and Sarah Wakefield, "Edible Backyards: A Qualitative Study of Household Food Growing and its Contributions to Food Security," *Agriculture and Human Values* 27 (2010): 1–15.

39. Kristian Larsen and Jason Gilliland, "Mapping the Evolution of 'Food Deserts' in a Canadian City: Supermarket Accessibility in London, Ontario, 1961–2005," *International Journal of Health Geographics* 7, no. 16 (2008): 1–16; Karen Smoyer-Tomic, John Spence, Carl Amrhein, "Food Deserts in the Prairies? Supermarket Accessibility and Neighbourhood Need in Edmonton, Canada," *The Professional Geographer* 58, no. 3 (2006): 307–26; Philippe Apparicio, Marie-Soleil Cloutier, and Richard Shearmur, "The Case of Montreal's Missing Food Deserts: Evaluation of Accessibility to Food Supermarkets," *International Journal of Health Geography* 6, no. 4 (2007): 1–13; Ian Clarke, et al., "Retail Competition and Consumer Choice: Contextualising the 'Food Deserts' Debate," *International Journal of Retail and Distribution Management* 32, no. 2 (2004): 89–99.

40. Lauren Baker, "Tending Cultural Landscapes and Food Citizenship in Toronto's Community Gardens," *Geographical Review* 94, no. 3 (2010): 305–25.

41. Betsy Donald, "Food Systems Planning and Sustainable Cities and Regions: The Role of the Firm in Sustainable Food Capitalism" *Regional Studies* 42, no. 9 (2008): 1251–62.

42. Examples of this kind of interdisciplinary collaboration include Mustafa Koc, et al., eds., *For Hunger-Proof Cities: Sustainable Urban Food Systems* (Ottawa: International Development Research Centre, 1999); Karen A. Franck, ed., "Food + the City," a special issue of *Architectural Design*, 75, no. 3 (May/June 2005).

43. Peter Atkins, Peter Lammel, and Derek J. Oddy, eds., *Food and the City in Europe since 1800* (London: Ashgate, 2007).

44. Megan Blake, Jody Mellor, and Lucy Crane, "Buying Local Food: Shopping Practices, Place and Consumption Networks in Defining Food as 'Local,'" *Annals of the Association of American Geographers* 100, no. 2 (2010): 409–26; Robert Feagan, "The Place of Food: Mapping Out the 'Local' in Local Food Systems," *Progress in Human Geography* 31, no. 1 (2007): 23–42.

45. For example, Brian Halweil, *Home Grown: The Case for Local Food in a Global Market*, Worldwatch Paper No. 163 (Washington, DC: The Worldwatch Institute, 2002). For a discussion of this dichotomy, see Susanne Freidberg, *Fresh: A Perishable History* (Cambridge, MA: Belknap Press, 2009), 280–83.

46. William Prichard, "Local and Global in Cyberspace: The Geographical Narratives of US Food Companies on the Internet," *Area* 31, no. 1 (March 1999): 9–17.

47. Shortridge and Shortridge, "Cultural Geography of American Foodways," 91–95. See also, Philip Crang, "It's Showtime: On the Workplace Geographies of Display in a Restaurant in Southeast England," *Environment and Planning D* 12 (1994): 675–704.

48. John Smithers, "Unpacking the Terms of Engagement with Local Food at the Farmers' Market: Insights from Ontario," *Journal of Rural Studies* 24, no. 3 (2008): 337–50.

49. David Goodman and Michael Watts, eds., *Globalising Food: Agrarian Questions and Global Restructuring* (London: Routledge, 1997); Michael Watts, "The Great Tablecloth: Bread and Butter Politics, and the Political Economy of Food and Poverty," in *A Handbook of Economic Geography*, ed. Gordon Clark, Meric Gertler and Maryann Feldmann (London: Oxford University Press, 2000), 195–215.

50. Ian Bowler, Christopher Bryant, and Chris Cocklin, *The Sustainability of Rural Systems: Geographical Interpretations* (Dordrecht, Netherlands: Kluwer, 2002); Kevin Morgan, Terry Marsden, and Jonathan Murdoch, *Worlds of Food: Place, Power, and Provenance in the Food Chain* (Oxford: Oxford University Press, 2006); Christina Stringer and Richard Le Heron, eds., *Agri-Food Commodity Chains and Globalising Networks* (Aldershot: Ashgate, 2008).

51. Michael Winter, "Geographies of Food: Agro-Food Geographies—Making Connections," *Progress in Human Geography* 27, no. 4 (2003): 505–13; idem, "Geographies of Food: Agro-Food Geographies—Farming, Food and Politics," *Progress in Human Geography* 28, no. 5 (2004): 664–70; George Henderson, "Nature and Fictitious Capital: The Historical Geography of an Agrarian Question," *Antipode* 30 (1998): 73–118; Terry Marsden, "Exploring Political Economy Approaches in Agriculture," *Area* 20, no. 4 (December 1988): 315–22; idem, "Agricultural Geography and the Political Economy Approach: A Review," *Economic Geography* 72, no. 4 (October 1996): 361–75.

52. Margaret Fitzsimmons, "The New Industrial Agriculture: The Regional Integration of Specialty Crop Production," *Economic Geography* 62 (1986): 334–53; John Smithers, Alan Joseph, and Matthew Armstrong, "Across the Divide (?): Reconciling Farm and Town Views of Agriculture–Community Linkages," *Journal of Rural Studies* 21, no. 3 (2005): 281–95; Daniel Block, "Making the Country Work for the City: Von Thünen's Ideas in Geography, Agricultural Economics and the Sociology of Agriculture," *American Journal of Economics and Sociology* 60, no. 1 (2003): 79–98.

53. Freidberg, *Fresh*.

54. Work on the dairy industry is of longstanding interest to American geographers. See Loyal Durand, Jr., "The Migration of Cheese Manufacture in the United States," *Annals of the Association of American Geographers* 42 (1952): 263–82; idem, "The Historical and Economic Geography of Dairying in the North Country of New York State," *Geographical Review* 57 (1967): 24–47. See also Gordon Fielding, "Dairying in Cities Designed to Keep People Out," *Professional Geographer* 14 (1962): 12–17; Daniel Block, "Public Health, Cooperatives, Local Regulation, and the Development of Modern Milk Policy: The Chicago Milkshed, 1900–1940," *Journal of Historical Geography* 35, no. 1 (January 2009): 128–53; idem, "Saving Milk Through Masculinity: Public Health Officers and Pure Milk, 1880–1930," *Food and Foodways* 13, no. 1/2 (2005): 115–34; idem, "Protecting and Connecting: Separation, Connection, and the U.S. Dairy Economy 1840–2002," *Journal for the Study of Food and Society* 6, no. 1 (Winter 2002): 22–30.

55. Otis Freeman, "Salmon Industry of the Pacific Coast," *Economic Geography* 11 (1935): 109–29; Michael Roche, "International Food Regimes: New Zealand's Place in the International Frozen Meat Trade, 1870–1935," *Historical Geography* 27 (1999): 129–51; Megan McKenna, Michael Roche, and Richard Le Heron, "An Apple a Day: Renegotiating Concepts, Revisiting Context in New Zealand's Pipfruit Industry," in *Restructuring*

Global and Regional Agricultures: Transformations in Australasian Agri-food Economies and Spaces, ed. David Burch, Jasper Goss, Geoffrey Lawrence (Aldershot: Ashgate, 1999), 41–59.

56. Julie Guthman, *Agrarian Dreams? The Paradox of Organic Farming in California* (Berkeley, California: University of California Press, 2004); idem, "Fast Food/Yuppie Food: Reflexive Taste and the Making of Yuppie Chow," *Social and Cultural Geography* 4 (2003): 45–58. For a review of how the concept of national health framed debates over diet and organicism in mid-twentieth-century England, see David Matless, "Bodies made of Grass made of Earth made of Bodies: Organicism, Diet and National Health in Mid-Twentieth-Century England," *Journal of Historical Geography* 27, no. 3 (July, 2001): 355–76.

57. Susanne Freidberg, "Cleaning Up Down South: Supermarkets, Ethical Trade and African Horticulture," *Social and Cultural Geography* 4 (2003): 353–68.

58. Damian Maye, Lewis Holloway, and Moya Kneafsey, eds., *Alternative Food Geographies: Representation and Practice* (Oxford: Elsevier, 2007).

59. Edmund M. Harris, "Eat Local? Constructions of Place in Alternative Food Politics," *Geography Compass* 4, no. 4 (2010): 355–69; David Watts, Brian Ilbery, and Damian Maye, "Making Re-connections in Agro-food Geography: Alternative Systems of Food Provision," *Progress in Human Geography* 29, no. 1 (2005): 22–40.

60. Maye, Holloway, and Kneafsey, *Alternative Food Geographies*, 1.

61. Peter Jackson, "Changing Families, Changing Food" (January 2009). [Online]. Available: http://www.shef.ac.uk/content/1/c6/05/09/93/CFCF_Final_Report_2008.pdf. [March 28, 2011].

62. Jody Mellor, Megan Blake, and Lucy Crane, "When I'm Doing a Dinner Party I Don't Go for the Tesco Cheeses; Gendered Class Distinctions, Friendship and Home Entertaining," *Food, Culture and Society* 13, no. 1 (2010): 115–34; Gill Valentine, "Eating In: Home, Consumption and Identity," *Sociological Review* 47 (1999): 491–524.

63. Peter Jackson, Neil Ward, and Polly Russell, "Moral Economies of Food and Geographies of Responsibility," *Transactions of the Institute of British Geographers* NS 34 (2008): 12–24; Peter Jackson, "Connections and Responsibilities: the Moral Geographies of Sugar," in Nützenadel and Trentman, *Food and Globalization*, 235–50. See also the response by Frank Trentman, "Before Fair Trade: Empire, Free Trade and the Moral Economies of Food in the Modern World," *Environment and Planning D: Society and Space* 25 (2007): 1079–1102.

64. This program is funded by the European Research Council; it began in 2009 and runs until 2012: http://www.sheffield.ac.uk/conanx/index.html. [March 28, 2011]

65. Neil Wrigley, Daniel Warm, and Barrie Margetts, "Deprivation, Diet, and Food-Retail Access: Findings from the Leeds 'Food Deserts' Study," *Environment and Planning A* 35, no. 1 (2003): 151–88.

66. Corinna Hawkes, "Uneven Dietary Development: Linking the Policies and Processes of Globalization with the Nutrition Transition, Obesity and Diet-Related Chronic Diseases," *Globalization and Health* 2, no. 4 (2006) [Online]. Available: http://www.globalizationandhealth.com/content/pdf/1744-8603-2-4.pdf. [March 28, 2011]; idem, "Government and Voluntary Policies on Nutrition Labelling: A Global Overview," in *Innovations in Food Labelling*, ed. Janice Albert (Cambridge: FAO/Woodhead Publishing, 2010), 37–58; idem, "The Influence of Trade Liberalization and Global Dietary Change: The Case of Vegetable Oils, Meat, and Highly Processed Food," in *Trade, Food, Diet and Health: Perspectives and Policy Options*, ed. Corinna Hawkes, et al. (Oxford: Wiley-Blackwell, 2010), 35–59.

Bibliography

Atkins, Peter. "Mapping Foodscapes." *Food & History* 3, no. 1 (2005): 267–80.

———, Peter Lammel, and Derek J. Oddy, eds. *Food and the City in Europe since 1800.* London: Ashgate, 2007.

Bell, David, and Gill Valentine, eds. *Consuming Geographies: We Are Where We Eat.* London: Routledge, 1997.

Carney, Judith, and Richard Nicholas Rosomoff. *In the Shadow of Slavery: Africa's Botanical Legacy in the Atlantic World.* Berkeley: University of California Press, 2009.

Freidberg, Susanne. *Fresh: A Perishable History.* Cambridge, MA: Harvard University Press, 2009.

Goodman, David, and Michael Watts, eds. *Globalising Food: Agrarian Questions and Global Restructuring.* London: Routledge, 1997.

Guthman, Julie. *Agrarian Dreams? The Paradox of Organic Farming in California.* Berkeley: University of California Press, 2004.

Hughes, Alex, and Suzanne Reimer, eds. *Geographies of Commodity Chains.* London: Routledge, 2004.

Morgan, Kevin, Terry Marsden, and Jonathan Murdoch. *Worlds of Food: Place, Power, and Provenance in the Food Chain.* Oxford: Oxford University Press, 2006.

Pitte, Jean-Robert, and Massimo Montanari, eds. *Les Frontières alimentaires.* Paris: CNRS Éditions, 2009.

Shortridge, Barbara, and James Shortridge. "Cultural Geography of American Foodways: An Annotated Bibliography." *Journal of Cultural Geography* 15 (1995): 79–108.

CHAPTER 10

CRITICAL NUTRITION STUDIES

CHARLOTTE BILTEKOFF

Urged by government health agencies, doctors, nutrition experts, and food marketers to think of diet as a primary avenue toward health and longevity, American consumers are clamoring for more information about what is in their food and guidance about what is good to eat.[1] Prodded at the same time by activists and reformers to think about food as a significant factor in the well-being of the environment, regional economies, and local communities, many people also want to know where their food comes from, how it was produced, by whom, and (sometimes) under what conditions. The space of public discourse around food is crowded with nutritional guides, ethical philosophies, labeling schemes, and food industry trends providing answers (often competing ones) to the persistent and apparently growing consumer quest to know more about what is good to eat. U.S. Department of Agriculture (USDA) nutritional guidelines, health claims on food packages related to specific diseases, organic certification, the local food movement, simplified ingredient labels, fair trade products, and front-of-package labeling schemes assessing the nutritional quality of packaged foods are but some of these concurrent responses to these questions. However, in this context of growing anxiety about eating right, what consumers really need is not ever more information about the nutritional content of food or where it comes from, but a more informed, educated, and critical relationship to dietary health and dietary advice. The essay explores the history and historiography of nutrition and dietary health in the United States since the late nineteenth century and illuminates an emerging body of scholarship that has the potential to contribute the tools needed for this new cultural literacy of dietary health.

My experience researching a century of American dietary advice has convinced me that the historical investigation of nutrition and dietary health is critical to establishing such a public literacy around the cultural politics of dietary health, and that this "critical dietary literacy" is exactly what is missing from our public discourse around food and health. Three things that I learned from my research have been especially important in shaping this conviction. First, dietary ideals are generally presumed to be objective reflections of nutritional truths but in fact they reflect social ideals; they communicate profoundly important and widely shared (at least among the middle class) ideas about what it means to be a good person and, by extension, a good citizen. Second, these dietary and social ideals reflect the values of middle-class reformers who express and advocate them. The language of dietary health has historically played an important role in establishing the identity and character of the American middle class and has done so in part by setting up an ongoing contrast between its members—responsible, good eaters—and the bad eaters among the lower classes whose dangerous diets require both scrutiny and intervention. Finally, the relative cultural and social importance of eating right—being a "good eater"—has grown consistently for a century and is now more pervasive and significant than ever before.[2] Given all of this, the social stakes involved in our dietary choices—involving identity, morality, and status—are as significant as or more so than the biomedical ones. And yet our public discourse about dietary health proceeds as if dietary advice is simply a means of conveying the facts of food and health. The nutrition community focuses on refining its understanding of the physiological properties of various foods; the alternative food movement attempts to redefine good food based on ethical production; and food manufactures incorporate elements of both in their quest for increasing revenue. Those of us engaged in the practice of food history can, and should, provide a way of understanding nutrition and dietary health as cultural practices.

The ability to identify and understand the social implications of discourses of dietary health has been circumscribed by a number of factors, including the popular view of dietary advice as a reflection of scientific facts that are distinctly free from cultural, political, and ideological content. But the modern science of nutrition, which is only about a century old, mapped onto an existing set of moral precepts about eating right and has only come to seem free from social and cultural content through a historical process. The imposition of a scientific framework of chemical analysis and numeric quantification made it possible to measure and assess a "good diet" in ways that seemed purely objective, but the science of nutrition actually incorporated many of the moral and ascetic elements that had governed eating since ancient times. The science of human nutrition that we are now familiar with began with the work of German chemists who, in the 1800s, established that food comprised different components with specific physiological functions (proteins, fats, carbohydrates, and mineral matter). Until the 1890s they had believed that a sufficient diet for both humans and animals was simply a matter of balancing these elements. But a good diet became more precisely measurable when, by the end of the century, the unit of energy called the calorie entered the equation. Wilbur Atwater, who had trained in Germany, became known as the "father of American nutrition." His work investigated the chemical components of foodstuffs and the process by which the body turned those foods into usable energy, using the caloric measure to quantify the value of food.[3]

While this work introduced a new kind of scientific classification and quantification to the question of what was good to eat, as John Coveney argues, it also remained consistent with earlier modes of ethical and religious assessment. Coveney explains that ancient Greeks practiced ethical comportment in the face of food pleasures, early Christians renounced food pleasures for god, and though the enlightenment introduced scientific and medical reasoning, moral and ascetic criteria continued to govern eating right from the sixteenth to the nineteenth century. For early nutritionists like Atwater, laboratory findings about the chemical composition of foods were inseparable from the aim of reining in impractical excesses among urban workers, reducing poverty, and contributing to a much needed improvement in character, morality, and social order. Nutrition provided a rational justification for the imperatives to be frugal, thrifty, and economical with nature that were all part of the earlier concerns of an ascetic Christianity.[4]

The modern science of nutrition has been constructed as an objective, value-free measure of the facts of food and health through means that include the writing of its history to elide early work that actively embraced the moral, political, and philosophical aspects of diet. In her essay, "Nutrition for the People," Harmke Kamminga argues that the establishment of nutrition as a separate science was predicated on the writing of a history of nutrition that was intentionally crafted to bolster the idea of scientific objectivity. She points to the erasure of the work of the nineteenth-century physiologist Jacob Moleschott, who considered the aims of scientific research to be "human well-being, dignity and freedom." Working at a time when the role of the scientists was not yet defined, he resisted the separation between the science and culture of nutrition and the distinction between producing scientific knowledge and using it in the public interest. He saw science as a "liberating force" and "food and diet as a political as much as a scientific issue." According to Kamminga, in the 1920s and 1930s, when histories of nutrition science began to appear, Moleschott and his views were intentionally ignored because values, politics, and philosophy were not considered part of scientific inquiry.[5] Nutrition thus fit within a larger cultural process through which science in general was framed as devoid of cultural and social content, speaking "truth" through processes of counting and calculation that were understood as objective and free of personal values.[6]Although the construction of science in general and the science of nutrition in particular may have limited critical analysis of the cultural aspects of dietary advice, changes in the culture of health and the significance of eating right, particularly over the last few decades, have made it increasingly important that we engage in critical debate about discourses of dietary health. After World War II the medical and public health communities shifted their focus from communicable diseases to the "chronic diseases of affluence," such as cancer, cardiovascular disease, and diabetes. *Lifestyle* became a keyword in health discourse, more parts of daily life came to be considered "health related," and health practices took on new significance for individuals. As Robert Crawford explains, the prevention of illness became a pervasive standard against which an expanding number of behaviors and phenomenon were judged.[7] He describes the emergence of a "new health consciousness" in which it was assumed that health must be achieved by individuals through their own persistent, informed effort. In this context of the new health consciousness, eating habits took center stage as a health related behavior. With the decline of major deficiency diseases by the end of World War II, nutrition researchers turned their focus to the role of diet in the prevention and treatment of chronic diseases and began to sound the alarm about the dangers of overweight and obesity.[8] At the nexus of these interrelated changes in the broader culture of health and the focus of dietary advice, eating right became more central to the notion of health and, therefore, more meaningful than ever in terms of morality, identity, and status.

This essay explores the history and historiography of nutrition and dietary health and discusses the potential of emerging work in what I am calling "critical nutrition studies" to provide the building blocks of a new kind of dietary literacy. I focus on the United States since the turn of the last century in order to emphasize the important role that studies of nutrition and dietary health can play in this context. The essay starts with a schematic overview of the major nutritional paradigms since the late nineteenth century to provide a basic understanding of the evolution of ideas about what constitutes a good diet over the last century. The next section shows the range of ways in which nutrition and dietary health have figured in the practice of history. The last section returns to the present moment of cultural intensity around the question of what to eat. It provides a brief overview of critical nutrition studies and argues that this work has the potential to reshape contemporary discourses of food and health by providing the foundation for a new "critical dietary literacy."

Modern Nutritional Paradigms

Three nutritional paradigms characterize the history of ideas about what constitutes a good diet over the course of the last century or so. The first of these is the *caloric paradigm,* or what historian Harvey Levenstein refers to as "New Nutrition."[9] Wilbur Atwater believed that the science of nutrition could improve diets, and therefore living standards, by giving people the knowledge they needed to eat efficiently. His work focused on quantifying the chemical components of American foods, from oysters to oats, and showing that the cost of food had no bearing on its nutrient quality. He also conducted novel experiments in a "calorimeter" to measure the human body's need for energy when engaged in various types of physical and mental labor. Atwater established what he called a "pecuniary economy" of food in the interest of teaching Americans—particularly the poor and immigrants crowding northeast urban centers—to choose the most "efficient" diet possible; the one that provided the most energy for work at the least cost.[10]

Atwater published widely, disseminating his idea of a good diet among the American middle class through USDA publications and a series of articles that ran in the popular monthly *The Century* in the late 1880s. In these articles, he painstakingly explained that the "best food," sold at the highest prices and having the finest flavor was not necessarily the most economical or the most healthful. The coal laborer who gave his family the best flour, sugar, and meat, paying extra for quality foods to save "pride and palate" while skimping on clothing and renting cheap living quarters in a crowded tenement, "was innocently committing an immense economic and hygienic blunder."[11] The eating habits of immigrants and workers were of particular concern to Awater and the female reformers who took up his work. In the 1890s domestic scientists, who would later be known as home economists, established public kitchens to teach the precepts of scientific nutrition to immigrants and the poor. Finding this audience "incorrigible," they shifted their focus to teaching the "intelligent classes" a scientific approach to the eating.[12]

World War I food programs assured that by the end of the war millions of people had become familiar with the basic tenets of early nutrition, but this nutritional logic was already being challenged by the discovery in the 1910s of odorless, tasteless, and previously undetected components of food that researchers named vitamins. Their link to deficiency diseases undermined the logic of early nutrition by revealing the fact that calories alone were not enough to promote health and sustain life. Vitamins ended the reign of the caloric measure, complicated the pecuniary economy of food, and caused the nutrition community to rethink whether or not Americans were really eating adequate diets.

The discovery of vitamins gave rise to the second major nutritional paradigm, named "The Newer Nutrition" by Elmer McCollum, whose experiments on rats put in motion the transition away from the caloric paradigm.[13] In 1908 he revealed an element of food that had not been detected in Atwater's work with human subjects. In 1911 another researcher, Casimir Funk, managed to isolate one of these nutrients, Vitamin B, and by 1912 McCollum had identified Vitamin A and linked its absence to vision and growth problems in rats. In 1916 he proved that the absence of Vitamin B was linked to the disease beriberi. Over the next ten years, a stream of discoveries about vitamins, minerals, and trace elements transformed the American concept of what constituted an adequate diet.[14] By the early 1920s the message of Newer Nutrition was sweeping the nation and enthralling the middle class, in large part because marketers mined its potential to sell familiar foods—such as Grape-Nuts, Fleischmann's Yeast, and Welch's Grape Juice—by using new health claims.[15]

During the Depression researchers armed with new knowledge about the dangers of vitamin deficiency but lacking adequate methods for assessing either the vitamin content of foods or the amount of each vitamin needed to sustain health began to produce alarming reports about the extent of dietary deficiency among the population. The government began to treat nutrition as a defense issue during the mobilization for World War II. It released the first ever recommended dietary allowances (RDAs) in 1941 and launched a national nutrition education campaign that translated the new RDAs into dietary advice that Americans were urged to follow in the name of victory. The RDAs reflected an ambitious view of what diet could do for the health of individuals (even those who were already adequately nourished) and the strength of the nation, thus setting the goal of "optimal nutrition" for the entire population.[16]

The end of World War II brought yet another major shift in nutritional thinking in the United States and the emergence of the third major nutritional paradigm of the century. The nutrition community recognized that the major vitamin deficiency diseases had for the most part been conquered, leading many to worry about the relevance of their field. As a prominent nutritionist later recalled, they were soon "rescued by obesity" and the beginning of the "chronic disease era."[17] By the late 1960s, nutritionists had positioned themselves as critical to solving "the health problems of adults in affluent society—the degenerative diseases of middle age," such as cancer, diabetes, and cardiovascular disease.[18] At the heart of this new nutritional paradigm, which Warren Belasco has named "negative nutrition," was the idea that some foods could contribute to or cause chronic diseases, especially if consumed in large quantities, and should be avoided or eaten sparingly.[19] The first major revisions in the U.S. RDAs since World War II, issued in 1969, included suggestions to limit the intake of highly caloric foods, fat, cholesterol, salt, sugar, and alcohol.[20] This new set of guidelines signaled a major change from earlier dietary advice, which encouraged Americans to eat more health-promoting foods. It also alarmed food processors, who feared the new paradigm would undermine profits and began lobbying to ensure that USDA advice said nothing negative about their products.[21]

As the nutrition paradigm shifted toward negative nutrition, obesity came to be seen as a chronic disease in its own right and considered a causal factor in others, including cancer, diabetes, and heart disease.[22] Insurance industry efforts to identify factors that correlated to early death, and therefore increased costs for the industry, motivated much of the research on obesity, but growing alarm about weight also resonated with cultural concerns about the postwar lifestyle. An article published in *The New York Times* in 1950 explained that obesity was becoming a national problem in large part because of "mechanical improvements" and declared, "Americans are getting fat on too much food and too little work."[23] Another complained that too many families were taking pride in overeating because "it proves they have the affluence to be overfed."[24] Concern about obesity escalated slowly but steadily throughout the postwar period, and surged in the mid 1990s when two studies showed that obesity rates had increased dramatically during the 1980s and early 1990s.[25] By 2001 the government launched a "war against obesity," and fighting fat became the major focus of the nutrition and public health communities.[26]

While the paradigm of negative nutrition clearly shaped the major nutritional preoccupation of our time, the obesity epidemic, it has also given rise to the distinct but related set of concerns about dietary health expressed by the alternative food movement. Today's calls for a more ethical and sustainable food system have their roots in the counterculture of the 1970s and the food culture, or "countercuisine, that was part of it."[27] The view of food embraced by hippies and radicals in the 1970s was entirely consistent with the central precept of negative nutrition—that some foods could be detrimental to health—and the implicit critique of the American lifestyle that pervaded the dietary response to chronic disease believed to be lifestyle-related. Contemporary activists seeking alternatives to the industrial food system have redefined dietary health to include not only what we eat but also how it is produced, and its effects not only on bodies but also on communities and the environment.

Historiography

Just as contemporary concerns about nutrition and dietary health are shaped by the legacy of the nutritional paradigms of the twentieth century, so too has contemporary scholarship on nutrition and dietary health been shaped by a historiographical legacy. The work of contemporary scholars builds on the range of methods and approaches that comprise the historiography of nutrition and dietary health. As this section seeks to show, each of these approaches is shaped by several interrelated factors, including professional training, transformations in historical practices, priorities, and assumptions, and differing understandings of science and the knowledge it produces. This brief overview is organized along two interdependent axes, moving relatively chronologically through the evolution of "the field" and also tracing a continuum of perspectives on the extent to which nutrition itself—its practice and its facts—is seen as a historical construct.

This schematic overview starts with *histories of nutrition* written by nutrition scientists. This work typically approaches nutrition science as a progressive effort to uncover the truth about food and the human body, tracing the development of scientific methods and discoveries while celebrating their positive impact on human health. Authors working in this vein recognize a sharp break between prescientific ideas about diet, with roots in philosophical and religious thought, and the era of scientific nutrition, which introduced objective experimental methods that answered persistent dietary questions and produced a body of factual knowledge that was then applied to reduce illness. A classic work of this kind, Elmer McCollum's *A History of Nutrition: The Sequence of Ideas in Nutrition Investigation* (1957), traces the evolution of ideas about nutrition from the prescientific through 1940. The work celebrates discoveries and advances in the field, grandly describing the rise of nutritional science as "one of the greatest events in human history."[28]

Nutritionists continue to document the accomplishments of their field in this mode, though usually in less grandiose terms. A 2009 article by Deanna Pucciarelli, for example, concludes that its "study and practice is relevant to humankind's biological and social successes."[29]

Social history began to take an interest in nutrition in the 1960s and 1970s as part of an effort to document the experience of ordinary people and their everyday lives. Concerned less with historical changes in the field of nutrition, social historians are interested in the data nutrition provides about the standards of living, which researchers link to other historical conditions. For example, scholars have used nutritional data to trace the impact of changes in nutrition status, food supply and dietary standards on the occurrence of deficiency diseases, rates of fertility and mortality, population growth, and worker productivity.[30] A well-known and highly controversial example of nutritional analysis in social history is Robert Fogel and Stanley Engerman's *Time on the Cross: The Economics of Negro Slavery* (1974), which argued that slavery was an economically efficient institution whose harshness and severity had been previously exaggerated. Using data about the total food supply to a specific plantation in 1860, they estimated the amount of food consumed by slaves actually exceeded the 1964 recommended daily allowance of major nutrients. After the Civil War, they argue, the diets of black sharecroppers deteriorated.[31] Nutritional data are also central to Thomas McKeown's argument that the rise in the world population from the 1700s onward resulted from broad social and economic changes—especially improvements in diet—rather than from specific public health and medical interventions.[32]

Nutrition and dietary health took on a different role in the work of historians influenced by the linguistic turn, the 1970s shift in the field away from the model of the natural sciences and toward interpretative approaches dealing with subjectivity and contextual meaning.[33] *Cultural history* generally focuses on understanding the meaning and significance of cultural practices and often includes attention to issues of power, identity, and ideology. In this context, nutrition is seen as a cultural practice that both shapes and is shaped by other cultural practices. The essays in *The Science and Culture of Nutrition, 1840–1940* exemplify this approach.[34] Cultural histories of food and eating published since the late 1980s have explored nutrition science in relation to eating habits, popular thinking, medical practice, scientific funding, government policy, and social movements. Harvey Levenstein's two volume history of eating habits in the United States is perhaps the best known and most influential work of this kind, exploring the individuals, institutional and professional structures, economic and political factors (including class), reform movements, industry imperatives, and government initiatives that influenced American eating habits during that time. The work is preoccupied with how food habits change (or do not) and focuses on what Levenstein sees as the particularly modern predilection among some people of changing—en masse—the eating habits of others. For Levenstein, and others working in this vein, nutritional knowledge evolves and is applied within a historical context that shapes and limits its impact.[35]

Influences including poststructuralist and science and technology studies have led to the relatively recent emergence of *critical nutrition studies*. Instead of exploring a reciprocal relationship between nutrition and its cultural context, this work approaches nutrition and dietary health as cultural constructs. Here beliefs about the empirical truth of science and the objective reality of the human body that anchor all of the work described above become the subject of critical inquiry. Scholars working in this vein consider nutrition itself—not just its practice but its content—as a product of history. Their approach is consistent with the broader impact of poststructuralist theory on the way in which history is viewed and conducted. Michel Foucualt's influence is particularly significant and evident in the way in which this type of work tends to be more genealogy than history, accounting for the production of common sense about subjectivity and the body and refusing to take for granted the existence of any kind of biomedical truth outside of the process of language, culture, and ideology.[36] But critical nutrition studies is also clearly shaped by the major insights of science and technology studies about production of scientific knowledge, and is practiced by scholars trained in a wide variety of fields including communication, rhetoric, public health, sociology, and cultural studies.[37] The final section of this essay explores this emerging work by focusing on two of its most salient insights and then discussing how these insights might reshape contemporary conversations about food and health and provide the tools for a new critical dietary literacy among scholars, dietary reformers, activists, and consumers.

Critical Nutrition Studies: Toward a New Dietary Literacy

Constructionist histories of nutrition and dietary health focus their interrogations on assumptions that are foundational to the work already described. The assumption that nutrition is an objective science that serves a need among individuals to seek self-improvement through increased knowledge about the relationship between food and health is the focus of inquiry for scholars more interested in understanding how this came to seem true and exploring the political and ideological significance of its apparent naturalness. The focus is on the interrelationship between society, subjectivity, and the body. Knowledge, meaning the "self," and the experience of embodiment are all considered the products of social processes. Scholars working from this perspective presume that the supposed objectivity of nutrition science is itself a cultural construct that serves ideological and political ends. The fundamental concern of critical nutrition studies is precisely to rethink the seeming neutrality and objectivity of nutrition facts. Two of its key insights are explored later in more detail: that nutrition is not only an empirical set of rules but also a system of moral measures, and that its presumably neutral quantitative strategies are themselves political and ideological.

One of the core insights to emerge so far from critical nutrition studies is that despite its seeming neutrality, the science of nutrition is absolutely inseparable from its moral content. Individuals have come to see learning and living by the rules of nutrition as something they do for their own health and well-being, but this scholarship suggests that eating right is in fact a social responsibility and a moral imperative. For scholars influenced by poststructuralism, the regulation of the diet based on scientific nutrition is neither inevitable nor objectively good, but rather a historical particularity that occurred in part because of the state's interests in the productivity of its citizens. For example Deborah Lupton, an Australian Cultural Studies scholar, rehearses the familiar history of evolving paradigms in nutritional thinking but interprets it differently, describing a process through which nutrition was constructed as a "problem" for the population. She describes the emergence of the modern science of nutrition as a process through which it became important for individuals to understand and live according to nutritional knowledge in the interest of their own well-being, explaining that by the late nineteenth century it was seen as "important for all individuals to live their lives according to nutritional wisdom." As diet became something for individuals to consciously manage in the name of health, the state also became concerned with promoting dietary health in the interest of military strength and economic efficiency. Therefore, she explains, diet "became a moral question, involving issues of an individual's capacity for self-control and work and the avoidance of waste and excess."[38]

Because the duty to use the facts of nutrition in the interest of self-improvement is presented as a moral and a social imperative, nutrition does more that simply inform, it shapes certain kinds of subjects and makes possible moral assessments of the self and others. John Coveney, an Australian professor of Public Health, shows how a series of social imperatives and moral panics shaped the history of dietary health and the ongoing "rationalization of food choice." He argues that nutrition is not only an empirical system that produces facts about what is good to eat but also an ethical one that provides the basis for the construction of "the modern subject of food choice." Coveney mines Foucault's work for its genealogy of nutrition and locates nutrition among the many population sciences that were developed during the Enlightenment. Discussing Atwater's work at the end of the nineteenth century, for example, Coveney points out that his pecuniary economy of food defined poor choices about what to eat not only as physiologically foolish, but also as morally problematic. Where more traditional histories take for granted the existence of scientists, social reformers, and individuals who become targets of nutritional improvement, Coveney explores the historical construction of the individual who has the capacity for making or recommending food choices. In other words, nutrition is both a science which provides rules about what is good to eat and an ethos through which individuals construct themselves, in relation to those rules, as certain kinds of subjects.[39]

Emerging work in critical nutrition studies has also established the political and ideological nature of nutritional quantification. Scholars have analyzed seemingly objective measures such as the calorie, recommended dietary allowances and the nutrition "facts" on food packages. They have determined that numbers—such as how many calories are in an apple or how many grams of protein an adult needs in a day—do not transparently represent facts of nutrition so much as they express values and construct particular truths about food, health, and eaters while disallowing others. Historian Nick Cullather explains: "Although few statistical measures seem more innocuous, the calorie has never been a neutral, objective measure of the contents of a dinner plate." He goes on to show that the purpose of the caloric measure was in fact to make possible the supervision of population welfare in the interest of the modernist state-building project. Ultimately, it was the calorie that made it possible to quantify the value of a diet and, therefore, to think about it in comparative and competitive terms vis-à-vis the diets of other social classes and nations. The calorie made it possible to quantify hunger and count the hungry, for example, and therefore led to the establishment of relationships between nations based on a seemingly objective measures of food surplus and deficit "that allowed Americans to see food as an instrument of power, and to envisage a 'world food problem' amenable to political and scientific intervention."[40]

Also concerned with the social implications of the quantitative strategies of nutrition, Australian social critic Gyorgy Scrinis has developed an influential critique of what he calls the ideology of nutritionism, a "reductive approach to diet" that has encouraged the public to view food solely in terms of its quantifiable nutritional content. Reducing food and diet to its biomedical effects removes individual foods from their broader contexts. Nutrient level information about food content becomes the dominant means of assessing the value of food, eclipsing the value of traditional cuisines, sensual experiences, and ecological effects. Scrinis also argues that the ideology of nutritionism serves food industry interests by providing an effective marketing tool while obscuring the distinction between whole foods and processed foods.[41]

Jessica Mudry builds on this critique of seemingly objective numeric measures of nutrition by analyzing one hundred years of USDA food guides, which she sees as producing a new reality through the imposition of a numeric language for the value of food. She argues that an epistemology of quantification replaces other claims to knowledge that may be less rational, sophisticated, or professional, thereby creating a new kind of eater. Like the modern subject of food choice described by Coveney, the eater that is interpolated by USDA advice about food is "ethically incomplete" and is expected to seek completion through the numeric language of food. The ideal eater imagined by USDA discourse eats according to the numbers, leading to "the loss or at least the erosion, of the richness and diversity of other reasons to eat and other kinds of assessment of health."[42]

Taken together, the emerging field of critical nutrition studies asks that we start from scratch when we approach questions of food and health. Once we adopt this paradigm we can no longer assume that nutrition facts are neutral or beneficent, that eating right is in our best interest, or that dietary reform itself is an unmitigated good. This unraveling of the taken for granted about food and health offers the opportunity to imagine the future of dietary health through a lens that is not distorted by unexamined assumptions and is instead realistic about the very serious political and ideological implications of how we both define and provide good food. How might these insights effect contemporary conversations about what is good to eat? I begin exploring the answer to this question here by considering how the work of critical nutrition studies might inform, or transform, the discourse of contemporary food politics.

The voices of public intellectuals and activists such Michael Pollan, Alice Waters, Marion Nestle, and Will Allen, the Slow Food Movement, the local foods movement, urban agriculturalists, and school lunch reformers are all contributing to a chorus that is questioning our systems of food production, distribution, and consumption and seeking alternatives that are more sustainable, ethical, and healthy. For the most part, however, these activists have yet to question many of the received ideas about dietary health that are integral to the status quo of American eating habits, or to acknowledge that the role of nutrition in our lives is the product of a historical process that is just as political, contingent, and significant as that of the food system itself. From the perspective of critical nutrition studies, to set the scientific facts of nutrition apart from interrogation because of their presumed objective authority is to fail to fully examine the food system itself, which is both brought into being and legitimated by nutritional thinking. What would happen if the political strategies of the alternative food movement were to include rethinking not just the farm to fork continuum, but also the "truths" about dietary health and what it means to eat right that anchor our production and consumption practices?

The current discourse of food politics does, to some extent, incorporate one of the major insights of critical nutrition studies; the view that nutritional quantification is not an objective measure of food value but rather a strategy that expresses a particular set of values while eclipsing others. This can be traced to skepticism toward scientific rationality that the movement inherited from the counterculture and its orientation around ecological, rather than nutritional, principles. Building on this foundation, Micheal Pollan adopted and popularized Scrinis's critique of nutritionism in his 2007 *New York Times Magazine* piece, "Unhappy Meals" and subsequent best selling book *In Defense of Food.*[43] In the context of today's food politics this critique of the ideology of nutritionism both emerges from and resonates with growing consumer ire at the food industry. For Pollan and his readers, nutritionism's most troubling effect has been to obscure the distinctions between food and what has come to pass as food by nature of its nutrient profile. Pollan describes a partnership between nutrition science and the food industry—the Nutrition Industrial Complex—that with the help of government legislation has, since the 1970s, transformed the food supply to reflect the ideological core of nutritionism; that food is nothing more than the sum of its nutrients.[44] In this context, he claims, "fake foods" have come to seem even more nutritious than "the real thing"[45] But according to Pollan impressive nutritional labels on fake foods don't add up to good diets. Ultimately, he argues, nutritionism fails to deliver because it does not properly account for the complexity of food, diets, or health.

Although this critique of nutritionism has to some extent been incorporated into the larger politics of the alternative food movement in the United States, the constructionist view of nutrition and dietary health that it represents has not been extended to other scientific claims about dietary health, particularly those related to obesity. Despite his criticism of nutritionism, for example, Pollan takes science based claims about obesity at face value, often using the fact of obesity to buttress his critique of the Nutrition Industrial Complex. Obesity registers as an objective fact among those who are fighting for better school lunches and access to farm fresh produce in "food deserts" based on the argument that such moves may help to mitigate the obesity epidemic in addition to securing a more sustainable food system and better tasting food. Food activists tend to share the dominant view of obesity as a killer disease and a rapidly growing threat to the health of individuals, the stability of the economy, the welfare of the nation.

This established view of obesity is grounded in part in a mythologized sense of the history of obesity that erases the complexity of the way in which obesity emerged as a cultural and medical preoccupation through a complex process that began at least a century ago. At the same time, the dominant historical narrative also obscures scientific debates about the etiology of obesity, and its relationship to morbidity and mortality, and replaces it with a simplistic image of an ever-growing danger to both individual health and the welfare of the nation. As Eric Oliver argues, this view was constructed and popularized in part by a series of maps that were originally released in 1989 by the Center for Disease Control and have been regularly updated and widely reproduced. The maps use different colors—from cool blues to alarming reds—to show rising rates of obesity and overweight in each state, with gradually darkening hues suggesting an ever-growing menace since 1985. Presented in a PowerPoint format the maps animate a lifeless set of data about statistical change over time and have convinced people, as Eric Oliver points out, that obesity is "infecting the population with virus-like speed."[46] Though the relationship between weight and health is fact a contested one the slides have worked in conjunction other medical, scientific, government, and media representations to secure a set of shared cultural convictions about obesity that remain largely unquestioned within current conversations about the politics of food.[47]

Using some of the same tools and premises as critical nutrition studies, however, the growing field of fat studies offers a more constructionist perspective on the history of dieting, body ideals, and the science of obesity. Fat studies scholars interrogate the factual basis of the obesity epidemic and reveal its political and ideological content. Many argue that the current obesity epidemic is in fact the result of moral panic that has been supported by questionable research and the manipulation of statistics.[48] Nonetheless, many of those people who are most invested in a critical reappraisal of contemporary eating habits not only take the fact of the obesity epidemic for granted but also use it as an alibi to legitimate their critique of the food system. As fat studies scholars and their allied fat activists would argue, however, they do so at the expense of fat people, who are vilified, marginalized, and oppressed by a supposedly beneficent effort to help them lead healthier lives.

Julie Guthman, for example, points out that when food activists decry the effects of the industrial food system on the nation's health, they tend to characterize fat people as dupes of the food system. This mindless consumption of bad food is set against the enlightened ethical eating of informed, thoughtful food activists, constructing a moral hierarchy that ultimately constrains the political possibilities of alternative food movement.[49] A critical nutrition studies that thinks broadly about the implications of what has become common sense about the relationship between food and health might make it possible to decouple critical thinking about the food system from unquestioning acceptance of obesity discourse, allowing for a more inclusive and productive food politics.

The tendency for contemporary food politics to rely on mythologized histories is also evident in the romantic sense of the past that pervades the movement. Pollan's injunction not to "eat anything your great-grandmother wouldn't recognize as food" invokes a more wholesome past.[50] Historian Rachel Laudan suggests that a mythologized history of food and health that relies on easy dichotomies between past and present, good and bad, natural and artificial may suit today's climate of food politics but obscures many of the reasons our food system has come to look as it does.[51]

The current critique of the industrial food system, legitimated by a simplistic view of history, has resulted in an exceedingly polarized debate about the future of food that pits the agri-food industry squarely against the interests of vulnerable consumers and the "real" food that they deserve. Consumers feel duped and threatened but cautiously optimistic that "voting with their forks" can lead to a major overhaul of a food system that does not share their interests. Food scientists and manufacturers feel unfairly vilified by the very people in whose interest they work but whose concerns and aspirations seem irrational and unrealistic.[52] A robust critical nutrition studies that illuminates the complex interplay of forces that have shaped both our food system and our beliefs about food and health may, however, offer a way toward a more productive common ground.

The insights of critical nutrition studies demand that we rethink many of our fundamental assumptions about dietary health in the context of contemporary food politics. By illuminating the moral content of dietary ideals and showing how discourses of a "good diet" create and uphold moral social hierarchies this work also gives us the tools that we need to think critically about dietary reform itself. The bad eaters in today's food politics are much like those in the other eras I have studied; by and large people of color and the poor whose behaviors are already considered threatening to the established social order and whose bad eating habits seem consistent with a general penchant for dangerous, deviant ways.[53] Pollan and Waters's injunctions to support an alternative food system by paying more for local and organic foods and spending more time growing, preparing, and savoring "real" food have incited charges of elitism among critics.[54] But critical nutrition studies suggests a far deeper set of concerns about these dietary ideals. It may not be possible to have dietary ideals that do not also express social ideals, but if we are going advocate for a more ethical food system we ought to take very seriously the politics—and ethics—of how we define good diets and good eaters. This same awareness will also ideally pervade the emerging Food Justice movement. As activist reorient the process of dietary reform around issues of access and equitability and engages underserved communities in the reform process critical dietary studies will ideally contribute to an acute awareness of the kind of power that is inherent in defining what is good to eat.[55]

Critical Dietary Literacy

Outside of the realm of alternative food politics, critical nutrition studies can and should also play a role in preparing food consumers to navigate an increasingly complex landscape of food and health. Grocery store aisles are packed with products that have been engineered and reformulated to promote health, and the food industry is preparing for, and creating, a future in which the kitchen cabinet will function more and more like a medicine cabinet. Products such as probiotic fruit juices and cholesterol lowering corn chips and novel health claims such as "antioxidant rich," "excellent source of omega-3 DHA," and "containing plant sterols" are altering the landscape of eating right. These food products—sometimes referred to as functional foods or neutraceuticals and always bearing health claims—are creating what some characterize as a much needed boost to food industry profits and others depict as a poorly regulated "wild west" for food consumers.[56] Critical nutrition studies is beginning to provide us with the tools to think through the ideological aspects of how health is being defined and capitalized on in these new market categories as well as the social, moral, political, economic, and even agricultural consequences. But there is much more work to be done here and elsewhere in our current food landscape to identify and deconstruct the assumptions about food and health that prevent us from clearly perceiving the values, beliefs, and ideologies that define dietary health, good food and what it means to "eat right."

Critical nutrition studies can contribute to a new set of competencies that would enable people to better analyze, evaluate, and create messages related to dietary health. Like media literacy, critical dietary literacy would expand our sense of literacy by treating dietary reform, dietary ideals, and conversations about dietary health as texts that require analysis. Ultimately, critical dietary literacy education would provide tools to help people examine assumptions about the relationship between food and health, think critically about the meaning of eating right, explore how structural factors such as funding models and industry interests influence public information, understand the framing of dietary problems in terms of social and individual responsibility, and analyze numbers, facts, and ideals as cultural, political, ideological. Beyond labels, health claims, nutrition facts and dietary advice, we need a new literacy through which to envision our world of "eating right" transformed by a collective rethinking of the common sense of dietary health.

Notes

1. Many thanks to the readers whose feedback has influenced this essay, especially the members of the University of California Studies of Food and the Body Multi Campus Research Program.

2. Charlotte Biltekoff, *Eating Right in America: Food, Health and Citizenship from Domestic Science to Obesity* (Durham: Duke University Press, forthcoming).

3. Harvey Levenstein, *Revolution at the Table: The Transformation of the American Diet* (New York: Oxford University Press, 1988), 46; John Coveney, *Food, Morals, and Meaning: The Pleasure and Anxiety of Eating* (New York: Routledge, 2000), 60.

4. Coveney, *Food, Morals, and Meaning*, 53–56; Nick Cullather, "The Foreign Policy of the Calorie," *American Historical Review* 112, no. 2 (2007): 342.

5. Harmke Kamminga, "Nutrition for the People," in *The Science and Culture of Nutrition, 1840–1940*, ed. Harmke Kamminga and Andrew Cunningham (Amsterdam: Rodopi, 1995).

6. Charles E. Rosenberg, *No Other Gods: On Science and American Social Thought* (Baltimore, MD: Johns Hopkins University Press, 1961), 6.

7. Robert Crawford, "Health as Meaningful Social Practice," *Health: An Interdisciplinary Journal for the Social Study of Health, Medicine, and Illness* 10, no. 4 (October 2006): 401–20.

8. Marion Nestle, *Food Politics: How the Food Industry Influences Nutrition and Health* (Berkeley: University of California Press, 2002); Harvey Levenstein, *Paradox of Plenty: A Social History of Eating in Modern America* (New York: Oxford University Press, 1993).

9. Levenstein, *Revolution at the Table*, 72–85.

10. Coveney, *Food, Morals, and Meaning*, 60; Levenstein, *Paradox of Plenty*, 46–49.

11. Wilbur O. Atwater, "Pecuniary Economy of Food: The Chemistry of Foods and Nutrition V," *The Century Illustrated Monthly Magazine* (November 1887 to April 1888): 445.

12. Levenstein, *Revolution at the Table*, 44–60; Ellen Richards, ed., *The Rumford Kitchen Leaflets: Plain Words About Food* (Boston: Rockwell and Churchill Press, 1899).

13. Elmer Verner McCollum, *The Knewer Knowledge of Nurition* (New York: Macmillan, 1918).

14. Levenstein, *Revolution at the Table*, 148.

15. Ibid, 150–56.

16. Food and Nutrition Board Committee on Diagnosis and Pathology of Nutritional Deficiencies, "Inadequate Diets and Nutritional Deficiencies in the United States: Their Prevalence and Significance," in *Bulletin of the National Research Council Number 109* (Washington, D.C.: National Research Council, National Academy of Sciences, 1943), 13.

17. David Mark Hegsted, "Recollections of Pioneers in Nutrition: Fifty Years in Nutrition," *Journal of the American College of Nutrition* 9, no. 4 (August 1990): 280–87.

18. Nestle, *Food Politics*, 39.

19. Warren Belasco, *Appetite for Change: How the Counter Culture Took on the Food Industry, 1966–1988* (Ithaca, NY: Cornell University Press, 1989), 174–76.

20. Nestle, *Food Politics*, 39.

21. Ibid, 38–50.

22. Among fat acceptance activists and fat studies scholars who challenge the factual premise of the so-called obesity epidemic and critique the negative social effects

of antiobesity discourse, "obesity" is a contested term. It is understood to medicalize a form of human diversity and do violence to fat people and it is therefore usually avoided or placed in scare quotes. Though I see critical nutrition studies as an ally to fat studies and share the concerns of those who problematize the term "obesity" I use it here without scare quotes in order to be consistent with the discourses I aim to represent.

23. "Overeating Laid to U.S.," *New York Times*, April 4, 1950.

24. "Overeating Called 'Compulsive'; Diet Held Only Way to Reduce," *New York Times*, October 21, 1950.

25. Ali H. Mokdad, et al., "The Spread of the Obesity Epidemic in the United States," *Journal of the American Medical Association* 282, no. 16 (October 1999): 1519–22.

26. U.S. Department of Health and Human Services, "The Surgeon General's Call to Action to Prevent and Decrease Overweight and Obesity" (Rockland, MD: U.S. Department of Health and Human Services, Public Health Service, Office of the Surgeon General, 2001).

27. Belasco, *Appetite for Change*, 4.

28. Elmer Verner McCollum, *A History of Nutrition: The Sequence of Ideas in Nutrition Investigations* (Boston: Houghton Mifflin 1957), 421.

29. Deanna L. Pucciarelli, "Early History and Evolution of Nutrition Science in the United States of America," *Family & Consumer Sciences Research Journal* 38, no. 2 (2009): 119–20.

30. Vivek Bammi, "Nutrition, the Historian, and Public Policy: A Case Study of U.S National Nutrition Policy in the 20th Century," *Journal of Social History* 14, no. 4 (1980): 627.

31. Robert Fogel and Stanley Engerman, *Time on the Cross: The Economics of Negro Slavery* (Boston: Little, Brown, 1974), 114–15, 261.

32. Thomas McKeown, *The Modern Rise of Population* (New York: Academic Press, 1976).

33. Victoria E. Bonnell and Lynn Hunt, eds., *Beyond the Cultural Turn: New Directions in the Study of Society and Culture* (Berkeley: University of California Press, 1999), 2.

34. Harmke Kamminga and Andrew Cunningham, "Introduction: The Science and Culture of Nutrition, 1840–1940," in *The Science and Culture of Nutrition*, 1.

35. Levenstein, *Revolution at the Table*; idem, *Paradox of Plenty.*

36. Michel Foucault, *Discipline and Punish: The Birth of the Prison* (New York: Vintage Press, 1979); idem, *The History of Sexuality: An Introduction Volume I*, trans. Robert Hurley (New York: Vintage Books, 1978); idem, *Power/Knowledge: Selected Interviews and Other Writings, 1972–1977* (New York: Pantheon, 1980).

37. Examples of influential work in Science and Technology Studies include, Ira H. Carmen, *Politics in the Laboratory: The Constitution of Human Genomics* (Madison: University of Wisconsin Press, 2004); Donna Haraway, *Primate Visions: Gender, Race, and Nature in the World of Modern Science* (New York: Routledge, 1989); Bruno Latour, *Science in Action: How to Follow Scientists and Engineers through Society* (Cambridge, MA: Harvard University Press, 1987).

38. Deborah Lupton, *Food, the Body and the Self* (London: Sage Publications, 1996), 6, 72, 73.

39. Coveney, *Food, Morals, and Meaning*, 1.

40. Cullather, "Foreign Policy," 338, 339.

41. Gyorgy Scrinis, "On the Ideology of Nutritionism," *Gastronomica* 8, no. 1 (2008): 39–48.

42. Jessica Mudry, *Measured Meals: Nutrition in America* (Albany: State University of New York Press, 2009), 18.

43. Michael Pollan, *In Defense of Food: An Eater's Manifesto* (New York: Penguin Press, 2008); Micheal Pollan, "Unhappy Meals," *New York Times*, January 28, 2007.

44. Pollan, *In Defense of Food*, 8, 32–34.

45. Ibid, 32.

46. Eric J. Oliver, *Fat Politics: The Real Story Behind America's Obesity Epidemic* (New York: Oxford University Press, 2006), 41–42.

47. For more on how the central claims of the obesity epidemic are contested ones: Paul Campos, *The Obesity Myth: Why America's Obsession with Weight Is Hazardous to Your Health* (New York: Gotham Books, 2004); Glenn A. Gaesser, *Big Fat Lies: The Truth About Your Weight and Your Health* (Carlsbad, California: Gurze, 2002); Michael Gard and Jan Wright, *The Obesity Epidemic: Science, Morality and Ideology* (London and New York: Routledge, 2005).

48. Paul Campos, et al., "The Epidemiology of Overweight and Obesity: Public Health Crisis or Moral Panic?," *International Journal of Epidemiology* 35, no. 1 (February 2006): 55–60; Kathleen LeBesco, *Revolting Bodies?: The Struggle to Redefine Fat Identity* (Amherst: University of Massachusetts Press, 2004); Gard and Wright, *The Obesity Epidemic.*

49. Julie Guthman, "Can't Stomach It: How Micheal Pollan et al. Made Me Want to Eat Cheetos," *Gastronomica* 7, no. 3 (Summer 2007): 75–79; idem, "Fast Food/Organic Food: Reflexive Tastes and the Making of 'Yuppie Chow,'" *Social and Cultural Geography* 4, no. 1 (2003): 45–58.

50. Pollan, *In Defense of Food*, 148–9.

51. Rachel Lauden, "A Plea for Culinary Modernism: Why We Should Love New, Fast, Processed Food," *Gastronomica* 1, no. 1 (2001): 36–44.

52. Eric A. Decker, "The Evolution of Processed Foods: Implications for the Food Scientist," in *Annual Meeting of the Institute of Food Scientists* (Anaheim, CA: Resourceful Recordings, 2009); Sally Squire, "Processed Food: Moving from Bad to Better in the News Media," in ibid; Robert E Bracket, "Implications for the Food Industry: The Evolution of Processed Foods and the Implications for Food Science," in ibid.

53. Biltekoff, *Eating Right in America.*

54. Ken Kelley, "Alice Waters," Mother Jones, [Online]. Available: http://www.motherjones.com/mother_jones/jf95/kelley.html. [February 21, 2011]. "Nurturing Connections with Farmers: An Interview with Alice Waters," *In Season* 1997. "Alice Waters' Crusade for Better Food," in *60 Minutes* (2009).

55. Patricia Allen, "Mining for Justice in the Food System: Perceptions, Practices, and Possibilities," *Agriculture and Human Values* 25, no. 2 (2008): 157–61.

56. Industry growth perspective: Peter Leighton, "Selling Wellness Leads to Greener Pastures," *Functional Ingredients*, November 1, 2002. Unregulated "wild west" perspective: Mark Lawrence and Mike Rayner, "Functional Foods and Health Claims: A Public Health Policy Perspective" *Public Health Nutrition* 1, no. 2 (1998): 75–82.

Bibliography

Biltekoff, Charlotte. *Eating Right in America: Food, Health and Citizenship from Domestic Science to Obesity.* Durham: Duke University Press, forthcoming.

Campos, Paul. *The Obesity Myth: Why America's Obsession with Weight Is Hazardous to Your Health*. New York: Gotham Books, 2004.
Coveney, John. *Food, Morals, and Meaning: The Pleasure and Anxiety of Eating*. New York: Routledge, 2000.
Crawford, Robert. "Health as Meaningful Social Practice." *Health: An Interdisciplinary Journal for the Social Study of Health, Medicine, and Illness* 10, no. 4 (2006): 401–20.
Cullather, Nick. "The Foreign Policy of the Calorie." *American Historical Review* 112, no. 2 (2007): 337–64.
Gard, Michael, and Jan Wright. *The Obesity Epidemic: Science, Morality and Ideology*. London: Routledge, 2005.
Kamminga, Harmke, and Andrew Cunningham, eds. *The Science and Culture of Nutrition, 1840–1940*. Amsterdam: Rodopi, 1995.
LeBesco, Kathleen. *Revolting Bodies? The Struggle to Redefine Fat Identity*. Amherst: University of Massachusetts Press, 2004.
Levenstein, Harvey. *Revolution at the Table: The Transformation of the American Diet*. New York: Oxford University Press, 1988.
Lupton, Deborah. *Food, the Body and the Self*. London: Sage Publications, 1996.
Mudry, Jessica. *Measured Meals: Nutrition in America*. Albany: State University of New York Press, 2009.
Scrinis, Gyorgy. "On the Ideology of Nutritionism." *Gastronomic* 8, no. 1 (2008): 39–48.

CHAPTER 11

TEACHING WITH FOOD

JONATHAN DEUTSCH AND
JEFFREY MILLER

SIFTING through about 1,000 pages of food syllabi and assignments from the past decade in the form of three editions of *Teaching Food: Agriculture, Food, and Society Syllabi and Course Materials Collection* from 2000, 2003, and 2010, colloquially known as the ASFS Syllabi Set, the reader cannot help but discern that the academic study of food, as it is practiced in the classroom, is a monkish fast, or perhaps a convoluted weight loss strategy (read Eric Schlosser's *Fast Food Nation*, discuss, lose appetite). This proliferation of instructional materials reveals that although food studies is thriving on campuses across North America, professors teach it, by and large, the way they teach most anything in the humanities and social sciences—by having students read about the subject outside of class, discuss it in class, and write about it in term papers and projects. Some food history classes incorporate actual food; many more do not, although some instructors may prefer not to mention their use of food in a document that will be forwarded to the dean and accreditors. Indeed, some syllabi go so far as to *prohibit* the presence of food in the food studies classroom, usually with a cut-and-paste policy explaining that the classroom space is in a library, "smart" classroom, or shiny new facility where food and drink are not allowed. Whether the professor or students note the irony we can only guess.

There are, of course, many exceptions to this pervasive words-only pedagogy. The best of these, we argue, use food not only as a subject for inquiry but also as a uniquely multisensory tool with which to investigate history, culture, and society. In this chapter we identify three levels of engagement with food in the classroom:

as a *lens* to explore diverse social and cultural issues, as a *topic* worthy of study in its own right, and as the physical *material* for academic inquiry and learning. Perusal of the ASFS Syllabi Set shows food being used in all three ways, from an illustrative point in a lecture to full-on engagement in a teaching kitchen, although the latter is decidedly the exception. These diverse approaches to food are matched by a wide range of disciplines in which food matters, running across the academic spectrum from history, philosophy, anthropology, geography, and sociology to gender studies and performance studies. In this chapter, we conflate the terms *food studies* and *food history* because of the multidisciplinary and interdisciplinary perspectives taken by food historians, both as scholars and teachers, in their approaches to sources and methods.

We would also like to emphasize that this chapter represents a collective effort—in writing syllabi, assignments, and pedagogical essays—by members of two established professional societies in the field of food studies. The Association for the Study of Food and Society (ASFS), founded in 1987, promotes interdisciplinary study in the field and publishes the journal *Food, Culture, & Society.* Since 1992, ASFS has been holding its annual meeting together with the Agriculture, Food and Human Values Society (AFHVS), which focuses more on agriculture and rural studies, and publishes the journal *Agriculture and Human Values.* Although centered largely in North America, both organizations have members on six continents. As editors of the 2010 (Miller) and 2003 (Deutsch) ASFS Syllabi Set, we have worked closely with these materials and reviewed the documents from all three editions again in the preparation of this chapter. We considered the syllabi and assignments as a data set and separately analyzed them, looking for themes as well as notable cases using a qualitative content analysis.[1]

Another point that we have observed is that food is largely a student-driven field, which has consequences for the ways that it is taught. Some of the reasons for student interest, and possibly for faculty's reluctance to use food directly, can be discerned from Paul Rozin's formative article showing food to be "Fundamental, Fun, Frightening and Far-Reaching."[2] Food is first of all an essential source of sustenance, and yet words are the currency of academe. Words record productive thinking and teaching—food is ephemeral. Second, food is fun, and students may sign up for a food history class as a moment of respite from weightier classes. For those same reasons, scholars who research or teach about food may risk trivialization by their colleagues and by hiring or tenure and promotion committees at some institutions. Third, food is frightening, and while undergraduates may feel a rush of excitement, the thought of allergens, knives, microbes, and boiling oil in the classroom is enough to send the most innovative higher education administrator cowering under the desk. Finally, the big secret: most professors talk better than they cook. While most food history professors rarely worry about their mastery of the Columbian exchange, they may feel out of their element leading the class through a cooking demonstration or exercise. Many are self-conscious about their own cooking—the assumption being that a scholar of food is surely a masterful cook. Do people assume art historians are great artists? Despite these reservations, food can enrich the educational experience as an analytical lens, as a valuable topic, and as a lively material.

Food as a Lens to Study Other Topics

Perhaps the most common place for food in the classroom, used at some point or other by virtually every instructor in the ASFS Syllabi Set, is as an example to illustrate points of interest, say, the decline of the Roman Empire as reflected by the vulgar feast of Petronius's *Satyricon*. At a more sophisticated level, the study of food can become an analytical lens, for example, an autoethnography of Thanksgiving dinner (a very popular assignment during fall semester in the United States and Canada). Such a project can serve many different ends—to examine gender and family dynamics in sociology, to ground the analysis of ritual in religious studies, or to stimulate discussion of nostalgia in American history. The attractions of such a pedagogical approach are obvious. Because each of us has a relationship with food—the same cannot be said for many other historical subjects, for example, military history—our own experiences with food may be starting points for explorations of complex topics—labor, globalization, nostalgia, ethnic identity, gender, and the family, to name a few. Yet ultimately, the rhythm of these classes is generally marked by shared discussions and outside reading and writing rather than by the sharing of actual foods.

As a glance through the table of contents of this handbook will reveal, there are many places where food is central to existing historical narratives, just as many analytical themes that can profitably be approached through food. The so-called "Neolithic revolution" and the rise of agriculture, the Columbian exchange and the intensification of early modern globalization, and the modern industrial era all entailed new methods of food production. In a similar fashion, the rise of nations and empires, the construction of racial and ethnic identities, and religious beliefs all hinge to a degree on shared or differentiated food consumption. As a result, college teachers have developed a wide range of assignments that use food as a prism to help students examine their own lives, explore the complex structures needed provision to modern world, and experience the different communities that make up our multicultural society.

Of the diverse assignments contained within the ASFS Syllabi Set, perhaps the greatest number rely on expressions of what Annie Hauck-Lawson calls the "food voice." There are many research strategies for interpreting personal identities and social relations through the ways people talk about food, whether in oral histories, interviews, ethnographies, or *charlas culinarias* ("kitchen chats"). In a similar fashion, the food voice offers a powerful medium for expressing individual perspectives on a range of issues, particularly for students who might otherwise feel reluctant to engage in class discussions. For example, in a religious studies class,

Commonly Used Classroom Activities Related to Food

Activity	Description	Sample Concepts Taught
Food Logs	Students record everything they eat over a set time period, usually three days, including two weekdays and one weekend day, a variation on nutrition's three-day dietary recall. Often notes regarding the social context in which the food is consumed (running to class, drinking beers with friends) are included alongside recorded foods.	Core versus peripheral foods, pervasiveness of some ingredients (corn, soy) in food system, deliberate versus "mindless" eating, influence of social group and mores on food choices, individual responses to common food environments.
Participant Observation in a Food Setting	Students conduct an ethnographic participant observation in a food-centric setting such as a farmers' market, full-service restaurant, fast food restaurant, cafeteria, or supermarket.	Ethnographic methods, consumers in relation to the food environment, the "third place," conventional and alternative food systems, health messaging in food environments
Commodity Chain Analysis	A single commodity (tomatoes, soybean oil, pork belly) or ingredients comprising a consumer packaged food (yogurt, tortillas, boxed macaroni and cheese) is traced from farm to retailer. Often two versions of the same product—one conventionally produced and one "ethically" produced are compared.	Food miles, conventional and alternative food systems, food marketing, consumer perceptions of health and nutrition, transparency and traceability in the food system, labor, globalization, food safety
Interview or Oral History	Students interview an ancestor regarding his/her past food habits and how foods and the food system have changed over time.	Nostalgia, changes in conventional and alternative food system, food and ethnic/cultural identity, food and memory
Personal Essays/Remembrances	Students write essays about meaningful foods from their childhood or remembrances of foods with which they hold strong associations.	Food and memory, food and identity, nostalgia, influence of food on self.

(Continued)

Activity	Description	Sample Concepts Taught
Cooking Food of a Particular Ethnic Group for Class	Students prepare a recipe from a particular cultural or subcultural group (usually not their own) and share information about the culture, tastes, and the recipe with the class	Cultural foods, cookery, comparative cultural foods, availability of ingredients, migration of food and people
Interview with Food Worker	Students interview a food worker such as a farmer, winemaker, artisan producer, or cook	Labor, conventional and alternative food systems, craft, food policy in practice
Ad Analysis	Students watch television ads or record food messaging they receive in their daily lives and perform a content analysis.	Food/health environment, food and media, policy, messaging
Service Learning	Students volunteer in food-related enterprise such as soup kitchen, health/nutrition awareness campaign or food bank.	Food policy in action, labor, conventional and alternative food systems, public health nutrition

Corrie Norman asked students to write down a food-based memory and then to interpret the memories of their classmates as a "cosmology," a particular form of creation story (which is often centered on food, such as Eve's apple) that serves to orient our lives by explaining who we are and why we are here. These memories often juxtaposed a sacred time of ritual family meals with the profane of everyday fast food.[3] Another project, developed by Lynn Walter, asked students to interview members of a food community, whether a community garden, restaurant, or soup kitchen. Such assignments encourage students to become more aware of the source of their food and the labor involved in producing it. Moreover, if preserved in an archival repository (such as the Southern Foodways Alliance online Oral History Project),[4] these interviews can provide a valuable primary source for future historians and students alike. In summary, many teachers have found that tapping into the food voice allows them to teach content more effectively by giving concrete expression to abstract concepts.

Sample Assignment: Interviews with Members of the Food Community

For at least one part of your term paper, you will conduct an interview with someone whose work involves your issue in a practical way. For example, you might interview a local farmer who is using sustainable agricultural practices; a restaurateur, community gardener, or grocer serving specific populations underserved by the predominant forms; someone involved in the development or promotion of new food products; people directing food banks or soup kitchens; leaders of community organizations addressing your issue; and so forth. Turn in a typed transcript of your interview with the paper in which you use the information from the interview.

Exercise from Lynn Walter—University of Wisconsin, Green Bay

One highly abstract system in particular, global capitalism, can be usefully studied through commodity chains analysis, which links the production and consumption of foods. Sidney Mintz's classic history of sugar, for example, is ubiquitous across the ASFS Syllabi Set. Another work, Deborah Barndt's study of the North American "tomato trail," reveals how the corporate pursuit of "flexible production" has marginalized and impoverished women on both ends of the supply chain, from migrant farm workers in Mexico to part-time cashiers in Canada.[5] Students can research these linkages for themselves by picking a particular food and following it around the world. A class project by David Fletcher at the California College of the Arts mapped out the "tacoshed," the area of land used to provision a San Francisco taco truck. In the process, students learned about the difficulty of calculating the environmental impact of food production.[6] Perhaps the most eye-opening lesson of such an assignment is just how difficult the research can be and how hard corporations work to cover their tracks.

Another place where food can provide an effective learning tool is in students' encounters with foreign cultures. Many young people find food so interesting precisely because of its potential for exoticism, hence the popularity of television shows such as Andrew Zimmern's *Bizarre Foods.* Philosopher Lisa Heldke has explained how these forms of culinary adventuring, whether in person or through virtual media, create the image that others are radically different from, and inferior to, ourselves. She encourages us to challenge the colonial power relations that are perpetuated by the pursuit of "authentic" folk foods as a resource to be extracted, refined, and profited from by chef-artists and corporations in the west.[7] Folklorist Lucy M. Long has also written about the pedagogical challenges of using food to explore ethnic boundaries, for example, through the many variants of chili served across the United States.[8] In her "ethnic market report," Deanna Pucciarelli encourages students to go shopping at an ethnic grocery or attend a cultural event and thereby become acquainted with foreign foods, thus rendering them less exotic to students.

Sample Assignment: Ethnic Market Report

Visit a local ethnic market [not of your background] or cultural event and write a two-page report describing your visit. Include in the report the date of the visit, location, culture represented; compare and contrast the market or event to a market or event that you usually frequent, what you learned, and how you could use it in your future career. If visiting a market, select three items you are not familiar with and ask the sales clerk (or farmer's market vendor) how the ingredients are typically used; include the information from the sales clerk.

Exercise from Deanna Pucciarelli—Ball State University

Food as a Topic

Whether food should be studied and taught as a subject in its own right or as a means to understand other subjects is a perennial point of discussion among scholars in the field, most notably, on the ASFS listserv; contributors generally conclude that the answer is both. Readers of this handbook may need little convincing of the importance of studying food, yet it is worthwhile to review some of the arguments for making food history a standard part of the curriculum. First, the production of food constituted the livelihood of most people in pre-industrial societies, particularly women, workers, and slaves; food can thus help ground an inclusive history that values their accomplishments. Second, the culture and symbolism of food provide rich texture to our understanding of past societies, whether among the elites who had a choice of what to eat or among those who often went without, and therefore valued food all the more. Third, studying the past can help students understand and improve contemporary social movements that center around food. By recognizing important pedagogical goals, we can begin to develop methods for teaching them most effectively.

Food matters first of all because its production and consumption was so central to everyday life. Before the industrial era, growing and processing food was the principal source of employment for the vast majority of all people. Although the gendered division of labor varied widely between societies, the intensely physical tasks of gathering, preparing, preserving, and sharing food were very much the fabric of daily life. These activities also connected rural people intimately to the natural world. That we have so little knowledge of this labor reflects the success of the food processing industry in its continual quest to add "value"—and raise prices—by distancing consumers from the source of their food, transforming our very understanding of chicken from a living being with feet and feathers into cellophane-wrapped parts, or better still, nondescript "nuggets."[9] Consumption, too, has changed dramatically in the western world in the last few centuries. With the advent of electronic-age cocooning, microwavable processed foods, and the ubiquitous drive-up window, eating has become a more solitary experience—something that was rarely the case in times past.

Beyond the foundations of subsistence, there is a cultural value to food that equally merits attention. Paul Freedman has noted the paradox that although historical diets and living standards have been central to professional research and teaching for half a century, the aesthetics and symbolism of food as recorded in menus and gastronomic literature were considered frivolous and elitist until quite recently.[10] By contrast, anthropologists at least since Mary Douglas have examined culinary tastes as a window for understanding some of the fundamental values of societies, and cultural historians have begun to follow their example. As Cathy Kaufman observed: "To understand ourselves, we should naturally begin with the food that constitutes the fabric of our existence. Yet every culture arrives at different solutions, uses different crops and cooking methods, and invents what amounts to a unique cuisine. These are to some extent predetermined by geography, technology, and a certain amount of luck. Nonetheless, every cuisine is a practical and artistic expression of the culture that created it. It embodies the values and aspirations of each society, its world outlook as well as its history."[11] By examining how people prepared food, studying what technologies they used to preserve it, understanding the patterns of commensality, and even trying to understand what food might have tasted like, we can get a much richer idea of the historical world we have lost.

Engaging with students' preexisting knowledge of food, particularly ideas based on the works of journalists and activists, offers yet another valuable focus in the classroom. Food has acquired a remarkable presence in contemporary public discourse. Students are often passionately engaged with local and sustainable movements, many have worked in restaurants or bakeries, and they may take a strong aesthetic interest in what they eat. Yet the even the most knowledgeable often have surprisingly little historical awareness. Modern food activists generally imagine a golden age of eating in the past that simply did not exist. Julie Guthman, Tracey Deutsch, and others have also observed that many of their political arguments focus on personal choices, often with a highly moralizing tone, that nonetheless do little to address wider economic and gender inequalities.[12] Helping students place their personal food politics in a broader historical and social perspective may actually contribute in the long run to a more democratic and sustainable food system.

To translate these goals into effective classroom practice, instructors face a number of important choices in sources, organization, and assignments. For textbooks, although there are now many excellent secondary works to choose from, broad surveys are often organized in idiosyncratic fashion.[13] This diversity of approaches is also reflected in historical monographs, which often take the form of biographies of individual commodities. For primary sources, translations of historical cookbooks have become increasingly available in print and online, yet there is still a need for a document reader that brings together a selection of the diverse types of sources used by historians of food and society. Meanwhile teachers have wide latitude for organizing the structure of the class, for there is little in the way of standard food history narrative to constrain them. Even the choice between a topical or chronological approach is open; in fact, instructors may prefer a combination of the two, using chronology to organize the premodern past while taking a topical approach for modern times. Some may paint the history of food in broad traditional strokes of politics, economy, society, and culture; a possible assignment for such a class might be the "famous domesticate presentation" created by Jeffrey Cole. Other instructors may prefer the example of social and gendered history to follow food into the domesticate sphere; oral history assignments employing the food voice might be more appropriate in this case. Yet whatever approaches that faculty take, we hope that they will be inspired to teach with and not just about food.

Sample Assignment: Famous Domesticate Presentation

You will be assigned a domesticated plant, such as the potato or tomato or sunflower, and asked to make a five-to-seven-minute class presentation. Your treatment should include a description of (1) the food's origins and domestication; (2) the spread of the food through migration, conquest, and trade; (3) common uses over time; and (4) a recipe for a dish containing the food. Be sure to make use of teaching aids. As a principal source, consult the *Cambridge World History of Food.* Recipes and supplemental information may be obtained elsewhere.

Exercise from Jeffrey Cole—Dowling College

Food as Material of Inquiry: The Ultimate Active Learning Tool

Research in education supports the idea that active learning strategies can have a strong impact on student learning.[14] The best active learning strategies tend to engage students in some type of activity that requires them to think about the activity in which they are engaging. Because food is multisensory—indeed, it is the only classroom medium we can think of that safely involves all five senses—students working with food have the opportunity to not only have their eyes and ears engaged, as they would when they discuss a text, for example, but their mouth, nose, and skin as well. Even beyond sensory perceptions, students may use physiological sensations related to food—hunger, satiety, queasiness, or salivation—to inform their experiences.

As has often been observed, everyone eats; therefore working with food both inside and outside of the classroom tends to readily engage students in the learning process. Already a century ago, John Dewey suggested that cooking is a powerful tool to get students to understand the reasons behind processes, thereby exposing them to experimental ways of thinking.[15] Food is a tool that is understood, and can be accessed, by every student in a classroom. The behaviors associated with food can illustrate the lessons of history at all levels, from the personal interactions of the smallest groups to the practices of entire populations. Further, because each of us eats and has strong memories, feelings, identifications, and viewpoints regarding various foodstuffs, food represents an important entry point or springboard to various concepts. Asking adult learners to start from their lived experiences in approaching new material is a cornerstone of adult education and culturally relevant curriculum.[16]

Yet despite its potential as an active learning tool, and of course its obvious relevance to food studies, food as a material seems not widely used in the classroom. While the ASFS Syllabi Set contains compelling examples of using food, one can flip through course after course, assignment after assignment with in-depth discussions of food the topic—reading about, talking about, writing about—with nary a mention of food the material—planting, harvesting, fishing, slaughtering, cleaning, cooking, smelling, tasting—as it relates to the class. This section considers some notable exceptions.

Even in the vast prairie lecture halls of the Big Ten, the strategic use of food can have a significant pedagogical impact. At the University of Illinois, anthropologist Martin Manalansan has begun his introductory class, Food, Culture, and Society, by handing out a fortune cookie to each of the 800 students who enrolled in a typical semester. Although a small bite, the cookie launched discussion of important themes such as the provenance of foods—since this quintessential "foreign" food was actually invented in the United States—as well as sexuality and exoticism. Coming on the first day, as an *amuse bouche* (pre-appetizer, literally "mouth amusement"), rather than as dessert at the end of the semester, it disrupted preconceived notions about the order of a meal and inspired students to think about the future of the class.

Likewise, at the University of Minnesota, Jeffrey Pilcher has hosted an "Aztec banquet" for students in his freshman world history survey. Rather than make hundreds of tamales (an undertaking better suited to the year-end holidays than a busy midsemester), he had students draw lots to determine their rank. A few lucky "nobles" feasted on tamales, while their "commoner" classmates got only a corn chip, thereby experiencing first-hand the inequalities of pre-Hispanic society. A kitchen-based variation of Pilcher's assignment challenges students to illustrate key concepts in food studies by preparing a menu around them. Faculty at the 2010 Association for the Study of Food and Society and Agriculture, Food and Human Values Society conference illustrated globalization, masculinities, and hegemony through cooking a course (appetizer, entrée, dessert) and asking their dinner companions to guess the theme, referencing clues on the plate and in the presentation.

One sample assignment that we find particularly compelling illustrates the pervasiveness of corn in the contemporary food system. While this topic is frequently taught across food studies courses, anthropologist Kelly Feltault's project allows the material to resonate for students. By restricting their access to all processed foods containing corn, Feltault uses the students' bodies as active learning laboratories not just to record data but also to have a multisensory and physiological connection that shows how difficult it has become to eat anything in America without this ubiquitous grain. This reflective piece invites a metacognitive understanding of the student experience.

Sample Assignment: Corn Food Challenge

After reading the units on Corn and Meat, go at least one week without eating any foods that contain corn in any form. So, that means no corn-fed beef or other meat, no corn tortilla chips or corn flakes, and most importantly NO corn syrup (processed foods, soda, juice, fast food, etc.). You must read labels and consider what you eat in restaurants for this challenge. Keep track in your Food Diary of what you eat, but also what you cannot eat that you normally do eat. Make notes of how you feel physically and otherwise in your Food Diary, and how difficult it is to not eat corn. Write a three-page paper describing how your diet changed and what difficulties you faced making this change; describe any physical or other changes you experienced; estimate how much corn is normally in your diet in a week. Discuss either the moral, cultural, or political economy of your corn-eating habit.

Exercise from Kelly Feltault—American University

Food history in particular is well suited for this kind of inquiry to promote heightened understanding by preparing and eating food. In a course on hunger the absence of food is logical, but fasting for a day and paying attention to cravings may help students understand first hand the paradox of obesity in food insecure households, or to relate more closely to those for whom a fast was both involuntary and multiday. On the other hand, it is possible to experience the possibilities and limitations of past cooking technologies through living history sites. With period technology, either antiques or reproductions, students can learn an entirely different method of cooking, such as manipulating the distance between the food and the fire rather than simply raising or lowering the heat with a turn of a knob as one would do these days. In his "Neolithic baking" project, Miller shows that with ingenuity and access to a kitchen, students can undertake quite elaborate "experiments" in historical cooking.

Sample Assignment: Neolithic Bakers

For this exercise you will need to access to a kitchen. No specialized equipment is required other than a way to grind grain. Ideally you can get access to some kind of stone grinder or metate, but a modern grain mill is fine, and in a pinch flour can be made in blender or food processor.

Purchase bulk grains at your local health food store or grocer with an extensive bulk foods section. Many stores now carry so-called "ancient grains" like teff, quinoa, faro, amaranth, spelt, and so forth, which add an aura to this activity. Have the students grind the grain into flours. This is a good place for a discussion on historical and modern technologies as students attempt to produce smooth flour out of whole grain. Allow them to play with blends if you desire. A discussion of proteins in flours and how they contribute to gluten development (and which ones do not) is also useful here. Once students have their flour ground, have them make dough by adding water and then shape small flat breads by hand. An upside down cast-iron skillet with a smooth bottom makes an excellent stand in for a hot rock, though for added authenticity, you could take your dough outside to a firepit and try that too. Have the students cook their flat bread on the heated skillet bottom. For contrast, you can have one group make bread with some type of leavener so students can see textural differences between the two styles.

There are many variants of products you can use in conjunction with this exercise. You might begin by attempting to capture wild yeast. This is an excellent exercise for helping students understand what has gone into the production of bread in history.

Exercise from Jeffrey Miller—Colorado State University

Another important lesson to be drawn from these hands-on activities lies in understanding the distance between written and oral cultures and filling in the silences in recipes. Historical recipes appear quite vague compared with the specific instructions contained in modern cookbooks. Authors assumed a degree of skill and basic cultural knowledge on the part of their readers, which made more detailed recipes unnecessary. Moreover, even illiterate cooks approached their task with an experimental attitude, constantly adjusting the recipe to adapt to the particular nature of the ingredients at hand. Cooks also paid attention to a wider range of sensory inputs than are accessible in a microwave oven; they felt, watched, listened, smelled, and of course tasted food as it cooked. Lynn Houston captures the improvisation involved in premodern cooking by asking students to cook a recipe from a literary source, where instructions may be described in emotional rather than scientific terms. Students are forced to take the initiative and interpret an unknown culture, one of the basic skills that we seek to teach students.

Sample Assignment: Food in Literature

For this assignment you will have to make one of the recipes included in one of the novels we are reading. In your presentation, you will tell the class about that process and analyze the directions given for the recipe. How did the dish turn out? Were you able to make the dish just as it was written or were there steps left out? If the author left something out, what was it and how is that significant? Were any of the ingredients hard to find? You will also do research on the food/dish or ingredients required to make the dish.

Exercise from Lynn Houston—California State University, Chico

Food also can be a useful tool in activities outside the confines of the classroom. Student activities that involve food can range from visiting a bodega in the students' own neighborhood to study abroad trips. Interestingly, instructors who, per their syllabi, fast during seminars on campus do a lot of farming, cooking, and eating with students when on the road. This may have more to do with the practical aspects of filling long days of instruction on a multiday tour rather than a couple of hours per week on campus, but travel also seems to liberate professors and students into fully immersing themselves in the food of the region by visiting producers, getting to know agriculture by helping with a harvest, cooking alongside local chefs, and eating and drinking together in an engaged and thoughtful way that we can only wish was done in more classes at home.

To be sure, there is much to be learned from pedagogy of food that is based on the seminar or lecture and discussion. If nothing else, it is the way most of *us* learned history (food and otherwise), and the importance, ubiquity, and relevance of food as a topic—perhaps further enhanced by students bringing in tastes to illuminate readings and build commensality—can make for a compelling class. But working with food—growing, harvesting, preparing, tasting—can also be a multisensory epistemological tool. It is here that the greatest potential for innovative and meaningful use of food in and beyond the classroom lies.

A Note on Logistics

As a practical matter, while food can be an ideal method for teaching any number of concepts, it also has drawbacks that are legal, medical, logistical, and financial. Among the legal obstacles to using food in the classroom are the needs for institutional insurance against the risk of injury or food-borne illness. In the United States, students who might have an accident while handling food—incidents like cutting or burning themselves—are generally covered by the university's insurance as long as they are in a supervised setting such as a food lab or official classroom experience. Such an incident related to the normal educational process should be handled no differently from a sprained ankle in a physical education course. Of course, historians rarely have access to such laboratories, and bringing food products into the educational setting can be harder than you might imagine. For instance, at a growing number of primary schools in the United States, homemade food is no longer permitted on campus due to the potential for unknown food ingredients that may lead to allergic reactions.

Students who go to off-campus experiences are much less likely to be covered by an institution's insurance policy, especially if these are not highly organized excursions made in school vehicles to a pre-approved location. Students who want to learn about food in an off-campus kitchen, but who are not an employee of the company, say in an unofficial unpaid internship, need to have personal insurance, as the company's worker's compensation insurance will not cover them. If the internship is part of the college curriculum, the institution's insurance or the institution's policy of requiring students to have personal insurance usually covers most situations.

There are also considerable medical questions to consider. Allergens are perhaps the most persistent concerns in the classroom setting. In postsecondary education, there is a certain responsibility for the student to self-identify, although this is much less true in primary and secondary schools. As we noted earlier, cuts, burns, and falls would likely be covered by an institution's insurance in most settings, but just the fact that these types of things might happen are cause for extra caution. A maxim from many culinary programs can be useful when instructing students as they work with food: "Act like everything in the kitchen can cut you, burn you, or trip you up."

Cost is another important issue, for food is rarely free. Sometimes donations can be gotten, but this introduces another set of chores. Will you take up a collection (frowned on at most institutions); is there funding available in your departmental budget; can you collect a lab fee? Institutions rarely give a second thought about requiring the students to buy hundreds of dollars of textbooks for a course but do not allow students to contribute a nominal amount for food in the classroom.

The ideal space for working with food as a hands-on tool is a kitchen on the institution's campus or perhaps even a modern tasting laboratory complete with sensory evaluation booths. Nevertheless, the lack of such facilities need not keep you from working with food altogether. There are many exercises that can be done with prepared or raw foods, including tastings, sensory analysis, visual demonstrations, and associational exercises.

Conclusion

Food is a versatile, tactile, and accessible tool that has many uses in the history classroom. As Sidney Mintz says, "the drive for food is more powerful than the sex drive, but we don't pay attention to it, because we are fed three times a day."[17] Every student in the history classroom has a personal relationship with food. They are engaged with it constantly outside of the classroom and can relate to it at multiple levels. Food is a lingua franca that every student can understand at some level. Using this relationship as a way to connect a student to the lessons of history can provide an effective entrée (if you will excuse the pun) into many periods, topics, and approaches to the teaching of history. Regardless of the level at which an educator can introduce it in the classroom—as a lens for exploring topics and themes, as a topic in its own right, or as a medium for inquiry—food can be a most useful tool in the history teacher's toolbox.

Notes

1. See Margot Ely, et al., *Doing Qualitative Research: Circles within Circles* (Philadelphia: Falmer, 1991).
2. Paul Rozin, "Food Is Fundamental, Fun, Frightening and Far-Reaching," *Social Research* 66, no. 1 (1999): 9–30.
3. Corrie Norman, "Nostalgia for Origins in a Fast Food Culture: Teaching with the Food Memories of Carolina College Women," *Food, Culture & Society* 15, no. 2 (June 2012).
4. "Southern Foodways Oral History." [Online]. Available: http://www.southernfoodways.com/documentary/oh/index.html. [January 12, 2011].
5. Sidney W. Mintz, *Sweetness and Power: The Place of Sugar in Modern History* (New York: Viking, 1985); Deborah Barndt, ed., *Women Working the NAFTA Food Chain: Women, Food, and Globalization* (Toronto: Second Story Press, 1999).
6. "Tacoshed," [Online]. Available: http://rebargroup.org/doxa/2010/02/tacoshed/. [March 15, 2012].
7. Lisa Heldke, *Exotic Appetites: Ruminations of a Food Adventurer* (New York: Routledge, 2003), 48–59.
8. Lucy M. Long, "Nourishing the Academic Imagination: The Use of Food in Teaching the Concept of Culture," *Food and Foodways* 9, no. 3–4 (December 2001): 235–62.
9. Warren Belaso, *Food: The Key Concepts* (Oxford: Berg, 2009), 4.
10. Paul Freedman, "Introduction: A New History of Cuisine," in *Food: The History of Taste*, ed. Paul Freedman (Berkeley: University of California Press, 2007), 7.

11. Cathy K. Kaufman, *Cooking in Ancient Civilizations* (Westport, CT: Greenwood Press, 2006), xxv.

12. Julie Guthman, "Commentary on Teaching Food: Why I am Fed Up with Michael Pollan et al.," *Agriculture and Human Values* 24, no. 2 (June 2007): 261–54; Tracey Deutsch, "Memories of Mothers in the Kitchen: Local Foods, History, and Women's Work," *Radical History Review* 110 (Spring 2011): 167–77.

13. See, for example, Giovanni Rebora, *Culture of the Fork: A Brief History of Food in Europe*, trans. Albert Sonnenfeld (New York: Columbia University Press, 1998); Felipe Fernández Armesto, *Near a Thousand Tables: A History of Food* (New York: New Press, 2002); Kenneth F. Kiple, *A Movable Feast: Ten Millennia of Food Globalization* (Cambridge: Cambridge University Press, 2007).

14. C. Charles C. Bonwell and James A. Eison, "Active Learning: Creating Excitement in the Classroom," *ASHEERIC Higher Education Report No. 1* (Washington, DC: George Washington University, 1991).

15. John Dewey, *The School and Society* (Chicago: University of Chicago Press, 1900), 32.

16. Jeffrey Miller, Jonathan Deutsch, and Yolanda Sealey-Ruiz, "Advancing Multicultural Education in Hospitality Education Through the Use of Food Studies Curricula," *Journal of Hospitality and Tourism Education* 16, no. 4 (2004): 45–51.

17. Quoted in J. Ruark, "A Place at the Table," *Chronicle of Higher Education* 45, no. 44 (July 9, 1999): A17.

Bibliography

Bender, Daniel, et al. "Eating in Class: Gastronomy, Taste, Nutrition, and Teaching Food History." *Radical History Review* 110 (Spring 2011): 197–216.

Bonnekessen, Barbara. "Food is Good to Teach: An Exploration of the Cultural Meanings of Food." *Food, Culture & Society* 13, no. 2 (June 2010): 279–95.

Deutsch, Jonthan, and Jeffrey Miller, eds. *Teaching Food: Agriculture, Food and Society Syllabi and Course Materials Collection*. 2000, 2003, 2010. http://www.food-culture.org/members/login.php?co=syllabi_set.php.

Deutsch, Jonathan, et al. "Food Voice in the Classroom: A Collection of Teaching Tools." *Food, Culture & Society* 7, no. 1 (Spring 2004): 107–45.

Deutsch, Jonathan, and Sarah Billingsley. *Culinary Improvisation: Skill Building Beyond the Mystery Basket Exercise*. New York: Pearson, 2010.

Guthman, Julie. "Commentary on Teaching Food: Why I am Fed Up with Michael Pollan et al." *Agriculture and Human Values* 24, no. 2 (June 2007): 261–54.

Heldke, Lisa. *Exotic Appetites: Ruminations of a Food Adventurer*. New York: Routledge, 2003.

Long, Lucy M. "Nourishing the Academic Imagination: The Use of Food in Teaching the Concept of Culture." *Food and Foodways* 9, no. 3–4 (December 2001): 235–62.

Miller, Jeffrey P., Jonathan Deutsch, and Yolanda Sealey-Ruiz. "Advancing Multicultural Education in Hospitality Education Through the Use of Food Studies Curricula." *Journal of Hospitality and Tourism Education* 16, no. 4 (2004): 45–51.

Norman, Corrie. "Nostalgia for Origins in a Fast Food Culture: Teaching with the Food Memories of Carolina College Women." *Food, Culture & Society* 15, no. 2 (June 2012): 261–76.

Parasecoli, Fabio. "Food and Pop Culture: Teaching Critical Theory Through Food." *Food, Culture & Society* 7, no. 1 (Spring 2004): 147–57.

PART III

THE MEANS OF PRODUCTION

CHAPTER 12

AGRICULTURAL PRODUCTION AND ENVIRONMENTAL HISTORY

STERLING EVANS

"HISTORY celebrates the battlefields whereon we meet our death, but scorns to speak of the plowed fields whereby we thrive. It knows the names of the kings' bastards but cannot tell us the origin of wheat. This is the way of human folly."[1] This statement, by nineteenth-century Provençal entomologist Jean Henri Fabre, speaks to a traditional bias by historians against studying food or the natural world more broadly, from both agricultural and environmental perspectives. Agricultural history, often called rural history in Europe, gained institutional legitimacy only in the 1920s, suffered a decline in the 1960s and 1970s, and has recently enjoyed a vigorous rebirth.[2] Environmental history emerged later still, in the 1960s, as a means to study the U.S. conservation history, and has grown into a thriving field for historians around the world and examines all time periods.[3] Both of these subdisciplines have allowed historians to tackle important questions about the past use of natural resources, farming, and land change over time, but they have had different historical trajectories, agendas, and audiences. Agricultural history has traditionally centered on the study of rural landscapes, societies, economies, and of agricultural production and technologies. Environmental history has taken a broader focus, adopting a more interdisciplinary research approach, offering both ecological and political analyses, and speaking more directly to the world's current environmental crises from a historical perspective.[4]

This chapter adopts an environmental approach to survey the development of human food production. Although long ignored by historians, subsistence has been a crucial theme from the earliest times to the rise of modern, industrial agriculture. Gathering and hunting peoples organized their seasonal migrations around the procurement of food. The advent of farming and herding allowed the emergence of urban, elite classes specializing in other activities, but food production remained the focus of the vast majority of the population in agrarian empires. Even today, agriculture accounts for US$1.3 trillion worth of business annually and continues to employ 1.3 billion people around the world, making it the largest industry on Earth. Likewise, about half of the habitable land on the planet is used for agriculture and livestock production, and globally, agricultural land use continues to increase at a rate of approximately 13 million hectares (32.1 million acres) a year, as has occurred annually for the past thirty years.[5] To interpret the consequences of this ever-increasing supply of and demand for food, environmental historians have relied on a wide array of multidisclipinary evidence and analysis, borrowing methodologies from anthropologists, archaeologists, paleontologists, geographers, biologists, ecologists, and other scientists.

This brief survey cannot hope to capture the complexity of scholarly debates surrounding the world history of human food production. Instead, it seeks to reconstruct what I. G. Simmons has called the distinct "cultural ecologies" of gatherer-hunter, agrarian, and industrial societies, while giving special attention to the transitions between these three basic modes of production.[6] A growing body of scholarship points to the evolutionary development within modern humans *(Homo sapiens sapiens)* of new abilities to conceptualize and transform their environment. The domestication of plants and animals arose from the conjuncture between human environmental intervention and social interaction at a decisive moment of climate change some 10,000 years before the present. Social change followed very slowly, but by the start of the Common Era, 2,000 years ago, humans had harnessed available solar power into highly productive complexes of staple crops, irrigated farming, and long-distance trade, thus establishing the foundations for agrarian empires in the Mediterranean basin, in South and East Asia, and in the Americas. Finally, in the early modern era, beginning about 500 years ago, nascent European empires extracted ever greater supplies of energy from new crop rotations, made possible by the Columbian Exchange, and from the forced labor migrations of Atlantic plantation slavery. These changes culminated with the development of technologies for burning fossil fuels and synthesizing nitrogen fertilizers from the atmosphere, thereby yielding a cultural ecology of industry, which remains dominant to the present.

Gatherers, Hunters, and the Environment

Humans and their hominid ancestors have been transforming environments to obtain food more efficiently for millions of years. Although the history of human evolution is far from settled, one prominent theory—the "expensive tissue" hypothesis—maintains that new food sources were critical to the development of humans as a species. The increasing substitution of more easily digestible animal proteins in place of plant foods protected by tough cellulose allowed the evolution of smaller digestive tracts and the shifting of energy to another "expensive tissue," the brain. "External digestion" through cooking and fermentation also rendered animal and plant foods more digestible. Primatologist Richard Wrangham, in a provocative book called, *Catching Fire* (2009), has even argued that cooking with fire provided a crucial stimulus to the evolution of *Homo erectus*, 1.8 million years ago, although more evidence of early cooking sites is needed to establish this claim definitively.[7]

In any event, modern humans had appeared in the highlands of East Africa some 100,000 years ago, and by about 70,000 years ago, small groups began to move out of Africa and occupy the Middle East, India, southern China, and the islands of Indonesia (and from there Australia), all environments where gathering and hunting of small game yielded sufficient resources to support life. Humans also advanced slowly northward and developed different production strategies in tune with local environments. The Americas were the last place to be occupied in this long history of human movement around the world because of the special adaptations needed for the harsh Siberian climate before groups could cross the Bering Strait to Alaska and beyond.[8] Of course it is reasonable to believe that some groups arrived much earlier to the Americas—as many Native American groups maintain—a theory corroborated by a great deal of archaeological evidence that predates the Bering crossings.[9]

Gatherer-hunter groups consumed an amazing range of foods, revealing a deep knowledge of local resources. In some regions of Africa, for example, early humans relied on over eighty important varieties of edible plants and fifty edible animals, including the mongongo nut, which contains five times the calories and ten times the protein of modern cereal crops. Ethnographic evidence suggests that hunting groups often sought to conserve resources to maintain subsistence over long periods of time by respecting sacred areas where killing animals was forbidden or by practicing rotational hunting to allow game populations to recover. Marine foods were also important in the diets of many gatherer-hunters. Stable isotope studies comparing the balance of carbon and nitrogen in skeletal remains have found that whereas Neanderthals ate a diet comparable to terrestrial carnivores, early humans consumed much more seafood. Some coastal and riverine areas provided such abundant supplies of fish and shellfish that they supported the earliest sedentary societies. Vast mounds of empty shells, dating back tens of thousands of years, provide silent testimony to generations of oyster aficionados. Yet most gatherer-hunter bands remained mobile, following elaborate paths of seasonal migration to take advantage of diverse resources. These foraging strategies helped to shape the organization of early human societies, encouraging multiple groups to gather in particular resource-rich places and times, for example, in river valleys during rainy seasons, only to disperse again during cold and dry seasons. Gatherers created sophisticated food processing technologies, including specialized grinding stones chosen to prepare most efficiently particular seeds. Hunters meanwhile jerked (sun dried) or smoked meat from animals to allow lengthy storage and rendered the fat from bones, which added essential vitamins and fatty acids to their diet.[10]

The assumption that early groups lived in some kind of harmony with nature and had only minimal impacts on regional ecosystems does not correspond with the archaeological record. Graeme Barker noted: "It would appear that, pretty much from the outset, modern humans were thinking about their environment and their place within it, putting their mark on the landscape, in very different ways from earlier species such as *Homo erectus* and Neanderthals."[11] Nevertheless, Edenic fantasies have persisted until modern times, as historians Richard White and William Cronon have written: "Depictions of Indians as savages wandering in the wilderness or as innocent children living gratefully off nature's bounty are cultural artifacts of Europe; they have little to do with the actual lives of Native Americans."[12]

Early humans transformed their environment most dramatically through overhunting of species, leading to what is known as the Pleistocene overkill—a theory that suggests that some animal species went extinct due in part to overhunting.[13] In North America alone, some two hundred genera of large mammals, including giant armadillos, large rodents, ancient species of deer, antelope, giant bison, and the enormous mastodons and woolly mammoths disappeared. As Simmons posits, already "climatically stressed animal populations were made extinct in the course of a southward expansion of human hunters."[14] In ancient Europe, likewise, climatic changes combined with overhunting led to the extinction of five herbivore mammals that were important food sources: the woolly mammoth and rhinoceros, the giant Irish elk, the musk ox, and the steppe bison. And in Australia, evidence shows that a whopping 86 percent of the original large animals on the continent went extinct over a period of 100,000 years, probably due to overhunting and habitat disturbance by aboriginals, since there were no major climatic changes (glacial advances or ice ages) to affect mammal populations. More recently, human colonization of isolated environments has led to the extinction from overhunting of birds in the Hawaiian Islands, of flightless birds like the kiwi and weka in New Zealand, and the pygmy hippopotamus in Madagascar.[15]

Gatherer groups left their own environmental impacts, especially with the use of fire. Early humans learned to use controlled burning to alter habitats and favor some annual plants over others. Ethnographic evidence from Africa shows how people cleared forested areas to encourage the growth of such food plants as yams and bananas. Native people on the Great Plains of North America used controlled fires to hinder the growth of trees, woody brush, and forbs that could interfere with the grassland ranges of bison and thus hinder the hunt. In California, native groups often used fire to manage forests, especially as some tree species depend on fire for cracking open nuts and pinecones to disseminate the seeds. Australian aboriginal groups actively used fire-sticks to clear land for hunting; in the early nineteenth century, they started an estimated 5,000 bush fires per year. The landscape change afforded by burns led to increased habitat for a variety of marsupial species that were then hunted and eaten. And in ancient England, humans learned that fire could be used to enlarge clearings and to rid areas of mature oak forests with high canopies. The new scrub landscape with lower leaves made browsing easier for deer—an important protein source—and thus increasing their populations.[16] As historian Joachim Radkau explains, "Virtually everywhere in the world, fire stands at the beginning of the drama of the relationship of humans to their environment." Nor did early humans set fires at random; "burning had its orderliness and technical culture."[17] Thus, fire was an important tool to help humans go from simple adaptation and subsistence to active management of environments.

According to Simmons, the "cultural ecology of gatherer-hunters" emerged from the global migrations of humans during periods of climatic change, like long dry periods and ice ages that signified a "world in transition" when "almost every feature of an ecosystem was changing." As the climate shifted from the last of Pleistocene ice age and the warmer, modern climate of the Holocene, around 12,000 years before the present, humans had "successfully adapted to rapid changes in climate and sea-level," by developing a wide variety of processes of food collection, or foraging. Simmons argues that these subsistence methods depended on energy relationships and had energy costs. Inputs such as solar energy for the production of seeds, nuts, fruit, and animal tissue, and how more energy was spent during migrations, were learned sets of knowledge folded into traditional wisdom about survival. Migration especially increased energy costs, and thus groups learned that fewer material possessions and fewer babies or children readily facilitated a move from one place to another, adjusting their lifeways accordingly.[18]

The question then arises, *why* abandon this way of life that served humans so well? Anthropologist Marshall Sahlins has pointed out that gatherer-hunters could generally support themselves working only a few hours daily, thus constituting a truly "affluent society," rich in leisure if not in material goods.[19] Studies of skeletal remains have shown gatherer-hunters to be healthier, on average, than agrarian populations, in large part because of their more diverse diets. Moreover, for thousands of years after the domestication of plants and animals, large numbers of humans did not settle into a sedentary existence but rather practiced mixed farming and foraging strategies. Each year they planted and harvested crops as part of seasonal migrations that also involved hunting and gathering. These patterns refute Victorian notions of history as a "ladder of progress" rising inexorably from nomadic barbarism to agrarian civilizations and then industrial modernity. Farmers did eventually displace gatherers and hunters, but not because of superior intelligence or vigor; instead, it was their greater ability to reproduce, an outcome that surely would have dismayed the Victorians.[20]

From Domestication to Agrarian Empires

"The transfer from dependence upon food collection to food production, from the usufruct of the wild to the reproduction of the tamed," I. G. Simmons explains, created a solar-based "cultural ecology of agriculture," subjecting different environments to forms of land management and manipulation. Founded on the domestication of a handful of species of plants and animals, this new ecology supported an exponential growth in population. Whereas in 10,000 B.C.E., the Earth supported perhaps 4 million humans, by 1750 C.E., on the eve of industrialization, that number had increased to 720 million. How this transition took place, and its environmental consequences, form the subject of this section.[21]

Scholars generally agree that the origins of agriculture lay in the climatic oscillations that occurred during the transition from the last ice age, the Pleistocene, to the modern climatic era, the Holocene, between 13,000 and 11,000 years ago. But the idea of a "Neolithic Revolution"—the invention and subsequent diffusion of agriculture out of a few favored "hearths of domestication"—has become increasingly untenable in light of archaeological evidence of diverse paths to agriculture by humans around the world. The Fertile Crescent along the Eastern Mediterranean and Mesopotamia still presents the earliest evidence for domesticated grains, emmer and einkorn wheat and barley, from around 9500 B.C.E. Rice cultivation probably developed independently, based on separate forms of wild rice, in the Ganges Valley of India and in the Yangzi Valley of China, where domesticated rice predominated over wild versions by around 7500 B.C.E. At about the same time, farther north, in the Huang He Valley of China, foragers had transformed wild grasses into foxtail and broomcorn millets. In the Americas, during the early Holocene, humans responded to the encroachment of forest on grassland in the Amazon and Caribbean basins by propagating wild tubers, the forerunners of cassava and sweet potatoes. These methods of propagation and selection were later used in the Andes Mountains to domesticate potatoes from local tubers that had lower yields or that were poisonous due to alkaloid content. Meanwhile, in Mesoamerica, maize was domesticated beginning around 7000 B.C.E. through the adaptation of a mutated version of the tropical grass teosinte.[22]

Yet for each of these "hearths," numerous other examples exist of parallel developments. Foragers in different parts of Africa independently domesticated versions of millet and rice as well as sorghum and teff. And in the New Guinea highlands, humans developed "forest management" systems utilizing bananas, sugar cane, sago, and taro. Based on his recent review of the archaeological literature on domestication, Barker noted "widespread evidence for modern humans in the Pleistocene, in every kind of environment, demonstrating examples of surprisingly 'interventionist' relationships to the landscapes they inhabited that in one form or another presaged the later relationships that we recognize as agriculture."[23]

Exactly how people learned to plant crops is probably unknowable for certain and no doubt different in every case. Much of it may have been a result of serendipity—observing that some specific plants, perhaps even those that had been tossed into garbage heaps—grew larger and had larger seed heads (the grains themselves) and then preserving those seeds, planting them, and raising them in an early form of selective breeding. Botanists meanwhile observe that wild relatives of crop plants grew best in disturbed areas (as weeds continue to do today), so that they started to take over a region—becoming "pioneer species" that colonize and compete against other plants. These heartier species thrived enough for people to harvest their seeds *en masse.*[24] Moreover, archaeologists suggest that domestication of plants began not with the intention of creating new ways of life but rather through more conservative attempts to preserve favored species that were threatened by climate change.[25] Jared Diamond insists that worldwide agricultural developments be considered not as a discovery, nor an invention, nor even a conscious choice, but rather how food (and fiber) production simply *evolved* "as a by-product of decisions made without awareness of their consequences" at the time.[26] Such an attitude is sound and goes far in understanding why agriculture developed differently across time and locations, and why perhaps it never evolved at all in some places.

Animal domestication also resulted from the human tendency toward environmental manipulation. Pleistocene examples of proto-herding can be found in Europe, where groups of hunters sought to avoid the problems of overhunting and skittish animals by managing herds of reindeer and red deer, adapting to the animals' own migration patterns, and culling them to produce a steady source of food of high-quality protein for their communities.[27] Archaeological and genetic evidence indicates that dogs were the first animal to be domesticated, for food, in East Asia some 15,000 years ago. The first true livestock were sheep and goats in the Fertile Crescent area of Mesopotamia, and pigs in China, both around 8000 B.C.E. Cattle were taken under human management in Mesopotamia, India, and probably North Africa as well, about the same time as chickens in southern China or Southeast Asia, around 6000 B.C.E. Other species, horses, donkeys, and water buffalo, were domesticated a couple of thousand of years later, llamas and alpacas (in the Andes of South America) around 3500 B.C.E. and camels (both in Arabia and Central Asia) around 2500 B.C.E.[28] Most animals were domesticated for meat; archaeologists now believe that milking cows, perhaps as part of a religious ceremony, began in Southwest Asia and spread slowly, in part because of adult lactose intolerance.[29]

The domestication of livestock was closely connected to improvements in technology, particularly the ability to make enclosures and clear pastures. Some scholars used to think that hunters morphed into herders and pastoralists out of necessity for a steady supply of meat, yet as famed geographer Carl Sauer and others have found, hunters were never domesticators and never had the know-how or the tools to develop fenced-in enclosures that herding requires. Another theory suggested that humans could raise infant animals orphaned from their mothers or captured in the wild as pets, and later expanded on that ability to herd large numbers of animals. But cattle and pigs have never really been good pet animals and herding takes different sets of skills and technologies than pet-raising.[30] Fence building and clearing fields of brush and trees for pastures required the use of sharp stone axes, especially double-headed ones, without which domestication would have failed. Clearing sparked ecological changes, with different plants thriving in the disturbed environment and with more rainfall leaching into the cleared fields changing the soil to be more acid, in which crops like wheat cannot survive.

However, plants that do thrive on acid soil were wild oats and rye, which herders learned made excellent feed for livestock. Later, more tools and forest resources for wood were needed to create early barns for storing wild grass (hay) and oats for winter feeding and to build stables to facilitate the handling of large animals, especially in winter. Thus, domesticating and herding livestock became a way of domesticating the environment. And as historian Lori Carlson has written, "It was through manipulating the natural world that they were able to maintain their control over cattle."[31]

In a similar fashion, cultural and intellectual adaptations spurred the expansion of farming. Cultivators developed specialized tools such as hoes to disturb the soil enough so seeds could sprout and extend their roots, and later to guard against weeds that could choke out the crops. They also developed reaping knives and sickles to aid in harvests. And with so much grain available, people needed to store supplies of it in large baskets or clay vessels, requiring other cultural and social skills to accommodate this requirement. Likewise, over time, farmers observed *when* to plant for optimal yields, and *which* specific plants produced the best grains in different soils. They then saved the seeds from those plants for future sowing, beginning the process of selective breeding. Some groups learned that various crops could exhaust the soil after two or three seasons, and thus either looked for new croplands to break, or learned that fields that had lain fallow could be productive later.[32] Cultivators, particularly in tropical areas, used swidden or slash-and-burn, clearing forests with stone axes and fire. In those fields, cereal crops initially did well due to the ash-enriched soil left from the burning, but many fields became exhausted with repeated use and insufficient manure and had to be abandoned, resulting in a secondary succession of bushes, brambles, and shrubs, and eventually second-growth forest, representing a significant ecological change in the region.[33] In temperate climes with sturdier soils, permanent fields in flood plains may have been more common in early agriculture.

The development of agricultural technology also included the choice of particular combinations of crops. Farmers practicing swidden agriculture in Mesoamerica had to keep clearing swaths of tropical forests, creating a patchwork of thousands of *milpas* (small corn fields) to produce enough maize to feed their growing villages and cities. But the Indians maximized the output of milpas by intercropping maize with beans and squashes. Beans, as legumes, served as a nitrogen fixer in the soils (slowing the process of soil exhaustion) and their vines took advantage of corn stalks on which to climb. In the same furrows or mounds, Indians planted various varieties of squashes whose leaves provided shade against the harsh sun to the young bean plants and whose natural enzymes served as an organic repellent against insects that could damage individual plants or ruin crops. This triad agroecological system, also known as the "three sisters," was remarkably efficient for food production, dietary diversity and nutrition, and soil replenishment. It was adopted by Indians throughout Mesoamerica and North America all the way into present-day New England and Canada, and continues to be used today by many Native farmers, especially in Mexico.

As Neolithic villages around the world grew over millennia into towns and agrarian empires, ever more advanced technologies were employed. Societies learned to replenish exhausted soils with marl (lime), composted manure from humans and domestic livestock, and guano (petrified bird and bat droppings rich in phosphates and nitrates). Starting in Mesopotamia, humans learned to manipulate rivers to provide an even supply of water for their fields instead of relying on sporadic rainfall. Terracing fields to limit erosion allowed the clearing of hilly terrain, colonizing new territory for farming populations. Such massive projects for moving water and earth went far in advancing city-states and became the basis of power in many societies. The social theorist and Asianist historian Karl Wittfogel studied the impact of irrigation on China to conclude that the control of water created a "hydraulic society" in the ancient world. The term, from his landmark book *Oriental Despotism* (1957), referred to the power bases and bureaucracies that developed in societies dependent on water projects and irrigation, suggesting that diverting rivers and engineering large-scale diversions to irrigate croplands necessitated a strong centralized state that could marshal the labor and finances to construct irrigation projects. A result was the development of hierarchical, authoritarian governments.[34]

Food processing technologies were just as important as farming skills for supporting civilizations. Fermented alcoholic beverages have been vital to societies for thousands of years both nutritionally and as a means of celebration. The transformation of raw animal milk into more digestible cheese and yogurt provided valuable sources of protein. The development of cuisines based on complementary cereals-legume complexes also increased the nutritional value of foods. Beans, chickpeas, lentils, and other legumes, in addition to adding nitrogen to the soil, provided valuable sources of vegetable proteins. Although legumes did not provide a complete chain of amino acids needed for human nutrition, when eaten together with staple grains such as rice and maize, they balanced the missing nutrients. Thus, the domestication of both soybeans in China and common beans in the Americas at the end of the second millennium B.C.E. spurred population growth and the emergence of complex societies. By the beginning of the Common Era, the first water powered mills had been developed in the Mediterranean for wheat and in China for rice.

For an illustration of the value of culinary processing in the rise of civilization, consider maize. The American staple contained a crucial nutritional flaw in the shortage of usable vitamin B3 (niacin), needed to prevent pellagra, a disease characterized by skin rash, intestinal problems, insanity, and death. Maize-based civilizations flourished only when cooks discovered alkali treatment, using limestone or wood ash, to free the chemically bound vitamin. In Mexico, at Teotihuacán (c. 250 B.C.E. to 750 C.E.), alkali-treated maize was eaten in griddlecakes called tortillas, while the independent invention of hominy in North America, near Cahokia around 800 C.E., allowed Mississippian culture to expand throughout the eastern woodlands.[35]

The rise of agrarian empires, with their artificial environments of single-species crops, left significant impacts on the natural world. Forest ecosystems suffered greatly from slash-and-burn deforestation, and habitat for wildlife and native plants often disappeared. The practice not only destroyed native plants that were part of the ground and forest cover, but exposed the soil to wind and rain that caused high rates of erosion and interfered with the land's natural nutrient restoration processes. Irrigation projects disrupted natural systems even more, often causing soil to be waterlogged, and thus ruined. They also changed the soil's mineral content due to salinization—a process that occurs in especially hot and dry climates (like Mesopotamia) when irrigated water in fields evaporates quickly leaving a residue of salt that kills crops. The growth of cities put exponentially more pressure, not just on local environments, but on ever broader foodsheds, as imperial capitals such as Rome, Hangzhou (near Shanghai), and Tenochtitlán (Mexico City) requisitioned food from subject peoples. There is evidence of city-states and empires around the world overextending the land's carrying capacity, leading to deforestation, ruined fields, and social collapse.[36]

Indeed, the costs of intensive agriculture may help to explain those regions where it never developed. Stuart Banner's wide-ranging comparative study, *Possessing the Pacific: Land, Settlers, and Indigenous People from Australia to Alaska*, examines cultural differences and the agricultural practices (or lack thereof) among Native groups around the Pacific Rim. Australian aboriginals and most Native Californians did not develop farming at all, and the Alaskan Natives and First Nations of British Columbia did so only in limited form. In contrast, Native peoples of the other six areas in his study, and especially the Maori of New Zealand and the Polynesians of Fiji and Tonga, practiced highly developed forms of agriculture. These varying lifeways shaped people's perceptions of and relationships with the natural world. The Maori, for example, maintained a spiritual relationship with the land, and believed that they belonging to it, rather than owning it.[37]

The development of agriculture gave humans increased power over nature, especially with the use of tools. Surplus food supplies led not only to a sedentary life and "advanced" cities and nation-states, but also to massive warfare between groups, increased social classes (between those who farmed and those who did not), dramatic increases in population (and at times, overpopulation beyond a region's carrying capacity), and the conversion of forests and meadows into fields and pastures across the world. Yet however profound the changes wrought by agrarian empires, they paled in comparison to the transformations of the industrial era.

Tropical Plantations and Industrial Farming

By 1492, the solar-based ecology of agrarian empires was approaching its natural limits, but in the succeeding centuries, global empires based in Europe discovered new ways of extracting energy from the landscape. Columbus's voyages to the Americas led to the integration of two highly efficient and in many ways complementary systems of agriculture, increasing food production around the world. Tropical plantations built on colonial lands and forced labor satisfied European demand for commodities that could not be raised at home. The resulting supply chains, and the multinational corporations that arose to manage them, allowed ever greater accumulation of capital. Finally, the development of steam engines allowed humans to burn fossil fuels, extracting ever greater supplies of energy. The creation of industrial diets, based on easily digestible sugars and fats, began to replace the cereal-legume complexes that had supported agrarian societies. During the twentieth century, the human population entered an even steeper period of growth, rising from 1.5 billion to more than 7 billion, even as the average weight of humans increased dramatically.

Environmental historian Alfred Crosby coined the phrase the "Columbian Exchange" to refer to the impact of Afro-Eurasian crops, livestock, and diseases on the Americas, and the return voyages of New World foods, especially maize, potatoes, and manioc, to the Old World. Crosby noted that the demographic collapse of American populations caused by unfamiliar diseases and colonial exploitation opened up vast regions for the cultivation of wheat and livestock. By contrast, the spread of productive American crops caused Old World populations to expand massively in the centuries after the encounter. Historians have since expanded on this thesis, providing more detailed analysis of the mechanisms through which Europeans carried out their "ecological imperialism," another term of Crosby's. For example, Elinor Melville showed the effects of European livestock on the Mexican ecology. Within a few decades after the conquest, sheep and cattle overran native fields, reproducing at a fantastic pace, and quickly exceeding the carrying capacity of the land. The formerly fertile land was denuded of vegetation, exposed to erosion, and rendered unfit for farming or herding. Another recent study, by James McCann, examined the spread of maize through Africa, at first entering particular cultural ecologies, and later, through colonialism, becoming the staple crop for much of the continent.[38]

The Columbian exchange had its most significant impact through the creation of tropical plantations, which presaged industrial capital accumulation and labor mobilization as well as the highly caloric modern diet. Anthropologist Eric Wolf has usefully defined a plantation as being "a capital-using unit employing a large labor force under close managerial supervision to produce a crop for sale." This labor regime is usually grouped in "gangs that carry out repetitive and physically demanding tasks under the watchful eye of foremen who enforce the required sequence and synchronization of tasks" similar to "the order and drill of an army"—a system that can be referred to as "military agriculture."[39] During the early modern period, these plantations relied overwhelmingly on enslaved Africans, more than ten million of whom were transported to the Americas from 1550 to 1850.[40] After the abolition of the Atlantic slave trade, indentured servants from Asia and other labor migrants increasingly replaced African workers.[41]

European powers advanced this system, first with logwood, cochineal, and indigo dyes from Brazil and Central America, and later with more large-scale production of sugar, tobacco, coffee, and rubber.

As Sidney Mintz has argued, sugar became the world's first manifestation of industrial agriculture. Botanically, sugar cane is a perennial grass whose stems are filled with watery and fibrous tissues filled with sugar. First domesticated in northern India around 300 B.C.E., it was carried to the Mediterranean by Arabic traders, and then to the New World by the Spanish and Portuguese. The production of sugar was a notoriously labor-intensive activity, particularly for field slaves, who worked in gangs under the tropical sun, armed with axe and hoe, planting, weeding, manuring, and eventually harvesting the cane. Yet plantations also required enormous investments of capital and technology in mills, which by the seventeenth century operated water-power rollers to crush the cane. Industrial scheduling was also needed to extract the greatest quantity of sugar juice from freshly cut cane. Soaring European demand for processed white sugar funded the growth of this industry. What had been an aristocratic item of conspicuous consumption in the Renaissance, with elaborate sugar sculptures prepared for banquets, worked its way down the social ladder to middle-class jams and candies, and by the nineteenth century sugar had reached the daily tea of English workers.[42]

The environmental consequences of tropical plantations were tremendous. Great amounts of land needed to be cleared of its natural vegetation for sugar plantations—forever altering the local ecology of Caribbean sugar islands and northeast Brazil by destroying millions of hectares of flora and habitat for fauna. Likewise, sugarcane production often causes severe soil degradation, making plantation owners constantly seeking to break more land into plantations. All of these considerations added many drastic environmental changes to plantation areas, especially in changing natural landscapes with their own degrees of biodiversity to ones of monocrop agriculture. Similar patterns of environmental change took place in other regions and crops. Coffee spread through Brazil in the nineteenth century, after sugar production had moved to lower-cost sites elsewhere, completing the destruction of an Atlantic rainforest that had once rivaled the Amazon in size and biodiversity. High incidences of agricultural pathogens and diseases occur when those commodities are grown not in dispersed and intercropped farms but in monoculture plantation environments, for example, banana plantations in Central America.[43] Eric Wolf has concluded forcefully: "the plantation is an invader, and its successful expansion is the fruit of successful invasions."[44]

Meanwhile, transnational commodity chains have formed increasingly complex webs that link labor, land, and markets around the world.[45] These systems depend not only on the production of valuable products like coffee or bananas, but also on new systems for transporting them from plantation to port and then on to distant markets. For example, in the late nineteenth-century refrigerated technology led to a global trade in chilled beef from the plains of North and South America, South Africa, and Australia to markets in Europe. More recently, air travel and container ships have facilitated the export of tropical fruits and out-of-season vegetables from countries in the Global South to affluent consumers in the Global North. In turn, these transport systems have been embedded in legal regimes and market economies that also serve to generate value for particular nations. Classical economists Adam Smith and David Ricardo argued that trading economies generated comparative advantage since the poorer nations would not need to invest large amounts of capital, which they did not have and would have to borrow at high interest, by continuing to trade in what they did have, minerals and agricultural products. Yet others have explained this scenario in different ways; sociologist Immanuel Wallerstein's World-Systems theory argued that industrial and colonial powers maintained a monopoly on capital to prevent resource-exporting colonies and dependent nations on the periphery from threatening their global power.[46]

Wheat, one of the first grains to be domesticated, illustrates the global links of modern agricultural production. One of the most significant environmental changes of the late nineteenth and early twentieth centuries has been the conversion of grasslands to wheat fields throughout large parts of Australia, North and South America, and Russia. This transformation was made possible by new machinery, including steam- and gasoline-powered tractors that could bust tough prairie sod and grasslands and plow them into wheat fields. Even earlier, in 1831, Cyrus McCormick's mechanical reaper had revolutionized the harvest, ending the back-breaking work of using of sickle and scythe. The addition of a binder, in the 1870s, mechanized the work of tying grain stalks into sheaves to dry before threshing. This created a sudden demand for twine to bind the international wheat harvest, launching the industrialization of fiber crops in the Philippines, East Africa, the Caribbean, and Brazil. For a time, around the turn of the twentieth century, Mexico's Yucatán Peninsula experienced an export boom because the native agave plants henequen and sisal produced exactly the right kind of twine fiber. The creation of henequen plantations transformed the landscape of Yucatán from an ecologically diverse deciduous scrub forest to a zone of commercial agriculture with rectilinear rows of agave plants, all for the growing demand of wheat elsewhere in the world. By 1950, however, combine harvesters (that both harvested and threshed wheat without the need to tie sheaves) displaced binders and ended the demand for twine fiber, leaving the Yucatán with a devastated landscape.[47]

Another vital contribution to industrial farming came from new sources of fertilizers, which were discovered in remote areas of South America in the nineteenth century and then synthesized chemically in the twentieth century. Guano was found in abundance on coastal Peru and Chile, where the driest climate on earth preserved vast quantities of shorebird dung for centuries. European fields fertilized with guano meant that fallowing was unnecessary, (for awhile, at least). Although surface deposits of guano were quickly depleted, nitrate mines were discovered nearby that allowed continued growth of European agriculture, while incurring other environmental calamities from mining in sensitive coastal regions.[48] Then, in the early twentieth century, German scientists Fritz Haber and Carl Bosch developed industrial methods to synthesize ammonia from the atmosphere and convert it into nitrate fertilizers.[49]

The environmental ramifications due to the production of food have increased even more in the last two hundred years. Some of the most dramatic conversion of natural ecosystems into croplands occurred during the last half of the nineteenth century and on into the twentieth. Historian John Richards has shown that from 1860 to 1920 farmers across the world developed 432 million hectares (or over one billion acres) of new cropland. The largest conversions occurred in North America with 164 million hectares, followed by 88 million in the former Soviet Union, 84 million in Asia, and 96 million hectares combined in Africa, Latin America, and Australia. Another 419 million hectares were added to that total in the next sixty years. Digesting these facts, Donald Worster lamented that much of the "one billion hectares of forests and grasslands that had been teeming with biological complexity... was lost in the simplifications of commercial agriculture."[50]

An Uncertain Future

William Cronon has observed that in writing environmental history we impose human morality on nature.[51] The above arguments fit into what he has called a declensionist narrative suggesting that throughout world history there has only been environmental decline and destruction. By contrast, a triumphalist narrative could celebrate the progressive accomplishments of gatherer-hunters, agrarian empires, and industrial farmers in subduing nature to human dominion. The latter analysis of course has its merits: People have to eat, and in developing the technology to obtain their daily bread, they have reshaped the earth. Moreover, with a global population that reached 7 billion by the year 2011 C.E., they have seemingly refuted doomsayers like Thomas Malthus, who in late eighteenth-century England warned that the world could never support such an expanding population.

Yet the triumphalist perspective cannot rest easy with the uncertainty of future climate change. Already in the twentieth century, the expansion of agriculture into the Great Plains of North America led to the Dust Bowl conditions of the mid-1930s—one of the greatest ecological disasters in the continent's history. By 1935, the wind, drought, and dust storms were so severe that over 13 million hectares (33 million acres), or about one-third of the Dust Bowl region, was denuded of plant life, and mountains of dust replaced what had been farm fields.[52] Most environmental historians agree that the Dust Bowl was caused by the great plow-up of the 1910s and 1920s. Famed ecologist Aldo Leopold's reference to the disaster as "wheating the land to death" was indicative of what Worster has called the "exploitative relationship with the earth" by investors, farmers, and millers.[53] Similar agro-ecological disasters in the second half of the twentieth century, including the tropical deforestation of the Global South and the crash of commercial fisheries, make us question the growing reliance on chemical pesticides and fertilizers and genetically modified crops.[54] In the twenty-first century there have been increasing calls for a more fair worldwide distribution of food, for a refocusing away from industrial agriculture that has particularly characterized world farming in the last forty years to giving more attention to small, sustainable farms, community farmer markets and even to redefining what food really is.[55]

Environmental historians have asked important questions and have added to the conversation about how we view the historical past, and what the role and place of nature has been in that understanding. Thus, it is not enough just to know the origin of wheat, as J. H. Fabre challenged us so long ago, but to understand the broader dimensions of food production on human societies and on the natural world over time.

Notes

1. The author wishes to thank Handbook editor Jeff Pilcher not only for his close attention to editing details here, but also for his wise suggestions on additional sources to consult, and for some very informed and useful ideas on focus and interpretation in this chapter. J. H. Fabre as quoted in John T. Schlebecker, *Whereby We Thrive: A History of American Farming, 1607–1972* (Ames: Iowa State University Press, 1975), 1.

2. The Agriculture History Society in the United States was founded in 1919, and its journal *Agricultural History* has been publishing articles since 1927. In Europe, rural history continues to enjoy widespread popularity, especially via the British Agricultural History Society (established in 1952) and its journal *Agricultural History Review*.

3. For summary and analysis on the origin and development of the field, see Richard White, "American Environmental History: The Development of a New Historical Field," *Pacific Historical Review* 54, no. 3 (August 1985): 297–335; Donald Worster, "Doing Environmental History," in *The Ends of the Earth: Perspectives on Modern Environmental History*, ed. Donald Worster (Cambridge: Cambridge University Press): 289–307; J. Donald Hughes, "Global Dimensions of Environmental History," *Pacific Historical Review* 70, no. 1 (Feb. 2001): 91–101; Richard White, "Environmental History: Watching a Historical Field Mature," *Pacific Historical Review* 70, no. 1 (February 2001): 103–111; and J. R. McNeill, "Observations on the Nature and Culture of Environmental History," *Environment and History* 42, no. 4 (December 2003): 5–43.

4. These were the conclusions of an important roundtable panel, "Working Fertile Ground: Environmental and Agricultural History in the New Millennium," at the Western History Association annual conference in St. Louis, Missouri, on October 12, 2006. Panelists included Claire Strom, Donald Worster, Donald Pisani, Deborah Fitzgerald, Mark Fiege, and Douglas Helms.

5. Jason Clay, *World Agriculture and Environment: A Commodity-by-Commodity Guide to Impacts and Practices* (Washington, DC: Island Press, 2004), 2, 3, 13.

6. I. G. Simmons, *Global Environmental History* (Chicago: University of Chicago Press, 2008).

7. Leslie C. Aiello and Peter Wheeler, "The Expensive-Tissue Hypothesis: The Brain and the Digestive System in Human and Primate Evolution," *Current Anthropology* 36, no. 2 (April 1995): 199–221; Martin Jones, *Feast: Why Humans Share Food* (Oxford: Oxford University Press, 2007), 79–87; Richard Wrangham, *Catching Fire: How Cooking Made Us Human* (New York: Basic Books, 2009).

8. For a summary, see Patrick Manning, *Migration in World History* (New York: Routledge, 2005).

9. For a good discussion, see Vine Deloria, Jr.'s essay "Low Bridge—Everybody Cross," in *Red Earth, White Lies: Native Americans and the Myth of Scientific Fact* (New York: Scribner, 1995), 67–92.

10. Clive Ponting, *A Green History of the World: The Environment and the Collapse of Great Civilizations* (New York: Penguin Books, 1991), 19–23; Alan K. Outram, "Hunter-Gatherers and the First Farmers: The Evolution of Taste in Prehistory," in *Food: The History of Taste*, ed. Paul Freedman (Berkeley: University of California Press, 2007), 35–61.

11. Graeme Barker, *The Agriculture Revolution in Prehistory: Why Did Foragers Become Farmers?* (Oxford: Oxford University Press, 2006), 396.

12. Richard White and William Cronon, "Ecological Change and Indian-White Relations," in *Handbook of North American Indians*, vol. 4, *History of Indian-White Relations*, ed. William C. Sturtevant (Washington: Smithsonian Institution, 1988), 417.

13. The controversial theory was first advanced by Paul S. Martin, "Prehistoric Overkill," in *Pleistocene Extinctions: The Search for a Cause*, ed. P.S. Martin and E.H. Wright, Jr. (New Haven: Yale University Press, 1967), 75–120. See also Donald K. Grayson and David J. Meltzer, "A Requiem for North American Overkill," *Journal of Archaeological Science* 30 (2003): 585–93. On Native beliefs toward the environment, see Raymond Pierotti and Daniel R. Wildcat, "Being Native to This Place," in *American Indians in American History, 1870–2001: A Companion Reader*, ed. Sterling Evans (Westport, CT: Praeger Publishers, 2002): 3–16.

14. Simmons, Environmental History, 4.

15. Ponting, *Green History of the World*, 33.

16. Simmons, *Environmental History*, 5; Stephen J. Pyne, *World Fire: The Culture of Fire on Earth* (Seattle: University of Washington Press, 1995), 11–12.

17. Joachim Radkau, *Nature and Power: A Global History of the Environment* (New York: Cambridge University Press, 2008), 42.

18. Simmons, *Global Environmental History*, 26, 27.

19. Marshall Sahlins, "The Original Affluent Society," in *Stone Age Economics* (New York: Aldine, 1972), 1–39.

20. Richard H. Steckel and Jerome C. Rose, ed., *The Backbone of History: Health and Nutrition in the Western Hemisphere* (Cambridge: Cambridge University Press, 2002); Jones, *Feast*, 170–75; Barker, *The Agricultural Revolution in Prehistory*, 4–9.

21. Simmons, *Global Environmental History*, 53–54.

22. Dolores R. Piperno and Deborah M. Pearsall, *The Origins of Agriculture in the Lowland Neotropics* (San Diego: Academic Press, 1998); Barker, *The Agricultural Revolution in Prehistory*, 104–48, 182–230.

23. Barker, *The Agricultural Revolution in Prehistory*, 221–22, 320–23, quote from 412.

24. Otto T. Solbrig and Dorothy J. Solbrig, *So Shall You Reap: Farming and Crops in Human Affairs* (Washington: Island Press, 1994), 17–18.

25. Jones, *Feast*, 142–49.

26. Jared Diamond, *Guns, Germs, and Steel: The Fates of Human Societies* (New York: Norton, 1999), 105–106.

27. Ponting, *A Green History of the World*, 26–35.

28. Frederick E. Zeuner, *A History of Domesticated Animals* (New York: Harper and Row, 1963); Carl O. Sauer, *Agricultural Origins and Dispersals: The Domestication

of Animals and Foodstuffs (Cambridge, MA: MIT Press, 1969); Laurie Winn Carlson, *Cattle: A Social History* (Chicago: Ivan Dee, 2001), 18–46; Kenneth F. Kiple and Kriemhild Conneè Ornelas, eds., *The Cambridge World History of Food*, 2 vols. (Cambridge: Cambridge University Press, 2000).

29. Carlson, *Cattle*, 18–20; Diamond, *Guns, Germs, and Steel*, 167.

30. Sauer, *Agricultural Origins and Dispersals*, 86; Carlson, *Cattle*, 19–20.

31. Zeuner, *A History of Domesticated Animals*, 35; Carlson, *Cattle*, 21.

32. Solbrig and Solbrig, *So Shall You Reap*, 14–15, 19, 28.

33. Radkau, *Nature and Power*, 41–45.

34. Karl Wittfogel, *Oriental Despotism: A Comparative Study of Total Power* (New Haven: Yale University Press, 1957). American environmental historian Donald Worster has applied the concept of "hydraulic societies" in, *Rivers of Empire: Water, Aridity, and the Growth of the American West* (New York: Oxford University Press, 1985).

35. S. H. Katz, M. L. Hediger, and L. A. Valleroy, "Traditional Maize Processing Techniques in the New World," *Science* 184 (1974): 765–73.

36. Clive Ponting, *A Green History of the World*, 68–87, 160–93; Simmons, *Global Environmental History*, 90–97; Radkau, *Nature and Power*, 71–77.

37. Stuart Banner, *Possessing the Pacific: Land, Settlers, and Indigenous People from Australia to Alaska* (Cambridge, MA: Harvard University Press, 2007), 55.

38. Alfred W. Crosby, Jr., *The Columbian Exchange: Biological Consequences of 1492* (Westport, CT: Greenwood Press, 1972); idem, *Ecological Imperialism: The Biological Expansion of Europe, 900–1900* (New York: Cambridge University Press, 1986); Elinor G. K. Melville, *A Plague of Sheep: Environmental Consequences of the Conquest of Mexico* (New York: Cambridge University Press, 1994); James C. McCann, *Maize and Grace: Africa's Encounter with a New World Crop, 1500–2000* (Cambridge, MA: Harvard University Press, 2005).

39. Eric Wolf, *Europe and the People without History* (Berkeley: University of California Press, 1997), 310–46, quotes from 315; Solbrig and Solbrig, *So Shall You Reap*, 143–161.

40. Philip D. Curtain, *The Rise and Fall of the Plantation Complex* (Cambridge: Cambridge University Press, 1998).

41. Wolf, *Europe and the People*, 315.

42. Sidney Mintz, *Sweetness and Power: The Place of Sugar in Modern History* (New York: Viking, 1985).

43. Richard Tucker, *Insatiable Appetites: The United States and the Ecological Degradation of the Tropical World* (Berkeley: University of California Press, 2000); Reinaldo Funes Monzote, *From Rainforest to Cane Field: An Environmental History since 1492*, trans. Alex Martin (Chapel Hill: University of North Carolina Press, 2008); John Soluri: *Banana Cultures: Agriculture, Consumption, and Environmental Change in Honduras and the United States* (Austin: University of Texas Press, 2005).

44. Wolf, *Europe and the People*, 315.

45. Terence K. Hopkins and Immanuel Wallerstein, "Commodity Chains in the World Economy Prior to 1800," *Review* 10, no. 1 (1986): 151–70; Steven Topik and Allen Wells, eds., *The Second Conquest of Latin America: Coffee, Henequen, and Oil during the Export Boom, 1850–1930* (Austin: University of Texas Press, 1998).

46. Immanuel Wallerstein, *The Modern World-System*, vol. 1, *Capitalist Agriculture and the Origins of the European World Economy in the Sixteenth Century* (New York: Academic Press, 1974).

47. Sterling Evans, *Bound in Twine: The History and Ecology of the Henequen-Wheat Complex for Mexico and the American and Canadian Plains, 1880–1950* (College Station: Texas A & M University Press, 2007).

48. Rory Miller and Robert Greenhill, "The Fertilizer Commodity Chains: Guano and Nitrate, 1840–1930," in *From Silver to Cocaine: Latin American Commodity Chains and the Building of the World Economy, 1500–2000*, ed. Steven Topik, Carlos Marichal, and Zephyr Frank (Durham: Duke University Press, 2006), 228–270.

49. Vaclav Smil, *Enriching the Earth: Fritz Haber, Carl Bosch, and the Transformation of World Food Production* (Cambridge, MA: MIT Press, 2001).

50. John Richards, "Global Patterns of Land Conversion," *Environment* 26, no. (November 1984), 6–13, 34–38; Worster, *The Ends of the Earth*, 15.

51. William Cronon, "A Place for Stories: Nature, History, and Narrative," *The Journal of American History* 78, no. 4 (March 1992): 1347–76.

52. Donald Worster, *Dust Bowl: The Southern Plains in the 1930s* (New York: Oxford University Press, 1979), 94.

53. Aldo Leopold, *A Sand County Almanac* (1949; repr., New York: Ballantine, 1990), 15; Worster, *Dust Bowl*, 93. For an alternate view, see Geoff Cunfer, *On the Great Plains: Agriculture and Environment* (College Station: Texas A & M University Press, 2005).

54. See, for example, Norman Wirzba, ed., *The Essential Agrarian Reader: The Failure of Culture, Community, and the Land* (Washington, DC: Shoemaker and Hoard, 2003).

55. See for example Andrew Kimbrell, ed., *The Fatal Harvest Reader: The Tragedy of Industrial Agriculture* (Washington, DC: Island Press, 2002); Eric Schlosser *Fast Food Nation: The Dark Side of the All-American Meal* (New York: Houghton Mifflin, 2001).

Bibliography

Banner, Stuart. *Possessing the Pacific: Land, Settlers, and Indigenous People from Australia to Alaska*. Cambridge, MA: Harvard University Press, 2007.

Crosby, Alfred W., Jr. *Ecological Imperialism: The Biological Expansion of Europe, 900–1900*. New York: Cambridge University Press, 1986.

Evans, Sterling. *Bound in Twine: The History and Ecology of the Henequen-Wheat Complex for Mexico and the American and Canadian Plains, 1880–1950*. College Station: Texas A & M University Press, 2007.

Funes Monzote, Reinaldo. *From Rainforest to Cane Field: An Environmental History since 1492*. Translated by Alex Martin. Chapel Hill: University of North Carolina Press, 2008.

Melville, Elinor G. K. *A Plague of Sheep: Environmental Consequences of the Conquest of Mexico*. New York: Cambridge University Press, 1994.

Ponting, Clive. *A Green History of the World: The Environment and the Collapse of Great Civilizations*. New York: Penguin Books, 1991.

Radkau, Joachim. *Nature and Power: A Global History of the Environment*. New York: Cambridge University Press, 2008.

Simmons, I. G. *Global Environmental History*. Chicago: University of Chicago Press, 2008.

Solbrig, Otto T., and Dorothy J. Solbrig. *So Shall You Reap: Farming and Crops in Human Affairs*. Washington, DC: Island Press, 1994.

CHAPTER 13

COOKBOOKS AS HISTORICAL DOCUMENTS

KEN ALBALA

HISTORIANS use cookbooks as primary source documents in much the same way they use any written record of the past. A primary source is a text written by someone in the past, rather than a secondary source, which is commentary by a historian upon the primary sources. A cookbook may be analyzed either in manuscript form or printed, in its original state or as a facsimile, as a modern edition or now increasingly as an online electronic version. There are certain advantages in using the original document, primarily bibliographical (to track publishing history, variant editions, etc.), but for most purposes a facsimile will suffice. A transcribed or translated version may have been significantly altered, with modernized spelling or even "adapted" for use in a modern kitchen, in which case it is practically useless as a record of the past. An exact facsimile of the original manuscript or book is always preferred, if not the original.

Original copies of historic manuscript and printed cookbooks over 100 years old are almost always kept in rare book rooms and special collections and must be consulted on site. Although almost all university libraries hold some old cookbooks, there are a number that have noted collections, such as the Schlesinger at Radcliffe College, The Clements at the University of Michigan, as well as the New York and Los Angeles Public Libraries. Practically all libraries now have online catalogues. To locate where a particular book may be held, WorldCat is extremely helpful. Cookbooks that have been reprinted can be easily purchased online or borrowed from a library, and there are publishers who specialize in such material: Prospect Books, Arnaldo Forni, Applewood, and Southover. To identify such books in the first place one should consult a bibliography such as Georges Vicaire's classic *Bibliographie Gastronomique* or Katherine Golden Bitting's *Gastronomic Bibliography*. There are also more recent and specialized bibliographic resources dealing with individual countries or periods, including Barbara Feret's *Gastronomical and Culinary Literature* and William Cagle's *American Books on Food and Drink 1739–1950*.

Historic cookbooks have been appearing increasingly on websites, in facsimile form, transcribed, and sometimes translated from foreign languages. A search on Google, including Google Books advanced search functions, is an excellent place to start, as are the Feeding America site from Michigan State, the Fons Grewe site from Barcelona, and the Biblioteque Nationale's Gallica site. If your university subscribes, you can also find dozens of historic cookbooks on Early English Books Online. Thomas Gloning's website also contains links to dozens of medieval and early modern cookbooks.

As might be expected, the closer one approaches the present, the richer the historical resources. For some cultures there remains no written record of culinary practices. Nonetheless, there are recipes on cuneiform tablets from ancient Mesopotamia (edited by Jean Bottéro), large fragments of Greek cookbooks (such as Archestratus), and complete texts from ancient China and Rome (the text attributed to Apicius). Several dozen medieval Islamic, European, and Asian cookbooks survive, and the number increases with each succeeding century. Modern historians have literally hundreds of thousands of cookbooks to consult ranging from tiny community cookbooks and personal recipe files to mammoth popular cookbooks issued in multiple expanded editions. It is important to note that the oldest of cookbooks are usually meant for the most elite readers, since literacy was a rarity. The more recent the cookbook, in general the broader the readership. Ancient and medieval texts were written mostly for courtly audiences. In the early modern period those of middling social rank in the city and country were addressed, and by the nineteenth century working classes, immigrants, and even the relatively poverty stricken were included.

It should also be pointed out that cookbooks are not the only primary source for food history. They are usually supplemented with corroborating evidence from tax and legal records, trade accounts, wills, diaries, census data, and even novels and paintings. There is also a large ancillary literature about food including diet books, agricultural texts, herbals, and catering manuals. These often contain rich and detailed information, but here we shall focus on the cookbook itself.

As with any document, the historian must attempt to answer five basic questions of provenance and purpose if possible. Who wrote the cookbook? What was the intended audience? Where was it produced and when? Why was it written? These are not always simple questions, as some cookbooks, especially manuscripts and *incunabulae* (the earliest printed books), are anonymous and may have been copied or printed without dates. From the mid-sixteenth century to the present such information is usually standard on the title page or colophon, but one must always remember that cookbooks went through many editions, which may differ significantly among different printings. Material may also have been pirated from other cookbooks directly, or slightly adapted and reworded. So the historian must never automatically assume that a recipe was written at the same time as the publication date of a book, or even the date on a manuscript. Without laws against plagiarism, it is safe to assume that recipes until very recently are borrowed versions of those the author found in another text or learned from another chef. This is probably more common even to this day than we like to admit. What this means is that the historian is rarely able to pinpoint a particular dish to a specific time and place. It is also usually safe to assume that a recipe has been cooked for some time before it arrives in print, though more modern cookbooks do consciously invent dishes and copyright them.

Perhaps the most important lesson to be learned is that cookbooks are rarely if ever accurate descriptions of what people actually ate at any given time and place. They are usually prescriptive literature, and thus reflect peoples' aspirations, or even merely the authors' expectations of what readers might like to know rather than actual culinary practice. Moreover, many cookbooks, in the past as today, are meant for armchair chefs and are read primarily for entertainment value rather than as practical guides for cooking food. Most cookbooks, especially early ones, would have been kept in a library, to be consulted by a literate elite rather than left to be sullied by a lowly cook. This makes them no less valuable as historical documents though.

Nor should any of these caveats prevent the historian from cooking historic recipes today. There is something palpably direct to be gained from tasting food from the past, in much the same way as one can learn from hearing a symphony on period instruments or viewing an old painting in a museum. The esthetic values that inform flavor preferences of the past are indeed very different from our own. Some ingredients people enjoyed would today be considered abhorrent; some flavors and textures bizarre if not disgusting. But this should not deter the intrepid investigator. Historians have been reluctant to cook from historic texts because, understandably, their training is in textual analysis rather than stirring the pot. But historical reenactors and living history displays have often successfully presented bygone cooking techniques to the public at historic sites, although today actually tasting the food is usually prohibited for insurance purposes. In any case, this is a viable use for historic cookbooks as long as one sticks to original equipment, fuel sources, and ingredients without substitution or adaptation. What one learns from such an exercise is a feeling for the embodied experience of physically carrying out certain culinary tasks and a direct apprehension of what the palates of our forebears might have experienced.

But what does a cookbook tell the traditional historian trained in textual analysis? Approaching the text is a process of sleuthing. First it is important to identify exactly what one wants to learn from a text. The culinary historian may simply be interested in what kinds of dishes were popular or found interesting in a particular period. Changing food preferences, modes of service and table settings, and manners and mealtimes are all important types of information that may be read prima facie directly from historic cookbooks, with the caveat again that they are not evidence of practice, but prescriptional. For direct evidence the historian must consult the archaeologist who digs up trash pits, the botanist who examines plant remains, and even the paleonutritionist who can describe an individual's diet from physical remains—sometimes by looking at stomach contents of a mummy. Even tiny biological samples reveal remarkably precise dietary information. For example, tests run on the sixteenth-century bodies in the Medici Chapel in Florence largely corroborated the picture painted by historians, of a noble diet heavy with meat, but also including a lot of fish for fast days.[1] The basic dietary information found in cookbooks is not therefore merely guesswork and speculation but can be used to help describe the history of dietary patterns, calories, and overall health.

On rare occasions the historian may find tell-tale stains on the pages of a cookbook that can be chemically analyzed as direct proof that someone tried a recipe at least once or twice. More often discovered are marginalia, and these are sometimes the most illuminating of all treasures discovered in cookbooks. Little comments, corrections to a recipe, or additions are positive evidence that someone interacted directly with the text and actually cooked the recipe. In modern manuscript recipe collections interpreters are often disheartened to find that the author copied the recipe from a newspaper or from the back of a can, but this, too, is good evidence that the recipe was found interesting and probably tested. In such cases, and of course in correspondence about cookbooks, we can feel more confident that the text describes actual meals eaten. The same goes for community cookbooks wherein contributors identify themselves, though that is no guarantee of originality.

Other types of information can be gleaned directly from the cookbook. The economic historian may simply look at the lists of ingredients to show what kinds of consumer goods would have been available at a given time, or what crops might have been produced locally on a farm or within a village. Some imported items, spices especially, traveled thousands of miles from their origin in what is today Indonesia to Europe, and their appearance in cookbooks gives reasonable assurance that they were available to some people. The presence of an ingredient, perhaps seafood in a book published in a land-locked region, provides evidence of a brisk internal trade network. Sometimes cookbooks also discuss prices, and this can be invaluable for historians reconstructing costs of living and inflation rates. And of course the mere appearance of certain ingredients is a great historical consequence, say, the first recipe for the tomato, which appears in Antonio Latini's *Lo Scalco alla Moderna* in the late seventeenth century.

The historian of material culture or technology will look at the equipment and cooking methods described in the recipes and be able to give a fairly accurate description of the kinds of tools that would have been available and used at least by some in a given time period. For example, cooking in an oven in some periods denotes substantial wealth and the ability to afford abundant firewood, while in others it would have been a matter of buying coal for an iron stove, or in others simply paying the electric bill. These are various ways the information in cookbooks may be read directly.

But there are also ways the historian can read between the lines of the recipes, so to speak, to answer questions that are not directly related to cooking or material culture but may deal with gender roles, issues of class, ethnicity, and race. Even topics such as politics, religion, and world view are revealed in the commentary found in cookbooks and sometimes embedded in what appears to be a simple recipe. The most valuable of cookbooks and related culinary texts also reveal what we might call complete food ideologies. By this is meant a way of thinking about the world that is part of a larger esthetic, political, or social mindset. For example, a vegetarian cookbook offers a specific ethical position about humans' relationship to animals. A diet cookbook may indicate the author's ideas about beauty and the human body and how society views overweight. A "quick and convenient" cookbook may also offer explicit details about people's daily routine and the values that are espoused in a family where both parents work and perhaps commute. The ideology also denotes a way of eating that promises some kind of transformation for the reader if he or she follows the directions prescribed. The dieter will lose weight, become more attractive, and perhaps find love. The convenient cook will escape drudgery, have free time for the children, and find familial happiness. In this way a food ideology is much like any other ideology, political or religious—it promises a better, more fulfilled life, moral rectitude, or even merely esteem among invited guests for one's culinary prowess, thus enhancing one's social standing.

But before jumping into these grander questions, methodologically it is important to approach the five basic questions first to contextualize the information contained in cookbooks. A detail in one period may mean something very different in another, for example a recipe calling for sugar in the fourteenth century denotes significant wealth, since it was still an expensive and fairly rare item, while a nineteenth-century recipe including sugar suggests something else, since it was by then cheap and affordable to the masses in most industrialized countries. A recipe that asks you to first kill your chicken offers hints about the audience, probably rural, that will not be spelled out clearly but can be easily read into the text. Thus it is important to gather as much information about the time and place before trying to answer the five basic questions.

To proceed: Who wrote the cookbook? More than the name of the author, one must ask, was this a professional chef or a home cook? Was this a dilettante writing for a leisured audience for entertainment or someone with direct practical cooking skills? Most important, was this a man or woman? Considering the author first, and they often describe themselves in the preface, is usually the best way to approach the other basic questions. For example, if the author has a noble title, such as Sir Kenelm Digby in seventeenth-century England, who speaks of his connections at court, the noble people who offered their own recipes for various quasi-medicinal alcoholic drinks, conserves, and candy, one can rightfully assume that the projected audience is much like author, or at least those who aspire to be like him. Digby was actually a famous scientist and many of the recipes call for equipment that would be beyond the budget of most households. Most likely his cookbook, *The Closet of Sir Kenelm Digby Opened* (closet here meaning secret laboratory kitchen), was meant for readers who cooked for leisure rather than basic meals to be served to a family. The recipes also reveal Digby's close connections to the continent, with a conscious Italianate bent, and his prominence as a Catholic in a country that had not only become Protestant but was frequently at war with Catholic Spain. In this case the author himself provides most of the clues for interpreting the recipes and their meaning.

Likewise, if we look at Fanny Farmer's *Boston Cooking-School Cook Book*, printed in many editions in the first decades of the twentieth century, we learn that the author ran a famous cooking school that treated recipes as scientific procedures to be followed exactly for predictable and reliable results. The cookbook offers these methods to regular housewives, who were instructed to apply the same principles to rationalize their own kitchens. Not coincidentally, standard measurements, cooking times, and procedures became requisite in cookbooks hereafter. But it is the author herself who explains the setting and purpose of the cookbook and the values to which her readership ascribed or aspired. Women of this period, domesticated in every sense of that word, were intent on making their realms as professional and scientific as any workplace. This afforded women's place in the home a certain dignity and seriousness of purpose. It elevated housework to a level, if not equal to men's work, then at least approaching it. The suffrage movement was gathering steam in these very years as well. The cookbook in this case offers concrete evidence of how women's roles were being redefined, even if they were not yet outside of the home.

Identifying the projected audience is the second question to be answered. Sometimes this is quite simple and stated directly in the title: *The Good Housewife's Handmaide for the Kitchen*, an anonymous work of the sixteenth century, or *Le Cuisinier Royale et Bourgeois* by François Massialot published in 1691,[2] which explains very clearly that dishes eaten by the king have been scaled down and made affordable and practical for urban households and a small number of guests. Likewise Charles Elmé Francatelli's *A Plain Cookery Book for the Working Classes* of 1861 makes absolutely clear that the book is intended for households on the strictest of budgets, with minimal equipment, who need good solid fare to fuel their bodies for difficult labor.[3] It also suggests that working class women, thrust into factories at a young age, may have not been trained by their mothers in basic cooking skills. Francatelli, as chef to Queen Victoria, essentially offers this cheap, small-format book as an act of charity. Like Soyer's *Shilling Cookbook for the Masses* of the same era, a superstar chef is offering his talents for the good of the nation at an affordable price, and in Soyer's case much of the proceeds went to charitable causes as well.

Sometimes, however, the projected audience and purpose are not stated directly but can be obliquely inferred from the details. The format of the cookbook is one good indication. A small affordable text is almost certainly aiming for a popular audience, whereas a large beautifully bound and illustrated quarto edition is most likely not. More recent cookbooks will also suggest a price, and one can be sure that a celebrity chef's glossy ode to his famous restaurant, Ferran Adrià's is a good example, priced at several hundred dollars, will only be purchased by the most avid fans with the largest wallets. A tiny, ten dollar paperback seeks a completely different crowd. The details within usually confirm this as well. But the point here is not merely to name the social and economic class the author has targeted. Usually a cookbook will also signal aspirational values. It will offer recipes that the target audience hopes to cook, using ingredients that will impress others, and often with the intention of rising beyond the audience's class and its values. For example, if a cookbook offers cheap popular ingredients cooked without complication or fuss, chances are it reveals very little about social emulation. But if the ingredients are expensive or rare, suggest some kind of gastronomic sophistication or savoir faire, then the author is guessing that those who buy it, and perhaps cook from it, want to better themselves.

Two very different examples will illustrate this point. In the court of sixteenth-century Ferrara Italy, the household steward of the duke named Christoforo di Messisbugo wrote a cookbook and list of foods served at magnificent banquets he personally presided over. The book is very clearly directed toward only the most magnificent and wealthy courts, since each banquet is designed to serve a mere fifty people or so with dozens upon dozens of courses with literally thousands of dishes. Ground pearls and gold leaf go into the food as well. Obviously one could read this text merely to marvel at the profligacy. But Messisbugo, himself having risen up the social ranks to be ennobled, very clearly understands there are managers in comparable courts who might not have the same culinary virtuosity, and who would be very interested in such a guide precisely to further their own careers. This is an aspirational text, written by and for professionals. But one can also very easily imagine rival courts, where nobles themselves, hoping not to look outdated or cheap with their own banquets, purchase such a book so as to instruct their household staff. It is precisely these social tensions, played out in competitive feasting, that are goaded by this cookbook. It is also precisely this emulation by slightly lower social classes and perhaps wealthy merchants that fuels innovation among cookbook authors, pushing them to increasing extravagance, expense, and complexity, merely to prevent the nouveau-riches and social upstarts from "passing" as nobles. That is, such cookbooks reveal enormous social anxieties among elites, and are often found side by side with sumptuary laws, specifying precisely how many courses may legally be served by people of various classes. None of this would have happened without great social mobility. Thus we have gained insight about the time and place and its values merely from reading between the lines of the recipe.

From a completely different time and place comes a small cookbook, the first to be written by a black man in the United States, entitled *Good Things to Eat* by Rufus Estes, published around 1911.[4] Estes was a professional chef, working at a time when it was fashionable to have a black man working in the kitchen. Some restaurants boasted this fact, and railroads hired blacks exclusively as Pullman Porters. One can only speculate why in an era long after the Civil War, when many blacks had migrated to Northern Cities, whites would actively seek out blacks as servants, and of course such images as Uncle Ben and Aunt Jemima would continue to persist in promoting such stereotypes through the entire century. In any case, Estes' story is one of rising above the conditions of his birth. He was born into slavery and came to work for the railroads and then as a professional chef for a powerful steel corporation. His audience is not immediately apparent. It may very well have been men in positions similar to his own, hoping to learn to cook and gain lucrative employment. In this case it would certainly be a book about social climbing and "making it" in a difficult world. But in all likelihood Estes' readers were also white, exactly the sort for whom Southern recipes recalled an era when whites owned blacks. To cook, or more likely have one's servants cook, such *authentic* black food is at some level constructing a fantasy of owning the people and their food. It is no less aspirational, nostalgically imagining a world that had disappeared, but in which one could nonetheless capture in a particular meal through the recipes of a man who was once a real slave.

The colonial cookbooks of British India, replete with kedgeree and curries, avidly read by those with no throngs of servants to dish up their afternoon tiffin, are also a way for readers to play out their fantasies of colonial domination, albeit at the level of the knife and fork. One might argue that all exotic cookbooks appeal to those for whom strange new tastes are a substitution for real foreign travel and real colonization. They are a way to appropriate the other by consuming their cultural products. And as in the other examples they aim toward people who generally don't have the wherewithal to go half way around the world to be served a meal. Most contemporary cooking magazines thrive especially on this kind of fantasy travel, eating weird and exotic foods, and of course on social climbing, *Gourmet* in particular.

When considering the audience, social emulation is not the only consideration. The author's intentions are equally important. Sometimes these are clearly enough driven by a political agenda. Take for example the classic Italian cookbook of Pellegrino Artusi *La Scienze in Cucina e L'arte di Mangiar Bene.*[5] It was first published in 1891 and written explicitly for the home cook, since the quantities feed a family, the ingredients are not expensive, and the techniques fairly uncomplicated. Artusi also explains that he is not in fact a cook, but has borrowed his recipes from experienced women around the country, indeed all throughout Italy with representative regional dishes, although the majority came from Emilia-Romagna and Tuscany. This differs from the vast majority of cookbooks written in nineteenth-century Italy, which were filled with French recipes and complex procedures only successfully carried out in professional kitchens with a large staff. Why then a consciously Italian cookbook for small households? The context reveals all here. This was only two decades after Italy had become a nation. This cookbook is an effort to build national unity by focusing on the native, authentic folk traditions of the various disparate regions, bringing them together as something uniquely Italian. If subsequent history is any indication, the project largely succeeded. Pasta, for example, became for the first time the staple first course everywhere, albeit industrially mass-manufactured.

The late nineteenth-century wave of nationalism witnessed a proliferation of books with precisely the same intent, to reject the international elite cookery so dominated by the French, and return to the peasant roots of native folk cookery. The same process led to a revival of folk music, folk costume, architecture and linguistic study. It is as if to be a proper nation one must have a national cuisine.

Similarly, cookbooks written for specific immigrant communities are a way to maintain and express identity when surrounded by the forces of assimilation. The early twentieth century produced scores of cookbooks that taught second or third generation descendants of immigrants the traditional recipes and skills that were in danger of being lost. They challenged the very idea of a "melting pot" in which all foreign cultural practices combined into a whitewashed American majority. Of course a political voice for such communities, made up largely of working classes, was also an item on the agenda. Suddenly there were Italian cookbooks, Jewish cookbooks, Polish and German cookbooks, and so forth. While these first appealed to people within these ethnic groups, increasingly those outside them also became interested. One must read closely for hints that outsiders are being welcomed in, for example if an ingredient must be explained, or if a recipe is adapted so it will appeal to mainstream tastes. *The Chinese-Japanese Cookbook* of 1914 by Sara Bosse and Onoto Watanna is an excellent example of this.[6] The authors explain that their Oriental dishes may sound strange and repugnant, but will appeal to American households if tried. In succeeding decades, of course many ethnic foods did go mainstream and cookbook authors constantly strive to offer the most authentic recipe, not bastardized for uninitiated palates but just as a *real* person from the country in question would make it. This in turn demeans the adaptive hybrid cuisines, Italian-American, Chinese-American, and so forth, which are then in turn rediscovered as viable and worthwhile cuisines in their own right.

All this is to say that understanding the context is crucial to interpreting the ethnic recipe as a historical document. Is it meant for insiders as an expression of identity or intended to appeal to outsiders as something new and exciting? Does it purport to be authentic as from the homeland or representing the practices of a new hybrid cuisine that is worthy of respect? Does it try to promulgate foods that one would find in ethnic restaurants, which one can make at home? These various contexts reveal the values, hopes, and aspirations of the potential reader: "I am proud to be Italian and want to maintain our family's heritage," or "I want real Italian food because I went on vacation there and the pizza was nothing like in the United States," or "I'm not a food snob and spaghetti and meatballs with gravy is perfectly delicious." The attitude of the cookbook clearly spells out where the author and potentially the readers are coming from.

Attitudes can also be classified by the author's stance toward the present. For example some cookbooks incorporate the newest gadgets—the microwave cookbook or food processor cookbook of the 1970s. Or cookbooks may offer recipes using canned goods, one written by Poppy Cannon, *The Can Opener Cookbook* of 1951, used them exclusively.[7] Cookbooks may value efficiency, ease of preparation, use of convenience foods, and often cater to an audience with minimal cooking skills. This suggests that readers did not learn basics at their mother's apron strings, and reflects larger changes in society: working mothers, students sent off to college eating cafeteria food and then perhaps suddenly faced with a kitchen and others to feed. The "dumbing down" of cookbooks in recent decades has been decried as symptomatic of the breakdown of the nuclear family, if such a thing ever existed. More likely it reflects a political agenda of what certain people would like—a family consisting of a married man and woman with 2.5 children, in which the woman handles the domestic chores. In any case, the quick, easy, and convenient cookbook reveals many of the most cherished values of mainstream American culture—speed is most important, food is merely fuel. It should taste good, but one should not be too concerned about where it comes from or what goes into it. Hence the popularity of fast food, quintessentially American, eaten on the go, by hand, with disposable containers.

But the exact opposite is also found in another type of cookbook, the nostalgic, slow, homey, laborious recipes meant to be shared among family and friends. Such cookbooks may be consciously Neo-Luddite, rejecting modern conveniences and gadgets in search of superior flavor, health, and perhaps concern for the environment. Here cooking is a usually a leisure activity and mastering a complicated dish is a major accomplishment for the weekend warrior cook, as often as not in recent decades a man. A related subgenre are what might be called macho cookbooks that encourage readers to handle large cuts of meat and offal, cook strange ingredients, and challenge the taste buds, often with searing hot chilies. Once again, one can read into the recipe values held by the potential audience.

Recent decades have also witnessed the emergence of cookbooks by celebrity chefs used essentially as a way to make money and promote a restaurant. The most popular cookbooks today are by TV chefs, which presumably attract viewers and advertising revenue, and they are often printed in astronomically large print runs. One must also take account of electronic recipe sites, blogs, podcasts, and a variety of new ways recipes are shared. Without venturing into an entire taxonomic system for cookbooks, perhaps a detailed analysis of a few examples will illustrate the methodology of historical analysis.

This is a fragment from the ancient cookbook of Archestratus written about 330 B.C. in Greek-speaking Sicily. It survives within the larger compendium of food by Athenaeus written several centuries later.

> Archestratus the Daedalus of tasty dishes in his Gastrology... says about the amia: The Amia. Prepare it by every method, in the autumn, when the Pleiad is sinking. Why recite it to you word for word, for you could not do it any harm even if you wished to? But if you desire to learn this too, my dear Moschus, the best way to present this fish I mean, then in fig leaves with not too much origano is the way. No cheese, no fancy nonsense. Simply place it with care in the fig leaves and tie them with rush-cord from above. Then put into hot ashes and use your intelligence to work out the time when it will be roasted: don't let it burn up. Let it come from lovely Byzantium if you wish to have the best, though you will get a good one if it is caught near here. The further from the Hellespont, the worse the

dish: if you travel over the glorious salt ways of the Aegean sea, it is no longer the same fish at all; rather it brings shame on my earlier praise.[8]

To start, we know the author's name, but little else about him other than the fact that five centuries after this was written it was still known and the author considered a *Daedalus*. The name means "an inventor"—the same who built his son Icarus wings. But Athenaeus in recording these words sounds somewhat sarcastic, and may be implying that being an inventor of tasty dishes is something a little silly, especially to be recorded in such grand language. We can also tell that Archestratus' words are cast in the form of a dialogue, with a teacher and master, a familiar enough arrangement for those who have read the Platonic dialogues. The recipe itself is absolutely simple, the amia is a kind of bonito or small relative of the tuna, wrapped in fig leaves. Why such simplicity? It appears as if Archestratus is reacting against common cooking methods, which in his opinion ruin the delicate flavor of the fish, by adding cheese and "fancy nonsense." He also believes most people overseason it with oregano. Most interesting, however, the author recommends where the best fish can be obtained. Byzantium is over 700 miles from Gela. Presumably fresh fish would never last such a trip, so this cosmopolitan author has been there himself, and has obviously tasted the fish elsewhere for comparison. And he even mentions the best season to eat them. What do we learn from this text? Foremost that this author and his readers prized connoisseurship. There were probably people who caught amia wherever they could, cooked it poorly and at the wrong time of year. But culinary wisdom dictates direct empirical experience, knowledge of how long to let it roast on the embers, and the understanding of how to appreciate food simply prepared and unadorned with excessive flavors. Today we would call this gastronomy, the art and science of understanding good food. Although few other culinary texts of this time have survived, we get an understanding of what ancient Greeks valued—not wealth, extravagance, or complexity, but true understanding of nature and the ability to transform it to the best effect.

Let us move to a completely different time and place for another practical exercise in cookbook analysis. Lydia Maria Francis Child's *The Frugal Housewife* was printed in Boston in 1829 and went through many further editions in the decades that follow. The subtitle, *Dedicated to Those Who Are Not Ashamed of Economy*, reveals much of the tenor of the book. The author also wrote novels and was active in the abolitionist movement, and her concern for the plight of the less fortunate comes through on every page of her cookbook. Most important, the book was the product of an economic depression, not unlike that a century later, and the prime cultural values espoused by the book, certainly indicative of this era, are stern self-sufficiency, resourcefulness, and independence. "Look to the grease-pot, and see that nothing is there which might have served to nourish your own family, or a poorer one." She is referring to drippings from bacon and the like, which should be recycled into other dishes rather than being thrown away or fed to pigs. Stale breadcrumbs should be used in puddings and broths.

Bread should be baked at home rather than bought; it is less convenient but much cheaper. This short selection practically speaks for itself on the virtues of frugality and doing it yourself.

> If you wish to salt fat pork, scald coarse salt in water and skim it, till the salt will no longer melt in the water. Pack your pork down in tight layers, salt every layer; when the brine is cool, cover the pork with it, and keep a heavy stone on the top to keep the pork under the brine. Look to it once in a while for the first few weeks, and if the salt has melted throw in some more. This brine, scalded and skimmed every time it is used, will continue good twenty years. The rind of the pork should be packed toward the edge of the barrel.
>
> It is good economy to salt your own beef as well as pork. Six pounds of coarse salt, eight ounces of brown sugar, a pint of molasses, and eight ounces of salt-petre are enough to boil in four gallons of water. Skim it clean while boiling. Put it to the beef cold; have enough to cover it, and be careful your beef never floats on the top. If it does not smell perfectly sweet, throw in more salt; if a scum rises upon it, scald and skim it again, and pour it on the beef when cold.[9]

One can also easily imagine that this advice would have been of excellent practical value for a family heading westward, both for homesteaders and prospectors. Reading between the lines we can also see that the projected audience is not only one concerned about expenses, but probably also a good sized family, since they are storing large quantities of meat. The do-it-yourself attitude also implies that one could, for more money, purchase preserved pork and beef, and this certainly would be more typical once large industrial packing firms such as Armour, Swift, and then Hormel began to supply the country via railroads. It is also interesting that once refrigerated railroad cars were able to supply fresh beef and pork year round, putting up large quantities of meat was no longer necessary, and such skills practically vanished.

The final example comes from a much more obscure cookbook, the *Libro del arte de cozina,* written by Domingo Hernandez de Maceras and published in 1607 in Salamanca, Spain. Its author identifies himself as the cook for the Colegio Mayor de San Salvador de Oviedo at the University of Salamanca, well known as the best place to study law. In other words, he is a college chef. It gives us a glimpse into a professional kitchen, and presumably was written as a guide for other chefs, though there are no measurements or indications of quantity so it could theoretically be used in ordinary households too. The author's comments are also fascinating because while he was certainly on a fixed budget for buying ingredients, he is trying to offer his students the most interesting fare he can. Spices, for example are used, though not in great quantity, as are other expensive ingredients. On the whole, the cooking is fairly straightforward and by the author's own testimony reflects dishes he actually served regularly in the college mess hall. It is also interesting to consider the students he was catering to. They are not nobility, who in Spain would inherit titles and positions and would not generally be educated, but rather younger sons of noble families, children of wealthy merchants and professionals. These are future *letrados*, lettered men who staffed the Imperial bureaucracy. So

Maceras, while trying to keep his costs in bounds, still tries to feed his charges well. By that, he thinks of not only good tasting food, but food that according to the current medical theories of the day would keep them in good health—varying the menu according to the seasons, and food that follows the dictates of the Roman Catholic Church, which set aside fast days throughout the calendar, and especially during the 40 days of Lent. The concerns that inform this cookbook are truly fascinating. Here is just one example of a Lenten dish. Incidentally, it is a delicious recipe as well.

> Spinach
>
> You must wash it very well, and put it to cook with salt, spices, and after it's cooked chop it on a board, and then squeeze out well, then put into a pot or casserole a half quartillo of oil, and some chopped garlic, that you fry in the oil, and add the spinach, and fry it all, and add raisins, and honey which is very sweet. Crush the spices and some garlic together, because greens require the flavor of garlic, and moisten the spices and garlic with a little water, and add to the spinach, mixing with all the condiments and cook, for you must serve it dry on the plate, and you can serve it in place of soup, and you can even serve it in a meal for Lent, and add a little vinegar.[10]

Notes

1. Gino Gornaciari, et al, "The 'gout' of the Medici, Grand Dukes of Florence: a palaeopathological study," *Rheumatology* 48, no. 4 (2009): 375–77.
2. François Massialot, *Le Cuisinier Royale et Bourgeois* (Paris: Charles de Sercy, 1691).
3. Charles Elmé Francatelli, *A Plain Cookery Book for the Working Classes* (London: Bosworth and Harrison, 1861).
4. Rufus Estes, *Good Things to Eat* (Chicago: By the Author, c. 1911).
5. Pellegrino Artusi, *Science in the Kitchen and the Art of Eating Well*, trans. Murtha Baca and Stephen Sartarelli (Toronto: University of Toronto Press, 1993 [1891]).
6. Sara Bosse and Onoto Watanna, *The Chinese-Japanese Cookbook* (Chicago: Rand McNally, 1914).
7. Poppy Cannon, *The Can-Opener Cookbook* (New York: Thomas J. Crowell, 1951).
8. Archestratus, *The Life of Luxury*, trans. John Wilkins and Shaun Hill (Totnes, Devon: Prospect Books. 1994), 73.
9. Lydia Maria Francis Child, *The Frugal Housewife*, 2nd ed. (Boston: Carter and Hendee, 1830), 9, 40.
10. Domingo Hernandez de Maceras, *Libro del arte de cozina* (Salamanca: Antonia Ramirez, 1607), 75 (author's translation).

Bibliography

Beck, Leonard N. *Two Loaf Givers or A Tour through the Gastronomic Libraries of Katherine Golden Bitting and Elizabeth Robins Pennel*. Washington, DC: Library of Congress, 1984.

Bower, Anne L., ed. *Recipes for Reading: Community Cookbooks, Stories, Histories.* Amherst: University of Massachusetts Press, 1997.

Floyd, Janet and Laurel Forster. *The Recipe Reader: Narratives, Contexts, Traditions.* Aldershot: Ashgate, 2003.

Gold, Carol. *Danish Cookbooks.* Seattle: University of Washington Press, 2007.

Haber, Barbara. *From Hardtack to Homefries: An Uncommon History of American Cooks and Meals.* New York: The Free Press, 2002.

Humble, Nicola. *Culinary Pleasures: Cookbooks and the Transformation of British Food.* London: Faber and Faber, 2005.

Lehmann, Gilly. *The British Housewife.* Totnes: Prospect Books, 2002.

Mendelson, Ann. *Stand Facing the Stove: The Story of the Women Who Gave America The Joy of Cooking.* New York: Henry Holt, 1996.

Mennell, Stephen. *All Manners of Food: Eating and Taste in England and France from the Middle Ages to the Present.* Oxford: Basil Blackwell, 1985.

Shapiro, Laura. *Perfection Salad: Women and Cooking at the Turn of the Century.* New York: Farrar, Straus and Girous, 1986.

Theophano, Janet. *Eat My Words: Reading Women's Lives through the Cookboks They Wrote.* New York: Palgrave, 2002.

Wheaton, Barbara Ketchum. *Savoring the Past: The French Kitchen and Table from 1300 to 1789.* New York: Simon and Schuster, 1983.

CHAPTER 14

FOOD AND EMPIRE

JAYEETA SHARMA

> "[W]hen it is winter with us, the sun somewhere else in the British Empire is reddening apples and putting the juice into oranges."
>
> —*Publicity write-up for an Empire Marketing Board poster*[1]

Between 1926 and 1933, the Empire Marketing Board used an array of advertisements, films, exhibits, and posters to send food products of empire into British homes. The real message of its publicity campaigns was that fruit from Australia or tea from India was not foreign. By dint of being imperial, such foods were also British. In buying and demanding them, the British consumer was consuming the products of her own garden. It is open to question, however, as to how much success the Board met in these specific efforts to promote intra-imperial consumption, indeed, whether those efforts were needed in the first place. Trading and colonial ventures of the early modern period had been inextricably tied to the dissemination of foods that were hitherto unfamiliar or uncommon. With the establishment of European empires and industrial societies, complex circuits spanned the globe that involved the production, distribution, and consumption of both new and old foods. Long before the Empire Marketing Board's campaign, a typical grocery list for metropolitan consumers already included products from every corner of empire, affordable to some degree for almost every one of its classes. The bounty of empire was less evident when it came to the diets and lives of those who inhabited the empire's peripheries.

The first section of the essay examines foods from Asia and America that were originally perceived as exotic in Europe, initially served as markers of elite status, and their gradual dissemination downwards. It also discusses how and why groups of people living in socially subordinate settings and geographically distant lands, adapted to strange foods imposed on them by the workings of the new European empires. The next section moves on to consider the role of long-distance trade and modern technologies in the creation and dissemination of new agro-industrial foods across networks of imperial knowledge and commodity circulation. The last section examines the circulation and adaptation of hitherto localized foods and their producers into imperial and postcolonial arenas, and goes on to explore the impact of the contemporary era's domination by global food corporations that serve in many ways as a new face of European and American empire.

Domesticated Exotics and Colonial Passages

In the 1920s, the agricultural geneticist Edward East noted: "Today one sits down to breakfast, spreads out a napkin of Irish linen, opens the meal with a banana from Central America, follows with a cereal of Minnesota sweetened with the product of Cuban cane, and ends with a Montana lamb chop and cup of Brazilian coffee. Our daily life is a trip around the world, yet the wonder of it gives us not a single thrill."[2] Locating the beginnings of such a culinary trip around the world necessitates going back a few centuries, to the early modern era, when European mercantilism and early capitalism were gradually transforming cultural encounters and power relations around the world, the era when foods from distant lands did thrill the Europeans who had access to them.

Paul Freedman's study of spices in the European imagination notes their centrality to medieval cookery and medicine. But he emphasizes that their prestige and versatility went well beyond such uses. Spices from the exotic, mysterious East were prized as symbols of material comfort and social prominence. The popular myth that spices were essential as preservatives for meat misunderstands the nature of medieval foodways and overstates the utility argument. Spices were important flavorings for sophisticated elite cookery of the medieval-era, in both Europe and Asia. But it was their scarcity and expense in medieval and early-modern Europe that made them, above all, markers of status expressed through conspicuous consumption.[3] In the case of one such spice, sugar, Sidney Mintz remarks that the elaborate marzipan subtleties at European royal banquets of the fourteen century were highly effective table-side displays of power and pelf, given sugar's rarity and cost in medieval times.[4] But by the sixteenth century, sugar's increased availability permitted even modest gentry and mercantile households to offer scaled-down sugar creations on festive occasions. As with sugar, most spices gradually increased in accessibility and moved down the social scale, even as early modern Europeans expanded direct contacts with the lands where they originated.

Paula de Vos's study of how the Spanish state sponsored a wide-ranging program for spice transplantation and cultivation provides an early example of how

European political powers began to employ colonial and scientific agents to further their food desires. Certainly, this Spanish program to extend the cultivation of spices met with limited success except for the Asian ginger-root transplanted into the Caribbean. Nonetheless, these Spanish endeavors in economic botany were important precursors of later British, Dutch, and French imperial quests that increasingly used scientific efforts to further the domestication of exotic or scarce foods.[5] In the case of spices, however, as expanding trading and plantation initiatives made them relatively affordable and plentiful, the European elite taste for heavily spiced dishes gradually receded. For instance, the intervention of sugar supplies from Caribbean plantations moved it from the category of rare spice to everyday condiment, from luxury to perceived necessity, from conspicuous consumption to invisible staple. Sugar's new abundance also enabled its new role as a companion to other foods, such as tea and coffee, which together created new tastes and habits for European consumers.

One of the important ways in which food history provides new insights into the processes of European exploration and colonization is by showing how newly available tropical foods quickly became markers of European conquests and elite status. One such food was the pineapple, whose very appearance as a delicious fruit with a forbidding exterior excited curiosity, admiration, and desire. Early Portuguese, Dutch, and English adventurers triumphantly carried back pineapples as conquering booty. Initially, it served as a royal prize, as in a 1668 banquet hosted by King Charles II of England for the French Ambassador where "the rare fruit called the King-pine" was displayed, possibly as an emblem of English dominion over contested Caribbean islands. Horticulturally minded aristocrats vied to build hothouses to breed superior examples. By the eighteenth century, pineapples appeared on North American tables, as decorative motif and food. The fruit continued to circle the globe as an object of culinary, social, and economic value along new and expanding currents of European and American commerce and colonization.[6]

Brian Cowan notes that simple contacts with new foods from overseas did not automatically bring actual assimilation into Old World dietary habits. Acceptance hinged on a host of factors, an important one being the European interest in new foods and drinks nurtured by influential scientific virtuosi such as the British physician and plant collector Sir Hans Sloane who introduced cocoa from Jamaica. This and other tropical crops first introduced into Europe as medicinal ingredients, tobacco, coffee, and tea, quickly entered the Galenic universe. Subsequently, they moved out of the medical domain into that of everyday tastes, first for elites and then more broadly. Often this was in a different mode from their original use, as for instance when Sloane added sugar and milk to cocoa to make drinking chocolate.

The complex interplays of gender, race, and class further shaped the domestic assimilation of such exotics. The marriage of the Portuguese princess Catharine of Braganza to Charles II gave a fashionable fillip to tea-drinking among English elites, celebrated in verse by the poet and parliamentarian, Edmund Waller. In keeping with the princess's patronage, eighteenth-century English society largely saw tea as a beverage that belonged to the world of upper-class feminine domesticity. Coffee by contrast, imported by the English East India Company from Mocha and by its Dutch counterpart from Java, was linked with masculine sociability. The Royal Society and Lloyd's Insurance Company were just two outposts of upper-class male associational culture in London that owed their origins to coffee-house sociability. For Europeans, coffee's imagined association with Turkey meant that coffee-houses often brandished the institutional sign of a Turk's Head.[7]

Once new exotics had entered into elite dietary routines, many filtered downwards in terms of price, availability, and social class. In a study of English overseas trade statistics where groceries included tea, coffee, rice, sugar, pepper, and other tropical products, in 1700, such former exotic commodities comprised 16.9 percent of all imports by official value; by 1800, their share rose to 34.9 percent.[8] Not all exotics gained popularity or acceptability, or even the same degree of success. An exhibit that aroused much curiosity at London's Great Exhibition of 1851 was that of a beverage called Paraguay "tea."[9] This was advertised as a cheap substitute for China tea, but the leaves could not be imported in sufficient quantity. Coffee, whose production was undertaken by all the European powers in their colonial hinterlands, retained its appeal for elite male society in Britain, but did not extend its appeal in the same manner as tea. The eventual success of tea for British consumers depended in large part on its successfully transcending class and gender lines.

Troy Bickham argues that the increasing domestication of tropical foods such as sugar, tea, tobacco, or coffee made them ubiquitous symbols of empire, as their advertisement, retail, preparation and consumption reflected and contributed to British perceptions of their nation's expanding reach across the world.[10] But, as Linda Colley reminds us, well into the early nineteenth century, the British hold over colonial possessions remained insecure.[11] In that light, the relatively early assimilation of imperial commodities into quotidian metropolitan lives takes on added significance, as assertions of dominion over non-European territories and non-white peoples that were as yet only partially under British sway.

Colonial and imperial networks played an important role in the spread and adoption of new foods not only into the metropole, but in their trans-migration into other parts of empire. A key example here is the New World's potato tuber, famously introduced by Elizabethan buccaneer-colonists into England, and by returning Spanish colonists into Spain and other parts of Europe. Despite the potato's early journey into the Old World, it was not until the late-eighteenth century that it entered the common diet of Europeans. Most notably, this took place in the colonized economy of Ireland where the potato came into its own as a cheap and prolific peasant staple that substituted for the Irish wheat harvests siphoned off by the English revenue machinery. The tragic consequences of the resultant dietary monoculture are well-known, most notably the Great Hunger of the mid-nineteenth century where the potato harvest's collapse and the colonial state's indifference led to the death of an estimated million and the emigration of at least another million. In New Zealand, its indigenous Maori population first encountered the potato as a tropical crop that had been acclimatized in Europe into a form capable of weathering temperate climes. John Fitzpatrick describes how the potato spread rapidly after 1801, through Maori kumara (sweet potato) growing techniques, and the close relationship between this new food and the new military dynamic whereby Maori forces challenged the British during the New Zealand Wars of 1843–1872.[12] At times, colonial authorities themselves played a key role in encouraging the production and consumption of such new foods. In India, the New World's potato arrived during the early modern era of Mughal rule, but did not come into vogue. Only after the British state launched agricultural improvement campaigns to popularize potato cultivation did it become an essential element of new pan-Indian diets, albeit as an addition to the vegetable repertoire supplement a grain-based diet, rather than as a staple or a carbohydrate as in Europe.[13]

Imperial laboring regimes and the lived encounters and power equations involved with them often played an important role in transforming and modifying food availability and dietary practices in a particular territory or among a particular people. The triangular trade in human beings and commodities across the Middle Passage transported salt cod from Canada and Newfoundland to the Caribbean even as it sent rum and sugar to Africa and Europe, and molasses to Newfoundland. In several cases, the actual adoption of a previously unknown food resulted from a lack of choice upon distant, inhospitable shores, or from penny-pinching by colonizing masters. For instance, Black Loyalists transplanted to Nova Scotia after the American Revolution and African slaves sent there after the War of 1812 encountered a lack of shelter and food that forced them to live off corn and molasses. The easy availability of cheap molasses, the byproduct of Caribbean sugar production, eventually made them an integral part of the diet of Newfoundland fisher communities. Similarly, French imperial networks imported huge quantities of Irish salt beef into Martinique and Guadeloupe. Its demand arose not from the slaves but from the French state that favored salt beef as the cheapest source of portable protein. On British plantations in the Caribbean, sugar laborers were provided the lowest-grade of Newfoundland salt cod as the only type of protein in their rations.[14]

Certainly, there were many occasions where colonized groups refused to cooperate with such dietary changes imposed from above. For instance, Caribbean plantation slaves managed to resist attempts by French and British colonists to introduce flour made from the transplanted Tahitian breadfruit tree, in place of imported wheat flour, perhaps the most ambitious Enlightenment era project of food substitution on record. Despite long lobbying for breadfruit introduction to replace the more expensive wheat, planters had made few arrangements to distribute it or instruct slave workers how to harvest, prepare, and cook the fruit. Also, slaves lacked protein sources, not starches since they already cultivated cassava, yam, and sweet potatoes in their own gardens. Interestingly, once slavery was abolished, breadfruit did make its way into the Caribbean diet, in new local dishes. After Slave Emancipation, straitened circumstances made dishes of breadfruit cou-cou, boiled breadfruit, steamed breadfruit, roasted breadfruit, and pickled breadfruit grudgingly acceptable, despite its unsavory link to planter coercion. As a Caribbean folklorist has it, such cheap and filling dishes "put food in the belly of a lot 'o poor people" who would otherwise have gone without.[15] As a poor person's staple, breadfruit retained its symbolic meaning as a "low" culture object.[16]

Thus, human ingenuity managed in diverse ways to transmute strange foodstuffs and culinary practices forced by imperial policies upon subaltern populations, into new dishes and cuisines. The conjunction of Newfoundland salt cod with an indigenous fruit used in slave kitchens created the now ubiquitous Caribbean dish, saltfish and ackee. Another group of post-Emancipation sugar workers, the indentured laborers imported from British-ruled India to Trinidad and Guyana, transmuted their homeland's flatbreads and accompaniments into a hybridized, portable dish that eventually became a ubiquitous street food in the Caribbean. This was the goat or pumpkin roti where the flatbread formed a burrito-like shell encasing the meat or vegetables and the spiced sauce in which they were cooked, a dish that could be easily taken to work.[17] At the other end of that Atlantic exchange, Newfoundlanders began to valorize molasses, formerly the food of scarcity, as a proud badge of regional identity enshrined in popular lore and song.[18] In such manner, many dishes, borne of necessity and hardship, gradually became creolized cultural markers or took on the role of society's iconic receptacles for nostalgia.

To conclude, from the seventeenth to the nineteenth centuries, many tropical and New World commodities made such the transition from expensive exotics to domesticated larder staples, even as European trading ventures were transformed into colonial empires and plantation producing cultures. Intrinsic to this transition was the altered social meaning of such commodities as the gradual rise of European political and economic power over distant lands brought the products of their landscapes and inhabitants into imperial circulatory circuits, aided by new technologies of production, distribution, and communication.

Industrial Foods: Circulation, Plenitude, and Hunger

In November 1909, the Hon. A. A. Kirkpatrick declared, "I look forward to the time when, with the aid of your kinsmen beyond the sea, we shall be able to make this Empire of ours self-supporting, so that in times of stress we shall be able to live in spite of anybody."[19] Kirkpatrick was then the Agent-General for South Australia and this was at a meeting of the Royal Colonial Institute in London, where the special subject for discussion was the resources and future prospects of Tasmania and Australia. His speech was preceded by glowing accounts of how trade in Antipodean fruit, fish, and wheat was raising the standard of living in Britain, the mother country. Following from this booster advocacy of imperial foods, this section of the essay explores the impact of long-distance trade and technological innovation in the diffusion of foods across empires and the creation of new agro-industrial foods that linked metropoles and colonies in ever more complicated networks of knowledge and commodity circulation.

At another meeting of the Royal Colonial Institute during the same year, a member presented a paper that described how the first Canadian apples had reached Britain in the 1860s, in a small speculative lot from an Ontario merchant. Fruit eventually became one of the mainstays of intra-imperial food trading networks. Prescient observations about this diversified food landscape at the heart of the empire came from the Indian traveler, N. L. Doss, who in 1893 published an account of his travels across England, Australia, New Zealand, Tasmania, and Ceylon. When Doss visited London's Covent Garden market in December, he exclaimed in surprise at the large quantities of fruit sold even at that inclement season. They included exotic varieties such as bananas and pineapples from the West Indies, oranges from Spain, Malta, and Joppa, as well as commoner pears and apples from Australia and Tasmania. By 1908, Canada exported 1,629,400 barrels of green and ripe apples, of which Great Britain received no less than 1,490,311 barrels.[20] Doss remarked that "subsequently when I visited those countries I found that this exportation of fruit to England forms a chief source of the income of the colonists."[21] He went on to observe that such a display of out-of-season fresh produce was unthinkable in his home city of Calcutta where only local fruits were available. Clearly, the imperial capital was, as yet, the most important destination for fresh foods from across empire. For those of its consumers who could buy them, these imperial food products transcended the limits of nature, time, and space.

The numerous pineapples that Doss admired at Covent Garden could only be an upper-class treat since they cost about six shillings each, in contrast to the humbler banana, sold at a penny. However, modern agro-industrial technology was about to change the aristocratic character of this tropical fruit, and many others. In 1901, the New England businessman James D. Dole arrived on Hawaii shortly after the kingdom was annexed by the United States. There, he conjured up a vision of pineapple cornucopia to add to its sugar fields: of "plantations and canneries and native workers and ships carrying cargoes of fruit to all the world."[22] By 1915, a host of Chinese, Japanese, Filipino, Hawaiian, Korean, and Portuguese men, women, and children worked in his fields and canning factories. In pursuance of his vision, Dole and other members of the Hawaiian Pineapple Growers' Association launched a spirited campaign from 1908–1912, at their headquarters in New York City, to send canned pineapple into the pantries and tables of middle-class homemakers. Pineapple was portrayed as the sanitary, convenient, and delicious embodiment of an island paradise in magazines such as the *Ladies Home Journal.* In 1939, the modernist artist Georgia O Keefe was enlisted to visit Hawaii and promote cans of Dole pineapple juice through her painting, *Pineapple Bud.* Sitting in their homes, European and American middle classes were being invited to savor the taste of the tropics, in the manner of past elites and pioneering empire-builders.

The foundation of Dole's American agro-industrial empire came from its utilization of innovations in food and transport technology that European powers had already initiated. In the development of industrial cuisine, the most important factors were developments in preserving (salting, pickling, biscuits, canning, freezing), mechanization (for production in both agriculture and in the factory, also for preparation, and distribution), retailing and wholesaling (commercial catering, branding, packaging, selling, advertising), and transport (railways, cargo ships). Imperial ambitions often drove the development of such innovations. For instance, the modern canning industry dates back to 1809 when a Parisian confectioner won the French government's prize for anyone who could preserve meats for its army and navy serving in distant and inhospitable lands. A British firm subsequently replaced the French use of glass bottles with cans made of iron sheets dipped in molten tin.[23] Subsequently, whether for European troops deployed up Egypt's Nile River, explorers seeking the Pole, or emissaries of the British Raj in India, canned foods ranging from green peas to steak and kidney pudding and potted beef became essential accoutrements of imperial ventures. In British India, canned foods and wine and spirits for European colonial consumers soon formed a significant part of the huge import bill that Indian nationalists resented as a "drain of wealth."

Two of the behemoths of modern food production, the canning industry and the production of biscuits were first directed to the needs of European travelers, explorers, armed forces, traders, and colonial officers overseas. Only after that first stage did the industrial production of canned and processed foods began to impinge upon the internal markets in Europe and local markets overseas. On seeing the awe-inspiring scale of the Huntly and Palmer's biscuit concern at Reading, the traveler Doss remarked that his countrymen and women in India were already familiar with the name of that English firm and its celebrated products. According to him, "there is scarcely a single-English speaking youth in Bengal who has not had a taste of these delicacies, however heterodox they may be as articles of food in the opinion of an orthodox Hindu."[24] The availability of condensed milk cans and ginger biscuits in colonial shops catering to Europeans made them visible to aspirational locals. For most inhabitants of British India, high costs and the presence of ritual barriers against unfamiliar foods rendered such industrial foods of empire practically unreachable. But the young were creative in their quests for such alluring novelties. In the small provincial town of Sibsagar, during the 1920s, European-style bread and biscuits were still forbidden foods for high-caste Hindu families but their school-going sons occasionally persuaded less ritual-bound Muslim classmates to provide them with illicit tastes. As the twentieth century wore on, their strangeness decreased as did ritual prohibitions. For instance, biscuits, initially new and expensive, became more affordable when locally manufactured. British India's first biscuit factory was the Britannia biscuit company, established in Calcutta in 1892, which expanded greatly with lucrative British government contracts during the world wars. Eventually, India became the world's second largest producer of biscuits, with products as varied as chocolate Bourbons to cumin biscuits, and the word finding quotidian use in every Indian language.[25]

The biggest impact of industrial-age technology on European and American food supplies came through its role in providing a reliable supply of fresh meat to consumers. Australian canned meat still fed British troops during the Boer War, as well as colonists in New Zealand, New Guinea, Fiji, China, India, Java, and Mauritius. Canned meat maintained empire's emissaries abroad but domestic consumers who yearned for fresh meat were deterred both by high prices and lack of availability. For Doss, meat, "the chief article of the Englishman's food," was a matter of deep interest. His wanderings around London convinced him of the extent to which England had become dependent on other countries for its meat. Until the late-nineteenth century, salted and cured pork products formed the bulk of American meat exports to Britain, since beef did not take well to curing. There also developed an Atlantic trade in live cattle, despite many difficulties. Meanwhile, experiments in meat refrigeration were underway in South America, the United States, France, and Australia. In 1874, the first cargo of beef was successfully shipped from the United States to England; in 1877, from Australia to England. By the end of the nineteenth century improvements in refrigeration facilities began to revolutionize the meat trade. Such improvements eventually realized the desire to have fresh meat available year-around at European markets.

In the United States, by the mid-nineteenth century, the tremendous expansion of the livestock industry brought huge changes in ecology and food patterns. The incursion of settlers' cattle into Western and Pacific coast grasslands accelerated the demise of the native bison that had already been precipitated by hunters supplying hides and other bison parts to new industrial enterprises. Andrew Isenberg shows that the hugely increased numbers of cattle in Wyoming and Montana, by the 1880s, corresponded to a fall in the bison population in the region to a few hundreds. Russel Barsh claims that the demise of the bison principally benefitted Western cattlemen of the industrial age, just as it destroyed the ecology and living cultures of Native American groups. Having connived at the destruction of the bison, the United States government became a major buyer of beef to feed the inhabitants of its new Native American reservations. Even from a nutritional viewpoint, this was a negative development since bison was much lower than beef in total fats and saturated fats. Coupled with the flour and sugar that made up the bulk of Native rations, this dietary regime was a slow disaster for such dislocated groups, the victims of internal colonialism and industrial expansion. Meanwhile, the demand for beef grew even greater as the westward expansion of railroads allowed emigrant trains, the army, and mining settlements to acquire supplies from a distance. The United States gradually became preoccupied with supplying this huge domestic demand.[26]

Australia, New Zealand, and Argentina eventually became Britain's main suppliers of meat. One of the early success stories in such long-distance oceanic trade was the Dunedin's ninety-eight-day voyage in 1882 sailing from New Zealand to London with 5,000 frozen mutton carcasses. Beef formed an important part of the new refrigerated trade, given its scarcity in England where there was an estimated single head of cattle for every seven people. Argentina soon acquired dominance in this market since well-to-do British consumers preferred its high-quality chilled beef and mutton. Hard-frozen Antipodean meats sold at cheaper prices to low-end British consumers. By 1911, the Argentine chilled beef industry was controlled by

British, Argentine, and American interests. During the First World War, deeming the Argentine meat supply to be of vital national importance for Britain, the British government even leased one of the main meat plants at Las Palmas, which it continued to operate for many years. In this manner, imperial circuits of meat supply became crucial to British consumers of the industrial age, as well as to the imperial economies that supplied them.[27]

Despite the abundance of such imperial foods in London markets, the reality was that price and income constraints still limited their everyday consumption to British society's higher ranks. Several tropical commodities—cocoa, sugar, tea, coffee—that became ubiquitous in Britain, were ones which provided affordable and quick calories for Britain's new industrial proletariat. The imperial history of these foods, which Mintz terms as "drug foods," requires inserting the experiences of labor mobilization and changes in imperial consumption—right into the British industrial and mass consumption revolutions. Tea, for instance, became indispensable for British consumers across class and gender lines with the wide availability of cheap empire-grown supplies from new Assam, Darjeeling, and Ceylon plantations, alongside the older, prestigious Chinese varieties. In contrast to slave-grown sugar whose consumption British Abolitionist opinion opposed, Indian tea, cultivated by ostensibly free laborers, lacked a clear binary that made visible the structures of oppressive colonial production. It needs to be remembered that tea was, for a long time, Indian only in its labor force and production sites; the British dominated its manufacture, distribution, and sale. The leaves were dispatched from British-owned plantations to be repackaged by grocery firms such as Lipton into boxes of English and Irish Breakfast Tea. Boosters of the East India Company's Indian tea exports argued that colonial control over tea production and distribution not only augmented British revenues but aided spread of civil virtues, whether among metropolitan working-classes or among India's "natives." In British India, the diffusion of tea-drinking was part of a distinct modern sensibility, heavily inflected by classed and gendered mores, and the expansion of public arenas. In rural Assam of the early twentieth century, local villagers tended to reserve market-purchased tea for important (usually male) visitors, while family members used milk from their cows for everyday consumption. In rural Bihar, many villagers classed tea with tobacco consumption, both practices predominantly associated with male public venues and cash outlays. In such societies where alcohol use invited social censure, tea gradually began to serve the purpose of a pint elsewhere, as a lubricant of public sociability.

To sum up, the story of industrial food needs to be told in a larger trans-national framework that takes into account the actions of empires and the European and American domination accompanying its rise. Inserting into a single frame such landmarks of food history as the demise of the American bison, emergence of California and Hawaii fruit farming, man-made Irish and Indian famines, indentured labor on Assam tea and Caribbean sugar plantations, and the rise of Australian and Argentine cattle industry, allows a new reading of histories of industrialization, imperialism, and food in a truly global manner.

Local and Global Foods: Empires and Their Aftermath

This final section of the essay discusses how imperial connections facilitated the process by which certain foods, Indian-style curry dishes for instance, gradually begun their journey towards global acceptance, albeit often in significantly changed forms. It explores how the diffusion and adaptation of previously localized and home-style foods into the global marketplace is tied to the movement of laboring bodies, often forced into mobility by the strains and stresses of successive deindustrialization, decolonization, the political conflicts and economic dislocations attending the birth and development of new nations from colonies. It further analyses how the globally linked production and circulation of foods in the postcolonial era have had a differential impact upon people and societies of the Global North and South, all in various ways the legatees of empire.

In 1897, G.P. Pillai, a resident of the Indian city of Madras, published his account of the West, titled *London and Paris Through Indian Spectacles*. Pillai reflected that it was a great advantage that one had no choice but to travel to England by sea since the voyage allowed colonized subjects to better adapt to metropolitan mores. "On board the steamer you begin to eat English dinners, you dress like Englishmen, you learn English manners, and become accustomed to English ways."[28] While his compatriot Doss was impressed by London's abundance of imperial produce, Pillai was awestruck by the city's restaurants and their splendidly versatile bills of fare. However, he was one with Doss in astonishment that London, the seat of British imperial power and pelf where all educated Indians aspired to travel and stay, could not produce a decent dish of "curry."

It seems paradoxically parochial that such cosmopolitan Indians as Doss and Pillai would seek out "curry and rice" when they visited Britain. The explanation seems to lie in the prominence that "curry" enjoyed in Victorian Britain. As early as 1747, Hannah Glasse produced the first known English recipe to make "a currey in the Indian way," in her book that claimed to instruct "the lower sort" in good household cookery.[29] By 1861, Isabella Beeton included no less than fourteen recipes for curry in her manual of household management, chiefly as a means to cook leftover meats by spicing them up with curry powder.[30] Troy Bickham argues that the explosion of cookbooks with such empire-related dishes allowed British consumers the opportunity to replicate and celebrate imperial experiences in their homes and clubs, just as consuming tea, coffee, cocoa, or sugar operated as an act of imperial participation through the performance of an everyday ritual.[31] However, the metropole's simulacrum of the empire's foodways appeared somewhat differently to those from its peripheries. Colonial visitors such as Doss and Pillai initially regarded the British popularity of curry as an appreciation of Indian tastes. In London, they eagerly sought curry as a familiar taste of home, but also as a taste of India in Britain. To their chagrin, they found that what they understood by the term curry was an altogether different food from the British versions then in circulation. The culinary historian Alan Davidson observed that until the eighteenth century, the English use of spices in cooking techniques made the East India Company representatives in India much more appreciative of Mughal-influenced ceremonial dishes than were their Raj successors. In keeping with such appreciation, Hannah Glasse's curry recipe of that era used aromatic whole spices such as coriander seeds. However, by the nineteenth-century visits of Doss and Pillai, this subtle spicing became bastardized into generic curry powder mixes, sold commercially, and loose inspiration from British-Indian cookbooks (e.g., Colonel Kenney-Herbert's recipe of 1885).[32] This food change mirrored the increased tendency of the British of the high imperial Raj to acquire distance from what they critically viewed as the dirt, disease, and backwardness of a tropical colony. Curry increasingly became a British meat dish with a small amount of rice cooked and served with it, rather than the South Asian dish of sauced meats cooked with spices and eaten as one of a number of sides with rice.[33] The curry that Doss and Pillai ate (and disliked) in London was a British appropriation of yet another tropical taste. Pillai wryly observed, "rice holds a subordinate place to curry here, while in India it is just the reverse. If curry is badly prepared, rice is worse cooked."[34]

Beyond the gaze of Doss and Pillai, curry in Britain was to change even more over the twentieth century, bound up with the changing destinies of the empire and its denizens. In the London that they visited, places where even remotely palatable Indian-style cooking might be available, such as the lascar's shipboard kitchen or the dockside areas of London and Bristol, were sufficiently on the margins that class conventions kept out middle-class visitors. Notwithstanding a few coffee-houses that purported to serve curry, it was only in the early-twentieth century that Asian immigrants opened the first "curry-house" restaurants, aimed at a British working-class and Indian sojourner clientele. They were followed in 1926 by an upper-class venture on Regent Street, Veeraswamy's restaurant. Its founder, Edward Palmer, who claimed to be the great-grandson of an English general and an Indian princess, had successfully run a Mughal Palace food stall at the Wembley Empire Exhibition.[35] His restaurant came to be known as "the ex-Indian higher serviceman's curry club." In 1935, Veeraswamy's was sold to a flamboyant businessman and Conservative M.P., Sir William Arthur Steward. A 1940s Veeraswamy menu offered five kinds of curry, but also the standard restaurant dishes of the time. Nostalgic Old India hands could relish mulligatawny soup with Madras chicken curry and rice as less intrepid companions dined on macaroni au gratin and supreme of turbot.[36]

Whether in Veeraswamy's kitchen and in the humble curry-houses of East London and Birmingham dockside areas, most makers of an emergent British Asian cuisine were former lascar seamen from the sea-faring region of Sylhet (then in East Bengal, now Bangladesh). Almost all lacked professional cooking skills, and in the gendered society of their homeland, few would ever have prepared food in the past, let alone the generic "curries" British consumers increasingly knew as Indian food.[37] Through the largely invisible, often illegal journeys of such migrants into the heart and hinterlands of the British Empire, hampered both by state regulations on free movement and the scarcity of essential ingredients, South Asian food in Britain began its historic journey through a hybridized landscape of circulating commodities, people, and foods. Political landmarks of decolonization such as the 1947 Partition of India into warring nation-states and the 1971 Bangladesh War engendered human trauma and further displacement into Britain's shores. Such events bequeathed Britain more cheap labor from its erstwhile colonies to make the dish its inhabitants knew as curry, in restaurants named after symbols of past Indo-Persian imperial glory, such as the Kohinoor and Taj Mahal.[38]

A broad consideration of the significant human and ecological costs of the expansion of industrial and imperial-era food production reveals that the repercussions were particularly widespread and severe upon colonized regions, going far beyond the health of individual populations. In Senegal, from the 1870s onwards, the imperatives of French metropolitan policies dictated that more than half the colony's land be diverted to the growing of a cash crop for export, ground-nuts. Instead of local food grains, Senegal's population was fed on imported rice surplus to requirements in French Indo-China. Local culinary mores soon changed to favor rice in lieu of indigenous grains such as millet and sorghum, which took more time to cook. The food legacy of empire was an enormous rice import bill that Senegal could ill afford. In British India, a range of imperial policies caused a drastic shift in commercial and livelihood patterns, and a steep rise in hunger. For instance, the rise in world demand for primary commodities and the British desire to meet them meant that the state encouraged the rapid spread of food-crops cultivated for export, whether tea or oilseeds or grains. All this expansion took place at the expense of subsistence crops that peasants previously grew for food. At the same time, India lost ground in traditional export areas such as textiles, hampered by imperial protectionist strategies such as high tariffs on Indian artisanal cotton goods entering Britain. Colonized India became an importer of British manufactured goods.[39] Indian economic historians described this as the deindustrialization of colonial India, the hidden face of the industrialization of imperial Britain. Rejecting neoclassical economic theories that portrayed this process as an inevitable working out of market forces, they saw this deindustrialization as wrought deliberately by colonial policies which destroyed through tariffs and high taxation India's traditional export-oriented craft production and created an agricultural sector with too many people to support for its ecological base. Other imperial policies which imposed laws restricting hunting and access to guns and ammunition for indigenous people not only resulted in the European monopoly of biological resources such as game but also increased food scarcities among local groups, limiting their access to readily available protein sources. Overall, whether in Asia, Africa, or Latin America, the age of empire saw the structural reshaping of colonial economies whose dangerous dependence on fluctuating world commodity prices created long-term conditions of stark income differentials and food hunger, both chronic and episodic.

From the late-nineteenth century onwards, the adoption of a free trade economy by Britain and the rapid industrialization of continental Europe, the United States, and Japan created a new level of demand for primary commodities and foodstuffs and transformed the world economy even as city dwellers and industrial populations in these countries began to receive cheap foods in relative abundance. It gradually became clear that such cheap foods were not necessarily healthy foods. In the nineteenth century, food concerns centered around the adulteration of everyday foodstuffs, sought to be addressed by legislation such as the Food Adulteration Bills, enacted in Britain between 1860 and 1899. Later, the focus shifted to the health ravages caused by new industrial-era diets. In a sensational expose, *The Nation's Larder* lecture series at London's Royal Institution showed that rats fed the usual working-class diet of white bread, margarine, tinned meat, vegetables boiled with soda, cheap tinned jam, tea, sugar, and a little milk eventually developed disease, discontent, and even cannibalism.[40] Despite the publicity given to such findings, the subsequent development of a globalizing food regime in the hands of major corporations did little to stem the spread of similarly unhealthy industrial eating habits.

By the mid-twentieth century, the workings of global multinational corporations and the supermarkets they established to control food from field to table made global food commerce a reality over large parts of the world. The same supermarket outlets could be found in Thailand as in Britain, as could fast-food chains. While the majority of consumers in the Global South still depended on small retailers and vendors, the aspirational images of the marketplace suffused the worldwide realms of food and popular culture. For the majority of food buyers in the Global North, the supermarket's cornucopia seemed to have finally realized the food dreams of plentiful uniformity first visualized during the age of empire. By the late-twentieth century, this new European and American world of cheap and convenient food received a series of shocks from food scares that ranged from salmonella to mad cow disease. These scares involved not just concerns about food quality and consumer health, but about the potential of industrial foods to cause human deaths and disabilities, and the seeming inability of either scientists or states to eradicate such risks. Consumer responses to such food scares varied. For those who lost trust in the supermarket and chain networks of globalized food, smaller purveyors of organic and free-trade certified goods, local foods, and farmers' produce, offered some semblance of an alternative, if not a truly viable one. For others, the response was to call for greater vigilance on the part of supermarkets and the state to purify the food supply. But such vigilance, even as it reassures the Global North, has had troubling consequences for people in the Global South. Susanne Freidberg in her study of transnational food commodity networks across Europe and Africa points out that the late-twentieth century anxieties about food safety and the bureaucratized regulations that neoliberal governing and food procuring institutions have generated, have served to exclude and discriminate against smaller primary producers, especially ones based in the Global South.[41]

The other face of a global food culture operates via the continued movements of people from former imperial peripheries who seek a better livelihood, and flee the political chaos that neo-globalization has often caused in those regions as they decolonize. While the cities of the Global South host huge numbers of internal migrants, the phenomenon of global migrants as purveyors of global foods is most visible in the Global North. That overseas laboring migrants gradually diversified public food cultures in the European and American world is as apparent to the layperson as to the academic. To offer just a few recent examples, the ambiguities and inequities inherent in their postcolonial homelands impelled Caribbean, Vietnamese, South Asian, and sub-Saharan migrants, to purvey home-cooking skills into precarious livelihoods in the new global cities where they sought refuge. It is almost a truism that every new wave of refugees into the Global North creates a new variety of "ethnic" eatery in New York, Toronto, or London, where formerly local foods such as the samosa or the empanada become transmuted into global foods.

Notes

1. I thank James Murton for this reference. James Murton, "John Bull and Sons: the Empire Marketing Board and the Creation of a British Imperial Food System," in *Edible Histories, Cultural Politics: Towards a Canadian Food History*, ed. Marlene Epp, Franca Iacovetta, and Valerie J. Korinek (Toronto: University of Toronto Press, 2012).

2. Edward P. Easty, *Mankind at the Crossroads* (New York: Charles Scribner's Sons, 1924), 64.

3. Paul Freedman, *Out of the East: Spices and the Medieval Imagination* (New Haven: Yale University Press, 2008), 1–5.

4. Sidney W. Mintz, *Sweetness and Power: The Place of Sugar in Modern History* (New York: Penguin, 1985).

5. Paula de Vos, "The Science of Spices: Empiricism and Economic Botany in the Early Spanish Empire." *Journal of World History* 17, no. 4 (2006): 399–427.

6. Gary Okihiro, *Pineapple Culture: A History of the Tropical and Temperate Zones*. Berkeley: University of California Press, 2009.

7. Brian Cowan, "New Worlds, New Tastes: Food Fashions after the Renaissance," in *Food: The History of Taste*, ed. Paul Freedman (Berkeley: University of California Press, 2007), 197–230.

8. Sidney W. Mintz, "Time, Sugar, and Sweetness," in *Food and Culture: A Reader*, ed. Carole Counihan and Penny Van Esterik (New York: Routledge, 1997), 363.

9. *Tallis's History and Description of the Crystal Palace and the Exhibition of the World's Industry in 1851* (London: John Tallis & Co., 1851).

10. Troy Bickham, "Eating the Empire: Intersections of Food, Cookery and Imperialism in Eighteenth-Century Britain," *Past and Present* 198 (February 2008): 71–109.

11. Linda Colley, *Captives: Britain, Empire and the World, 1600–1850* (London: Pimlico, 2003).

12. John Fitzpatrick, "The Columbian Exchange and the Two Colonizations of Aotearoa New Zealand," *Food, Culture, and Society* 10, no. 2 (Summer 2007): 211–38.

13. Sucheta Mazumdar, "The Impact of New World Food Crops on the Diet and Economy of China and India, 1600–1900," in *Food in Global History*, ed. Raymond Grew (Boulder, CO: Westview Press, 1999), 58–78.

14. Bertie Mandelblatt, "A Transatlantic Commodity. Irish Salt Beef in the French Atlantic World," *History Workshop Journal* 63 (2007): 18–47.

15. Austin Clarke, *Pig Tails 'n Breadfruit: Rituals of Slave Food* (Kingston: Ian Randle Publishers, 1999), 113–14.

16. Elizabeth DeLoughrey, "Globalizing the Routes of Breadfruit and Other Bounties," *Journal of Colonialism and Colonial History* 8, no. 3 (Winter 2007): np.

17. Mimi Sheller, *Consuming the Caribbean: From Arawaks to Zombies* (London: Routledge, 2003).

18. Diane Tye, "A Poor Man's Meal: Molasses in Atlantic Canada," *Food, Culture, and Society* 11, no. 3 (September 2008): 335–53.

19. "Tasmania: Its Resources and Future," *Journal of the Royal Colonial Institute* 1, no. 1 (January 1910), np.

20. "Colonial Fruit," ibid.

21. N. L. Doss, *Reminiscences, English and Australasian. Being an Account of a Visit to England, Australia, New Zealand, Tasmania, Ceylon etc* (Calcutta: M. C. Bhowmick, 1893), 64.

22. Quoted in Okihiro, *Pineapple Culture*, 129.

23. Jack Goody, *Cooking, Cuisine, and Class. A Study in Comparative Sociology* (Cambridge: Cambridge University Press, 1982).

24. Doss, *Reminiscences, English and Australasian*, 103.

25. K. T. Achaya, *The Food Industries of British India* (New Delhi: Oxford University Press, 1994).

26. Andrew C. Isenberg, *The Destruction of the Bison* (New York: Cambridge University Press, 2000); Russel L. Barsh, "The Substitution of Cattle for Bison on the Great Plains," in *The Struggle for the Land. Indigenous Insight and Industrial Empire in the Semi Arid World*, ed. Paul A. Olson (Lincoln: University of Nebraska Press, 1990), 103–26; Jeffrey M. Pilcher, "Empire of the 'Jungle': The Rise of an Atlantic Refrigerated Beef Industry, 1880–1920," *Food, Culture, and Society* 7, no. 2 (Fall 2004): 63–78.

27. Richard Perren, *The Meat Trade in Britain, 1840–1914* (London: Routledge & Kegan Paul, 1978).

28. G. Paramaswaran Pillai, *London and Paris through Indian Spectacles* (Madras: Vaijayanti Press, 1897), 9.

29. Hannah Glasse, *The Art of Cookery made Plain and Easy* (London: W. Strahan, 1747), 101.

30. Isabella Beeton, *The Book of Household Management* (London: Jonathan Cape, 1861).

31. Bickham, "Eating the Empire," 198.

32. Alan Davidson, "Curry" and "Curry Powder," in *The Oxford Companion to Food* (Oxford: Oxford University Press, 2006), 236–37.

33. Eliza Fay, *Original Letters from India* (New York: NYRB Classics, 2010), 181.

34. Pillai, *London and Paris Through Indian Spectacles*, 12.

35. "Veeraswamy." [Online]. Available: http://www.veeraswamy.com/. [February 25, 2011].

36. *The Times* (London). February 3, 1949: 2.

37. Lizzie Collingham, *Curry: A Tale of Cooks and Conquerors* (Oxford: Oxford University Press, 2006).

38. Ben Highmore, "The Taj Mahal in the High Street: The Indian Restaurant as Diasporic Popular Culture in Britain," *Food, Culture, and Society* 12, no. 2 (June 2009): 173–190.

39. K. N. Chaudhuri, "Foreign Trade and Balance of Payments," in *The Cambridge Economic History of India*, ed. Tapan Raychoudhuri, 2 vols. (New Delhi: Cambridge University Press, 1983), 2:828.

40. Christopher Driver, *The British at Table* (London: Chatto & Windus, 1983), 18.

41. Susanne Freidberg, *French Beans and Food Scares: Culture and Commerce in an Anxious Age* (New York: Oxford University Press, 2004).

Bibliography

Achaya, K. T. *The Food Industries of British India*. New Delhi: Oxford University Press, 1994.

Collingham, Lizzie. *Curry: A Tale of Cooks and Conquerors*. Oxford: Oxford University Press, 2006.

Counihan, Carole and Penny Van Esterik, eds. *Food and Culture: A Reader*. New York: Routledge, 1997.

Davidson, Alan. *The Oxford Companion to Food*. Oxford: Oxford University Press, 2006.

Epp, Marlene, Franca Iacovetta, and Valerie J. Korinek, eds. *Edible Histories, Cultural Politics: Towards a Canadian Food History*. Toronto: University of Toronto Press, 2012.

Freedman, Paul, ed. *Food: The History of Taste*. Berkeley: University of California Press, 2007.

Freedman, Paul. *Out of the East: Spices and the Medieval Imagination*. New Haven: Yale University Press, 2008.

Freidberg, Susanne. *French Beans and Food Scares: Culture and Commerce in an Anxious Age*. New York: Oxford University Press, 2004.

Goody, Jack. *Cooking, Cuisine, and Class: A Study in Comparative Sociology*. Cambridge: Cambridge University Press, 1982.

Grew, Raymond, ed. *Food in Global History*. Boulder, CO: Westview Press, 1999.

Mintz, Sidney W. *Sweetness and Power: The Place of Sugar in Modern History*. New York: Viking, 1985.

Okihiro, Gary. *Pineapple Culture: A History of the Tropical and Temperate Zones*. Berkeley: University of California Press, 2009.

CHAPTER 15

INDUSTRIAL FOOD

GABRIELLA M. PETRICK

THE process of industrialization is a topic that has had much ink spilled over it. Works by Walter Licht, Louis Galambos, Alan Trachenberg, Olivier Zunz, and Alfred Chandler are essential reading in any American history survey course.[1] These authors deftly illustrate that between 1880 and 1930 much of American life changed based on industrial output and increased wages. These decades have been characterized as both "Hell with the lid taken off" and the consumer revolution.[2] Historians of technology, business, the environment, medicine, consumption, and labor have all weighed in on this grand transformation. What has been missing until recently is sustained attention to how industrialization changed the foods available to Americans. While food has not been completely neglected, especially by agricultural historians, connections between the industrialization process, changing food habits, and provisioning urban centers are relatively new to the historiography. It is especially important to understand the forces that pushed Americans to shift their food choices from a bread and cereal based diet into one that was not only more varied (meat, milk, lettuce, peas, oranges, bananas, and peaches) but also ultimately a more industrial one.

Before we examine what Americans were eating in the first half of the twentieth century, we first need to define what is and is not an industrial food. While one can certainly make a good argument that flour milled in large factories or lard processed in Chicago slaughterhouses were industrial foods, when historians, and more recently, popular writers like Michael Pollan and Eric Schlosser, have written about the industrial diet they generally mean more highly processed foods. In keeping with this notion, I define industrial foods as foods that are mass produced in a factory setting and require no or very little cooking to make them edible. These foods are also generally highly portable due to their packaging. Some examples include commercially canned goods; frozen foods; breads, cakes, and pies purchased at bakeries or groceries and supermarkets; cake mixes; pastry and pie shell mixes; jams and jellies; ice cream; hot and cold cereals; and instant mashed potatoes. While other foods such as milk, meat, fresh fruits and vegetables, fats and oils, flour, sugar, eggs, and other dairy products are clearly part of an industrial complex, for our purposes they will be considered as fresh or minimally processed foods. When viewed in this fashion, it becomes clear that industrial food is not a product of either the Gilded Age or the Progressive Era, but rather of the Cold War and the Baby Boom Generation.

Food Industrialization: Bridging Historiographies

Food history is a relatively new subfield with a number of important works published in the mid-2000s, yet there were a few scholars as early as the 1940s who thought about food as being fundamental to the American experience. In this section, I want to examine how a variety of scholars have written about technology and industrialization in relation to food. Although not all of these scholars would define themselves as food historians, by thinking about their contribution in relationship to food we can better understand how and why American eating habits changed.

Any examination of food in the United States must address two of the earliest food scholars, Richard Osborne Cummings and Oscar Edward Anderson. Richard Osborn Cummings's 1940 book, *The American and His Food: A History of Food Habits in the United States* builds on his previous book *The American Ice Industry and the Development of Refrigeration 1790–1860.*[3] In *The American and His Food,* Cummings examines the very broad dietary habits of Americans from 1789 to 1940. For the most part, he chronicles the changing foodstuffs available to Americans and how health improved based on these shifting food habits. While industrialization and technology are not one of the major themes of the book, he does examine how technological change and improved scientific knowledge influenced American nutrition and foodways. He speaks very broadly about refrigeration, canning, pasteurization, and food adulteration, largely as these technologies affected urban health. Ultimately, what is most significant about Cummings work is his focus on provisioning cities, which required fundamentally different techniques to secure wholesome food than a more rural or town centered population.

Unlike Cummings's work on the ice industry and refrigeration, Oscar Edward Anderson's *History of Refrigeration in America* clearly lays out the importance of cold to the industrializing process in the latter half of the nineteenth century and its ever more central role to food production in the twentieth.[4] Ice and refrigeration not only kept milk and beer cold, but they also facilitated the movement of a vast array of foods from the hinterlands into urban centers. Anderson traces the transition from natural ice to industrial ice production and then explains how ice-making technologies were transformed into mechanical systems for cooling packinghouses, warehouses and ultimately the development of home refrigerators. Anderson stresses that historians cannot underestimate the importance of reliable refrigeration in reshaping the various systems required to supply Americans with both fresh and industrial foods. The other contribution Anderson makes, particularly to the history of technology, is that he opens up the "black box" of what is commonly referred to as the cold chain, showing how the technologies were modified and disseminated through the early postwar period.

A contemporary of Cummings and Anderson, architectural theorist and art historian Siegfried Giedion has had a surprising influence on historians of technology and industrialization. Most relevant for historians of food is his work on the mechanization of grain harvesting, flour milling, bread baking, and meat slaughtering. According to Giedion, automating these processes not only fed urban populations, but also contributed to a mass production ethos, which he characterized as a "split between thought and feeling." While being sensitive to the extent to which humans could master nature, Giedion is the first to truly critique mechanized and later industrialized foods. He believes the tools and technologies for creating bread and disassembling meat have interrupted "our contact with organic forces" and by 1948 created "a paralyzed, torn, chaotic condition" which was "increasingly menaced as the tie with basic human values became frayed." In addition to his critique of mechanizing the organic, historians of food can heed his call to study "anonymous history" through the materiality of the world whether it be a can of peas or bag of tortillas.[5]

Equally important are a number of historians who have made contributions to the scholarship on food industrialization through their examination of other topics. Alfred D. Chandler's classic work *The Visible Hand* is helpful for understanding the changing structure of capitalism.[6] Chandler sees food companies as fulfilling a need to feed expanding urban centers while they simultaneously created key brands and marketing and distribution strategies during the consumer revolution. Chandler's emphasis on vertical integration and the expansion of many food companies including Swift, Armour, Heinz, and National Biscuit Company (NABISCO) illustrate how the industry shifted from proprietorships to corporations as well as the controls these companies required to ensure that their product met both sanitary and flavor standards. For Chandler, the quality and consistency of industrial food production required a shift to managerial capitalism in addition to industry consolidation. However, Chandler does overstate the extent to which many foods were industrialized, largely because he was more interested in business structures than technological processes. That said, his emphasis on infrastructure (railroads and telegraphs), development, and dissemination illustrates how multiple technological systems were essential to the development of mass-produced foods, an important element of the industrializing process that is largely missing from the early food literature. Furthermore, his observation that branding and marketing were key elements in the emergence of ubiquitous mass-produced consumer goods exemplifies the shift toward a more consumer-oriented economy.

Similarly, both David Hounshell and William Cronon provide insights into the emergence of industrial food production in the late nineteenth century. Hounshell's work focuses on technological change in the machine tool industry and the question of how standard interchangeable parts came about. Here Hounshell provides a window into how the reaper and the disassembly line changed food production in the United States. For the purposes of food historians, the adoption of the McCormick reaper enabled larger fields of wheat and other grains to be cultivated, which spurred the growth of large flour mills in the upper Midwest. These mills made flour and bread much less expensive. The decrease in the cost of staples such as bread enabled Americans to alter their diets to include a wider variety of foods, including beef, fruits, and vegetables, in the first decades of the twentieth century. Additionally, relating the disassembly line to the assembly line links early food technologies to the large process of industrialization as technology was transferred from one industry to another. In fact, the Fordist assembly line (where parts came to workers) was pioneered in large can-making factories such as American Can and large canneries such as Campbell's and Heinz.

Cronon, an environmental historian, provides a complimentary account of both the reaper and the disassembly line. Largely interested in the spatial dynamics between urban centers and agricultural hinterlands, he argues that trains, grain elevators, and disassembly lines compacted the landscape, forging tighter links between rural producers and urban consumers. Thus technologies such as trains and telegraphy facilitated the growth of both eastern industrial centers and the exploitation of rich agricultural soils of the trans-Mississippi west in the years after the Civil War. These links enabled large-scale food processors to become an integral part of America's food systems by drawing products from rural into urban areas. Cronon also argues that as raw products flowed from west to east, industrial products flowed from east to west, thereby creating a dynamic that benefited both farmers and city dwellers, although he certainly does not see industrialization and the increasing marginalization of farmers as unproblematic.[7] Both Hounshell and Cronon build on Giedion's work—Hounshell from a technological perspective and Cronon from a spatial perspective.

As historians of technology and the environment have helped us better understand how food became industrial, so have historians of medicine and social movements. From a consumer's point of view, the period between the Civil War and World War I was an era fraught with anxiety over how to acquire pure, nutritious, and wholesome food products. Perhaps the most well-known commentary on the problems with food at the turn of the twentieth century is Upton Sinclair's *The Jungle* (1906).[8] The disgust, horror, and outrage directed toward Chicago meatpackers upon the book's publication signaled a generalized anxiety and the distrust consumers had with food produced in anonymous places. Historians James Harvey Young, Nancy Tomes, and Loraine Swainston Goodwin have all illustrated how the urbanizing process made acquiring and consuming all manners of food (from meat to milk to apples, flour and canned goods) an anxiety provoking process, especially for the women who were largely responsible for purchasing and cooking the family's meals.[9] As Goodwin notes, the lack of a federal agency to oversee food, drink, and drugs was "undermining the physical, mental and moral health of the nation" at the turn of the last century.[10] This consumer-oriented view presents a dramatically different narrative of food and industrialization than many that focus on the role of Harvey Wiley and large food companies. Collectively, these works argue that small producers were the cause of foodborne contamination and illness and that women saw large producers as protecting them from harm. The brand-name and sanitary packaging became an assurance that the products inside were safe. Cooperation and coordination among club women, government chemists, state and local public health officials, large corporations and muckraking journalists forced a reluctant federal government to regulate the safety of food. While the Pure Food, Drink, and Drugs Act of 1906 did not completely eliminate either food contamination or foodborne illness, it did help begin to ease the public's fear of food made in distant factories.

Unlike the above works, food historians Sidney W. Mintz and Harvey A. Levenstein view food industrialization more negatively. In *Sweetness and Power*, Mintz explores the nexus between the metropolis and the colony through Britain's desire for sugar. By focusing on sugar as an export commodity, Mintz examines how political and economic power was wielded between the colonial West Indies and Britain from the seventeenth to the nineteenth centuries. For Mintz, the rise of the British factory system reinforced Caribbean sugar production. He explains, "Cheaper sugar came at a time when its increased consumption was guaranteed not by the sugar habit itself, but by the factory world and machine rhythms which were the background of its use."[11] Mintz concludes that ready access to cheap calories (in the form of sugar) fueled industrial economies and ultimately ceded control over of the foods people ate to large corporations, thus changing not only what people ate but also separating the source of food production from the locus of its consumption. Additionally, Britain's taste for cheap sugar ultimately oppressed and impoverished those who made it. While the plantation system established by the British in its Caribbean colonies was unquestionably brutal, the extent to which sugar was consumed in any great quantity by British factory workers simply does not bear out empirically when production is calculated on a per capita basis.[12] In fact, sugar was not a principle source of calories for factory workers, bread and butter were.

Harvey Levenstein, by contrast, places the emergence of an industrial diet in the United State between 1880 and 1930. For Levenstein the transition to industrial food required a new ideological framework based on a better scientific and medical understanding of human nutrition and diet, a set of dietary missionaries, and an urban working class that depended on food imported from the countryside. Although largely a history of nutritional thinking, Levenstein discusses the class tensions between progressive-era diet reformers and working-class eaters. Like many labor historians, Levenstein argues that factory work eroded working-class craft and skill. He notes, "In food as in petroleum, iron and steel, quests for technological innovations to reduce costs and eliminate dependence on skilled, artisanal labor went hand in hand with drives to merge and consolidate business in order to gain control of market forces."[13] Levenstein is clearly drawing on Chandler, but as Roger Horowitz points out, food production—particularly in the meat industry—was skilled.[14] By not paying more attention to the differences among food products and only looking at industry growth, Levenstein misinterprets both the extent of industrialization in food plants as well as the skill required by workers in canning, meat packing, cheese making, ice cream, and condiment production.

This is not to say that producers did not improve efficiency in many factories through the application of new technologies. Yet food historians need to pay greater attention to the biological and organleptic characteristics of each food product to determine the extent to which it could be industrialized given the technologies available; that is, both the product and the process matter. Furthermore, in his chapter on the growth of large food processing companies, Levenstein overstates the importance of advertising in new food products, claiming that advertising had a more important impact on dietary change by World War I than the taste, price, or purity of the foods.[15]

More recently, however, authors such as Roger Horowitz, J. L Anderson, E. Melanie DuPuis, and Shane Hamilton provide more a complicated picture of the transformation of commodities like meat and milk into mass-market commodities and essentially overturn Levenstein's claims. Taken as a whole these works account for the biological and cultural complexities of food thus prying open the black box of industrial food production and providing a more nuanced understanding of the industrial transformation taking place in twentieth century America.[16]

In *Putting Meat on the American Table*, Roger Horowitz illustrates how meat resists subordination to industrial processing. Confounding the irregularities and perishability of meat that make it difficult to mechanize is the potential for meat to cause illness and death if not handled properly. Throughout his study, Horowitz shows how various forms of meat were transformed into quasi-industrial products depending on how successful packers were in developing and applying new production techniques. Equally important to processing techniques were consumers' ideas of what was and what was not meat. A good example of this conflict was consumers' rejection of frozen beef because it looked brown rather than the cherry-red color of freshly cut meat. Despite an industry campaign to educate consumers, the women who purchased meat for their families refused to buy frozen beef because to them brown meat was spoiled.

Horowitz reveals the complexity of industrial meat by examining not only the nature of domestic meat production, but also how urbanization and industrialization altered Americans' relationship to their food. Through a series of case studies devoted to various meats, including beef, pork, hot dogs, and chicken, Horowitz examines the difficult and often uneasy tensions among living organisms, food production, technological change, and eating habits. In one particularly illuminating example, Horowitz traces the transformation of pork from a cured to a fresh meat, largely due to the proliferation of inexpensive fresh beef. Quite literally,

Americans' taste for salted barrel pork disappeared as meat packers shipped large quantities of beef to urban markets in the late nineteenth century. With a cultural preference for beef, pork producers needed to rethink the nature of pork and ultimately settled on a product that was more like beef than bacon or ham in flavor, texture, and appearance.

Horowitz also makes an important methodological contribution to food history. Unlike previous food historians, he utilizes consumer data in conjunction with business records to support his arguments on the changing nature of meat in industrial society. By using this approach, he writes a more balanced history of production that identifies the constraints both producers and consumers faced, and continue to face, when selling or buying meat. The book also begins to fill a deficiency in the historiography of food systems, allowing historians of business, consumption, technology, science, and food to begin to understand the economic and technological factors in addition to the cultural boundaries that have influenced and constrained industrial meat production and consumption.[17]

J. L. Anderson's "Lard to Lean: Making the Meat-Type Hog in Post-World War II America," extends Horowitz's analysis of pork production in the United States. It seems that despite their best efforts to make pork a rival of beef, pork producers never could inspire Americans to increase their consumption. What is striking in Anderson's work is the lengths to which hog producers went to alter the morphology of pigs, that is, to create a lean, meat-based pig. One of the most significant historical points that Anderson makes is the importance of pigs as producers of fat, in the form of lard, before the Second World War. Anderson corrects the misconception that hydrogenated fats such as vegetable shortening and margarine overtook animal fats early in the century by explaining that in 1940, lard was still a high-priced commodity on which hog farmers could bank. In the postwar era, however, Americans began to worry about the amount of fat in their diets and in their meat, thus prompting the development of a hog that was twenty-five percent leaner than its antecedents a mere three decades earlier.

Anderson also notes that competition from chicken was not the sole reason pork consumption remained stagnant, although it was certainly an important factor. In fact, by producing a leaner pig, pork manufacturers actually changed the experience of eating pork. Consumers found leaner pork to be, by turn, watery (when raw) and dry (when cooked). As Anderson explains, "new" pork could not be cooked as long as "old" pork or it dried-out. Yet, consumers fearful of contracting trichinosis refused to cook pork as processors and home economists instructed, often making pork unpalatable when compared to either chicken or beef. Whether or not the threat of trichinosis was real was moot by 1950 because the public simply refused to eat more pork. By explicitly relating the biology of the post-war pig to the flavor of pork on dining room tables, Anderson reminds us that taste and flavor are as important to food history as processes and marketing. No amount of marketing or advertising seemed to alter Americans' preferences for particular meats, namely beef and later chicken. Together Horowitz and Anderson show how pig farmers struggled to make pork a regular part of the American diet from the mid-nineteenth century to today.

This greater sensitivity to taste illustrates consumers' agency in determining their food choices and moves the history of food industrialization beyond the hegemony of corporate advertising and mass-marketing.[18]

E. Melanie DuPuis's *Nature's Perfect Food: How Milk Became America's Drink* bridges cultural ideologies and technological innovations in an effort to understand the rise and fall of milk consumption in the United States. A cultural geographer, DuPuis uses historical sources to explain how milk became a steady and naturalized part of the American diet. Her analysis of the debate surrounding pasteurization highlights the tensions around new food technologies. The fact that a new technology, pasteurization, was not readily accepted but rather was contested and incompletely adopted, based on both political and economic wrangling, should encourage food historians to look for these types of debates and tensions when writing about new food technologies. Also, her regional analysis of the economic power dairy farmers exerted over milk prices contradicts the notion that there was or is a unified system rather than a set of regional systems that interact in a variety of political and economic ways. This regional analysis does not deny that many commodities have come to be dominated by large national and multinational processors over the last forty years, but the transition has never been simple or monolithic, thus providing an opportunity to examine the historical contingencies of food industrialization based on regional differences.[19]

Shane Hamilton's work on trucking in the twentieth century similarly complicates our notion of a food system rather than a set of distinct systems. In particular, his analysis of milk and meat trucking from the 1940s through the 1970s illustrates how new highways, especially during the 1950s and 1960s, allowed food processors to move closer to the farm and truck goods directly to suburban supermarkets, thus eliminating warehouses. Sidestepping the teamsters and regional storage facilities ultimately reduced the cost of meat and milk for most Americans. It also brought industry to the rural hinterlands, expanding the scale of production and forcing smaller farmers out of agriculture. Furthermore, Hamilton describes how urbanization forced potential farmers off the land and onto the road, if they wanted to maintain their rural roots. By combining agricultural policy, technological change, and infrastructure development, Hamilton shows how large dairies and meatpackers were able to consolidate these industries, drive down the cost of food, and fulfill the dream of abundant food for all Americans, even as it created monopoly power and eroded the wages of many rural workers. [20]

By taking a closer look at the industrialization process of specific foods, a more nuanced and complex understanding of how various political, cultural, and economic forces have shaped a variety of food systems becomes evident. The above studies allow us to begin to pull a complex set of systems apart to better understand how and why Americans eat what they do. What is largely missing from these studies is an analysis of which industrial foods American ate most frequently. As the case studies below will show, examining underutilized consumption data can provide a more complete picture of dietary change and industrial food consumption in the United States over the twentieth century.

Using Home Economics Research to Tell the Story of the American Diet

In reading these classic works on food history, it is easy to see why the period between 1880 and 1930 is seen as pivotal in the shift to an industrial diet dominated by corporations. If one looks at industry data, the growth during this period is, indeed, dramatic. Production of flour, canned goods, oranges, raisins, lettuce, cereals (hot and cold) all explode. Yet, it is a rare occurrence, Horowitz being the exception, that historians calculate this growth on a per capita basis. Ultimately, it is only possible to determine when Americans began to eat large quantities of industrialized food when industry and consumption data are combined. As most historians of the American diet have shown, the industry data is plentiful and relatively easy to find and use. The consumer data, however, is much more elusive and complicated.

There are several sets of historical resources available to determine what foods consumers were eating throughout the twentieth century. Largely based on the efforts of home economists to catalogue what Americans ate, these sources generally fall at three distinct levels of analysis. The broadest set of consumer data was collected by the Bureau of Home Economics at the U.S. Department of Agriculture. Historical studies date back to 1948, when statistician and home economist Marguerite C. Burk led a team of researchers to determine what Americans were eating. This dataset is based on "disappearing" figures. What this means is that the researchers complied data on every sector of food production and then adjusted that figure for other uses, such as feeding livestock, canning, and exports. The remaining food was assumed to be available for retail purchase.[21] These data basically enumerate the amount of food flowing from farm to table. While not a perfect measure, because it tends to overestimate per capita consumption and underestimate home-produced foods, it does illustrate national trends in the quantity and variety of foods Americans ate in the first half of the twentieth century.

The second level of consumption data and analysis was also collected by home economists, most often in conjunction with state Agricultural Extension efforts, but the Home Economics Research Bureau (also known as the Bureau of Home Economics) also produced regional consumption data. These studies generally sought to understand what consumers were purchasing and/or producing for themselves to evaluate the nutritional health of a community, state, or region. In these studies home economists generally went into the homes of individuals and tracked what they purchased, ate, and discarded over the course of a week. Researchers also collected a variety of socioeconomic data.[22]

The final type of source is the actual food consumption survey home economists collected from families across the United States. While the most detailed of the three sources, household food surveys were rarely saved after the completion of larger studies and are not as readily available as other sources. While the national and regional reports can often be found in libraries or via interlibrary loan, the actual surveys tend to be in archives. Taken together, these sources allow us to reconstruct how industrialization reshaped American eating habits.

Calculating the National Diet

By using the USDA's *Consumption of Food in the United States 1909–1948*, historians are able to identify the most commonly consumed foods in the first half of the twentieth century. Generally, what these data reveal is that before 1950, most Americans ate very little industrial food. They also show that processed foods tended to be consumed by the affluent much more frequently than by poor or working-class American. Of particular importance for historians are the general trends in fresh versus processed foods because these data upend both the historiographic and contemporary literature on food.

In examining the tables within the report, it becomes evident that there were certain foods that Americans ate at far higher rates than others. The first table illustrates these changes.[23] Milk and dairy products, fruits and vegetables, grain products, meat, and potatoes, dominated daily consumption. Generally fruits and vegetables were becoming more important while potatoes and grain products were becoming less so. Meats, fats, eggs, dry beans, and sugar (1930 was an outlier) were all relatively stable with a slight upward trend.[24]

Approximate Consumption of Food Per Capita in the United States by Major Food Groups (in Pounds)

Year	Dairy products, excluding butter	Meats	Fats	Potatoes (white and sweet)	Citrus fruit and tomatoes	Leafy green and yellow vegetables	Other vegetables and fruits	Grain products	Sugar and syrups
1909	388	161	59	204	44	76	209	291	84
1920	389	145	58	162	53	88	224	248	101
1930	385	139	67	144	60	88	216	227	124
1940	391	149	70	138	94	104	233	191	107
1948	431	158	65	115	105	114	234	171	106

We can further mine this report for even more detailed observations. For instance, the three most important fresh fruits in the American diet between 1909 and 1948 were apples, bananas, and peaches.[25] While these charts do not answer why eating habits were changing, they do provide evidence of change, which can be further explored. Americans also ate a wide variety of minor fruits in smaller quantities, shown in the second chart. The next most common fruits were grapes, pears, and strawberries in that order. If we look at fresh vegetable consumption, in the next chart, we see very similar patterns, that is, like fruits there were a few favored vegetables that dominated the national palate.[26]

Per Capita Consumption of Major Fresh Fruits in the United States, 1909–1948[27]

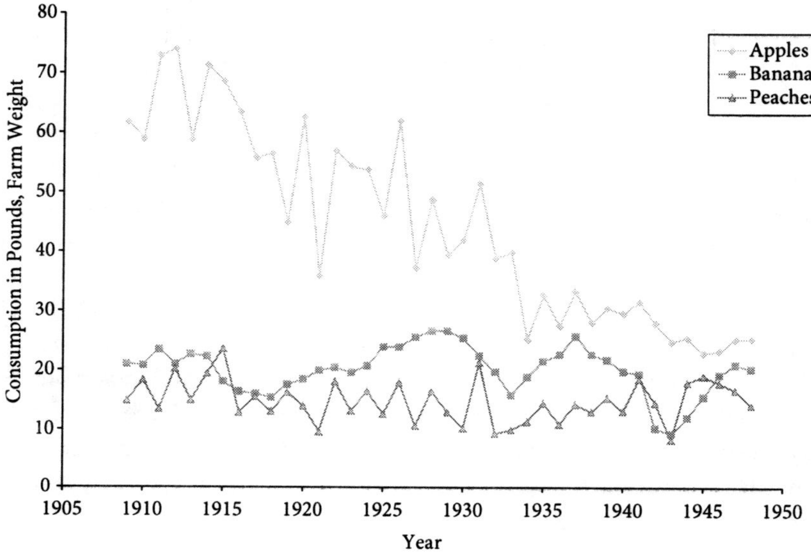

Per Capita Consumption of Minor Fresh Fruits in the United States, 1909–1948[28]

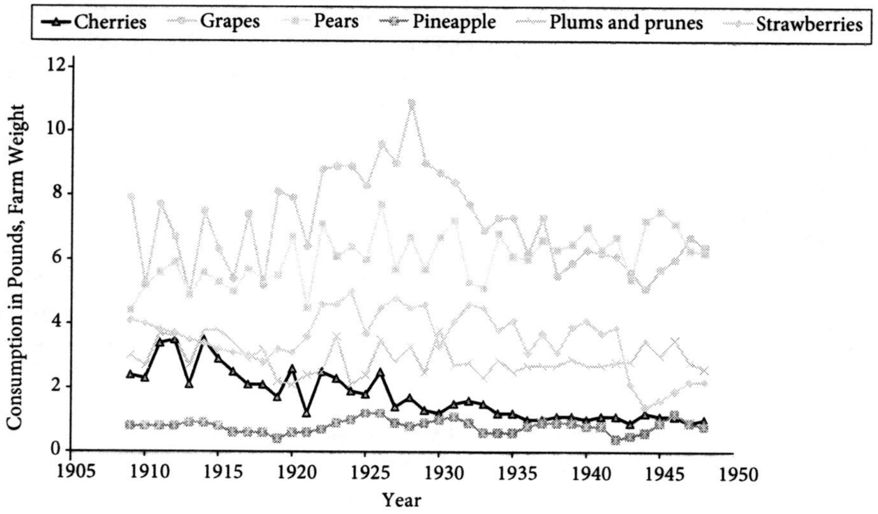

Per Capita Consumption of Fresh Vegetables in the United States, 1918–1948[29]

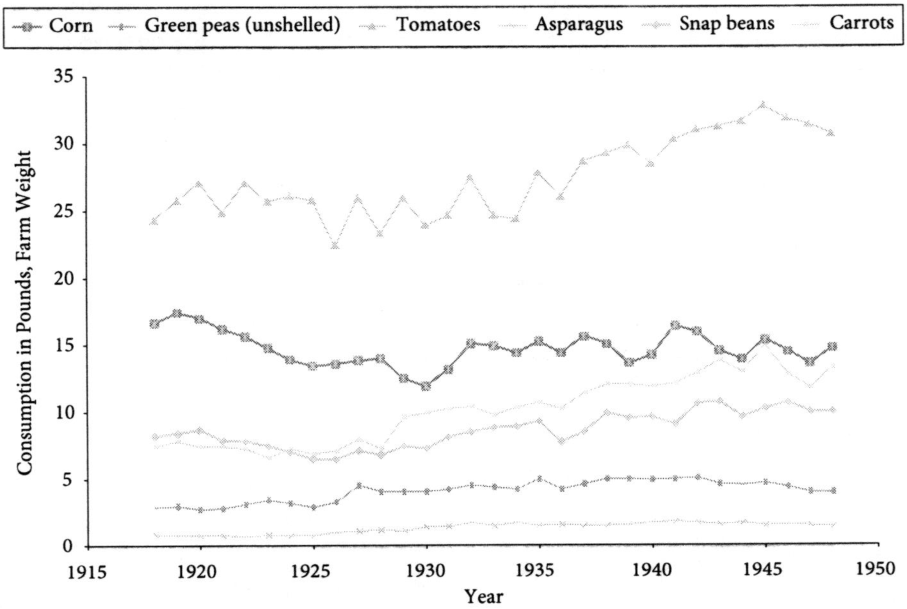

When we compare the amount of fresh foods consumed to canned goods, for instance, we see that canned food was not prevalent in the American diet, as suggested by many historians.[30] So while there was definitely significant growth in the industry and some American were certainly eating a lot more canned foods, one would not call them a ubiquitous part of the diet especially when compared to other foodstuffs, like fresh fruits and vegetables, milk, potatoes, meat, or farinaceous products. It is also striking that only a few foodstuffs consistently dominate canned food consumption. These are tomatoes, corn, peas, canned soups (after 1935), peaches, and pineapple. The most consumed canned fruits and vegetables either have short seasons, as in the case of tomatoes, corn, peas, and peaches, or are impossible for most people to get locally, as in the case of pineapple. Peas are really the only product between the turn of the century and 1950 that consumers chose to eat in greater quantities processed than fresh. Whereas canned and fresh pea consumption in 1925 was roughly equal at about five-pounds per capita, by 1940 most Americans ate about six-pounds per year canned and only two-pounds per year fresh.[31] By 1975, Americans ate very few fresh peas at approximately 0.2 pounds per year. Both canned and frozen pea consumption increased by 1975 to 4.1 pounds and 1.9 pounds per capita per year respectively.[32]

A more speculative aspect of this study is the consumption data based on income.[33] The researchers illustrate the relationship between income and food consumption based on dietary surveys from 1935–1936 and 1942, which were derived from in-home interviews by home economists. While we should not take the per capita consumption of an individual foodstuff as absolute, that is, we should be skeptical that the average American earning between $1,500 and $1,999 ate exactly 16.2 pounds of canned tomatoes, the power of the table is the comparison between relative quantities of fresh versus processed food eaten as well as the relative increase in processed food with income. Historians can discern the trends and general increase in processed food consumption from this data. Fresh foods were a far more important component of the diet than processed foods, across all income categories. If we also think about one of the most popular industrial foods, canned tomatoes, even at the highest income bracket (20.4 pound per capita), the average American ate less than one ounce per day, whereas they consumed more than a pint of milk, roughly half a pound of meat, and a bit more than three ounces of fresh green vegetables daily. Based on this 1948 national study and additional national studies in 1952 and 1954, it is very difficult to conclude that the American diet was industrial, but it is certainly fair to say that most Americans did use processed foods, mostly in the form of canned foods, and that they were being eaten on a more frequent basis in the early postwar although they did not comprise a major food source.[34]

Per Capita Consumption of Canned Fruits in the United States, 1909–1948

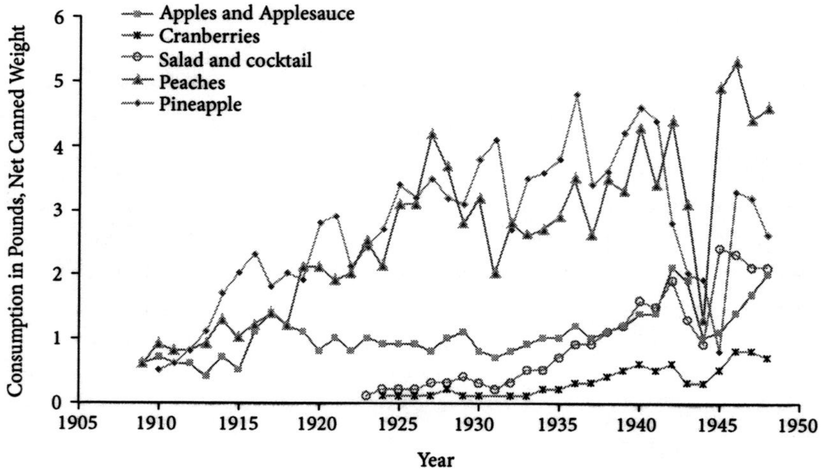

Per Capita Consumption of Canned Vegetables in the United States, 1909–1949

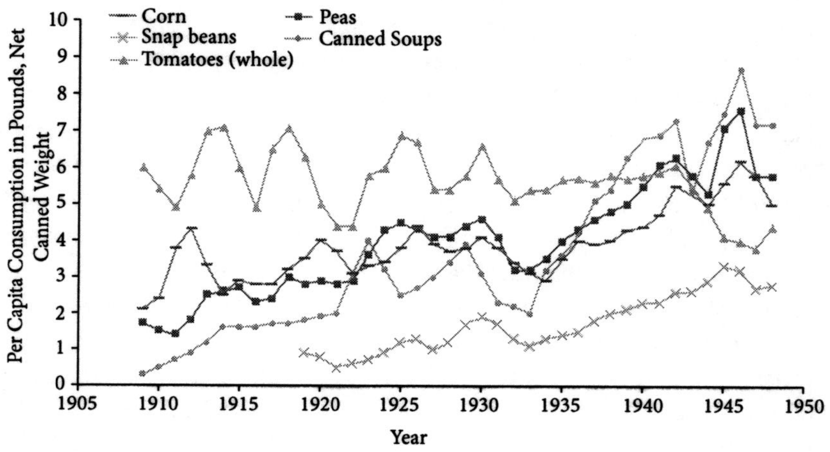

Accounting for Regional and Economic Variation

While we have some sense of national food consumption, these studies do not account for regional food preferences and have a hard time capturing home production. Regional food data, that analyzes both production and consumption, helps us better understand who had access and the economic means to purchase industrial food products. One such study examined family food production in five southern states. By paying attention to the land tenure of rural farmers, both black and white, this study suggests that urban populations likely purchased more factory produced foods than did rural populations. The study also illustrates the importance of home produced meat, dairy, and canned fruits, vegetables, pickles, jams and jellies in rural Americans' lives. The study looks at African American and white farmers in the mountains of Tennessee (general farming), the Mississippi River Delta of Arkansas and Mississippi (cotton farming), and farmers in Virginia and South Carolina (flue-cured tobacco). Note that there was only one African American family in the Tennessee group and more African American farmers (200) than white farmers (108) in the Cotton region. Tobacco farmers were relatively evenly split between African Americans and white farmers, 144 and 157 respectively.[35]

This dataset tell us a few things. Farmers in Tennessee and the tobacco regions produced more food to feed themselves than they purchased. And even relatively poor cotton farmers produced a significant amount of the foods they ate. In 1947 cotton farmers, on average, spent $501 on food and produced $353 for home consumption. Tobacco farmers spent $452 on food and produced $672 worth of food and Tennessee farmers spent $357 on food and produced $777.[36] Home-produced food fell into several general categories: milk and milk products; meat; produce; eggs; rabbits, game and fish; cereals; potatoes; honey, syrup and sorghum; and nuts. Animal products were by far the most commonly home-produced foods. In the cotton and mountain areas milk and milk products predominated while in the tobacco region meat ruled.[37] Although less important than either milk or meat, produce (both vegetables and fruits) was the third most significant home-produced item.[38] What was not eaten fresh was canned to be eaten later. Farmers in the mountain region canned the most. White farmers and black farm owners in the cotton and tobacco regions canned considerable amounts of produce.[39] Black sharecroppers in the cotton region were a notable exception to home production. These sharecroppers were the least likely to can and produced the lowest level of milk and meat products, although they frequently fished to supplement their diets.[40] These sharecroppers were also the poorest farmers in the study. Thus race, income and volume of home-processed and canned foods were directly correlated.

While this study singles out specific sub-categories of food in each region, tabulated data provide a more detailed accounting of the kind and volume of home-produced foods. These types of data help food historians distinguish subtle food preference even within a region. For example the most commonly raised or hunted meats were pork, chicken fryers, other types of chicken—probably tough laying hens—rabbits, and fish. But examining the more inclusive data shows that veal, beef, lamb, mutton, goat, other game, ducks, and turkeys were also eaten by a small number of households. It also reveals that both cotton region black and white farm owners were the most likely to raise beef for home consumption, 20 percent and 35 percent respectively. White and black renters and sharecroppers in the tobacco and cotton regions were the least likely to raise cattle for meat.[41] A particularly interesting finding was that mountain farmers were the only group that made cottage cheese, most probably a legacy of their Northern European heritage.[42] Cornmeal and grits were common in the tobacco and mountain regions and a large quantity of wheat was produced by a relatively small number of tobacco farmers.[43] All farmers produced radishes, but eggplant was only grown in the cotton and tobacco regions, with white farm owners growing the most. Tomatoes were one of the most important crops. Sweet corn, field peas, cabbage, and green, wax, and snap beans were also grown in large quantities. Lesser vegetables (generally grown in quantities of less than 100 pounds per household) included lettuce, English peas, greens, turnips, beets, okra, carrots, squash, cucumbers, peppers, and onions. Canned pickles, soup vegetables, and mixed vegetable also graced the tables of these families.[44] Home fruit production was generally less important than vegetable production. Home-grown fruits included watermelons, other melons and cantaloupe, apples, figs, grapes, peaches, pears, plums, rhubarb, berries, and other miscellaneous fruits. Watermelons were by far the most important crop, with peaches and apples (depending on the region) at a distant second.[45] The wealthiest farmers had great variety in their diets while the poorest had a much more limited one. The poorest African American sharecroppers depended on local grocers for their food more than other farmers, although these foods were likely not industrial.[46]

Tracking Household Choices

The most fine-grained data we have are individual dietary surveys. These are essentially the raw material of most nutritional and cost of living surveys the USDA and state extension agencies collected. Unlike national and regional reports, individual surveys are much more difficult to find and are the most challenging datasets to use. Although it is possible to create a database from the surveys to quantify dietary change, I find these surveys helpful in telling stories about individual families.

For example, in May 1936, one African American family of four in Portsmouth, Virginia, home of the Norfolk Navy Yard, purchased all of its food at a full-service grocery. Full-service groceries, unlike cash-and-carry or chain stores, extended credit to customers, which allowed families without ready cash to regularly purchase food between paychecks and settle their accounts on a weekly, bi-weekly or monthly basis. The husband of this family was atypical in that he worked all thirteen weeks of the quarter. Many others in the study had two or more weeks of unemployment during the quarter. The husband was a skilled worker and worked as a machinist in a soybean factory while his wife worked exclusively in the home cooking, cleaning and taking care of their four-year-old daughter.[47] Their fifteen-year-old son was still in school rather than working in a shop like his father, which would not have been at all unusual at the time. By contrast, an older neighbor down the street worked in "domestic service" one day a week and she took in a lodger at $30 per week but did not cook for him. She purchased her groceries at a cash-and-carry store, save for milk, which she apparently did not buy. In fact, she and her husband did not consume any mike during the week of the survey. Her husband, who was sixty-five, was a laborer on the railroad.[48] While not particularly detailed, the information on the surveys helps us sketch the lives of these families in relation to their food habits.

We not only get a sense of what these families were eating, but the rhythm of their diet and shopping patterns. The stay-at-home mother had 8 pounds of flour, 4 ounces of butter, 8 ounces of oatmeal, 4 ounces of relish, 3 pounds of sugar, 1 pint of Mores mustard and 4 pounds of potatoes in her home at the beginning of the survey on Monday, May 11. On Tuesday she purchased 2 cans of beans, a loaf of white bread, a jelly roll (7 ounces), a pound of Fluffo lard, and 1 pound of fresh pork chops. On Wednesday she purchase a loaf of bread, a pound of sugar, 4 ounces of boiled ham, anther jelly roll, and 12 ounces of strawberries. Thursday brought another 12 ounces of strawberries, a pound and a half of round steak, a cake of yeast, 2 pounds of potatoes and a third jelly roll. Friday she bought a can of Libby's corned beef, a dozen eggs, a box of Diamond tea, 4 pounds of dressed fish, 3 pounds of cabbage, a pound and a half of smoked meat (probably a few ham hocks) and 5 pounds of fresh peas. On Saturday, the biggest shopping day of the week, she purchased a loaf of white bread, a two-and-a-half pound fryer chicken, a can of pineapple, a pound of salt pork, 5 pounds of sugar, 6 pounds of flour, a dozen eggs, 4 pounds of potatoes, a pound of butter, a cake of yeast, and another 5 pounds of fresh peas. She did not shop on Sunday. On the following Monday, she bought 6 lemons, 5 pounds of sugar, and a loaf of white bread. She did not shop on Tuesday.[49] While she purchased bread and cakes frequently, given the lard, butter, flour, yeast and eggs she purchased, she also probably made biscuits and/or some bread. She also clearly bought fruits and vegetables in season as well as making commercially canned foods a regular, but not extensive part of her family's diet. It seems that she only planned meals a day or two ahead and that fresh vegetables and meat were a relatively small portion of their diet. While the family of four ate a few canned foods, the older couple only bought a single can of condensed milk during the survey week.[50]

An extended family of seven from Claremont, New Hampshire (a mill town about ninety miles from Nashua and just south and west of the White Mountains) had similar shopping patterns, but ate very different foods. Here donuts, cakes, cookies, crackers, cinnamon buns, homemade apple pie were eaten throughout the week. Unlike the families in Portsmouth, Virginia this family had three quarts of milk delivered every day. They also ate ground beef, beef tripe, ham to bake, boiled ham, corn flakes, fresh pork chops, fresh pork rib roast, canned peaches, and Jell-O gelatin. A grown son, his wife and their daughter in addition to a second son lived with the family.

The grown children contributed to household by paying $130 a quarter for their lodging and board. It does not appear that this family baked as frequently as the Virginia families given the comparatively small quantities of flour and sugar purchased and the large quantity of baked goods they purchased.[51] While this large family purchased a single box of corn flakes, another Claremont family bought shredded wheat and Wheaties, the same week in late April. Canned sardines were occasionally purchased by a few families in the area. Oranges and grapefruits were eaten although only one family purchased them during the mid-March survey. Another unusual family ate a can of asparagus, canned peas, fresh spinach and celery one week in late March.[52]

While this is only a very brief look at a specific set of surveys, these records help us better understand the food choices many working-class Americans made in the mid-1930s. They also provide more detail about how and where families acquired the foods they ate, highlighting regional and ethnic food preferences and shopping patterns. Even in looking at this small number of surveys we can see some similarities. For example, all the families ate foods rich in carbohydrates and a seemingly high amount of fat and sugar, whether in jelly rolls or donuts. Meats were eaten in smaller quantities than fish, but most meals seem to have had meat or fish. Fruits and vegetables were not necessarily an everyday affair and tended to be seasonal. Yet, food inventories taken in June from San Francisco, California tended to be higher in fresh and canned produce as well as having a more varied and well-stocked pantry than the families in Virginia and New Hampshire.[53] Taken as a whole, it is striking how even the individual surveys reinforce both the national and regional data on food consumption, while giving us a much more intimate look inside American homes.

Epilogue

Walk into any grocery store, supermarket, or gas station and there is no doubt that today the American diet is truly industrial. There are aisles of canned goods, frozen dinners, soda and snack foods, baked goods and ready to eat "fresh" salsa and hummus. Even our vegetables seem industrial. "Baby" carrots ready to eat out of the bag or boxes of triple washed salad greens. Like so many aspects of American industrialization, industrializing the American diet was an iterative process based not only on what was technologically possible but also on what consumers were willing to purchase on a regular basis. An industrial diet was ultimately a confluence of cultural, social, and technological change by the early 1980s. Increasingly sophisticated polymers and plastics that could protect foods better were developed throughout the 1960s and 1970s and perhaps reached an apogee with the two-liter plastic (polyethylene terephthalate or PET) soda bottle in the late 1970s. Microwave ovens at home and work made heating frozen meals convenient. Duel income families looking for short cuts to dinner, especially for working women with little time to shop and cook. More singles living alone, divorced men and women, and "latch-key kids" all found feeding themselves ready-made foods from grocery stories, gas stations, and a variety of restaurants attractive. Deindustrialization and riots from the late 1960s through the early 1990s also changed the way the poorest Americans ate as supermarkets pulled out of the most troubled neighborhoods, leaving few fresh choices. While it is doubtful that most Americans will turn their backs on industrial foods, the new emphasis on more healthful choices may once again reshape the food industry and the American diet.

Notes

1. Walter Licht, *Industrializing America: Nineteenth Century* (Baltimore, MD: Johns Hopkins University Press, 1995); Louis Galambos, *Competition and Cooperation* (Baltimore, MD: Johns Hopkins University Press, 1966); and Louis Galambos and Joseph A. Pratt, *The Rise of the Corporate Commonwealth: U.S. Business and Public Policy in the Twentieth Century* (Baltimore, MD: Johns Hopkins University Press, 1988); Olivier Zunz, *Why the American Century?* (Chicago: University of Chicago Press, 1998); and Alfred D. Chandler, *The Visible Hand: The Managerial Revolution in American Business* (Cambridge, MA: Harvard University Press, 1977).

2. James Parton, "Pittsburg" *The Atlantic Monthly*, January 1868 [Online]. Available: http://www.pittsburghinwords.org/james_parton.html. [January 31, 2011]

3. Richard Osborne Cummings, *The American Ice Industry and the Development of Refrigeration, 1790–1860* (Cambridge, MA: Harvard University Press, 1940).

4. Anderson. *Refrigeration in America: A History of a New Technology and Its Impact* (Princeton, NJ: Princeton University Press, 1953).

5. Siegfried Giedion, *Mechanization Takes Command: A Contribution to Anonymous History* (New York: Oxford University Press, 1948), v, 6.

6. Alfred D. Chandler, Jr., *The Visible Hand: The Managerial Revolution in American Business* (Cambridge, MA: Belknap Press, 1977).

7. William Cronon, *Nature's Metropolis: Chicago and the Great West* (New York: W. W. Norton, 1991), 55–108, 207–62.

8. Upton Sinclair, *The Jungle* (New York: Doubleday, Page, 1906).

9. James Harvey Young, *Pure Food: Securing the Pure Food and Drugs Act of 1906* (Princeton, NJ: Princeton University Press, 1989); Nancy Tomes, *Gospel of Germs: Men, Women and the Microbe in American Life* (Cambridge, MA: Harvard University Press, 1998); Lorine Swainston Goodwin, *The Pure Food, Drink, and Drugs Crusaders, 1879–1914* (Jefferson, NC: McFarland, 1999).

10. Goodwin, *Pure Food, Drink, and Drugs*, 1.

11. Sidney W. Mintz, *Sweetness and Power: The Place of Sugar in Modern History* (New York: Viking Books, 1985), 166.

12. Mintz states that between 1800–1809 annual British sugar consumption was 18 pounds per capita, which translates into less than two tablespoons of sugar a day or 96 calories per day per capita, see page 67 and note 165 on page 252. Sugar consumption was only slightly higher in 1835 at roughly 22 pounds per year. By 1937, when per capita consumption of sugar in all forms was approximated at 4.9 ounces per day, it constituted only 16 percent of a then standard 3000 calorie per day dietary requirement. While no one would dispute that sugar consumption dramatically increased throughout both the nineteenth and twentieth centuries, to say that it fueled the industrial revolution is a vast over statement. By contrast, U.S. consumption in 1909 was 84 pounds per capita and by 1948 had risen to 106 per capita or 4.6 ounces per day. See *Consumption of Food in the United States, 1909–1948*, Miscellaneous Publication No. 691 USDA (Washington, DC: Government Printing Office, 1949), 120.

13. Harvey Levenstein, *Revolution at the Table: The Transformation of the American Diet* (New York: Oxford University Press, 1988), 32.

14. Roger Horowitz, *Putting Meat on the American Table: Taste Technology, Transformation* (Baltimore, MD: Johns Hopkins University Press, 2006), 144.

15. Levenstein, *Revolution at the Table*, 30–43. For a very different interpretation of the rise of early industrial foods see Gabriella M. Petrick, "'Purity as Life': H. J. Heinz, Religious Sentiment and the Beginning of the Industrial Diet," *History and Technology* 27, no. 1 (2011): 37–64.

16. Two valuable collections of this new literature are Warren Belasco and Philip Scranton, eds., *Food Nations: Selling Taste in Consumer Societies* (New York: Routledge, 2001); Warren Belasco and Roger Horowitz, eds., *Food Chains: From Farmyard to Shopping Cart* (Philadelphia: University of Pennsylvania Press, 2009).

17. Horowitz, *Putting Meat on the American Table.*

18. J. L. Anderson, *Industrializing the Corn Belt: Agriculture, Technology, and Environment, 1945–1972* (DeKalb: Northern Illinois University Press, 2008).

19. E. Melanie DuPuis, *Nature's Perfect Food: How Milk Became American's Drink* (New York: New York University Press, 2002).

20. Shane Hamilton, *Trucking Country: The Road to America's Wal-Mart Economy* (Princeton, NJ: Princeton University Press, 2008).

21. *Consumption of Food in the United States*, 1.

22. Two examples are Southern Cooperative Experimentation Stations, *Family Food Consumption in Three Types of Farming Areas of the South: I An Analysis of 1947 Food Data* Southern Cooperative Series Bulletin 7, Bureau of Home Economics and Nutrition, USDA (Washington, DC: Government Printing Office, 1950); and Faith Clark, Janet Murray, Gertrude S. Weiss, and Evelyn Grossman, *Food Consumption of Urban Families in the United States with an Appraisal of Methods and Analysis* Agricultural Information Bulletin No. 132, Home Economics Branch, Agricultural Research Service, USDA (Washington, DC: Government Printing Office, 1954).

23. Derived from Table 38, *Consumption of Food in the United States*, 120.

24. Derived from Table 38, *Consumption of Food in the United States*, 120.

25. Although there is no clear reason for the dramatic decline in apple consumption after the depression, disaggregation of civilian and military food consumption may account for some of the decline. Blight or farmers simply curtailing production due to unfavorable economic condition are other likely factors. Interestingly, both bananas and peaches enjoyed remarkably stable consumption over the same period.

26. These first three charts are derived from Table 10, *Consumption of Food in the United States*, 75, 80.

27. Derived from Table 10, *Consumption of Food in the United States*, 75.

28. Derived from Table 10, *Consumption of Food in the United States*, 75.

29. Derived from Table 15, *Consumption of Food in the United States*, 80.

30. Derived from Table 11, *Consumption of Food in the United States*, 75. Data from 1909–1942 are based on pack-year data (June to June) while date from 1943–1948 is based on calendar year data.

31. Donald K. Tressler and Clifford F. Evers, *The Freezing and Preservation of Foods* (Westport, CT: AVI Publishing Company, 1977), 116.

32. Ibid.

33. Table 16, *Consumption of Food in the United States*, 81.

34. *Supplement for 1954 to Consumption of Food in the United States, 1909–1952*, Agricultural Handbook No. 62, Agricultural Marketing Service, USDA (Washington, DC: Government Printing Office, 1955).

35. Southern Cooperative Experiment Stations, *Family Food Consumption*, 10.

36. Ibid, 12.

37. Ibid, 24.

38. Ibid, 25

39. Ibid.

40. Ibid, 25–28.

41. Ibid, 121.

42. Ibid, 120.

43. Ibid.

44. Ibid, 125–29

45. Ibid, 129–31.

46. Ibid, 107–18.

47. Records of the Bureau of Labor Statistics, Record of Food Consumption for One Week, 1934–1937 National Archives and Records Administration, College Park, MD, Record Group 257, Entry 33, Box 48.

48. Ibid.

49. Ibid.

50. Ibid.

51. Ibid, Box 25.

52. Ibid, Box 24.

53. Ibid, Box 30.

Bibliography

Anderson, Oscar Edward. *Refrigeration in America: A History of a New Technology and its Impact*. Princeton, NJ: Princeton University Press, 1953.

Belasco, Warren and Roger Horowitz, eds. *Food Chains: From Farmyard to Shopping Cart*. Philadelphia: University of Pennsylvania Press, 2009.

Chandler, Alfred D. *The Visible Hand: The Managerial Revolution in American Business*. Cambridge, MA: The Belknap Press, 1977.

Hamilton, Shane. *Trucking Country: The Road to America's Wal-Mart Economy*. Princeton, NJ: Princeton University Press, 2008.

Horowitz, Roger. *Putting Meat on the American Table: Taste, Technology, Transformation*. Baltimore, MD: Johns Hopkins University Press, 2006.

Levenstein, Harvey. *Revolution at the Table: The Transformation of the American Diet*. New York: Oxford University Press, 1988.

Mintz, Sidney. *Sweetness and Power: The Place of Sugar in Modern History*. New York: Viking Books, 1985.

CHAPTER 16

FAST FOOD

STEVE PENFOLD

If fast food has an origins story, it would probably start in 1948, when Dick and Maurice McDonald redesigned their successful restaurant. Since 1940, the brothers had operated a typical drive-in stand in San Bernadino, California, hawking burgers, hot dogs, and barbeque sandwiches, delivered by female cars hops to the parking lot, which teenagers had made into a popular hangout. The brothers did well, but they remained frustrated: car hops were too expensive, teenagers were too rowdy, and the whole operation was too slow. In 1948, then, they redesigned the outlet, reducing the menu from twenty-five items to nine, lowering prices, standardizing portions and condiments, assigning specific tasks to each worker, and downloading labor to their customers through self-service. At first, the story goes, no one was impressed. Customers didn't understand the new system so they sat in their cars, honking their horns to page the now departed car hops. The teenagers drifted away and sales plummeted. Eventually, however, local families and nearby workers arrived, lines bulged, and people started noticing. A national restaurant magazine profiled the brothers in 1952, and soon prospective hamburger makers arrived to check out the operation, reproducing it as far away as Florida and Arizona.[1]

One of the visitors was Ray Kroc of Chicago, Illinois. He had spent thirty years selling supplies to restaurants, including the Multimixer, a piece of American ingenuity that could mix five milkshakes at a time. Kroc was amazed to notice that the brothers, with a single outlet, had purchased *eight* Multimixers, so he flew to California to see the McDonald operation for himself. He was impressed. "This had to be the most amazing merchandising operation I had ever seen," he recalled. "Visions of McDonald's restaurants dotting the crossroads all over the country paraded through my brain." The brothers had little interest in expanding on their own, but Kroc convinced them that he could be their national franchising agent.

Contract in hand, Kroc told his wife the news. She wasn't enthusiastic, but this hardly slowed him down. Kroc was pure entrepreneurial masculinity: he titled his autobiography, *Grinding It Out*; his personal credo was "Press On"; he took every task with a hard-driving, take-no-prisoners attitude. Under Kroc's leadership, McDonald's grew from his first outlet near Chicago to over 300 locations in 44 states by 1961, when he bought out the brothers for $2.7 million.[2] Over the next decade, the chain established its dominance in the United States, spread to Canada, and began its march to global hegemony.

Like many origins stories, the often-repeated tale of Kroc and the McDonald brothers is at once convenient and inaccurate. An origins story necessarily highlights a clear moment of genesis and invention, but fast food history rarely worked that way. Few of the brothers' "innovations" were entirely new. Most societies have some version of quick and convenient food, from street carts through crêpe stands to fish and chip shops, and even in America, fast food had much longer genealogies. Before World War Two, diners served cheap food to customers on the go, hot dog stands specialized in a few products for a self-serve clientele, White Castle sold standardized burgers in cities across the United States, and Howard Johnson's built an impressive chain aimed at roadside markets. This longer history is important, but most of the largest and most recognized companies emerged, like McDonald's, in the postwar period. Colonel Sanders hit the road in 1954 to sell his Kentucky Fried Chicken (KFC) recipe full time. Burger King started in Florida that same year and was franchising nationally by 1961. Glen Bell founded Taco Bell in California in 1962, following several experiments with small taco chains in the 1950s.[3] The list goes on. Indeed, as of 1999, seven of the ten largest fast food chains in the United States—and most of the largest in the world—traced their origins to the decade and a half after 1948.[4]

Of course, starting a history of fast food with a story about McDonald's has an additional advantage, since the company is the largest, most important, and most studied chain. McDonald's is, to paraphrase Lenin, the highest stage of fast food: widely copied in the industry, carrying enormous symbolic weight in the global imagination, and serving as the touchstone of an ongoing scholarly conversation about larger economic, social, and cultural processes. In *Jihad vs. McWorld*, Benjamin Barber famously used McDonald's as a symbol of the increasing power of global mass culture. George Ritzer's "McDonaldization thesis" traced the extension of efficiency, predictability, and control from McDonald's to many spheres of life. Ritzer later extended the idea to the world by coining the term "grobalization," which describes "the imperialistic ambitions of nations, corporations, organizations, and the like and their desire, indeed need, to impose themselves on various geographic areas."[5] By contrast, ethnographic studies focused on the reception of fast food by consumers. *Golden Arches East*[6], in which six anthropologists studied McDonald's in East Asia, is the best-known, but fast food ethnography has spread almost as far as fast food itself, with scholars, like hamburger makers, adapting international ideas to many local contexts. If these scholars agree that fast food is a quintessential form of American and global culture, the keywords of this reception literature are nonetheless accommodation, hybridity, and "glocalization," highlighting reciprocal processes of meaning creation. Other scholars, like Joe Kincheloe and Douglas Kellner, have called for versions of a "multi-perspectivist" approach: since McDonald's operates at many levels—production, consumption, marketing, symbolism—a full understanding requires many analytic tools.[7]

This chapter takes up this point about multiple perspectives and adds another. Four decades of McStudy have produced rich and nuanced portraits of McDonald's; with a few notable exceptions, scholars have lavished less attention on other chains. Indeed, at times, the agenda-setting power of McDonald's has served to distort more than illuminate, focusing attention on fast food's leading edge and most powerful agent rather than the full range of companies and experiences. Historians have an additional concern—to chart change over time and to place business and cultural developments in their social and historical context. In this sense, we might read the McDonald's origins story in another way, as a starting point that hints at some key themes but only imperfectly describes the broader history of fast food. The brothers specialized in a small number of familiar foods. They applied systematic thinking to production. Their new outlet had a social life, fitting into existing and emerging cultures of age, family, leisure and consumption. Kroc built these basic insights into a large chain. These themes—expansion, taste, systems, and social life—might form the basic ingredients of a global history of fast food, one that has similarities to the McDonald's story but has distinctive elements as well.

McEverywhere: Expansion[8]

Ray Kroc could not understand the McDonalds' lack of drive. He knew their operation had national potential, but the brothers were content—they owned a big house, bought a new Cadillac every year, and didn't want the hassles of expansion. "[This] approach," recalled Kroc, "was utterly foreign to my thinking." For Kroc, when you have a good idea, you press on, grind it out, and build your "personal monument to free enterprise." His autobiography is a capitalist manifesto, filled with entrepreneurial rhetoric, stories of pluck and determination, and masculine metaphors of intense competition. "It is ridiculous to call this an industry," Kroc told *Institutions* magazine in 1972. "This is rat eat rat, dog eat dog. I'll kill 'em before they kill me. You're talking about the American way of survival of the fittest."[9] Like Kroc, the founders of fast food lived in a largely male world of entrepreneurship, travelling constantly, doing deals on a handshake, even judging family life by how it supported their business vision. The good wife joined the crusade or took care of the home front; the bad wife complained about financial insecurity and absent fathers. Above all, the founders of fast food measured themselves by the growth of their chains, speaking of their business in personal terms—my monument to free enterprise, my baby—and constantly charted the growth of their competitors. Over time, through corporate acquisition or evolution, entrepreneurial masculinity gave way to bureaucracy, stockholders, boards of directors, and specialized knowledge, but from the early days, fast food had an expansionist imperative.

From its origins in the mid-1950s, fast food spread widely, rapidly and continuously, crossing regional boundaries within the United States and pushing outward into the world. "America the beautiful, let me sing of thee," Ada Louise Huxtable wrote sarcastically in 1971, "Burger King and Dairy Queen from sea to shining sea."[10] Yet fast food's American hegemony had only just begun: the 1970s marked a new phase of more intensive growth that would take it beyond suburban roadsides to truly national status, covering small towns, inner cities, central business districts, hospitals, universities, and every other imaginable crevice in the foodscape.[11] By 1971, moreover, fast food had already pushed well beyond America's shores. Many chains crossed the border into Canada even before they had thoroughly covered the United States—Dairy Queen in 1953, KFC in 1959, and many others in the 1960s. If geographic proximity and cultural similarity made Canadian growth relatively seamless, fast food was going further afield by the mid-1960s. KFC landed in Britain in 1964, Germany and Australia in 1968, and Japan in 1970. McDonald's sold its first developmental license (covering the Caribbean) in 1965, opened its first international outlet (located in Canada) in 1967, and set up a formal International Division two years later. From these early beachheads, international growth accelerated as North American markets approached saturation in the 1980s. Fast food moved to many more places (McDonald's was in 20 countries in 1980 and 89 in 1995) while each place got more fast food (France had 109 fast food outlets in 1980 and over 2000 by 1991; in 2000, Thailand hosted 300 KFCs, 300 Dairy Queens, 102 McDonald's, 115 Pizza Huts, 170 Dunkin Donuts).[12]

While big companies grew systematically, the *idea* of fast food expanded in a less predictable process of copying and borrowing, a dynamic that might be called (in an Internet age) "going viral." "Most everybody copied McDonald's," recalled one of the founders of Burger Queen, which began in Louisville in 1961. "If I had looked at McDonald's and saw someone turning hamburgers while he was hanging by his feet I would have copied it."[13] KFC similarly attracted copies, bearing names like Kansas Fried Chicken, Ozark Fried Chicken, and Cincinnati Fried Chicken. Internationally, fast food sometimes first spread to new markets not by American chain penetration but by local entrepreneurs importing the idea. In the Philippines, Tony Tan Caktiong and his brothers founded Jollybee in the mid-1970s, emulating McDonald's in technique, prices, products, and even color schemes.[14] Once American chains arrived, copying often accelerated. After McDonald's set up in Japan and France in the early 1970s, several local entrepreneurs opened hamburger chains in both places, adopting American-sounding names like Magic Burger and MOS Burger. Another pattern of viral growth was adapting the fast food idea to new foods. Taco Bell emerged in this way, founded by Glen Bell, who owned a small hamburger stand not far from the McDonald brothers' original outlet in San Bernadino. Bell was looking for a unique product that was amenable to the

McDonald's model, so he dipped into the cuisine of local Mexican migrants. In 2000, an Israeli entrepreneur did the same to falafel, founding a chain that featured retro-styled outlets and industrial-rolled balls. The croissant underwent a similar process in France.[15]

Fast food, then, grew extensively, intensively, virally and, above all, rapidly. Within a half century, the form spread widely though unevenly across the globe. Indeed, even for American companies, global operations exerted increasing economic importance: by 2001, both KFC and McDonald's earned over half their profits from their international subsidiaries.[16] Yet it is important to put such figures in context: fast food did not always enter the global economy through direct American expansion, and while some international versions spread beyond their initial home countries—Israel's falafel chain Ma'oz to Europe and Japan's MOS Burger to several Asian markets—they made hardly any dent on the American foodscape. Fast food spread widely, but it flowed one way.[17] While new and exotic foods frequently entered mainstream North American diets, foreign fast food chains were never the agent of transformation. In the Empire of the French Fry, the McColonies have yet to conquer the metropole.

Meat, Potatoes and Money: Taste

From its early years, the fast food revolution built on tensions between standardization and variation, familiarity and novelty, adaptation and education. It began with the simple formula that *Time* magazine dubbed "meat, potatoes, and money."[18] Early menus were small, rarely more than a dozen items, and each company specialized in one line, with hamburgers and chicken leading the way and secondary products including donuts, tacos, hot dogs, and pizza.[19] These products were perfectly suited to the time. Between the 1950s and the 1980s, per capita consumption of almost every core fast food ingredient increased dramatically: beef (35 percent), chicken (121 percent), and cheese (179 percent).[20] Even potato consumption, declining in the four decades before 1950, made a comeback in the fast food era, having been saved, in part, by French fries.[21] Drinks were also important. In the half-century after 1950, soft drink consumption in the United States increased almost four times. More important, drinks were the most profitable items on the menu, with low costs for both raw materials and labor. "[Y]ou can say we at McDonald's are thankful that people drink with their sandwiches," McDonald's president Fred Turner noted in 1973.[22]

In bringing these various ingredients together into tasty food, fast food chains combined familiarity with products adjusted for mainstream American tastes. By the interwar years, the hot dog had been stripped of its roots in ethnic sausages by years of exposure at amusement parks and baseball stadiums, while chains like White Castle had so thoroughly naturalized the hamburger that it was placed alongside apple pie as the symbolic American food. The donut, which had several regional and ethnic designations in the nineteenth century, was similarly standardized and nationalized, becoming a generic snack of the urban working class—the poor man's rich food—by the 1930s.[23] Other fast foods crossed culinary boundaries. By the time Glen Bell arrived on the scene, street vendors had made tacos popular in urban California, but the product had hardly entered the American mainstream. Glen Bell's first wife rather unsupportively summed up the culinary dilemma, suggesting that white consumers would not eat spicy Mexican food while blander flavors would only serve to alienate local Mexicans. As an alternative, she proposed Bell return to his more secure job reading gas meters. To stay in the mainstream, Bell toned down the spices, and when Taco Bell later spread to Florida, it educated consumers by combining nationalist references with analogies to familiar foods: "The All American Taco: The Cheeseburger that Goes Crunch."[24] Fried chicken was in between: hardly unknown across the United States, but with enough regional caché that Sanders put "Kentucky" in his brand name as he took his food national. The Colonel crossed gender boundaries even more decisively, taking fried chicken out of the female world of home kitchens to the commercial world of masculine entrepreneurship.[25]

Over time, for many reasons, menus expanded. In the 1960s, chains performed various "upsizings," from the Big Mac to Red Barn's Barnbuster, mainly to compete with Burger King's Whopper. In the 1970s, new offerings (like McDonald's breakfast) targeted different "day-parts." In the 1980s, chains added supposedly healthier options like grilled chicken, muffins, or salads. Other changes flowed from the need to balance mass-market aspirations against culinary diversity on the ground. When Pizza Hut moved from its Midwest base to the northeast, it confronted regional diversity: consumers preferred the thick crusts of ubiquitous immigrant-owned pizzerias to the thin crusts of the new chain, so the company developed chewier alternatives. Companies also struggled to deal with cultural difference. McDonald's Cincinnati franchisee developed the Filet O' Fish to appeal to Catholic consumers, who were bypassing his all-beef menu on meatless Fridays. Thirty years later, with African Americans representing one quarter of sales, KFC's "urban restaurants" began offering "menu additions that reflect local tastes," including so-called "soul sides" like sweet potato pie and collard greens.[26] At the end of this broad process of product creep, menus were much larger and more complicated, but the foundation remained the same—meat, dairy, starch, salt, and sugar—with most chains creating "variety through the combination of standardized materials."[27]

International menus paralleled this North American pattern of variation within standardization. As fast food went global from the 1960s to the 1990s, world meat consumption increased almost 50 percent per capita. The pattern, of course, was very uneven, both across space and between various products. Chicken was becoming the closest thing to the global flesh although consumption varied both between and within countries where fast food was expanding. In China, for example, total chicken consumption was impressive, but typically higher in cities and in the southeast.[28] Beef was even more complicated. In Britain, beef itself was common but hamburgers had a poor reputation; in Australia, consumers preferred meat pies; in many other places, beef was completely unfamiliar. Everywhere, hamburger chains resorted to heavy advertising to convert local populations. But even when the hamburger was widely adopted, it often underwent a "category shift." In Asia, where local notions of a filling meal required rice and a vegetable or meat topping, consumers adopted the burger as a snack rather than a meal and as bread rather than meat.[29]

As journalists tirelessly point out, chains also adjusted menus and ingredients to local palates. McDonald's sells mutton in India, falafels in Egypt, and pork burgers in Thailand; KFC offers pumpkin porridge in Beijing; Wendy's serves corn chowder in Japan; Taco Bell pours beer in Puerto Rico; Pizza Hut uses mutton in Malaysia. This list goes on (and on and on . . .). Menu expansion was more a constant tension than an automatic imperative, so it played out unevenly across chains and over time. KFC thoroughly localized flavors in China, but the basic idea was still to fry chicken in seasoned batter. McDonalds' early attempts to adapt to local palates often failed, and the chain became convinced that menu standardization was the best strategy in the long term, though the insight was unevenly applied (with more adjustment in India than Japan, for example).[30] Even James Watson, who emphasized local diversity in consumer reception, noted that "the structure of the McDonald's menu remains essentially uniform the world over: main course burger/sandwich, fries, and a drink—overwhelmingly Coca-Cola. The keystone of this winning combination is . . . the fries. The main course may vary widely . . . but the signature innovation of McDonald's—thin, elongated fries cut from russet potatoes—is ever-present and consumed world-wide."[31] Two parents at a Mexican Taco Bell agreed, dismissing the tacos and burritos—"we've never had a taco with rice and fried potatoes"—but noting that their daughter "loved the fries."[32] The culinary politics of local authenticity were always complex. "This doesn't taste like the real thing, does it?" complained one woman at a Mexican Taco Bell. "What I wanted was those big taco shells stuffed with salad and Kraft cheese and all kinds of stuff, like what you get in Texas."[33]

In many ways, moving from menu expansion to grand, universal conclusions about homogenization or diversity is a fool's errand. Context is key: adding a hamburger to local cuisines might bring more variety; if fried chicken replaced existing foods, the result might be homogenization; expanding menus to include local flavors could theoretically homogenize and diversify diets at the same time. But all these dynamics would miss the most important point: in culinary terms, fast food's defining feature is not homogenization or diversity of taste, but standardization of products. Theoretically, fast food could expand to almost any simple edible, so long as outlets produced each particular item in identical form across space and over time. Whether the specific food is a burger or a taco, based on mutton or beef, or flavored with ketchup or curry, the system remains.

Techno-Burger: Systems[34]

Food became fast food through the application of technology and technocracy. Entrepreneurs like Ray Kroc spoke the language of mass production and thought in terms of rationalized systems. "We put the hamburger on the assembly line," Kroc famously remarked, a phrase that was more metaphorically evocative than descriptively accurate. Burger King and Burger Chef used automatic broilers,[35] and while most chains adopted specialized equipment like ketchup guns, pressure cookers, and French fry timers, human beings did most of the work, including feeding cookers, assembling burgers, and dipping donuts. Chains subjected these tasks to intense study, setting up streamlined production systems by dividing labor into the smallest units. No one just made a hamburger and fries: there were grill men, dressing men, frying men, drink men, and counter men, each with rigidly defined duties. "[T]he ketchup is applied by spreading it evenly in a spiral circular motion over the pickles, starting near the outside edge," sociologist Ester Reiter reported after a stint at Burger King in the late 1970s. "[S]even seconds are allotted to placing the fry basket in the fry pot... five seconds to filling the first bag in the bagging cycle, and three seconds to packing each subsequent one."[36] Despite Kroc's assembly line rhetoric, such stopwatch capitalism and ketchup choreography owed more to Frederick Taylor than to Henry Ford. Back in Ford's time, Taylor conducted detailed experiments on work, carefully charting workers' movements to improve efficiency, eliminate discretion from labor processes, and codify every task into a series of rules that management could control and enforce. Like Taylor, early fast food leaders prayed at the altar of the One Best Way. "Herein," began an early McDonald's operations manual, "lies *the* successful method...There isn't any compromising."[37]

Through franchising, chains applied the same vision to the entire outlet. Under this system, a franchisor sells to a franchisee the right to operate a business according to certain rules. This could entail a range of relationships: Burger King and Wendy's sold large territories to big franchisees; other companies drew in petty entrepreneurs from the middle or working class, who marshaled family economies to buy a single outlet, perhaps growing to two or more over a number of years. Taco Bell's first franchisee was typical, a Los Angeles cop who bought the outlet with a loan from the Police Credit Union and a second mortgage on his house.[38] Franchisees liked the system because it promised independence with security and economies of scale; franchisors because it allowed rapid expansion with little capital and because an owner-operator was often more motivated than a mere manager. To achieve this balance, franchisors controlled their franchisees, training them in centralized facilities (like McDonald's Hamburger University or Burger King's Whopper College), issuing operating manuals that detailed everything from food costs to cleaning washrooms, checking up through ongoing inspections, and promising termination of the franchise for failure to comply. Chains also limited franchisee discretion by controlling food before it even entered the outlets.

McDonald's used its buying power to compel bakers to precut buns, meat suppliers to conform to chain specifications, and potato farmers to alter their growing and storage practices. Others chains controlled inputs by controlling distribution.

Fast food's particular mix of technology and technocracy flowed from the structure of the business—a sort of Taylorized cottage industry that balanced economies of scale against a powerful pull to the small. Because fast food entrepreneurs served hot food and smiles to customers who were waiting, they needed small shops dispersed across space and staffed by human beings; because the chains sought rapid expansion and rigid uniformity, they needed a way to extend their industrial systems and operational control across wide geographies. Tensions were endemic, and making fast food could be a constant battle—between chains and franchisees, managers and workers, systems and individuals, rationality and humanity. "Operational control can only work when a franchisor understands he is constantly battling the ingrained habits of people," explained George Sukornyk, president of Harvey's Hamburgers, an early leader in Canada. "Unless he prevents it by regular supervision, his franchisees and their employees will revert to the various habits they have acquired through their lives."[39] Few companies did well in the long term without taking Sukornyk's insight to heart.

Indeed, in some ways, the tendency over time was toward greater control, particularly as menus grew, corporate infrastructures expanded, and operations became more complicated. At McDonald's, the manual grew from 75 pages in 1958 to over 750 by the mid-1990s. By 1981, Burger King's computer system regulated exact staff allocation—down to the specific task—based on projected sales, a job previously performed by managers based on experience and judgment.[40] Even before this, chains transferred more preparation to industrial processors. After the late 1960s, hamburger chains converted to frozen patties and French fries, while pizza companies developed prerolled, frozen crusts, delivered from a central commissary to each outlet.[41] In a parallel process, fast food companies took up serious research—McDonald's as early as the 1960s and other companies somewhat later—making taste a creature of food science.[42] Not only was such industrial and scientific manufacture cheaper, it ensured more direct, central control over portion, taste, and quality, eliminating all but the most basic processes of local preparation. "My job is I, like, basically make the tacos!" commented one Taco Bell employee in 2000. "The meat comes in boxes that have bags inside, and those bags you boil to heat up the meat. That's how you make tacos."[43]

Such McDonaldized systems traveled well across space and through time in almost complete defiance of culinary traditions, regulatory structures, and other local variables. One multi-country study of fast food labor discovered that many practices varied (wage rates, scheduling, worker demographics, systems of representation), but these local wrinkles affected few fundamental changes in lines of authority, production systems, or basic labor conditions. "[T]he kitchen is the heart of our business and our formula varies little," noted one McDonald's official. "This allows the McDonald's experience in Paris, Texas, to match that of Paris, France."[44] This systematic similarity went beyond kitchens to corporate cultures. While most companies recruited local partners and executives—"We live here. We're Chinese. We see what people prefer," claimed Ben Koo of KFC-China[45]—they generally preferred local partners and executives who, in the words of boosterish McDonald's historian John Love, "are not traditionalists in their homeland... and have affinity for American business practices and American entrepreneurs." At KFC-China, the so-called Taiwan Gang of executives combined Chinese backgrounds, western educations, and fast food experience. Once selected, moreover, chains funneled executives through corporate training procedures.[46]

This kind of corporate "glocalism" was paralleled in supply chains. The larger companies loudly proclaimed their preference for local supplies, which they considered more stable and better for public relations. Local food systems often made the goal impossible, however. The best French fry potato, for example, doesn't grow everywhere (it needs to be extra long with a high solid content), so an international trade in frozen fries soon developed, totaling almost 2 million tons by 1998, dominated by the Netherlands (shipping mainly to Europe), the United States (shipping mainly to Asia), and Canada (shipping mainly to the United States). At the same time, chains worked to build "local" supplies through the global movement of capital, knowledge, and technique. In India, McCain Foods (a global food processor) adapted a Canadian potato (the Shepody, itself the product of scientific breeding in a government-funded lab) to local climactic conditions by first planting a master crop in the Himalayan Mountains, harvesting it in September, replanting it elsewhere, reharvesting it in March, and finally shipping the crop to a McCain plant for processing. To induce Indian farmers to sign on, McCain set up a demonstration farm and negotiated guaranteed prices. Of course, potato diasporas were hardly new. Since at least the sixteenth century, the humble tuber moved in trans-Atlantic networks of trade, migration, and knowledge. But if the Indian Shepody updated a longstanding dynamic of agricultural and economic change, "local supplies" could also be McDonaldized. Science and capital could even overcome climate and season, with the economic power of fast food serving as the underlying engine of change. By 2010, McDonald's expected to use 3500 tons of potatoes at its 200 Indian outlets.[47]

Still, McDonaldization was never automatic or inevitable. To reproduce it across space and over time required constant nurturing and repetition. Here, the human element often intervened. While all the big chains shared the technocratic ideal, rationality was not automatic on the ground. "Burger Chef had similar rules on quality, service, and cleanliness," recalled Ohio franchisee Jack Roshman, "but we just didn't get it done as effectively as McDonald's."[48] Burger Chef collapsed in the 1970s, but even some successful companies, like Dairy Queen and Burger King, diluted their on-the-ground control by selling large territorial franchises, setting up multiple layers between head office and outlet. Similarly, fast food's first global beachheads were often haphazard and uncontrolled. KFC arrived in Hong Kong in 1973 but withdrew two years later, owing to poor locations, inconsistent product quality, and uncertain marketing practices; the company returned in the mid-1980s with more stringent controls.[49] Even McDonald's lost control of its operations in

France, where the chain eventually had to fight an extended legal battle to claim back its license from a poor national operator.[50] If large chains sometimes had problems putting procedures into practice, smaller companies often adopted only parts of the fast food model, lacking the scope and scale to fully McDonaldize their operations. In Cincinnati by the late 1970s, several small chains served a fast food version of the local chili recipe (spiced with cinnamon), including manufacture in central commissaries and locations that stressed convenience, but they were hardly technocratic operations. Indeed, at one chain, the owner still mixed the spices at home in his basement.[51]

Nor were the objects of rational control completely passive. Franchisees resisted, forming councils to represent their interests, challenging company policy, even suing their own franchisors. Workers also resisted, including hundreds of efforts to unionize specific outlets across the world. Unionization usually failed, but workers resisted in smaller ways—stealing food, slowing down, and talking back, a process described most evocatively in Robin Kelley's *Race Rebels*.[52] Recognizing such limitations is not to deny the power of McDonaldization as a process, but to try to reconcile the techno-burger with the intensely human history of fast food. Work was de-skilled but competence remained a source of pride for many workers. Recruitment strategies were both systematic and social, marshalling formal procedures like applications and the personal networks of ethnicity, family, and friendship. Service work was difficult to totally codify, and rational scripts could have unanticipated effects. Even highly technocratic systems played out in cultural terms, often entailing informal gender divisions between front-of-house service and back-of-house production. Rational systems of production and authority were interwoven with human and historical processes.[53]

History from the Bucket Up: Social Life

Fast food was more than a meal: companies set up outlets that were simple in design, but had a rich social history, one that was influenced by marketing strategies and broader cultural dynamics. In the United States, eating out increased from less than quarter to over a third of the average food dollar in the three decades after 1954, a trend driven by rising affluence and women working outside the home.[54] But even a "housewife" could appreciate the merit of a meal in a bucket. "Colonel Sanders is a woman's best friend," KFC reminded Americans in 1968. "[He] fixes Sunday dinner seven days a week. For weary wives. For working women. All you do is pick it up."[55] In this sense, North American fast food emerged at the intersection of the key postwar booms—economic, baby, and suburban—that converged in what marketers called the "mass-class market," middle-income families who made up over half the population by the mid-1950s. Given the racial geography of American cities at the time, the typical fast food family was usually (though not always) white. According to historian Jeffrey Pilcher, for example, the early growth of Taco Bell around Los Angeles was one part of a "geographic shift" of taco shops "into the white suburbs of Glendale, Pasadena, and the San Fernando Valley."[56]

Reaching this market meant constructing a commercial speech that articulated the cultural codes of white middle class families—convenience, cleanliness, civility, and domesticity—in several different spheres of operation, from menu through architecture to advertising. Convenience meant big parking lots, speed of service, and easy-to-eat hand-held food, but also fitting into middle class routines. Fast food outlets were almost completely unlike a formal restaurant. Widely advertised "No Tipping" policies made meals cheaper but also implied a more casual social relationship between server and customer. In this sense, the policy reinforced two distinctive features of fast food convenience—affordability and informality. In the early days, almost everyone offered *something* under 20 cents, with the 15-cent hamburger leading the way. McDonald's "All-American Meal" (a burger, fries and milkshake), which set the standard, cost 45 cents in 1960 (put another way, four All American meals cost the average family less than 40 minutes of paid labor). Outlets also invited middle class families with come-as-you-are informality and child-friendliness.

Sanitized was another middle-class keyword. Not only did chains ruthlessly enforce cleanliness (Kroc famously remarked, "if you have time to lean you have time to clean"), but they sanitized their outlets in cultural terms as well. Though McDonald's attracted many teenagers, Kroc aimed to "clean up" the rowdy image of the drive-in by banning jukeboxes and female employees and by preaching the value of community involvement. "Our theme is kinda synonymous with Sunday School, the Girl Scouts, and the YMCA," Kroc told *Newsweek* in 1965. "McDonald's is clean and wholesome. It is for the family with youngsters."[57] Taco Bell took a different route to the same cultural end, adapting an immigrant street food to the "theme park" culture of California's Anglo suburbanites. Outlets played on stereotyped "Mexotica," including architectural elements like arches and bell towers and carnivalesque Grand Openings featuring spotlights and Mariachi bands.[58] At KFC, the Colonel's image as genteel patriarch significantly sanitized Sanders own personality (he was a rather opinionated fellow[59]) and highlighted the most culturally innocuous image of a white southerner at the time.

Above all, fast food chains projected images of family and domesticity, a "food is love" strategy that resonated with parents who wanted to treat their kids and to get a break at the same time: "If you're too busy to fix lunch today," read one early ad, "why not come to McDonald's? The kids will love it." Chains also spoke directly to children. Television ads frequently constructed children as agents, with taglines like "Kids Bring their Families to Burger Chef," while outlets themselves served as training grounds for consumption, with straws and condiments at child level, step stools to reach the order counter, and by the 1970s, Playlands and other child-friendly features.[60] Ronald McDonald was the highest stage of such childhood spectacles. He started life as a product pitchman in Washington D.C. in 1963, but soon became part of a sophisticated national strategy to construct McDonald's as an idealized childhood experience. Other chains invented their own mascots (like the animated "Burger King"), but backed by massive advertising spending (McDonald's spent $40 million on television ads in 1972 and over $1 billion by 1985), this kinder, gentler Ronald swept the country. As early as 1973, 97 percent of American children recognized Ronald. Even when the baby boom waned and companies segmented their marketing to reach young adults and teens, most chains extended these child-focused strategies in the 1970s and beyond, churning out fun meals and big-money tie-ins with Walt Disney and Star Wars.[61]

When fast food chains located outside white middle class suburbs, as they did increasingly by the late 1960s, they confronted different social dynamics. In 1969, a coalition of African American organizations picketed four McDonald's outlets in Cleveland, arguing the chain should sell the stores to African Americans to reflect the local neighborhood.[62] McDonald's eventually began affirmative action programs to attract minority franchisees, including so-called "zebra partnerships" (white investors, black operators), but the Cleveland dispute was only one part a broader struggle that ran from local areas to national politics. In 1982, Jesse Jackson's Operation PUSH negotiated an accord with KFC-parent Heublein, including assistance to open 112 black-owned outlets. For PUSH, franchising was a potential form of black economic development, but for fast food companies, it was just good business. By the mid-1980s, African Americans spent $8.4 billion on food away from the home. "Blacks account for an important part of our domestic sales," Heublein's president remarked, "and we support those who support us."[63] Marketing was another wing of this strategy. In 1973, McDonald's hired a black-oriented advertising agency; Burger King followed suit a decade later. The McDonald's agency, Burrell-McCain, translated the chain's commercial speech into more meaningful African American idioms, including unique slogans (replacing "You Deserve a Break Today" with "McDonald's is Good to Have Around") and commercials featuring idealized scenes of black family life.[64] By the mid-1990s, many chains extended these strategies to Hispanic Americans.[65]

As it travelled globally, fast food intersected with a parallel cultural politics of similarity and difference. Scholars traced fast food's global popularity to various manifestations of a cosmopolitan consuming class around the world. In France, McDonald's appealed to bourgeois consumers as a new expression of the longstanding appeal of American modernity. In Asia, fast food reached the emerging "new rich," who took up conspicuous consumption as a symbol of their growing wealth and power. "The numbers are just staggering," claimed KFC Vice President Steve Provost, noting that as many as 250 million Chinese residents would enter the middle class in the following decade. "All those people are going to buy TVs, buy cars, and eat fast food."[66] Fast food's global popularity was also tied to changing family and generational dynamics, particularly the emergence of children as consumers, a kind of globalized version of food is love. "Britain seems full of middle class parents protesting that they only go to McDonald's because the kids drag them there," *The Times of London* reported in 1983. "Two year olds are seen climbing out of push chairs to pull their mothers in." Across the world, it seemed, parents were chained to the consumer desire of their children. "I do not eat it because I want to," complained a fast food customer in Ecuador, "but because of my children."[67] Parents at a Chinese KFC echoed these complaints. Having discovered that Chinese children influenced 69 percent of consumer purchases and controlled almost $5 billion in buying power a year, KFC-China reached out through sporting events, essay competitions and partnerships with schools and teachers. Such marketing strategies worked because of broader social changes, particularly declining fertility rates and the rise of "Little Emperors," a supposedly spoiled generation of only-children.[68]

The correlation of fast food's global march and changing dynamics of class, family and age should not suggest a simple diffusion of North American ideas. Corporate officials often referred to fast food consumers as "middle class," but such terms—problematic enough in North America—should not evoke images of a stable mass-class market. Fast food consumers generally formed a small slice of local populations, typically urban and affluent. When McDonald's arrived in Moscow, a meal of a Big Mac, fries, and drink cost the average Soviet worker about half a day's wage; in Mexico, the basic McDonald's burger cost two times the price of *torta*, the staple of working men's eating out.[69] As mass marketers, fast food chains wanted to serve everyone, but reaching "ordinary consumers" was never simple, particularly in the unstable global economy of the 1990s. Many companies pulled out of Russia; McDonald's closed restaurants in Bolivia, Paraguay, and Trinidad; Taco Bell's first Mexican outlet failed. Nor were global family dynamics uniform—even when reaching out to children, chains translated their commercial speech into local dialects. In Asia, Aunt McDonald joined Ronald McDonald, who became Donald (which is easier to pronounce). When KFC discovered that Beijing children saw Colonel Sanders as a "dour grandfather," the chain developed Chicky, a colorfully dressed character with baseball cap turned sideways.[70]

Nor did American products necessarily bring American practices, as several studies of local reception have pointed out. Self-service, it turned out, did not come naturally. "[T]here is a considerable melee in front of the bank of cash registers," Peter Stephenson observed in a Netherlands McDonald's, "where a swarm of children and a few lumbering adults are all trying to gain the recognition of... McDonald's employees... Several people in front of me begin to wave their order forms aloft, and when the 'service person' asks, 'Who is next?'; they simultaneously yell, 'me!'"[71] In Japan, consumers shared their food, passing hamburgers from person to person and placing fries in the centre of the table for collective dining, practices that scholars traced to the importance of commensality in local meals.[72] Fast food companies embraced such practices: after arriving in Hong Kong in 1981, Pizza Hut advertised pizza as the only western food that could be eaten "Chinese style."[73]

Even fast food's American origins did not produce stable meanings. Fast food often arrived as part of local ideas of America, particularly modernity, informality and affluence. Workers at Hungary's Alamo Chicken thought fast food represented "an 'Amerika' which had never lived through the traumas of the Second World War, had never experienced the confines of Communism, and where—it was remarked (in acknowledged exaggeration)—'there is a millionaire on nearly every street corner.'"[74] These American associations never disappeared, but over time fast food also became ordinary, familiar and routine. Within a decade of its arrival in Beijing, KFC attracted adjectives like convenient, child-friendly, and clean more than hip, modern, and novel.[75] When McDonald's arrived in Japan, the hamburger was so exotic that the chain's local director resorted to parody to extol its virtues: "The reason Japanese people are so short and have yellow skins is because they have eaten nothing but fish and rice for two thousand years. If we eat McDonald's hamburgers and potatoes for a thousand years, we will become taller, our skin will become white, and our hair blond." Yet two decades later, when ethnologists asked 1500 Japanese informants to name the representative national food, the hamburger ranked number two (behind instant ramen).[76]

This process of "domestification" emerged from both marketing strategy and social practice. Not only did chains consistently highlight their efforts to be local, they also aimed to be ordinary, a sensible strategy for mass marketers, but one that could cause problems. In Russia, McDonald's opened rubles-only restaurants, which fit with the chain's social vision but also meant profits could not be easily transferred out of the country. "[T]he entire thrust of McDonald's is that it is a place for everyone," recalled George Cohon. "I could see that excluding the bulk of the Soviet population by insisting on hard currency would be... like opening a McDonald's in a mall in some small North American town and telling people they had to wear tuxedos and ball gowns."[77] On the ground, marketing intersected with social practice. On one level, this process was mundane—after a number of years, an outlet was just "there" so origins became less important, even unknown. One Japanese informant reported her excitement at seeing a Mister Donut in Pittsburgh; she had previously thought the chain was Japanese. But domestification could run deeper. Melissa Caldwell describes the "*nashification*" of McDonald's in Moscow (playing on the word "*nash*," which can mean "ours" or "familiar/ordinary"). Over time, hamburgers ceased to be novel and exotic. "I am used to them," one Russian college student reported. "They are tasty and easy to buy." More intriguingly, *nashification* took fast food beyond the outlets themselves. A milkshake craze hit Moscow in the 1990s, spreading to high end restaurants, sidewalk food stalls, and even into forms of home consumption, an area normally confined to "authentically Russian" cooking.[78]

In this sense, domestification could highlight change as much as continuity. Fast food could bring new tastes into culinary cultures that were themselves dynamic and changing, or even alter broader foodservice practices. Many scholars point out, for example, that fast food outlets raised consumer expectations around restaurant cleanliness, spreading the gospel of relentless sanitation to many other retailers.[79] If such examples of continuity and change were widespread, they did not necessarily represent a shift from American novelty to local routine; instead, meanings ran together with varied resonance to different groups. "The first time I went [to McDonald's], it was like I was visiting the United States," claimed one French youth, perfectly capturing the mix of spectacle and routine at the heart of global fast food, "then it became normal, but it is still interesting."[80] Nor was domestification always uniform—in Japan, grandfathers were more likely than grandmothers to see fast food as foreign, the latter having taken their grandchildren to the outlets more often.[81]

Of course, not everyone was happy with American fast food. In 1999, French farmer and activist José Bové famously bulldozed a half-built McDonald's, marshalling arguments that merged critiques of scientific food, *malbouffe* (junk food), neoliberal trade regimes, and American cultural influence, choosing a McDonald's for its symbolic and practical value (as a prominent American company and as a key part of the modern food system). In Italy, Carlo Petrini launched Slow Food in response to the opening of a McDonald's outlet in Rome. Yet another response to homogenization was local food revivals. In Thailand, for example, some upper and middle class consumers turned to *chiiwajid*, a blend of Buddhist philosophy and popular nutritional science that urged consuming food in its natural form. A parallel trend was the revival of "traditional" and "folk" cuisines, stressing local ingredients and "cooking like grandmother," actively promoted by public health authorities and expressed in a mini-industry of cookbooks, restaurants, and street stalls. In such cases, resistance took for the form not just of rejection but creation, inventing traditions that played the local-authentic against the global-industrial, often leavened with a healthy dose of anti-Americanism.[82]

In many ways, however, fast food counter-revolution was shared—indeed, pioneered—in America. In the 1970s, small town and urban residents launched campaigns to block outlets, charging fast food with disrupting (in the words of one Brooklyn city councilor) "the delicate balance between the community and commercial establishments."[83] American critics also attacked the food. "McDonald's food is irredeemably horrible," New York food critic Mimi Sheraton disdained during a fast food fight in 1974. "It is ground, kneaded, and extruded by heavy machinery that compacts it so that the texture is somewhat like that of a baloney sausage."[84] At the same time, ethnic and community food revivals swept the United States, often seeking, in the words of historian Donna Gabaccia, to recouple "ethnic food with community-oriented business values... [B]ureaucratic encounters in Pizza Hut simply could not satisfy customers who associated ethnic food with ethnic businessmen—and with their personal approach to customer service."[85] Twenty years later, Slow Food had many North American devotees, who fused the idea with other forms of culinary backlash.[86] Criticisms were not all snobby. By the late 1970s, several fast food "urban legends" circulated in the United States. Kentucky Fried Rat told of an unwitting consumer served rodent meat by a prankster employee. Another variant claimed that the Ku Klux Klan owned Church's Chicken (which had several outlets in inner city neighborhoods) and added chemicals to its food to cause sterility among African American men. If Slow Food focused on taste and urban legends on contamination, both evoked the sense of "eater's alienation" that resulted from impersonal fast food.[87]

Other attacks on fast food focused on health, one part of the growing movement against highly processed foods that began in the mid-1960s and accelerated in the 1970s.[88] Activist groups like Action for Children's Television targeted fast food advertising, but adult health was also in the mix. Wealthy industrialist and heart-attack survivor Phil Solokof crystallized many such critiques in a series of full-page ads, provocatively titled, "The Poisoning of America." "McDonald's, Your Hamburgers Have Too Much Fat!" declared one ad in 1990.[89] More and more, "obesity" became the keyword of this fast food debate. Several studies linked rising obesity to fast food diets in America and abroad, where "globesity" came to rival malnutrition as a problem.[90] Since weight is at once a measurable standard of size, a function of social factors, and a cultural construction about body image, obesity discourse often blended the clear and the confused, the educational and the judgmental, the statistical and the stereotypical. In 1992, Alice Waters attacked Bill Clinton's McDonaldized diet, fusing questions of good taste, public health, and political economy by urging the President to eat "food that is delicious, wholesome and responsibly produced." A decade later, an American journalist chronicled obesity rates amongst minority groups by profiling the eating habits of inner city drug dealers, surely an unhelpful place to begin a rational discussion of race, diet, and health.[91] Throughout this process, the fast foodscape showed a certain ambiguity, as companies added healthy options like salads and fruit, sold bigger portions, and pitched meat eating in commercials with overtly masculine narratives.[92]

The Empire of the French Fry

Almost five decades after Kroc met the McDonalds, Eric Schlosser's *Fast Food Nation* hit American bookshelves to critical and popular acclaim. In many ways, it was the highest stage of fast food counter-revolution, combining almost every strategy of critique into a single book. Schlosser covered a wide range of topics, from production through consumption to health, in a style that combined moral outrage, evocative story telling, deep research, and reasoned empiricism. He generally avoided populist celebration or snobby dismissal, keeping his focus on the historical backdrop to fast food, the corporate manipulation of taste, and the hidden effects of industrial production. The book quickly entered the global economy of fast food counter-revolution, translated into twenty languages and fictionalized in a popular movie—an American product travelling to the world.[93]

But if fast food and *Fast Food Nation* both circulated through the global cultural economy, the comparison is obviously facetious, except to point out that America is a complicated metropole, at least where fast food is concerned. Fast food chains emerged at the intersection of postwar booms in the United States, spreading their standardized products across the country with remarkable speed. In spite of its association with American culture—or perhaps because of its association with American culture—fast food pushed beyond the United States very quickly, driven by the systematic growth of American chains and adaptations by local entrepreneurs. As it expanded internationally, fast food became intertwined with the social dynamics of family, class, and taste, as well as the multidimensional cultural politics of "America abroad," a mix of imperialism, resistance, desire, and adaptation. Yet there was a parallel complexity in "America at home"—even if most Americans ate fast food, the dynamics of race, taste, class and culture segmented the foodscape and produced varied results. Questions of reception, difference, and resistance seem as legitimate for America as they are for Asia or Europe.

The point can be broader: fast food is ubiquitous, familiar, and routine, but it is hardly one dimensional. Fast food history was at once bureaucratic, technological, entrepreneurial, and human; our historical tools must be organizational, economic, social, and cultural. Each of these approaches requires a different analytic balance: if the cultural meaning of fast food is negotiated between the marketing imperatives of chains and the social worlds of consumers, labor relations seem much less analytically nuanced and allow much less space for human agency. As Joe Kincheloe and others point out, the McDonaldization thesis works well as a description of fast food systems (although we can never assume that control is total or that McDonald's set the practice for all chains at all times), but we need more flexible tools for other issues. For historians, an additional danger is reading fast food's current state back into its historical evolution, missing change over time and social context.

The most difficult issue, however, is figuring out the relationship between the different levels of analysis. For narrative or analytic convenience, we can separate fast food history into distinct categories like structure (corporations, rationalization, labor, etc.) and culture (symbol, sign, icon, etc.) or divide it into themes like expansion, taste, systems, and social life. In practice, however, they all intersect in a bag of French fries, a falafel, a family meal, or a fast food outlet. On the ground, moreover, peeling apart political economy and culture or rational systems and social practice seems difficult. Tastes and social life show some diversity, but rational systems, rapid expansion, and economic power put cultural reception on the table in the first place. At the same time, while rationality was a consistent and powerful dynamic, it relied on human imagination and enforcement. Similarly, expansion was rapid and continuous, but it occurred because American chains and local entrepreneurs sold familiar products and well-known tastes as much as they aimed to remake local culinary cultures. In the Empire of the French Fry, the sun never sets on power, efficiency, or complexity.

Notes

1. John Love, *McDonald's: Behind the Arches* (New York: Bantam Books, 1995), 9–29.
2. Ray Kroc with Robert Anderson, *Grinding It Out* (New York: St Martin's Paperbacks, 1977), 8–10, 72–3, 123.
3. John Jakle and Keith Sculle, *Fast Food: Roadside Restaurants in the Automobile Age* (Baltimore, MD: Johns Hopkins University Press, 1999), 20–40, 73–78, 100–13, 186–89.
4. *Nation's Restaurant News*, July 15, 1999, 133.

5. Benjamin Barber, *Jihad vs. McWorld* (New York: Times Books, 1996); George Ritzer, *The McDonaldization of Society*, rev. ed. (Thousand Oaks, CA: Pine Forge Press, 2004), 12–15, 164.

6. James Watson, ed., *Golden Arches East: McDonald's in East Asia* (Stanford: Stanford University Press, 1997).

7. Douglas Kellner, "Theorizing/Resisting McDonald's: A Multi-Perspectivist Approach" in *Resisting McDonaldization*, ed. Barry Smart (Thousand Oaks, CA: Sage, 1999), 186–206; Joe Kincheloe, *The Sign of the Burger: McDonald's and the Culture of Power* (Philadelphia: Temple University Press, 2002).

8. Paul Ariès, *Les Fils de McDo: Le McDonaldisation du Monde* (Paris: L'Harmattan, 1997), 48.

9. Kroc, *Grinding*, 12; "Rat eat rat" cited in Ester Reiter, *Making Fast Food: Out of the Frying Pan and into the Fryer* (Montréal: McGill-Queen's University Press, 1993), 47.

10. Ada Louise Huxtable, "Pow! It's Good-by History, Hello Hamburger," *New York Times*, March 21, 1971, D23.

11. Stan Luxemburg, *Roadside Empires: How the Chains Franchised America* (New York: Viking, 1985), 203–9.

12. Steve Penfold, "Selling by the Carload: the Early Years of Fast Food in Canada" in *Creating Postwar Canada, 1945–75*, ed. Magda Fahrni and Robert Rutherdale (Vancouver: UBC Press, 2008); *Newsday*, November 30, 1986, 8; Rick Fantasia, "Fast Food in France," *Theory and Society* 24 (1995): 203; Clulanee Thianthai, "Cosmopolitan Food Beliefs and Changing Eating Habits in Bangkok" (Ph.D. diss., University of Oregon, 2003), 84.

13. Luxembrug, *Roadside Empires*, 76–77, citing George Clark.

14. Ty Matejowsky, "Global Tastes, Local Contexts: An Ethnographic Account of Fast Food Expansion in San Fernando City, the Philippines" in *Fast Food/Slow Food: The Cultural Economy of the Global Food System*, ed. Richard Wilk (Lanham, MD: Altamira Press, 2006), 153–54.

15. Uri Ram, "Glocommodification: How the Global Consumers the Local—McDonald's in Israel," *Current Sociology* 52, no. 1 (January 2004): 12–14.

16. Eric Schlosser, *Fast Food Nation: The Dark Side of the All-American Meal* (New York: Harper Collins, 2001), 229.

17. See Ram, "Glocommodification," 12–14.

18. "Meat, Potatoes and Money," *Time*, November 3, 1961.

19. D. Daryl Wyckoff and E Earl Sasser, *The Chain Restaurant Industry* (Lexington MA: Lexington Books, 1978), xxxi–xxxii.

20. USDA, *Agriculture Fact Book, 2001–2*, Tables 2.1, 2.2, 2.6, [Online]. Available: http://www.usda.gov/factbook/. [March 3, 2010].

21. James Lang, *Notes of a Potato Watcher* (College Station: Texas A&M University Press, 2001), 43–46.

22. Ernest Holsendolph, "Keeping McDonald's Out in Front," *New York Times*, December 30, 1973, 83.

23. David Hogan, *Selling 'Em by the Sack: White Caste and the Creation of American Food* (New York: New York University Press, 1997); Paul Mullins, *Glazed America: A History of the Doughnut* (Gainesville: University Press of Florida, 2008), 31–49, 53–62.

24. Baldwin, *Taco Titan*, xx, 54–5; Jeffrey Pilcher, "Was the Taco Invented in Southern California?" *Gastronomica* 8, no. 1 (2008): 35–36; Taco Bell advertisement in *St Petersburg Evening Independent*, July 5, 1972, 10B.

25. Donna Gabaccia, *We Are What We Eat: Ethnic Food and the Making of Americans* (Cambridge, MA: Harvard University Press, 1998), 171; Psyche A. Williams-

Forson, *Building Houses Out of Chicken Legs: Black Women, Food, and Power* (Chapel Hill: University of North Carolina Press, 2006).

26. Gabaccia, *We Are What We Eat*, 197; Love, *Behind the Arches*, 226–27; *Advertising Age*, May 31, 1993, 3, 46.

27. K. Yasumuro, "Conceptualizing an Adaptable Marketing System," cited in Stephen Taylor, Sheena Smith, and Phil Lyon, "McDonaldization and Consumer Choice in the Future: An Illusion or the Next Marketing Revolution" in *McDonaldization Revisted: Critical Essays in Consumer Culture*, ed. Mark Alfino, John Caputo, and Robin Wynyard (Westport, CT: Praeger, 1998), 112.

28. Warren Liu, *KFC in China* (Honoken, NJ: Wiley & Sons, 2008), 62.

29. Yunxiang Yan, "McDonald's in Beijing: The Localization of Americana" in Watson, *Golden Arches East*, 45.

30. Love, *Behind the Arches*, 418–45.

31. James Watson, "Introduction," in Watson, *Golden Arches East*, 24.

32. Lisa Taleuchi Cullen, "Kentucky Fried Rice" *Time*, January 17, 2008.

33. Cited in Jeffrey Pilcher, "Taco Bell, Maseca and Slow Food: A Postmodern Apocalypse for Mexico's Peasant Cuisine?" in Wilk, *Fast Food/Slow Food*, 74.

34. Theodore Levitt, "Production-Line Approach to Service," *Harvard Business Review* (September-October 1972): 44.

35. McLamore, *Burger King*, 19–20, 35–6; Scott R. Sanders, *Burger Chef* (Charleston: Arcadia Publishing, 2009), 8–9.

36. Reiter, *Making Fast Food*, 100.

37. Love, *Behind the Arches*, 141.

38. Baldwin, *Taco Titan*, 109–10.

39. *Canadian Hotel and Restaurant*, May 15, 1968, 44, 47.

40. Love, *Behind the Arches*, 140; Reiter, *Making Fast Food*, 116–20.

41. Love, *Behind the Arches*, 324–36; Harvey Levenstein, *Paradox of Plenty: A Social History of Eating in Modern America* (New York: Oxford University Press, 1993), 231.

42. Eric Schlosser, *Fast Food Nation: The Dark Side of the All-American Meal* (New York: Harper Collins, 2001); Love, *Behind the Arches*, 124–26.

43. Cited in Pilcher, "Taco Bell, Maseca, and Slow Food," 74.

44. Tony Royle and Brian Towers, eds., *Labour Relations in the Global Fast Food Industry* (London: Routledge, 2002), 192–203; Brad Task of McDonald's to Marshall Fishwick, cited in Fishwick, "Ray and Ronald Girdle the Globe" *Journal of American Culture* 18, no. 1 (Spring 1995): 20.

45. *Time*, November 17, 2003.

46. Love, *Behind the Arches*, 429–30; Warren Liu, *KFC in China*, 24–29.

47. Charles Plummer, "French Fries Driving Globalization of Frozen Potato Industry" *Frozen Food Digest*, December 2002; *Business Week*, April 5, 2009. On the potato more generally, Linda Murray Berzok, "Potato" in *Encyclopedia of Food and Culture*, ed. Solomon Katz (New York: Scribner, 2003), 108–16. Other products would reveal slightly different economic geographies. There is little serious scholarly work on the global supply chains of fast food. Some earlier attempts to chart the global effects of fast food resulted in the so-called "hamburger thesis," with which scholars tied beef consumption in America to deforestization in Latin America (an argument that was often more rhetorically provocative than analytically nuanced and has since been modified and qualified). For a review and update, see Mark Edelman, "Rethinking the Hamburger Thesis: Deforestation and the Crisis of Central America's Beef," in *The Social Causes of Environmental Destruction in Latin America*, ed. Michael Painter and William Durham (Ann Arbor: University of Michigan Press, 1995), 25–62.

48. Love, *Behind the Arches*, 114–5.

49. Liu, *KFC in China*, 18–20.

50. Li Lan and Mahmood A. Khan, "Hong Kong's Fast Food Industry: An Overview," *Cornell Hotel and Restarant Administration Quarterly* 36, no. 3 (June 1995): 36; Fantasia, "Fast Food in France," 206.

51. Timothy Charles Lloyd, "The Cincinnati Chili Culinary Complex" *Western Folklore* 40, no. 1 (January 1981): 28–40. See also André Czeglédy, "Manufacturing the New Consumerism: Fast-Food Restaurants in Postsocialist Hungary" in *Markets and Moralities: Ethnographies of Postsocialism*, ed. Ruth Mandel and Caroline Humphrey (New York: Berg, 2002).

52. Luxemburg, *Roadside Empires*, 252–78; Royle and Towers, *Labour Relations*; Robin D. G. Kelley, *Race Rebels: Culture, Politics, and the Black Working Class* (New York: Free Press, 1996).

53. Royle and Towers, *Labour Relations*; Robin Leidner, *Fast Food, Fast Talk: Service Work and the Routinization of Everyday Life* (Berkeley: University of California Press, 1993); Jennifer Parker Talwar, *Fast Food, Fast Track: Immigrants, Big Business, and the American Dream* (Cambridge: Westview Press, 2002); Czeglédy, "Manufacturing the New Consumerism," 156–57.

54. Levenstein, *Paradox of Plenty*, 105, 233.

55. KFC ad in *Better Homes and Gardens*, November 1968.

56. Pilcher, "Was the Taco Invented," 35.

57. Kroc cited in Toerpe, "Small Fry," 107. The ban on female employees was lifted in 1968.

58. Baldwin, *Taco Titan*, 99–101, 110–11; Pilcher, "Was the Taco Invented," 35–36.

59. John Ed Pearce, *The Colonel: The Captivating Biography of the Dynamic Founder of a Fast-Food Empire* (Garden City, NY: Doubleday, 1982).

60. Katherine Parkin, *Food is Love: Advertising and Gender Roles in Modern America* (Philadelphia: University of Pennsylvania Press, 2006); Sanders, *Burger Chef*, 77–91; Toerpe, "Small Fry," 90–92.

61. Toerpe, "Small Fry," 161–70, 217; James Helmer, "Love on a Bun: How McDonald's Won the Burger Wars," *Journal of Popular Culture* 26, no. 2 (Fall 1992): 85–97.

62. Love, *Behind the Arches*, 359–60; Lawrence Brisker, "Black Power and Black Leaders: A Study of Black Leadership in Cleveland, Ohio" (Ph.D. diss., Case Western Reserve University, 1977), 230–66; Frederick Benbow, "A Study of the Boycott of McDonald Hamburger Restaurants in Cleveland, Ohio in 1969" (Ph.D. diss., Union Graduate School, 1976).

63. *Jet*, April 5, 1982, 6.

64. Jason Chambers, *Madison Avenue and the Color Line* (Philadelphia: University of Pennsylvania Press, 2008), 246–47.

65. *Advertising Age*, May 31, 1993, 3, 46; "Fast Food Firms Learn Lessons of El Mercado," *Los Angeles Times*, October 18, 1996, A1.

66. Fantasia, "Fast Food in France" 213–15; Richard Robinson and David Goodman, "The New Rich in Asia," in *The New Rich in Asia: Mobile Phones, McDonald's, and Middle Class Revolution*, ed. Robinson and Goodman (New York: Routledge, 1996), 1–18; *Nation's Restaurant News*, February 14, 1994.

67. *The Times* (London), October 17, 1983, cited in Karen DeBres, "Burgers for Britain: A Cultural Geography of McDonald's UK," *Journal of Cultural Geography* 22, no. 2 (Spring/Summer 2005): 130–31; Mireya Fuerra, "Fast Food Creolization in Ecuador: How Consumers Have Received the Fast Food Concept in their Culture" (M.Sc. Thesis, University of Guelph, 2002), 168, 181.

68. Eriberto P. Lozada Jr., "Globalized Childhood? Kentucky Fried Chicken in Beijing" in *Feeding China's Little Emperors: Food, Children, and Social Change*, ed. Jun Jing (Stanford: Stanford University Press, 2000), 118, 128–29.

69. *New York Times*, January 28, 1990, 1; William Stockton, "The Big Mac Goes to Mexico," *New York Times*, November 2, 1985, 35.

70. Watson, "Introduction," 19; Lozada "Globalized Childhood?" 116, 119.

71. Peter Stephenson, "Going to McDonald's in Leiden: Reflections on the Concept of Self and Society in the Netherlands," *Ethos* 17, no. 2 (June 1989): 231–32.

72. John Traphagan and L. Keith Brown, "Fast food and Intergenerational Commensality in Japan," *Ethnology* 41, no. 2 (Spring 2002): 127–30.

73. Lan and Khan, "Hong Kong's Fast Food Industry," 39.

74. Czeglédy, "Manufacturing the New Consumerism," 160.

75. Lozada, "Globalized Childhood?" 132.

76. Love, *Behind the Arches*, 423; Traphagan and Brown, "Fast Food and Intergenerational Commensality," 131.

77. Cohon, *To Russia With Fries*, 85–86.

78. Melissa Caldwell, "Domesticating the French Fry: McDonald's and Consumerism in Moscow," *Journal of Consumer Culture* 4, no. 1 (2004): 15.

79. Watson, *Golden Arches East.*

80. Cited in Marianne Debouzy, "Working for McDonald's, France: Resistance to the Americanization of Work," *International Labour and Working Class History* 70 (Fall 2006): 127.

81. Traphagan and Brown, "Fast food and Intergenerational Commensality," 121.

82. David Ellwood, "French Anti-Americanism and McDonald's," *History Today* (February 2001): 34–36; Thianthai, "Cosmopolitan Food Beliefs," 90–95.

83. For a sampling, see *New York Times*, August 18, 1974, 78; May 5, 1974, L102; October 3, 1983, A16; February 26, 1986, B1.

84. Cited in Love, *Behind the Arches*, 362.

85. Gabaccia, *We Are What We Eat*, 198; Warren Belasco, "Ethnic Fast Foods: The Corporate Melting Pot," *Food and Foodways* 2 (1987): 1–30.

86. Charlotte Anne Biltekoff, "Hidden Hunger: Eating and Citizenship from Domestic Science to the Fat Epidemic" (Ph.D. diss., Brown University, 2006), 166–68.

87. Gary Fine, "Kentucky Fried Rat: Legends and Modern Society," *Journal of the Folklore Institute* 17, no. 2/3 (May 1980): 222–43; Patricia Turner, "Church's Fried Chicken and the Klan: A Rhetorical Analysis of Rumor in the Black Community," *Western Folklore* 46, no. 4 (October 1987): 294–306.

88. Levenstein, *Paradox of Plenty*, 195–212, 237–55.

89. *New York Times*, April 4, 1990, A21. Solokof had earlier taken on industrial food processors. Leon Jaroff, "A Crusader from the Heartland," *Time*, March 25, 1991, 56–9. On criticisms of advertising to children, see Toerpe, "Small Fry," 232–46.

90. Ty Matejowsky, "Fast Food and Nutritional Perceptions in the Age of 'Globesity': Perspectives from the Provincial Philippines," *Food and Foodways* 17 (2009): 29–32.

91. "Hail to the Chief," *Washington Post*, December 11, 1992, A26; "Habit Forming," *Wall Street Journal*, December 19, 1990, A1.

92. Smara Joy Neilson and Barry M. Popkin, "Patterns in Food Portion Sizes, 1977–88," *Journal of the American Medical Association* 289 (January 23/29, 2003): 450–53; Carrie Packwood Freeman and Debra Merksin, "Having it His Way: The Construction of Masculinity in Fast-Fast Food TV Advertising," in *Food for Thought:*

Essays on Eating and Culture, ed. Lawrence Rubin (Jefferson NC: McFarland & Co., 2008), 277–93.

93. Schlosser, *Fast Food Nation*.

Bibliography

Jakle, John, and Keith Sculle. *Fast Food: Roadside Restaurants in the Automobile Age*. Baltimore, MD: Johns Hopkins University Press, 1999.

Reiter, Ester. *Making Fast Food: Out of the Frying Pan and into the Fryer*. Montréal: McGill-Queen's University Press, 1993.

Schlosser, Eric. *Fast Food Nation: The Dark Side of the All-American Meal*. New York: Harper Collins, 2001.

Smart, Barry, ed. *Resisting McDonaldization*. Thousand Oaks, CA: Sage, 1999.

Watson, James, ed. *Golden Arches East: McDonald's in East Asia*. Stanford: Stanford University Press, 1997.

PART IV

THE CIRCULATION OF FOOD

CHAPTER 17

FOOD, MOBILITY, AND WORLD HISTORY

DONNA R. GABACCIA

As a scholarly field, food studies is understandably torn between efforts to understand the general, on the one hand, and the particular, on the other. All living beings must eat—a universal, biologically based fact of animal life—while cooking with heat numbers among a small cluster of general, yet learned and taught, behaviors that are so common that they are understood to distinguish humans from other animals.[1] Nor is cooking with fire the only universal but not instinctive food-related practice that can be identified, for all humans also cooperate and use tools in order to provision, prepare, eat, and share food.[2] In all times and places, general practices are so intimately interwoven with the physiological, natural, and biological as well as the social, cultural, political, and economic dimensions of human life that studying food also usually makes obvious just how distinctive and particular each human society is.

This essay explores scholarship connecting the histories of food and of human mobility in order to think about how and under what circumstances food practices "spread" or "diffuse" among many or all human societies. One subset of scholarly studies focuses on how the search for food itself encourages people to move and on what the generalizing or particularizing consequences of their moves have been. A much wider swathe of scholarship instead uses human movement to explain how particular foods, food practices, and food technologies have "traveled" to become widely used across a wide variety of groups. Because both histories, in differing ways, seek to understand general phenomena in human culinary life, both also encourage analysis at rather grand temporal or spatial scales. These are the scales most often embraced by world historians, those historians who claim as their subjects all human life on Earth, and not just the histories of literate peoples over the past five thousand years.[3] How have scholars tackled the study of food as part of world histories? Often enough, as this chapter demonstrates, the most recent world histories have linked histories of food with histories of mobility in order to trace and describe what we currently call globalization.

My basic argument, then, is that recent enthusiasm for mapping webs of connections among the culturally distinct societies of the six continents over the *longue durée* of human life on Earth is beginning to make the study of food a more central theme in world history. Such histories allow us to understand in far more intricate detail and in analytically powerful ways the relationship of the general and particular in culinary culture. World histories increasingly point to trade, to human migrations, and to media as the mechanisms by which particular foods, food practices, food technologies, and food knowledge travel across space, time, and cultural boundaries to become general. This means that attention to the mobility of commodities and of people and a new-found awareness of the changing and increasingly mediated technologies of long-distance communication promise to remove from food studies specifically and from world histories more generally the still-all-too-common explanation encouraged by vague references to the "spread" or "expansion" of both people and their culinary cultures. Abstractions like these are the unacknowledged legacy for world history of nineteenth-century anthropological theorizing about "diffusion."

To observe that humans, food, or human food practices spread, diffuse, or expand over time and across space is to describe badly and to explain nothing. Fortunately, few of the best recent works of world history, including those included in this volume, depend exclusively upon such explanatory abstractions. Much of the best recent work instead carefully traces the mobility of people and their culinary ideas and preferences as an element of globalization. Students of food in world history will understand very differently the "spread" of sugar plantations or the "diffusion" of sugar consumption across time and space if they learn it as a history of human agency, of human inequalities, and of human choices, which is to say, through a focus on social interaction across cultural borders.[4] Often enough it was human beings—slave traders and their coerced migrant slaves, runaways, investors, landowners, factors, sailors, merchants, and ship captains—who made possible the diffusion, expansion, or spread of commodities, ideas, and food practices that we now understood to be the Columbian exchange of crops, seeds, luxury foodstuffs, and scientific or culinary treatises. Only rarely in food history can we identify the culinary equivalent of the exact moment when Sigmund Freud, anticipating his disembarkation in New York in 1909, supposedly told Carl Jung that the Americans about to learn of his psychoanalytical ideas "don't realize that we are bringing them the plague."[5] Still, a focus on the lives of border-crossing, mobile humans, along with detailed histories of technologies of mediated knowledge transfers, build the firmest foundation for writing a social and cultural history of globalization. It will certainly guarantee that our histories of globalization are human histories, driven by sentient and strategizing humans, rather than by abstract structures or forces.

Food and Mobility in Recent World Histories

Food studies have only quite recently found a secure place in local and national histories yet food historians have already made important contributions to studies of nation building.[6] The study of food is also a relatively recent development in world history. Following the early work of Arnold Toynbee,[7] world history—which was primarily a teaching, not a research field through most of the 1950s, 1960s and 1970s—focused mainly on the cyclical and almost predictable processes of rise and decline of distinct "civilizations."[8] Of course it would have been possible to describe Toynbee's twenty-six civilizations—including those he called Hellenic, Sinic, Polynesian, and Eskimo—through their distinctive foodways, but Toynbee's causal framework for explaining the consolidation and collapse of civilizations attributed greater importance to militarism and to the changing nature of elites than to glacial shifts in everyday material culture. Such topics were central to the work of the Annales school, by contrast, and by the 1990s there had been concerted efforts to understand civilizations through their foods and to explore food history through the rise and fall of civilizations.[9]

Modern and updated textbooks that continue to use histories of discrete civilizations to introduce students to world history, especially for the years before 1500, still seem at first glance to teach contemporary readers relatively little about food, even though such studies of civilizations, nations, and local societies are now more readily available.[10] Nevertheless, embedded in most such textbooks is an implicit understanding of a particular relationship of mobility with food production and consumption. World historians still understand human civilization to have originated in a Neolithic revolution giving rise to agrarian food production and thus a distinctive new food regime.[11] They describe civilization as characterized by urbanism, which is also understood to rest, exclusively and necessarily, on the production of food surpluses through something called settled agriculture, which means, in practice, the extraction of surpluses from subordinated and sedentary cultivators (called peasants) of grain by an equally sedentary elite. In this view, however, civilizations are also understood to be characterized by long-distance trade, usually in luxury goods, although these are rarely described as food items until after the year 1000, when authors turn their attentions to the spice trade. However, as Paul Freedman's work hints, luxury foods had a far longer history of being exchanged across long distances; this trade in foods is a reminder of an alternative, long-lived, and equally "civilized" food regime—one that scholars today associate with "expanding" global markets and the "extension" of commodity chains and that they view as linking independent societies in far-flung parts of the world into hierarchies of unequal power within a world system.[12] Thus, the medium of writing—the third distinctive characteristic of human civilizations—is the only one of civilization's three defining characteristics that is not linked directly to food production or food exchange and, with them, to patterns in human mobility. (The indirect linkages of writing to food and mobility—records of planting and harvests to extract surpluses or of trade items—are obvious enough.)[13]

By focusing on civilizations, world historians have long marginalized and at times even ignored both the most important and longest-lived of human food regimes and, with it, the ubiquity of human mobility. Until quite recently, significant proportions of humans obtained their food not through agriculture or trade but rather through foraging (sometimes also called hunting-gathering) and herding (sometimes also called pastoralism or nomadic pastoralism). Both food regimes rested on considerable, normative, regular, and patterned, if also circular and repetitive migrations. Whether called hunting-gathering, foraging, or pastoralism, mobile food regimes have been the focus of disciplines other than history, and their study has drawn on methods quite different from those traditionally employed by historians.[14] One unintended consequence of this sharp divide between scholarship on foraging and agriculture is that early civilizations are still—wrongly, I believe—too easily portrayed as overwhelmingly sedentary. Civilizational world histories certainly have acknowledged trade as a constituent element of civilizations but their pages are filled with accounts of the wars and military campaigns by which civilizations purportedly rose and fell. Neither activity occurred without the "mobilization" of large numbers of men and equally large quantities of food provisions and other material resources, but world historians otherwise show surprisingly little interest in human mobility of any kind. They have tended to portray civilizations as if they were composed of bounded territories occupied by largely sedentary cultivators, rulers, and religious leaders.[15]

This assumption that civilized peoples were largely immobile has sometimes been labeled as sedentism or sedentarism.[16] Sedentism not only renders invisible and uninteresting the importance of foragers and herders,[17] but it also makes the merchants and religious proselytizers who followed trade routes or the laborers who traveled long distances to build Egypt's pyramids or the Great Wall of China seem far more exceptional and marginal than they may have been. Scholarly preferences for sedentism are probably best understood as one of the unexamined and powerful ideological products of civilizations, which celebrate their own ways of life, including their agrarian food regimes, as superior. Sedentism suggests also that mobile people—and this is probably how the rulers of civilizations generally saw them too—were aberrant, threatening outsiders. They were, to use the ubiquitous terminologies of the early civilizations themselves, "barbarians" and "invaders." This distinction between sedentary civilized persons and mobile barbarians was sometimes even exemplified in culinary terms, for example in the early Chinese distinction between "cooked" (sinified) and "uncooked" (nomadic and culturally other) barbarians.[18]

Thus, in *The Heritage of World Civilizations*, a textbook organized around the civilizational tradition of world history, food figures briefly and predictably in discussions of the earliest or Paleolithic ("Stone Age") humans, who are described as being dependent on nature for their food. A colorful map, with bright orange arrows (labeled as "colonization routes") introduces students to "The Spread of

Modern Humans," while on the adjoining page, authors note that it was hunters following game, for example to North America, that produced this spread, which they label both a migration and a colonization.[19] Following the text's discussions of the Neolithic or agrarian revolution and the grains (barley, wheat, rice) that provided the basis for life in the earliest settled, civilized societies, attention to how people acquired and processed their foods, and thus to changing food regimes, almost completely disappears.

Individual rulers, capital cities, and political events dominate the index of *The Heritage of World Civilizations*. Warfare as much as trade (and considerably more than migration) does merit space in the textbook's index as a significant form of contact between civilizations. But the volume offers no general index entry on food; beyond the Neolithic revolution, its attention to food is limited to its discussion of the early modern cultivation of sugar and to a single reference to the modern United Fruit Company. Its sole index reference to migration, furthermore, points readers to a discussion of the world after 1945, suggesting that mobility on a global scale distinguishes our own world from past times—a fallacy to which I will return in the conclusion.

Only with the rejection of sedentism can we begin to write world histories that give proper place to the trade routes and commodity chains of the early civilizations or to the long-term importance of the nomadic pastoralists who often—and the hunter-gatherers and foragers who sometimes—became rather extensively involved in both. Arguably, *The Heritage of World Civilizations* reflects older understandings of world history. As is well documented in works published in the early 2000s by Patrick Manning and Ross Dunn, world history had moved decidedly away from Toynbee's narrative of successive civilizations during the 1990s.[20] The teaching of world history at universities became more common in this decade and world history also found some acceptance as a research field, with its own professional associations and journals. Most important, the "new world history" scholarship extended its chronological reach more enthusiastically into prehistory, and it became methodologically more diverse and more interdisciplinary as it did so. Responding to 1990s-era discussions of globalization, world historians also began to shift the main research focus of the field to the changing and thickening network of connections among the world regions and peoples and the accompanying changes in human relationships to the natural world over the very *longue durée* of human life on Earth. Although it was scarcely the intention of world historians (who were, and still are, generally far more interested in debating William McNeill's thesis about the rise of the West or the relationship of the West and the rest than in contributing to food studies),[21] both a more expansive world history chronology (for example David Christian's "Big History"[22]) and new intellectual interests in globalization generated rich new opportunities for linking the study of mobility to histories of food with a focus on cultural dynamics.[23] World history thus began to move decisively and sometimes also self-consciously away from the sedentism of much civilizational world history.

That both migration and food—along with other aspects of culture—figure far more prominently in world history today than they did twenty years ago is documented by the first edition of the *Berkshire Encyclopedia of World History*. Published in 2005, this five-volume reference work includes a general entry on food by Adrian Carton. The entry is organized tightly around the theme of exchange. According to Carton: "The act of exchanging food connects human beings with other species, with other human beings across diverse geographical regions, and with a notion of a divine being," making food "an integral part of world history on both biological and cultural levels." Not only is food "central to cultural identity," Carton acknowledges, both that human life is always "socially organized around the search for nutrition." He describes the agrarian revolution as an important "shift from food collection to food production," accompanied by a comparable shift from spatially extensive to spatially intensive technologies of production—an implicit recognition of changes in human mobility.[24] But the shift, he argues further, contributed to increasing food exchanges through trade. Carton especially emphasizes that early trade *within* societies involved the exchange of staples (wheat, millet, rice), while exotic luxury foods figured more prominently in long-distance trade, at least until the nineteenth century. (Surprisingly, given his broader attention to trade, Carton seems little interested in the traders, their agency, or the particular cultural dynamics associated with trade.) A section on the Columbian exchange (which is described as "new webs of commercial exchange," involving potatoes, maize, and wheat, sugar, and somewhat later, coffee and tea) is followed by discussion of the industrialization of food production and of colonization, which beautifully integrates the slave trade and the mobile, if coerced, slave labor that made both possible. As he turns to modern histories of overpopulation and to subsequent processes of industrialization, Carton makes it clear that basic staples replaced luxury foods as the most important foodstuffs traded over long distances by 1930, but he fails to explain why trade in foodstuffs then diminished, as he asserts it did, in the latter half of the twentieth century. Neither does he suggest that such a change in food exchanges may have been linked with changes in human mobility (although in fact, rates of international migration—although not the mobility of military personnel—did drop off sharply between the 1930s and the 1970s.)[25]

And there is more. In addition to Carton's essay, readers of the *Berkshire Encyclopedia of World History* will find detailed entries on the agrarian revolution, on the relationship of nutrition and disease, on Paleolithic and modern foraging, on the Columbian exchange, on famine, on pastoral, nomadic, and horticultural societies and on many widely-traded individual food items such as salt, tea, coffee, sugar, alcohol, and cereals. The article on nutrition and disease by Mark Cohen is particularly trenchant in its observations about the relation of food and mobility. Calling attention to the sedentist bias of earlier scholarship, Cohen strongly implies that celebrations of settled peoples as civilized mainly worked to paint their foodways as superior—a point that the history of nutrition and disease cannot support. On the contrary, evidence suggests that historic foragers were better nourished and far less troubled by parasites and parasitic diseases than the modern poor precisely because foragers were more mobile and lived across larger, and more thinly populated, territories.[26]

Contemporaneous with the *Berkshire Encyclopedia,* two short works of synthesis published in the Routledge series Themes in World History, edited by Peter Stearns, outlined even more fully an emerging scholarly grasp on the relation of mobility and food. Patrick Manning's *Migration in World History* (2005) and Jeffrey M. Pilcher's *Food in World History* (2006) were undoubtedly solicited by Stearns to explore completely separate questions and themes.[27] Yet they overlapped more than one might have expected, especially in their attention to food and mobility.[28] These two works are a good introduction to the questions that world historians of food now need to address more fully.

With little earlier evidence of any interest at all in the history of food, Patrick Manning's volume resembles Adrian Carton to an amazing degree, especially in his linkage of food and mobility among early humans. Manning, like Carton, adopts a capacious temporal framework that focuses greater attention than the civilizational studies on both the role of food in the "spread" of early humans around the Earth and to the changing material culture of humans in far-flung corners of the world as a result of the Columbian exchange between 1400 and 1700.

In his book, Manning makes a bold claim in asserting that migration itself has been an important engine of social change, suggesting that humans are a mobile species and that their mobility differs from that of other animals because humans also learn from each other, and their societies develop progressively as individual migrants cross cultural boundaries, enter culturally different communities and produce cultural innovation. As he describes them, early humans "spread" largely through their food-searching activities, traveling by foot or by boat along river valleys, sea coasts, and mountain valleys in search of fish or game. When he turns to the era of the Columbian exchange, Manning, again like Carton, effectively links the movements of migrants and merchants with the worldwide transfer of various foodstuffs. Only when Manning turns to the modern world does his attention to food and foodways, and to material culture generally, falter, as if interactions around food had ceased with the early modern era—a possibility that Pilcher's book clearly precludes.

Unlike Manning and the *Berkshire Encyclopedia,* with its entries still focused predominantly on food and foodways in the pre-historic and pre-industrial eras, Pilcher's *Food in World History* offers far greater attention to the world during and after the Columbian exchange. Pilcher's five themes are "the ongoing diffusion of foodstuffs," over the *longue durée* of human history, tensions between pastoralists and agriculturists, class distinctions based on access to and preparation of food, the way in which food defines social identities, whether gendered or cultural, and the role of modern nation states in determining production and allocating food. Pilcher situates his analysis within debates over globalization (although he misses a chance to note how globalization revived early scholarly concepts about mechanisms of cultural change that are reflected, presumably unselfconsciously, in his own use of terms such as "spread" and "diffusion"). As an historian, he boldly asserts, "If 'globalization' is taken to mean the intensification of cultural and trade connections then clearly it has been ongoing for centuries, at least in culinary forms."[29]

Pilcher's distinction between the civilizations of China and Rome—which, in differing ways, both used food habits and metaphors to distinguish themselves from barbarians understood to be more mobile in their living habits—and of the Arabs of the Middle East and North Africa—whose multi-ethnic cuisines were instead built on the mobile lifestyles of traders and nomadic herders—makes the sedentism of earlier civilizational approaches particularly obvious and problematic. God and halal, not specific foods or sedentism, Pilcher notes of the Muslim world, distinguished believers from non-believers. Pilcher thus helps us both to understand the cultural origins of sedentism and to document how culinary identities intersect differently with mobility in different times and places.

Much like Carton and others, Pilcher's account of the slave, sugar, and spice trades rests on an understanding that human agency and human mobility—and not the vague abstraction of "diffusion"—explain the Columbian exchange—a point also reinforced and beautifully illustrated recently by Rebecca Earle.[30] Pilcher's comparative treatment of famine should help any reader to understand why Ireland and China produced so many migrants and his especially useful chapters on the mobility that undergirded both empire-building and the forging of migrant cuisines in the nineteenth century serve as a nice counterpart to his chapter on culinary nation building, which treats cooks and eaters as more territorially bounded. Only the main themes of his twentieth-century chapters—notably guns and butter, the Green Revolution, and McDonald's—fail to develop further his otherwise acute sensitivity to human mobility, a failing mitigated in part by his attention to culinary pluralism as a product of revived migrations of laborers and refugees by century's end.

Collectively, Manning and Pilcher provide powerful examples of the advantages of examining the movements of food and food-related beliefs, symbols, and practices in tandem with and embedded within the histories of movement, migration, trade, and border-crossing. In their chapters on the nineteenth and twentieth centuries, both authors devote considerable attention to the cultural (and in the case of Pilcher, culinary) dynamics that have accompanied the mass movements of people as emigrants and as immigrants. Assimilation, acculturation, borrowing, and cultural pluralism are central themes in both works, despite their ostensibly quite different subject matters. Both authors want to offer an explanation for why and how particular cultural practices and beliefs—in the case of Pilcher this literally means foodstuffs, food practices, food technologies, and food beliefs—become general among large numbers of otherwise quite different but interconnected human societies. Both however have hesitated to analyze the relationship of mobility and food in our own times.

Unlike Pilcher, Manning assiduously avoids the language of diffusion, in part because he also offers a critique of it. Manning states firmly that analysts who rely on simple terms such as "'diffusion' and 'spread' to describe the movements of foods, textiles, musical styles, and religious belief" do not provide a good explanation of cultural change.[31] Manning suggests that those hoping to understand general cultural traits among humans should begin by distinguishing between the "carrying" and the "borrowing" of culture. His examples of this conceptual distinction, it is worth noting, are drawn from food studies.

We have seen that world histories of food and mobility as exemplified by Pilcher and Manning occurred as part of a shift from an older civilizational to a newer, relational agenda for world historians. This shift has also made the intellectual legacy of anthropological diffusionism both more visible and more problematic. Neither the Neolithic revolution, the long-term prevalence and persistence and then disappearance of foraging and nomadic pastoralism, the Columbian exchange, the plantation complex, globalization, McDonaldization, nor particular food regimes spread, diffused, or expanded automatically or by themselves. The challenge for writers of world histories of food is to begin to describe and to analyze how exactly human beings, human choices, and human strategies resulted in particular customs and beliefs becoming general ones. In taking up this challenge, scholars might find it helpful to grapple a bit more explicitly with the legacy of anthropological diffusionism, as their colleagues in anthropology have had little choice but to do over the past century.

Diffusion is still a word that can raise anthropologists' hackles because of their discipline's role in justifying nineteenth-century racism, imperialism, and evolutionary theory. Yet it is also still possible for anthropologists to define diffusionism rather dryly and neutrally as "the process by which discrete culture traits are transferred from one society to another, through migration, trade, war, or other contact."[32] The diffusionists of the past developed competing and controversial hypotheses about how cultures expanded and spread. A century ago, for example, anthropologists battled over the possibility that general or shared elements of human culture all originated in a single place (or "hearth") or in several sites (which included many of the early civilizations Toynbee would recognize—in the river valleys of the Nile, Indus, Ganges, Huang He, and Yangtze, and in Mesopotamia, Mesoamerica, and West Africa). Some argued instead that general human cultural traits were products of independent inventions accomplished by equally capable but isolated human groups faced with similar ecological, demographic, or environmental challenges in diverse locations. (For understandable reasons, battles between diffusionists and advocates of independent invention proved especially intense among specialists trying to understand life in pre-historic North America.) Yet historians of anthropology also acknowledge that debates over diffusionism gradually gave way to analysis of the cultural dynamics—assimilation and acculturation, for example—most often associated with post-1500 migrations, much as they are now also in the world histories of Pilcher and Manning.

Thus rather than regard the legacy of diffusionism as an enemy to be conquered or overcome, scholars might instead review and evaluate the distinctions and typologies developed by anthropologists as they seek to understand more completely how particular cultural elements become general through the course of world history. According to some early anthropological theorists, diffusion created "culture circles," which were characterized by predictable cultural dynamics between core, domain, sphere, and outlier societies—a way of thinking that eerily prefigured Immanuel Wallerstein's World Systems framework, which is frequently used by today's world historians.[33] Also prefiguring Manning's plea for distinguishing between cases of carrying and borrowing, early diffusionists sometimes distinguished among direct diffusion (borrowing between adjacent societies—that is, without extensive long-distance migrations or trade), forced or expansion diffusion (which modern scholars would probably term either colonization or conquest, and which most often involves movements of powerful people), and indirect diffusion (when the ideas of one culture are carried to new places by middlemen, media, or people of a different culture). Other theorists have identified relocation diffusion to describe an idea or innovation that moves so far—presumably with mobile people who function as middle men or through mediated borrowing—that its origins elsewhere or in another culture are eventually forgotten.[34] Sigmund Freud also certainly understood a final type—contagious diffusion—which occurs through person-to-person or even mediated contacts with no need for extensive human mobility beyond the arrival of an initiating "germ" (in his case, his own ideas and lectures at Clark University).

Clearly, the linkage of mobility and food is a complex one, and both world historians of migration and world historians of food seek not only to describe it, but also to analyze with a new respect for human agency some of the same cultural dynamics that fascinated early diffusionists. They especially share with the diffusionists a desire to understand how particular and particularistic foods, food practices, food technologies, and food-related knowledge traveled or were invented and borrowed across space, time, and cultural boundaries. What most distinguishes the best recent studies from those of the early diffusionists is their interest in human agency, human choices, and human creativity and in the ways that humans respond to constraints and limits. Thus, even when they use the methods of the social sciences, the latest scholarship on food and mobility serves the intellectual and philosophical agenda of humanists, broadly understood.

Toward a Cultural History of Global Food

How can scholars advance the writing a cultural world history of globalization by further expanding our understanding of the linkage of food and mobility? I conclude this paper by considering three particularly promising arenas for research—one from early prehistory, one from the great international migrations of the nineteenth and twentieth centuries, and one from our own era—thus viewing, from a distinctive perspective, some of the scholarly literature introduced and reviewed by Sterling Evans, Yong Chen, and Steve Penfold.[35]

No field of study offers as much promise for advancing our understanding of the relationship of the general and the particular in culinary studies than the multidisciplinary field of scholarship focused on the colonization of the Earth by *Homo sapiens* foragers. Based largely on the methods of historical linguistics, Manning created a chronology of human migrations that described *Homo sapiens* emerging in Africa around 200,000 years ago. He then traced their migration over a period of some 30,000 years between 70,000 to 40,000 years ago into old-world tropical settings. Manning's mobile humans then peopled temperate and colder northern and, finally, American regions between 40,000 and 15,000 years ago.[36] Much remains to be learned about the importance of food for these early movements. Some research suggests, for example, how changing diets, increasing brain size, and upright stature interacted powerfully to raise human calorie requirements, thus nudging early humans toward greater mobility over wider foraging territories than had been characteristic of other primates.[37] Manning's chronology also suggests that migratory humans already knew the use of fire and that humans did indeed carry this knowledge of fire—along with practices such as sharing and the use of tools—with them as they traveled out of eastern Africa, turning these into general practices that have persisted down to the present.

Still, there is a conundrum at the heart of Manning's analysis of the spread of humans to every corner of the Earth. If humans are a mobile species, and mobility is in some sense instinctual as he seems to assert, why did Manning in his analysis also so clearly argue that early humans traveled in search of food? (Dirk Hoerder's recent short essays on migrations over the *longue durée* have been even more explicit in linking human migration to food-seeking practices.[38]) Sterling Evans suggests a much richer story—one in which changing climate, food resources unevenly distributed across diverse ecologies, and environmental change all sparked migration, not as a matter of instinct but of human decision making in response to changing material and ecological conditions.[39] Many other scholars also force us to consider the irrationality of early humans, by pointing to human groups that repeatedly overhunted, overfished, or overforaged, producing diminishing caloric returns from familiar territories and forcing kin groups to split periodically, a practice accompanied by the movement of new fractions of colonizers onto unoccupied, if adjacent territories, with better or at least different food resources.[40] Early humans responded to the world around them—sometimes with positive and sometimes with negative consequences for their diets and the habitats they occupied. As this suggests, even scholars working with extremely fragmentary evidence about the food practices of very early human beings treat them as decision makers, as "thoughtful" as well as hungry foragers.[41]

This means that for all the importance of the considerable common store of culinary knowledge that early humans carried with them, their moves into and through changing and new ecosystems continuously generated new food habits, and the material, culinary foundations for amazing cultural diversity over time and space. Indeed, almost all archaeological studies of prehistoric foragers and ethnographic studies of more recent foragers have emphasized the wide array of animals, plants, and seeds that humans have learned about and transformed into food, using an ever-proliferating variety of tools, fuels, and cooking, preserving, and processing techniques. The creativity of mobile, thoughtful human colonizers of unpopulated territories resulted not in rigid human homogeneity but rather in cultural diversity, a diversity that mattered even more as once-independent and isolated groups began to intermingle, opening possibilities for the kinds of cross-community migrations that Manning finds to have been the engine of human history. Under conditions that earlier scholars have labeled as "civilization," borrowing became as important, if not more important, than carrying, and possibilities for mutual culinary adaptations between interacting human groups began to complicate further what earlier scholars understood as diffusion or expansion.

If we fast-forward through early civilizations, emerging systems of long-distance trade, and the early modern Columbian exchange to the era of the mass international migrations of the nineteenth and twentieth centuries, we arrive at yet another site for creative work on the relationship of the general and the particular in food history. Pausing briefly, it is helpful first to contrast scholarly studies of food and mobility in the era of the mass migrations to the studies of food and mobility during the Columbian exchange. In both eras, foodstuffs and people are described as traveling in large volumes but the balance of scholarly attention to mobile foods and mobile bodies differs. Studies of the Columbian exchange have focused mainly on the transportation and trade of foodstuffs along trading routes organized and managed by imperial middlemen (often Jews or Genoese) in an almost-classic case of "indirect diffusion." With time, Turks, Italians, Spaniards, and the Chinese learned to cultivate and eat new-world crops such as potatoes, corn, and chile peppers. But since the Mesoamericans who had elaborated a culture of corn did not travel with their foodstuffs, and since middlemen did not always understand or adopt the foodways of the New World, knowledge of *nixtamalization* (alkaline processing) was lost along the trade routes, and old-world corn eaters eventually suffered from the dietary deficiency disease pellagra, as Mexicans never had. Nevertheless, scholars who have argued for an active role for slaves in carrying seeds, foods, and cultivation and culinary knowledge out of Africa to the Americas have faced sharp resistance.[42] To a considerable extent, the Columbian exchange is told as a story of borrowed commodities and of indirect diffusion by minority European traders or imperial conquest rather than as a story of familiar culinary knowledge carried and transmitted by migratory Americans or Africans.

By contrast, students of food and mobility during the nineteenth and early-twentieth-century era of mass migrations have instead made immigrants—as eaters, cooks and consumers—central historical actors. In doing so, they have mostly ignored the larger circuits of import and export trade, commerce, and governmental regulation of trade through tariffs in which the migrants were embedded and at times, intimately involved. (Unfortunately, one of the few studies that directly connects migration to international trade during the nineteenth century not only concentrates exclusively on the United States, but also practically ignores trade in food.[43]) Instead of writing world histories, Hasia Diner, Krishnendu Ray, and others have resembled Yong Chen in situating their studies of mobility and foodways within histories of racial and ethnic formation and nation building, most often in a single nation of immigrants such as the United States.[44]

A world historian might better begin with some of the observations made about this era by Carton in his entry in the *Berkshire Encyclopedia of World History.* The concomitant rise of industrialized food production, empire-building, and long-distance trade of the nineteenth and early-twentieth centuries made international migrants both producers and consumers of basic foodstuffs and both people and food traveled in growing volumes over long distances. Some of the immigrants that settled and cultivated grain on the Argentine Pampas and in the American Midwest literally had relatives who consumed these foods in the far-away, industrializing cities where they too had migrated in search of work. Similarly, the urban, proletarian migrants helped to feed the colonial enclaves from which mobile empire builders ruled. Italian migrants carried pizza to Argentina and America while British *sahibs* and *memsahibs* (male and female colonists in India) introduced a taste for curry to their friends in the United Kingdom. By exploring linkages among circulating migrants (as both carriers and borrowers of culinary knowledge), merchants, and the organization of food import and export trade, scholars could determine whether the relation of food and mobility in the nineteenth century represented a continuation, reversal, or transformation of the cultural dynamics of the better-understood Columbian exchange.

Carton's observations about the industrialization of both the production and processing of food also introduced a new impetus for the homogenization of foods and food practices across societies and cultures in the era of the mass migrations. Yet studies of food and migration within particular national contexts have instead established that nineteenth-century culinary standardization—in the form of mass production and large-scale trade of standardized food commodities, the industrialization of food processing, and mass export of standardized processed products—failed to produce culinary homogeneity. There was no global McDonaldization in the era of the mass international migrations. Instead high levels of human mobility helped to guarantee that diverse foods, tastes, and practices traveled just as extensively and as widely as a narrow range of mass-produced foodstuffs. Whereas theorists of assimilation in host countries may have dreamed that immigrants would quickly "borrow" the cultural practices and foodstuffs of natives, in fact, natives often borrowed as much from immigrants as immigrants did from each other or from natives.[45] Cross-community migrations, to use Manning's term, resulted in considerable culinary inventiveness (think "chop suey sandwiches" and "Cincinnati Chili"), creolization, and hybridization. In the United States, regional differences survived the standardizing onslaught of industrial foods and the growing popularity of the consumption of standardized nationally distributed products such as ground beef or canned pickles, and they did so, in part, because of their distinctive histories of immigration. Diffusionists' earlier notions of carrying, borrowing, and conquest seem far too simple to describe the cultural dynamics set off by massive international migration and trading in foodstuffs in the nineteenth and early-twentieth centuries.[46]

Although scholars again today refer to our own times as "The Age of Migration," it seems that the balance of mass-produced, standardized and corporate foods—symbolized by McDonald's—and the circulation of diverse tastes, foods, and food practices with migrant consumers has altered since the nineteenth-century era of mass migration.[47] While migrants certainly continue to carry, borrow, invent, adapt, and mix the foods and practices they know and encounter on their travels—and are almost certainly again changing the regional cuisines of the United States—the most important factors in moving fast-food production and consumption worldwide have not been migrants and refugees. On the contrary, Steven Penfold makes it rather clear that after entrepreneurs visited the somewhat sedentary and unambitious McDonald brothers in San Bernardino, and after a rather frenetic period of travel by Ray Kroc, McDonald's production schemes became a form of knowledge easily transmitted through print and other media. Writes Penfold, "the *idea* of fast food expanded in a less predictable process of copying and borrowing, a dynamic that might be called (in an Internet age) 'going viral'" and even internationally, "fast food sometimes first spread to new markets not by American chain penetration but by local entrepreneurs importing the idea."[48] Once again, however, the borrowing and carrying of culinary ideas, whether learned through tourism, migration, or more often through media and corporate networks of communication, did not result in standardization. As fast foods "spread" internationally, theorists quickly identified a cultural dynamic they termed "glocalization." It describes the naturalization of McDonald's in diverse settings through the use of local food sources, the transformation of the beef patty through adaptation to local taste, and accommodations to local consumer practices. Because fast food did not travel with American migrants, furthermore, but rather through media and corporate decentralized franchising, the result has occasionally been a kind of relocation diffusion: In Korea, for example, children consuming fast food pizza believe they are eating American and not Italian food.

The three cases explored briefly here suggest that each of the food regimes considered—foraging, international commerce in staple foodstuffs, and McDonaldization—has been associated with a distinctive mobility regime. Viewed over the *longue durée* of human mobility in world history, human movements may have been a more powerful factor in prehistory and during the period of the mass migrations than during either the Columbian exchange or our own times. (Of course, given the very different ways in which scholars have framed their studies of various periods—focusing sometimes exclusively on food commerce without considering the human movements that facilitate it; other times only on migration, neglecting commerce—this finding may only reflect scholarly conventions, not patterns of human life in any of these eras.) In all three eras, furthermore, it seems obvious that as some particular food practices became more general or as they "spread" or "diffused" across human societies and geographical territories, the cultural processes that scholars once described as expansion, spread, or diffusion typically also resulted in considerable innovation and differentiation. Scholars have elaborated a more complex, and also sometimes confusing array of terms—from glocalization to hybridity—to describe how and in what ways culinary innovation occurred. But only in the few cases mentioned do such cultural dynamics fit comfortably into older typologies of diffusionism. Human-centered studies of what was once called diffusion have highlighted dynamics that did not figure prominently in older theorizing and that seem to call for a fresh round of typologizing, for those scholars so inclined to this theoretical work.

In several of the cases discussed here it has been possible to identify quite specifically the sentient and creative humans who were responsible for the creation of new particularisms. These particularisms in turn have made changing human societies in every time and in every place appear as unique and distinctive, despite their increasing commonalities and connections. Whether these particularisms are understood as culinary diffusion, globalization, standardization, or homogenization, humans can share much even as they persistently differentiate among themselves as producers, processors, and consumers of food. As much as any other field of research, food studies thus promises to keep humans at the center of world history and at the center of our understanding of globalization, guaranteeing that globalization will not become the twenty-first century equivalent of the mechanistic or teleological explanation for historical change that diffusionism once offered.

Notes

1. Richard Wrangham, *Catching Fire: How Cooking Made Us Human* (New York: Basic Books, 2009).

2. See for example, Martin Jones, *Feast: Why Humans Share Food* (Oxford: Oxford University Press, 2007).

3. I view world historians as interested in analyzing the very long-term dynamics of human life on earth; I view global historians as committed to exploring the more immediate roots of the contemporary global moment. Both perspectives are valuable but the former is more useful for those intrigued by the intersection of mobility and food as an important factor in creating culinary commonalities across cultures and societies.

4. As they do learn about it, for example in Sidney W. Mintz, *Sweetness and Power: The Place of Sugar in Modern History* (New York: Viking Books, 1985).

5. Cited in Russell Jacoby, "When Freud came to America," *The Chronicle of Higher Education*, September 21, 2009. [Online]. Available: http://chronicle.com/article/Freuds-Visit-to-Clark-U/48424/. [January 10, 2011].

6. Alison K. Smith, "National Cuisines," in *Oxford Handbook of Food History*, ed. Jeffrey M. Pilcher (New York: Oxford University Press, 2012), 444–60.

7. See the influential Arnold Toynbee, *A Study of History*, 12 vols. (London: Oxford University Press, 1934–61).

8. Nor were Toynbee and his followers alone in this fascination: see also H.G. Wells, *A Short History of the World* (New York: The Macmillan & Co., 1922); Oswald Spengler, *The Decline of the* West, trans. Charles Francis Atkinson, 2 vols. (New York: Alfred A. Knopf, 1922).

9. Jean-Louis Flandrin, Massino Montanari, and Albert Sonnenfeld, eds., *Food: A Culinary History from Antiquity to the Present*, trans. Clarissa Botsford, et al. (New York: Columbia University Press, 1999), is very much an analysis of the culinary civilizations adjoining the Mediterranean. Jared Diamond may have omitted food from his title but the central argument of his *Guns, Germs and Steel: The Fates of Human Societies* (New York: W.W. Norton, 1997), is that that Euro-Asian civilizations enjoyed a "head-start" with long-term consequences through their early domestication of plants and animals. See also Evan Fraser and Andrew Rinas, *Empires of Foods: Feast, Famine, and the Rise and Fall of Civilizations* (New York: Simon and Schuster, 2010), which is in more obvious dialogue with newer world histories that focus on the movements, connections and commerce that link civilizations.

10. Here, I use as a recent exemplar, Albert M. Craig, et al., *The Heritage of World Civilizations*, 8th ed. (Upper Saddle River, NJ: Pearson Prentice Hall, 2009).

11. Studies of this Neolithic or agrarian revolution have generated fierce controversies, although without exerting much impact on the writers of world history texts. Three studies that trace changing interpretations across time are Mark Cohen, *The Food Crisis in Prehistory: Overpopulation and the Origins of Agriculture (*New Haven: Yale University Press, 1977); David Rindos, *The Origins of Agriculture: An Evolutionary Perspective* (Orlando: Academic Press, 1984); Graeme Barker, *The Agricultural Revolution in Prehistory: Why did Foragers become Farmers?* (Oxford: Oxford University Press, 2006).

12. Marijke van der Veen, "When is Food a Luxury?" *World Archaeology* 34, no. 3 (2003): 405–27; Paul Freedman, *Out of the East: Spices* and the *Medieval Imagination* (New Haven: Yale University Press, 2008).

13. Most definitions of civilization offered in world history textbooks can be traced to the work of V. Gorden Childe. See David Russell Harris and Vere Gordon Childe, eds., *The Archaeology of V. Gordon Childe: Contemporary Perspectives* (Chicago: University of Chicago, 1994).

14. Nomadic pastoralist societies, which emerged in tandem with settled agricultural civilizations and developed their own empires over time, largely as a result of their superior military prowess (itself the product of superior technologies of mobility), have found their historians. See Peter B. Golden, "Nomads and Sedentary Societies in Medieval Eurasia," in *Agricultural and Pastoral Societies in Ancient and Classical History*, ed. Michael Adas (Philadelphia: Temple University Press, 2001), 71–115. Foragers, by contrast, continue to be the subjects of anthropology and archaeology, not history.

15. For a recent study that insists on including soldiers, combatants, and "camp followers" among the mobile of civilized warfare, see Jan Lucassen and Leo Lucassen, "The Mobility Transition Revisited, 1500–1900: What the Case of Europe can Offer to Global History," *Journal of Global History* 4 (2009): 347–77.

16. The term is most commonly used and debated by archaeologists. See for example Robert L. Kelly, "Mobility/Sedentism: Concepts, Archaeological Measures, and Effects," *Annual Review of Anthropology* 21 (October 1992): 43–66.

17. For an early effort to explain the long-term persistence of foraging, see Marshall Sahlins, *Stone Age Economics* (London: Tavistock Publications, 1974).

18. Norman J. Girardot, *Myth and Meaning in Early Taoism: The Theme of Chaos* (Berkeley: University of California Press 1983), 130.

19. Craig, *Heritage of World Civilizations*, 6–9.

20. Patrick Manning, *Navigating World History: Historians Create a Global Past* (New York: Palgrave-Macmillan, 2003); Ross Dunn, ed., *The New World History: A Teacher's Companion* (Boston and New York: Bedford/St. Martin's, 2000).

21. William McNeill, *The Rise of the West: A History of the Human Community* (1963; repr., Chicago: University of Chicago Press, 1991).

22. David Christian, *Maps of Time: An Introduction to Big History* (Berkeley: University of California Press, 2004).

23. Jerry Bentley and Herbert Ziegler, *Traditions and Encounters: A Global Perspective on the Past*, 3rd ed. (New York: McGraw-Hill, 2005); Edward H. Judge and John W. Langdon, *Connections: A World History* (Upper Saddle River, NJ: Pearson Education, 2009); Trevor Getz and Richard Hoffman, *Exchanges: A Global History Reader* (Upper Saddle River, NJ: Prentice Pearson, 2009).

24. Adrian Carton, "Food," in *Berkshire Encyclopedia of World History*, ed. William McNeill (Great Barrington: Berkshire Publishing, 2005), 757–63.

25. Dirk Hoerder, *Cultures in Contact: World Migrations in the Second Millennium* (Durham: Duke University Press, 2002).

26. See also Clark Spencer Larsen, "Dietary Reconstruction and Nutritional Assessment of Past Peoples. The Bioanthropological Record," in *The Cambridge World History of Food*, ed. Kenneth F. Kiple and Kriemhild Coneè Ornelas, 2 vols. (Cambridge: Cambridge University Press, 2000), 1:13–34.

27. Jeffrey M. Pilcher, *Food in World History* (New York: Routledge, 2006); Patrick Manning, *Migration in World History* (New York: Routledge, 2005).

28. A connection that is scarcely problematized, by contrast, in Kiple and Ornelas, *The Cambridge World History of Food*.

29. Pilcher, *Food in World History*, 6.

30. Rebecca Earle, "The Columbian Exchange," in Pilcher, *Oxford Handbook of Food History*, 341–57.

31. Manning, *Migration in World History*, 126.

32. Peter J. Hugill, "Diffusion," in *Encyclopedia of Cultural Anthropology*, ed. David Levinson and Melvin Ember (New York: Henry Holt and Company, 1996), 344–45; Robert H. Winthrop, *Dictionary of Concepts in Cultural Anthropology* (New York: Greenwood, 1991), 82; Gail King and Meghan Wright, "Diffusionism and Acculturation," in *Anthropological Theories: A Guide Prepared for Students by Students*, ed. M. D. Murphy. [Online]. Available: http://www.as.ua.edu/ant/cultures/cultures.php?culture=Diffusionism%2520and%2520Acculturation. [March 12, 2011].

33. Walter Dostal and Andre Gingrich, "German and Austrian Anthropology," *Encyclopedia of Social and Cultural Anthropology*, ed. Alan Barnard and Jonathan Spencer (London: Routledge, 1996), 262–65.

34. King and Wright, "Diffusionism and Acculturation."

35. Sterling Evans, "Agricultural Production and Environmental History," in Pilcher, *Oxford Handbook of Food History*, 209–26; Yong Chen, "Food, Race, and Ethnicity," in ibid, 428–43; and Penfold, "Fast Food," in ibid, 279–301.

36. Manning, *Migration in World History*.

37. See for example Leslie C. Aiello and Peter Wheeler, "The Expensive-Tissue Hypothesis: The Brain and the Digestive System in Human and Primate Evolution," *Current Anthropology* 36, no. 2 (April 1995): 199–221.

38. Christiane Harzig and Dirk Hoerder, *What is Migration History?* (Cambridge: Polity Press, 2009), ch. 2.

39. Evans, "Agricultural Production and Environmental History," in Pilcher, *Oxford Handbook of Food History*, 209–26.

40. Suggestive of some of this research is James L. Boone, "Subsistence Strategies and Early Human Population History: An Evolutionary Ecological Perspective," *World Archaeology* 34, no. 1 (June 2002): 6–25; P. Jeffrey Brantingham, "Measuring Forager Mobility," *Current Anthropology* 47, no. 3 (June 2006): 435–59; Gary Hanes, "The Catastrophic Extinction of North American Mammoths and Mastodonts," *World Archaeology* 33, no. 3 (February 2002): 391–416; Marcello A. Mannino and Kenneth D. Thomas, "Depletion of a Resource? The Impact of Prehistoric Human Foraging on Intertidal Mollusc Communities," *World Archaeology* 33, no. 3 (February 2002): 452–74.

41. Steven J. Mithen, *Thoughtful Foragers: A Study of Prehistoric Decision Making* (Cambridge: Cambridge University Press, 1990).

42. Judith A Carney and Richard Nicholas Rosomoff, *In the Shadow of Slavery: Africa's Botanical Legacy in the Atlantic World* (Berkeley: University of California Press, 2010). See also Frederick Douglass Opie, *Hog and Hominy: Soul Food from Africa to America* (New York: Columbia University Press, 2008).

43. Donna R. Gabaccia, *Foreign Relations: Global Perspectives on American Immigration* (Princeton, NJ: Princeton University Press, 2012). New work may help to correct this problem. See Elizabeth Zanoni, "Gendered Geographies of Consumption and Migration: Commercial and Migratory Links between Italy, the U.S., and Argentina, 1880–1940" (Ph.D. diss., University of Minnesota, 2011).

44. Chen, "Food, Race and Ethnicity"; Andrew Coe, *Chop Suey: A Cultural History of Chinese Food in the United States* (New York: Oxford University Press, 2009); Krishnendu Ray, *The Migrant's Table: Meals and Memories in Bengali-American Households* (Philadelphia: Temple University, 2004); Hasia Diner, *Hungering for America: Italian, Irish and Jewish Foodways in the Age of Migration* (Cambridge, MA: Harvard University Press, 2002); Donna R. Gabaccia, *We Are What We Eat: Ethnic Food and the Making of Americans* (Cambridge, MA: Harvard University Press, 1998).

45. This was certainly one of the main themes of my own, *We Are What We Eat*.

46. See, for example, "Migrations, pratiques alimentaires et rapports sociaux: Quand continuité n'est pas reproduction, discontinuité n'est pas rupture," a special issue of *Anthropology of Food* 7 (December 2010).

47. Stephen Castles and Mark J. Miller, *The Age of Migration* (New York: Guilford Publication, 2008).

48. Penfold, "Fast Food."

Bibliography

Crosby, Alfred W. Jr. *The Columbian Exchange: Biological and Cultural Consequences of 1492*. Westport, CT: Greenwood Press, 1972.

Davidson, Alan, ed. *Oxford Symposium. Food in Motion. The Migration of Foodstuffs and Cookery Techniques*. Leeds: Prospect Books, 1983.

Diamond, Jared. *Guns, Germs, and Steel: The Fates of Human Societies*. New York: Norton, 1999.

Fernández-Armesto, Felipe. *Near a Thousand Tables: A History of Food*. New York: Free Press, 2002.

Friedmann, Harriet. "Food." In *Dictionary of Transnational History*, edited by Akira Iriye and Pierre-Yves Saunier, 416–22. New York: Palgrave-Macmillan, 2009.
Kiple, Kenneth F. *A Movable Feast: Ten Millennia of Food Globalization*. Cambridge: Cambridge University Press, 2007.
Kiple, Kenneth F., and Kriemhild Coneè Ornelas, eds. *The Cambridge World History of Food*. 2 vols. Cambridge: Cambridge University Press, 2000.
Pilcher, Jeffrey. *Food in World History*. New York: Routledge, 2006.
Wilk, Richard R., ed. *Fast Food/Slow Food: The Cultural Economy of the Global Food System*. Lanham, MD: Altamira Press, 2006.

CHAPTER 18

THE MEDIEVAL SPICE TRADE

PAUL FREEDMAN

THE insatiable European demand for spices in the late Middle Ages (A.D.1200–1500) is perhaps the most important and best-known example of great historic change brought about by consumer preference. The fateful European voyages of discovery and subsequent colonization were launched not to locate basic, vitally important commodities such as grain, but for aromatic products to provide flavor and an aura of healthful and gracious refinement to food and drink in order to enhance what we would term "lifestyle." The journeys of Columbus, Da Gama, and their successors were organized with a number of goals in mind, including the quest for gold and silver and the possibility of finding Christian rulers beyond the realms of Islam who might aid in combating the Turks. But among the principal motives was to find where spices came from and to obtain them for a price far below what the Venetians or Genoese supplied via the market ports of the Muslim Middle East. A considerable amount of lore, learning, navigational technique, financial backing, and economic theorization were mobilized to acquire what were thought to be extremely desirable exotic fragrances and condiments which, it was widely believed, were far more plentiful in their magical and mysterious countries of origin than in the constricted markets of Europe.

The importance of the spice trade to the history of food is not simply in the commercial routes and speculation about how to expand them, but in the reasons for the extraordinary demand in the first place. It is obvious that modern European cuisine does not require or even tolerate very much in the way of tropical spices. The development of what became classic French cuisine in the seventeenth and eighteenth centuries was defined in part by a rejection of an earlier highly flavored and complicated spectrum of tastes imparted by cinnamon, cloves, saffron and the like. Medieval and Renaissance cuisine was dismissed as "Arabic" and "childish" and a richer more intense type of sauce was developed made with distillates of meat juices and flavored not with hot or sharp spices but with shallots, truffles, and European herbs. In North Africa, the Middle East, India, or Indonesia, spice dealers handle what seems to Europeans an astonishing variety and quantity of spices, and consumers buy on a routine day what might be a lifetime's supply in France. Outside of desserts (a kind of home in exile for spices such as cinnamon, cardamom, or nutmeg), there are only a few European niches for particular spices. Saffron is necessary for some types of paella, or *lotte au safran*, or *risotto Milanese*, but these are very specific preparations, not part of a generalized culinary practice. Pepper managed to survive as a common spice (although even here European usage is small), and sugar, considered a spice in the Middle Ages, would have an unusual and prosperous future, but for the most part the success of European discovery of the spice lands and control of the spice routes would be followed by the increasing irrelevance of spices. This evanescence of the taste for a piquant cuisine impedes our present understanding of the basis for the earlier popularity of spices.

Understanding the medieval demand for spices involves describing medieval preference in cuisine and an appreciation for its fairly radical difference from European taste of the last several centuries. Medieval spices would have other uses, however, besides cooking. In addition to their role in sauces and other edible uses, spices were regarded as healthful. They were important ingredients in drugs. Equally important, spices were useful to bring equilibrium to the body's humors which were prone to imbalance. Depending on individual temperament, the four vital fluids constituting the humors were easily thrown out of harmony by such things as the properties of different foods. Blood, bile, black bile (melancholia), and phlegm corresponded to combination of hot, dry, moist and cold. As many kinds of meat and fish were cold and/or wet, the generally hot and dry properties of spices balanced their humoral influences.

As part of their gastronomic and medical aura, spices were above all exotic. They came from far away; their wonderful fragrance evoked received ideas about India derived from classical learning. To this image of the Orient was conjoined a Biblically derived Christian conception of the fragrant earthly Paradise and its Eastern location. Spices conferred a kind of social prestige and status was closely joined to the ability to provide a fragrant environment including, but not limited to, food. They were in some sense magical, not merely mundane cooking ingredients. The most expensive spices such as ambergris, musk, or camphor were used in perfumes, as preventive medicines to ward off disease emanating from pestilential smells, and as fragrances to scent rooms or adorn wealthy persons. They might also have some use in cuisine, especially in formulae for spiced wines. This versatility was part of the allure of spices, but it was a heightened, otherworldly utility that conferred a kind of well-being, spiritually as well as physically. The closest modern parallel might be the sense of "wellness" that constitutes a kind of health and freedom from ambiguous diseases difficult to describe, a malaise such as "stress" as opposed to calm, purity, fragrance, and harmony. In particular the notion that fragrance is both mentally and physically healthful, the underlying idea behind aromatherapy, is close to a medieval picture of the broad significance and meaning of aromatic luxury products.

Inclusion of fragrant but only marginally edible exotica such as musk or ambergris leads one to ask what was meant by "spices" in the Middle Ages if this category was prized for reasons that went outside of cooking. The Florentine merchant Francesco Balducci Pegolotti in about 1340 listed no fewer than 288 spices in his handbook *La pratica della mercatura*. Allowing for different types or grades of the same substance (three grades of mastic, three of ginger, for example), there are 193 different substances mentioned. What they have in common is that they are imported, not perishable, and have a high unit value (a small amount is valuable and so, unlike iron, timber, or wheat, spices do not require bulk transport to make a profit). Pegolotti includes a number of dye products, wax, and cotton, but the vast majority of his *speziere* are aromatic. They may require some grinding or scraping to reveal their fragrance, but this is what gives them value.

Spices are distinguished from herbs because they are imported and are much more valuable. Herbs were also used in preparing food and were featured in medical lists of remedies, but they were locally cultivated or gathered and so were thought of as green, even if they were sometimes saved in dried form. They might be sold in markets, but by farmers or foragers, rather than appearing in the urban shops of apothecaries, spicers, or grocers. Herbs were not inferior to spices in flavoring food and had some medicinal and quasi-medicinal uses that spices could not duplicate. Poisons, witchcraft, and love potions required herbs, not spices, but herbs were either non-commercial or at the low end of mercantile value. They were domestic, not imported.

Spices in Medieval Gastronomy

Spices were ubiquitous in medieval gastronomy and also in medieval pharmacology. They were condiments but also cures and preventives for disease. The fields of cooking and medicine are always related in the sense that good health is associated with adhering to dietary rules and bad health is often thought to be due to dietary abuse or imbalance. At various times the proximity of food consumption to perceptions of illness and its causes is more or less. In the mid-twentieth century, it was assumed that drugs could (or soon would) treat any kind of disease or nutritional insufficiency. It was even a common belief of food industry planners that home cooking would soon be eliminated in favor of well-balanced, nutritionally enhanced frozen or concentrated meals. In this setting food and medicine were widely separated and the sole purpose of dietary advice was to lose or manage weight. By the late twentieth century anxiety over obesity, food processing, the practices of the food industry, and changes in attitudes towards freshness, seasonality, and the environment encouraged the return of a more historically typical association of food with health and, more especially, of illness with poor dietary practices. Not only are certain foods regarded as dangerous (those processed with high fructose corn syrup, for example) or beneficial (oat bran, flax seed), but ideas of imbalance versus equilibrium or of toxicity versus purity affect the perception of a blurred frontier between medicine and food. This makes it easier than in the recent past to imagine something of the medieval view of the world in which spices were not only flavoring ingredients but healthful, balancing, and prestigious as well. Their contribution to wellness and refinement was enhanced by their exotic origins, their high price, and their association with the sacred. If the Garden of Eden abounded in spices, if the bodies of saints could be identified by their aromatic fragrance (as opposed to the usual stench of decay), then food that was perfumed with spices and aromatic medicines must have powers that favorably influenced the body, mind, and even the spirit or soul.

Nevertheless, all this elite versatility notwithstanding, spices were real flavors. Medieval cuisine was richly piquant not because of medical or nutritional lore or the desire to display wealth but because of a taste for the spices themselves. The culinary aesthetic of medieval Europe was synthetic rather than analytic, to use the terms Massimo Montanari has outlined in a general discussion of culinary categories.[1] Synthetic in the sense that what the cook strives for is a palate or spectrum of flavors in each dish rather than enhancing the basic ingredients. Modern European cuisine is analytic and has broken with this medieval tradition by exalting the quality of ingredients, maintaining their integrity and identifiable look and taste throughout the preparation process, and by intensifying rather than covering or blending the principle constituents. Most cuisines of India are synthetic in that the sauce is what distinguishes a dish and it might be applied to different kinds of meat or vegetables so that the taste of the dish is determined more by a complexity of ingredients and savors than by its primary basis. When in 1656 Nicolas de Bonnefons wrote that "a cabbage soup should taste entirely of cabbage, a leek soup of leeks, a turnip soup of turnips," he was asserting the primacy of the basic ingredients over the seasonings, the easily separable components of analytic cuisine, over the blended mysteries of the synthetic. He concludes quite clearly: "food should taste like what it is."[2]

The excessive use of spices (which eventually came to mean almost *any* use of spices) was a capital offence according to the new authenticity championed by French chefs in the seventeenth century. The novelty of this culinary philosophy and the backwardness of the rest of Europe can be seen in the accounts of travelers such as the marquis of Coulanges who found German cuisine in 1657 marred by peculiar spice, fruit, and meat combinations, or Gaspard d'Hauteville's impressions of Poland at around the same time where the food was redolent of nutmeg, cinnamon, saffron, and sugar. Advocates of the new style rejected not only foreign backwardness but also their own earlier French traditions. The anonymous L.S.R., author of *L'Art de bien traiter* (1674), dismisses even his innovative predecessor La Varenne for excessive use of spices and for too many flavors, a practice "more willingly tolerated among the Arabs... than in a refined atmosphere such as ours, where propriety, delicacy, and good taste [reign]."[3] In all these examples there is an explicit or implicit denunciation of what had been the fashion—the medieval taste for highly spiced, sweet, and complicated sauces.

The modern French chefs' contempt for medieval cuisine based on its supposedly "Arabic" character is understandable to the extent that medieval European recipes seem to partake of an Arabic, Persian, and even Indian aesthetic. The use of perfumed ingredients such as rosewater, a fondness for dried fruit, sugar in sauces and sugared confections, or almond milk, seem to indicate borrowings from the Near East. New vegetables such as spinach and artichokes or the bitter oranges and pomegranates of Andalusia were clearly introduced from the Muslim world. Yet there is substantial disagreement about how direct was the dependence of European medieval preferences on the cuisine of Islamic cultures. It is hard to find North African, Near Eastern, or Persian dishes transferred or picked up by European recipe books. Even where reference is made to "Saracen style" or "Saracen sauce," there is no connection, or perhaps the color red is associated with Islam. Concoctions dubbed "Saracen" might even include pork or other clearly non-Muslim ingredients.[4]

With regard to spices, the peculiarities of medieval recipes do in a general sense reflect an Eastern aesthetic. Spices are used in mixtures and combinations, not singly in the modern Western manner. They appear across the menu, in savory as well as in sweet dishes and often in combination with sugar and vinegar so the savory/sweet contrast is, from a modern standpoint, blurred. And finally, spices are used in large quantities in medieval recipes. While recipes don't usually specify amounts and it won't do to exaggerate and think of medieval cuisine as simply overwhelmed indiscriminately with spices, the accounts of households and provisions for individual meals show that spices were not subtle or barely visible but rather major flavors in a majority of recipe collections. For the totality of medieval cookbooks (about 150 survive, all from the thirteenth through fifteenth centuries), 75 percent of the recipes call for spices and no less than 90 percent of English medieval cookbooks require spices.[5]

The widespread use of varied spices fits with an overall set of medieval culinary preferences. In general, medieval cuisine emphasized artifice rather than simplicity and complex taste combinations (sweet and sour, for example) rather than intense concentration on primary elements. It took delight in special effects including not only perfumed and piquant flavors but color, *trompe l'oeil*, and magnificence. Pepper, saffron, cinnamon, and ginger and sugar were the most common spices used in medieval cooking and made up the bulk of what was imported from the East into the Mediterranean. However, one of the remarkable aspects of the medieval fondness for spices was the variety of piquant ingredients called for by the recipes and supplied by the merchants. Nutmeg and cloves were imported from tiny islands in the Moluccan archipelago of what is now eastern Indonesia. They were highly prized and quite expensive. Other spices commonly used are all but unknown in Europe in North America today outside Asian ethnic enclaves.

Galangal, zedoary, and long-pepper (an Indian spice not in fact related to black pepper) were well-known in medieval Paris but have been absent there now for centuries. Malagueta pepper, which came from West Africa and not from East Asia, was called "grains of Paradise" in what must be considered an early example of successful marketing or "branding." It took France in particular by storm in the thirteenth and fourteenth centuries before dying out completely by the sixteenth century.

Both the royal cook Taillevent and the upper bourgeois author of *Le Ménagier de Paris* employ about twenty different spices in their recipes, and Taillevent gives a list of what the cook needs to have on hand. There were also different spice mixtures such as *poudre noir* or *poudre marchant* that resemble Indian masalas or North African and Middle Eastern multiple spice combinations such as the Moroccan *ras el hanout*.

Some aromatic ingredients that we think of as perfume or medicine were used in cooking. Musk and camphor scented confectionaries, for example. But this became more current in the Renaissance where even ambergris, the most precious spice of all and used for medicinal purification for the most part, was used to scent and flavor banquet dishes.

Spices and Health

The sharp or fragrant smell and taste of spices provided not only delight but was supposed to impart health benefits to medieval food. There is no current equivalent to the dual appeal of spices since for the most part delightful foods are now deemed unhealthful and what is healthful is not particularly expensive or searched after. The beneficial health effects of spices were thought to be twofold. They were in the first place considered medicines and supposed to have curative properties for various disorders. At the same time, however, their culinary and pharmaceutical uses overlapped more closely than this as spices were thought to provide a necessary balance to many kinds of meat and fish and were associated with good digestion, the prevention of illness, and bodily equilibrium.

Medieval pharmaceutical manuals list hundreds of basic medicinal ingredients, known as "simples." All spices used in cooking also appear in lists of effective drugs and in many instances, as with sugar for example, their medicinal use preceded their diffusion as culinary ingredients. According to a twelfth-century manual, pepper helps reduce chest congestion and relieves asthma. Cinnamon soothes digestive problems and when heated in wine heals decaying gums.[6]

Pharmacists also dispensed combined medicines that consisted of several or even dozens of aromatic products. Among the most celebrated drug mixtures was theriac, a panacea that consisted of no less than eighty-three ingredients according to the recipe of Montpellier, a town with a famous medical faculty.[7]

Pharmacists had a great variety of aromatics as well as mineral and animal products. A postmortem inventory of the contents of a pharmacists' shop in Barcelona dating from 1353 includes over a hundred spices, herbs, and compound preparations such as lapis lazuli, crushed pearls, musk, and dried squid. It even contains what was termed "mummy," which was exuded from embalmed (preferably Middle Eastern) corpses and had the consistency of pitch and, not surprisingly, an unpleasant smell.[8] It was indicated in the treatment of bleeding and the healing of wounds.[9] Thus relatively ordinary cooking spices were deemed effective, along with stranger ingredients.

Fragrance in itself was considered a preventive to the spread of disease. To the extent that illness was thought to spread by foul odors, attractive perfumes and aromatics were used to create a healthful environment. Bad air—"miasma" from swamps, sewage, dead animals, and industrial effluents and processes (notably from tanning or smelting)—was to be repulsed by perfumed substances including edible spices such as nutmeg as well as ambergris, camphor, musk, and the like. Rooms were scented with fresh or burned herbs, spices, and incense. There were portable fragrance compounds that could accompany the cautious and affluent citizen into the insalubrious streets. Pomanders (from *pomme d'ambre* = "ambergris apple") were metal open-work balls that could contain mixtures of spices and they were carried around on a chain or in the hand. Doctors and pharmacists recommended different pomander mixtures according to the disease to be guarded against. Even the terrible Black Death was thought to be at least to some extent weakened by the beneficent scent of mace, sandalwood, myrrh, storax, and, above all, ambergris.[10]

Spices also had a disease-preventive role in the preparation of food and were important in achieving the balance of humors considered necessary for health. The four bodily humors were supposed to be in balance so that none of them predominated. Illness resulted from disproportionate humoral interaction and theories of the influence of humors were derived from Greek and Roman medicine. Everyone had a slight tendency or *temperament* that produced some excess of phlegm, yellow bile, black bile, or blood. Thus a person might be phlegmatic, sanguine, bilious, or melancholic by nature. Doctors, in order to recommend diets to fit their patients, needed to know these temperamental facts to be able to adjust for them. A person with a slight tendency towards melancholia (favoring black bile) should be careful about foods that were humorally cold and dry, for it was not only human physiology but the food consumed by humans that had humoral tendencies and imbalances. Beef, a cold and dry food, should either be avoided by those of a melancholic temperament, or cooked in such a way as to neutralize the humoral bias of the basic ingredient.

Cooking methods and added ingredients such as spices served to advance or temper humoral properties. Roasting and frying made foods warmer, so pork should be prepared in one of these ways as it was cold and moist, but roast beef was considered less healthful than boiled beef as it was already dry enough to begin with.

Spices were in general regarded as hot and dry and as meat tended to be cold and moist, spices were ideal accompaniments. The spices were most often delivered in the form of sauces. Although meat broths might be used in the cooking process and in making some sauces, it was more common for the sauce to be prepared separately from the meat it accompanied. This was, in part, in order to make the counteracting humoral effect of the spices stronger. It was therefore a key innovation of what was to become classic French cuisine to enshrine the reduction of meat juices as the key to sauce preparation, a break with medieval practice. Medieval sauces were sharp rather than rich, thin rather than velvety, complex rather than intense.

There is some intuitive logic to the complicated world of humoral theory found in the appeal of notions of equilibrium, as can be seen in contemporary schemes of balance as well as traditional Chinese and Indian dietary lore. The fundamental attributes of cold, hot, moist, and dry also can be seen to correspond to the nature of certain foods, and thus it is not surprising that fish would be considered, for the most part, cold and wet. But there are many basic ingredients that might seem similar but that were thought to have rather different humoral characters. Grape products had contrasting humoral qualities depending on their preparation so that while wine was warm and dry, vinegar was very cold and mildly dry. Must was warm and moist while verjuice (the juice of unripe grapes) was the opposite: cold and dry. Within the overall properties of dryness and heat, spices differed in degree. Nutmeg was hot and dry to the second degree but pepper was very hot (fourth degree) but similarly dry to the second degree. Ginger was unusual in that it was moist as well as hot.

The use of spices in cuisine and medicine by no means exhausts their significance in the Middle Ages. As already stated, spices were unusually versatile luxury products in that they were both tasty and healthful, elegant in secular settings yet linked with the sacred. Their aura was enhanced and closely related to their distant and often mysterious origins which justified their high price and significance as markers of social status. In the remaining sections of this essay we discuss the origins, routes, and prices of these precious yet widely diffused commodities.

Origins and Imagined Origins

As already mentioned, spices were defined, or at least conceived, as aromatic products imported from far off, indeed from lands not very clearly perceived by their European end users. Spices obtained some of their aura of exotic desirability because they came from India, but where "India" actually was remained mysterious, part of a complicated but not consistently articulated "East." The conquests of Alexander the Great and tenuous though continuous Hellenistic and Roman communication with India bequeathed to the Middle Ages a strong if largely fanciful impression of India as a land of fabulous wealth, as well as sinister wonders of nature. Jewels, gold, and spices abounded in India, but so did monstrous semi-human peoples, poisonous snakes, and off-putting customs. The alluring and the perilous were side by side, so that pepper was reputed to come from Indian forests where snakes "guarded" the trees. In order to drive away the snakes and harvest the pepper, the groves had to be burned. This explained both the high price of pepper and the wrinkled, desiccated appearance of the peppercorns. Similarly, diamonds were plentiful in certain gorges in India, but could not be retrieved by men because of the presence of snakes. Instead, eagles were trained to fetch meat thrown down into the gorges, to which the diamonds supposedly stuck.[11] Such stories might function as merchants' tales to obscure the actual origins of precious commodities or to justify and enhance their value. They also reflect some sense of the exotic as a combination of the precious and the dangerous, a feeling sufficiently deep that it was not limited to distorted European notions of India but proliferated in India itself in thinking about valuable substances.[12]

Combining Biblical and classical lore, the medieval era produced a considerable body of "wonders of the East" literature which was enriched rather than supplanted by accounts of travelers who actually managed to reach India, beginning with Marco Polo in the late thirteenth century. On world maps the farthest eastern reaches were usually occupied by the earthly Paradise (inaccessible to humanity after the Fall, but still a terrestrial place) and India. On one of the most famous of these maps, the Hereford Map drawn in about 1300, Paradise is an island off the eastern edge of the world and India occupies the nearest part of the mainland. It has 5,000 cities and peoples of "unbelievably various ritual practice and dress" including Pygmies and one-legged humanoids. There is a pepper forest, an abundance of jewels and precious metals, but also all manner of wild animals including dragons.[13]

The ancient and Christian geography of Asia was gradually undermined, or at least complicated, by the unanticipated consequences of the Mongol invasions of the thirteenth century. Once the terrifying threat of annihilation by an irresistible enemy faded, Europeans started to take advantage of the sway held by one set of rulers over thousands of miles of territory. The so-called "Pax Mongolica" made it possible to traverse the route from Europe as far as China and the Pacific Ocean. An ultimately fateful if at the time unremarked discovery of one of these early travelers, the Franciscan William of Rubruck, was the relative positions of India and China. Reporting on his journey which had lasted from 1253 to 1255, William noted that envoys from India at the court of Möngke Khan said that their home was west rather than east of the Mongol capital of Karakorum. He confirmed this by riding westward with the emissaries for a considerable distance before their ways diverged.[14]

Marco Polo visited India on his slow return from China and he not only gave an accurate (if rather vague) sense of India's location in relation to the rest of Asia but was the first to observe that many spices originated further east of India and that Indian ports were centers of both local spice harvests and aromatic products that came from even further away (from a European perspective). In the fourteenth century there were a few adventurous European traders resident in India as well as China, Persia, and what is now Turkestan.[15] Information about the islands east of India, which came to be known as the "Indies," became sufficiently precise so that even individual islands of the Moluccas were identified with particular spices. Relying on an account of the voyage of Niccolò de' Conti, the Florentine humanist Poggio Bracciolini describes Banda (an island "near the shadows") as the source of cloves.[16]

Certain spices, such as nutmeg and cloves, had a very restricted habitat, in this case eastern Indonesia. For others there were perceived quality differences so that the best camphor came from Borneo and the best cinnamon from Ceylon. The medieval European impression that India was the source of spices was accurate to the extent that most of what came to Europe went through India if it did not originate there.

There were some exceptional spices that did not follow this pattern. Mastic, a resinous product of a plant in the pistachio family, is to this day produced only on the Greek island of Chios. Saffron grew in many parts of Europe including England, Spain, France, and Italy. Its high value was related to the laborious process of harvesting it rather than the rarity of the plant or the distance of its natural habitat. Malagueta pepper or "grains of Paradise" grew in West Africa as the Portuguese discovered in the mid-fifteenth century. Nevertheless, the main spice routes were from East and South Asia to other points. Europe was by no means the largest buyer of spices and in terms of the actual trade routes, India must be regarded as central rather than distant, in Janet Abu-Lughod's phrase, "on the way to everywhere" instead of at the world map's extreme margin.[17]

Routes

From India, Indochina, and Indonesia, spices were exported to China, the Middle East, Central Asia, and Europe. The latter was a relatively small player in this global (or at least old-world global) commerce. Marco Polo claimed that for every ship that left Alexandria loaded with pepper for Europe, one hundred ships arrived in China through the port of Çaiton (Quanzhou).[18] This is not useful as any sort of exact measure of trade volume but does put Europe in a modest perspective. Notwithstanding the superior population and economy of China, a considerable volume of spices did arrive in Europe, usually but not always via the Red Sea and Egyptian ports. Archaeological excavation has shown how important the Red Sea coast was for the Roman Empire's monsoon trade with India, which was principally organized around the importation of pepper.[19] The Cairo Geniza documents provide evidence for the activities of Jewish merchants of the eleventh and twelfth centuries who brought all manner of spices from India to Egypt with Aden as the most important intermediary port.[20]

From the West coast of India, especially Malabar and Gujarat, spices were exported to Mediterranean Europe most often via the Red Sea or Persian Gulf. From the ninth until the twelfth century Constantinople was an important center for the supply of spices to Western Europe. These arrived at the Persian Gulf and were then shipped overland through Baghdad or other Persian cities. With the triumph of the First Crusade in 1099, eastern Mediterranean ports in Christian hands, notably Acre, obtained some of this trade. In both the Byzantine and crusader cases, there were Muslim intermediaries but the ports of entry into the Mediterranean were Christian cities. This ceased to be the case after the fall of Acre in 1291 and the consequent end of a crusader presence on the mainland. Christian Cyprus was still an important destination for spice merchants from Barcelona and other western port cities. But now Alexandria, Beirut, and Damascus handled the transfer of spices from Islamic to Christian worlds and the Christian merchants defied, or more often skirted, papal prohibitions on commercial dealings with Islam.

There was some fluctuation in routes, however, especially because of the impact of the Mongols. In the late-thirteenth and early-fourteenth centuries, the near destruction of the Islamic states of Western Asia and the Mongol control over Central Asia encouraged an overland trade in spices, silks, and other eastern commodities. At this point the trade in spices followed the western parts of the famed Silk Road, joining it not in China (which was not a supplier but rather consumer of spices) but rather via Tabriz, Bokhara or Samarkand. The slowness and effort of land transport was offset by the security provided by the Mongol rulers. For this overland commerce, the Black Sea became the site for transfer to European merchants, specifically such places as sub-Byzantine Trebizond or the Genoese base at Caffa in the Crimea.

The eclipse of the Mongols was evident by the second part of the fourteenth century. They lost their hold over China to the resurgent Ming emperors and they assimilated their religion and rulership in Persia to Islam and local powers during the course of the fourteenth century. By 1400 Europeans were completely dependent on Islamic potentates, such as the Mamluk sultans of Egypt or the Ottoman rulers of the northeastern Mediterranean, for the trade in spices. This was more than satisfactory to the Venetians and Genoese who simply passed on to European consumers whatever prices the market or the rulers imposed. The high cost of spices and the control of the trade by Muslims did excite the interest of commercial and religious strategists to figure out ways of either defeating Islam by, for example, a blockade of the Red Sea, or by going around the Muslim-controlled zones to reach India and the Indies directly. The rulers of these lands were widely assumed to be either pagans, or sympathetic to Christians, or perhaps already Christians. Legends of Prester John, the Christian priest-king of "the Three Indias," combined tales of the fabulous wealth of the East with wishful thinking about an alliance of Christian powers that would outflank and surround Islam. In the first part of the fifteenth century, Emmanuel Piloti argued that Alexandria and Cairo were the key to the entire economy of the Levant because of the spice trade. If they could be conquered (a task Piloti considered not very difficult if the Venetian navy could be enlisted), the entire Muslim economy would collapse. Piloti argued that the spice trade was so important and Cairo's role as its entrepôt was such, that whoever held the city could be considered the effective lord of Christendom as well as the indirect ruler of the places where the spices came from.[21] This bellicose strategy to claim the spice trade would not, in the end, find powerful backers. The schemes that launched Columbus and Da Gama were to bypass Islam and corner the spice trade at its source. They involved an equally imaginative but far more flexible sense of geopolitical strategy, but also a similarly grim view of commerce as potentially a form of strangling one's adversary. When the Portuguese located the Moluccan "Spice Islands" in 1511–1513 and conquered Malacca on the Malay Straits, there was a new appreciation of the routes and vulnerabilities of the global spice trade, summarized by the pithy observation of Tomás Pires: "whoever holds Malacca has his hands on the throat of Venice."[22]

Prices

Spices were expensive commodities, routinely likened to precious metals and gems although they were more ephemeral than these as they were consumed either in food, as medicines, or as scents. They were non-perishable products of a high unit value so that it was profitable to carry them in relatively small quantities over immense distances. How profitable is difficult to determine as is everything connected with ascribing a price for spices comprehensible in our contemporary terms. An additional difficulty is that the vast spaces traversed by the spices imported into Europe meant that the number of transfers and middlemen increased the total difference between price at origin and the price for retail customer, and distributed profits in a way that makes them even more difficult to reckon. At the end of the Middle Ages, specifically from 1496 to 1498, the price of cloves in Venice was on the order of one hundred times the cost of purchasing them in the Moluccan islands where they grew.[23] Venice in turn flourished because it charged considerably more than what it had cost its merchants to purchase things such as cloves in the Levant. For the early fifteenth century the Venetian markup for cloves was 72 percent.[24] Spices sold in northern Europe, or in fact anywhere beyond the Mediterranean ports, would have been subject to further transport and profit-taking charges. The Nuremberg cartographer Martin Behaim, who designed a world globe in 1492, posited twelve stages in the journey made by spices from their East Indian origins to "our land." His sense of trade routes and entrepôts is quite unreliable as regards East Asia—he says spices move from Java or Borneo to Ceylon and are then handled by merchants from Malaya and Sumatra—but his sense of the distance and complexity involved and their commercial consequences is perceptive. With each change in carriage and jurisdiction new charges were added so that between the customs duties, real transport costs, and realized opportunities for profit, Behaim observes, it is "no wonder spices for us cost their weight in gold."[25]

All spices were luxuries, but individual spices differed greatly in cost. Pepper, ginger, cinnamon, and sugar were the least expensive. Cloves and nutmeg were considerably more valuable, perhaps three times the price of pepper. Saffron was ten to fifteen times the price of pepper and the most extravagantly expensive spices were medicinal perfumes such as ambergris, musk, and camphor.

Perceptions of the relative value of different spices seem to have changed, at least to the extent that pepper came to be seen as so widely available that it lost some of its aristocratic image. In a fifteenth-century medical treatise wrongly attributed to Arnau de Vilanova, pepper is described as appropriate for rustics, and this is confirmed by the poet Eustache Deschamps, writing in 1404, who complains about rural inns where they serve unpleasant and lowly cabbage and leeks seasoned with copious amounts of black pepper.[26] Was pepper really so inexpensive that peasants routinely seasoned their meager fare with it? We know that spices were available in small towns and markets, not just in large cities, and agricultural tenants were sufficiently tied to a market economy so that they occasionally paid small but not insignificant quantities of pepper to their landlords as tokens of their tenancy or as rent.

In addition to the differential in value among spices, there were considerable fluctuations in prices due to changes in supply and in conjectured supply (i.e. perceived shortages, future hedging and, speculation). Thus at the great wholesale center of Alexandria in 1355 pepper sold for 163 gold dinars per *sporta* (the equivalent of about 500 modern pounds), but in 1386 the same quantity was priced at only 60 dinars. These shifts in turn affected retail prices, which were equally unstable.[27]

In a meticulous and exhaustive study of prices in late-medieval and early-modern Antwerp, Herman Van der Wee charts the price of an Antwerp pound of pepper at the annual St. Bavo's Fair between 1385 and 1400 in a range between 9.50 Flemish groats (and 9.50 Brabant groats) at the low end, and 19.00 Flemish groats (21.08 Brabant groats) at the upper. Ginger cost from 10.67 Flemish groats (12 Brabant) to 36 Flemish groats (66 Brabant) per pound. Cinnamon and sugar are in a similar price range while cloves for the same period were never lower than 31 Flemish groats (31 Brabant) and reached a maximum of 57 Flemish groats (95.33 Brabant). Saffron had a striking fluctuation: a low of 70 Flemish groats in 1395, down from a high of 198 in 1389 and 110 Brabant groats in 1395 to 291.33 just three years later in 1398.[28]

Attempts to chart a long-term trend in spice prices have proved intriguing but controversial. Frederic Lane, the great historian of Venice, claimed that the price of pepper rose during the reign of the Mamluk sultan of Egypt al-Ashraf Barsbay (1422–1438) as he severely limited the supply in order to impose a price hike. After his death, however, prices fell throughout the rest of the century. This calculation has been questioned, but not definitively refuted.[29] At any rate, at the time of the early Portuguese voyages to India, the differential between point of origin and European wholesale price was still such that Da Gama's second trip (1502–1503) netted a 400 percent profit for 1,700 tons of spices, mostly pepper.[30]

It is difficult to get a sense of what the retail price of spices meant in terms that can be related to modern prices. It won't do simply to come up with a conversion of a medieval transaction extrapolated into our currencies. This is because of the inconsistencies of not only medieval prices but also of medieval coins and values as well as the availability of other options and the cultural significance placed on spices. Thus spices are still expensive, but they offer no particular social or cultural benefit to the consumer, whereas in the Middle Ages such things as spices, clothes, horses, or silver utensils were prominent as items of status and ostentation. One approach is to figure out the price of spices in comparison with other goods and measured against the purchasing power of an average wage earner. John Munro has undertaken the task of comparing the average daily earnings of a master craftsman such as a mason or carpenter with the price of luxury commodities over a very long time span.[31] Using spice prices in Antwerp and London, Munro has found that in 1200 it took nearly fourteen days' pay to buy a pound of pepper and 8.6 days for a pound of ginger. Compare this to 1875, when the figure for a pound of pepper is a mere 0.1 days (although ginger was still relatively high at 1.6 days). At the present, it requires a mere fifteen minutes to earn the price of a pound of pepper, ginger, or cinnamon. The craftsman's daily wage of approximately eight pence in London in the year 1439 could buy eight gallons of milk or two bushels of coal. Seven yards of good wool cloth cost ten days' salary while a pound of cloves required four and a half days' work.

Naturally spices weren't purchased in such large quantities except by the wealthiest and largest households, anymore than they would be now. A medieval person of moderate affluence could afford a certain number of judiciously determined luxuries, including, if he or she wished, an assortment of culinary and medicinal spices. The most dramatic decline in spice prices occurred from the late Roman Empire (when according to Munro's data spices really were extravagantly expensive) to the establishment of regular Mediterranean trade with the temporary success of the crusades and the longer-term accomplishments of the Italian and other merchant entrepreneurs.

Conclusion

I have tried to suggest that the popularity of spices in the Middle Ages was more extensive and had other bases than their use in cooking. This is not by any means intended to obscure their importance to the peculiar aesthetic of medieval cuisine but rather to indicate how food choices are influenced by ideas about health, sophistication, and the exotic. The spice trade is often and rightly considered a prime example of the way in which commercial quests can drive historical shifts of immense and reverberating significance. What is often ignored is why in this case there was such a powerful demand in the first place, for which any number of efforts would be made to overcome the limitations (and expense) of the supply. Readers of this handbook do not have to be convinced of the importance of the history of culinary taste and innovation, but the historiographically well-plowed subject of the spice trade deserves to be looked at in greater detail in terms of the influence of taste, luxuries, and even a species of frivolity and erroneous speculation on historical change.

Notes

1. Alberto Capatti and Massimo Montanari, *Italian Cuisine: A Cultural History*, trans. Aine O'Healy (New York: Columbia University Press, 2003), 86–87.
2. Susan Pinkard, *A Revolution in Taste: The Rise of French Cuisine, 1650–1800* (Cambridge: Cambridge University Press, 2009), 62.
3. Ibid, 125–26.
4. Bruno Laurioux, "Le goût médiévale est-il Arabe? À propos de la 'Saracen Connection'," in Laurioux, *Une histoire culinaire du Moyen Âge* (Paris: Honoré Champion, 2005), 305–35; *The Neapolitan Recipe Collection: Cuoco Napolitano*, ed. and trans. Terence Scully (Ann Arbor: University of Michigan Press, 2000), 68.
5. Bruno Luarioux, "De l'usage des épices dans l'alimentation médiévale," *Médiévales* 5 (1983): 16–17.
6. *Das Arzneidrogenbuch "Circa instans" in einer Fassung des XIII. Jahrhunderts aus der Universitätsbibliothek Erlangen*, ed. Hans Wölfel (Hamburg: Preilipper, 1939), 33–34, 91–92.
7. François Granel, "La Thériaque de Montpellier," *Revue d'histoire de la pharmacie* 64, no. 228 (1976): 75–83.
8. Tomás López Pizcueta, "Los bienes de un farmacéutico barcelonés del siglo XIV: Francesc de Camp," *Acta Medievalia* 13 (1992): 17–73.
9. Michael Camille, "The Corpse in the Garden: *Mumia* in Medieval Herbal Illustrations," *Micrologus* 7 (1999): 297–318.
10. John M. Riddle, "Pomum Ambrae: Amber and Ambergris in Plague Remedies," *Sudhoffs Archiv für Geschichte der Medizin und der Naturwissenschaften* 48 (1964): 111–22.
11. Paul Freedman, *Out of the East: Spices and the Medieval Imagination* (New Haven: Yale University Press, 2008), 133–36.
12. James McHugh, "The Incense Trees of the Land of Emeralds: Exotic Material Culture of *Kāmaśāstra*," *Journal of Indian Philosophy* 39 (2011): 63–100.
13. Scott D. Westrem, *The Hereford Map* (Turnhout: Brepols, 2001), 27–33.
14. William of Rubruck, *The Mission of Friar William of Rubruck*, ed. Peter Jackson and David Morgan (London: Hakluyt Society, 1990), 247.
15. Robert Lopez, "Da Venezia a Delhi nel Trecento," in Lopez, *Su e giù per la storia di Genova* (Genoa: Università di Genova, 1975), 137–59; idem, "European Merchants in the Medieval Indies," *Journal of Economic History* 3 (1943): 164–84; idem, "In quibuscumque mondi partibus'," in *Miscellanea di storia italiana e mediterranea per Nino Lamboglia* (Genoa: N.p., 1978), 345–54.
16. Poggio Bracciolini, *De L'Inde: Les voyages de Niccolò de' Conti*, ed. and trans. Michèle Guéret-Laferté (Turnhout: Brepols, 2004), 117. In fact Banda produced nutmeg rather than cloves. Niccolò said nutmeg came from an unidentifiable island called "Sondai." This information would be reproduced in the world map of Fra Mauro of

Venice, completed in 1459, Piero Falchetta, *Fra Mauro's World Map* (Turnhout: Brepols, 2006), 210, 305–7.

17. Janet L. Abu-Lughod, *Before European Hegemony: The World System, A.D. 1250–1350* (New York: Oxford University Press, 1989), 260–86.

18. Marco Polo, *Le devisement du monde*, ed. Jean-Claude Delcos and Claude Roussel, vol. 5 (Geneva: Droz, 2006), 129–30.

19. Gary K. Young, *Rome's Eastern Trade: International Commerce and Imperial Policy, 31 B.C.—A.D. 305* (London: Routledge, 2001), 27–89.

20. S. D. Goitein and Mordechai Akiva Friedman, *India Traders of the Middle Ages: Documents from the Cairo Geniza (India Book, Part One)* (Leiden: Brill, 2008). There are at least 26 records that mention spices, dated between 1097 and 1199.

21. *Traité d'Emmanuel Piloti sur le Passage en Terre Sainte (1420)*, ed. Pierre-Herman Dopp (Louvain and Paris: E. Nauwelaerts, 1958), especially 111–18. The date of the treatise is probably later, around 1440 according to Aline Durel, *L'imaginaire des épices: Itlaie médiévale, Orient lointain, XIVe-XVIe siècles* (Paris: L'Harmattan, 2006), 202.

22. Jack Turner, *Spice: The History of a Temptation* (New York: Knopf, 2004), 27.

23. David Bulbeck, et al., *Southeast Asian Exports Since the Fourteenth Century: Cloves, Pepper, Coffee, and Sugar* (Leiden: KITLV Press, 1998), 26.

24. Eliyahu Ashtor, "Profits from Trade with the Levant in the Fifteenth Century," *Bulletin of the School of Oriental and African Studies* 38 (1975): 265–67; reprint, *Studies on the Levantine Trade in the Middle Ages* (London: Variorum Reprints, 1978).

25. E. G. Ravenstein, *Martin Behaim, His Life and His Globe* (London: G. Philip & Son, 1908), 90.

26. Arnau de Vilanova, *Opera nuperrima revisa ...* (Lyon, 1520), folio 137ʳ, col. A; Eustache Deschamps, *Oeuvres complètes*, ed. Marquis de Queux de Saint-Hilaire and Gaston Raymond, vol. 7 (Paris: Fermin Didot, 1891), 88–90.

27. Eliyahu Ashtor, *Histoire des prix et des salaires dans l'Orient médiévasl* (Paris: S.E.V.P.E.N., 1969), 324–25.

28. Herman Van der Wee, *The Growth of the Antwerp Market and the European Economy (Fourteenth-Sixteenth Centuries)*, vol. 1 (Louvain: Nijhoff, 1963), appendix 26, 306–31.

29. Frederic Lane, "Pepper Prices Before Da Gama," *Journal of Economic History* 28 (1968): 590–97; Jeffrey G. Williamson and Kevin H. O'Rourke, "Did Vasco da Gama Matter for European Markets?" *Economic History Review* 62 (2009): 655–84.

30. Sanjay Subrahmanyam, *The Career and Legend of Vasco da Gama* (Cambridge: Cambridge University Press, 1997), 184.

31. John Munro, "The Consumption of Spices and Their Costs in Late-Medieval and Early-Modern Europe: Luxuries or Necessities?" Rev. 2005. [Online]. Available: http://www.economics.utoronto.ca/munro5/SPICES1.pdf. [February 9, 2011]. This lecture was revised from earlier talks given in 1983 and 1988 as noted on the first page of the latest version. See also the Munro's chart of spice prices and craftsmen's wages in *Silk Roads, China Ships: An Exhibition of East-West Trade* (Toronto: Royal Ontario Museum, 1983), 162.

Bibliography

Ashtor, Eliyahu. *East-West Trade in the Medieval Mediterranean*. London: Variorum Reprints, 1986.

Freedman, Paul. *Out of the East: Spices and the Medieval Imagination*. New Haven: Yale University Press, 2008.
Keay, John. *The Spice Route: A History*. Berkeley: University of California Press, 2006.
Krondl, Michael. *The Taste of Conquest: The Rise and Fall of the Three Great Cities of Spice*. New York: Ballantine Books, 2007.
Turner, Jack. *Spice: The History of a Temptation*. New York: Vintage, 2004.

CHAPTER 19

THE COLUMBIAN EXCHANGE

REBECCA EARLE

"BEFORE the Columbian Exchange, there were no oranges in Florida, no bananas in Ecuador, no paprika in Hungary, no tomatoes in Italy, no coffee in Colombia, no pineapples in Hawaii, no rubber trees in Africa, no cattle in Texas, no donkeys in Mexico, no chili peppers in Thailand and India, no cigarettes in France, and no chocolate in Switzerland."[1] Thus a well-known online encyclopedia summarizes the significance of the Columbian Exchange, the flow of plants, animals, and microbes across the Atlantic Ocean and beyond, set in motion by Columbus's arrival in the Americas in 1492. Clearly, a world untouched by the Columbian Exchange would look (and taste) very different from the world we know.

The term "Columbian Exchange" was coined in 1972 by the historian Alfred Crosby to designate the process of biological diffusion triggered by Europe's colonization of the Americas. Crosby's *The Columbian Exchange: Biological and Cultural Consequences of 1492* detailed the wide-ranging consequences of the transfer of diseases, plants, and animals that followed in the wake of 1492. The book, essentially a series of interlocking essays, examined the impact of old-world plants and animals on the Americas, the global dissemination of new-world foods, and the ways in which European colonization was entangled with the transmission of pathogens. Crosby traced the routes that introduced paprika to Hungary, horses to the Apache, and syphilis to unfortunate lovers, while at the same time championing the importance of attending to such exchanges. He argued forcefully that the most significant consequences of European colonization of the New World were biological in nature.

Early reactions to the book reveal that the novelty of Crosby's approach and the unfamiliar nature of his material posed challenges to readers. Struggling to process the counter-intuitive fact that the familiar potato is a native of South America, one reviewer asserted that Crosby had explained the process whereby Europeans introduced the potato to the Americas—although *The Columbian Exchange* makes clear that potatoes were an important *new-world* product.[2] This pardonable confusion indicates the depth of the botanical transformation wrought by European settlement of the Americas: foods that in the sixteenth century were exotic imports to Europe (not to mention North America) are now considered native to both regions. Such initial confusion notwithstanding, Crosby's insistence on the centrality of biological change to the history of European colonization has been widely accepted. Scholars are in accord that the Columbian Exchange altered global food systems in dramatic and unexpected ways. The manner in which these alterations occurred reflects the larger processes of European expansion and colonization in which the Columbian Exchange was embedded. At the same time, its impact also illustrates how these larger processes were refracted at the local level into the diets of individual people. Before discussing these matters, however, it will be useful to survey briefly the principal culinary actors in the Columbian Exchange's cast of characters.

Foods New and Old

Let us begin with the New World. For reasons to be discussed later in this essay, Crosby divided the New World's distinctive culinary offerings into two basic categories: starches and everything else. The most important new-world starches are maize, manioc, potato, and sweet potato. Indigenous cultures from the Hopi to the Incas were structured around the cultivation of these crops, which were the objects of religious veneration whose similarity to Christian ritual sometimes disconcerted European settlers.[3] Maize was grown in many parts of the Americas, where it was often processed into food through a distinctive and time-consuming process known as nixtamalization, whereby maize kernels are soaked in a solution of calcium carbonate prior to being ground into a soft paste. Nixtamalization greatly increases the nutritional value of maize, particularly when it is eaten in combination with complimentary proteins such as the kidney beans also native to the New World. Manioc, which flourishes in tropical and subtropical regions, comes in sweet and bitter varieties, the latter requiring complex processing to remove the poisonous juice it contains. Potatoes and the botanically unrelated sweet potatoes, together with a variety of other tubers, roots, and grains such as quinoa, rounded out the array of starchy carbohydrates that sustained indigenous communities both before and after 1492.

The Americas were also home to many vegetables that have subsequently assumed important positions in cuisines from Italy to India. Notable among these are the tomato, the chile pepper, and pumpkins and squashes of the genus

Cucurbita. Settlers also encountered a mouth-watering variety of fruits, which in tropical regions produced fruit with a frequency unknown in Europe. Spanish conquistadors rhapsodized about the delectable pineapples, guavas, cherimoyas, and avocados, whose flavor they proclaimed to be superior to those of all other fruits. And then there was cacao, from which Amerindians prepared a peculiar frothy beverage that constituted Western Europe's first encounter with caffeine. Settlers quickly developed a taste for the drink, whether flavored with the native vanilla pod or with sugar. For Mesoamerican cultures the drink represented not simply a refreshing and healthful beverage but a semi-sacred substance with its own attendant deities.[4]

The absence of meats from this list is notable. There were plenty of new-world animals unknown in the Old World, including vampire bats and jaguars, but other than the turkey, none acquired significance in terms of the post-Columbian Exchange diet. Even the guinea pig, widely eaten in the Andes, spread around the world not as a food but as a pet. In addition there were many other items eaten by Amerindians that settlers roundly rejected. Human flesh topped the list of such un-foods, which also included spiders, snakes, algae, and the little worms that grow in the agave cactus. Settlers found it surprising that Amerindians persisted in eating insects and algae even after Europeans had introduced their obviously superior foodstuffs, which were as intimately linked to European culture as were maize and cacao to the indigenous world.[5]

Most significant among European foodstuffs were wheat and wine. Since the days of the ancient Greeks wheat bread and wine had for Europeans been associated with civilization and health. In addition, Catholic doctrine declared that these were the only substances that through the mystery of transubstantiation could be transformed into the body and blood of Christ. Bread and wine thus represented and ensured both physical and spiritual health.[6] Spaniards accordingly planted wheat and vines everywhere they went, although to their chagrin these crops often failed to prosper.[7] Protestants such as the French Huguenots who voyaged to Brazil in the 1540s were happy to conduct the sacrament of communion using local substitutes such as manioc, but they too longed for the healthful and familiar taste of wheat bread.[8] Bread stood at the center of the culinary regimes of all Western European countries, and settlers relied upon it. When they landed in South America in the late eighteenth century the Spanish Franciscan Juan de Santa Gertrudis Serra and his companions were fêted with an abundance of stewed and roast fowl, plantains, manioc, sweet potatoes and maize cakes. Serra however recorded that he and his fellow Franciscans "did not know how to eat without bread."[9] A meal without bread was not a meal; "I realized," Serra wrote, "that bread was sustenance to those who were brought up on it." Serra's view was widely shared. Writing from Mexico in the late sixteenth century, Beatriz de Carvallar complained to her father back in Spain that her new homeland lacked proper bread. While she admitted that there were plenty of other tasty things, these did not, in her view, compensate for the central, fundamental problem of not having bread.[10] All the pineapples in the world could not make up for that.

In addition to sowing wheat and planting vines Spanish settlers also introduced many other old-world plants and animals to the Americas. Radishes, chickpeas, melons, cabbage, olive trees, and watercress were planted up and down the Indies, while from the 1490s conquistadors were leaving breeding pairs of cattle, horses, pigs, and goats on Caribbean islands (and later on the mainland) with the hope of populating them with livestock for future use. As a result, by the 1590s old-world oranges were growing in the Andes and Iberian sheep were beginning to reduce the landscape in parts of Mexico to barren stubble.[11]

Settlers undertook these measures not simply because they were nostalgic for the foods of home but also because they hoped that their usual diet would help protect them against the rigors of travel to an alien climate. The understanding of the human body common in early modern Europe accorded diet a pivotal importance in the maintenance of health.[12] Diet helped maintain the body's humors in their accustomed balance, and provided a powerful corrective to the destabilizing effects of travel and other disruptive changes. Familiar foods could also help cure the nostalgia that was acknowledged to afflict colonists, which many writers believed posed almost as much of a danger to travelers as did disease and an unfamiliar climate. Equally important, diet was, in the estimation of early settlers, the principal reason why Amerindians looked and behaved so differently from Spaniards. Amerindians, explained one Spanish doctor, "don't have the same humors as us because they don't eat the same foods."[13] Eating too much indigenous food was likely not only to induce illness but perhaps also to fill the European body with dangerous indigenous humors. European foods were thus doubly important to colonizers. They symbolized the central elements of the European culture that they hoped to reproduce, and they helped protect the European body against disease and disintegration. It was for this combination of reasons that settlers assiduously planted wheat, barley, radishes, and cabbage and introduced sheep and cattle into the new-world landscape.[14]

In addition to attempting in this way to "Europeanize" the American landscape—to use another of Crosby's terms—settlers also introduced a number of commercial crops and animals which radically transformed the history of the hemisphere.[15] Paramount among these are sugar and coffee. Sugar, a native of New Guinea, had long been known in Europe, but only with the acquisition of suitable American colonies were Europeans able to produce it on a semi-industrial scale through the use of slave labor. From the sixteenth to the early nineteenth century the Americas dominated world sugar production, helped by an amenable climate and an abundant supply of slaves. Europe's voracious demand for sugar fuelled the transatlantic slave trade, which dragged some ten million Africans to Brazil and the Caribbean, where they labored in the hellish environment of the new-world sugar plantation. Some indication of working conditions may be gleaned from the fact that the expected lifespan of a slave on a sugar plantation was about fifteen years. Not without reason did abolitionists proclaim that sugar was made with blood.[16]

Coffee, a native of Yemen, was cultivated from the eighteenth century in the Americas, where it was likewise grown as a commercial crop, initially using slave labor. During much of the eighteenth century world coffee production centered on the West Indies; by the 1780s the tiny French colony of Saint-Domingue was producing nearly half the world's coffee.[17] The Haitian Revolution of 1791–1804 which overthrew both French rule and slavery in Saint Domingue, marked the end of the Caribbean's primacy in coffee production. After the revolution, significant quantities of coffee were grown in the Caribbean only in Cuba, Puerto Rico, and Jamaica. By the mid-nineteenth century the spotlight had shifted to Brazil, which has subsequently dominated world production. In 1906, 82 percent of the world's coffee harvest came from Brazil, which continues to produce more coffee than its two nearest competitors combined.[18] "They've got an awful lot of coffee in Brazil," was the jaunty refrain of one song popular in the 1940s.[19] It was not simply that Brazil responded to an existing demand for coffee. Rather, as the historian Steven Topik has shown, Brazil helped create that demand "by producing enough coffee cheaply enough to make it affordable for members of North America's and Europe's working classes."[20] The global popularity of coffee is thus at least in part a consequence of the Columbian Exchange. In the Americas, coffee has left a complex legacy. Some scholars argue that, unlike sugar, the crop helped bring democracy and strong government to the region. Others insist that like sugar, it instead left a heritage of inequality and poverty.[21]

Rice was another old-world food introduced into the Americas as a commercial crop, again grown during its early history with unfree labor. The expertise that made commercial rice cultivation possible may have derived from the very enslaved people who waded through sodden rice fields of Georgia and the Carolinas planting seedlings. It has been argued that the technical knowledge behind rice cultivation in the Americas came from West Africa, which had a long tradition of growing rice. Although scholars continue to debate the precise role of enslaved Africans in creating commercial rice culture in the Americas, it is clear that the transfer of seeds or crops alone is only part of the story of the Columbian Exchange.[22] We need also to consider the associated systems of cultivation, processing, and preparation that support their consumption. Rice grains without the necessary agricultural expertise, like bitter manioc roots without the grating technique that removes the poisonous juice, are of only limited use. The introduction of maize to Africa and Europe without the attendant technology of nixtamalization illustrates well the fact that crops do not always travel together with these larger systems.

Enslaved Africans and their descendants also cultivated many other African food crops in the New World, from yams and black eyed peas to watermelon and plantains. These foods were grown in the provision grounds that slaves were sometimes able to maintain, in the gardens of maroon communities, and also on the lands of free blacks. The attempt to consider the contributions of subaltern groups such as slaves to the Columbian Exchange—Crosby focused largely on the actions of European elites and semi-elites—raises interesting methodological challenges, and the precise mechanisms that brought these plants to the New World remain sketchy. Nonetheless, as the geographer Judith Carney has shown, these crops formed part of a distinctive African culinary tradition even as they intermingled with new-world foods that were themselves being introduced to West Africa in the early modern era in large part as a result of the slave trade. Many Africans arriving in the Americas would thus already have been familiar with staples such as maize and manioc, which had been cultivated in West Africa from the sixteenth century.[23]

The bananas and plantains that were cultivated in provision grounds, and which had been introduced into the Americas in the early colonial era (the Spanish chronicler Gonzalo Fernández de Oviedo reported that uncounted numbers were growing in the Caribbean by the 1540s), came in due course to constitute another important commercial crop.[24] Beginning in the late nineteenth century, banana entrepreneurs, often from the United States, established commercial concerns that exported bananas from Central America and the circum-Caribbean to North American markets. In a number of cases these companies came to play an important political role that matched or overshadowed their economic role. The instrumentality of the United Fruit Company to the 1954 overthrow of President Jacobo Arbenz of Guatemala is well-established, and readers of the Colombian writer Gabriel García Márquez's *One Hundred Years of Solitude* will be familiar with the fictionalized account of a massacre carried out by a banana company on Colombia's Caribbean coast.[25] At the same time, the history of the banana in Latin America is not simply a tale of foreign domination and political intrigue. As is indicated above, bananas were and are eaten by a wide cross-section of the population; indeed most bananas grown in the Americas are not produced for export, but rather for domestic consumption.[26]

New-world ranching was a further consequence of the Colombian Exchange. Prior to the arrival of Europeans the Americas were home to many animals absolutely unknown in the Old World, but very few of these proved suitable for domestication as a source of either food or labor. Europeans not only introduced goats, sheep, pigs, cattle, horses, and mules, which in the absence of competition flourished to a degree that settlers found astounding, but also imported European traditions of animal husbandry and stock rearing. The result was vast hordes of cattle and horses that roamed the prairies from the Rockies to Río de la Plata, and made possible the world of the cowboy. The environmental consequences of this development were striking. As the historian Elinor Melville has shown, sheep quickly desiccated the landscape of highland central Mexico after their introduction in the sixteenth century, and cattle ranching contributed to deforestation in the Amazon.[27] Ranching had other destructive consequences. It generally competed with indigenous agriculture in an unequal struggle that resulted in the loss of much communally held village land. Moreover, herds tended to trample unfenced indigenous agricultural plots. Crosby indeed asserted that if the post-conquest American landscape were viewed from outer space it might look like an attempt to replace Amerindians with cattle.

Beyond foodstuffs the Columbian Exchange also introduced other things to the New World. Settlers to begin with brought many plants and animals that were not intended as foods. Horses, although edible, were employed primarily as a useful form of transport in a region entirely lacking in draft animals, and cattle were often raised for their hides rather than their meat. Nor were all imports intentional. Crosby placed particular emphasis on the role of disease in facilitating the Spanish conquest, and the spread of human pathogens between the Old and New World has undoubtedly been an important factor in the history of both regions. In addition, colonists inadvertently introduced many weeds and pests. Phylloxera and Dutch elm disease continued a process set in motion in 1492.

Such transfers, as well as the intimate connections between slavery and sugar cultivation, indicate the wide-ranging significance of the Columbian Exchange on the history of both the Old and New Worlds. In the Americas, in particular, the introduction of new diseases, together with export agriculture and ranching, had clear and dramatic effects on the lives of millions of people, as well as on the landscape. What, however, of the impact on global diets? The Columbian Exchange dramatically altered eating practices around the world. That process of transformation began with the many individual encounters between Europeans and Amerindians that followed Columbus's arrival in the Caribbean in 1492.

From Early Encounters to New World Cultural Nationalism

The earliest accounts of post-1492 new-world culinary encounters indicate that while hungry Europeans were resigned to eating indigenous foodstuffs when their own supplies gave out, Amerindians often responded to European food with suspicion. The chronicler Oviedo recorded many cases in which European explorers offered food to Amerindians, only to have it rejected. Describing one encounter between Joan de Areyzaga and some Patagonians, Oviedo reported that the Spanish "gave them very good food, fish and meat, but they did not want the bread, which those giants will not eat, nor did they want wine."[28] Spanish settlers were generally disappointed by the lack of enthusiasm with which indigenous people greeted their most prized foods. Settlers in Hispaniola complained that locals ate roots, "which they prefer to the foods that the Christians give them."[29] "They don't care at all for our bread," observed another astonished writer.[30] The Spanish, in contrast, were not always in a position to be so choosy, although they worried that too much indigenous food would prove dangerous. Hernando de Soto sustained himself in his trek across the U.S. south with maize cakes and scallions provided by local Indians.[31]

Both Europeans and Amerindians tried to make sense of the new foods they encountered by comparing them to more familiar foods. Spaniards routinely likened new-world fruits and vegetables to European ones, in an attempt to overcome their novelty. "Avocado is like a pear, guava is like an apple, pineapple is like a quince," explained one writer in the sixteenth century.[32] Amerindians did the same.

The Aztecs dubbed black pepper *caxtillan chilli*, or "Castile chile," while wheat was *castillan tlaolli* or *caxtillan centli*, "Castile maize." Carrots were *caxtillan camotli*, "Castile sweet potato." Almond trees were described as "a certain Castilian tree from which things resembling peanuts grow."[33] Language analysis indeed provides insights into both the reception and the global dissemination of these new foods. The terms for maize in various East African languages indicate that the grain must have arrived in that region by sea, while in Europe its exotic qualities were signaled by names such as *granoturco* [Turkish wheat] or *blé sarazin* [Saracen wheat] that associated it the Moors or Turks.[34] The important role played by the Portuguese in introducing new-world foodstuffs into India is similarly reflected etymologically. For instance, the name for pineapple in a number of Indian languages is "ananas," exactly as it is in Portuguese.[35]

The initial resistance with which Amerindians reportedly greeted European foods changed slowly. It is clear that in some cases indigenous people viewed European foodstuffs as part of the larger process of colonial oppression. Amerindians on the island of Cubagua cut down the orange trees planted in the garden of a Franciscan monastery during a rebellion, while the leaders of the 1680 Pueblo Revolt in New Mexico ordered their followers to "burn the seeds which the Spaniards sowed and to plant only maize and beans, which were the crops of our ancestors."[36] Nonetheless, many indigenous communities did come to embrace at least some elements of the European culinary repertoire. Reports from Peru indicate that as early as the 1580s Andean villages were growing European crops such as lettuce, cabbage, radishes, peas, onions, garlic, beans, mustard, and turnips.[37] Chickens and pigs, which did not trample maize fields to the same extent as cattle, were widely adopted, and colonists often complained that Amerindians were excessively fond of European alcohols.[38] Spaniards, in turn, incorporated all sorts of new tastes into their diets. In Spanish America chroniclers and travelers noted the widespread consumption by settlers of "*atole*, *pinole*, scalded plantains, butter of the *cacao*, puddings made of Indian maize, with a bit of fowl or fresh pork in them seasoned with much red biting chilli," and other local delicacies such as chocolate.[39] And from the 1570s sailors on ships returning from the Indies were sometimes provisioned with bread made from maize or cassava in place of the regulation hardtack, although they complained vociferously that it caused all manner of digestive disturbances.[40] English colonists in New England adapted their familiar steamed and boiled puddings to the use of maize meal, although like Spanish settlers they worried about the effects of prolonged consumption of Indian foods.[41] In addition to incorporating indigenous ingredients Europeans adopted many indigenous cooking techniques. Colonial recipe collections instruct the cook to grind spices on indigenous grindstones, cook meats on indigenous griddles and boil food until it "makes a sound like a cooked tamal."[42] At the same time, as in all parts of the world, in the colonial Americas diet also played an important role as a marker of status and caste. A taste for "Indian" foods such as guinea pig was a sure sign of low-status indigenous identity, and after the ending of colonial rule generations of policy-makers recommended that Amerindians be obliged to eat more "civilized" foods, so as to reduce their indigenousness and increase their overall level of culture. The process of culinary transformation that occurred in the centuries after 1492 took place in the context of hierarchical colonial and postcolonial power structures that valorized certain peoples and their foods, and disdained others.[43]

In the twentieth century the idea that during the colonial era European and indigenous culinary practices began to blend became a central element of nationalist mythology in many Latin American countries. While elite nineteenth-century nationalists often complained that Amerindians constituted a leaden weight on the emergent nation because they stubbornly refused to embrace such elements of "modernity" as individual landownership, by the early twentieth century Latin American nationalist ideology began to advance an image of the nation as a blend of European and indigenous (and to a lesser extent African) traditions.[44] Blended foods served as an effective symbol of blended nations. Nationalists in many different Latin American countries began to celebrate the unique culinary traditions that supposedly emerged in the colonial era, when cooks great and small combined old- and new-world ingredients in their own personal Columbian Exchanges. As the historians Jeffrey Pilcher and Rachel Laudan have shown, often these stories reveal a willful misunderstanding of the complexities of colonial history, but they nonetheless serve as powerful emblems of a vision of the nation as essentially mixed. "Mexican cooking is, as we ourselves are, the product of the joining of two peoples and two cultures," reads the preface to one Mexican cookbook.[45] In Mexico *mole poblano*, a poultry dish dressed with a complex savory sauce combining many spices as well as chocolate, is often hailed as a quintessentially Mexican dish precisely because it combines indigenous ingredients (turkey, chocolate, chiles) with European ones such as cumin and nuts, just as Mexico itself is a blend of European and indigenous cultures—Mexico's African heritage rarely figures significantly in such culinary metaphors. *Mole*, explained one Mexican writer, resulted from "a cultural process explained by geography, the economy, politics, and above all the formation of a new way of thinking. Cooking, as a mixture of all of these, became the source of the most transcendent phenomenon of the nineteenth century in Mexico: the birth of a nation."[46] Such hybrid foods are thus read within the language of nationalism as potent symbols of the nation itself. Many other Latin American countries have similarly iconic foods which are said in one way or another to reflect the ethnic and cultural *mestizaje* celebrated by contemporary nationalism. Culinary nationalism thus reverses Brillat-Savarin's dictum, to proclaim "we eat what we are."

New Diets for the Old World

New-world foods transformed the old-world diet. Tomatoes, potatoes, hot peppers, squashes and chocolate are now such integral components of the old-world diet that incredulity often greets the observation that these foodstuffs were introduced no more than five hundred years ago. Meals as varied as the British Christmas dinner and Indian *saag aloo* rely on new-world ingredients such as turkey, potatoes, and chiles for their characteristic taste and ingredients. Crosby provided extensive evidence of the culinary transformations wrought in the Old World by the Columbian Exchange, and it is difficult to think of a regional or national cuisine untouched by its effects.

The particular routes whereby these foods spread around the world are intimately connected to the history of European exploration and colonization. It was Portuguese traders who brought the chile pepper to the Indian subcontinent, where it came to form a central element of the flavor complexes of many of the region's cuisines. Indeed, chiles are now so deeply embedded in the subcontinent's diet that most possess names linking them to particular parts of India, rather than to their ancestral home in the Americas.[47] Most likely the Portuguese also introduced maize into West Africa, where it was used to provision slaving ships at the same time that it began to form a significant part of the local diet.[48] The chocolate habit spread across Europe in routes carved out by the Hapsburg dynasty; aristocrats in Austria used their connections in Spain to commission private shipments of cacao, and artisans in Madrid were drinking chocolate for breakfast at a time when it was still a luxury item in England.[49] Foods rarely travel independently of the larger forces that shape both global and local history. For example, although new-world foods were introduced into both China and India in the late sixteenth century, the histories of their subsequent cultivation in these two regions differ considerably, as the historian Sucheta Mazumdar has shown. In China crops such as sweet potatoes were quickly incorporated into the agricultural and culinary system, most probably because the heavy pressure on agricultural land led farmers to seek more intensive forms of cultivation and more efficient crops. In the Indian subcontinent, in contrast, the greater availability of agricultural land retarded their adoption until colonialism transformed landholding patterns.[50] In general, however, we know far more about the dissemination of new-world foods across Europe then we do about the equivalent processes in Asia and Africa, although a number of scholars have made important contributions to altering this situation.[51]

The depth of the changes that new-world foods wrought on the diet of Europeans, in particular, subtly modifies the observation by the distinguished historian John Elliott that European colonization of the New World provoked only limited interest among the inhabitants of early modern Europe. Elliott's "blunted impact" thesis emphasizes the muted response of savants outside the Iberian peninsula to the new vistas opened up in the west, which he shows did not result in any radical transformation of epistemologies.[52] Nonetheless, whatever the scholarly reaction to the existence of the New World, peasants in Ireland and the Veneto quickly adopted potatoes and maize as staple crops, perhaps because they recognized their superior calorific qualities. Although food historians sometimes claim that European peasantry was hopelessly conservative, and so refused to eat new foods until obliged to do so by visionary aristocrats, peasants were in fact no less interested in new food crops than were elites. The suspicion with which some European botanists greeted these new foods—the English herbalist John Gerard had described maize as "more convenient food for swine than for men"—was not matched by an equivalent disdain among the hungry poor.[53] Similarly, it was peasants, rather than elites, who were responsible for the incorporation of sweet potatoes and maize into the Chinese diet. Peasants embraced these new foods because they grew well, required far less labor than did rice, and are very calorific. This allowed land that had previously been used for subsistence farming to be devoted to the cultivation of cash crops, which in turn had dramatic effects on China's agricultural economy and population.[54]

Indeed, it is this latter aspect of the Columbian Exchange that Crosby singled out in the penultimate chapter of *The Columbian Exchange*. Crosby asserted that, notwithstanding the importance of the tomato to Italian cuisine and the hot pepper to Hungary, it was new-world starches that truly transformed world history. New-world carbohydrates such as maize, manioc, potatoes and sweet potatoes, he suggested, contributed to the tremendous demographic growth that has characterized global history over the last five hundred years. "Is there a connection between Christopher Columbus and the population explosion?" Crosby asked.[55] The answer, he concluded, was a cautious yes. New-world starches are certainly more calorific than those of the Old World—potatoes produce 7.5 million calories per hectare, whereas wheat produces only 4.2—and crops such as manioc adapt well to a range of growing conditions. Crosby reminded readers not only of the importance of the potato to Ireland but of the sweet potato to Japan and China, and maize and manioc to many parts of Africa. Now, as at the time Crosby wrote, the majority of the world's sweet potatoes are cultivated in China, not the Caribbean where they originated, and Nigeria produces more manioc than anywhere in the Americas. Calories derived from maize constitute a higher percentage of the national diet in Zambia than in Mexico or Guatemala.[56] Clearly these crops have integrated themselves into the food systems of many parts of the world. Other scholars have supported Crosby's contention that improved nutrition, resulting at least in part from the dissemination of new-world crops, is behind demographic growth, although this is by no means universally accepted as an explanation.[57] Indeed, the dissemination of new-world crops may in some cases have contributed as much to worsening health conditions as to improvements. When processed with lime using traditional Mesoamerican techniques maize is a nutritious foodstuff. When eaten without having been nixtamalized, however, it is deficient in niacin and people reliant on a diet of unnixtamalized maize are at risk of developing pellagra. Although maize spread across the world in the centuries after 1492, the time-consuming and apparently unnecessary process of nixtamalization did not travel with it, and so maize consumption in both Africa and Italy has been associated with pellagra. More recently, maize has come under attack not for its links to deficiency diseases but rather for its entanglement with agribusiness in the U.S., where it is cultivated on an industrial scale and makes its way into an astonishing number of processed foods.[58]

Legacies

Since its publication in 1972, Alfred Crosby's *Columbian Exchange* has continued to generate rich scholarship on the biological consequences of European colonial expansion. It is clear that our understanding of the age of exploration, and its colonial aftermath, must embrace the history of the biological exchanges these set in motion. It is moreover clear that the ramifications of these biological exchanges were far-reaching. Diets around the world altered dramatically in the centuries after 1492. Today the evidence of this transformation is almost limitless, ranging as it does from Bombay potatoes and vanilla ice cream to flour tortillas and the many varieties of fufu. Whether or not the spread of new-world cultigens contributed to the demographic growth that has characterized the last five hundred years, the Columbian Exchange has indubitably changed what people eat and constitutes an early example of the globalization that continues to the present day.

A thick history of the processes through which new-world foods were accepted, adopted or rejected in the Old World is still being written. It appears that sometimes new foods were accepted readily precisely because they resembled familiar foodstuffs; the speedy adoption of new-world beans in some parts of Europe is probably an example of this.[59] In other cases novelty seems to have been part of the appeal. Frothy, stimulating chocolate was not like anything Europeans had previously encountered, but Spanish settlers soon developed a taste for it, helped, perhaps, by its high status within indigenous cultures. Our understanding of the dynamics motivating these processes of adoption and rejection nonetheless remains in many cases rather sketchy. It is clear however that the older story of suspicious early modern Europeans mistrusting new-world foods is inadequate. Sweet potatoes were being grown, and eaten, in Spain by the late sixteenth century, at the same time that Venetians were embracing maize over millet. Seventeenth-century English recipe collections include nonchalant references to chocolate and potatoes, although it has often been claimed that until the eighteenth century most Europeans rejected potatoes because they believed them to be poisonous.[60] Early modern Europeans were not all the culinary troglodytes they have been depicted as being.

The intimate ties that link these dietary transformations to the history of colonialism should not be overlooked. More cacao is now cultivated in Africa than in its ancestral home of Mesoamerica because European colonists deliberately introduced the crop to that continent. Coffee was introduced into the Americas in a similar attempt to situate control over production more firmly in the hands of Western European colonial powers. The history of the Columbian Exchange is also entangled with that of slavery. The introduction of both African crops into the Americas and new-world foods into West Africa was driven largely by the transatlantic slave trade, which inadvertently "Africanized" new-world diets at the same time as it brought new foods to West Africa. As the historians Judith Carney and Nicholas Rosomoff have noted, "discussions of Columbian Exchange crop introductions to Africa thus should not be divorced from their role in enabling the commerce in human beings."[61] Clearly, the Columbian Exchange should not be viewed simply as a global recipe exchange.

In sum, the history of the Columbian Exchange must encompass both the excitement with which early European colonists tasted pineapples and the relentless labor of the new-world sugar plantation. It should include spicy stir-fried sweet potatoes and chicken paprikash, as well as that hybrid entity known as Mexican food. It is very unlikely that anyone reading this book has remained untouched by the changes first set in motion by the Columbian Exchange, which, as Crosby himself remarked, continue to make their effects felt in the present day.

Notes

1. "Columbian Exchange," Wikipedia [Online]. Available: http://en.wikipedia.org/wiki/Columbian_Exchange. [February 27, 2011].

2. Edward Barry, "Review of *The Columbian Exchange*," *American Historical Review* 80, no. 1 (1975): 67. Crosby's discussion of the origins of the potato was far from being the most innovative feature of *The Columbian Exchange*. See Redcliffe Salaman's *The History and Social Influence of the Potato* (Cambridge: Cambridge University Press, 1949).

3. For an introduction to the pre-conquest diet see Sophie Coe, *America's First Cuisines* (Austin: University of Texas Press, 1994).

4. Salaman, *The History and Social Influence of the Potato*; Betty Fussell, *The Story of Corn* (New York: Knopf, 1992); Nelson Foster and Linda S. Cordell, eds., *Chilies to Chocolate: Food the Americas Gave the World* (Tucson: University of Arizona Press, 1992); Janet Long, ed., *Conquista y comida. Consecuencias del encuentro de dos mundos* (Mexico City: Universidad Nacional Autónoma de México, 1997); Marcy Norton, *Sacred Gifts, Profane Pleasures: A History of Tobacco and Chocolate in the Atlantic World* (Ithaca, NY: Cornell University Press, 2008).

5. For guinea pigs see Edmundo Morales, *The Guinea Pig: Healing, Food and Ritual in the Andes* (Tucson: University of Arizona Press, 1995); Eduardo Archetti, *Guinea Pigs: Food, Symbol and Conflict of Knowledge in Ecuador* (Oxford: Oxford University Press, 1997).

6. Jean-Louis Flandrin, Massimo Montanari and Albert Sonnenfeld, eds., *Food: A Culinary History from Antiquity to the Present*, trans. Clarissa Botsford (New York: Columbia University Press, 1999); Thomas Aquinas, *Summa Theologica of St. Thomas Aquinas*, c.1265–74, trans. Fathers of the English Dominican Province, third part, question 74 [Online]. Available: http://www.newadvent.org/summa/. [February 27, 2011]; Miri Rubin, *Corpus Christi: The Eucharist in Late Medieval Culture* (Cambridge: Cambridge University Press, 1991), 37–49.

7. In addition, the Spanish crown periodically forbade the cultivation of vines so as to prevent competition with imported Peninsular wines. See for example Instrucciones al Marqués de Cañete, 1591, *Los virreyes españoles en América durante el gobierno de la casa de Austria*, ed. Lewis Hanke, 7 vols., Biblioteca de Autores Españoles vols. 280–86 (Madrid: Editorial Atlas, 1978), 1:274; Clarence Henry Haring, *Trade and Navigation between Spain and the Indies* (Gloucester: Peter Smith, 1964), 125.

8. Jean de Léry, *History of a Voyage to the Land of Brazil*, trans. and ed. Janet Whatley (Berkeley: University of California Press, 1992 [1580]), 49 (chap. 6).

9. Fray Juan de Santa Gertrudis Serra, *Maravillas de la naturaleza*, 2 vols. (c.1771; reprint: Bogotá: Empresa Nacional de Publicaciones, 1956), vol. 1, chapter 3. Biblioteca

Luis Angel Arango Virtual [Online]. Available: http://www.lablaa.org/blaavirtual/faunayflora/mara/indice.htm. [February 27, 2011].

10. Beatriz de Carvallar to Lorenzo Martínez de Carvallar, Mexico, March 10, 1574, *Cartas privadas de emigrantes a Indias, 1540–1616*, ed. Enrique Otte (Mexico City: Fondo de Cultura Económica, 1996), 85.

11. Elinor G. K. Melville, *A Plague of Sheep: Environmental Consequences of the Conquest of Mexico* (Cambridge: Cambridge University Press, 1994); William Dunmire, *Gardens of New Spain: How Mediterranean Plants and Foods Changed America* (Austin: University of Texas Press, 2004).

12. Ken Albala, *Eating Right in the Renaissance* (Berkeley: University of California Press, 2002); Carmen Peña and Fernando Girón, *La prevención de la enfermedad en la España bajo medieval* (Granada: Universidad de Granada, 2006).

13. Pedrarias de Benavídez, *Secretos de chirurgia, especial de las enfermedades de morbo gallico y lamparones y mirrarchia* (Valladolid, 1567), 26–7.

14. Rebecca Earle, "'If You Eat Their Food . . . ': Diets and Bodies in Early Colonial Spanish America," *American Historical Review* 115, no. 3 (2010): 688–713.

15. Alfred Crosby, *Ecological Imperialism: The Biological Expansion of Europe, 900–1900* (Cambridge: Canto, 1986).

16. Richard Dunn, *Sugar and Slaves: The Rise of the Planter Class in the English West Indies, 1624–1713* (New York: W.W. Norton, 1972); Sidney W. Mintz, *Sweetness and Power: The Place of Sugar in Modern History* (New York: Viking Books, 1985); Stuart Schwartz, "Plantations and Peripheries," in *Colonial Brazil*, ed. Leslie Bethell (Cambridge: Cambridge University Press, 1987), 67–144.

17. Steven Topik, "Coffee," in *The Second Conquest of Latin America: Coffee, Henequen and Oil during the Export Boom, 1850–1930*, ed. Steven Topik and Allan Wells (Austin: University of Texas Press, 1998), 41.

18. Steven Topik, "Where is the Coffee? Coffee and Brazilian Identity," *Luso-Brazilian Review* 36, no. 2 (1999): 87.

19. "The Coffee Song" (Lyrics: Bob Hilliard/Music: Dick Miles), 1946.

20. Topik, "Coffee," 62.

21. See for example Charles Bergquist, *Coffee and Conflict in Colombia, 1886–1910* (Durham: Duke University Press, 1978); William Roseberry, Lowell Gudmundson, and Mario Samper, eds., *Coffee, Society and Power in Latin America* (Baltimore: Johns Hopkins Press, 1995).

22. For the "black rice" debate see Judith Carney, *Black Rice: The African Origins of Rice Cultivation in the Americas* (Cambridge, MA: Harvard University Press, 2001); David Eltis, Philip Morgan, and David Richardson, "Agency and Diaspora in Atlantic History: Reassessing the African Contribution to Rice Cultivation in the Americas," *American Historical Review* 112, no. 5 (2007): 1329–58; "*AHR* Exchange: The Question of Black Rice," *American Historical Review* 115, no. 1 (2010): 123–71.

23. Judith Carney and Richard Rosomoff, *In the Shadow of Slavery: Africa's Botanical Legacy in the Atlantic World* (Berkeley: University of California Press, 2009).

24. Gonzalo Fernández de Oviedo, *Historia general y natural de las Indias*, ed. Juan Pérez de Tudela Bueso, 5 vols., Biblioteca de Autores Españoles 117–121 (1535–1557; reprint: Madrid: Editorial Atlas, 1959), 1:248 (book 8, chap. 1).

25. Stephen Schlesinger and Stephen Kinzer, *Bitter Fruit: The Untold Story of the American Coup in Guatemala* (New York: Anchor, 1982); Walter LaFeber, *Inevitable Revolutions: The United States in Central America* (New York: W.W. Norton, 1984); Gabriel García Márquez, *One Hundred Years of Solitude*, trans. Gregory Rabassa (London: Picador, 1970).

26. Mark Moberg and Steve Striffler, "Introduction," in *Banana Wars: Power, Production and History in the Americas*, ed. Steve Striffler and Mark Moberg (Durham: Duke University Press, 2003), 9.

27. Jeremy Rifkin, *Beyond Beef: the Rise and Fall of the Cattle Culture* (New York: Plume, 1993); Melville, *A Plague of Sheep*; Richard Tucker, *Insatiable Appetite: The United States and the Ecological Degradation of the Tropical World* (Lanham, MD: Rowman and Littlefield, 2007).

28. Fernández de Oviedo, *Historia general y natural*, 2:248 (book 20, chap. 8).

29. "Interrogatorio Jeronimiano" (1517), in *Los dominicos y las encomiendas de indios de la isla Española*, ed. Emilio Rodríguez Demorizi (Santo Domingo: Academia Dominicana de la Historia, 1971), 298.

30. Juan Botero Benes, *Relaciones universales*, trans. Diego de Aguiar (Valladolid, 1603), 134 (part 1, book 4).

31. Fernández de Oviedo, *Historia general y natural*, 2:164 (book 17, chap. 25).

32. Juan López de Velasco, *Geografía y descripción universal de las Indias*, ed. Cesáreo Fernández-Duro (c. 1574; repr., Madrid, 1894); "De los arboles de las Indias," Biblioteca Luis Angel Arango Virtual [Online]. Available: http://www.lablaa.org/bibliotecavirtual.htm. [January 5, 2012].

33. James Lockhart, *The Nahuas after the Spanish Conquest: A Social and Cultural History of the Indians of Central Mexico, Sixteenth through Eighteenth Centuries* (Stanford: Stanford University Press, 1992), 276; *Vocabulario trilingüe, castellano, latino y mexicano*, Newberry Library, Ayer ms. 1478; Mary Clayton, personal communications, July 2007 and May 2010.

34. James McCann, *Maize and Grace: Africa's Encounter with a New World Crop, 1500–2000* (Cambridge, MA: Harvard University Press, 2005), 33–34; Stanley Brandes, "Maize as a Culinary Mystery," *Ethnology* 31, no. 4 (1992): 331–36.

35. Sucheta Mazumdar, "The Impact of New World Food Crops on the Diet and Economy of China and India, 1600–1900," in *Food in Global History*, ed. Raymond Grew (Boulder, CO: Westview Press, 1999), 60.

36. Fernández de Oviedo, *Historia general y natural*, 2:196 (book 19, chap. 3); Ramón Gutiérrez, *When Jesus Came, the Corn Mothers Went Away: Marriage, Sexuality, and Power in New Mexico, 1500–1846* (Stanford: Stanford University Press, 1991), 136. Thanks to Deborah Toner for this latter reference.

37. "Descripción que se hizo en la Provincia de Xauxa por la Instrucción de S.M.," 1582, in *Relaciones geográficas de las Indias: Perú*, ed. Marcos Jiménez de la Espada, 3 vols., Biblioteca de Autores Españoles 183–185 (Madrid: Editorial Atlas, 1965), 1:171.

38. Fernández de Oviedo, *Historia general y natural*, 2:373, 382 (book 23, chaps. 12, 15); Diego de Landa, *Relación de las cosas de Yucatán*, ed. Angel María Garibay (1574; reprint: Mexico City: Editorial Porrua, 1973), 57, 133; Bernardo de Vargas Machuca, "Descripción breve de todas las Indias occidentales," *Milicia y descripción de las Indias*, 2 vols. (1599; repr., Madrid, 1892), 2:92; Rebecca Earle, "Algunos pensamientos sobre 'el indio borracho' en el imaginario criollo," *Revista de Estudios Sociales* 29 (2008): 18–27.

39. Thomas Gage, *The English-American: A New Survey of the West Indies, 1648*, ed. A. P. Newton (Guatemala City: El Patio, 1946), 197–8. *Pinole* is a mixture of maize and cacao, while *atole* is a maize porridge.

40. John Super, "Spanish Diet in the Atlantic Crossing, the 1570s," *Terra Incognitae* 16 (1984): 60–63.

41. For anxieties see for example Joyce Chaplin, "Natural Philosophy and an Early Racial Idiom in North America: Comparing English and Indian Bodies," *William and Mary Quarterly*, 3rd series, 54, no. 1 (1997): 229–252.

42. Anon., *Recetario novohispano, México, siglo XVIII*, prologue Elisa Vargas Lugo (Mexico City: Conaculta, 2004), 14, 39, 44, 45, 47, 51, 50 (for quote), 52, 55, 60.

43. Jeffrey Pilcher, *¡Que vivan los tamales! Food and the Making of Mexican Identity* (Albuquerque: University of New Mexico Press, 1998).

44. Marilyn Miller, *The Rise and Fall of the Cosmic Race: The Cult of Mestizaje in Latin America* (Austin: University of Texas Press, 2004).

45. Quote from Ana M. de Benítez, *Pre-Hispanic Cooking/Cocina prehispánica* (Mexico City: Ediciones Euroamericanas, 1974), 7; Jeffrey Pilcher and Rachel Laudan, "Chiles, Chocolate, and Race in New Spain: Glancing Backward to Spain or Looking Forward to Mexico?," *Eighteenth-Century Life* 23 (1999): 59–70.

46. Lorenzo Luna cited in Boris Berenzon Gorn, "Historia y cocina: las fronteras de lo efímero", in *Historia y universidad: Homenaje a Lorenzo Mario Luna*, ed. Enrique González González (Mexico City: Universidad Nacional Autónoma de México, 1996), 252.

47. I am grateful to Shirin Rai for advice about Hindi and Tamil names for chile.

48. Lizzie Collingham, *Curry: A Biography of a Dish* (London: Chatto and Windus, 2005); McCann, *Maize and Grace.*

49. Bianca Lindorfer, "Discovering Taste: Spain, Austria, and the Spread of Chocolate Consumption Among the Austrian Aristocracy, 1650–1700," *Food and History* 7, no. 1 (2010): 35–52; Irene Fattacciu, "Cacao: From an Exotic Curiosity to a Spanish Commodity. The Diffusion of New Patterns of Consumption in Eighteenth-century Spain," *Food and History* 7, no. 1 (2010): 53–78.

50. Mazumdar, "The Impact of New World Food Crops," 58–78.

51. Ibid; McCann, *Maize and Grace*; Carney and Rosomoff, *In the Shadow of Slavery.*

52. John Elliott, "Renaissance Europe and America: A Blunted Impact?," in *First Images of America: The Impact of the New World on the Old*, ed. Fredi Chiappelli, 2 vols. (Berkeley: University of California Press, 1976), 1:11–23.

53. John Gerard, *The Herbal or General History of Plants. The Complete 1633 Edition as Revised and Enlarged by Thomas Johnson* (New York: Dover, 1975), 82–83.

54. Mazumdar, "The Impact of New World Food Crops," 58–78.

55. Crosby, *The Columbian Exchange*, 166.

56. "Food and Agricultural Commodities Production," Food and Agriculture Organisation of the United Nations. [Online]. Available: http://faostat.fao.org/site/339/default.aspx. [February 27, 2011]; McCann, *Maize and Grace*, 9.

57. Massimo Livi-Bacci, *A Concise History of World Population* (Oxford: Blackwell, 2007), 67–69.

58. Daphne Roe, *A Plague of Corn: The Social History of Pellagra* (Ithaca, NY: Cornell University Press, 1973); Michael Pollan, *An Omnivore's Dilemma: A Natural History of Four Meals* (London: Penguin, 2006).

59. Ken Albala, *Beans: A History* (Oxford: Berg, 2007).

60. Francisco Nuñez de Oria, *Regimiento y aviso de sanidad, que trata de todos los generos de alimentos y del regimiento della* (Medina del Campo, 1586), 43r; José de Acosta, *Natural and Moral History of the Indies*, trans. Frances López-Morillas (1590; reprint: Durham: Duke University Press, 2002), 202; Nicholas Monardes, *Joyfull News out of the New-found Worlde* (London: E. Allde, 1596), 104; Antonio Regueiro y González-Barros, "La flora americana en la España del siglo XVI," in *América y la España del siglo XVI*, ed. Francisco de Solano and Fermín del Pino, 2 vols. (Madrid: Consejo Superior de Investigaciones Científicas, 1982), 1:209; Sara Pennell, "Recipes and Reception: Tracking

'New World' Foodstuffs in Early Modern British Culinary Texts, c. 1650–1750," *Food and History* 7, no. 1 (2010): 11–34.

61. Carney and Rosomoff, *In the Shadow of Slavery*, 57.

Bibliography

Carney, Judith, and Richard Rosomoff. *In the Shadow of Slavery: Africa's Botanical Legacy in the Atlantic World.* Berkeley: University of California Press, 2009.

Crosby, Alfred W, Jr. *The Columbian Exchange: Biological and Cultural Consequences of 1492.* Westport, CT: Greenwood Press, 1972.

Earle, Rebecca. "'If You Eat Their Food . . . ': Diets and Bodies in Early Colonial Spanish America." *American Historical Review* 115, no. 3 (2010): 688–713.

Foster, Nelson, and Linda S. Cordell, eds. *Chilies to Chocolate: Food the Americas Gave the World.* Tucson: University of Arizona Press, 1992.

Long, Janet, ed. *Conquista y comida. Consecuencias del encuentro de dos mundos.* Mexico City: Universidad Nacional Autónoma de México, 1997.

Mazumdar, Sucheta. "The Impact of New World Food Crops on the Diet and Economy of China and India, 1600–1900." In *Food in Global History*, edited by Raymond Grew, 58–78. Boulder, CO: Westview Press, 1999.

McCann, James. *Maize and Grace: Africa's Encounter with a New World Crop, 1500–2000.* Cambridge, MA: Harvard University Press, 2005.

Melville, Elinor. *A Plague of Sheep: Environmental Consequences of the Conquest of Mexico.* Cambridge: Cambridge University Press, 1994.

Norton, Marcy. *Sacred Gifts, Profane Pleasures: A History of Tobacco and Chocolate in the Atlantic World.* Ithaca, NY: Cornell University Press, 2008.

Pilcher, Jeffrey M. *¡Que vivan los tamales! Food and the Making of Mexican Identity.* Albuquerque: University of New Mexico Press, 1998.

Salaman, Redcliffe. *The History and Social Influence of the Potato*, Cambridge: Cambridge University Press, 1949.

Warman, Arturo. *Corn and Capitalism: How a Botanical Bastard Grew to Global Dominance.* Translated by Nancy Westrate. Chapel Hill: University of North Carolina Press, 2003.

CHAPTER 20

FOOD, TIME, AND HISTORY

ELIAS MANDALA

> [T]ime's arrow and time's cycle is, if you will, a great dichotomy because each of its poles captures, by its essence, a theme so central to intellectual (and practical) life that Western people who hope to understand history must wrestle intimately with both—for time's arrow is the intelligibility of distinct and irreversible events, while time's cycle is the intelligibility of timeless order and lawlike structure. We must have both.
>
> —Stephen J. Gould, *Time's Arrow Time's Cycle*[1]

WHEN peasants in rural Malawi speak of food, they are not only concerned about its availability, but also about its role in connecting people. Villagers interact with one another in different ways as they select the seeds, plant them, weed the young plants and protect them from marauding animals and birds, harvest their crops, and store them; and women pound the grain to make flour for a meal, which, with beer, can also feed the spirits in a ritual meal. Food acquires varying social identities on its journey from the field to the table, and at each point it connects members of the community in different ways.[2] In the African countryside, food has a social biography.

This social biography is both cyclical and linear. It is linear since a planted seed goes through increasing degrees of maturity before reaching a digestible state. But the same movement is also cyclical from the viewpoint of the farmer. At each stage of the plant's life, a peasant engages in orderly practices that she has learned and practiced many times before as a member of the community. Thus, although villagers are fully aware of the linear movement of the crop, in their debates about food they highlight the cyclical. And the two dominant principles of sharing food in rural Malawi also privilege order and the repetitive. The first, the "golden-age" theory, rests on the ideal that every member of the community deserves access to food, and the second, the "alternative vision," highlights the limited nature of those rights.

Both the alternative vision and the golden-age theory fall within what the geologist, paleontologist, and zoologist Stephen J. Gould of Harvard University called "time's cycle" or "the intelligibility of timeless order and lawlike structure."[3] As aspects of time's cycle, the golden-age theory and the alternative vision address the problem of order and represent peasants' collective protest against what Mircea Eliade, the historian of religion, philosopher, and professor at the University of Chicago, appropriately called the "terror of history"—here, of terrifying events like famine.[4] Both theories are about orderly and the more routine aspects of social life, including seasons, abundance and hunger.

The old Mang'anja of Malawi referred to seasonal hunger as *njala* in distinction from *chaola* or famine, a one-time event. Drought may precipitate, but it does not cause, *chaola*. Drought only becomes famine in the context of a political crisis that disables key elements of the preventive (or limiting) scheme, as during the slave raids of the early 1860s and the transition to British rule in the first part of the twentieth century. However, to understand this terror of history, one has to take account of the underpinning daily and seasonal routines. To write the history of a Malawi food system is to tell a story that is both cumulative and repetitive; a story about irreversible change and about days and seasons.

The Season

Malawi has three seasons: the cold and dry *(masika)*, hot and dry *(chilimwe)*, and rainy or wet *(dzinja)*, running from May to August, September to November, and December to April respectively. These are the naturally constituted divisions of the year, but from an economic, sociological, and political point of view, the year only has two significant periods: the cold and dry and rainy or wet seasons. There is little or no agricultural activity on the main fields on drylands during the hot and dry season, when men would typically repair their houses and granaries while women would make pots and plaster their houses. The dry season is also the time of communal fishing, hunting, and preparatory work on the drylands and, wherever possible, some farming on the floodplains. Then comes the rainy or wet season, which is a period of generalized hunger *(njala)* and hard work in the main fields on the drylands. As their plants progress toward maturity, peasants repeat the sowing and weeding processes most of them had done many other times before.

A household's ties to the village community contract during the rainy season. Farming in Malawi is, for all practical purposes, a household-based enterprise, with the larger community appearing only intermittently during such operations as field preparation. But the household itself becomes internally divided as the community takes a back seat. Most procedures in the field separated the able-bodied members from the young, aged, and the infirm. As the stronger members head for the fields, those not physically fit for cultivation remain in the village. Cultivation, which confirms a household's rights to land, divides and isolates this unit of production.

As they work in their fields, villagers recreate the natural world in its diversity. Whenever possible, peasants maintain several fields in different ecological zones. Under the universal African intercropping regime, they plant different crops in the same field and at the same time. Villagers also stagger the planting process, sowing different crops or different varieties of the same crop at different moments during the same growing season. An ideal peasant field in fact replicates the natural landscape, with different plants in different stages of growth.[5]

By cultivating different fields, mixing crops of differing properties, and by staggering the sowing process, villagers simultaneously assume and avoid risk. Samuel Popkin and James Scott, separately, simplified reality in their claims that peasants can only be rational actors and risk-takers or moral actors who systematically avoid risk.[6] Peasants are social actors like the interpreters themselves. Like members of other social classes, peasants both assume and avoid risk, depending on the context. Their risk-avoiding and risk-taking strategies are as subject to historical context as are their experiences of hunger, another major theme of the rainy growing season.

Villagers treat *chaola* or famine as a subset of the larger phenomenon of food deficits, and seasonal hunger *(njala)* as another. Moreover, while famine is catastrophic and irreversible, *njala* is not. *Njala* belongs to cyclical time, revisiting poor households every rainy season.[7]

Every year, a large segment of the rural poor suffers a food gap, especially during the month or so before the new harvest. Daily routines change. Instead of two or three meals, poor households often survive on one meal a day. These meals are made from less nutritious or culturally less desirable foods.[8] The deficits tend to strengthen people's ties with relatives located in distant, food-surplus areas to the same extent that they strain a household's relations with its immediate neighbors. People find it difficult to share food procured in distant places with neighbors. The rainy season puts the golden-age theory on trial. Inter-household suspicions and tensions place in jeopardy the more vulnerable members of the community, particularly non-working elders and the young. The death rate among children under the age of five tends to soar during the rainy season in rural Africa while the elderly face their own challenges.

Hungry, non-working elders often become victims of violence and harassment within the family. Seasonal hunger undermines their position as custodians of agricultural expertise because they do not take an active role in the ongoing struggles for survival. They become a burden, and a dangerous burden, when children begin to die. Instead of producing food, elders "eat" future producers; in rural Malawi thought, they are witches, who do not deserve to live. This dark and ugly side of the peasant world becomes especially obvious when economic distress exacerbates seasonal hunger, as during the Great Depression of the early 1930s. In a powerful reminder of the slave raids of the 1860s, elderly men and women of the Great Depression lost the protection of their children, wandering between Malawi and Mozambique. Many died in the search for food and shelter.[9]

While seasonal hunger or *njala* may be a new phenomenon in some communities, in others it predates Africa's incorporation into the world economy. Moreover, it remains impossible to tell whether scarcity has become more or less acute in such communities. It is difficult to settle the question because while some of the new developments have exacerbated *njala*'s impact, others, like access to new food markets, have softened its edges. The important point though is that regardless of the many shifts in its economic context, seasonal hunger remains for many households a predictable event. Villagers trapped in this form of hunger cannot hope to break the cycle; *njala* is a conservative force. It strains but does not subvert the rules of sharing as famine does. *Njala* instead creates future disasters while allowing its victims to cope with the present. Not only are hungry peasants less effective workers, but some mechanisms they employ to survive *njala*, like working in other people's fields for food, take them away from their own fields. A garden full of weeds this year guarantees the return of *njala* next season. Only radical change in rural technology and, especially, in peasant-state relations can break the cycle of *njala*. The histories of India, South Africa and Zimbabwe show how it is easier to end *chaola* famine than to eradicate *njala*; *njala* is a more stubborn and endemic form of hunger than the news-making famine.

Turning attention from *chaola* to *njala* makes one realize that Africa's food experiences are not as unique as they look under the lens of famine. While the West and parts of the Third World have effectively conquered *chaola* famine, structural hunger remains the experience of the poor in every class society. Preharvest shortages among poor villagers in the Third World are as much driven by inequality as is the endemic hunger of low-income earners in the developed First World. Everywhere low-wage earners scale down their standards of living toward the end of each pay period. While famine exaggerates Africa's otherness, *njala* draws attention to the common destiny of the poor in all class societies. Moreover, the fact that they go hungry while others have full stomachs highlights the need to treat scarcity as the flip side of plenty. This coexistence is as true today as it was in the pre-colonial era. Then, as now, villagers endure the horrors of scarcity as social and thinking actors, fully aware of the abundance other social classes enjoy even at the height of the hunger, as well as during the generalized plenty of the harvest season.

With their granaries full after harvest, villagers turn the harvest season into a time for rebuilding relationships weakened by *njala* and teaching order to the new generation in major rites of passage, particularly those of puberty and the ceremonies held for a person about nine months after his or her death. Moreover, cooking and brewing beer for these celebrations provide a forum for women to collectively retool their expertise as food processors. Cooked food reassembles and reenergizes the community without regard to age, sex, or social status. Villagers in Malawi believe that the spirits of the dead join the community of the living in the generalized merriment, eating and drinking their own specially prepared foods and drinks. Food is not only about filling the stomach. It is also about nourishing social relationships and about connecting the living with the dead. This is the final stage in food's long journey and at this point it loses its purely physical attributes; it becomes holy nourishment. The golden-age theory finds its fullest expression in these ritual meals. But as true reflections of social reality, the festivities also solemnize inequality and the structural conflict between social juniors—on the move from being "animals" to various gradations of "humanness"—and their social elders and earthly representatives of the departed spirits. The harvest season reconstitutes and provides the community the social and ideological energies for its self-reproduction on a daily basis. The daily meal stands at the core of these routines, routines that need to be understood in their own right.

The Day

It is possible to use moments of extreme want as a window to the everyday; moments of dire need can illuminate daily structures. In poor households, for example, seasonal hunger does heighten underlying tension between the able-bodied and past or future workers. Some issues that barely catch the eye in good times do indeed become visible in moments of hardship. It would, however, be simplistic to assume that knowledge of the unique will always illuminate the routine.[10] Extraordinary events shed light on some, but not all, aspects of the routine, and they do so from a particular angle. Peasants would, in particular, remind the researcher of the stories about the countrywide famine of 1921–1923. Like the one before it in 1861–1863, this *chaola* transformed the struggle for survival so broadly as to make all sorts of food the focus of conflict, including plants from the bush. But because villagers do not ordinarily fight for such plants, exclusive reliance on famine as a window to the everyday would be misleading; it could lead scholars to view the extraordinary events of the moment as part of the everyday. It is therefore important to understand daily routines like eating in their own right.

Eating is of course a supra-seasonal activity, whose organization is never left to chance or the idiosyncrasies of individual actors. When an adult peasant woman in rural Malawi wakes up in the morning, she knows, with the certainty of death, that she will prepare and cook food that day. Peasants do not inhabit a world in which they can pull from cupboards and refrigerators pre-boiled rice, tinned vegetables, instant cereals, or cooked food. Women process everything before it reaches an edible state. Every day, peasant women organize their day around the preparation of the daily meal, which is the most inclusive of activities, bringing together every member of the community regardless of their role in production. Around cooked food, the able-bodied meet both future and past workers as equals.

A standard eating group in rural Malawi would have two sections, one consisting of men and teenage boys and the other of women, girls of all ages, and children under the age of five of both sexes. One component of their meal is stiff porridge (*nsima*), made with the flour of maize, millet, sorghum, or cassava. Boiled or roasted cassava and sweet potatoes sometimes substitute for porridge. In relation to the carbohydrate-delivering porridge or its substitutes, everyone is equal. There are no discriminatory rules guiding the distribution of this component of the meal. If there are any, it is the principle that gives each according to their needs and, perhaps, the dexterity involved in seizing and swallowing a morsel from the undivided mound of porridge. Porridge (or its substitutes) is the salient if unspoken target of the golden-age theory's declaration that every member of the community has an inalienable right to food. As one Chewa proverb affirms, everyone "has a right to that which is in the pot."[11]

The golden-age theory gives way to the alternative vision in the distribution of the second component of the daily meal: *ndiwo* (the American "stew," English "relish," or academics' "side dish"), the protein-deliverer. Three principles guide the unequal distribution of *ndiwo* between adult males, on the one hand, and women and the young, on the other. The first bars women from certain types of *ndiwo*, although the list of such foods is short if not nonexistent nowadays. The second places *ndiwo* relishes in different grades, starting with the meat group on top, and followed in a descending order by fish, vegetables, and simple salt. Villagers expect women and children to eat the lower grades in the event the more desirable type of *ndiwo* cannot feed everyone. The third and probably most pervasive form of differentiation categorizes some parts of fish and meat as distinctively "female" and others as "male." Thus, according to elderly women, the outspoken explicators of this practice (in keeping with an old Malawian adage that "only those on the rough edges of society can remember its evils"[12]), every meal becomes "feast" for men and elders with their established rights to better portions of *ndiwo*, and "famine" for the women and children without those same rights. The old Chewa-speaking peoples of Malawi condensed the alternative vision in the proverb that "The joys of being a community come to an end when you have to share the *ndiwo*."[13] "Feast" and "famine" can coexist and conflict is inherent in every meal regardless of its form.

The hierarchical alternative vision is used to regulate ndiwo distribution in both the single-household and the communal meals *(chidyerano)*. Almost coterminous with the unit of production, the single-household meal featured a wife, her husband, and dependent children. Outsiders joined this group mostly as kin or dependents of the wife or husband. By contrast, the communal meal, which is no longer practiced nowadays, brought together for the purpose of eating several independent households primarily on the basis of neighborhood. Kinship was a secondary determinant. Under some communal arrangements, one participating household brought to the table one meal for everyone to eat; under others, all households cooked something for the common meal. The communal meal not only protected poor families but it also brought greater variety to the meal than the single-household eating plans, which are notorious for the monotony of their porridge ingredients.

Today, villagers locate the origins of the communal meal in times of plenty as well as in times of hunger. Both moments encourage sharing, one because there is so much food to go around and the other because there is so little. Peasants also hold two views about the end of the nutritionally richer communal meal. According to golden-age theorists, the single-household meal has become the dominant regime as a result of long-term, structural deterioration in the food supply. There is no communal meal today because there is not enough food to go around. Women politely disagree, bringing up conflict over the *ndiwo* as the root cause.[14] The communal meal comes to an end when, they argue, some households eat alone inside their houses the more desirable kinds of *ndiwo*, bringing to the common table only the less desirable. When other households discover this, they retaliate and place the communal meal at risk. The *ndiwo* holds an important key to understanding structural conflicts between and within households.

It is not difficult to see why the *ndiwo* relish, rather than porridge, should stand at the center of conflict. On the one hand, relish gives any meal its distinctive character, and on the other, it is the more variable element with its ingredients varying according to seasons and location. Moreover, unlike the ingredients of porridge, most items forming *ndiwo* are perishable; it is the scarcer resource. Peasants have to be continuously creative to provide stew for their families.

The fact that married women are the primary providers of *ndiwo* on a daily basis brings up interesting research questions for the historian of food. One needs to know for example, how men, who were never in the kitchen, were able to enforce the ideals of the alternative vision on a daily basis. One answer I would hazard is that they relied on custom and, by inference, on women as the principal transmitters of tradition from one to another generation of women. And the system worked because the female accomplices in oppressing women were not ordinary women. They were elders, enjoying some of the privileges of their male counterparts. Like their crops, people too changed their social identities with time. Having become "men," female elders were friends of order vis-à-vis the younger generation, the internal enemies of order.

During the past hundred years, the internal enemies of order have received new allies in the form of Christianity, western education, and in general, the faceless but powerful force they call money. The history of Malawi shows how these external enemies of order have strengthened the hand of the internal enemies. The alliance has transformed and weakened the old ways of teaching order. As a result, many young wives today are not conversant with nor practice the oppressive charter regulating the *ndiwo*. For the most part, the alternative vision today survives mostly as a guide to social behavior and discourse among the elderly. They are the custodians of order, who now spend their lives worried about what they consider the disorderly conduct of the younger generation of new wives and mothers who are either ignorant or openly flout the old ways of doing order.

Disorder

To highlight order, as in the preceding pages, is not to ignore disorder, the irreversibility of time, or the "terror" of history. It is only to underscore the fact that even as we go through the chaos of aging, there are certain regularities underneath this disorder. In real life, order only exists as part of disorder. Mircea Eliade admits that much when he says that archaic cultures tolerate unidirectional history—and its randomness; they know that random disasters will occur, and *chaola* famine is one of these.

Peasants regard *chaola* as an irreversible event not only because it signifies the absence of food, but also because it subverts the rules of sharing. Hunger becomes famine when its victims apply the principles of sharing *ndiwo* to every kind of food, including that from the bush. Every famine is about *both* the absence *and* the presence of food and not simply the absence of food. In no era do people suffer *chaola* like animals; in every famine people experience the pangs of hunger with full knowledge of the existence and meaning of abundance. *Chaola* is the absolute negation of the ordinary, which is one reason villagers give it proper names, which they never give to drought or *njala* seasonal hunger (they do, however, give proper names to certain types of flooding). These are not the kind of names people give to their children in remembrance or in an attempt to recreate the social identities of their ancestors. Famine names embody the conditions under which those terrors of history occurred. They are historical markers against which villagers date other events like the birth of someone. These are all matters relative to time's arrow, although not necessarily the Whiggish sense of time stretched back beyond memory and forward toward a goal. But, these are the kinds of linear schemes that allow most people, including those in the West, to lead meaningful lives.[15] The dominance of cyclical time in peasants' debates does not preclude conceptions of linear time and its catastrophes.[16] Cyclical time does not lead an independent life apart from linear time.

Repetitive processes make sense only in terms of the irreversible. Indeed, one can go even further. Archaic people idealize the predictable so much precisely because the enemies of order are, in some ways, more real in their world than in industrialized societies. Floods and drought threaten the order of the season and make the possibility of a *chaola* famine an ever-present danger. Late rains that delay planting have taught villagers to do seasonal work with flexibility, resisting official dictates for strict deadlines.[17] But even a perfect season is only so in its contradictions. The rainy season becomes an ideal season even as it increases the level or intensity of agricultural work, promising a future of plenty against the backdrop of present seasonal hunger. Different kinds of tensions also characterize the harvest season of plenty. Abundance promotes competing methods of teaching order, while every ritual meal unites the community by dividing it along the lines of gender, age, and social status. After leaving these great festivals, villagers confront an equally chaotic day. As in other types of society, in peasant communities order is not always far from disorder. It would be simplistic to view order as a separate social reality distinct from disorder.

Order and disorder cohabit the same peasant world and indeed the very daily practices that are otherwise orderly. Daily work in the fields supports the unity of the able-bodied members of the household to the same degree that it sets them against the elderly and children not strong enough to hoe. Moreover, the able-bodied can deviate from established farming practices by becoming specialists. Equally fragile is the order of the daily meal. First, there are conflicting institutionalized options of taking it. Villagers can eat as members of one or several households (*chidyerano*). Second, whatever form it may take, the daily meal both unifies the community through the application of the principles of the golden-age theory, while dividing the same through the alternative vision. Every meal opposes male elders against the women and children of the same community. The orderly food regime of the preceding pages operates as a terrain of conflict, with its own internal dynamics working for change.

Therefore, the question facing the student is not whether a food regime can or did change. One can take change for granted. In any age, tradition-respecting peasants are also potential rebels and risk-takers. The real question is whether, or to what extent can rebels transform the disorder of today into the order of tomorrow. And to see that, one needs to insert the food system into its wider field. Liberals are absolutely right to insist on the need for context. However, they commit a fundamental error in limiting the historical context to the so-called "transition" from "pre-capitalist" to "capitalist" forms of social organization—a grand teleology that, by its nature, cannot address the more critical and routine aspects of a food system. They ignore the simple fact that as social actors we experience the disorder of aging in an orderly fashion. Even the richest of Africa's kings and life-presidents do not change their dining tables, cooking utensils, or toilets each day they get older and wealthier. We, therefore, need *both* time's arrow and time's cycle to understand the history of food, an important dimension of the history of the human producer and consumer.

Conclusion

The golden-age theory and alternative vision illuminate the unity and the inequality of consumers. But, the fact that the tensions one observes at mealtime represent the culmination of a series of principles of inclusion and exclusion starting from the time of opening the fields, means that at each stage in its development a food system creates both friends and enemies of existing order. In short, any food regime is subject to change and Gould's formulation provides a framework for raising questions about that change.

Gould himself was keenly aware of the pitfalls of dichotomies. The two metaphors are not meant to close debate around two "opposing interpretations."[18] On the contrary, the metaphors help open debate in much the same way as the golden-age theory and the alternative vision do. One can see an assortment of time signatures between the two poles. Gould's method provides a more powerful tool for understanding history than the familiar genuflection to "change and continuity," which typically allows historians to drop into the frozen category of "continuity" anything they cannot plot along time's arrow. By contrast, Gould's metaphors permit a fruitful discussion of *different* laws of historical motion. The cycle cannot be about the "changeless" because of its inherent relationship to the arrow. The interdependence between the two would allow the researcher to raise fundamentally different questions than those that allow researchers to postulate transitions from one era to another, but not the days and seasons constituting the transition.

Inserting the days and seasons into an investigation of a food system can slow and complicate the arrow's flight. It can let the historian postulate the operation of multiple trajectories within a food system. One can begin to think of a regime whose components progress at varying speeds. The sociological aspects can for instance lag behind the technical and technological. Peasants may learn new ways of surviving seasonal hunger, as through new food markets, without necessarily transforming their ideas about sharing. One may also be able to see reversible change in developments that had at one point looked like linear trends. During the first four decades of the twentieth century, peasant cotton growers in Malawi appeared to be headed toward becoming yeoman farmers, the ultimate goal of British social engineering in the colony. But ecological change, in the context of adverse market forces starting with the Great Depression, interrupted the flight of the arrow. Villagers retreated and the tendency toward becoming cotton specialists who grew nothing else fizzled away.[19]

Finally, Gould's insights can permit a researcher to anticipate a situation in which a system reaches an impasse, a state of unresolved tensions reflecting, among other things, the fact that the enemies of order are not always strong enough to overwhelm the friends of order. Gould's model has analytical space for such an outcome. Time's arrow and time's cycle is a dynamic model, opening a researcher's eyes to the possibilities of multiple historical trajectories operating at the same time but not necessarily at the same speed or in the same direction.

Notes

1. Stephen J. Gould, *Time's Arrow Time's Cycle: Myth and Metaphor in the Discovery of Geological Time* (Cambridge: Harvard University Press, 1987), 15–16. Emphasis added.

2. Elias Mandala, *The End of Chidyerano: A History of Food and Everyday Life in Malawi, 1860–2004* (Portsmouth, NH: Heinemann, 2005), 203–238.

3. Gould, *Time's Arrow Time's Cycle*, 16.

4. Mircea Eliade, *The Myth of Eternal Return: Or, Cosmos and History*, trans. Willard R. Trask (Princeton: Princeton University Press 1991 [1949]).

5. Ibid, 165–202.

6. James C. Scott, *The Moral Economy of the Peasant: Rebellion and Subsistence in Southeast Asia* (New Haven: Yale University Press, 1976); Samuel L. Popkin, *The Rational Peasant: The Political Economy of Rural Society in Vietnam* (Berkeley: University of California Press, 1979).

7. See, for instance, J. U. Ogbu, "Seasonal Hunger in Tropical Africa as a Cultural Phenomenon," *Africa* 13, no. 4 (1973): 317–32; Audrey. I. Richards, *Land, Labour and Diet in Northern Rhodesia: An Economic Study of the Bemba Tribe* (1939, reprint: London: For International African Institute by Oxford University Press, 1952); idem, *Hunger and Work in a Savage Tribe* (London: Oxford University Press, 1932). But not so in the 1970s and 1980s. This leads one to suspect that some of the "famines" mentioned in the crisis literature belong to the class of seasonal hunger. The temptation to conflate these cyclical events with "famine," a one-time episode, must have been especially strong among historians bent on proving how capitalism fomented hunger in Africa.

8. Ogbu, "Seasonal Hunger in Tropical Africa," 317–32; Richards, *Land, Labour and Diet*; idem, *Hunger and Work*. A Ph.D. dissertation by Dr. Chrissie Chawanje-Mughogho, shows the lack of congruence between the cultural and "scientific" definition of what is good food for the body. In southern Malawi people consider *nyika* roots as an inferior product, eaten only by the poor in times of hunger. But Dr. Chawanje-Mughogho has discovered that these roots, found in the marshes of the Tchiri River, are a storehouse of nutrients and vitamins.

9. Mandala, *Work and Control*, 173.

10. Interview conducted by Elias Mandala with Mrs. Sigresi Lingstonya Zachepa and Venancio Zachepa, Njereza Village, TA Kasisi, Chikwawa, Malawi, on July 8, 1995. She was the one who raised my awareness of the seasonal and everyday dimensions of food.

11. African Way of Life Club (Kachebere Major Seminary), "Bantu Wisdom: A Collection of Proverbs" (Unpublished manuscript), 20, item 142.

12. This is a liberal translation of the more colorful proverb: "Wodya nyemba ndi wodya madeya, amaiwala ndi wodya nyemba." A close-to-literal rendering would run as: "[Between] those who ate [good] beans and those who ate bran only those who ate bran will remember [what they ate]"—also a powerful reminder of the centrality of food to rural thought.

13. This is a liberal translation of: "Ali awiri si mantha, kuipira kutha ndiwo m'mbale." A literal translation would run something like this: "Being two causes no fear, but it finishes relish in the plate."

14. Interviews: by Edward Pereira Tembo with Mrs. Leni Pereira, Chitsa Village, T.A, Tengani, Nsanje District, Malawi, November 5, 1991; Elias Mandala with Arnold Kukhala, Jambo Village, T.A. Mbenje, Nsanje District, July 2, 1995.

15. See Robin Horton, *Patterns of Thought in Africa and the West: Essays on Magic, Religion and Science* (Cambridge: Cambridge University Press, 1993); John S. Mbiti, *African Religions and Philosophy* (New York: Anchor Books, 1970).

16. Some kind of eschatology seems to be a key element of the witchcraft eradication (or *mchape*) complex. While officially sponsored religions like the Mbona rain cult

project villagers to one well defined future, namely, a future that was already realized in the "golden" age, *mchape* specialists operating on the fringes of established order, could promise a future with a goal. For a parallel with modern millenarian movements, see Karen Fields, "Antinomian Conduct at the Millennium: Metaphorical Conceptions of Time in Social Science and Social Life," in *The Political Dimensions of Religion*, ed. Said Amir Arjomand (Albany: State University of New York Press, 1993), 157–68. Time's arrow may not have dominated African cosmologies; but it often showed up, as an uninvited guest, in times of trouble to highlight the meaning of the ordinary.

17. Which often landed them into trouble with government officials, who insisted on strict and factory-like work schedules.

18. Gould, *Time's Arrow Time's Cycle*, 8.

19. Mandala, *End of Chidyerano*, 131–63.

Bibliography

Eliade, Mircea. *The Myth of Eternal Return: Or, Cosmos and History.* Translated by Willard R. Trask. 1949, reprint: Princeton, NJ: Princeton University Press 1991.

Gould, Stephen J. *Time's Arrow Time's Cycle: Myth and Metaphor in the Discovery of Geological Time.* Cambridge, MA: Harvard University Press, 1987.

Mandala, Elias C. *The End of Chidyerano: A History of Food and Everyday Life in Malawi, 1860–2004.* Portsmouth, NH: Heinemann, 2005.

Ogbu, J. U. "Seasonal Hunger in Tropical Africa as a Cultural Phenomenon." *Africa* 13, no. 4 (1973): 317–32.

CHAPTER 21

FOOD REGIMES

ANDRÉ MAGNAN

Food scholars face the difficult task of explaining the evolution of a global food system that brings distant social actors, ecologies, and places into new, complex, and often contradictory relations. Among the key challenges is to provide an account of food system change that is at once theoretically sophisticated, historically grounded, and holistic in its perspective. Anchored in historical political economy, food regimes analysis is a leading example of this type of approach. The food regimes perspective interprets agriculture and food in relation to the development of capitalism on a global scale, and sees social change as the outcome of struggles among social movements, capital, and states. Its key strengths are its historicity, methodological holism, and ability to connect and interpret processes of local and global change. In this chapter, I review the theoretical, empirical, and methodological contributions of food regimes analysis, and highlight some of the latest developments in food regime theorizing and research.

Emerging from the political economy of agriculture tradition,[1] food regimes analysis was originally developed as a means of contextualizing the restructuring of agriculture and food in the late twentieth century in world-historical terms. By the 1980s, major shifts in the world food trade generated increasing interest in the global restructuring of food production, consumption, and distribution. These processes became a focus of international scholarship, generating several collected volumes on the restructuring of agrofood commodity chains in a new international division of labor.[2] Much of this research focused on the emergence of counter-seasonal international commodity chains for fresh fruits and vegetables and their role in the agro-export strategies of countries in the Global South.[3] Other research tracked the growing power and influence of transnational corporations in agrofood sectors upstream (e.g., seeds and chemicals) and downstream (processing, distribution, and retain) from farming.[4] These various strands of research in the political economy tradition provided inspiration to—and an empirical basis from which to construct—the food regimes approach.

Harriet Friedmann and Philip McMichael introduced the concept of food regimes in an article that interpreted the changing role of agriculture and food in global capitalist development since 1870. The formation of a world market in wheat—the first for a food staple—marked a radical rupture in the history of food provisioning, as entire populations (e.g., the United Kingdom) became dependent on distant supplies of food for survival, and food exchanges bound together states, farmers, and eaters in new ways. According to Friedmann and McMichael, this development made possible the emergence of the first international food regime, a historically specific set of rules, institutions, and practices that regulated food and agriculture on a world scale under British hegemony. In the article, they traced the rise and fall of two historical food regimes, showing how changing patterns of food production, consumption, and distribution related to the evolution of the state system, changing international divisions of labor, and the increasingly strong links between agrofood and industrial sectors. In turn, they suggested that the structural changes to the world-economy of the 1970s had ushered in a crisis of food regime relations manifested in trade conflicts among key agricultural exporters, the Third World debt crisis, and volatility in international markets. Contemporary processes of agrofood restructuring could therefore be traced to conflicts and contradictions arising from the breakdown of the last stable food regime.[5]

Food regimes analysis has been applied to several substantive areas of social change in the global agrofood system. In the 1990s, it was used to interpret the intense process of contestation involved in establishing new rules for international trade in agriculture. This literature suggested that the politics of food and agriculture were changing because of increasing corporate power, the decline of farm lobbies, and a shift from public to corporate forms of regulation of the agrofood sector.[6] Another key substantive focus consisted of explaining how the global food system created internationally coordinated commodity complexes that tended to erase the "particularities of time and place in both agriculture and diets" under restructuring led by agrofood corporations.[7] Some scholars used food regimes as a point of departure for empirical studies of regional or national agrofood sectors, especially in the antipodes.[8]

Since the mid-2000s, there has been something of a resurgence of food regimes research, as scholars have tried to come to grips with a rapidly evolving global agriculture and food sector. Scholars such as David Burch and Geoffrey Lawrence have used the food regimes concept to make sense of the increasing power of food retailers over many aspects of the global food system, especially their use of private standards to create quality-differentiated market segments and consolidate their control over global supply chains.[9] Friedmann and McMichael have interpreted what has come to be called the "retailing revolution" in the context of global class relations and ecological crisis.[10] In 2009, the journal *Agriculture and Human Values* published a special issue on food regimes, with innovative theoretical and empirical perspectives on the applicability of the concept to the present conjuncture.[11]

I return to this recent scholarship below in my review of on-going debates over the status of a third food regime.

Food Regime Theory

The concept of food regimes combined two strands of macro-sociological theory: regulationism and world-systems theory. French regulation theory emphasizes how different moments in capitalist history tend to combine particular forms of accumulation with stabilizing social and political institutions. According to the regulationist perspective, capitalist societies have evolved through several historical regimes of accumulation, each with its own underlying logic and conditions of stability.[12] The food regimes concept applied the regulationist approach specifically to the realm of agriculture and food, and extended it from the national to the world-historical scale by combining it with a world-systems interpretation of social change.[13] World-systems theory conceives of social change as occurring from the dynamic interplay of global capital accumulation and a hierarchical system of states, over successive periods of hegemony (economic, social, and political leadership vested in a dominant state) and transition.[14] By combining these theoretical strands, the food regimes approach has sought to develop a lens for analyzing the transformation of food sectors at multiple, interpenetrating scales.

As a "framing concept," food regimes locate processes of global and local change in historical narratives describing periods of stability and crisis in global agrofood relations.[15] Stable food regimes have emerged when key actors—farmers, consumers, states, and capital—agree on implicit rules tying them into predictable relations of food production, consumption and trade. Historically, food regimes have been underwritten by the influence of a hegemonic power, the United Kingdom until 1914, and the United States between 1945 and 1973. Although food regimes may be relatively stable for decades, they contain internal contradictions which, during periods of system-wide crisis, may turn into open conflicts among key actors. Under these conditions, the implicit rules governing the previous food regime unravel as actors advance new agendas and interpretations of reality. In the transitions between food regimes, competing interests struggle over new arrangements, with a particularly important role played by social movements, which are understood to serve as "engines of regime crisis and formation."[16] Though social movements can be influential, food regime rules are contested in a field structured by unequal relations of power and property.

The food regimes approach has been among the most influential framing tools in agrofood studies. Some scholars have been critical, however, of food regimes and political economy approaches for presenting an overly determinist portrayal of capitalist accumulation as a force of transformation in the agrofood system. As it applies to food regimes, this critique called into question the legitimacy of assuming the coherence of food regimes over particular historical periods. In doing so, critics contend, the food regimes approach glosses over national and regional particularities of restructuring and political contestation. Michael Watts and David Goodman, for instance, remained relatively agnostic about the trajectory of change in the agrofood system, claiming that key differences between the globalization of industrial sectors and of the agrofood sector mean that "the agro-food sector is clearly *not* global in any simple sense."[17] Likewise, they expressed skepticism about the significance of Friedmann's claim that multilateral trade rules serve as a mechanism of "private global regulation"[18] of agrofood relations. Other debates have focused on appropriate ways to theorize the nature-society nexus in accounts of agrofood change. Goodman criticized political economy and associated approaches for perpetuating a nature-society dualism embedded in "modernist ontology." As an alternative, he proposed using Bruno Latour's actor-network theory to analyze agrofood networks as nature-culture hybrids emerging from the interaction of both human and non-human "actants."[19]

Yet food regimes analysis is considerably more open-ended than it is sometimes given credit for, even as it retains an emphasis on processes of commodification and accumulation that are central dynamics of capitalist political economy. In food regimes analysis, agrofood relations are neither totally contingent, nor determined by abstract economic forces, but arise from the interplay of historical social structures and social actors. The rise, fall, and transformation of successive historical food regimes occurs in the broad framework of an evolving capitalist political-economy, subject to changing social, technological, and ecological bases of organization. While avoiding determinism, the key is to pay attention to the *historicity* of political-economic change. Processes of change are understood to be structured by a "unity in time" that links the local to the world-historical across periods of stability and change.[20]

The food regimes approach is also fundamentally *comparative*. This comparative dimension allows different processes of change occurring across space and time to be interpreted in their diversity, in their connection to each other, and as part of an evolving whole. At its best, food regimes analysis therefore privileges neither "unity" nor "heterogeneity," but uses world-historical accounts to contextualize particular instances of change.[21] Critics of food regimes and allied approaches mistakenly confuse the *scale* (macro) and *scope* (holistic) of analysis with determinism. Contrary to the view of these critics, the food regimes approach does take into account both "contingency and politics," especially in the way the detailed reconstruction of periods of stability and contestation in global agrofood relations emphasizes the struggle among historical actors, with uncertain outcomes.[22]

Finally, food regime analyses have addressed nature-society relations by underscoring the ecological foundations and contradictions of historical food regimes.[23] Drawing especially on the environmental histories of Alfred Crosby and William Cronon, Friedmann has traced the radical transformation that agriculture has wrought on relations between humans, other living organisms, and ecosystems. Ecological conditions at both the nexus of production and consumption are understood to structure and constrain food regime change. [24]

Food Regime Methodology

The food regimes approach provides historical narratives used to organize and interpret agrofood system change, but also methodological prescriptions for historical-comparative research. Indeed, McMichael has suggested that, with its development over the last two decades, the food regimes perspective has become as much an analytical lens as a historical accounting of agrofood system change. As an analytical lens, food regime analysis identifies "significant relationships and contradictions in capitalist processes across time and space," focusing on the centrality of food and agriculture to capitalist dynamics.[25] Methodologically, food regimes analysis calls for a holistic, non-determinist historical interpretation of evolving social and ecological relations. The most important methodological influences on food regimes research are commodity chain analysis and McMichael's own version of historical-comparative analysis, called incorporated comparison.[26]

Originally formalized as a method by William Friedland, commodity chain analysis traces the relations tying social actors into networks of production and consumption, usually for a single commodity or commodity complex. Here, economic exchanges are interpreted as social relations of *power.* As such, commodity chain analysis challenges mainstream economic discourses that abstract economic relations from their social basis. Commodity chain approaches gained currency in the mid-1980s, a period during which global changes such as the shift in power from states to corporations called into question the centrality of the nation-state as the basic unit of analysis in macro-historical sociology. Development scholars saw in commodity chain analysis an approach that "could grasp the evolving organizational aspects of international trade, the linkages that animate it, the coordination that makes it possible, and the new global bodies that regulate it." [27]

Commodity chain analysis became a leading approach in world-systems sociology, as scholars applied the approach to historical change in international commodity chains. This usage gave the approach an explicitly global focus, with *global* commodity chains conceived of as "sets of interorganizational networks clustered around one commodity or product, linking households, enterprises, and states to one another within the world-economy." The key is to understand how social relations among unequal actors shape global economic processes, requiring an analysis that "probes above and below the level of the nation-state."[28] Scholars have applied these insights to many agrofood commodities; for example, Deborah Barndt's analysis of North American commodity chains for tomatoes—from migrant women workers in Mexico, to Northern consumers, and women workers in retail—revealed the class-based, racialized and gendered patterns of inequality bound up in commodity chain relations.[29]

Although it does not rely on a formalized commodity chain methodology, food regimes analysis is consistent with this approach in the sense that it traces production-consumption relations globally.[30] Food regimes scholars have, for instance, emphasized the importance of different commodity complexes to the character of historical food regimes. Food regimes analysis goes further, however, by interpreting the broader relations organizing food production, consumption, and distribution in historical constellations of power and accumulation.

This holistic, historical political economy approach is a form of "incorporated comparison." McMichael conceives of this method as a type of historical-comparative analysis that locates instances of social change in geographical and chronological contexts while avoiding the reification of social structures and historical processes. It does so by interpreting change among system parts in relation to the transformation of a contingent, evolving whole (e.g., food regimes). Rather than assuming the existence of a pre-conceived, "all-encompassing" whole, incorporated comparison allows for the possibility of qualitative change in parts and wholes over time, and explores how the parts of a system *construct* the whole in historical relations. In essence, McMichael suggests that the whole be treated as an "emergent totality"—less an empirical entity than a "conceptual *procedure*... in which the whole is discovered through analysis of the mutual conditioning of parts."[31] Here, comparison becomes the substance of inquiry rather than its goal.

Consistent with incorporated comparison, food regime analysis proposes structured historical narratives—always subject to reinterpretation—that help situate the conditions of conflict and stability characterizing agrofood relations in a given moment. In food regime analysis, historical parts form the basis of comparison, but are also understood to construct the whole (food regimes) historically. In turn, food regimes analyses track successive periods of stability and change as a lens on the historical evolution of the whole. In this way, it differs from approaches to agrofood studies giving priority to heterogeneity and contingency.[32]

While food regimes analysis originally focused on specifying periods of stability in the rules governing food production, consumption and trade, more recent work has emphasized periods of *transition* and political contestation. Indeed, the question of whether or not a new food regime is emerging (or has emerged) is perhaps less important than the need to clearly delineate the disintegration of old relations and the emergence of new relations.[33] This way of viewing food regimes deploys the concept as an analytic lens, used to "pose specific questions about the structuring processes in the global political-economy, and/or global food relations, at any particular moment."[34] The key is to avoid structural or historical reductionism in articulating historical food regimes and the real world contests among social actors that lead to food regime change.

Food Regime History

Food regime accounts detailing periods of historical stability called regimes and change through crisis or transition have been elaborated many times elsewhere. In this overview of food regime history, I highlight the essential features of the first and second food regimes, and comment on debates over the emergence of a third food regime. The first international food regime (1870–1914) emerged from the consolidation of the food staples trade linking the settler-states of North America and Australasia to European imperial powers.[35] In this new international division of labor, settler-states exported to Europe the products of temperate agriculture, especially wheat and meat, in exchange for capital, manufactured goods, and migrants. Cheap imports of grain and meat from settler-states served as "wage foods" for European working classes, reducing the cost of industrialization, and helping to diffuse discontent. At the same time, the spread of temperate agriculture from Europe to settler-states provided a relief valve to population pressure in Europe, as streams of European migrants poured into the settler-states. In turn, settler-states, beginning with the United States, used agricultural exports to Europe in a process of territorial expansion and settlement linked to national projects of development.

The division of labor between settler-states and Europe emerged alongside an older yet, in the late-nineteenth century, expanding division of labor between European powers and their colonies of "occupation."[36] In contrast to settler-states, these colonies were directly administered by colonial powers and specialized in producing tropical and sub-tropical crops including sugar, coffee, tea, tobacco, and cocoa, many of which had assumed a new importance in working class European diets.[37] This international division of labor produced a climatic and geographical complementarity between Europe and the colonies of occupation. By contrast, the trade between the imperial powers and the settler-states produced *competition* between independent nation-states producing many of the same products.

The United Kingdom's hegemonic role in the capitalist world-economy underpinned the first food regime, as the gold standard played a key role in regulating international currencies and trade. The United Kingdom was also central to food regime relations because it was the largest single food importer during this period, a result of its radical experiment with food import dependence beginning with the repeal of the Corn Laws in the 1840s. Here it sacrificed the interests of landed property for industrial capital, and exported capital and manufactured goods under its free trade policy.

The first food regime produced a number of institutional innovations and legacies that transformed social and ecological relations in European and settler-states and restructured the state-system. First, it created a class of commercial farming households (the "family farm") dependent on the unpaid labor of women, men, and children, and as a result, able to undercut the price at which food could be produced in Europe.[38] These farm households were dependent on distant export markets and at the mercy of the private interests, including railways, banks, and grain merchants as well as states that organized the grain trade. Second, and related, the structural inequalities faced by farming households generated a distinctive farm politics expressed in new agrarian social movements.[39] Third, the first food regime drove changes to the state-system. By instituting international (as opposed to mercantile) trade and competition, the new international division of labor produced "a system of independent, liberal national states."[40]

These states would attempt to model the U.S. experience, where the expansion of agricultural production complemented industrialization, on the path to national development.

The internal tensions of the first food regime—of which there were both ecological and social strands—led to regime crisis between 1925 and 1945. The stabilizing influence of U.K. hegemony declined following World War I and the end of the gold standard as the world reserve currency. When world grain prices collapsed in the mid-1920s—a prelude to the generalized economic collapse of the Depression—farming households experienced acute dislocation and hardship.[41] This was compounded by the dustbowl conditions of the 1930s, which revealed the shaky ecological foundations of settler agriculture. Under intensive wheat farming, the virgin soils of the North American plains were rapidly depleted of their nutrients, leaving them extremely vulnerable to drought and erosion. Meanwhile, the experiences of the two world wars revealed the vulnerability that came with heavy food import dependence in the United Kingdom

In response to the economic disaster that had befallen the agricultural sector, U.S. governments implemented commodity programs under the New Deal. Rather than directly subsidizing farm incomes, commodity programs instituted price supports that encouraged production. The particular form taken by U.S. domestic agricultural policy of this era was only one available alternative, and was to prove extremely consequential to the eventual structure of the second food regime.[42] Economic depression in world agricultural markets drew a second government response in the form of international commodity agreements, which were intended to match world supply to demand among key importers and exporters. Yet, just as agreement neared on an international wheat deal, talks were suspended by the outbreak of World War II in 1939.[43]

In re-establishing the conditions for stability after the war, states, social movements, and capital drew on some of the innovations, including farm programs and state marketing boards spawned in the crisis of the first food regime and invented altogether new relations such as food aid. Friedmann has called the second food regime "mercantile-industrial" in order to account for its twin dynamics: 1. politically constructed international trade, and 2. the rise of an industrialized agrofood sector, eventually to be dominated by large agrofood corporations. In both of these dimensions, the mercantile-industrial food regime was fundamentally shaped by U.S. hegemony. After the war, the United States sought to retain depression-era commodity programs as a means of stabilizing farm incomes. Commodity programs produced, as a side-effect, large agricultural *surpluses,* and the need to deal with these surpluses came to dominate the establishment of international food regime rules. Most significantly, food and agriculture were excluded from the General Agreement on Tariffs and Trade (GATT), the postwar multilateral framework for liberalizing trade among industrialized countries, at the request of the United States. This allowed the United States to retain domestic commodity-programs, which were incompatible with the GATT since they depended on the use of both import controls and export subsidies.[44]

With the exceptional status given to agriculture, the new food regime came to be characterized by non-market or state-state transfers of food and agricultural goods. Nowhere was this clearer than with the invention of "food aid." Beginning with the Marshall Plan for European reconstruction, the United States found an outlet for its agricultural surpluses in massive shipments of food aid. However, as Europe replicated the U.S. model of agricultural regulation and protected its domestic food sector, American export opportunities declined. The solution to this problem was found in extending food aid to the decolonizing Third World, accomplished through U.S. Public-Law 480 of 1954, which permitted recipient countries to pay for food shipments in local currency, allowing them to import large quantities of grain (mostly wheat) at discounted rates, and without access to U.S. dollars. In this way, U.S. surpluses, in the form of food aid, contributed directly the postwar project of Third World industrialization. Given the new role for the dollar as world reserve currency, the United States was uniquely positioned to use food aid as a mechanism of surplus disposal.[45] Food aid not only served domestic agricultural policy, but allowed the United States to pursue foreign policy goals. In the context of Cold War rivalry, food aid cemented geo-political ties with key Third World states, and contributed to wider anti-communist strategic goals. As the Cold War intensified, the First World and the communist Second World became mutually exclusive trading blocs. This embargo, referred to as the Cold War dam, provided one condition under which U.S. surpluses persisted, and was thus a key structural feature of food the second food regime. In the Third World, food aid created dependence on cheap imports and shifted eating habits towards wheat-centered diets, which later precipitated severe crises under changed conditions in the 1970s.[46]

Government farm programs and state-sponsored modernization of agricultural production provided for the second—*industrial*—character of the postwar food regime. With agricultural price supports, farmers were encouraged to maximize production, and did so through industrial intensification. Building on the introduction of farm machinery in the first food regime, farmers adopted chemical fertilizers, pesticides, and new crop varieties and completed the process of mechanization by adopting tractors on a large scale. Large national and eventually transnational agro-input corporations became a significant industrial sector, as capital selectively appropriated aspects of agricultural production and reintroduced them as external inputs, shifting from animal manure and draft power to chemical fertilizers and tractors.[47]

Meanwhile, cheap agricultural commodities fed into new agrofood complexes, generating large agribusiness corporations on the output side of agriculture. The "livestock complex" turned agricultural commodities into industrial inputs in the manufacture of animal feeds for intensive meat production. This process began in the United States, where soy, introduced to North America in the early-twentieth century, and high-yielding maize hybrids became important feed crops, in turn fuelling increased meat consumption, one of the hallmarks of the postwar diet. The livestock sector became internationally integrated when, in exchange for European protection of its wheat industry, the European Economic Community exempted U.S. animal feed from import duties.[48] Led by the multinational grain merchants and feed processors, who integrated specialized crop production, processing, and meat production, the livestock sector eventually became transnational, with global sourcing of raw materials and sales into class-differentiated global markets, providing quality cuts for wealthy consumers in the First World, and low-quality products for Third World markets.[49]

The second key commodity complex of the mercantile-industrial food regime was "durable foods." Although the first industrially manufactured foods such as canned fruit and vegetables were introduced during the first food regime, markets for such foods exploded after World War II as food manufacturing became a powerful industrial sector in its own right. Food processing and manufacturing industries devised many new standardized food products, including packaged and frozen foods, turning commodity crops such as soy, maize and wheat into inputs for industrial production. Large, national food manufacturing companies—producing branded goods—were ascendant during this period. Food processing and manufacturing went hand in hand with the emergence of new forms of retail, particularly the supermarket format, which first emerged in the United States before World War II, but became dominant in the postwar period.[50] Together, processed foods and the supermarket came to epitomize the cheap food economy of the second food regime, premised on generalized, though not universal, standardization of diets.

Like the livestock complex, the durable foods complex became transnationally integrated as national agrofood capitals became international giants. Using increasingly sophisticated food science and technology, food corporations diversified the sources of their raw materials by substituting the products of tropical agriculture in the Third World (e.g., palm oil) for temperate inputs (soy, maize) used as generic fats and sweeteners. This shift undermined the colonial division of labor between temperate and tropical agriculture, and eroded traditional Third World agro-exports.

The mercantile-industrial food regime entered into prolonged crisis in 1973, when massive structural changes to world grain markets undermined its stability. Though this was a sudden rupture, its origins lay in the internal contradictions of the postwar food regime. First, the power of the farm lobby declined as the efficiency gains of industrial agriculture allowed for fewer and fewer farmers in larger operations to continually increase production. Second, Third World countries faced declining terms of trade for their traditional exports just as their food import dependency increased, leaving them extremely vulnerable to debt and hunger. Third, the agrofood corporations spawned by the food regime outgrew the paradigm of national regulation and state-led trading rules that governed food and agriculture, and began to push for liberalization. Fourth, as Europe replicated the U.S. model and protected its domestic agricultural sector, it came eventually to face the same problem of surpluses, and by the 1970s sought outlets through which to increase its exports.

These contradictions were laid bare as the Soviet Union entered the world market, in 1972, with a huge demand for grain, breaching the Cold War dam. The effect was, virtually overnight, to eliminate the grain surpluses that had underpinned the food regime and had been a source of U.S. power. The historic U.S.-Soviet grain deal of 1972 caused a dramatic price spike which, combined with the oil crisis of the early 1970s, created a food crisis with global repercussions. Dependent on cheap supplies of wheat and facing the evaporation of markets for their traditional exports, Third World countries faced increasing hunger, debt, and social instability. The United States shifted away from food aid and towards commercial sales, just as competition among exporters became increasingly fierce. Meanwhile, the U.S. government responded to the end of surpluses by encouraging farmers to expand production, which they did enthusiastically, and by borrowing heavily. When surpluses and price volatility returned later in the decade, heavily indebted farmers faced a financial crisis, laying the foundation for the farm income crisis of the last thirty years.

These events marked the breakdown of consensus around food regime relations on national and international scales. On the national scale, the postwar alliance between the state and the class of independent farmers eroded, as deficit politics prompted many neoliberal governments to scale back public spending on agriculture.[51] At the same time, farm politics became more fractionated and marginal, as farmers became increasingly differentiated by size and commodity, and continued to decline in number.[52] On the international scene, food aid was reframed as "dumping" and subsequently scaled-down and tied more strictly to humanitarian goals. The decline of food aid prompted criticism of U.S. and European trade policies, especially the use of export subsidies to increase or maintain market share, which came widely to be seen as destructive. Secondary exporters including Canada, New Zealand, Australia, and Argentina, which could not afford to compete in the subsidy game, formed a loose alliance called the Cairns group seeking to liberalize agricultural trade. These tensions and conflicts ultimately culminated in a push to incorporate agriculture into the framework for multilateral trade negotiations under the GATT. This was accomplished during the Uruguay Round of GATT negotiations, begun in 1986 and completed in 1994.

With the completion of the Uruguay Round, agriculture was formally integrated into the global free trade agenda and given a powerful new enforcement mechanism, the World Trade Organization (WTO). The WTO's Agreement on Agriculture included provisions for reducing agricultural import tariffs (the minimum market access rules), and curtailing both export subsidies and domestic agricultural subsidies. Implementation of global free trade in agriculture has proceeded only haltingly, however, as the United States and the European Union have been reluctant to meaningfully reduce export subsidies, and as key agro-exporters from the South led by Brazil have pressed their own agenda. In 2003, the Doha round of WTO negotiations foundered on the intractability of agricultural trade, as a bloc of Southern countries made a show of force and walked out of the negotiations.

A Third Food Regime? Interpreting Current Agrofood Relations

Food regime scholars have taken the on-going conflicts around the regulation of agriculture and food—expressed in the collapse of WTO negotiations, persistent global hunger, food price volatility, farm crises, food safety scares, and the environmental critique of industrial agriculture—as signs that the crisis conditions which emerged in the 1970s have never been fully resolved. Under these conditions, there has been a longstanding debate over whether or not a third food regime has emerged, and, if it has, what its key tendencies and contradictions might be. In this section, I review this debate, highlighting some of the new and innovative perspectives on food regime theory and history that have emerged from it.

Friedmann has argued that recent strands of agrofood change—particularly supermarket-led restructuring and international environmental and food politics—have combined to produce the "lineaments" of a third food regime.[53] In her view, these new relations signal that we are in a period of food regime transition, though the stabilization of these new relations—given social and ecological tensions inherent in them—is uncertain. Her thesis hinges on the spectacular rise of supermarket power and changing food politics over the last three decades. Supermarket chains—now large, often transnational corporations—have consolidated their power over agrofood commodity chains by implementing new, private quality standards that both respond to and construct consumer demand for quality-differentiated foods. Partly, this strategy has emerged from the introduction of "own brand"[54] products, which has allowed supermarkets to become increasingly involved in food manufacturing, and to compete directly with suppliers of branded food products. This has provided supermarkets with greater control over product design, more leverage over contracted suppliers, and a strategic advantage in the introduction of new products and market segments such as ready to eat meals.[55] Meanwhile, consumer anxiety over food safety, new genetic technologies, and health and nutrition have created new social movements and market segments including natural and organic foods.

The key characteristics of a potentially new food regime are thus the proliferation of private food standards, supermarket power, and consumer-led food politics. Supermarket-designed private standards have been superimposed on scaled-down public food standards, at once providing for new conditions of stability and accumulation in the global agrofood system and generating new inter-state and class relations. Because privately regulated supply chains respond to consumer demands that, broadly speaking, represent "green" issues of health and sustainability, Friedmann has called the emergent food regime *corporate-environmental*. Under the conditions of supermarket power, "private capitals... create their own carefully regulated supply chains containing just those *higher* standards that cannot be sustained in inter-governmental negotiations." To these quality chains is paired a parallel network of supply chains for standardized, lower-end commodities destined for poorer consumers, representing the majority of the world's eaters. Contrary to the universalizing thrust of the mercantile-industrial food regime, the emerging food regime is characterized by diverging quality conventions, likely to deepen existing global inequalities in consumption standards. The reconfiguration of agrofood relations also implies new forms of marginalization and integration for producers and regions, as they stake their fortunes, with varying success, on becoming "quality export sites."[56]

McMichael, for his part, has argued that, despite containing inherent contradictions and crisis tendencies, a third, corporate, food regime has emerged. The corporate food regime is conceived of as a project for instituting a "world agriculture," a global agrofood system in which the "dumping of subsidized food surpluses and growing agribusiness access to land, labor, and markets in the Global South clears the way for corporate-driven food supply chains binding together a (selective) global consumer class."[57] The main "vehicle" behind this transformation is agricultural trade liberalization through the WTO, which has tended to pry open markets in the Global South to cheap agrofood commodities from the North, commodify and privatize agricultural knowledge and resources, and undermine peasant agriculture. The WTO's Agreement on Agriculture is also the framework through which powerful Northern states maintain their "corporate-mercantilist comparative advantage" in relation to the South. By and large, Northern agro-exporting states have succeeded in manipulating WTO rules in such a way as to exempt them from meaningfully reducing their farm subsidies, even as Southern states are forbidden from providing support to their beleaguered farm sectors.

The corporate food regime produces deep social and ecological dislocations, including the displacement and marginalization of peasant farmers, growing global hunger, the depletion of soils, and growing CO_2 emissions. These have generated a counter-movement, however, in the form of diverse "food sovereignty" movements. As articulated by the transnational peasants' movement, La Via Campesina, food sovereignty places the rights of farmers—to a decent livelihood and to control over agricultural resources—and eaters—to culturally appropriate, nutritious, and ecologically benign food sources—ahead of the profit imperatives of corporate agriculture. McMichael sees in food sovereignty movements the kernel of an alternative modernity, centered on socially and ecologically embedded agriculture and food systems.

Other scholars have also taken up the debate. William Pritchard has suggested that the collapse of the WTO's Doha round, in 2008 is indicative of the failure to consolidate a third, corporate food regime. Indeed, he argues that the protracted conflicts over incorporating agriculture into the WTO are best thought of as attempts to resolve contradictions carried over from the collapse of the second food regime—what he calls the "long hangover." In the late 1980s, much debate revolved around whether the WTO might constitute the basis for a new, privatized mode of regulating agriculture on a global scale. In the two decades since then, however, it has become apparent that WTO rules have failed to resolve tensions among key exporters, and indeed, have created new conflicts. Far from eliminating Northern protectionism, the WTO's Agreement on Agriculture has become a mechanism for legitimizing it, if only implicitly. Combined with the forced liberalization of Southern agriculture, the result was "to aggravate already-existing uneven opportunities in the world food system." By the early 2000s, this led to mounting grievances among countries of the Global South, especially emerging agro-exporting powerhouses such as Brazil. Conflicts between Northern and Southern power blocs ultimately derailed further agricultural trade liberalization with the collapse of the Doha Round. To Pritchard, this suggests that the WTO served more as an "arena of contestation" than "the institutional architecture" necessary to meld competing interests into a stable food regime.[58]

Hugh Campbell, meanwhile, has suggested that environmental food auditing systems, as they have been developed over the last twenty years by retail capital, could form the basis of a more ecologically rational food regime. The standard ecological critique of the contemporary global food system has been that it revolves around "food from nowhere"—cheap agrofood commodities for which the origins and ecological and social conditions of production are hidden. Campbell picks up from Friedmann's notion of the corporate-environmental food regime to suggest that the emergence of quality-differentiated, privately regulated commodity chains supplying affluent consumers can be thought of as producing "food from somewhere." With heightened cultural awareness of food issues and the ecological costs of cheap food, food corporations have begun to develop complex standards and auditing procedures that incorporate ecological feedbacks (information flows that allow social actors to respond to environmental changes). To the extent that these feedbacks allow food systems to reduce the ecological burden of food production and distribution, they may pave the way for greater sustainability. There is a contradiction at the heart of these emerging relations, however, in that "food from somewhere" assumes its cultural legitimacy from being defined in opposition to "food from nowhere."[59]

Two other recent reflections on food regimes have sought to move the perspective forward. Burch and Lawrence interpret recent scholarship on the transformation of the agrofood food system in light of the changing dynamics of the wider capitalist economy. Here, they argue, food scholars must pay close attention to the increasing dominance of global finance capital—empowered by the deregulation of international money flows since the 1980s—in shaping global economic processes. This process of "financialization" is profoundly transforming agrofood supply chains as "finance capital is not simply underwriting the corporate control of land and resources overseas by companies in the agri-food supply chain, but is emerging as part of a wider process in which finance capital is directly and independently applied in a variety of ways—that is, in speculation as well as productive investment."[60] Food regime scholars must therefore understand how finance capital is remaking the food system, just as food corporations become increasingly financialized, that is, involved in activities such as banking and financial speculation.

Finally, Jane Dixon revisits food regime history through the lens of nutrition science, public policy, and diets, revealing how different manifestations of the state-science nexus have served to legitimize and regulate consumption relations. Her argument is that contemporary food politics reflect a breakdown of previously unquestioned assumptions linking industrial foods as sources of cheap calories to health and affluence. In the current political and cultural climate, however, attempts to address the flaws of the industrial diet have been co-opted by private interests. Here, large "life sciences" corporations have come to exert increasing influence over nutrition science and diets by framing these issues in terms of "the enumeration, enrichment and promotion of both single foods and national food supplies in terms of nutrient values profile" in dietary fads such as "superfoods."[61]

Conclusion

The food regimes perspective offers a way of reading the history of agriculture and food in global capitalist relations since the nineteenth century. Food regimes scholars have suggested that this history has been characterized by alternating periods of stability and crisis linked to broader processes of change in global capitalism. To date, there have been two historical food regimes, with scholars disagreeing on whether or not a new food regime has crystallized. Rather than undermining the food regimes perspective, however, these debates may represent "different vantage points in understanding the structuring relations in, and multiple dimensions of, the agrofood system."[62] By continually interpreting and re-interpreting the contradictions, conflicts, and possibilities inherent in the twenty-first century food system in historical terms, the food regimes approach will contribute to important societal debates about the future of food and farming.

Notes

1. Frederick Buttel and Howard Newby, ed., *The Rural Sociology of the Advanced Societies: Critical Perspectives* (London: Croom Helm, 1980); Frederick Buttel, Olaf Larson, and Gilbert Gillespie, *The Sociology of Agriculture* (New York: Greenwood Press, 1990); William H. Friedland, et al, *Towards a New Political Economy of Agriculture* (Boulder, CO: Westview Press, 1991).

2. William H. Friedland, "Commodity Systems Analysis: An Approach to the Sociology of Agriculture," in *Research In Rural Sociology and Development: A Research Annual*, ed. H. K. Schwarzweller (Oxfordshire: Elsevier, 1984), 221–35; Alessandro Bonanno, et al, eds., *From Columbus to ConAgra: The Globalization of Agriculture and Food* (Lawrence, Kansas: University Press of Kansas, 1994); Philip McMichael, ed., *The Global Restructuring of Agro-food Systems* (Ithaca, NY: Cornell University Press, 1994); David Goodman and Michael Watts, eds., *Globalising Food: Agrarian Questions and Global Restructuring* (New York: Routledge, 1997).

3. William H. Friedland, "The Global Fresh Fruit and Vegetable System: An Industrial Organization Analysis," in McMichael, *The Global Restructuring of Agro-food* Systems, 173–89; William H. Friedland, "The New Globalization: The Case of Fresh Produce," in Bonnano, *From Columbus to ConAgra*, 210–31; Luis Llambi, "Comparative Advantages and Disadvantages in Latin American Non-Traditional Fruit and Vegetable Exports," in McMichael, *The Global Restructuring of Agro-food Systems*, 190–213; Laura Raynolds, "The Restructuring of Third World Agro-Exports: Changing Production Relations in the Dominican Republic," in ibid, 214–37.

4. William Heffernan, "Concentration of Ownership And Control in Agriculture," in *Hungry for Profit: The Agribusiness Threat to Farmers, Food, and the Environment*, ed. Fred Magdoff, John Bellamy Foster, and Frederick H. Buttel (New York: Monthly Review Press, 2000), 61–75; William Heffernan and Douglas Constance, "Transnational Corporations and the Globalization of the Food System," in Bonnano, *From Columbus to ConAgra*, 29–51.

5. Harriet Friedmann and Philip McMichael, "Agriculture and the State System: The Rise and Decline of National Agricultures, 1870 to the Present," *Sociologia Ruralis* 29, no. 2 (1989): 93–117.

6. Harriet Friedmann, "The Political Economy of Food: A Global Crisis," *New Left Review* 197 (1993): 29–57; Philip McMichael and David Myhre, "Global Regulation vs. the Nation State: Agro-Food Systems and the New Politics of Capital," *Capital and Class* 43 (1991): 83–105.

7. Harriet Friedmann, "Distance and Durability: Shaky Foundations of the World Food Economy," in McMichael, *The Global Restructuring of Agro-Food Systems*, 272.

8. Richard Le Heron, *Globalized Agriculture, Political Choice* (New York: Pergamon Press, 1993); William Pritchard, "The Emerging Contours of the Third Food Regime: Evidence from Australian Dairy and Wheat Sectors," *Economic Geography* 74, no. 1 (1998): 64–74; Michael Roche, "International Food Regimes: New Zealand's Place in the International Frozen Meat Trade, 1870–1935," *Historical Geography* 27 (1999): 129–51.

9. David Burch and Geoffrey Lawrence, "Supermarket Own Brands, Supply Chains and the Transformation of the Agri-Food System," *International Journal of the Sociology of Agriculture and Food* 13, no. 1 (2005): 267–79.

10. Harriet Friedmann, "From Colonialism to Green Capitalism: Social Movements and Emergence of Food Regimes," in Buttel and McMichael, *New Directions in the Sociology of Global Development*, 227–64; Philip McMichael and Harriet Friedmann, "Situating the 'Retailing Revolution,'" in *Supermarkets and Agri-Food Supply Chains*, ed. David Burch and Geoffrey Lawrence (Northampton, MA: Edward Elgar, 2007), 219–319.

11. Jane Dixon and Hugh Campbell, eds., "Symposium on Food Regime Analysis," *Agriculture and Human Values* 26, no. 4 (December 2009).

12. See Michel Aglietta, *A Theory of Capitalist Regulation* (London: New Left Books, 1979).

13. The world-systems perspective was first presented in Immanuel Wallerstein, *The Modern World System*, vol. 1 (New York: Academic Press, 1974).

14. Giovanni Arrighi, *The Long Twentieth Century: Money, Power, and the Origins of Our Times* (New York: Verso, 1994).

15. William Pritchard, "Food regimes," in *The International Encyclopedia of Human Geography*, ed. R. Kitchin and N. Thrift (London: Elsevier, 2009), 225.

16. Friedmann "From Colonialism to Green Capitalism," 229.

17. David Goodman and Michael Watts, "Reconfiguring the Rural or Fording the Divide? Capitalist Restructuring and the Global Agro-Food System," *The Journal of Peasant Studies* 22, no. 1 (1994): 14, 18–26, 37–38.

18. Friedmann, "The Political Economy of Food," 52.

19. David Goodman, "Agro-Food Studies in the 'Age of Ecology': Nature, Corporeality, Bio-Politics," *Sociologia Ruralis* 39, no. 1 (1999): 17–38; Bruno Latour, *We Have Never Been Modern* (Cambridge, MA: Harvard University Press, 1993).

20. McMichael, *The Global Restructuring of Agro-food Systems*, 3.

21. Ibid, 13.

22. Jane Collins, "New Directions in Commodity Chain Analysis of Global Development Processes," in Buttel and McMichael, *New Directions in the Sociology of Global Development*, 9.

23. Hugh Campbell, "Breaking New Ground in Food Regime Theory: Corporate Environmentalism, Ecological Feedbacks and the 'Food from Somewhere' Regime," *Agriculture and Human Values* 26 (2009): 309–19.

24. Alfred W. Crosby, *Ecological Imperialism: The Biological Expansion of Europe, 900–1900* (Cambridge: Cambridge University Press, 1986); William Cronon, *Nature's Metropolis: Chicago and the Great West.* (New York: W. W. Norton and Company, 1991); Harriet Friedmann, "Circles of Growing and Eating: the Political Ecology of Food and Agriculture," in *Food in Global History*, ed. Raymond Grew (Boulder, CO: Westview Press, 1999), 33–57.

25. Philip McMichael, "A Food Regime Geneaology," *The Journal of Peasant Studies* 36, no. 1 (2009): 163.

26. Philip McMichael, "Incorporating Comparison within a World-Historical Perspective: An Alternative Comparative Method," *American Sociological Review* 55, no. 3 (1990): 385–97.

27. Collins, "New Directions in Commodity Chain Analysis," 4.

28. Gary Gereffi and Miguel Korzeniewicz, eds., *Commodity Chains and Global Capitalism* (Westport, CT: Praeger, 1994), 2.

29. Deborah Barndt, *Tangled Routes: Women, Work, and Globalization on the Tomato Trail* (Lanham, MD: Rowman & Littlefield, 2002).

30. See Collins, "New Directions in Commodity Chain Analysis," 8–9.

31. McMichael, "Incorporating Comparison," 389, 391.

32. E.g., Goodman and Watts, *Globalising Food.*

33. McMichael and Friedmann, "Situating the 'Retail Revolution'," 292.

34. McMichael, "A Food Regime Genealogy," 148.

35. Friedmann and McMichael, "Agriculture and the State System."

36. Ibid, 97.

37. For the case of sugar, see Sydney Mintz, *Sweetness and Power: The Place of Sugar in Modern History* (New York: Viking Press, 1985).

38. Harriet Friedmann, "Simple Commodity Production and Wage Labour in the American Plains," *Journal of Peasant Studies* 6 (1978): 70–100.

39. Seymour Martin Lipset, *Agrarian Socialism: The Cooperative Commonwealth Federation in Saskatchewan* (Berkeley: University of California Press, 1971); Murray Knuttila and Bob Stirling, eds., *The Prairie Agrarian Movement Revisited* (Regina: Canadian Plains Research Centre, 2007).

40. Friedmann and McMichael, "Agriculture and the State System," 94.

41. John Conway, *The West: The History of a Region in Confederation*, 3rd ed. (Toronto: James Lorimer & Company, 2006).

42. Friedmann, "From Colonialism to Green Capitalism," 237–40.

43. C. F. Wilson, *A Century of Canadian Grain* (Saskatoon: Western Producer Books, 1978), 628.

44. Friedmann, "From Colonialism to Green Capitalism"; idem, "The Political Economy of Food," 32–35.

45. Friedmann and McMichael, "Agriculture and the State System," 104.

46. Friemann, "The Political Economy of Food," 38–39.

47. David Goodman, Bernardo Sorj, and John Wilkinson, *From Farming to Biotechnology: A Theory of Agro-Industrial Development* (New York: Basil Blackwell, 1987).

48. Friedmann, "Distance and Durability," 269.

49. Friedmann and McMichael, "Agriculture and the State System," 107–8.

50. Kim Humphery, *Shelf Life: Supermarkets and the Changing Cultures of Consumption* (Cambridge: Cambridge University Press, 1998).

51. The important exceptions have been the European Union and the United States, whose intransigence in reducing agricultural subsidies has, since the 1980s, been among the most contentious issues in the project of agricultural trade liberalization.

52. Anthony Winson, *The Intimate Commodity Food and the Development of the Agro-Industrial Complex in Canada* (Toronto: Garamond Press, 1992), 90–92.

53. Friedmann, "From Colonialism to Green Capitalism," 227–64.

54. Also referred to as generic, no-name, and supermarket brand products.

55. Burch and Lawrence, "Supermarket Own Brands," 1–28.

56. Friedmann, "From Colonialism to Green Capitalism," 253–57.

57. Philip McMichael, "Global Development and the Corporate Food Regime," in Buttel and McMichael, *New Directions in the Sociology of Global Development*, 270.

58. Bill Pritchard, "The Long Hangover from the Second Food Regime: A World-Historical Interpretation of the Collapse of the WTO Doha Round," *Agriculture and Human Values* 26 (2009): 297, 301, 306.

59. Hugh Campbell, "Breaking New Ground in Food Regime Theory," 312, 317.

60. David Burch and Geoffrey Lawrence, "Towards a Third Food Regime: Behind the Transformation," *Agriculture and Human Values* 26, no. 4 (2009): 268.

61. Jane Dixon, "From the Imperial to the Empty Calorie: How Nutrition Relations Underpin Food Regime Transitions," *Agriculture and Human Values* 26, no. 4 (2009): 321.

62. McMichael, "A Food Regime Genealogy," 163.

Bibliography

Bonanno, Alessandro, et al., eds. *From Columbus to ConAgra: The Globalization of Agriculture and Food*. Lawrence: University Press of Kansas, 1994.

Burch, David, and Geoffrey Lawrence. "Supermarket Own Brands, Supply Chains and the Transformation of the Agri-Food System." *International Journal of the Sociology of Agriculture and Food* 13, no. 1 (2005): 1–28.

Campbell, Hugh. "Breaking New Ground in Food Regime Theory: Corporate Environmentalism, Ecological Feedbacks and the 'Food from Somewhere' Regime." *Agriculture and Human Values* 26, no. 4 (2009): 309–19.

Collins, Jane. "New Directions in Commodity Chain Analysis of Global Development Processes." In *New Directions in the Sociology of Global Development*, edited by Frederick Buttel and Philip McMichael, 3–17. Oxford: Elsevier, 2005.

Dixon, Jane. "From the Imperial to the Empty Calorie: How Nutrition Relations Underpin Food Regime Transitions." *Agriculture and Human Values* 26, no. 4 (2009): 321–33.

Friedmann, Harriet. "Distance and Durability: Shaky Foundations of the World Food Economy." In *The Global Restructuring of Agro-Food Systems*, edited by Philip McMichael, 258–75. Ithaca, NY: Cornell University Press, 1994.

Friedmann, Harriet. "From Colonialism to Green Capitalism: Social Movements and Emergence of Food Regimes." In *New Directions in the Sociology of Global Development*, edited by Frederick Buttel and Philip McMichael, 227–64. Oxford: Elsevier, 2005.

Friedmann, Harriet, and Philip McMichael. "Agriculture and the State System: The Rise and Decline of National Agricultures, 1870 To The Present." *Sociologia Ruralis* 29, no. 2 (1989): 93–117.

McMichael, Philip, ed. *The Global Restructuring of Agro-food Systems*. Ithaca, NY: Cornell University Press, 1994.

McMichael, Philip. "Global Development and the Corporate Food Regime." In *New Directions in the Sociology of Global Development*, edited by Frederick Buttel and Philip McMichael, 265–300. Oxford: Elsevier, 2005.

McMichael, Philip. "A Food Regime Geneaology." *The Journal of Peasant Studies* 36, no. 1 (2009): 139–69.

Pritchard, Bill. "The Long Hangover from the Second Food Regime: A World-Historical Interpretation of the Collapse of the WTO Doha Round." *Agriculture and Human Values* 26, no. 4 (2009): 297–307.

CHAPTER 22

CULINARY TOURISM

LUCY M. LONG

CULINARY tourism is both a scholarly field of study and a growing trend within the tourism industry. It is defined as adventurous eating, eating out of curiosity, exploring other cultures through food, intentionally participating in the foodways of an "other," and developing food as tourist destination and attraction.[1] Also referred to as gastronomic tourism, tasting tourism, and simply food tourism, it is seen as tourism in which experiencing a specific food is the primary motivation for travel.[2]

This essay offers an overview of these perspectives, using a folkloristic framework for understanding tourist behaviors as a way a balancing the exotic and the familiar. A product of both world history and contemporary mass culture, culinary tourism reflects the globalization of food production and consumption as well as issues surrounding tourism in general. Questions of authenticity, commodification of tradition, identity construction, intellectual property, and intangible heritage, and the ecological, economic, and cultural sustainability of food cultures in response to tourism are hotly debated. In some minds, culinary tourism offers solutions to some of these issues by suggesting a framework for exploring other people's connections to food, as well as offering strategies to insure cultural, economic, and ecological sustainability.[3]

Origins of Culinary Tourism: Eating out of Curiosity

People have always eaten food out of curiosity, both for sustenance and to explore new tastes. Food scholar Fabio Parasecoli quotes sociologist Claude Fischler and psychologist Paul Rozin in describing two conflicting impulses that have propelled the development of new foods and new cuisines: *neophilia*, "the curiosity to try new food, based in humans' omnivorous nature," and *neophobia*, "the concurrent fear of being poisoned."[4] Such curiosity has been a driving force in the history of food, introducing new ingredients, recipes, preparation methods, and cooking styles. Culinary tourism suggests the process by which novelty is incorporated into a food culture by the movement from exotic to edible to familiar and finally to palatable. New foods are perceived as strange and different (exotic) and possibly not edible. Once they are perceived as an item that can be eaten (familiar), then evaluations of its tastiness can be made. Chinese food in the United States, for example, was initially seen as too exotic to be considered food when first experienced by California gold rush miners in the mid-1800s. Once Americans got used to the idea of eating it, it became a part of their familiar "culinary universe," and taste preferences might then determine their choice of consuming it, rather than fear that it was too unknown. Similarly, restaurant owners might then add something exotic in order to stir curiosity again. This may explain the common pattern seen in the United States in which Cantonese-style Chinese restaurants are first accepted, then are followed in some areas by restaurants offering various regional styles of Chinese food. Donna Gabaccia makes cross-ethnic dining central to her interpretation of American food in *We Are What We Eat* (1998).[5]

World historian Felipe Fernández-Armesto suggests a similarly long view of culinary tourism in his book *Near a Thousand Tables: A History of Food* (2002). He identifies eight "revolutions," or paradigmatic shifts in the ways humans use and think about food, including the rise of agriculture and herding, the development of cooking and manners, and long-distance trade and industrialization. These transitions are not successive chronological periods, but tend to overlap, survive in pockets of populations, and leave behind vestiges of each stage. His history suggests that "eating out of curiosity/exploratory eating" has always occurred but in different manners and with different meanings. In the eighth and final phase, the postindustrial, Fernández-Armesto helps to explain the emergence of culinary tourism as an intentional exploration of the "other" for the purpose of pleasure and satisfying curiosity. This phase is characterized by "the internationalization of the palate and the rise of fusion cookery reflect[ing] multiculturalism."[6]

The industrial world offered new mobility to people to cross cultural boundaries—both voluntarily for pleasure, education, or commerce and involuntarily for safety, health, lifestyle, or occupational opportunities. This has literally brought together individuals from different backgrounds to living in close proximity and sharing their everyday lives, including their foodways. We smell our neighbors' dinner cooking; we see new vegetables in the supermarkets; we visit restaurants serving cuisines completely foreign to us—these all make us curious about things we might not have known even existed before. Geographer David Harvey characterizes the state of the modern world, particularly since the 1950s, as one of "space-time compression."[7] Food cultures are also compressed in the sense that many of us (particularly in the United States) now have access to ingredients, dishes, cooking styles, and food philosophies from across the world. Although literature and travel writing might have piqued our curiosity before, we can now actually satisfy that curiosity and experience these new foods. This intentional mixing of ingredients and styles has created numerous fusion dishes and even cuisines. Simultaneously, hybrid dishes have emerged from expediency (cost, availability, ease of preparation) that then may become the focus of curiosity. Reactions against industrialization could also encourage culinary experimentation, particularly with foods that were seen as more authentic and natural. The countercultural revolutions of the 1960s and 1970s saw an openness to new cultures and new experiences as well as a celebration of diversity and nonconformity, all of which helped open up peoples' palates to new tastes.[8]

Eating out of curiosity now occurs in a wide variety of forms—commercial and public as well as informal and private. They also include educational explorations into other cultures and places as well as pleasurable excursions into new tastes. Contemporary global culture encourages adventurous eating, and numerous new products featuring "exotic" foods are being marketing in grocery stores and restaurants.

Cookbooks and other culinary literature could perhaps be seen as the first virtual media for culinary tourism, offering readers a window into other people's food. Although these were originally meant to function as primers for cooking skills and housewifery, they also offered vicarious eating, enabling readers to imagine new tastes. Many cookbooks today include portraits of the culture surrounding the recipes, giving histories, biographies, maps, and luscious photographs that whet the appetite. Cookbooks featuring regional food traditions are particularly popular throughout the United States and Europe. Even though many of these present gourmet updates of traditional recipes or innovative recipes using local ingredients, they also reflect a shift toward looking inward to explore the complexities within a nation, as well as a concern with place as significant to human experience. Food writing moved in the early 1990s from reviewing restaurants to exploring the pleasures of new foods and new cuisines, as well as accounts of travels for and with food. Today, food periodicals frequently feature exotic (or at least, new) foods and ingredients, along with new ways of cooking and serving food. For example, the cover of the January 2007 issue of *Food and Wine* heralds "100 tastes you must try in 2007." Even non–food-centered periodicals often include foods or eating experiences based on culinary curiosity. During the 2008 Beijing Olympics, a major fashion magazine included an article in which the author describes how "after a few wrong turns, [he] finds his way to some of China's most delicious, authentic, and innovative cuisine—and the perfect roast duck."[9]

New media have also been primary venues for satisfying one's curiosity about food. Televised cooking shows, like cookery books, opened new culinary worlds for thousands of people who would never be able to travel to experience those foods. Julia Child, though not the first television chef, broke new ground in 1963 with the premier of her program, *The French Chef*, in which she showed American housewives how to "tame" gourmet French cooking. Cooking shows, though popular, tended to remain the domain of day-time programming for stay-at-home adults (wives, particularly) until the Food Network was established in 1993. This brought new foods and cuisines into the home and helped transform the perception of cooking from a domestic chore into a culinary art. By 2004, cooking shows were wildly popular among all ages and genders, and the Food Network created shows dedicated to exploring new and exotic foods. One of the most popular culinary adventure shows was Anthony Bourdain's *A Cook's Tour*, which aired in 2001 and 2002, and visited locales ranging from Tokyo and Southeast Asia, to Portugal and the Basque region of Spain, Mexico, Kansas City, Brazil, and Australia.

Films, like television, have always included food and eating as part of the setting for action and as metaphors for characters' emotions and relationships. *My Dinner with Andre* (1981), for example, consisted entirely of two characters talking over a meal. Films that focused on food preparation and consumption, though, tended to be rare, and even in the 2010, there are a limited number that actually center action and character development around food. *Babette's Feast*, (1987), about a woman who cooks for a Danish community of ascetics, has inspired adventuresome home cooks to recreate her nineteenth-century Parisian banquet. Another film that uses eating our of curiosity as a theme is *Sideways* (2004), an American comedy in which two middle-aged men travel through California's wine country, exploring possibilities in their own lives as they explore wine and fine dining. Numerous other films have stirred audiences' curiosity about food and cooking, most notably, *Big Night* (1996), *Eat, Drink, Man, Woman* (1994), and the award winning, *Julie and Julia* (2009).

Also riding this wave is an emerging genre of literature made up of memoirs and fiction based on exploring food. Memoirs, in particular, have become popular and usually use food as a tangible way to organize and make sense of memories. Often set as an exploration of food in a new place, this exploration is a metaphor for discovery of the self. Some of the most influential ones include, M. F. K. Fisher's *The Gastronomical Me* (1989), Peter Mayle's *A Year in Provence* (1991), and Ruth Reichl's *Tender at the Bone: Growing Up at the Table* (1998) and *Comfort Me with Apples: More Adventures at the Table* (2001). Of particular relevance to culinary tourism is Jeffrey Steingarten's *The Man Who Ate Everything* (1997), in which the author, food critic for *Vogue* magazine, sets out to taste and learn about foods that he disliked. Even though he does not acquire a liking for them, he eats them out of curiosity, a sense of adventure, and an exploration of his own culinary universe. More recently, Barbara Kingsolver's *Animal, Vegetable, Miracle* (2007) explores a year of living off of locally produced food in the Virginia mountains, tapping into more recent concerns about connecting one's food to environmental and community sustainability. A similar thread in many of these memoirs is a search for identity, family, and community through food. An excellent example is food scholar and writer Laura Schenone's *The Lost Ravioli Recipes of Hoboken: A Search for Food and Family* (2008), in which a desire to learn to make ravioli like her grandmother did takes the author on a culinary tour through Italy—and a discovery of herself.

Restaurants, cooking classes, and folklife festivals also cater to the search for new culinary pleasures. Eating out in the United States has become much more common today, not just for special occasions but also for nourishment, and is a major source of entertainment. As palates become more cosmopolitan, restaurants offer more and more tastes, oftentimes adding dishes from a variety of culinary cultures to the menus. A brochure for an exclusive restaurant in the Washington, D.C. area, for example, boldly claims: "Tour the world's finest cuisines, presented with flair and accompanied by premium spirits and wines." As our tastes have broadened, cooking classes and "tasting" events have become popular. Classes in the United States may still focus on culinary skills drawn from French cooking, but many now focus on learning techniques and styles from cultures across the globe. These often teach iconic dishes (Chinese stir fry, Japanese sushi, Thai noodles) that have become popular through the restaurant scene so that they can be reproduced at home. Since food is a window into culture, eating out of curiosity can also be a way of exploring the culture surrounding a food. Educators, museums, and other cultural institutions and culture scholars have long used food to introduce belief systems, aesthetics, lifestyles, and traditions of other cultures. For example, the Smithsonian Institution's annual Folklife Festival includes foodways as an integral part of every cultural group presented at the festival. Many people come because they are curious about particular foods, and leave with an understanding that food is a much more complex—and richer—topic than they realized.

Food in the Tourism Industry

The tourism industry was slow to recognize the potential of food as an attraction and destination, treating it instead as one part of "hospitality services." This is understandable, however, if we define tourism as travel for pleasure, and realize that the hardships and dangers early travelers had to endure rarely made it a pleasurable experience. A number of cultures have traditions of people traveling to places specifically to eat the food produced there. Northern Spain, for example, is famous for the varieties of beans associated with each village, and knowledgeable eaters travel to restaurants in those regions serving specialty dishes made from those beans. Consumers insist that the beans taste differently if transported elsewhere, and that a full appreciation of them requires consuming them in situ, in the place they are grown. Wine, similarly, has attracted consumers who want to sample the wine in its place of origin and production. Such travels can perhaps more accurately be called food pilgrimages since they include an element of seeking the authentic as an almost sacred quest for knowledge and personal transformation.[10]

The countries most associated with both domestic and international culinary tourism are France, Italy, and Spain. All have highly developed cuisines, as well as native populations that are knowledgeable and willing to travel within their own countries for food experiences. They also boast historical and contemporary cultures of wine consumption, often tied to strong family traditions of vineyards and vintners. Today, Australia, New Zealand, China, Thailand, and Singapore have become major food destinations. Canada and the United States are also vying for their share of the tourism market. In most cases, wine tourism is leading the way in the tourism industry bringing in tourists usually willing and able to pay for higher-priced hospitality services. This has encouraged the development of fine-dining, gourmet food establishments, and, in some instances, is forming the basis for the emergence of new cuisines—for example, the Niagara region of Canada, Southern Appalachia in the United States, and the New Global Cuisine based in Hong Kong.[11]

Individual businesses within the tourism industry are developing products in response to recognizing this interest. Wineries and restaurants, for example, began promoting themselves as tourist destinations, often adding overnight accommodations for guests. In the early 2000s, travel companies began including food as a focus, offering tours to famous restaurants or to eating experiences in regions well known for their food, and in the 2000s, businesses emerged that focused on culinary tours. With names such as Culinary Adventures, The Globetrotting Gourmet, Crete's Culinary Sanctuaries, and A Cook's Tour, these companies are obviously focusing on food as a destination. Guidebooks and travel brochures are also emphasizing food. For example, the *Lonely Planet—World Food* series is specifically "for people who live to eat, drink and travel with local recipes and culinary dictionary."[12] These include maps, photos, recipes, and cultural and historical context so that readers can explore the food culture knowledgeably and respectfully.

New Zealand, Australia, Great Britain, and Canada have led the way in establishing culinary tourism within the tourism industry, and have tied industry developments with scholarly research and assessment on the subject. Each nation has established its own organizations overseeing culinary tourism. The United States has been slower to recognize food's potential, and has tended to focus more on the business and management side with less attention to cultural issues. For example, the International Culinary Tourism Association, based in Oregon, focuses on strategies for creating and marketing products and offers expensive certification programs for members.[13]

Although tourism initiatives are becoming more aware of the potential for everyday foods to attract visitors, their emphasis is primarily on fine-dining, innovative foods that deliver satisfying taste experiences and justify tourist expenditures. Any food associated with a place, however, can become the focus of culinary tourism, for example, maple syrup in New England, beef in Argentina, lobster in Maine, crawfish in Louisiana, or grits in the Southern United States. Some cities become associated with particular foods—Cincinnati chili, Kansas City or Memphis barbecue, Boston baked beans, Philadelphia cheese steak—and are using those foods in their tourism marketing. Tourists frequently intentionally eat those foods in order to better "experience the place," and restaurants catering to tourists frequently market the foods in that way. Iconic foods are also featured on tourist souvenirs such as clothing, key chains, and other trinkets.

Culinary tourism is closely related to other varieties of tourism. It can be included under cultural tourism, in which tourists travel to experience another culture. In these instances, food is used as a way to discover everyday life as well as to share a sense of community with members of that culture (or with the tour group). Festivals often offer sites for cultural tourism, presenting specialty dishes intentionally selected to represent a cuisine. Also closely related is agritourism, which consists of farm tours, possibly observing or participating in farm activities, such as milking cows or harvesting a crop, or tours of food processing and manufacturing establishments, such as canneries, cheese making, or factories. For obvious reasons, agritourism tends to focus on rural areas, while culinary tourism is frequently urban with access to restaurants.

Heritage tourism is also relevant to culinary tourism. Living history museums, notably Colonial Williamsburg in Virginia and Plimouth Plantation in Massachusetts, often allow for the exploration of foodways of the past with demonstrations of food preparation. Interpreters may give explanations along with such activities as cutting apples, baking bread, or working in the garden. In some venues, visitors are given the opportunity to participate or to at least taste some of the results. Extreme tourism, in which tourists test boundaries of safety or social and cultural appropriateness, sometimes includes food, involving ingredients not usually considered "normal" or edible in the tourist's home culture. Ecotourism, in which the focus is on exploring the natural environment without damaging it, can be related to culinary tourism by including meals utilizing locally produced and organic foods. Culinary tourism is also frequently now tied to sustainable tourism, offering a way to keep money in host communities, provide employment to local residents, and teach understanding of the culture among tourists. Later I will discuss the ways it attempts to resolve the twin challenges of tourism: competitiveness and endurance of resources.

Culinary Tourism—Scholarly Literature

Scholarship on the intersection of tourism and food is surprisingly recent, with the late 1990s and early 2000s marking the publication of most foundational studies. Research initially divided into two strands. The first was humanities-based, using qualitative, ethnographic research that explored both food and tourism as socio-cultural constructions. The focus tended to be the meanings and impacts of those constructions. The second strand was an applied one, using social science, business, and marketing models with quantitative methods to clarify and resolve issues surrounding food within the tourism industry. Although these two strands still exist, sometimes in opposition to each other, tourism scholars and individuals working within the industry (particularly outside the United States, notably in Canada, Australia, New Zealand, and Great Britain) have recently recognized the need to bridge the two. Research on sustainable tourism tends to merge the two approaches.

Geographer Wilbur Zelinsky was perhaps the first scholar to discuss the concept, which he termed "gastronomic tourism." In a 1985 article, he used a novel quantitative method of surveying telephone book listings of ethnic restaurants to map culinary regions in the United States and Canada. His research was concerned with explaining the prevalence of particular ethnic groups as restaurateurs.[14] Nevertheless, a number of scholars within the humanities picked up on the term and sought to explore the meanings of "eating the other."[15] For example, a cultural studies dissertation by Jay Ann Cox examined Mexican foods in an Arizona folklife festival as well as the stereotypes presented in salsa advertisements.[16] *Consuming Geographies: We Are Where We Eat*, by David Bell and Gill Valentine, offers excellent summaries and critiques of various theories and publications. They use the phrase "kitchen table tourism" to refer to the possibilities offered by modern technology (specifically, the Internet) for vicariously experiencing other food cultures. Their chapter on the global explores numerous issues involved in culinary tourism from a cultural geography perspective.[17] Another excellent discussion of these issues is provided by cultural studies scholars Bob Ashley, Joanne Hollows, Steve Jones, and Ben Taylor in their important food studies text, *Food and Cultural Studies*. Among other things, they address the application of Pierre Bourdieu's notion of social distinction as an explanation for the modern trend in acquiring knowledge of the culinary other as cultural capital to assert identity and class difference. They point out that multiple interpretations should be recognized, and that consuming the other is tied to numerous cultural processes. Their delineation of five of those offers a useful model for research: production, regulation, representation, identity, and consumption.[18]

Zilenski's work on restaurants established those institutions as significant sites for food and tourism. Numerous publications touch on this intersection without referring specifically to tourism, and my own formulation of culinary tourism grew out of research on Korean restaurants in the United States.[19] The edited volume by anthropologists David Beriss and David Sutton, *The Restaurants Book: Ethnographies of Where We Eat*, also uses restaurants as the "ideal postmodern institutions" for exploring the many challenges facing us today, including tourism.[20]

I first used the term "culinary tourism" in 1996 conference papers at the Association for the Study of Food and Society and the American Folklore Society. The favorable reception by colleagues led to a journal article in 1998, and an edited volume, *Culinary Tourism: Eating and Otherness*, in which I offered a framework for broadening our understandings of both tourism and food as cultural, social, and personal constructions. My definition of culinary tourism draws from folklore, sociolinguistics, cultural anthropology, and philosophy of aesthetics: "the intentional, exploratory participation in the foodways of an other—participation including the consumption, preparation, and presentation of a food item, cuisine, meal system, or eating style considered to belong to a culinary system not one's own." From this perspective, culinary tourism deals with the negotiation of exotic and familiar foods by individuals—tourists as well as producers. Foods have to be different enough to elicit curiosity, but familiar enough to be considered edible. Also, exoticness or "otherness" is a matter of personal perspective involving multiple factors. Culture, ethnicity, region, time (past, future, and festive), ethos or religion, socioeconomic class, gender, and age can all offer foods that are different for an eater. For example, kosher foods might be exotic for non-Jews; alcohol for under-age teenagers; stews cooked in an iron kettle over an open fire for modern day eaters; vegetarian foods for an omnivore; quiche for "real men."

This approach to otherness expands the possibilities of what foods are available for tourism. I adapt John Urry's "tourist gaze"[21] as a way of seeing the potential exoticness in common, everyday foods, moving beyond gourmet dishes to recognizing the potential meaningfulness of the everyday—"exoticizing the familiar." My model for culinary tourism also shifts the focus from food (the product that is consumed) to foodways, the total network of activities surrounding food and eating. This network includes procurement, preservation, preparation, presentation, consumption styles, contexts for eating, cleaning up, conceptualizations about food, and symbolic performances. Individuals attach different meanings to foods partly because they have different memories associated with these components. For example, a fish caught in the local river during a family vacation might be the same product as one shipped in from a commercial distributor, but it carries memories of people and events that give it different emotional weights. The model also suggests that venues for tourism extend beyond the usual sites for consumption of food to include a variety of venues, both virtual and "real": cookbooks, cookware shops and catalogues, grocery stores, films, literature, television cooking shows, advertising, festivals, farms, classes, and so on. The folkloristic approach to culinary tourism recognizes that aesthetic and sensory memories shape individual's responses to new experiences, and that individuals constantly reconstruct their perceptions of identity, community, and culture.

Culturally grounded food studies scholars also began addressing culinary tourism in the mid-1990s. The 11th conference on The International Commission for Ethnological Food Research held in Cyprus in 1996 focused on the role of colonization in culinary tourism as well as connections between migrations, immigrations, and the geographic distribution of particular foods and foodways. The proceedings were published in 1998, edited by Irish folklorist Patricia Lysaght, and articles provide historical as well as ethnographic perspectives. A more recent exploration of these issues can be found in a special issue of *Food, Culture and Society*, titled "Food Journeys: Culinary Travels in Time and Space." Articles in this volume explore "a wider range of temporal and figurative journeys," using travel "as a metaphor for reflection, memory, exchange and otherness." They utilize a critical theory approach recognizing that "accounts of eating practices therefore have an intimate and intricate relationship with colonial discourse, and with differential power relations in general."[22] In this publication, Kaori O'Connor analyzes food as not only a central tourist attraction but also a metaphor for the tourist identity that has developed around Hawaii, while Daisy Tam uses Bourdieu to develop a theory of Slow Food that actually centers the self as part of a system with responsibility to the rest of that system, a positioning that forces individuals to look outward and that holds the possibility for culinary tourism to enable positive shifts in human's relationships to others.[23]

Meanwhile, scholarship within tourism studies began addressing food as an attraction and destination in the mid-1990s. Scholars in the United Kingdom, Australia, and New Zealand defined food tourism as a particular genre of tourism having as its primary motivation "the desire to experience a particular type of food or the produce of a specific region."[24] This definition was later expanded to include "visitation to primary and secondary food producers, food festivals, restaurants and specific locations for which food tasting and/or experiencing the attribute of specialist food production regions are the primary motivating factor for travel."[25] Thus, a volume on wine tourism offered a cross-disciplinary perspective drawing from business, social science, and policy approaches. A 2003 work, *Food Tourism Around the World*, also edited by Hall and Sharples, explored motivations, models, and implications for culinary identity as well as regional economic development. The book offers management and marketing perspectives but also recognize the role of culture as a useful tool for marketing. The authors also focus on location as significant to food tourism, stating that even though it can be "exported" it still retains a spatial fixity: "The tourists must go to the location of production in order to consume the local fare and become food tourists."[26] This conclusion differs from the humanities approach in which individuals can explore other foods through a variety of venues without actually traveling away from home.

Another influential volume, *Tourism and Gastronomy* (2002), edited by Anne-Mette Hjalager and Greg Richards, examines gastronomic tourism as a force for economic development and cultural transformation. Authors discuss issues such as the potential for gastronomy and tourism to serve as radical, activist disciplines, the importance of intellectual property, regional and national identities, and the connections between globalization and localization. The editors conclude by pointing out that tourism and gastronomy are both emerging disciplines with similar dichotomies in practice from small-scale, artisanal production to industrial mass production. They also call upon globalization to be interpreted as a potentially beneficial force, noting that fears of it fail to recognize the dynamic character of both gastronomy and tourism. Portugal's protectionist stance toward globalization has, in their opinion, stifled the local food culture. By contrast, Spain's ability to develop brand names for regional cuisines not only allows for more creativity but is also more realistic.

In another formative publication, Priscilla Boniface has sought to explain why food and drink have recently become attractions in their own right, placing the question in historical context as well as a contemporary reaction to industrialization, modernity, and globalization. She suggests that this shift represents more than just the discovery of a new niche in tourism. It is a shift in the culture of tourism itself, implying that tourism is no longer based on a separation from the quotidian, but instead a blending between holiday and the everyday. Taking a cultural perspective on "tasting tourism," Boniface recognizes that culture drives tourism, which in turn provides a medium through which society works out issues of identity and power. Building upon the ideas of cultural critic Henri Lefebvre, who emphasized the disconnection of modern man to his modes of production and even consumption, Boniface sees food tourism as a seeking of authentic experiences through food—resulting from the peculiarities of modern life. Boniface raises the possibility, though, that this very modernity is what makes us recognize and appreciate the past, the rural, and the non-industrialized. Finally, she identifies five "driving forces" acting as motivations for food tourism: anxieties over food safety and social uncertainty; a need to show distinction, affluence and individualism; curiosity and wish for knowledge and discovery; the need to feel grounded amid globalization; and the requirement for sensory and tactile pleasure. Her work is particularly useful for humanities scholars of culinary tourism who are exploring the constructions of the meanings of culinary tourism.[27]

The publications mentioned previously emphasize the positive opportunities offered by recognizing food in tourism, but a 2004 article by Erik Cohen and Nir Avieli points out that food can also be an obstacle to tourism. In this useful assessment of the state of food tourism both as an industry and a field of scholarship, they observe that unpleasant food experiences can lead to cultural misunderstandings and that the use of food as an attraction can actually have harmful effects on the host culture.[28] By 2010, scholarship in tourism recognizes culinary tourism not only as a significant industry trend but also as a subject crucial for understanding the implications of tourist productions and behaviors.

Issues

Many of the issues surrounding culinary tourism concern tourism in general. Although food presents some unique challenges, it also offers a medium for exploring these issues. Because it is so multifaceted and easily holds a variety of meanings simultaneously, food helps in understanding the complexities of tourism as both a human impulse and an industry building upon that impulse. This section first addresses some of the common criticisms of tourism and then explores the two biggest challenges facing culinary tourism in the future: competitiveness and sustainability.

One of the most fundamental criticisms is that tourism is categorically a colonialist enterprise in which individuals with power and wealth exploit other cultures for their own pleasure, entertainment, or edification. That exploitation means that individual members of other cultures are stripped of their personhood and perceived as less than the tourist. Similarly, tourism puts "others" on display, turning them into an object to be looked upon. This issue in culinary tourism translates into asking what it means to eat an "other," a food perceived to be exotic or somehow different from one's own food culture. Eating does not necessarily lead to understanding or respect for that culture.[29] My formulation of culinary tourism as a means of developing an experiential understanding of the humanity of others also addresses this concern. By approaching food, a basic and universal need, as a cultural, social, and personal construction, we can identify our commonalities as well as the logic behind our differences.[30]

Philosopher, Lisa Heldke, addresses the colonialist issue in her book, *Exotic Appetites: Ruminations of a Food Adventurer* (2003). She points out that eating other cuisines poses a philosophical dilemma. On one hand, it represents imperialism in that it is only with wealth that we are able to experiment with food. But, she continues, "for me to decide to eat only foods of my own ethnicity is to close my doors, not to allow any foreign influence in. It is also a decision to impoverish my life by remaining ignorant of other cultures." Her answer is to continually question ourselves—our motivations, our responses, our attitudes and relationships to that food and the people behind them: "we cannot eat just once and be done with it. The meanings of our actions do not remain constant, but shift and change with the changes in their context." This consciousness allows us to become "anticolonialist food adventurers."[31]

A recent trend in culinary tourism initiatives may reflect a shift in attitude among tourists that reflects awareness Heldke encourages. Cooking classes and educational culinary tours turn tourists into students of that culture. Although these types of activities tend to be high-priced, and the knowledge these tourists gain might be for their own enhancement "back home," they are acting in a way that reverses the typical host-tourist relationship. In this case, the host has knowledge and skills that the guests want and respect, and many individuals involved in such tourism feel that it creates a more equitable relationship than the usual tourism one. To describe this particular attitude of respect, even reverence, for the food of an "other," I have suggested the term "food pilgrimage." Individuals on food pilgrimages seek original contexts in which to experience a food cultural as authentically as possible. Seeing the food "in situ" offers the opportunity to understand it as a whole system connected to a specific time, place, and people. Such tours can lead to a "transcendent" experience with food, and food "pilgrims" often feel that they have undergone a positive transformation in some way.

Another major criticism of tourism is that it leads to a weakening of cultural identity, that, by putting a culture on display as part of a tourist attraction, that culture becomes a commodity, and identity becomes little more than a brand name. Proponents of tourism, however, point out that individuals frequently become more aware of their identity through tourist activities. Furthermore, if tourists are respectful of that identity and show an appreciation for it, they can actually encourage pride and a desire to preserve identity. Kevin Meethan, for example, states that tourism actually reinforces "locality, or the specificity of places and cultures."[32]

Since foodways are an expression of identity, culinary tourism offers an especially potent means of affirming that identity. George Ritzer's work on McDonaldization asserts that globalization has often stimulated local cuisine rather than stifled it, and Richard Wilk observes that tourism in Belize has recently encouraged the development of a Belizean cuisine.[33]

These positive interpretations of tourism make sense if we think of "differential identity" as identities constructed out of contrast with another identity. The differences between cultures help us identify what characterizes them, and which of those characteristics are significant. Culinary tourism plays a role in this process by emphasizing the unique foodways of a culture. This happens on a variety of levels. Regional identities based on real or imagined attachments to a geographic space can actually be recognized as well as constructed through food. Barbecue has become iconic of the American South, and scholars are now demonstrating that variations in barbecue meats and sauces reflect regional differences within that larger region.[34] Food can also offer a commonality around which individuals can feel a sense of attachment to a place, so that consuming that food becomes a symbolic means of acting upon that attachment. Clambakes in New England often serve that purpose as well as others.[35] Furthermore, food is also being used to develop a definition of a region. A new cuisine is developing in Southern Appalachia, for example, that features local produce and foods from nature—mountain trout, blackberries, morels. In order to appeal to culinary tourists, these foods are sometimes "fancied up" and removed from their cultural histories. Grits, for example, might be referred to as "Appalachia polenta," or "traditional" foods such as fried green tomatoes and ripened tomato slices are paired with fresh mozzarella and basil leaves.[36]

Ethnic identities have also been constructed and affirmed through culinary tourism. Restaurants, festivals, church fairs, and cookbooks all offer venues for culinary tourists to experience these foods.[37] Tourism also allows for ethnic identity to be situational, a highlighting of that identity rather than others also held by the hosts. For example a Middle-Eastern restaurant in Detroit where there is a large population of Lebanese-Americans, might be run by family who has lived in the United States for several generations and intermarried with non-Lebanese, but for purposes of the restaurant, they highlight their Lebanese ancestry. Similarly, since Korean food was slow to be accepted in the United States outside major cities on the east and west coasts, many Koreans highlighted their Asian heritage and opened restaurants serving Chinese or Japanese foods. There are numerous other examples of ethnic foods that were initially exotic tourist items that have become familiar and accepted within mainstream food culture and have perhaps then led to both a recognition of that ethnicity and further exploration of that cuisine—Italian pizza, Mexican tacos, Spanish tapas, Chinese chop suey and chow mein, Thai pad thai, and so on.

The adaption of foods for culinary tourism reflects another frequent criticism of tourism in general, that it manipulates cultural traditions, commodifying and "trinketizing" (turning them into trivial souvenir objects), stripping them of their original meanings and cultural power. Also, as a force in globalization, tourism is correspondingly leading to homogenization of cultural differences. Since many tourists seek familiar foods when they travel, popular restaurant chains have been established throughout the world, in some cases supplanting local food practices and spawning local imitations. Some scholars have challenged the interpretation that this leads to homogeneity. James Watson, for example, has demonstrated that McDonald's in Asian countries are given culturally specific meanings and functions by local residents.[38]

Culinary tourism can actually be a force in encouraging both globalization and the affirmation and preservation of local foods since such tourists actively seek foods different from their familiar ones. Tourists can provide practical incentives for maintaining culinary traditions by creating markets for them. This leads to "tourist cuisines or dishes," that are either inventions of new dishes or adaptations of traditional ones in order accommodate tourist tastes and expectations. For example, restaurants in southern Appalachia now offer updated versions of traditional foods such as grits and cornbread, using organic or exotic ingredients. Similarly, chefs in Singapore have developed a new fusion cuisine specifically in response to tourists. Emphasis also tends to be on celebratory foods rather than common, everyday ones since these are often considered more distinctive, tastier, and higher priced. This can then dilute the meanings of that food. The luau in Hawaii, for example, has become a tourist production with stereotypical foods, shifting from the sacred meanings held within the community to simply a party and feast for the tourists.[39]

The tendency to adapt foods for tourists raises questions about authenticity, a quality felt by some tourism scholars to be a primary motivation for many tourists.[40] Authenticity, however, presupposes that there exists an original, pure version of a food culture that has remained static and free of outside influences. Recognition of the dynamic nature of culture in general has led instead to questions concerning how to define a food culture, how to preserve it without also stifling it, and ownership of it.

Food is now recognized as intangible heritage and, as such, can be protected under international law. UNESCO includes it as part of cultural heritage. Preservation of this heritage, however, is very complex, as seen in the example of a town in Italy, Lucca, which attempted to ban all ethnic foods in restaurants in order to preserve their local specialties. Critics pointed out that the cuisine they were trying to protect had itself been developed from "foreign" foods originally (tomatoes, for example). Also, some local residents protested, saying that they wanted to be able to be innovative and creative in their food preparation and consumption. Again, the role of tourism was seen in this discussion as both an affirmation of the food heritage and a threat to it.

Food is also now recognized as intellectual property, meaning that ownership is being contested for cuisines, recipes, cooking styles, and even ingredients. Geographical indicators are used in many countries to designate the accurate origin of a food product, beginning with France, which established the Appellation d' Origine Controllee in the early 1900s to protect cheeses and wines. This is based on the older concept of *terroir* ("taste of place") and allows regions to claim certain types of produce as belonging to them. An arm of the government also sets standards by which any produce from a designated region can carry an AOC stamp of approval. Such geographical indicators directly benefit and are benefited by the culinary tourism industry in that they guarantee quality and authenticity. Tourism marketing then tends to treat them as a brand by which products can be known.

Many scholars of tourism now call for a more nuanced view of tourism that acknowledges these criticisms but also recognizes that tourism can offer both benefits and costs to all participants involved either directly or indirectly. Participants include tourists (guests), the host community, the government of the host community, the tourism suppliers or businesses connected to supply, and the natural environment. Each participant has their own perspective, so that what benefits one may be a cost or harmful to another. To further complicate matters, definitions of success might differ according to each perspective. As tourism scholar, Erve Chambers notes, tourism is complex, involving numerous players who construct their own meanings from tourist activities.[41] Although, more powerful nations and individuals have the opportunity to develop infrastructures and financial capital for a tourism industry, these "contradictions of tourism" exist regardless of who the tourist is.

These concerns are being addressed in the field of sustainable tourism, which argues that by carefully managing the resources for tourism (local economies, ecologies, and cultures) the tourism industry will not only help those resources endure but will also sustain itself. Culinary tourism offers a potentially powerful tool for sustainability. Similar to Slow Food's vision of promoting food that is "good, clean, and fair," it can encourage culinary "destinations" and "attractions" that are locally produced with environmentally friendly methods, and provide employment for members of the host culture. An issue arises from the culinary tourism industry's frequent focus on gourmet ingredients or preparation methods appealing to elite, high-paying customers. In order to be competitive in the tourism marketplace, businesses need to offer something that is distinctive and unique and also has the highest margin between profit and production possible. This can mean that producers (chefs, farmers, restaurant managers) are brought in from outside the local culture, sometimes creating "leakage" (profits leave the host community) and culturally unsustainable products. For example, a gourmet restaurant in a small, culinarily conservative town, might bring in the occasional outside customer but not appeal to local eaters. Rather than creating an appreciation for local food culture, the tourism actually dismisses it. The folkloristic approach to culinary tourism attempts to counteract this possibility by promoting an understanding of the host culture's cultural history, placing their food traditions within that history, and presenting them in ways that emphasize their local meanings. The Bowling Green Culinary Tourism Trail is a successful example of this "exoticizing the familiar." Another approach to ensuring that culinary tourism is sustainable calls for a number of local food producers and distributers to collaborate, ideally with other public and private sectors to offer a systematically planned destination with a diversity of attractions. A cooperative of growers in Michigan provides an excellent example of such "clustering," as it is called in the tourism industry.

Conclusion

As both a scholarly field of study and an initiative within the tourism industry, culinary tourism is complex and multifaceted. It also offers unique insights into not only numerous issues facing us today, but also possibilities for resolving those issues. Perhaps of utmost significance is its potential for encouraging the recognition of the power of food. It reflects our personal and cultural histories and ties us to all the external and internal forces shaping our lives. As food scholar Fabio Parasecoli points out in relation to food and tourism: "A deeper awareness of the political, non-neutral nature of semiotic processes defining codes and modalities of cultural exchange can help tourists to shift their location not only physically, but also culturally. Having a better grasp of the various signifying networks that make tourists define a phenomenon, in our case a dish or a product, as 'typical' or 'local' might help them learn how to occupy the subject position of the otherness, without losing the awareness of their own location."[42] As such, culinary tourism offers the opportunity to explore not only other foods and cultures but also our own lives through food.

Notes

1. Respectively, Lisa M. Heldke, *Exotic Appetites: Ruminations of a Food Adventurer* (New York: Routledge, 2003); Lucy M. Long, ed., *Culinary Tourism* (Lexington: University Press of Kentucky, 2004); C. Michael Hall, et al., eds., *Food Tourism Around the World: Development, Management and Markets* (London: Butterworth-Heinemann, 2003).

2. Ane-Mette Hjalager and Greg Richards, eds., *Tourism and Gastronomy* (London: Routledge, 2002); Priscilla Boniface, *Tasting Tourism: Travelling for Food Drink* (Aldershot: Ashgate, 2003); C. Michael Hall and Liz Sharples, "The Consumption of Experiences or the Experience of Consumption? An Introduction to the Tourism of Taste," in Hall, et al., *Food Tourism Around the World*, 1–24.

3. Long, *Culinary Tourism*, 37–44; C. Michael Hall and Liz Sharples, *Food and Wine Festivals and Events Around the World* (London: Butterworth-Heinemann, 2008).

4. Fabio Parasecoli, *Bite Me: Food in Popular Culture* (Oxford: Berg, 2008), 142.

5. Donna R. Gabaccia, *We Are What We Eat: Ethnic Food and the Making of Americans* (Cambridge, MA: Harvard University Press, 1998).

6. Felipe Fernández-Armesto, *Near a Thousand Tables: A History of Food* (New York: Free Press, 2002), 223.

7. David Harvey, *The Condition of Postmodernity: An Enquiry into the Origins of Cultural Change* (Oxford: Blackwell, 1989).

8. Warren Belasco, *Appetite for Change: How the Counterculture Took on the Food Industry* (1989; repr., Ithaca, NY: Cornell University Press, 1993).

9. Jeffrey Steingarten, "Lost in Beijing," *Vogue* (June 2008): 178–181, 203.

10. Lucy M. Long, "Food Pilgrimages: Seeking the Authentic and Sacred in Food" (paper presented at the annual meeting of the Association for the Study of Food and Society, Boston, MA, June 2006).

11. David J. Telfer and Atsuko Hashioto, "Food Tourism in the Niagara Region: The Development of a Nouvelle Cuisine," in Hall, et al., *Food Tourism Around the World*, 158–77; Lucy M. Long, "Culinary Tourism and the Emergence of an Appalachian Cuisine: Exploring the Foodscape of Asheville, NC," *North Carolina Folklore Journal* 57, no. 1 (2010): 4–19; Rosario Scarpato, "Sustainable Gastronomy as a Tourist Product," in Hjalager and Richards, *Tourism and Gastronomy*, 132–53.

12. See, for example, Bruce Geddes, *Lonely Planet World Food Mexico* (Hawthorn, Australia: Lonely Planet, 2000).

13. For more information on ICTA, see Eric Wolf, *Culinary Tourism: The Hidden Harvest* (Dubuque, IA: Kendall Hunt Publishing, 2006).

14. Wilbur Zelinsky, "The Roving Palate: North America's Ethnic Restaurant Cuisines," *Geoforum* 16, no. 1 (1985): 51.

15. Rogert Abrahams, "Equal Opportunity Eating: A Structural Excursus on Things of the Mouth," in *Ethnic and Regional Foodways in the United States: The Performance of Group Identity*, ed. Linda Keller Brown and Kay Mussell (Knoxville: University of Tennessee Press, 1984), 19–36.

16. Jay Ann Cox, "Eating the Other: Ethnicity and the Market for Authentic Mexican Food in Tucson, Arizona" (Ph.D. diss., University of Arizona, 1993).

17. David Bell and Gill Valentine, *Consuming Geographies: We Are Where We Eat* (London: Routledge, 1997), 6, 185–207.

18. Bob Ashley, et al., *Food and Cultural Studies* (London: Routledge, 2004), vii.

19. Brown and Mussell, *Ethnic and Regional Foodways*; Lucy M. Long, "Culinary Tourism: A Folkloristic Perspective on Eating and Otherness," *Journal of Southern Folklore* 55, no. 30 (1998): 181–203.

20. David Beriss and David Sutton, eds., *The Restaurants Book: Ethnographies of Where We Eat* (Oxford: Berg, 2007).

21. John Urry, *The Tourist Gaze: Leisure and Travel in Contemporary Societies* (London: Sage, 1990).

22. Daisy Tam and Nicola Frost, eds., "Food Journeys: Culinary Travels in Time and Space," *Food, Culture and Society* 11, no. 2 (2008): 129.

23. Kaori O'Connor, "The Hawaiian Luau: Food as Tradition, Transgression, Transformation and Travel," *Food, Culture and Society* 11, no. 2 (2008): 149–72; Daisy Tam, "'Slow Journeys," *Food, Culture and Society* 11, no. 2 (2008): 207–18.

24. C. Michael Hall, "Wine Tourism in New Zealand," in *Tourism Down Under II: Towards A More Sustainable Tourism*, ed. G. Kearsley (Otago: University of Otago Centre for Tourism, 1996), 109–19.

25. C. Michael Hall and R. Mitchell, "Wine and Food Tourism," in *Special Interest Tourism: Context and Cases*, ed. N. Douglas and R. Derrett (New York: Wiley, 2001), 308.

26. Hall, et al., *Food Tourism Around the World*, 10.

27. Boniface, *Tasting Tourism*, 23–25.

28. Erik Cohen and Nir Avieli, "Food in Tourism: Attraction and Impediment," *Annals of Tourism Research* 31, no. 4 (2004): 755–78.

29. Amy Bentley, "From Culinary Other to Mainstream American: Meanings and Uses of Southwestern Cuisine," in Long, *Culinary Tourism*, 209–25; Abrahams, "Equal Opportunity Eating," 19–36.

30. Long, *Culinary Tourism*, 32–34.

31. Heldke, *Exotic Appetites*, 163, 172.

32. Kevin Meethan, *Tourism in a Global Society: Place, Culture, Consumption* (Basinstoke: Palgrave, 2001), 114.

33. Richard Wilk, *Home Cooking in the Global Village: Caribbean Food from Buccaneers to Ecotourists* (Oxford: Berg, 2006), 172; George Ritzer, *The McDonaldization of Society* (Thousand Oaks, CA: Pine Forge Press, 1993).

34. Lolis Eric Elie, ed., *Cornbread Nation 2: The United States of Barbecue* (Chapel Hill: University of North Carolina Press, 2009); Lucy M. Long, *Regional American Food Culture* (Santa Barbara, CA: Greenwood Press, 2009), 138–39.

35. Kathy Neustadt, *Clambake: A History and Celebration of an American Tradition* (Amherst: University of Massachusetts Press, 1992).

36. Long, "Culinary Tourism," 4–19.

37. Susan Kalcik, "Ethnic Foodways in America: Symbol and the Performance of Identity," in Brown and Mussell, *Ethnic and Regional Foodways*, 37–65.

38. James L. Watson, ed., *Golden Arches East: McDonald's in East Asia* (Stanford: Stanford University Press, 1997).

39. O'Connor, "The Hawaiian Luau," 149–71.

40. Dean MacCannell, *The Tourist: A New Theory of the Leisure Class* (New York: Schocken, 1989).

41. Erve Chambers, *Native Tours: The Anthropology of Travel and Tourism* (Prospect Heights, IL: Waveland Press, 2000), 122.

42. Parasecoli, *Bite Me*, 144–45.

Bibliography

Boniface Priscilla. *Tasting Tourism: Travelling for Food Drink*. Aldershot: Ashgate, 2003.

Hall, C. Michael, and Liz Sharples. *Food and Wine Festivals and Events Around the World*. London: Butterworth-Heinemann, 2008.

Hall, C. Michael, et al. *Wine Tourism Around the World: Development, Management and Markets*. London: Butterworth Heinemann, 2002.

Hall, C. Michael, et al. *Food Tourism Around the World: Development, Management and Markets*. London: Butterworth-Heinemann, 2003.

Heldke, Lisa M. *Exotic Appetites: Ruminations of a Food Adventurer*. New York: Routledge, 2003.

Hjalager, Ane-Mette, and Greg Richards, eds. *Tourism and Gastronomy*. London: Routledge, 2002.

Long, Lucy M. "Culinary Tourism: A Folkloristic Perspective on Eating and Otherness." *Southern Folklore* 55, no. 3 (1998): 181–204.

______. "Culinary Tourism and the Emergence of an Appalachian Cuisine: Exploring the Foodscape of Asheville, NC." *North Carolina Folklore Journal* 57, no. 1 (2010): 4–19.

______, ed. *Culinary Tourism*. Lexington: University Press of Kentucky, 2004.

Lysaght, Patricia, ed. *Food and the Traveller: Migration, Immigration, Tourism and Ethnic Food*. Cyprus: Intercollegiate Press, 1998.

Wilk, Richard. *Home Cooking in the Global Village: Caribbean Food from Buccaneers to Ecotourists*. Oxford: Berg, 2006.

Wolf, Erik. *Culinary Tourism: The Hidden Harvest*. Dubuque, IA: Kendall Hunt Publishing, 2006.

PART V

COMMUNITIES OF CONSUMPTION

CHAPTER 23

FOOD AND RELIGION

CORRIE E. NORMAN

In the beginning, there was food—at least according to the creation stories of many religious traditions. From Brahman cooking the world into existence to Adam, Eve, and the apple, religious peoples have related to their gods, each other, and the world through food. They have made meaning while making dinner, whether in rituals such as Christian Communion and Hindu deity feedings or in eating everyday according to the *kashrut* or *halal* codes of Judaism and Islam. They continue to do so, often spicing up the old stories with new ingredients in season for new cultural and historical contexts. Thus there is almost always something fresh on the menu for those interested in the relationship between food and religion, as well as much worth chewing over again and again.

Food was important at the beginning of the academic study of religion too. Among its formative works in the early twentieth century were the lectures of William Robertson Smith on the origins of ancient Hebrew religion. The first of those lectures focused on the importance of feasting to the development of communal identity, including the community's relationship to its deity.[1]

Scholars in religion have rarely followed that early interest in food. It has been left largely to colleagues in anthropology and sociology to tell us about the relationships between religion and food. Mary Douglas is the most influential. Her theories on the relationships of food and purity and particularly the social meanings encoded in Hebrew dietary laws have come to shape the study of food. They have even shaped the study of religion. Yet while her works are on every (good) religious studies program's reading list, few students of religion have applied them to studying food.[2]

Where Douglas's work has propelled interest in religion and food, it has taken a very different trajectory from Smith's for the most part. Douglas, like Smith, is primarily interested in the connections between food and communal identity. (So is almost everyone writing about food and religion since, if not before, her.) Smith began with feasting, but Douglas's early work particularly underlined the importance of food "abominations." Scholars in anthropology and out these days are far more fascinated with fasting and forbidden food than with calorie-laden religious foodways. The compelling nature of Douglas's theories aside, this is not surprising in a cultural context that might be defined by its own obsessions with dieting.

An obvious place for the beginning student to turn for all-things-religion is the *Encyclopedia of Religion*. The entry on food in the 2005 edition begins with religious "food customs" characterized narrowly as "dietary laws, food taboos, and the religious and social environments that have molded them." And while the essay goes on to cover a broader range, beginning and ending with sections that feature ancient taboos, modern alcohol prohibitions, and contemporary vegetarianism illustrate how the relationship between food and religion has become primarily—and narrowly—understood.[3]

As estimable a food scholar as E. N. Anderson, in his introduction to food and culture, writes almost exclusively about taboo in his chapter on religion.[4] That Anderson even devoted a chapter to it is remarkable, however. For another tendency has been to ignore religion or talk about it as something else. One of the best collections of essays on food, an entry point for many students into the study of food in the United States, contains articles on foodways in religious communities, sacred spaces, and holidays but most give no attention to their religious contexts or character.[5] The same thing happens in food journalism and popular writing. One well-respected food writer quotes from the Upanishads and the Bible to show how food has been used "for illuminating broader subjects, especially sexuality." Despite his sources, he never mentions religion.[6]

More than being overshadowed by a fascination with sex (but not unrelated to it usually), religion's relationship to food has been reduced to "bad influence." This is particularly true in the United States, where scholarly and popular volumes on food blame "bad food" on "Puritanism" in the culture's "guilt-ridden," "sin-obsessed" religious history. It all came home to me a few years ago, when I posted a notice about a project on the list-serve of the Association for the Study of Food and Society. Having very carefully explained that I am studying, not advocating, certain religious phenomena, I still got the following responses: an angry diatribe about the evils of religion from a scholar whose parents have joined a "Jewish-vegetarian cult," several queries about fasting (not the topic of the post), and one sympathetic warning about "food people" being "uncomfortable" with religion.

To be sure, taboo and fasting are important subjects and we have by no means exhausted them. The complex intertwining of religion, food and sex, or more precisely gender roles, is certainly a fruitful field of inquiry. Indeed next to and often alongside food prohibitions, it is the most popular subject in current food and religion scholarship. And of course, religious phenomena may well be interpreted as something else and they can lead to negative consequences worthy of critical examination. These are, however, far from all that should be on the table when it comes to chewing over the foodways of religious peoples.

Short of shaming us as absentee hosts or advocating that we take over the party, I believe scholars in Religious Studies need to be more present at that table. At the time I received those wary responses from ASFS members, I could locate only one other member of that interdisciplinary organization in the field of Religious Studies. We should do lunch more often with each other as well. Often described as "interdisciplinary," in practice the study of religion is more accurately "multi-disciplinary," made up of various methodologies and sub-fields, most focused on particular religious traditions. A Buddhism scholar working on food may remain unaware of the research of an Islamicist working on similar themes, at least until publication. This is one reason why so many of the articles on food and religion are, while informative, too thinly descriptive.

Part of the challenge for scholars in Religious Studies—and for others who might look to us for information on religion and food—is that we cannot agree on one recipe for religion. And even when we do, we may wind up with something half-baked. The prevailing assumption in Religious Studies of religion as a "meaning-making process," some have argued, tempts scholars to privilege the analytical and abstract over physical or practice-oriented aspects of religion. For a subject such as food in religious practice, that is hardly a balanced diet. Major theorists of religion have given little guidance when it comes to making sense of foodways, even when their topics have been as food-related. Caroline Walker Bynum's study of medieval women and food is the rare work in Religious Studies that serves as a model approach for scholars of food in a variety of subfields in religion, as well as other disciplines.[7]

One of the axioms of Religious Studies has been that it must be comparative in nature: "to know only one tradition is to know none." Prompted in part by Jonathan Z. Smith and others, scholars of religion who are interested in working across traditions and historical contexts have become alert to the risks of comparison, to the "evils" of universalizing, and even worse, essentializing their subjects. These are valid concerns but they may also contribute to a reluctance to say anymore about food and religion than what the *Encyclopedia of Religion* surmises: food is significant in religions and is "as varied as humanity itself."[8]

Thus, we have not moved far beyond the early (and still useful) volume of essays published in the *Journal of the American Academy of Religion* in 1995, a collection of works on food in various traditions, from Mayan to Sufi, Sephardic to African American Christian.[9] Yet there is a kernel of hope exemplified in that and subsequent volumes on religious foodways. First, they are among the indicators that scholars of religion are discovering food. The 2010 Annual Meeting of the American Academy of Religion solicited papers on food for sessions in Chinese Religions and Womanist and Ritual Studies and advertised a pre-conference workshop on "Food, Justice, and Sustainability." The AAR's "Religion, Food, and Eating" seminar began in 2007 and will culminate in 2012 with a volume on food and religion in North America.[10]

We may soon reach critical mass. As more information is gathered and processed in collaborative forums, we can expect not only more description of religious food phenomena but also sound comparative analysis and new methods of thinking with food that may not only expand our understanding of religious foodways but also of religion period. Especially promising is the turn toward ritual and performance studies. As Philip P. Arnold, editor of a volume of the *Journal of Ritual Studies* devoted to "religious dimensions of food" explains, "Food moves the scholar from the mundane to cosmological and back again." Foodways run the gamut of religious experience and should be studied in their breadth. As Arnold suggests, thinking with food about religion helps Religious Studies come to a fuller understanding of its subject.[11]

If all this happens, scholars of religion may find dinner companions eager to partake in what they bring to the table. In just the last few years, more serious and balanced accounts of religion and food have appeared in newspapers and magazines, along with even more unbridled but wistfully positive nostalgia about religious foodways. It is not uncommon to find a *Gastronomica* or *Saveur* article that covers a religious community without condemning it or making it seem strange. There is a renewed interest in what might best be called a spiritual side to food. Revisiting the ethics and practices of traditional religions is an emerging aspect of the "food revolution."[12]

Awareness of the growing number of offerings from Religious Studies, however, has not yet increased. Just last winter, another query on the ASFS list-serve asked for resources for developing a course on religion and food. Someone suggested a dated but still useful anthropology of food and several interesting literary examples. Except for the promise of a forthcoming anthology on food in faith traditions, there was no mention of resources from Religious Studies. So this essay, in part, hopes to serve as something of an extended answer to that request, focusing on contributions from the field. Many of these will be of more use to researchers than students in a general education course or someone with an interest in food but little background in religion. I will point out helpful "starting places" where I can. It also aims to introduce those with expertise in Religious Studies to the study of foodways relevant to their work, whether in Religious Studies or in another field. Anthropology still offers more for some traditions and contexts.

With apologies to those who prefer a thematic treatment (the three I have already mentioned—social identity, dietary restriction, gender—dominate and intertwine in almost every case), I still think it makes sense to discuss work on religious foodways via the major religious traditions. They are contested categories themselves and analysis of foodways may indeed muddle them further, as well as mark their boundaries. Hinduism, Buddhism, Islam, Judaism and Christianity, however, remain primary constructs for scholars of religious foodways, as well as feasting and fasting religious peoples. So what follows is a hearty menu for those ravenously hungry for information on food and religion writ large and a series of smaller plates for those interested in specific traditions. This is hardly a balanced discussion, however, because there has not been equal attention to all traditions. In some cases, I mention practically everything that has been published in English. For other traditions, there is enough from which to pick and choose.

It would be remiss not to mention some works that fall outside of the large traditions I cover. Along with anthropologist Anna Meig's work on religion in New Guinea, Philip P. Arnold's, *Eating Landscape* (1999), about Aztec culture and its colonial interpreters, is important not only for its subject matter but also as a rare multi-disciplinary analysis (archeology, linguistics, history of religions, geography). The structural analysis of Oglala food rituals by Douglas disciples William K. and Marla M. N. Powers should be on the religion and food reading list too.[13]

A few works in Religious Studies that are not food-focused but that treat it integrally as a part of religious expression are important resources. Anyone interested in foodways and religion would be well advised to pick up Robert Orsi's *The Madonna of 115th Street* (1986), Karen McCarthy Brown's study of Vodou practitioner *Mama Lola* (1991), or David Carrasco's *City of Sacrifice: Violence From the Aztec Empire to the Modern Americas* (1999).[14]

And ironically perhaps, some secular manifestations of religious expression through foodways have received closer readings than many overtly religious ones. Anorectic adolescent girls "starving for salvation," wine connoisseurs and gourmets who behave religiously about tasting and cooking, and secular vegetarian activists who turn to Christian theological rhetoric to justify their reform agenda stretch the boundaries of our notions of religion, as well as the lines between the religious traditions from which they draw and the foodways they follow.[15]

Hinduism and Food

It has been said that Hinduism has some 330 million gods, give or take a few. Its food traditions are no less colorful and plenteous. For those unfamiliar with Hindu traditions, a good introduction to some important food-related themes by religious insider and exemplar Raja Deekshitar is in the *Encyclopedia of Food and Culture* (2003).[16] Added to the bounteous foodways that Hinduism offers researchers are those of other traditions indigenous to India such as Jainism. Add these traditions in diaspora and there is even more fertile field.

Scholarship on Hindu food traditions has tended to concentrate on food restrictions and asceticism, whatever the particular context. And dealing with the particular—whether regional, sectarian, etc—has been the trend of scholarship. As R.S. Khare has recently complained, there is "dearth" of "comprehensive" work on food in Hinduism.[17] While the tremendous and fascinating variety and intense description of "smaller" pictures captured the interest of scholars of religion and others justifiably, this is a sad irony. For according to Khare, *anna* (food) in Hinduism, is all-encompassing. It "weaves together crucial philosophical ideas, religious values, and ritual traditions with, first a distinct moral order, moral economy, caste custom and ritual schemes."[18]

Khare has made it his life's work to look comprehensively at Hindu—and more broadly Indian—culture and the centrality of foodways. Rarely has a food scholar been able to command such an expansive knowledge about such a complex and multi-faceted topic. In Khare's own writings and edited volumes that range from religious symbolism to social caste and agricultural policy, he attempts to maintain a balance between food in thought and practice, to acknowledge diversity of practice but also to remind of the hold of ancient ideas and traditions on contemporary realities and always argues that there is a "comprehensiveness" to the meanings and practices of food in the "Hindu World." While some of his work is of a structuralist approach now out of fashion, it is still useful for understanding social relationships that have emerged from a complex series of religious, social, and other factors. Given, as he notes, the "rarity" of history of religions approaches to *anna*, his work is still the best beginning point for those interest in studying food and religion in Hindu contexts.[19]

While not a work on food per se, Charles Malamoud's study of sacrifice and associated ritual acts as revealed in Vedic texts should be of interest to food scholars for its argument about the power of metaphor and ritual practice involving foodways. Even in its very origins according to early cosmologies, Brahman, "cooked" the world into existence. Cooking, argues Malamoud, arises as a central metaphor for many aspects of ritual activity and identity.[20]

Other scholars have honed in on the significance of foodways for understanding social, economic and religious factors in particular settings. Carol Appadurai Breckenridge's essay in Khare and Rao does so for a South Indian pilgrimage center in a period spanning the fourteenth through seventeenth centuries. Also in a South India setting, Arjun Appadurai's analysis of the "gastro-politics" of Tamil Brahmins offers insight into the complex and sometimes contradictory ways in which the combination of religion and food work to construct social relations and boundaries. James Laidlaw's book on Jains in Jaipur is another contemporary example.[21]

Jainism makes an obvious subject for the study of food especially given the restrictions on diet that come from *ahimsa*, or the prohibition against taking life in any form be it a cow or root vegetable, and its role in maintaining not only personal but also communal purity. On the other end of the food spectrum, the feasts of Krishna devotees have attracted scholarly attention. Paul Toomey has examined the role of feasting at a Krishna pilgrimage site in North India (Braj) and looked comparatively at foodways and their meanings in two Krishnaite sects. Eliot Singer's 1984 essay on the multiple meanings of food and especially the use of food in evangelism among Krishnas in the United States is still a useful introduction to the complex relationship of foodways, immigration, and religious identity and expression in pluralistic religious environments.[22]

That is a topic of ongoing discussion. A number of articles have appeared recently that look at the roles of foodways in indigenous Indian traditions as they develop in new contexts. Many of these works are preliminary and lean more toward description than analysis. While we await further development and research, however, the best of these serve up fresh thinking about food in community formation and preservation of identity and are approachable for non-specialists. Among those are Martin Woods' essay on the significance of food miracles in Gujarati communities in the United Kindom and New Zealand and Anne Vallely's study of the "semiotics of the diaspora diet" for immigrant Jains that draws from the work of Roland Barthes. Also of interest is Kathryn McClymond's essay on negotiating foodways in temple communities formed by immigrants with varying traditions in Atlanta, Georgia. Her description of the mix not only of various Indian traditions but also of Indian traditions with the dominant Christian culture of the American South (Hindu potluck dinners!) is fascinating.[23]

The works mentioned so far largely focus on temple worship or public foodways. But equally important are the "private" aspects of food and religion that take place in domestic space and in which women are often the primary agents. Anne McKenzie Pearson's book on the surprisingly complex and arguably empowering role of periodic fasting in the lives of Hindu women stands out here. And while not an academic work, Chitrita Banerji's vivid and astute memoir of food practices in Bengal is a must for those interested in the powerful combination of food and religion for women in India or elsewhere (and a useful classroom tool).[24]

Buddhism and Food

From multiple editions of the ancient *Instructions for the Tenzo* to the cookbooks of spiritual leader and cook Edward Espe Brown, there is enormous popular interest in Buddhism (especially but not exclusively Zen) and food. So where is the scholarly interest? Besides the relevant essays in the Khare and Rao volumes mentioned earlier, Emiko Ohnuki-Tierney's study of the meaning of rice in Japan should be of interest to religion scholars for its examination of food and worldview across time.[25]

For those interested in an overview, anthropologist Penny Van Esterik's essay in the *Encyclopedia of Food and Culture* is perhaps the best place to start. Her more recent book on food in Southeast Asia, part of the Greenwood series on food in various cultures, is a good primer on all-things-food in that region, including religious foodways. She has also provided one of the best essays on food and women's agency in religious communities in which they might appear to have little authority, as well as a fascinating look at an important aspect of daily life in Thai Buddhism.[26]

Most of the publications are almost two decades old, however. There is encouragement from the number of conference papers and paper sessions devoted to food and Buddhism, but we await full-length studies. Two approaches that are especially promising appear in recent articles. First is the examination of foodways and relations between religious traditions, particularly as a means of expressing religious identity in a pluralistic or religiously competitive context. Ellen Posman shows how food provides a pathway between Judaism and Buddhism for many who embrace common dietary concerns in contemporary America.[27] Katherine E. Ulrich's article on dietary polemics ("food fights") in sixth through eleventh-century South India among Hindus, Buddhists, and Jains is an ambitious and tight reading of ancient texts and a welcome examination of traditions in formation and the use of foodways as defining tools—both defining in and out. In this context, according to Ulrich, dietary differences took "center stage" in "the process of building boundaries" between these emerging religious cultures. "By targeting what they regarded as unacceptable or reprehensible," she surmises, "they implicitly highlighted what was acceptable or even laudable. By condemning other communities, real or imagined, they constructed themselves."[28]

Second, Philip P. Arnold's examination of the relationship between practice and "ideology" in an essay on food in Thai Buddhism is that exemplary work in history of religions that is "too rare," as Khare put it. It comes close, for Thai Buddhism, to the kind of comprehensive approach that Khare advocated.[29] A scholar primarily of Mesoamerican religious traditions who also writes about methodology, Arnold examines "disparate" theoretical and ritual contexts of Thai Buddhism to find "a coherent religious view which integrates ritual, myth, doctrine, and folk beliefs with reference to eating and giving food."[30]

Islam and Food

To date, there is very little accessible scholarship on religion and foodways in Islamic cultures despite the centrality of foodways in Islamic texts and traditions and the variety of cultural settings in which they figure. For those interested in analysis of Islamic law and theology related to food, there are a few articles, most pointing to the significance of these texts and their interpretations for Muslim identity formation.[31] For those who need a general introduction to Islam and food, Paul Fieldhouse's article in the *Encyclopedia of Food and Culture* is the place to begin.[32]

Given that fasting is one of the five pillars of Islam and scholarship on religion and food tends to privilege food restrictions anyway, there is a surprising emphasis on the balance of eating and food avoidance in Islam in the available literature. The balance is attributed both to principles innate in Islamic food teachings and to complex ways in which Muslims—particularly, Muslims in minority contexts and Muslim women practicing "informal" traditions associated with Ramadan—negotiate their social contexts, as well as the "official" traditions. Valeria Hoffman's essay on Sufism and food emphasizes that Sufi interpretation of the Koran and Hadith lead to a balanced mix of charity in the form of cooking and serving food, fasting, and feasting. All linked together, she argues, by gratitude to Allah. (By the way, for those unfamiliar with the rich food traditions of Sufism or looking for a creative classroom example of foodways, Kathleen Seidel's on-line Sufi cookbook and art gallery is a must-see.)[33]

Christopher Murphy's work on Muslim feasts in "Old Delhi," still perhaps the best analysis of Muslim foodways in a specific context, describes how feasts negotiate identity and community for the Muslim minority there both internally and among "non-Muslim neighbors." The Muslim values of piety, honor, hospitality, and charity are emphasized in varying combinations on different holiday occasions. For example, honor and hospitality are emphasized in marriage feasts while piety and charity feature in Ramadan fast-breaking meals. The balance of these values in feasting and fasting traditions also functions to mediate the place of Muslims in society by expressing and resolving contradictions at the same time. For example, ritual sacrifice binds these North Indian Muslims to all Muslims doing the same ritual at the same time. The community also is extended beyond Islamic identity in this event, however, when sacrificed meat is offered to non-Muslim neighbors and the poor, as well as family in accordance with the value on charity.[34]

As with Hindism and Buddhism, the spiritual and social dynamics in Muslim women's fasting practices has attracted attention. In anthropologist Marjo Buitelaar's study of Moroccan women's Ramadan activities, fasting stands out as a "more manifest" public expression than most Islamic rites for women, "in which men appear to be the leading actors." Yet much of the leadership of women in fasting periods involves cooking, giving food, and even eating in the permitted fast breaks and conclusions. The feast-fast balance is paralleled in the mix of "normal" private and "exceptional" public roles of women during Ramadan as well. Going outside their homes to give food alms or "exchanging Ramadan delicacies," are "local practices" that put women in the public sphere. They are also, argues Buitelaar, examples of the "informal Islam of women that go beyond but do not contradict 'official'" teaching.[35]

The embrace of Islam by many African Americans has created a fascinating example of how food symbolism can endure, be transformed, or be rejected all at the same time. Doris Witt's magisterial study of foodways, political rhetoric, and identity, *Black Hunger*, includes a discussion on how "soul food" was associated not only with the dominant racist Christian culture but also emasculation of black men. Drawing also on concerns about health, some Muslim leaders blamed black women who colluded with the oppressors in cooking their menfolk to death. A more recent article in *Cultural Anthropology* examines how African American converts understand eating in accordance with Islamic teachings on purity to free themselves from "the heritage of slavery" symbolized in "soul food," as well as "western" materialism and unhealthy eating practices.[36]

Judaism and Food

More thought has been given to the origins of the ancient Hebrew dietary laws than any other religion-related food topic. Driven mostly outside the study of religion and tied up in methodological conundrums, the discussion has been well rehearsed.[37]

Scholars of religion by and large have rejected materialist explanations that focus on animal husbandry, health or economy and have more or less followed Mary Douglas's theories proposing connections between prohibitions against eating certain animals, most famously pigs, and a particular loathing of anomalies observed in them by early Hebrew culture. Douglas herself, as well as others, developed and even rejected aspects of her theory over time. Milgrom (and Douglas in revision) have shifted the focus from anomalies like the cloven hooves of pigs to "ethical, humanitarian principles" behind other types of prohibitions such as ingesting blood or cooking a calf in its mother's milk. But in general today, most follow Douglas's notion that the dietary laws "encode" a notion of holiness or purity that is basic to Israelite self-understanding as a holy society separate from others.[38]

Moving beyond those now old debates, essay collections and monographs in the last decade have explored what the ancient Israelites did and did not eat, most often as a context for important theological and social themes. While much of this work focuses on food as a literary device in the early Hebrew texts, there is a welcome trend toward a well-rounded methodological and topical eclecticism as exemplified in Nathan McDonald's recent book covering food, memory and history (something more religion scholars ought to explore), political theology and food, and archeology of diet among other topics.[39]

Attention is increasingly directed beyond the ancient texts to communities for which their directives are givens, or at least givens to be negotiated in the process of negotiating identity. How have Jews in various contexts developed, defended, rejected or revised those rules? Beyond them, how do foodways mark differences between Jews and others, or Jews and other Jews? As in other areas of food studies, answers to these questions are coming piece by piece, place by place.

A good example of the territories being covered is the volume of papers simply called *Food and Judaism* in the Studies in Jewish Civilization series. Offerings come from folklorists, culinary and social historians and even a "TV personality," Joan Nathan. Religion is as well represented here as other fields. From "Russian Jewish Foodscapes of New York" to "Southern Jewish Foodways" and Jewish cookbooks from Nebraska, North American terrain is particularly well covered. Vegetarianism and "just" eating, topics of increasing interest in many Jewish communities, are the focus of three articles. The "kosherization" of Jewish ethnic foods in various settings is discussed, as is food as spiritual symbol and vehicle, particularly in sectarian movements such as Hasidism. Articles on women as "gatekeepers" of Jewish identity in their kitchens emphasize levels of authority sometimes at odds with each other, split between public and private realms and along gender lines. An essay on polemics involving early modern garlic consumption is one of two essays that examine food as expression of difference and accommodation with outsiders.[40]

David Kraemer's *Jewish Eating and Identity Through the Ages* (2007) aims "to interpret Jewish eating practices in these many ages as keys to understanding current Jewish identities." A readable volume (serviceable in an undergraduate classroom), it covers similar themes and sometimes the same territory as *Food and Judaism*. Kraemer argues that *kashrut* separates, as well as unites Jews in many contexts, from sixteenth-century Poland where the separation of milk and meat separated "pious" and "common" Jews from each other to ever-stricter readings of *kashrut* that separate the "ultra-orthodox" from the "non-observant" today. He explains "negotiation" with *kashrut* as often being "rejection and preservation" at the same time, as in the development of "kosher style" in American delicatessens.[41]

While both volumes expand the range of study beyond biblical texts and early Judaism, both pay attention to them as well. Kraemer's book emphasizes the significance of developments in the early rabbinic period. Following Catherine Bell's ritualization theory, he underlines the important of ritual blessing rather than kosher meat restrictions, as the "culturally specific strategy" that made Jewish meals Jewish. While focusing on ritual, however, Kraemer also underlines context. Jews of this period shared much in common with others in Hellenistic culture; the commonalties and differences in meal forms can tell us much about identity formation.[42]

Therein lies the most fruitful trajectory for understanding the significance of food and meals in Judaism in the last decade. As Jonathan Brumberg-Kraus puts it in an excellent summary of generally accepted ideas about Jewish meals in the Hellenistic period, meals are "midrash," actively interpretive vehicles that work out what Judaism is through their gestures and words.[43]

Brumberg-Kraus is part of perhaps the most exciting effort to understand the roles of food in religion at present. Over two decades ago, anthropologist Gillian Feeley-Harnak and a few scholars of early Judaism and Christianity began to understand the parallel development of Jewish and Christian meal traditions as significant for the parallel development of the two religions.[44] But methodological and technological advances and a flowering of research both in Jewish and Christian origins and food and meals in Greco-Roman culture spurred a fresh attempt at this in the last decade.

The Greco-Roman Meals Seminar of the Society of Biblical Literature, begun in 2002, "explores meals as a window into social and religious life in the Greco-Roman world and as a pivotal consideration in understanding early Christianity and Judaism," according to its very useful website. Focusing on the "banquet form and ideology" and how it was adapted in early Christian and Jewish settings to express social development, the seminar is a collaborative, comparative effort that employs methods from other areas of food studies to advance its goals. Most of the working papers are available on the website. Some of the work even takes place on-line via its discussion forum. At this writing in Fall 2010, proposed conclusions are posted and being discussed by seminar members with the goal of reaching a consensus of conclusions at the Society's Annual Meeting.[45]

The legacy of such work is already evident in the very recent book on food in early rabbinic texts by seminar member Jordan Rosenblum.[46] This insightful, engagingly written volume promises to be joined soon by new works of other seminar members. Moving beyond the context of the Greco-Roman meals seminar and into previously unexplored territory is David M. Freidenreich's forthcoming work on food and identity in medieval Jewish, Christian, and Islamic law.[47] Together, these readable, methodologically sophisticated, comparatively sensitive works of new scholars point toward a promising future for Jewish food studies.

Christianity and Food

A number of works in the last decade began to examine the role of food and diet in the development of early Christianity as reflected in the literature of the New Testament and other early Christian writings. Their topics included debates over whether to eat food offered to Roman deities or keep Jewish dietary laws, asceticism and eating, what eating and meals might tell us about gender in early Christian society, and the role of table fellowship in early Christian socialization.[48] Two English-language books and one German, however, have precipitated a fresh flowering of developments. Along with the work of German scholar Matthias Klinghardt, Dennis Smith's *From Symposium to Eucharist: The Banquet in the Early Christian World* (2003) prompted the formation of the Greco-Roman Seminar and brought meals in the life of early Christianity to the forefront of research on early Christianity. Smith sets New Testament meals clearly in the Greco-Roman banquet tradition "in its structures and ethics."[49] While concurring about their link to the common Hellenistic banquet, Andrew McGowan's *Ascetic Eucharist* (1999) reveals the diversity of early Christian meal practices. Fish and cheese, as well as bread and wine, served as ritual foods for some Christian groups, for example. McGowan's work has emphasized among other things how early Christians used varying dietary "strategies" to achieve spiritual goals of their communities. He also provides the clearest introduction to the role of meals and food in early Christianity, readily accessible for undergraduate classes, in his essay "Food, Ritual, and Power."[50]

These works and the ongoing work in the Greco-Roman Meals Seminar are showing us a much different meal than the one seen in churches today or that had been assumed by scholars when most looked backward through the lens of the later Eucharist with its formalized liturgy to New Testament meals. What we now know is that early Christians came together to worship and eat, at the same time and table, well into the third century. When they came to table, argues Seminar member Hal Taussig in his 2009 book, *In the Beginning was the Meal: Social Experimentation and Early Christian Identity*, they were working out who they were as they ate. Following Jonathan Z. Smith's thinking about rituals as means of performing and coping with problems, Taussig explains how the table became the primary place to act out social relations in flux.[51]

While the ritual Eucharist and everyday meals became separated, there was still a direct connection for at least some Christians. For scholars who have studied the Eucharist, as well as theologians who tried to explain it, that connection has been buried under other concerns. Caroline Walker Bynum's study of medieval women mystics and the significance of food, *Holy Feast, Holy Fast* (1987), resurrected it.[52]

Bynum's analysis of the interrelationship of gender-prescribed roles of feeding, fasting, and eating and the mystics' identification with Christ's humanity and suffering in Eucharistic devotion is now a model for the study of food's importance in religious experience.

While *Holy Feast, Holy Fast* propelled interest in medieval Christianity and particularly women's mysticism, it remains a contribution without peer in the study of food and Christianity post-antiquity. Those who have followed Bynum have seldom treated the connection between feeding, eating and spiritual experience as judiciously or provided any new insight. Rachel Fulton's essay on tasting and spirituality is one welcome exception in Medieval Studies.[53]

What Bynum's work did forerun is the interest in dietary restriction, whether fasting, dieting, or rejecting certain foods, by scholars studying a tradition characterized by its relative lack of food rules. Some have focused on the perpetuation of *kashrut* in Christian communities from the Celts to Vietnamese Protestants despite "normative" Christianity's rejection of them.[54] Vegetarianism has received more attention and rightly so given its attraction for many Christian sects and reform programs. The variety it has attracted over time is well documented in the recent volume of essays edited by Rachel Muers and David Grummet. Another volume illustrates the breadth of connection between diet and utopian or reformist ideals in America, in and outside of Christianity and the meat-eating divide.[55].

Understanding historical practices of fasting, especially its more bizarre (to most of us anyway) aspects, may have been more undermined than enlightened by attempts to relate them to modern dietary issues. Rudolf Bell's book on "anorectic" nuns preceded Bynum's far more nuanced study.[56] Essays that document interest in diet, health, and holiness are mounting up but Marie Griffith's study of contemporary "Christian dieting movements" and their historical precedents in a variety of American Protestant groups that advocated disciplining the appetite is the best source.[57]

But what of Christian holiday feasting, community dinners, food fairs, and all those casserole dishes? What about charitable feeding and hunger (not due to fasting or dieting)? There is surprisingly little on these or similar topics and a virtual silence on them (in English) outside of the North American context. At that, Daniel Sack is the only scholar who has tried to draw a big picture of eating and feeding in mainstream American Protestantism.[58] A few others have covered smaller, regional, or ethnic communities. Patricia Curran's study of food and change in a women's monastic community post Vatican II remains the only book-length study of food in a Catholic community after the Middle Ages of which I am aware. Those interested in how food bridges and blurs religious and secular culture should read Wade Clark Roof's analysis of the two at play in the barbecue and bible belt of the American South.[59]

While diet manuals are receiving due attention in Religious Studies, church cookbooks have piqued the interest primarily of social historians and literature scholars mining sources of women's history. Scholars of Christianity have rarely taken notice of these. Worthy of mention is Matthew Bailey-Dick's article on

Mennonite cookbooks that illustrates how significant they can be not only as records of self-understanding but also for defining groups to outsiders who know them only through recipes and the worldviews they encode.[60]

This is just one example of how we have been depriving ourselves. For all the good morsels on our plates (even if most have been low fat so far), scholars of religion and others who realize food's significance as religious expression should be reading recipes, as well as food rules and ritual manuals. Perhaps the recipes *are* ritual manuals that can tell us more about what is in this rich mixture we call religion and how it is cooked up and served forth.

NOTES

1. W. R. Smith, *Lectures on the Religion of the Semites: Their Fundamental Institutions*, 3rd ed. (London: A. & C. Black, 1927). A good summary of Smith's influence and the historiography on food in biblical studies appears in Nathan McDonald, *Not Bread Alone: The Uses of Food in the Old Testament* (New York: Oxford, 2008), 1–17.

2. Among the relevant works are Mary Douglas, *Purity and Danger* (New York: Oxford, 1966); idem, "Deciphering a Meal," in *Myth, Symbol and Culture*, ed. Clifford Geertz (New York: Norton, 1971), 61–81; idem, *Leviticus as Literature* (New York: Oxford, 1999).

3. James E. Latham (1987) and Peter Gardella (2005), "Food," in *Encyclopedia of Religion*, ed. Lindsay Jones, 2nd ed. (Macmilan Reference USA, 2005), 5:3167–75. For another introduction to the topic, see Corrie E. Norman, "Religion and Food," in *Encyclopedia of Food and Culture*, ed. Solomon Katz (New York: Scribner's, 2003), 3:171–6. [Online]. Available: http://www.enotes.com/food-encyclopedia/religion-food. [November 20, 2010].

4. E. N. Anderson, *Everyone Eats: Understanding Food and Culture* (New York: NYU Press, 2005), 155–61.

5. Carole M. Counihan, ed., *Food in the USA: A Reader* (New York: Rutledge, 2002). For more on this and writings on food and religion in the United States, see Corrie E. Norman, "Reading Foodways as Faithways in Contemporary America" in *Faith in America: Changes, Challenges, and New Directions*, ed. Charles H. Lippy (Westport, CT: Praeger, 2006), 2:213–36, esp. 217–20.

6. Mark Kurlansky, *Choice Cuts: A Savory Selection of Food Writing from Around the World and Throughout History* (New York: Ballantine, 2002), 1–2.

7. Caroline Walker Bynum, *Holy Feast, Holy Fast: The Religious Significance of Food to Medieval Women* (Berkeley: University of California Press, 1987).

8. For example Jonathan Z. Smith, *Imagining Religion* (Chicago: University of Chicago Press, 1982). Latham and Gardella, "Food," 3167.

9. *The Journal of the American Academy of Religion* 63, no. 3 (1995).

10. "American Association of Religion" [Online]. Available: https://www.aarweb.org/Meetings/Annual_Meeting/Program_Units/PUCS/Website/main.asp?PUNum=AARPU181. [November 20, 2010].

11. Philip P. Arnold, "Religious Dimensions of Food: An Introduction," *Journal of Ritual Studies* 14, no. 1 (2000): 4–5.

12. In journalism, see for example Samantha M. Shapiro, "Kosher Wars," *New York Times Magazine*, October 9, 2008 [Online]. Available: http://www.nytimes.com/2008/10/12/magazine/12kosher-t.html. [November 11, 2010]. On religion in food magazines, see Norman, "Reading." For example, H.C. Chehabi, "How Caviar Turned Out to be Halal," *Gastronomica* 7, no. 2 (2007): 17–23; and Leah Koenig, "Reaping the Faith," *Gastronomica* 8, no. 1 (2008): 80–84, on two Muslim farmers and the connection between their faith and sustainable foodways. Number 70 of the 2010 "*Saveur* 100" is a church dinner: Theresa Wolke, "Sacred Heart Church Ravioli Dinner," *Saveur* (January/February 2010): 62.

13. Anna Meigs, *Food, Sex, and Pollution: A New Guinea Religion* (New Brunswick: Rutgers University Press, 1988); Philip P. Arnold, *Eating Landscape: Aztec and European Occupation of Tlalocan* (Boulder: University Press of Colorado, 1999); William K. and Marla M.N. Powers, "Metaphysical Aspects of an Oglala Food System," in *Food in the Social Order: Studies of Food and Festivities in Three American Communities*, ed. Mary Douglas (Washington, DC: Sage Foundation, 1994), 40–96.

14. Robert Orsi, *The Madonna of 115th Street: Faith and Community in Italian Harlem, 1880–1950* (New Haven: Yale University Press, 1986); Karen McCarthy-Brown, *Mama Lola: A Vodou Priestess in Brooklyn* (Berkeley: University of California Press, 1991); David Carrasco, *City of Sacrifice: Violence From the Aztec Empire to the Modern Americas*, (Boston: Beacon Press, 1999), esp. ch. 6, "We Eat the Gods and Gods Eat Us."

15. Michelle Lelwica, *Starving for Salvation* (New York: Oxford, 1999); Norman, "Reading Foodways as Faithways"; Robert Fuller, *Religion and Wine* (Knoxville: University of Tennessee Press, 1994); James R. T. E. Gregory, "A Lutheranism of the Table: Religion and the Victorian Vegetarians" in *Eating and Believing: Interdisciplinary Perspectives on Vegetarianism and Theology*, ed. Rachel Muers and David Grumett (New York: T&T Clark, 2008), 135–52.

16. Raja Deekshitar, "Fasting and Abstinence: Hinduism and Buddhism" in Katz, *Encyclopedia of Food and Culture*, 1:611–612, [Online]. Available: http://www.enotes.com/food-encyclopedia/hinduism-buddhism. [November 20, 2010].

17. R. S. Khare, "Anna," in *The Hindu World*, ed. Sushil Mittal and Gene Thursby (New York: Rutledge, 2004), 407–28, 408. Also, R. S. Khare, *Annambrahman: Cultural Models, Meanings, and Aesthetics of Hindu Food* (Albany: State of New York Press, 1992).

18. Khare, "Anna," 408–11, on historiography.

19. See for example the range of essays in R. S. Khare, ed., *The Eternal Food: Gastronomic Ideas and Experiences of Hindus and Buddhists*, (Albany: State University of New York Press, 1992). Khare, "Anna," 410, particularly recommends from this volume A. K. Ramanujan, "Food for Thought: Toward an Anthology of Hindu Food Images," 221–50, as a comprehensive overview. Also R. S. Khare and M. S. A. Rao, eds., *Food, Society, and Culture: Aspects in South Asian Food Systems* (Durham, NC: Carolina Academic Press, 1986).

20. Khare, "Anna," 410. Charles Malamoud, *Cooking the World: Ritual and Thought in Ancient India*, trans. David White (New York: Oxford, 1998), 24–53.

21. Carol Appadurai Breckenridge, "Food, Politics, and Pilgrimage in South India, 1350–1650 AD," in Khare and Rao, *Food, Society, and Culture*, 21–53. Arjun Appadurai, "Gastro Politics in Hindu South Asia," *American Ethnologist* 8, no. 3 (1981): 494–511. Also useful is Appadurai's, "How to Make a National Cuisine: Cookbooks in Contemporary India," *Comparative Studies* 30, no. 1 (1988): 3–24. James Laidlaw, *Riches and Renunciation: Religion, Economy, and Society among the Jains* (Oxford: Oxford University Press, 1995).

22. Eliot A. Singer, "Conversion Through Foodways Enculturation: The Meaning of Eating in an American Hindu Sect" in *Ethnic and Regional Foodways in the United States: The Performance of Group Identity*, ed. Linda Keller Brown and Kay Mussell, (Knoxville: University of Tennessee Press, 1984), 195–214. Three works by Paul M. Toomey, *Food from the Mouth of Krishna: Feast and Festivities in a North Indian Pilgrimage Center* (Hindustan Publishing, 1994); "Food From the Mouth of Krishna: Socio-Religious Aspects of Sacred Food in Two Krishniate Sects," in Khare and Rao, *Food, Society, and Culture*, 55–83; and "Mountain of Food, Mountain of Love: Ritual Inversion in the Annakuta Feast at Mount Govardhan" in Khare, *Eternal Food*, 117–45.

23. Kathryn McClymond, "You are Where You Eat: Negotiating Hindu Utopias in Atlanta," in *Eating in Eden: Food in American Utopias*, ed. Martha Finch and Etta Madden (Lincoln: University of Nebraska Press, 2006), 89–106; Martin Wood, "Divine Appetites: Food Miracles, Authority and Religious Identities in the Gujarati Hindu Diaspora," *Journal of Contemporary Religion*, 23, no. 3 (2008): 337–53; Anne Vallely, "The Jain Plate: Semiotics of the Diaspora Diet," in *South Asians in the Diaspora*, ed. Knut Jacobsen and Pratap Kumar (Boston: Brill, 2004), 3–22.

24. Anne McKenzie Pearson, *Because It Gives Me Peace of Mind: Ritual Fasts in the Religious Lives of Hindu Women* (Binghampton: State University of New York Press, 1996); Chitrita Banerji, *Feeding the Gods: Memories of Food and Culture in Bengal* (Seagull, 2006).

25. Khare, *Eternal Food*; Khare and Rao, *Food, Society, and Culture*; Emiko Ohnuki-Tierney, *Rice as Self: Japanese Identities through Time* (Princeton, NJ: Princeton University Press, 1993).

26. Penny Van Esterik, "Buddhism," in Katz, *Encyclopedia of Food and Culture*, 1:269–71, also at http://www.enotes.com/food-encyclopedia/buddhism; idem, *Food and Culture in Southeast Asia* (Westport, CT: Greenwood Publishing Group, 2008); idem, "Feeding Their Faith: Recipe Knowledge among Thai Buddhist Women," *Food and Foodways* 1 (1986): 197–215, republished in *Food and Gender: Identity and Power*, ed. Carol M. Counihan and Steven L. Kaplan (Newark, N.J.: Harwood Academic Press, 1998), 81–97.

27. Ellen Posman, "Veggie Burger in Paradise: Food as World Transformer in Contemporary American Buddhism and Judaism," in Finch and Madden, *Eating in Eden*, 239–57.

28. Katherine E. Ulrich, "Food Fights" among Buddhist, Hindu, and Jain Dietary Polemics in South India," History of Religions, 46, no. 3 (2007): 228–61, 229, 261.

29. Philip P. Arnold, "Eating and Giving Food: The Material Necessity of Interpretation in Thai Buddhism," *Journal of Ritual Studies* 14, no. 1 (2000): 6–22.

30. Ibid, 6.

31. Mohammed Hocine Benkheira "Artificial Death, Canonical Death: Ritual Slaughter in Islam" *Food and Foodways* 8, no. 4 (2000), 227–52; Michael Cook, "Early Islamic Dietary Law," *Jerusalem Studies in Arabic and Islam* 7 (1986): 217–77; idem, "Magician Cheese: An Archaic Problem in Islamic Law," *Bulletin of the School of Oriental and African Studies* 47 (1984): 449–67; Myhammad Khalid Masud, "Food and the Notion of Purity in the *fatw* Literature," in *La alimentación en las culturas Islamicas*, ed. Manuela Marin and David Waines (Madrid: Agencia Español de Coopercaión Internacional, 1994), 89–110.

32. Paul Fieldhouse, "Islam," in Katz, *Encyclopedia of Food and Culture*, 2:293–98. [Online]. Available: http://www.enotes.com/food-encyclopedia/sunni-islam. [November 20, 2010].

33. Kathleen Seidl, *Serving the Guest: A Sufi Cookbook and Art Gallery* [Online]. Available: http://www.superluminal.com/cookbook. [November 20, 2010]. Valerie J. Hoffman, "Eating and Fasting for God in Sufi Tradition," *Journal of the American Academy of Religion* 63, no. 3 (1995): 201–30.

34. Christopher P.H. Murphy, "Piety and Honor: The Meaning of Muslim Feasts in Old Delhi," in Khare and Rao, *Food, Society, and Culture*, 85–119.

35. Marjo Buitelaar, *Feasting and Fasting in Morocco: Women's Participation in Ramadan* (Oxford: Berg 1993), 180.

36. Doris Witt, *Black Hunger: Food and Politics of US Identity* (New York: Oxford, 1999); Carolyn Rouse and Janet Hoskins, "Purity, Soul Food, and Sunni Islam: Explorations at the Intersection of Consumption and Resistance," *Cultural Anthropology* 19, no. 2 (2004): 226–49.

37. For reviews of the important literature and debate, see McDonald, *Not Bread Alone*, 18–28, and David Kraemer, *Jewish Eating and Identity Through the Ages* (New York: Routledge, 2007), 12–19.

38. Kraemer, *Jewish Eating and Identity*, 17–9. The best-known materialist interpretation is Marvin Harris, *Good to Eat: Riddles of Food and Culture* (Prospect Heights, IL: Waveland, 1985). Jacob Milgrom, "Leviticus 1–16," in *The Anchor Bible* (New York: Doubleday 1991).

39. McDonald, *Not Bread Alone*, 7–13, outlines and critiques the bibliography well. Especially of interest is Athalya Brenner and Jan Willem van Henten, eds., *Food and Drink in the Biblical Worlds. Semeia* 86 (Atlanta: Society of Biblical Literature, 2001).

40. Leonard J. Greenspoon, Ronald A. Simkins, and Jean Axelrad Cahan, eds. *Food and Judaism. Studies in Jewish Civilization* 15 (Omaha, NE: Creighton University Press, 2005). Among the book-length studies of some of these themes are Marcie Cohen Ferris, *Matzoh Ball Gumbo: Culinary Tales of the Jewish South* (Chapel Hill: University of North Carolina Press, 2005); Eliezer Diamond, *Holy Men and Hunger Artists: Fasting and Asceticism in Rabbinic Culture* (New York: Oxford University Press, 2004).

41. Kraemer, *Jewish Eating and Identity*, 87ff, 153ff, and 140ff.

42. Ibid, 74–76.

43. Jonathan Brumberg-Kraus, "'Meals as Midrash': A Survey of Meals in Jewish Studies Scholarship," available in PDF form in 2002 as "Meals and Jewish Studies" at the Greco-Roman Meals Seminar" [Online]. Available: http://www.philipharland.com/meals/GrecoRomanMealsSeminar.htm. [November 20, 2010].

44. Gilliam Feeley-Harnik, *The Lord's Table: The Meaning of Food in Early Judaism and Christianity* (Washington, DC: Smithsonian Institution Press, 1981); Paul F. Bradshaw and Lawrence A. Hoffman, eds., *Passover and Easter: Origin and History to Modern Times* (South Bend, IN: University of Notre Dame Press, 1999).

45. Jonathan D. Brumberg-Kraus, Susan Marks, and Jordan Rosenblum, "Table as Generative Locus for Social Formation in Early Judaism," available in PDF form under Session 3, 2010 [Online]. Available: http://www.philipharland.com/meals/GrecoRomanMealsSeminar.htm. [November 20, 2010].

46. Jordan D. Rosenblum, *Food and Identity in Early Rabbinic Judaism* (Cambridge: Cambridge University Press, 2010).

47. David M. Freidenreich, has number of forthcoming articles on food and a book manuscript in progress based on his dissertation, "Foreign Food: A Comparatively-Enriched Analysis of Jewish Christian and Islamic Law" (Ph.D. dissertation, Columbia University, 2006).

48. Among significant works are Willi Braun, *Feasting and Social Rhetoric in Luke 14* (Cambridge: Cambridge University Press, 1995); Kathleen Corley, *Private Women, Public Meals: Social Conflict in the Synoptic Tradition* (Peabody, MA: Hendrickson, 1993); Teresa M. Shaw, *The Burden of the Flesh: Fasting and Sexuality in Early Christianity* (Minneapolis: Fortress Press, 1998). One article that stands out is Blake Leylerle, "Clement of Alexandria on the Important of Table Etiquette," *Journal of Early Christian Studies* 3 (1995): 123–41.

49. Matthias Klinghardt, *Gemeinschaftsmahl und Mahlgemeinschaft: Soziologie und Liturgie frühchristlicher Mahlfeiern* (Tübingen: A. Francke Verlag, 1996). Dennis E. Smith, *From Symposium to Eucharist: The Banquet in the Early Christian World* (Minneapolis: Augsburg Fortress, 2003), 6–7, 285.

50. Andrew McGowan, *Ascetic Eucharists: Food and Drink in Early Christian Ritual Meals* (New York: Oxford, 1999); idem, "Discipline and Diet: Feeding the Martyrs in Roman Carthage," *Harvard Theological Review* 96, no. 4 (2003): 455–76, 472 cited here; idem, "Food, Ritual, and Power," in *A People's History of Christianity: Late Ancient Christianity*, ed. Virginia Burrus (Minneapolis Augsburg Fortress, 2005), 145–64. A bibliography of McGowen's works on food appears on the Greco Roman Meals Seminar website under Session Two, 2007.

51. See Matthias Klinghardt and Dennis Smith, "Rethinking Last Supper/Lord's Supper in the New Testament"; Andrew McGowen and Lillian Larsen, "Toward a Profile of Eucharistic Origins" under Sessions 1 and 2, 2010, Greco-Roman Meals website. Hal Taussig, *In the Beginning was the Meal: Social Experimentation and Early Christian Identity* (Minneapolis, MN: Fortress Press, 2009), 19–20, 66–67.

52. Bynum, *Holy Feast, Holy Fast*.

53. Rachel Fulton, "'Taste and See That the Lord is Sweet': The Flavor of God in the Monastic West," *Journal of Religion* 86, no. 2 (April 2006): 169–204.

54. David Grumett, "Mosaic Food Rules in Celtic Spirituality in Ireland," in Muers and Grumett, *Eating and Believing*, 31–43. Nir Avieli, "At Christmas We Don't Like Pork, Just Like the Maccabbees: Festive Food and Religious Identity at the Protestant Christmas Picnic in Hoi An," *Journal of Material Culture* 14, no. 2 (2009): 219–41.

55. Muers and Grumett, *Eating and Believing*; Finch and Madden, *Eating in Eden*.

56. Rudolph M. Bell, *Holy Anorexia* (Chicago: University of Chicago Press, 1985). See also Margaret R. Miles, "Religion and Food: The Case of Eating Disorders," *Journal of the American Academy of Religion* 63, no. 3 (1995): 549–64.

57. R. Marie Griffith. *Born Again Bodies: Flesh and Spirit in American Christianity* (Berkeley: University of California Press, 2004).

58. Daniel Sack, *Whitebread Protestants: Food and Religion in American Culture* (New York: St. Martin's Press, 2000).

59. Patricia Curran, *Grace Before Meals: Food Ritual and Bodily Discipline in Convent Culture* (Urbana: University of Illinois Press, 1989); Wade Clark Roof, "Blood in the Barbecue? Food and Faith in the American South," in *God in the Details: American Religion in Popular Culture*, ed. Eric M. Mazur and Kate McCarthy (New York: Routledge, 2001), 109–21.

60. For example, see Ann Romines, "Growing Up with Methodist Cookbooks," in *Recipes for Reading: Community Cookbooks, Stories, Histories*, ed. Anne L. Bower (Amherst: University of Massachusetts Press, 1997), 75–88. Matthew Bailey-Dick, "The Kitchenhood of All Believers: A Journey into the Discourse of Mennonite Cookbooks." *Mennonite Quarterly Review* 79 (2005): 153–79.

BIBLIOGRAPHY

Arnold, Philip P., ed. "Religious Dimensions of Food." Special Issue of *Journal of Ritual Studies* 14, no. 1 (2000).

Bynum, Caroline Walker. *Holy Feast, Holy Fast: The Religious Significance of Food to Medieval Women*. Berkeley: University of California Press, 1987.

Greenspoon, Leonard J., et al, eds. *Food and Judaism*. Studies in Jewish Civilization 15. Omaha, NE: Creighton University Press, 2005.

Griffith, R. Marie. *Born Again Bodies: Flesh and Spirit in American Christianity*. Berkeley: University of California Press, 2004.

Khare, R. S., ed. *The Eternal Food: Gastronomic Ideas and Experiences of Hindus and Buddhists*. Albany: State University of New York Press, 1992.

Khare, R. S. "Anna." In *The Hindu World*, edited by Sushil Mittal and Gene Thursby, 407–28. New York: Rutledge, 2004.

Kraemer, David. *Jewish Eating and Identity Through the Ages*. New York: Rutledge, 2007.

McGowen, Andrew. "Food, Ritual, and Power." In *A People's History of Christianity: Late Ancient Christianity*, edited by Virginia Burrus, 145–64. Minneapolis: Augsburg Fortress, 2005.

McKenzie Pearson, Anne. *Because It Gives Me Peace of Mind: Ritual Fasts in the Religious Lives of Hindu Women*. Binghampton: State University of New York Press, 1996.

Miles, Margaret R., ed. "Food and Religion." Special Issue of *The Journal of the American Academy of Religion* 63, no. 3 (1995).

Sack, Daniel. *Whitebread Protestants: Food and Religion in American Culture*. New York: St. Martin's Press, 2000.

Smith, Dennis E. *From Symposium to Eucharist: The Banquet in the Early Christian World*. Minneapolis: Augsburg Fortress, 2003.

CHAPTER 24

FOOD, RACE, AND ETHNICITY

YONG CHEN

A Chinese sage noted more than two thousand years ago that food and sex were the most basic human desires. Since Freud, our understanding of human sexuality has advanced greatly. By comparison, the importance of food remains underappreciated. Food is the most basic need of the human body, and what we eat and how we eat bespeaks our relationship with the natural environment. But its importance extends beyond physical necessity to reflect the multitude of relationships that we form with others as individuals, communities, and nations. Individuals and societies have embedded political, socioeconomic, and cultural meaning in food. Our notions about what is edible and desirable and what is not convey deeply rooted ideas about ourselves and powerful ideologies about our relations with others. The old saying, "we are what we eat," has inspired an often-unspoken corollary that those who eat differently are not like us. Thus, food has played an important role as a marker of identity throughout history.

Although humans have always separated "us" from "them," the ways they do so have changed over time. In the modern era, notions of difference have been cloaked in the seemingly scientific language of race and ethnicity. Nineteenth-century authors varied in the categories they used—some defined at least three separate races in Europe alone—but their taxonomies shared a common belief that racial characteristics were inherited at birth and could not be changed.[1] In the twentieth century, as the scientific basis for racial distinction was revealed to be fraudulent, scholars increasingly used the notion of ethnicity to indicate group differences that derived from more mutable cultural patterns such as food and language. In popular usage in the United States and Britain, there has been a tendency to use the word *race* in discussions of black-white relations, while ethnicity is reserved for relationships among non-black groups. Yet the boundaries between these two categories easily become blurred through a process of "racialization," which emerges from the perception of difference, both physical and cultural, of a particular group from the mainstream. Chinese Americans, for instance, were long regarded as an inferior race with both distinct physical features and despicable cultural characteristics. Such fluidity in the use of these two words helps explain why in popular culture, all non-mainstream cuisines, including those of African Americans, are called "ethnic" food.

The racialization of foodways derived from a number of sources, not only the association of particular groups with foodstuffs, but also the forced production of foods by slaves and servants for the consumption and enjoyment of others. In social contexts, where racial differences entailed discrepancy in power, food and food systems have facilitated and symbolized the political oppression and economic exploitation of racial and ethnic minorities. At the same time, however, minorities have used food as a symbol of resistance and even as an effective weapon against their oppressors.

Modern racialization is paralleled by other connections between food, identity, and power that have recurred throughout human history. The dichotomy of "pure" and "polluted," noted by Mary Douglas, establishes both the centrality and the socially constructed nature of our ideas about the edibility of food. The Jews, for instance, have used dietary restrictions to define themselves as the chosen people. Moreover, the cultural differences articulated through food are often hierarchical, reflecting discrepancies in power. In his study of myth in the indigenous communities in South America, Claude Lévi-Strauss has explored "the raw" and "the cooked" as binary categories to characterize the difference between nature and culture in a stratified way, with nature representing the emotional and instinctive, while culture was associated with the rational and intellectual. In China, for example, during the Qing Dynasty (1646–1911), the native people of Taiwan were classified into "raw" and "cooked" depending on their degree of acculturation. Modern national consciousness is also articulated in terms of food, creating emotional bonds between insiders and excluding those considered unfit for the nation. Emiko Ohnuki-Tierney has described how rice became an icon of the national identity of the Japanese, who regard "rice as our food" and "rice paddies as our land."[2]

As socially constructed categories, race and ethnicity vary from one society to another. This essay focuses on the United States, where a particularly complicated set of racial and ethnic patterns emerged historically from the mixing of diverse European settlers and non-white peoples. Food provides special insights into the complexities of race and ethnicity in American history. Politically, mainstream society has persistently targeted the culinary traditions of racialized groups in an effort to transform or exclude them. In so doing, food became a powerful metaphor and tool of those seeking to define and redefine the racial character of the nation. The racial and ethnic hierarchies that evolved in this process also mirrored the socioeconomic inequalities in food consumption and production patterns. Such inequalities reveal the intersections of race and ethnicity with class and gender.

This essay seeks to provide a historical narrative of the connections between food, race, and ethnicity based on both primary research and secondary sources. The colonial roots of American regional cooking emerged as status-conscious early modern settlers sought to recreate European societies in the New World. The demands of subsistence in a frontier society made them dependent on Native American and African foods, but they nevertheless transformed these goods to make them fit within European categories of health and status. In the nineteenth century, the so-called "old stock" descendants of earlier settlers sought to exclude or assimilate new immigrants from Europe, Asia, and Latin America. These efforts often took the form of "food fights," struggles for national identity between that pitted Anglo, industrial foods against the supposed unhealthy and unsanitary foods of newcomers. Earlier patterns of exclusion and inequality continued into the twentieth century, even as assimilated versions of ethnic foods gained widespread popularity. Eventually, corporate versions were challenged in the marketplace by the foods of new migrants, particularly after the passage of immigration reform in 1965. Despite recurring patterns of exclusion and assimilation, the emerging scholarship on food, race, and ethnicity has not yet become a settled field of inquiry. This essay will seek to provide an introduction to basic concepts, important studies, and ongoing debates.

The Cultural and Gastronomical Roots of Mainstream America

In encounters with non-Anglo cultures, early settlers were determined to maintain their own supremacy and to remain loyal to Anglo cultural roots, particularly their traditional foods. The decimation of American Indian populations through warfare and disease opened abundant land for raising crops and livestock. Moreover, African slaves provided a skilled agricultural labor force that was acclimated to the intense summer conditions of the southern colonies. With these advantages, settlers gained wide access to those British dietary staples of beef, beer, and bread by the mid-eighteenth century. The gentry and merchants could even import luxury goods such as Madeira, cookbooks, tableware, and tea. Nevertheless, culinary blending had already begun to take place, mixing European with Native and African foods. To preserve their own sense of purity, the colonists began a longstanding tradition of repressing the historical memory of non-European cultural contributions.

The uneasy culinary relationship between European colonists and American Indians revolved around maize. In the harsh first winters, colonists at both Jamestown and Plymouth depended for survival on corn produced by local Indians. Yet Trudy Eden, in her book *The Early American Table* (2008), explains the great lengths that early settlers went to avoid eating it, a reluctance based on the belief that ingesting American foods would literally transform their European bodies into Indian bodies.[3] Instead, the settlers sought to transform maize, adopting it to their cultural norms. They planted the seeds in neat rows in the proper English manner, rather than intercropped with beans and squash according to Indian practices. Moreover, they prepared it European-style by feeding it to livestock, cooking it as cornbread or johnnycake, and distilling it into whiskey. Still, the most common method of consumption, indeed, the staple food in British North America, hominy, utilized native alkaline processing technologies to maximize the plant's nutritional value. Rather than acknowledge this debt, settlers condemned the Indians as uncivilized, in part because of different gender roles; women cultivated the soil while men went off to hunt, a frivolous, aristocratic pursuit in British eyes.[4] Nevertheless, colonists profited from Native hunting skills by exchanging valuable pelts for distilled spirits, thereby contributing to a new stereotype of the "drunken Indian."[5]

African slaves also had a profound and historically overlooked role in the creation and development of British foods, both in the American colonies and in the metropolis. Sidney Mintz, in his seminal work *Sweetness and Power* (1985), tells how the emergence of sugar as a coveted commodity and an increasingly present food was a racialized process: its production by African slaves for European consumers.[6] Judith Carney has described the role of African slaves in the creation of another important colonial staple, rice. Noting important continuities between West African and Carolina rice agriculture, she concluded that British colonial planters relied on their slaves for the knowledge, as well as the labor, to construct elaborate networks of levies and floodgates for growing rice in the wetlands around Charleston. The skilled work of African women was equally indispensable for milling the rice with mortar and pestle, a backbreaking chore that also required considerable dexterity.[7] Together with coauthor Richard Rosomoff, Carney has recently offered a broad survey of the impact of African foods, farming, and cooking methods on the Americas. While pointing to the ways that slave ship provisioning and slave subsistence production facilitated the survival of African skills under the yoke of slavery, the authors also seek to recover the historical memory of this African connection from hegemonic accounts that attribute agricultural innovation exclusively to European planters.[8]

The silencing of African American cooks, as well as the historiographical controversy surrounding Carney's "black rice thesis," is due in part to the dehumanizing consequences of plantation slavery. Yet many scholars have noted the ability of slaves to utilize "weapons of the weak" such as self-provisioning and theft to preserve agency within the oppressive system. Particularly in the decades prior to abolition, planters came to depend for subsistence on slave market vendors, giving them a measure of power and, in the words of Mintz, a "taste of freedom."[9]

Diverse European settlers also contributed to cultural diversity within British North America, yet they too were largely assimilated into a hegemonic colonial cuisine. Germans, Dutch, and Swedes introduced to the Middle Colonies a range of dishes, including sausage, sauerkraut, waffles, and scrapple. In the South, meanwhile, as Marcie Cohen Ferris has explained in her delightful book *Matzoh Ball Gumbo* (2005), Jewish residents of early Charleston and Savannah negotiated regional and religious identities at the table, adapting the prescriptions of kashrut to the demands of Southern hospitality.[10] James McWilliams concludes: "One of the most exceptional characteristics of colonial British America, in fact, was its ability to absorb non-English immigrants while simultaneously allowing them to selectively preserve and adopt culinary practices to a very British society."[11]

Even after declaring political independence from Britain, the English-speaking colonists maintained their allegiance to Anglo foodways and their suspicion of foreign items. Regional cooking traditions became increasingly prominent in the culinary literature that emerged in the early republic. Works such as Amelia Simmons's *American Cookery* (1796), Lucy Emerson's *The New England Cookery* (1808), and Mary Randolph's *The Virginia Housewife* (1838) largely obliterated the role of Native Americans and the native roots of New World foods that remained the centerpiece of mainstream America. Thus, corn became known as a southern food, and tomatoes became Italian. Harvey Levenstein describes this process as a form of "British-American culinary conservatism," while quoting a British-American television personality as saying: "A Briton telling an American about cooking is like the blind leading the one-eyed."[12] In a still-unrivaled social history, *Revolution at the Table* (1988), Levenstein offers ample evidence that the persistence of bland, white American foodways was rooted in efforts to preserve a sense of racial purity. Such efforts, however, would confront challenges in the years that followed from a succession of new migrants.

Exclusion and Assimilation in the Nineteenth Century

During "the century of immigration," from the 1820s to the 1920s, millions of newcomers arrived in the United States, predominantly from Europe. The historical memory of a "nation of immigrants" conjures a welcoming attitude: "Give me your tired, your poor . . . " in the hopeful words of Emma Lazarus, enshrined at the base of the Statue of Liberty. In fact, the "huddled masses" were precisely the ones that white leaders feared as a threat to the nation's racial purity. Historian Erika Lee has observed that this period marks the rise of the United States as a "gatekeeper" nation, excluding first the Chinese, then progressively more groups, culminating with the highly restrictive immigration quota laws of the 1920s.[13] The labor demands of industrialization made complete restriction impossible in the decades around the turn of the century, but reformers insisted on assimilating those immigrants who were admitted into proper notions of civilization, starting with their cooking habits. The bland British diet promoted by home economists, however, had little appeal to new immigrants, who transplanted their traditional cuisines and ultimately enriched the national culture.

The Irish immigrants who fled the Great Famine illustrate the racialization of foreigners in mid-nineteenth-century America. As colonial subjects since the sixteenth century, the Irish had long been considered inferior by the British, and newspaper illustrations often depicted them as equivalent to blacks. Their Catholic religion also set the Irish apart from the largely Protestant Anglo elite. Nevertheless, their labor was in great demand, particularly as domestic servants for middle-class households. The abundant ridicule and criticism of the Irish servant girl in cartoons and cookbooks magnified the prevalence of both the Irish servant girl as a racialized occupation and of anti-Irish prejudice. For example, *The American Woman's Home* (1869), coauthored by the domestic educators and abolitionist campaigners Catherine Beecher and Harriet Beecher Stowe, contained obvious Anglo biases toward the Irish servant girl, whom they referred to as "a creature of immense bone and muscle, but of heavy, unawakened brain."[14] Here, the prejudice also has a class basis in references to the peasantry. Hasia Diner, in her masterful study of immigrant foodways, offers further evidence of Anglo Americans' distrust: "Rhetorical associations between Irish servant women and culinary disasters abounded in private writing and journalism."[15]

The case of Chinese food also offers valuable insights into the racialization of minority groups and their foods, as well as the deep cultural roots of racism and prejudice. Already in the early nineteenth century, China represented the largest potential market for American manufactured goods and the largest field for Christian evangelical missionaries. Through these early encounters, Americans developed a lasting image of Chinese as an exotic, backward people with deplorable foodways. S. Wells Williams, who arrived as a missionary printer in 1833, captured Western perceptions: "the articles of food which the Chinese eat, and the mode and ceremonies attending their feasts, have aided much in giving them the old character they bear abroad." He continued: "Travelers have so often spoken of birdsnest soup, canine hams, and grimalkin fricassees, rats, snakes, worms, and other culinary novelties, served up in equally strange ways, that their readers get the idea that these articles form as large a proportion of the food as their description does of the narrative."[16]

As Chinese immigrants arrived in the United States, beginning with the California Gold Rush of 1849, their food habits became the target of derision both by elite Anglo restrictionists and by labor leaders who feared competition from so-called "coolie" workers. Eager to maintain its racial character as an Anglo nation, journalists projected Chinese food as a threat to the bodily health of the nation. A satirical article from 1854 reported: "A California paper gives the following as a bill of fare at a Chinese restaurant in that city: 'Cat Cutlet, 25 cents; Griddled Rats, 6 cents; Dog Soup, 12 cents; Roast Dog, 18 cents; Dog Pie, 6 cents.'"[17] The notion that Chinese food contained rat meat became a popular urban legend, and its reverberations can still be heard today. Union leaders meanwhile feared that competition from Chinese subsisting on rice would drive down the wages of white workers, making it impossible for them to afford a proper diet of meat. In 1902, the American Federation of Labor published an influential pamphlet entitled: *Some Reasons for Chinese Exclusion: Meat vs. Rice: American Manhood against Asiatic Coolieism: Which Shall Survive?*[18] For white Americans, meat represented material abundance, power, and masculinity, while rice was associated with scarcity, weakness, and femininity. Thus, foods were not only racialized but also gendered. The Chinese Exclusion Act of 1882 responded to these fears by forbidding Chinese workers from entering the country and reaffirming the racist principle that Chinese immigrants could not become naturalized citizens.

Domestic cookery became an important battlefield in a turn-of-the-century food fight to define the American nation. In *Revolution at the Table*, Harvey Levenstein has told this story based on the works of Progressive-era food reformers and home economists, who sought to educate immigrant women to prepare healthy, economical, and most importantly American foods. A pot roast and boiled vegetables fit their cultural notions of a proper meal; a bowl of spaghetti with tomato sauce and grated cheese did not. For Levenstein, this dietary revolution followed a declensionist narrative of corruption through industrialization and assimilation. Hasia Diner examines the same historical moment in her book *Hungering for America* (2001), but from the perspective of European immigrants. Through a careful reading of immigrant memoirs, she challenges simplistic accounts of Americanization, noting that generational conflicts and social mobility *within* ethnic communities were more important sources of change than the campaigns of food reformers. She explains that foods contributed to dualistic identities, maintaining ethnic traditions in some situations while adopting national affiliations in others. Ultimately, she provides a classic immigrant tale of Old World hunger overcome by moving to America.

Levenstein makes an important point that with the rise of the food processing industry at the end of the nineteenth century, pure food became associated with neatly packaged, canned, and branded items marketed by national firms. Yet not all industrial foods were created equal, as Donna Gabaccia has shown in a prosopographic study of the ethnic origins of food entrepreneurs. The industries targeted by muckraking journalists such as Upton Sinclair were largely run by immigrant businessmen, most notably, meatpacking, with prominent Scots, Irish, and Jewish leaders. Progressive-era outrage also focused on alcohol, produced by German brewers in the Midwest and Italian and Central European vintners in California, and destined for predominantly urban, immigrant consumers. By contrast, market sectors dominated by Anglo firms such as milling and baking became exemplars of national development. Thus, Progressivism and Prohibition reflected, in part, a xenophobic attempt to protect the nation from undesirable outsiders.[19]

The racialization of industrial foods involved exclusion and subjugation on the one hand, and the creation of idealized white domestic models on the other. Betty Crocker, invented in 1921 by the Washburn-Crosby Company, which seven years later merged with other mills to create the world's largest flour company, served to communicate with consumers and to advertise General Mills products. An unmistakably Anglo presence on the radio and in print, she did her job effectively, and in 1945, *Fortune* magazine ranked her as the second most popular woman after Eleanor Roosevelt, calling her "America's First Lady of Food."[20] In comparison to this caretaker of family and racial identity, African American women were portrayed as paid cooks and housekeepers. Before creating Betty Crocker, Washburn-Crosby had used advertising images of a "mystic Mammy."[21] The best known of such figures was of course Aunt Jemima, also created by Midwestern flour millers to sell pancake mix in the late nineteenth century. Based on a minstrelsy act, perhaps performed originally by a white man in blackface and drag, the advertisements appropriated the iconography of slavery for modern capitalism. Doris Witt explains: "Aunt Jemima pancake mix not only contributed to the widespread naturalization of black women's culinary abilities, in effect, denying that their cooking as slaves and domestic servants was a form of expropriated labor, but they also enabled the product's purchasers to disavow knowledge of the labor... of an emergent class of factory food workers, many of them immigrant women."[22]

African American foodways were subject to ridicule in an attempt to maintain white supremacy following the abolition of slavery. Psyche Williams-Forson has examined the pervasive and denigrating image of the black as a chicken thief, a petty crime which nevertheless conveyed the supposed illicit desire of blacks to possess all the white man's property, including white women. Black men were even anthropomorphized into chickens through the figure of "Zip Coon," a dandy who preened like a cock in fancy but shabby clothes, and served to mock blacks with aspirations. Yet despite the pervasive racism, Williams-Forson shows how cooking and serving chickens could provide a source of power and income for blacks.[23] In a similar fashion, Itai Vardi has analyzed the widespread practice of eating contests—watermelons were a particular favorite—staged by white promoters to assert control over black bodies and thereby shape racial perceptions. Yet beyond this constructionist framework of race relations, Vardi like Williams-Forson employs bell hooks' concept of the "oppositional gaze" to explore how blacks reversed these power relations. Mickey Baker, who took part as a youth in one such eating contest in 1930s Kentucky, felt disgusted by the grotesque behavior of the white audience: "crackers, watching the watermelon gobbling and seed-spitting up on stage. They were farting with pleasure. Literally falling in the aisles of the theater."[24]

Other minority groups were subject to expropriation and demonization in their food habits. Michael Wise has discussed the process of food colonialism on the Blackfeet Indian Reservation in Montana, where government agents sought to restructure patterns of subsistence to instill capitalist patterns of wage labor. The shift from hunting wild buffalo to herding domesticated cattle and the construction of a reservation slaughterhouse sought to cleanse the Blackfeet diet of its predatory past. This colonial project had a gendered component as well in the establishment of a butcher shop which de-legitimated the traditionally female labor of preparing meat and replaced indigenous recipes such as "dupuyer," a form of buffalo bacon, with dishes more acceptable to European sensibilities.[25] Health reformers in San

Antonio, Texas, waged a similar campaign against Mexican street vendors known as "chili queens." Unlike the Blackfeet, the chili vendors provided the city with a valuable tourist attraction, which allowed them to maintain their business despite police harassment. Eventually their foods were appropriated in the form of chili powder and canned tamales by businessmen outside the ethnic community, and by the 1940s, health officials had closed their open-air restaurants.[26]

Notwithstanding the ongoing harassment of ethnic food production, the white American elite arguably failed in their hegemonic goal of maintaining the supremacy of Anglo foods in the nineteenth century. Donna Gabaccia, in her book *We Are What We Eat* (1998), has shown the extent to which migrants have shaped American eating habits. Although the WASP upper class cringed at the thought of Chinese, Italian, Jewish, or Mexican food, ethnic dishes gradually entered the mainstream from the bottom up as marginalized white groups including Bohemians and workers recognized the value of tasty and affordable foods.[27] What began with working-class cosmopolitanism eventually became a hallmark of middle-class American dining,[28] even though racialized inequality persisted throughout the twentieth century.

Ethnic Succession and "Food Deserts" in the Twentieth Century

American race relations in the twentieth century have been marked by historic civil rights movements and by persistent segregation and inequality in access to food. Ethnic food gained wider acceptance in the middle decades of the century, at precisely the moment when the number of foreign born in the United States fell as a consequence of 1920s restrictions and the Great Depression, which prompted the informal exclusion of Latin American migrants, who had been exempt from the 1920s restrictive quotas. As the children of white migrants moved out of ethnic enclaves into mainstream communities, they began to assimilate in their dietary patterns as well, although often maintaining symbolic ties to the homeland through special celebratory meals. By the third generation, many white ethnics felt a desire to reclaim their identity. A resurgence of newcomers after the 1965 immigration reform provided ample opportunities to sample diverse ethnic cuisines, but middle-class consumers often turned instead to suburban grocery stores and theme restaurants. Racialized minorities remained largely excluded from the mainstream, and their segregated urban and rural neighborhoods were particularly poorly supplied with healthy food options. Fast food chains and government commodity support programs became important sources of food, leading to some of the highest levels of food-related disease in the country. Thus, race-based inequality has remained a constant fact in the realm of food consumption.

The United States government persisted in efforts to promote Anglo foodways among the wider population. During World War II, National Research Council's Committee on Food Habits generated numerous studies of American food habits with an eye toward assimilating outsiders and promoting these foodways globally in the postwar era. The committee's executive secretary, the renowned cultural anthropologist Margaret Mead, identified the nature of mainstream food in the following manner: "Being American is a matter of abstention from foreign ways, foreign food, foreign idea, foreign accents, foreign vices. So whisky drinking becomes identified with the Irish and, by coincidence, with Catholics, beer drinking with Germans, and marijuana with black musicians."[29] The military also sanctioned and institutionalized a racialized division of labor in food production. In 1932, the U.S. Navy began to recruit African Americans, but only to serve as messmen.[30] Filipinos have been cast in similarly subordinate roles. In 1970, according to Yen Espiritu, "of the 16,669 Filipinos in the U.S. Navy, 80 percent were in the steward rating."[31]

The domestic consumption of ethnic foods remained an important definer of family and community identity for many, but these patterns changed considerably from one generation to the next. An important study of Italian-American foodways in Philadelphia by Judith Goode, Janet Theophano, and Karen Curtis found that ethnic and American foods were consumed in differing formats: one-pot meals with gravy tended to follow a modified Italian pattern while platters of segregated meat and vegetables featured American items. These meals were served in alternation according to regular weekly routines. Religious feasts and fasts also served as occasions for preserving Italian traditions. Nevertheless, younger generations often showed great reluctance to consume particular items such as organ meats and smelt that were considered inedible by mainstream Americans. The authors observed that families could be highly idiosyncratic in the manner of cooking, rapidly transforming Italian village cooking styles, and challenging the idea that an ethnic community was unified around particular flavor principles.[32] Iconic dishes can still remain as symbols of ethnicity, however, even when they have gone out of fashion in the home country. For example, the descendents of Norwegian immigrants in Minnesota still make a distinctive thin potato pancake called *lefse*, and when they served it to a visiting diplomat's wife, they were nonplussed to learn that the dish was considered a museum piece in contemporary Norway.[33]

Scholars have also sought to determine the patterns followed by ethnic restaurants. Geographer Wilbur Zelinsky developed a valuable methodology for mapping ethnic restaurants using telephone books. He found, not surprisingly, that the three most popular cuisines, Chinese, Italian, and Mexican, made up fully 70 percent of the total in the United States. Comparing these numbers with population data, he concluded that entrepreneurial cooks were more important than ethnic dining communities, most notably in the case of Chinese restaurants, which had achieved a near universal presence in North America despite quite modest populations in most regions.[34] Donna Gabaccia has pointed to the importance of migratory gender ratios in determining the presence of ethnic restaurants. The groups that became the leading source of restaurants in the twentieth century, the three mentioned before plus Greeks, were all characterized by predominantly male migrants, for whom inexpensive commercial foods provided a substitute for domestic cooking. By contrast, more gender-balanced migrations, such as Poles, Germans, Jews, and Irish opened fewer restaurants, and their culinary impact came more from groceries and delis.[35]

Patterns of ethnic succession, whereby new migrant groups take over low-status service niches formerly filled by earlier immigrants, have also shaped the restaurant industry. Krishnendu Ray has discerned two separate processes at work in determining the status of ethnic restaurants in the United States and the ethnic origins of workers in the industry. Challenging notions that particular groups were inclined toward restaurant work, he argued instead for a theory based on social forces exerted by mainstream society. In particular, he concluded that restaurants gained status in inverse proportion to the number of actual immigrants in the country. Thus, the relative scarcity and wealth of Japanese compared to Chinese migrants helped sushi to gain more favor than dim sum in contemporary America. At the same time, the presence of low-skilled jobs in professional kitchen attracted recent labor migrants, positions now filled largely by new arrivals from Latin America.[36] Meanwhile, Haiming Liu and Lianlian Lin have observed another pattern of ethnic succession, not between different ethnic groups, but rather in the transformation of a particular group's foodways with new migrations from the home country. Nineteenth-century Chinese migrants came predominantly from the Guangzhou region of southern China, better known to Americans as Canton. After 1965, as new migrants arrived from Sichuan, Shanghai, and Beijing, their regional specialties replaced the older assimilated version of Cantonese, at least among discerning consumers in Chinatowns.[37]

The invention of "soul food" illustrates another interesting pattern of culinary tourism within and beyond the African American community. The Great Migration of southern sharecroppers to northern industrial jobs began at the turn of the century and reached a high point around World War II. When they arrived in northern communities, existing urban black professionals in Harlem and Hyde Park looked down at first on the catfish, collards, and chitterlings eaten by rustic newcomers. Nevertheless, the nostalgia felt by migrants, combined with the continued segregation suffered in the north, made home-style cafes and cafeterias into havens of commensality in Harlem and Chicago. As the Black Power movement gained strength in the 1960s, middle-class African Americans suddenly embraced the authenticity of soul food as a largely imagined slave diet in order to avoid criticism for assimilation. Often overlooked in considerations of soul food is the immigrant presence, which was first highlighted by Frederick Douglas Opie. In a recent history, Opie noted not only the influence of Caribbean cooking as early as the 1920s and 1930s, but also the growing importance of ethnic succession, as Harlem soul food restaurants have been taken over by recent immigrants, most famously, the Red Rooster opened by Ethiopian-Swedish celebrity chef Marcus Samuelsson.[38]

One common thread running through the presentation and consumption of ethnic food in America has been a desire for authenticity, which has been met in a number of different ways. Shun Lu and Gary Alan Fine have examined the delicate balance that Chinese restaurateurs face in marketing their dishes as authentic outside the ethnic community. As cultural entrepreneurs, they offer "novel culinary traditions [that] must be situated so as to seem simultaneously exotic and familiar: distinguishable from mainstream cuisine (and thus desirable) yet able to be assimilated as edible creations."[39] Warren Belasco has demonstrated how this balance between exoticism and familiarity was mastered by corporate food processors and restaurant chains, whose ersatz versions of authenticity largely succeeded in coopting the ethnic revival and the counterculture movements of the 1960s and 1970s. For example, General Mills gave Betty Crocker a makeover, transforming her into a multiracial, multiethnic figure calculated to appeal, in the words of Marilyn Halter, to "a rainbow coalition of consumers."[40] Marie Sarita Gaytán's recent study of Mexican restaurants has emphasized the importance of *inauthenticity*, as well as authenticity, in the narratives and performances of ethnicity. She offers a valuable typology distinguishing between authenticity that is commemorative of the ethnic community or Americanized to appeal to mainstream consumers, and inauthenticity that is embraced by ethnics seeking a hybrid identity or by corporations to cleanse a cuisine of its foreignness.[41]

Contemporary neoliberal policies, paradoxically intended to subsidize large agribusiness while limiting government support for minority populations, have extended the racialization of foodways and undermined the nutritional health of historically excluded groups. The proliferation of fast food restaurants, purveying goods made cheap by commodity supports, have spread through urban centers in the last few decades, even as full-service restaurants and supermarkets have fled to the suburbs, transforming these impoverished slums into "food desert," areas where it is difficult to obtain fresh, healthy foods. At the same time, as Charlotte Biltekoff explains elsewhere in this volume, experts have sought to moralize the discourse on healthy eating and to pass off onto consumers blame for the poor "choices" they are supposedly making. The complexity of this issue can be seen in recent local government initiatives, such as the vote taken on July 29, 2008, by the Los Angeles City to ban for one year new fast food restaurants in poor, minority neighborhoods in South Los Angeles. Compared to the more affluent, Anglo Westside of the city, these neighborhoods have a far greater concentration of fast food places and a much higher rate of obesity. Nevertheless, the one-year moratorium, which was to be voted as a permanent policy by the city council in December 2010, generated criticism as a form of "paternalism" and a restriction on consumer choice.[42] But no one denies the prevalence of poor nutritional health and obesity among racial minorities. Meanwhile, anthropologist Gary Paul Nabham, commenting on the high prevalence of diabetes among American Indians subsisting on commodity surpluses assistance programs, has called for a return to a traditional indigenous diet.[43] Perhaps the one thing can be safely concluded from the contradictory discourse coming from all sides of the political spectrum is that racialization and inequality remain intractable elements of American foodways in the twenty-first century.

In Short

Racial inequality has remained a constant in the history of American foodways through the labor relations that produce it, the access to healthy diets, and the status accorded to particular foods. Nevertheless, there have been clear historical changes in the forms of racial oppression, as well as in the ways that minority groups have resisted it. Colonial patterns of bland British cooking began to be replaced in the nineteenth century by equally nondescript industrial, mass-produced food. By the twentieth century, corporate advertising had begun to see profits from marketing to minorities. Yet counter-hegemonic trends were also in place from early on. Certainly by the great proletarian migrations of the nineteenth century, a critical mass of workers had begun to challenge the supremacy of Anglo models and to eat across the boundaries of race and ethnicity. Although the process of ethnic succession led to the incorporation of many groups into the mainstream middle class, the continued influx of new immigrants offered alternatives to the bland offerings of corporate foods. As the diverse scholarship cited in this essay shows, food has great potential for helping us understand the processes of racial formation and transformation in America.

Notes

1. Ivan Hannaford, *Race: The History of an Idea in the West* (Baltimore, MD: Johns Hopkins University Press, 1996), 329.

2. Emiko Ohnuki-Tierney, *Rice as Self: Japanese Identities through Time* (Princeton, NJ: Princeton University Press, 1993), 4.

3. Trudy Eden, *The Early American Table: Food and Society in the New World* (DeKalb: Northern Illinois University Press, 2008), 22, 58–77. Similar fears of culinary and racial blending among Spanish conquistadors were described by Rebecca Earle, "'If You Eat Their Food . . . ': Diets and Bodies in Early Colonial Spanish America," *American Historical Review* 115, no. 3 (June 2010): 688–713.

4. James E. McWilliams, *A Revolution in Eating: How the Quest for Food Shaped America* (New York: Columbia University Press, 2005), 82–84.

5. On the construction of the "drunken Indian," see Peter C. Mancall, *Deadly Medicine: Indians and Alcohol in Early America* (Ithaca, NY: Cornell University Press, 1995).

6. Sidney W. Mintz, *Sweetness and Power: The Place of Sugar in Modern History* (New York: Viking, 1985).

7. Judith A. Carney, *Black Rice: The African Origins of Rice Cultivation in the Americas* (Cambridge, MA: Harvard University Press, 2001).

8. Judith A. Carney and Richard Nicholas Rosomoff, *In the Shadow of Slavery: Africa's Botanical Legacy in the Atlantic World* (Berkeley: University of California Press, 2009).

9. Sidney W. Mintz, *Tasting Food, Tasting Freedom: Excursions into Eating, Culture, and the Past* (Boston: Beacon Press, 1996), 33–49; Eugene Genovese, *Roll, Jordan, Roll: The World the Slaves Made* (New York: Vintage Books, 1976), 540–59; Charles Joyner, *Down by the Riverside: A South Carolina Slave Community* (Urbana: University of Illinois Press, 1984), 106, 129–30; Psyche A. Williams-Forson, *Building Houses Out of Chicken Legs: Black Women, Food, and Power* (Chapel Hill: University of North Carolina Press, 2006), 13–37. On the "black rice" controversy, see the exchange in the *American Historical Review* 115, no. 1 (February 2010).

10. Marcie Cohen Ferris, *Matzoh Ball Gumbo: Culinary Tales of the Jewish South* (Chapel Hill: University of North Carolina Press, 2005).

11. McWilliams, *A Revolution in Eating*, 181.

12. Harvey A. Levenstein, *Revolution at the Table: The Transformation of the American Diet* (New York: Oxford University Press), 4.

13. Erika Lee, *At America's Gates: Chinese Immigration During the Exclusion Era, 1882–1943* (Chapel Hill: University of North Carolina Press, 2003).

14. Catharine Esther Beecher and Harriet Beecher Stowe, *The American Woman's Home* (New York: J. B. Ford and Company, 1869), 311.

15. Hasia Diner, *Hungering for America: Italian, Irish, and Jewish Foodways in the Age of Migration* (Cambridge, MA: Harvard University Press, 2001), 118.

16. S. Wells Williams, *The Middle Kingdom*, 2 vols. (1895; reprint, New York: Paragon Book Reprint Corp., 1966), 1:771. See also J. A. G. Roberts, *China to Chinatown: Chinese Food in the West* (London: Reaktion, 2002); Andrew Coe, *Chop Suey: A Cultural History of Chinese Food in the United States* (New York: Oxford University Press, 2009), 32.

17. *Gleason's Pictorial Drawing—Room Companion* 6, no. 3 (January 21, 1854): 47.

18. American Federation of Labor, *Some Reasons for Chinese Exclusion: Meat vs. Rice: American Manhood against Asiatic Coolieism: Which Shall Survive?* (Washington, DC: Government Printing Office, 1902).

19. Donna R. Gabaccia, "As American as Budweiser and Pickles? Nation-Building in American Food Industries," in *Food Nations: Selling Taste in Consumer Societies*, ed. Warren Belasco and Philip Scranton (New York: Routledge, 2002), 175–93.

20. Susan Marks, *Finding Betty Crocker: The Secret Life of America's First Lady of Food* (Waterville, ME: Thorndike Press, 2005), 116. See also Katherine J. Parker, *Food Is Love: Food Advertising and Gender Roles in America* (Philadelphia: University of Pennsylvania, 2006).

21. Alice A. Deck, "'Now Then—Who Said Biscuits': The Black Woman Cook as Fetish in American Advertising," in *Kitchen Culture in America: Popular Representations of Food, Gender, and Race*, ed. Sherrie A. Inness (Philadelphia: University of Pennsylvania Press, 2001), 69.

22. Doris Witt, *Black Hunger: Food and the Politics of U.S. Identity* (New York: Oxford University Press, 1999), 36–37.

23. Williams-Forson, *Building Houses out of Chicken Legs*, 26–37, 50–70.

24. Quoted in Itai Vardi, "Feeding Race: Eating Contests, the Black Body, and the Social Production of Group Boundaries Through Amusement in Turn of the Twentieth Century America," *Food, Culture & Society* 13, no. 3 (September 2010): 380.

25. Michael Wise, "Colonial Beef and the Blackfeet Reservation Slaughterhouse, 1879–1895," *Radical History Review* 110 (Spring 2011): 59–82.

26. Jeffrey M. Pilcher, "Who Chased Out the 'Chili Queens'? Gender, Race, and Urban Reform in San Antonio, Texas, 1880–1943," *Food and Foodways* 16, no. 3 (July 2008): 173–200.

27. A similar pattern emerged among the working classes of Manchester according to Tamara Ketabgian, "Foreign Tastes and 'Manchester Tea-Parties': Eating and Drinking with the Victorian Lower Order," in *Consuming Culture in the Long Nineteenth Century*, ed. Tamara S. Wagner and Narin Hassan (New York: Rowman & Littlefield, 2007), 125–39.

28. On middle-class cosmopolitanism, see Andrew Haley, *Turning the Tables: Restaurants and the Rise of the American Middle Class* (Chapel Hill: University of North Carolina Press, 2011).

29. Margaret Mead, "Ethnicity and Anthropology in America," in *Ethnic Identity: Cultural Continuity and Change*, ed. George A. DeVos and Lola Romanucci-Ross (Palo Alto, CA: AltaMira Press, 1995), 313. See also idem, "The Problem of Changing Food Habits," in *Food and Culture: A Reader*, ed. Carole Counihan and Penny Van Esterik, 2nd ed. (New York: Routledge, 2008), 21.

30. Richard E. Miller, *The Messman Chronicles: African Americans in the U.S. Navy, 1932–1943* (Annapolis, MD: Naval Institute Press, 2004).

31. Yen Espiritu, *Filipino American Lives* (Philadelphia: Temple University Press, 1995), 16; Ray L. Burdeos, *Filipinos in the U.S. Navy & Coast Guard During the Vietnam War* (Bloomington, IN: AuthorHouse, 2008).

32. Judith Goode, Janet Theophano, and Karen Curtis, "A Framework for the Analysis of Continuity and Change in Shared Sociocultural Rules for Food Use: The Italian-American Pattern," in *Ethnic and Regional Foodways in the United States: The Performance of Group Identity*, ed. Linda Keller Brown and Kay Mussell (Knoxville: University of Tennessee Press, 1984), 66–88.

33. Traci Marie Kelly, "Honoring Helga, 'The Little Lefse Maker': Regional Food as Social Marker, Tradition, and Art," in *Cooking Lessons: The Politics of Gender and Food*, ed. Sherrie A. Inness (Lanham, MD: Rowman and Littlefield, 2001), 22.

34. Wilbur Zelinsky, "The Roving Palate: North America's Ethnic Restaurant Cuisines," *Geoforum* 16, no. 1 (1985): 51–72.

35. Gabaccia, *We Are What We Eat*, 80–81.

36. Krishnendu Ray, "Ethnic Succession and the New American Restaurant Cuisine," in *The Restaurants Book: Ethnographies of Where We Eat*, ed. David Beriss and David Sutton (Oxford: Berg, 2007), 97–114.

37. Haiming Liu and Lianlian Lin, "Food, Culinary Identity, and Transnational Culture: Chinese Restaurant Business in Southern California," *Journal of Asian American Studies* 12, no. 2 (June 2009): 135–62.

38. Frederick Douglas Opie, *Hog and Hominy: Soul Food from Africa to America* (New York: Columbia University Press, 2008). See also Tracy N. Poe, "The Origins of Soul Food in Black Urban Identity: Chicago, 1915–1947," *American Studies International* 37, no. 1 (February 1999): 4–33.

39. Shun Lu and Gary Allen Fine, "The Presentation of Ethnic Authenticity: Chinese Food as a Social Accomplishment," *Sociological Quarterly* 36, no. 3 (Summer 1995): 536.

40. Marilyn Halter, *Shopping for Identity: The Marketing of Ethnicity* (New York: Schocken Books, 2000), 180; Warren Belasco, "Ethnic Fast Foods: The Corporate Melting Pot," *Food and Foodways* 2 (1987): 1–30.

41. Marie Sarita Gaytán, "From Sombreros to Sincronizadas: Authenticity, Ethnicity, and the Mexican Restaurant Industry," *Journal of Contemporary Ethnography* 37, no. 3 (June 2008): 314–41. See also Liora Gvion and Naomi Trostler, "From Spaghetti and Meatballs through Hawaiian Pizza to Sushi: The Changing Nature of Ethnicity in American Restaurants," *Journal of Popular Culture* 41, no. 6 (2008): 950–74.

42. Robert Creighton, "Cheeseburgers, Race, and Paternalism: Los Angeles' Ban on Fast Food Restaurants," *Journal of Legal Medicine* 30:2 (2009): 249–67; Abby Wisse Schachter, "Our Year of Lost Liberty," *Jewish Chronicle* 49, no. 33 (December 25, 2008): 6; Charlotte Biltekoff, "Critical Nutrition Studies," in *Oxford Handbook of Food History*, ed. Jeffrey M. Pilcher (New York: Oxford University Press, 2012), 172–90.

43. Gary Paul Nabhan, "Rooting Out the Causes of Disease: Why Diabetes is So Common Among Desert Dwellers," in Counihan and Van Esterik, *Food and Culture*, 369–80.

Bibliography

Belasco, Warren. "Ethnic Fast Foods: The Corporate Melting Pot." *Food and Foodways* 2 (1987): 1–30.

Brown, Linda Keller, and Kay Mussell, eds. *Ethnic and Regional Foodways in the United States: The Performance of Group Identity*. Knoxville: University of Tennessee Press, 1984.

Carney, Judith A. *Black Rice: The African Origins of Rice Cultivation in the Americas*. Cambridge, MA: Harvard University Press, 2001.

Diner, Hasia R. *Hungering for America: Italian, Irish, and Jewish Foodways in the Age of Migration*. Cambridge, MA: Harvard University Press, 2001.

Ferris, Marcie Cohen. *Matzoh Ball Gumbo: Culinary Tales of the Jewish South*. Chapel Hill: University of North Carolina Press, 2005.

Gabaccia, Donna. *We Are What We Eat: Ethnic Food and the Making of Americans*. Cambridge, MA: Harvard University Press, 1998.

Levenstein, Harvey A. *Revolution at the Table: The Transformation of the American Diet*. New York: Oxford University Press, 1988.

Lu, Shun, and Gary Allen Fine. "The Presentation of Ethnic Authenticity: Chinese Food as a Social Accomplishment." *Sociological Quarterly* 36, no. 3 (Summer 1995): 535–53.

Opie, Fredrick Douglass. *Hogs and Hominy: Soul Food from Africa to America*. New York: Columbia University Press, 2008.

Poe, Tracy N. "The Origins of Soul Food in Black Urban Identity: Chicago, 1914–1947." *American Studies International* 37, no. 1 (February 1999): 4–33.

Williams-Forson, Psyche A. *Building Houses Out of Chicken Legs: Black Women, Food, and Power*. Chapel Hill: University of North Carolina Press, 2006.

Witt, Doris. *Black Hunger: Food and the Politics of U.S. Identity*. New York: Oxford University Press, 1999.

CHAPTER 25

NATIONAL CUISINES

ALISON K. SMITH

In 2005, the Council of Europe published a glossy, heavily illustrated volume celebrating the "culinary cultures of Europe," with the stated aim of presenting readers with "a kaleidoscope of essays describing the food of forty European nations."[1] In his introduction, Fabio Parasecoli describes the created nature of national cuisines, and the many "signifying networks [that] define the key concepts of tradition and authenticity, which play a paramount role in constructing what is 'typical,' hence defining local, regional or even national identities." These signifiers include ingredients, techniques, trade, location, time and media, all of which create variations and, eventually, differences that are read as national. Furthermore, he notes, "since these qualities are supposed to catch the 'essence of a certain food or foodway,' it is precisely around these supposed essences that all the identification and exclusion processes are actually built."[2] In other words, national cuisines, particularly as understood in the recent past, reflect the influence of cultural and economic changes on the diets of individuals and societies.

The organization of the rest of the volume seems to affirm this notion; rather than grouping nations by region, or articles by focus, the editors simply list the forty nations in alphabetical order, as if emphasizing the idea that "national" divisions are simply arbitrary. And some authors of individual articles have a great deal of fun with the notion that national cuisines are created ideas that encompass whole rituals of the social life of peoples, in one case relating them to modern art, in another to cinema, in a third to general thoughts about the practice of eating. Based on these articles, a reader might conclude that national cuisines are now readily understood as constructed artifacts of national movements, with a certain persistence, but also possible to dismiss. Elements of the introduction and conclusion buttress this ideal, pointing out the complicated place of national cuisines in the world of globalization (and, in the European context, of pan-European administration). New products—or, perhaps, even more, once scarce but now readily available products—and new modes of consumption, via international franchises, create changes across national lines, and these articles can be read as evidence of the strength of such forces.

But despite this side of the volume, just as many articles take a very different approach, one much more tied to the kinds of nationalist exploration and cultural description that rose as "nations" became subjects of inquiry in the nineteenth century. In some cases, they simply list "national," "authentic," or "traditional" foods, in others, slightly more sophisticated analysis still essentially comes down to a description of a particular series of different foods and dishes. To a certain extent, all these authors view national cuisines as obvious, as real artifacts of age-old tradition, largely unchanged. In so doing, they hew closely to a conception of national cuisines as easily defined by a list of foods, recognized by all members of the nation, and capable of serving as ambassador for the nation to the outside world. Furthermore, the persistence of this kind of identification of national cuisines, as apparently simple lists of nationally significant foods, shows the limits of globalization to overcome differences in eating habits. Indeed, it may in fact show that globalization can harden the conception of national foods by politicizing the local. When faced with the threat of obsolescence from new products, new consumption patterns, and even new ethical constructs, national cuisines can be extremely resilient, thanks to the efforts of both individual proselytizers such as cookbook authors, slow food proponents, and restaurateurs, who seek to preserve older patterns of consumption, and also of nation states acting in the interests of specific agricultural producers or agricultural products, both to preserve the economic health of their nations, and also to preserve national particularities. This sort of "gastronationalism" underlay the 2005 decision of the French government to name foie gras part of the "officially-protected cultural and gastronomic patrimony" of the nation, formally recognizing this element of cuisine as central to France's conception of itself.[3]

The following discussion will first look at the general development of national cuisines out of a series of different possible building blocks, and then switch to a case study of one particular national cuisine that was developed in concert with ideas of the nation. The first section begins with a discussion of the raw ingredients, as it were, of regional cuisines. It then progresses to a discussion of the various ways that those regional cuisines were transformed into national cuisines, and the purposes behind such transformations—to unify a nation, to present a nation to the outside world, or to speak to diasporic or migrant communities. It ends with a discussion of the ways that those very forces, particularly in the modern world of global trade and high levels of migration, also alter national cuisines. The final section looks at one case study: Russia. In this place, nearly all the elements discussed in the first section can be seen; conceptions of "tradition," new products and modes of production and consumption brought about by trade and other contacts with foreigners, conscious discussion of a national cuisine, and conscious efforts to codify that cuisine. As a result, Russia presents a case study that shows well the broad array of influences on national cuisines.

Ingredients: The Building Blocks of National Cuisines

Within the world of social science, the idea that nations are not age-old institutions, but instead more recently created bodies, has become the standard. Nations are "imagined communities" built in part out of "invented traditions," but they also often exert powerful real influence over their members.[4] National cuisines, therefore, are best understood as collections of prepared dishes, created out of agricultural, trade, regional, local, family, and religious differences and traditions, and presented to a public—sometimes to introduce a nation to its own members, sometimes to introduce that nation to the outside world, and sometimes to preserve the memory of a nation in an immigrant population—through cookbooks, other media, restaurants, and specific goods.[5] Furthermore, national cuisines are composed of real foods that have real meanings, but that are not necessarily synonymous either with all the foods actually eaten by all citizens of a given nation or with actual age-old tradition in a given place. Instead, they have been built, sometimes consciously, sometimes not, out of the history of given nations, with all the complications such a construction implies. And, too, national cuisines are not static, but can be transformed without necessarily losing their essential "national" character.

Because nations (with the exception of purely diasporic nations) are associated with specific geographic spaces, national cuisines first of all develop out of the agricultural practices and products of those spaces. This source of differentiation starts with the different flora and fauna of the new and old worlds and then becomes more complex through the very different agricultural zones of individuals continents. Given the central role played by starchy foods in most common diets, one major source of difference between regions comes from the very different agricultural sources of those foods across and between continents. The rice of Asia gives way to the varied cereal grains of Europe, and the potato and corn of the Americas. Within and between these large regions come other agricultural divisions that create culinary differences. The olives of the Mediterranean give way to the seed oils of northern Europe in one direction, and to the *ghee* of India in another. The tropical fruits of equatorial climates give way to hardier fruits and rougher vegetables in colder regions. And, often, these basic building blocks of cuisine are imbued with significance by the compilers of national cuisines.[6] Little is more Russian than its buckwheat porridge, more Ethiopian than its fermented bread of teff, or more Peruvian than its potatoes. Basic agricultural products—which may well be shared with regional neighbors—eventually come to be seen as particularly important to the national culture.

Even looking only at these base identifiers, varied technologies of cooking have already intervened in the basic food supply to create locally specific patterns of eating. Cooking transforms the raw into something not only digestible, but imbued with cultural significance, and variations in the methods of that transformation, in the specific techniques of cooking, create regional variations in cuisines. While basic combinations of starch, meat, and vegetable might be common across many regions, the specifics of their preparation—and particularly the vessels in which they are cooked—become imbued with national significance. The tagine itself makes a basic stew into a specific regional dish, the wok stir fries instead of sautés, and ovens of various structures and fuel create differences between lavash, naan, and ciabatta. Thus, not only do different technologies and techniques create difference between regions, but they start to create difference within regions, as well, which means the beginnings of more specific geographic and cultural identifications.

Few conceptions of national cuisines, however, grow solely out of the "age old" or "native" agricultural products or cooking techniques of given regions, in large part because trade and other contacts between peoples have long altered both agricultural practices and food habits. Goods have moved from place to place and have been adopted into local traditions, at times being completely incorporated into a new conception of the "native." In some places, New World crops virtually eradicated older foods, with varying degrees of influence on the eventual creation of a "national" cuisine. The New World crops cassava and corn triumphed over native millet and sorghum across much of Africa. In this case, instead of creating the basis for national (or other) culinary differentiation, the new crops brought with them a certain common ground in culinary practices that demonstrates cultural diffusion and uniformity across a wide swath of the continent. Meanwhile, in Britain, new access to cane sugar—something made possible through colonial expansion in the New World and the rise of plantation agriculture, not through the introduction of a new crop to Britain itself—brought about a revolution in eating and drinking habits. Not only did sugar and its products triumph over older sweeteners, and help a new "national" drink—tea—find success, but a taste for sweetness became a dominant part of British dietary preferences, and a feature that diverged from dietary preferences on the continent.[7]

New crops or goods did not have to eradicate older ones in order to influence diets in significant, but not necessarily uniform, ways. In many cases, new ingredients were incorporated into diets to such an extent that they became imbued with cultural significance—the potato pancake, the tomato, or pepper sauce—but in others, older crops remained startlingly resilient. In the New World, as colonizers brought with them foods from home, the resulting confrontation of two food worlds added new levels of insider/outsider to the possible sources of food-based social differentiation. In Mexico—and Latin America more generally—wheat and corn became markers of social and ethnic distinction, and read as essentially part of different images of the "people" and the nation. In the nineteenth century, creole elites viewed corn as the backward food of the native population, while wheat spoke to them of the modernity of their new nations.[8] And in other places, the interaction between new and old was yet more complicated. Despite its success in the fields of the country, corn, for one, failed to alter significantly cuisine in Ethiopia, where a strong conception of a unique national cuisine had developed in conjunction with Ethiopia's conception of itself as an independent nation. Of course, even given the resilience of native grains such as teff on the Ethiopian table, the cuisine was hardly pristine. An earlier example of the power of trade networks—the spice trade—had long influenced eating patterns in the country.[9] And this particular example demonstrates the complicated ways in which trade networks and other contacts alter eating habits, at times creating significant change, at times missing the mark.

One reason that new products and techniques may not be accepted into an area is that cultural norms also to a large extent guide individual tastes—both preferred tastes and conceptions of unacceptable or disgusting foods. In any given location, not every ingredient that can in principle be eaten necessarily is adopted into regular use; nor is every possible method of cooking or preserving food used in every place. Instead, tastes, often but not always based in cultural practices, guide these distinctions. Preferences for bitter, acid, or fermented tastes develop in different cultures, and affect the array of foods deemed acceptable within. These may owe something to local practices of preserving foods, as the various common methods—pickling, fermenting, salting, smoking—create these strong flavors. These preferences can also serve as markings against outsiders, as recognition of what others might deem disgusting can actually serve to increase the symbolic importance of a given dish. Scotland's famed haggis—oatmeal and offal cooked inside a sheep's stomach (though now usually in a sausage casing)—is a prime example. Its perceived loathsomeness to outsiders played an important role in its ascension to the position of most Scottish of Scottish foods, as it stood for the particular hardiness of Scotland's people against their culinarily weaker English foes.

Religion, which often serves as a source of differentiation and division between cultures, does so in part by defining acceptable and unacceptable foods. Many religions mark foods as clean or unclean: as Lenten or not, as kosher or trefah, as halal or haram. These distinctions can be particularly strong markers of outsider and insider status, because of the visceral quality of their identification with purity and sin. In some cases, these distinctions therefore play particularly strong roles in defining cultures against other cultures. But they can also create divisions within societies that may create difficulties for those seeking to define nations through cuisine. In India, dietary guidelines are more strongly associated with specific castes than with Hinduism in general; as a result, reifying a particular national cuisine based broadly in Hinduism has been challenging, as some foods that have become strongly associated with "Indian cuisine," such as highly spiced foods, are unacceptable to some religiously orthodox members of the society. One result has been a tendency to focus attention on one religious association with food: the need to protect literal sacred cows, in opposition to beef-eating Muslims. But this association, as Swijendra Narayan Jha both pointed out and suffered from, was located more in recent nationalist politics than in supposedly ancient writings.[10] In other cases, different religions can be united in food rules—and even in food preferences—but very much divided in other ways. Judaism and Islam share certain dietary restrictions in principle, and in the modern middle east a love for falafel in practice, but these commonalities if anything serve to provoke division rather than assuage it, as, for example, satirized in the short film *West Bank Story* (2005).[11]

Religion not only marks certain foods as clean or unclean, but it also gives rise to calendars of festivals—and as a result, of festive foods. These festive foods often come to play particularly important roles in the definition of national cuisines, in large part because they serve a unifying function within given national groups. Their very out-of-the-ordinariness already gives them a special place in individual diets, something rare and therefore anticipated and expected. They become markers of these particular holidays, and the larger emotional world those holidays bring. Because they are associated with regular but rare events, too, they serve as a temporal unifier—they bring together the past and the present in a very real way. Additionally, festive foods may be (in principle, at least) among the only foods shared widely across stratified societies. In societies with different eating patterns between the masses and the elite, festive foods can create a common bond across class. Furthermore, festive foods can create bonds within diasporic nations and immigrant communities, as well. Festivals and holidays bring members of far-flung families and societies together, sometimes literally, sometimes figuratively, both to worship and to enjoy particular festive foods.[12]

There are yet other sources of differentiation even within a single self-defined (or internationally recognized) nation. On the smallest scale, all "traditional" foods are really family foods as much as anything else; traditional recipes are simply those passed through generations, often via a single family. As a result, there are many possible variations of any single dish associated with a particular group, and not inevitably a quintessential version that can stand for all the members of a group. Furthermore, social stratification means that there is often significant variation among normal diets within a given region. Peasant foods and elite foods diverge, in part through new, more expensive ingredients, in part through new, more labor-intensive techniques. Jack Goody suggests, in particular, that "the higher cuisine also incorporates and transforms what, from the national standpoint, is the regional food of peasants and the cooking of exotic foreigners."[13] Defining a national cuisine, therefore requires both overcoming these sources of differentiation and, often, teasing out a conception of "national" cuisine within a context that has already been altered by foreign practices and foods.

Method: From Raw Ingredients to National Cuisines

All these sources of variation do not necessarily add up to national cuisines. They do create distinctly different cuisines in different regions, and in principle, any region that self-identifies as a nation may call its cuisine a national one. In practice, though, defining a national cuisine requires grappling both with overarching regional similarities that blur national boundaries from the outside, and with the possibility that a single nation comprises multiple regions or other social or cultural sources of differentiation from within. When nations are part of larger regions with similar food patterns, building a national cuisine requires identifying certain parts of those larger patterns as uniquely belonging to that particular nation. When nations contain within them multiple regions with significant local identities, including local foodways, or dramatically different social groups with distinct ways of eating, building the national cuisine requires taking on a similar task, but this time either of identifying those foods that can stand for the nation as a whole, or of identifying (or creating) something new that stands apart from those many separate cuisines.

The twin powers of print and industrial capitalism provide the mechanism for the process of defining national cuisines. Just as print is essential to the creation of nations, as Eric Hobsbawm and Benedict Anderson suggest, print helps transform these regional, class, or family foods into a national cuisine—that is, a creation that helps define a nation in the eyes of its own members or of the world.[14] First and foremost are cookbooks, which both bring together separate foods into coherent wholes, and also refine what might once have been a whole series of different versions into a single accepted dish. While only some cookbook authors explicitly try to create national cuisines in a single volume, many others contribute pieces to the production of a national cuisine through their works. Enough cookbooks that feature the same basic recipes over and over, particularly if they discuss nationhood in the process, help create these national cuisines. And as Stephen Mennell points out, the cookbooks (and the press surrounding them) produced in different nations do not just eventually codify an array of dishes or modes of eating particular to given nations, but they can furthermore be read as indicative of significant differences between those nations more generally.[15] That is, cookbooks and culinary writings illuminate not just the foods that make up national cuisines, but the nations themselves.

At the same time, new forms of economic production—revolutions in agriculture and food industries, as well as the growth of public eating establishments run by new kinds of entrepreneurs—also helped reify certain foods, dishes, and manners of consumption as particular to and appropriate for a given nation. Hans J. Teuteberg has noted that industrialization alone had a whole cascading series of effects on diet: factory work altered meal patterns, the diet of the middle classes became dominant in newly central towns, and new food technologies such as canning changed the ubiquity of various foods.[16] In so doing, industrialization served to create more uniform patterns of eating in particular areas, often newly defined as nations, helping to create a new sense of national uniformity. At times, too, entrepreneurs and others more explicitly sought to identify their products as "national" in order to build new markets. In modern nations, consumption societies nearly one and all, "it seems that 'national cuisines' may be most important to the people who stand to profit the most from their construction, especially politicians, food marketers, and other food professionals.... It also seems clear that the idea of national cuisine is quite modern, even though the claim may seek to root itself in assertions of tradition, custom, soul, *terroir*."[17]

This junction of print and trade creates national cuisines in ways that speak to multiple audiences. First and foremost, they help to present conceptions of national cuisines, often simultaneously with other conceptions of the nation, to the citizens of these nations. Cuisine becomes one of possibly many invented traditions that help support the nation. This inward orientation happens in both "old" and "new" nations. In parts of England with a history of distinct regional foods, the early modern period brought new printed cookbooks that helped to develop a more general sense of English cookery appropriate for people of middle status. In so doing, they supported the concept of identification with a broadly English social group rather than with a region that united people of different social standings. In the late nineteenth century, Pellegrino Artusi, the author of *Science in the Kitchen and the Art of Eating Well* (1891), wanted to describe the food of his new nation as something unified and unique—which meant something other than regional peasant food and heavily French elite food that then separately dominated. The cookbook sought to overcome regional divisions, class differences, and even a disjuncture between past and present, although in practice, the dishes of Tuscany and Emilia-Romagna predominated. In so doing, it helped to create a new unified history of Italian cooking that supported the new nation, which reinforcing unequal power relations within it, particularly between north and south.[18]

The national shift can also serve to look outward, to present nations to a wider international audience. The rise of French cuisine as an international elite standard—in fact, as the other against which Italian and English foods were at least partly defined—is certainly the most successful melding of national image and cuisine in the minds of outsiders, in large part because of its ability to present a coherent national image that had, at least initially, little to do with what most French people ate. The rise of *La Cuisinière Royale et Bourgoise* in the eighteenth century, and then of the famed master chefs such as Carême in the early nineteenth, gave French elite cuisine a new and broader market—the middle class, not just the aristocracy—and a new way to spread to them—through cookbook after cookbook, printed in France and translated and reprinted abroad.[19] Furthermore, it was not just the printed cookbook, or even gastronomic literatures more generally, that spread the notion of this unified, national French cuisine. Instead, so too did innovations in the world of trade, particularly the rise of the restaurant as a site for the transmission of cuisine to both a domestic and a foreign audience and the development of new and marketable conceptions of national authenticity based in the French land and landscape itself—the *terroir*.[20] The result was a widely understood conception of France and French culinary culture that overcame regional differences, and furthermore stood for a particular identification of France and the rise of the bourgeoisie.

These multiple audiences for conceptions of national cuisines interacted—and continue to interact—in complicated ways in postcolonial nations. As Benedict Anderson notes, the "creole pioneers" who led national revolutions in the Americas at the turn of the nineteenth century based their new nations largely on administrative units left over from colonial times, a history that complicated the process of establishing national traditions and cultures. As a result, these nations saw, in a way, multiple conceptions of their national cuisines. For much of the nineteenth century, the literate few were of European descent, and the cookbooks that addressed them spoke more to the worldwide influence of French cuisine (as well as a rejection of Spanish precedent) than to the foods of the wider populace. In the twentieth century, however, those wider populaces gained both political power, and a greater role in the development of national cuisines. They are joined by the twentieth-century wave of postcolonial nations, which have slowly sought to do much the same: either defining a new national cuisine out of multiple possible internal variations, or by separating out something uniquely national from a wider regional, or even continental, conception of cuisine.[21]

For some of these postcolonial nations, a third possible market for notions of national cuisines can play an important role: diasporic nations or immigrant populations more generally who seek to preserve the memory of an earlier identity. For many immigrant groups, print and trade entrepreneurs help them navigate the conflicting pressures to assimilate and to keep up their national cuisines in sometimes hostile situations. Immigrants find their cuisines to be markers either of their continued separateness or of the persistence of earlier identities. One way this manifests itself is in the blurry line between "national" and "ethnic" cuisines. In many cases, cuisines that might be defined as national within their home nations are transformed into "ethnic" foods when taken out of their place of origin. But the very fact that this is not universal suggests that this is simply a semantic difference. Furthermore, in some cases, the fact that a cuisine is maintained in immigration helps to create a sense of nationality where none existed before. Immigrants can find themselves defining their foods as specifically national, not simply as part of a larger regional tradition. According to Richard Wilk, exactly that sort of development occurred with immigrant communities from Belize. Although Belize had developed a distinct cuisine long before, it was only in its immigrant communities that a real discourse of that cuisine as a national one, as opposed to a variation on a regional one, developed.[22] In these cases, food allows individuals to maintain their national identity outside their national space—and perhaps the importance of this role helps to crystallize the boundaries of these national cuisines.

Perhaps because the definition of national cuisines is so dependent on multiple variables, from economic production to cultural norms to understandings of time to geographical location, those very definitions are themselves far from static. For one, the urge to build new nations is hardly dead, and separatist groups often focus on the very elements of cultural nationalism, including cuisine, to find reason for their political demands of autonomy. But even developed conceptions of national cuisines can shift over time, either by adopting new foods and norms, or by rejecting older ones. This can be tricky. One example at once highlights not only the persistence of the notion of national cuisines among immigrant communities, but also the possibilities of shifting national norms. Anne J. Kershen has noted, in regards to the foods of immigrant communities within Britain (itself a tricky created national conception), that "all too often the receiving society has a simplistic and superficial interpretation of food and identity. Irrespective of the transcultural changes which have *Anglicised* and transformed the curry, it is," she claims, "still perceived as an Indian dish."[23] Her emphasis on "Anglicized" indicates the tension within this development. Curry is at once a sign of the persistence of some national Indian identity, and also transformed into something demonstrating Englishness.

Such new interventions into national cuisines are not always accepted as truly national, and are instead often seen as signs of decay, or objects of derision. But they do transform the ways that individuals within nations eat, and in some cases those transformations are serious enough to be accepted as indicative of a new stage in national cuisines. More generally, as global foodways have intervened in domestic ones in many ways, and as technology has changed, conceptions of national cuisines have had to come to terms with the fact that even the most "authentic" of them include these interventions from the present. The past may be present in conceptions of national cuisines, but these conceptions are only successful if the past is effectively united with the present.

Variation: From Russian Cooking to Russian Cuisine

When the historian Reggie Zelnick published an interpretation of Russian history via borsch, he was clearly enjoying a chance to play games both with perceptions of Russian history and with perceptions of the stodginess of Russian food. Borsch, he claims, tongue planted firmly in cheek, created dissension within the Russian state during the Time of Troubles, became a focus of Peter the Great's Westernizing disdain (which earned him the title of anti-Borsch), and played a particular role through the imagined early Soviet New Gastronomic Policy. But as joking as his description is, his claimed starting point—"to outline, however briefly, the ways in which a broadly conceived social history of Russian soup might some day contribute to our understanding of the development of Russian politics and society"—is actually quite an apt one.[24] And, moreover, the idea that Russian soup, or at least Russian cooking more generally, was connected to understandings of Russian politics and society was well understood by Russians of the past. Indeed, starting in the late eighteenth century, when Russian elites began to question whether, given their recent Westward orientation, they truly belonged to the same society as the rest of the Russian people, the development of a written idea of Russian cooking went hand in hand with concerns over the state of the Russian nation and of the state of the Russian empire. Cuisine, in essence, became a place of contestation over what it meant to be Russian.

The history of Russian cooking as a national cuisine, rather like the history of the Russian nation itself, in many ways begins with the reforms of Peter the Great (r. 1682–1725) at the beginning of the eighteenth century. Of course later nationalists drew heavily on their imagined version of the pre-Petrine past in service of building up their notions of the authentically Russian, but they also generally understood that past as just that: the past, severed from the present by the great man and his actions. In particular, the most visible result of Peter's reforms was the creation of an elite society whose Westernized culture was increasingly removed from that of the "traditional" masses, debatably more so than in other European societies. This opposition became a central concern of many members of Russia's intelligentsia over the next centuries, as members of that elite had to struggle to find commonalities with the larger world of Russia, and to interpret their new nation (for many saw "Russia" as beginning only with Peter) as both something belonging to the present and to that forgotten past.

Toward the end of the eighteenth century, as a nationalist consciousness began to develop among some members of Russia's elite, those men began to think about Russian food, and cuisine more generally, as centrally important to conceptions of Russian culture. First, and perhaps best remembered, were those conservative nobles who discussed food in the process of negatively comparing the current habits of Russia's elite society to the more moderate and fitting habits of the Russian past. Writing in the 1780s, at the height of the reign of Catherine the Great (1762–1796), M. M. Shcherbatov saw changes in eating habits as part and parcel of the "corruption of morals" that were the focus of his ire. Russian nobles now ate food that was far too luxurious in its preparation and ingredients, and far too removed from the dishes of the past. According to Shcherbatov, those dishes had been "numerous, but all made up of simple things." Furthermore, in olden days, the consumption of food had been almost a purely domestic action, as nobles ate modestly at home, with perhaps a few close relatives as guests. But already in the time of Peter the Great, Shcherbatov complained, certain powerful nobles began to open their dining rooms to others, and in so doing, to bring in the far more complicated dishes featuring imported foods that were meant to show off their power and wealth rather than the health of their domestic economy. In the current reign, while Catherine herself was "even too moderate" in her eating habits, her favorite, Prince Potemkin, had brought the degree of luxury and immoderacy on noble tables to its apogee, even to the point of gluttony.[25] In so doing, he exemplified the way that the nobility (and its eating habits) had become unnaturally un-national.

Railing against the luxury of modern times, however, did little to develop a conception of a cuisine suitable for the modern nation, particularly given the importance of national cuisines in representing the nation both to members of the nation and to outsiders. Shcherbatov, thanks to a rather unappetizing description of pre-Petrine noble food (mostly simple preparations and virtually no spices or seasonings, for example), did not give his audience a true alternative to what he saw as the unacceptable excess of modern times, but other writers began to think of food in terms that could be better developed into a more positive recommendation. At nearly the same time Shcherbatov wrote his critique, another Russian, Ivan Boltin, wrote a similarly scathing critique—but this time, not of Russian society, but of a French traveler's view of that society. Boltin realized that the traveler, LeClerc, saw

"Russian cuisine" as part of Russia's present, not Russia's past, but also as belonging to Russia's peasants, not its elite. This presented a problem, in part because LeClerc got things wrong, and in part because looking only at Russia's peasants failed to present a cuisine worthy of standing for Russia internationally. Boltin took on the first question, and corrected numerous misunderstandings of LeClerc; that Russians ate little bread, "which is generally poorly prepared and poorly baked," for example, or that Russian peasants ate their *shchi* (cabbage soup) with oils then considered fit only to lubricate machinery. Boltin decried these claims. Russia had excellent bread, and lots of it, he wrote, and furthermore, while peasants certainly ate seed and nut oils during Lenten fasts, the quality of those oils was high. LeClerc also erred in his description of particularly Russian foods. He listed two fish dishes (one of which was not a prepared dish, but rather a type of fish) and aspic as the most characteristic of Russian foods, a claim Boltin found ridiculous. Clearly, he wrote, everyone knew that *shchi* was the most Russian of Russian foods.[26] LeClerc was again wrong—but again, Boltin had hardly given a new basis for considering Russian cuisine as a national one.

The task of creating a positive definition of Russian cuisine was left to Vasilii Levshin, one of Russia's first cookbook compilers and authors. In the mid 1790s, Levshin published a multi-volume *Cooking Dictionary*, in which he included the first written account of a modern Russian national cuisine. Russian cooking was but one of many national cuisines considered in the larger project—the title promised French, German, Dutch, Spanish, English, Austrian, Berlin, Bohemian, and Saxon cuisines, as well—and it was listed last among all the constituent elements of the larger dictionary, but its inclusion in this list of other possible national cuisines was an important step in recognizing Russian cuisine, and perhaps by extension Russian culture, as worthy of a nation. Levshin also took seriously the process of defining this Russian cuisine. In some ways he echoed writers such as Shcherbatov, describing how "simple foods, prepared from ingredients found in the fatherland," had given way on the tables of Russia's nobles to "those of foreign soils, quite complicated . . . stuffed with many spices," and lamenting the fact that there had not yet been full written instructions for Russian cooking, and that as a result "Russian dishes" had been almost completely forgotten. At the same time, however, Levshin provided his readers with a formal definition of Russian cuisine, based less on specific "traditional" foods, and more on other organizing principles. Levshin organized the section using two sources of order: the Orthodox fasting calendar, which demanded Lenten foods without animal products at all, or with fish but no milk or eggs; and a specific order of courses: a cold dish, a soup or other hot dish, a stew or roast, and a filled pastry. Some specifically Russian foods did appear in these lists, particularly soups (including the ubiquitous *shchi*) and pastries, but Levshin made it clear that the larger ideas of Orthodoxy and a particular style of meal were just as important to defining cuisine as Russian.

What was only a minor issue in the late eighteenth century became a major one in the middle of the nineteenth century, as Russianness itself became a center of state and intelligentsia concern. During the reign of Nicholas I (1825–1855), the Ministry of Education sought to spread a love for "Orthodoxy, Autocracy, and Nationality," a trinity that came to be known as "Official Nationality," among the Empire's subjects. It was easy to define Orthodoxy and autocracy, but nationality proved to be a more complicated concept, one that led to explorations of nationality and popular culture becoming common among both intellectuals seeking to support the current regime and the Slavophiles and Westernizers who debated the relative values of Russian traditions and Western influences as they strove to imagine a better future Russia. At the same time, during Nicholas' reign several years of famine or near-famine conditions brought food, both its production and consumption, into Russian public consciousness in a new way. The national character of agriculture became a political issue, as ideas of traditional agricultural practices came up against visions of a modernized, internationally prominent agricultural powerhouse in Europe. But, too, Nicholas' reign saw significant worry over bare necessity and the ability of Russia's peasants to feed themselves. One result, and by far the longest-lasting result of the concern over agriculture, was a series of state-sponsored measures to encourage increased potato production. Although these measures had limited success during these early decades of the nineteenth century, by the early twentieth century potatoes had become standard in Russian fields and on Russian tables.

Related to these agricultural concerns, and to new conceptions of the political power of nationalism, was a new interest in Russian cuisine. In general debates about the nation, some writers imbued certain foods (onions and garlic) and dishes (*shchi*, again) with particular national significance. The noted conservative nationalist publicist Faddei Bulgarin in particular devoted many articles and, in one journal, an entire regular column, to cooking, and in particular addressed the question of Russian cuisine. Even more importantly, during the 1840s a new school of Russian cookbook writing became dominant, one that was explicitly national, and explicitly aimed at Russia's variant of a middle class—the group more generally considered as among the prime consumers of nationalist ideals during the nineteenth century. In particular, K. A. Avdeeva, the sister of another important publicist, became the most popular cookbook author in the country by using an explicitly Russian tone—she labeled herself an "experienced Russian housewife," a figure who claimed authority over questions of national cuisine. In content, Avdeeva maintained Levshin's structure based in Orthodoxy and a particular order of courses, but also she expanded the array of "Russian" dishes by including "foods that have come into use among Russians." This arrangement—including focus on the middle, on women as interpreters of Russianness, and on integrating new foods into what was now defined as Russian—joined with Levshin's earlier codification to create a new standard for Russian national cuisine in an age of nationalism.

Thus, by the middle of the nineteenth century, "Russian cooking," or "Russian cuisine," had been identified and codified. That seemed to be enough for cookbook writers, who dropped explicit references to Russianness in their titles. No longer were cookbooks labeled as by or for Russians—their simple existence within Russia seemed enough. But Russian cuisine did continue to play an important role in the rampant Russophilia of the late Imperial period. During this period, official love of all things old Russian manifested itself not just in architectural styles and fancy dress balls, but also in Imperial dinners touting their national components. The menus printed to commemorate such dinners were lavishly decorated in the then-popular "Russian style," with images of ancient knights and ladies, decorations borrowing from older architectural designs, and old-fashioned lettering. In content, they also continue to show much the same "Russian cuisine" that had been defined by mid-century, as they include dishes both "national" and not, but the integration of image and food—as Muscovite iconography accompanied a listing of cabbage soup, roast fowl, asparagus and ice cream, say—emphasized the ability of Russian cuisine to incorporate these disparate elements.

With the revolutions of 1917 and the coming of a new Soviet state, one that at least in principle valued a new Soviet identity above any national one, Russian cooking as a discrete cuisine should perhaps have faded away. Instead, in part due to the relatively closed economic world of the Soviet Union, the new state found conceptions of Russian cooking as a national cuisine to be remarkably persistent. While new institutions of "social nutrition"—everything from restaurants to cafeterias to kiosks on the street—never fully replaced home cooking, they became centers of a new standardization of cuisine, controlled (at least in principle) by local culinary soviets and increasingly featuring the same array of salads, soups, and pastries described in cookbooks written for their use. Furthermore, as cookbooks of the era suggest, much of this newly standardized cuisine was in essence a particular vision of Russian national cuisine. Even broadly "Soviet" cookbooks for the home cook, such as the *Book of Tasty and Healthy Food*, which appeared in multiple editions from the late 1930s on, continued to describe certain foods and habits as particularly Russian. Just as authors from Boltin on had suggested that cabbage soup was the most essentially Russian of all foods, the authors of the Soviet work informed their readers that "Russian cuisine is distinguished by a particularly rich array of possible soups, and *shchi* [and others] make up the characteristic particularity of Russian cooking."[27] The consistency of reference to what was essentially tradition, even in a state that in principle broke with tradition, suggests the power of these national identifications even after nations themselves are transformed.

In the newly revived Russia left in the aftermath of the fall of the Soviet Union, the national cuisine has received significant new attention, again in sometimes explicitly nationalist ways. While new foods and goods have flooded Russian markets and transformed the foodways that many Russians experience, at least at a remove—sushi restaurants, for example, have become a striking part of urban landscapes in the early 2000s—Russian cuisine, even a deliberately self-conscious Russian cuisine, has persisted as an important force. Fast food franchises based around *bliny* and buckwheat porridge create a nationalist counterpart to the McDonald's on the corner, as servers use nineteenth century terms of respect in addressing customers, and menu items are named after old-time heroes. Even more explicitly nationalist are advertisements for *kvas*, a peculiarly Russian non-alcoholic beverage, which suggest that buyers say "No—to Cola-nization." Of course many Russians eat foods from well beyond the "traditionally Russian," but the persistence of these tropes highlights the both the resilience of concepts of national cuisines, and in particular their ability to adapt, to new foods, to new economies, and to new audiences.

National cuisines suffer from, as the authors of *Food and Cultural Studies* have put it, "problematic obviousness."[28] On the one hand, many people find it easy to describe what they see as their national cuisine—or, at times, other people's national cuisines. But on the other hand, few of those accounts perfectly align, and instead they are likely to contain a whole series of differences that make constructing a perfect representation different. Those differences, however, highlight the constructed, and yet powerful, nature of national cuisines. They represent the many layers of meaning incorporated into a supposedly obvious set of dishes: the interactions between economics, religion, climate, culture, and politics that give rise both to nations and to national cuisines. They also account for the ability of national cuisines to adapt, as people and goods move around the world, bringing new foods and techniques to old places (or vice versa). At the same time, the obviousness of national cuisines speaks to their power and persistence. Because they are understood as basic components of nations, they have a particular pull on national consciousness. They can be mobilized in support of the nation, to preserve identities, to fight off economic incursions, or to demonstrate the power of a nation to attract outsiders. In the end, they are much like the results of any recipe: made out of real ingredients, transformed by human care and preparation into something unique, something that, because of distinctions in taste, both divides and unites people.

NOTES

1. Terry Davis, "Preface," in *Culinary Cultures of Europe: Identity, Diversity and Dialogue*, ed. Darra Goldstein and Kathrin Merkle (Strasbourg: Council of Europe Publishing, 2005), 9.

2. Fabio Parasecoli, "Food: Identity and Diversity," in ibid, 14.

3. Michaela DeSoucey, "Gastronationalism: Food Traditions and Authenticity Politics in the European Union," *American Sociological Review* 75, no. 3 (2010): 444.

4. Benedict Anderson, *Imagined Communities: Reflections on the Origin and Spread of Nationalism*, rev. ed. (London: Verso, 1991).

5. Arjun Appadurai, "How to Make a National Cuisine: Cookbooks in Contemporary India," *Comparative Studies in Society and History* 30, no. 1 (1988): 3–24.

6. See, for example, Emiko Ohnuki-Tierney, *Rice as Self: Japanese Identities through Time* (Princeton, NJ: Princeton University Press, 1993).

7. Sidney Mintz, *Sweetness and Power: The Place of Sugar in Modern History* (New York: Viking, 1985).

8. Jeffrey M. Pilcher, *¡Que vivan los tamales! Food and the Making of Mexican Identity* (Albuquerque: University of New Mexico Press, 1998).

9. James C. McCann, *Stirring the Pot: A History of African Cuisine* (Athens: Ohio University Press, 2009).

10. D. N. Jha, *The Myth of the Holy Cow*, new ed. (London: Verso, 2004).

11. Yael Raviv, "Falafel: A National Icon," *Gastronomica* 3, no. 3 (Summer 2003): 20–25.

12. Linda Keller Brown and Kay Mussell, eds., *Ethnic and Regional Foodways in the United States: The Performance of Group Identity* (Knoxville: University of Tennessee Press, 1984).

13. Jack Goody, *Cooking, Cuisine, and Class: A Study in Comparative Sociology* (Cambridge: Cambridge University Press, 1982), 105.

14. E. J. Hobsbawm, *Nations and Nationalism since 1780: Programme, Myth, Reality* (Cambridge: Cambridge University Press, 1990); Anderson, *Imagined Communities*.

15. Stephen Mennell, *All Manners of Food: Eating and Taste in England and France from the Middle Ages to the Present*, 2nd ed. (Urbana: University of Illinois Press, 1996).

16. Hans J. Teuteberg, "The General Relationship between Diet and Industrialization," in *European Diet from Pre-Industrial to Modern Times*, ed. Elborg and Robert Forster (New York: Harper & Row, 1975), 61–110. See also Katarzyna Cwiertka, *Modern Japanese Cuisine: Food, Power, and National Identity* (London: Reaktion Books, 2006).

17. Warren Belasco, "Food Matters: Perspectives on an Emerging Field," in *Food Nations: Selling Taste in Consumer Societies*, ed. Warren Belasco and Philip Scranton (New York: Routledge, 2002), 12

18. Luigi Ballerini, "Introduction: A as in Artusi, G as in Gentleman and Gastronome," in Pellegrino Artusi, *Science in the Kitchen and the Art of Eating Well*, trans. Murtha Baca and Stephen Sartarelli (Toronto: University of Toronto Press, 2003 [1891]), xv, xix.

19. Priscilla Parkhurst Ferguson, "A Cultural Field in the Making: Gastronomy in Nineteenth-Century France," *The American Journal of Sociology* 104, no. 3 (November 1998): 597–641; idem, *Accounting for Taste: The Triumph of French Cuisine* (Chicago: University of Chicago Press, 2004); idem, "Culinary Nationalism," *Gastronomica* 10, no. 1 (2010): 102–9; François Massialot, *Le Cuisinier Royale et Bourgeois* (Paris: Charles de Sercy, 1691).

20. Rebecca L. Spang, *The Invention of the Restaurant: Paris and Modern Gastronomic Culture* (Cambridge, MA: Harvard University Press, 2000); Kolleen M. Guy, *When Champagne Became French: Wine and the Making of a National Identity* (Baltimore, MD: Johns Hopkins University Press, 2003).

21. Appadurai, "How to Make"; Igor Cusack, "African Cuisines: Recipes for Nation-Building," *Journal of African Studies* 13, no. 2 (2000): 207–25.

22. Richard Wilk, "Food and Nationalism: The Origins of 'Belizean Food'," in Belasco and Scranton, *Food Nations*, 80.

23. Anne J. Kershen, "Introduction: Food in the Migrant Experience," in *Food in the Migrant Experience*, ed. Anne J. Kershen (Aldershot: Ashgate, 2002), 7.

24. Reginald E. Zelnik, "Wie es Eigentlich Gegessen: Some Curious Thoughts on the Role of Borsch in Russian History," in *For Want of a Horse: Choice and Chance in History*, ed. John M. Merriman (Lexington: The Stephen Greene Press, 1985), 77–90.

25. Prince M. M. Shcherbatov, *On the Corruption of Morals in Russia*, trans. and ed. A. Lentin (Cambridge: Cambridge University Press, 1969), 120–22, 128, 142, 244–46 (my translations).

26. Ivan Boltin, *Primechaniia na istoriiu drevniia i nyneshniia Rossii G. Leklerka [Notes on G. LeClerc's History of Ancient and Modern Russia]*, vol. II (St. Petersburg: Gornoe Uchilishche, 1788), 370–71, 374, 408, 410–11.

27. *Kniga o vkusnoi i zdorovoi pishche [The Book of Tasty and Healthy Food]*, 8th ed. (Moscow: Legkaia i pishchevaia promyshlennost', 1982), 47, 85. See also V. V. Pokhlebkin, *Kukhnia veka [Cuisine of the Century]* (Moscow: Polifakt, 2000).

28. Bob Ashley, Joanne Hollows, Steve Jones, and Ben Taylor, *Food and Cultural Studies* (London: Routledge, 2004), 76.

Bibliography

Appadurai, Arjun. "How to Make a National Cuisine: Cookbooks in Contemporary India." *Comparative Studies in Society and History* 30, no. 1 (January 1988): 3–24.

Cusack, Igor. "African Cuisines: Recipes for Nation-building." *Journal of African Studies* 13, no. 2 (2000): 207–25.

DeSoucey, Michaela. "Gastronationalism: Food Traditions and Authenticity Politics in the European Union." *American Sociological Review* 75, no. 3 (2010): 432–55.

Ferguson, Priscilla Parkhurst. *Accounting for Taste: The Triumph of French Cuisine.* Chicago: University of Chicago Press, 2004.

Guy, Kolleen M. *When Champagne Became French: Wine and the Making of a National Identity.* Baltimore, MD: Johns Hopkins University Press, 2003.

Karaosmanoğlu, Defne. "Surviving the Global Market: Turkish Cuisine 'Under Construction'." *Food, Culture and Society* 10, no. 3 (Fall 2007): 425–48.

Ohnuki-Tierney, Emiko. *Rice as Self: Japanese Identities through Time.* Princeton, NJ: Princeton University Press, 1993.

Pilcher, Jeffrey M. *¡Que vivan los tamales! Food and the Making of Mexican Identity.* Albuquerque: University of New Mexico Press, 1998.

Pujol, Anton. "Cosmopolitan Taste: The Morphing of the New Catalan Cuisine." *Food, Culture and Society* 12, no. 4 (December 2009): 437–55.

Rogers, Ben. *Beef and Liberty.* London: Chatto & Windus, 2003.

Scholliers, Peter, and Anneke Geyzen. "Upgrading the Local: Belgian Cuisine in Global Waves." *Gastronomica* 10, no. 3 (2010): 49–54.

Smith, Alison K. *Recipes for Russia: Food and Nationhood under the Tsars.* DeKalb: Northern Illinois University Press, 2008.

CHAPTER 26

FOOD AND ETHICAL CONSUMPTION

RACHEL A. ANKENY

THE usual narrative about food consumption would lead us to believe that over the course of history, most people have made relatively simple choices about what to eat and drink, often without giving much thought to their choices or the values underlying them. Food choices have often been viewed as matters of personal preference rather than something with moral dimensions, unlike actions that have more obvious potential to harm other people such as lying, cheating, or stealing. The relative lack of explicit attention to ethical issues associated with food likely has occurred because people's decisions traditionally arose from a combination of factors such as availability, convenience, cost, habit, and more rarely, actual choice or preference, and hence in some sense their choices were largely out of their control.

A deeper historical exploration reveals that although most of the labels associated with food ethics are neologisms, many of the key issues are not new: some indigenous and traditional societies had codes about who was permitted to kill animals, when, and why (for example, only in times of extreme need and not for routine consumption). In many traditional religions including Judaism, Christianity, Islam, Buddhism, and Hinduism, there are limitations on what can be eaten or about when certain foods should be eaten and the permissibility, as well as the morality, of particular types of consumption decisions. Some scholars have blamed our neglect of historical recognition of these issues on the tendency in the Christian era to focus on gluttony, categorized in Catholicism as one of the seven cardinal sins, rather than the range of other moral issues related to food.[1]

In the modern developed world, where food is relatively plentiful and society is affluent, there is growing awareness that our choices about what foodstuffs to consume are more complex than a simple response to an empty stomach. The problem of "what to eat" has changed: we are faced not with an absence of choice about how to obtain even the basics but what often can appear to be an overwhelming range of options. We are variously encouraged to eat local, seasonal, wild, organic, fair trade, or sustainable foodstuffs; to consider whether our foods have been produced in humane or sustainable ways, or have contributed to climate change due to production of what are now known as "food miles"; to boycott companies or industries viewed as behaving in morally irresponsible ways; or more generally, to buy and eat responsibly. So-called "ethicureans," for example, promote eating well while also seeking foods that are sustainable, organic, local, and/or ethical (now known as SOLE foods).[2] Representatives of some religious denominations have argued that ethical decision-making needs to be extended to food choices. In 2005, the Archbishop of Canterbury (the leader of the Church of England) recommended sustainable food consumption and waste reduction, as well as eco-friendly and fair trade product choices, and even organic bread and wine for communion.[3]

Despite these exhortations, trying to make ethical food decisions is a complex matter and can result in contradictory outcomes: fair trade and organic products often travel long distances to market, for instance. It is unclear whether local products have positive effects on the environment, or how the effects of such purchases can be assessed. Even defining "ethical consumerism" is a vexed issue: it is clear that the turn toward ethical consumption cannot be described in terms of a set of shared values, beliefs, or politics on the part of its practitioners. Some argue that ethical consumerism should be generally distinguished from political consumerism (e.g., forms of activism, consumer organizations with particular political aims, and so on),[4] and from responsible or conscientious consumption, which are claimed to have features that are distinctively contemporary and which engage with broader critiques of the excesses of modern life.[5]

Ethical consumerism is probably best understood as a catch-all phrase that covers a range of tendencies, rather than a coherent set of practices.[6] Ethical consumption, in turn, can be viewed as "a political phenomenon in which everyday consumption practices are reconstituted as the sites for citizenly acts that reach beyond the realm of consumption *per se*."[7] Consumption can be a space in which citizen-consumers pursue their conceptualizations of the good life, for instance in making choices that reflect their concerns for fair trade, environmental issues, and so on.[8] Ethical consumerism is a subset of the wider alternative consumption movements that flourished in the second half of the twentieth century, which some claim emerged as a reaction to the Reagan and Thatcher eras.[9]

For purposes of this chapter, "ethical food consumerism" is taken to describe a set of diverse and often conflicting food choices that are voluntary and outwardly directed as a result of the actor's beliefs about his or her values, responsibilities, and so on. A decision not to eat meat products or foodstuffs containing genetically modified organisms solely for health reasons would not be considered as part of this category, nor would the purchase of fair trade cocoa because it tastes better than alternatives but without regard to the fact that it is produced under fair conditions for workers.

Studying ethical food consumption requires not only examining what people buy and consume but why they make particular types of food choices, as developing an account of people's motivations is essential to understanding this category of consumption. Consequently, scholarship on ethical food consumerism utilizes diverse methods, including those of the social sciences, environmental studies, marketing and business, and philosophy. Discussions about these issues often occur outside of the context of food studies narrowly construed (so for instance in explorations of consumerism, corporate governance, or globalization). It relies on a range of types of source materials, many of which are ephemeral and popular in nature such as menus and advertising, as well as governmental policies, dietary surveys, and more traditional scholarly source materials, which often are limited in terms of content relating to people's motivations. Hence any scholar attempting to trace the history of ethical food consumption faces considerable methodological challenges.

This chapter aims to outline the major topics associated with contemporary food ethics arising from these various disciplinary perspectives, seeks to articulate underlying themes and continuities within recent popular and scholarly discussions of ethical food consumerism, as well as analyzing the very notion of "ethical food consumption." It proposes that the main difference between contemporary and historic discussions of food ethics can be found in the strengthening connection between identity and ethical food choices, which in turn has reshaped our understandings of ethical food choices.

Vegetarianism and Veganism

As a food choice, there perhaps is no category with more varied motivations underlying it than vegetarianism. Empirical studies of contemporary forms of vegetarianism have found that animal welfare concerns are commonly reported by its adherents, along with personal concerns for health.[10] Ethical vegetarians typically avoid consumption of meat in order to minimize harm to animals, and often make sudden changes in their food choices to support their beliefs in animal welfare in order to bring their actions in alignment with their moral beliefs.[11] In contrast, health vegetarians typically avoid meat in order to lose weight, or to pursue various benefits to their personal well-being that they associate with vegetarianism. Health vegetarians often make more gradual conversions to vegetarianism than ethical vegetarians.[12]

The term "vegetarian" appears to date to the late 1830s (and hence the notion of identifying oneself explicitly through this dietary choice is a recent one), but the idea of a vegetarian diet was present in ancient times. Those who partook of such a diet were sometimes formerly called Pythagoreans, after the early Greek philosopher who argued against consumption of animal flesh.[13] Vegetarianism also has a long history within certain religious traditions such as Hinduism and Buddhism.[14] In Hinduism, for instance, avoiding all meat, but beef in particular, is related both to religious beliefs such as the transmigration of the soul but also arguably ethical ideas about the sacred nature of the cow. Buddhism generally bans intentional killing, including of animals for consumption, and ties this prohibition to the moral precept of compassion and non-harm of others. However, its core texts do not explicitly address the consumption of flesh from animals that are already dead, so many modern-day Buddhists are not strict vegetarians.

A growing subcategory of ethical vegetarians is composed of those who reduce or avoid meat consumption due to concerns about the potential negative environmental impacts of meat consumption and production.[15] Yet another subcategory of ethical vegetarians (which perhaps could be termed feminist ethical vegetarians) includes people concerned not only with animal welfare but with the systems of patriarchy promoted by the production of meat for food and its consumption.[16] A higher percentage of vegetarians are women, although this is usually attributed to a mix of factors, including greater concern on average for health and diet rather than a set of shared moral beliefs. However, feminist critics such as Kathryn Paxson George have noted that calls for universal ethical vegetarianism rely on assumption of the male as the norm for human beings, and hence results in ageism, sexism, and classism.[17]

Veganism in its current forms is a more recent movement, dating formally only to the mid-1900s, though adhering to a "bloodless diet" has a much longer history.[18] It took its name from the first and last letters of "vegetarian": as its originator Donald Watson indicated, "veganism starts with vegetarianism and carries it through to its logical conclusion."[19] Advocates of veganism view it as a natural extension of moral vegetarianism, inasmuch as their refusal to consume all animal products (including eggs and dairy products such as cheese, butter, and milk) is taken as a stand against all forms of animal exploitation. Although veganism was initially thought to be extreme even by many within the vegetarian movement, nowadays veganism is often viewed as an ideal to which many vegetarians aspire.[20]

There are a variety of lines of criticism about vegetarianism and veganism in particular, ranging from concerns about whether it is a healthy choice to questions about whether it is evolutionarily appropriate to avoid all animal products. There is a long intellectual history from Aristotle onward supporting the natural hierarchy of men over animals (and women), and the inferior nature of these other beings.[21] More recently some scholars such as Roger Scruton have argued that advocating vegetarianism has become a new form of extremist religion among some adherents, and so instead we should attempt to reduce our meat consumption and to consume conscientiously.[22] Hence as Leon Kass and others claim, we must become more aware of the spiritual and moral values associated with food, rather than just seeing food as fuel, and hence it is most effective and meaningful to focus on the quality of our eating habits (including how they can foster relationships and communities) rather than on the elimination of one type of foodstuff.[23]

Animal Welfare

Increasing numbers of people avoid certain types of products, or seek out others, because of their desire not to contribute to cruelty or abuse of animals.[24] The classic example of this type of ethical consumption decision is the rejection of eating veal due to the conditions under which these cows are raised, described as inhumane because of early separation of calves from their mothers, deliberate inhibition of growth through an unnatural diet and other means, and severe limits on the space in which the calves are raised in order to limit muscle development and produce a more tender product. These conditions often result in animals which are much more susceptible to high levels of stress and disease.[25] Graphic documentation about these rearing conditions and their effects became widely available in the United States, the United Kingdom, and elsewhere in Europe in the 1980s, and veal sales have declined significantly in many Western countries since that time.[26] The American Veal Association has plans to phase out the use of crates for raising veal by 2017, and demand for free-raised veal is rapidly increasing.

A more recent controversy surrounds foie gras, a food product made from the liver of a duck or goose that has been specially fattened, typically through force feeding of corn in a process known as gavage. A number of countries (including Israel, Italy, and the United Kingdom) and the state of California directly or indirectly ban the force feeding of animals for non-medical purposes. The production of foie gras is prohibited by treaty by the Council of Europe's European Convention for the Protection of Animals kept for Farming Purposes "except where it is current practice."[27]

Animal welfare concerns also often underlie a number of positive consumption decisions, and have fostered the recent proliferation of a range of new product categories, certification schemes, and labels, such as free-range, cage-free, or humane eggs, poultry, and meat products. Critics note that the legal regulations defining these categories are different or non-existent depending on the jurisdiction, and the labels used are oftentimes highly misleading.[28] A variety of labels have been developed to attempt to accurately describe the conditions under which chickens live, such as "barn-roaming" (chickens which do not range freely but live in barns rather than restrictive cages), as well as improved methods for measuring welfare.[29] These categories often are misinterpreted by consumers, who might interpret them as indicating that the animals only feed on grass and other natural products, which is not necessarily the case even if they are "free-range." Other major ethical consumption categories include dolphin-safe tuna and other types of fish, and grass-fed beef, which bring with them similar definitional problems in some locales, along with conflicting interpretations by consumers.

Local Consumption

Reconnecting consumers to the origins of their foodstuffs through personal contact at farmers' markets, labeling which provides detailed information about production methods and locales, and standards for recording and communicating provenance through official or more informal labels has been claimed to be a leitmotiv of ethical consumption.[30] A range of settings that promote local consumption have grown in popularity in recent years, including farmers' markets, farm door sales, community-supported agriculture, and community gardens, accompanied by increasing use of the label "locavore."[31] Often local consumption is promoted in conjunction with seasonal foods and a return to self-sufficiency through kitchen gardens and similar small-scale modes of production for personal use, as in the novelist Barbara Kingsolver's recent tome (coauthored with her daughter and husband) about their attempts to grow most of their food and eat seasonally.[32]

The general concept of buying local has an extremely long history: it is arguable that most food that was purchased or even bartered in traditional societies was locally-produced, except exotic or luxury goods such as spices. Explicit promotion of local products repeatedly has occurred in a number of places as an expression of nationalism.[33] For instance, in India, the pre-Gandhi Swadeshi ("self-sufficiency") movement in the early 1900s urged people to buy Indian products and boycott British ones, including foodstuffs, in order to combat British imperialism.[34] Contemporary promotion of local eating is not typically based in nationalism, but tends to be focused on a smaller conception of the "local," including focus on a defined radius as seen in promotion of the "100-mile diet."[35]

The Slow Food movement, which began in Italy in 1986 through its predecessor organization Arcigola's resistance to the opening of a McDonald's outlet in Rome, has a particular emphasis on the local.[36] This movement has since expanded to more than 130 countries. Adherents seek to preserve traditional and regional cuisine and food-related practices, as well as to encourage sustainable agriculture characteristic of local ecosystems through seed banks and the "Ark of Taste," an international catalogue of heritage foods and local food traditions which have been identified as in danger of extinction. As part of the broader Slow movement, Slow Food retains an overarching agenda in opposition to globalization.[37] Critics rightly note that the formal Slow Food movement is rather amorphous and non-unified, and can be viewed as promoting an elitist view of the "right way" to eat, particularly given its focus on cultural and other forms of "authenticity," specialized culinary traditions, and gastronomic pleasure.[38]

Several overlapping ethical rationales underlie most local eating philosophies: first, buying local keeps your money in your local community, and hence strengthens those communities economically and otherwise. Buying local, for instance at farm doors or farmers' markets, can allow the building of relationships based on understanding and trust, which further contribute to the strength of the community. Consumption of local foods supports small, family farms, many of which have become endangered by the growth of multinational corporations, rising costs of agriculture, and so on. A final ethical rationale for buying local is that it can help protect the environment by reducing food miles, packaging, and waste.

The validity of these rationales needs to be carefully assessed within the particular context of particular consumption decisions, and with regard to a range of other factors. For instance buying local produce outside of the usual growing season can contribute to more carbon dioxide emissions (as hothouse production can be very inefficient) than buying imported goods grown in warmer climates.[39] Scholars such as Gwendolyn Blue note that the turn toward local eating is embedded in neoliberal forms of governance and helps to reinforce these problematic institutions.[40] In addition, focusing narrowly on the local can result, as Claire C. Hinrichs puts it, in "a conflation of spatial relations for social ones,"[41] and create romanticized and elitist illusions of human connectedness rather than real, sustainable communities. Finally, being a "locavore" has become a sort of identity claim for those seeking to be ethical food consumers.

Organic Foods

Organic foods are generally defined as those grown without the use of "artificial" or non-organic components such as pesticides and fertilizers, and processed without using irradiation, solvents, or food additives. Regulations about precisely what can be labeled as "organic" differ from place to place, including the percentage of the overall product which must be organically-produced for it to be labeled as such. Some regulations specifically make reference to environmental conditions, such as the 1990 U.S. Organic Foods Production Act and related regulations which explicitly discuss the integration of cultural, biological, and mechanical practices to foster cycling of resources, promote ecological balance, and conserve biodiversity. In most countries, organic produce may not be genetically modified, and in many locations antibiotics and growth hormone cannot be used for livestock to be considered organic. Costs for organic products are usually considerably higher than their conventional counterparts.

As with vegetarianism, those who pursue organic diets typically have differing motivations, some of which are connected to health or others to the perception of organic foods as safer, fresher, or of higher quality, while still others buy organics primarily for what they view as environmental reasons. The obvious rationale for the latter group is that less fertilizer and pesticide use is likely to result in less environmental damage and also less health risks for farm workers. Organic growers need to sustain diverse ecosystems in order to maintain their crops, and thus use natural means for pest control (such as animals or insects), which in turn also has positive environmental effects. Finally, organic farms use less energy and produce less waste (for instance, packaging associated with synthetic ingredients used in conventional farming). In some cases supporting organic production also allows support for local agriculture as, until recently, organic products were largely available only at farm doors or through farmers' markets.

As with most of the previous categories of ethical foods, the "organic" label also has considerable meaning for the shaping of oneself as a particular sort of consumer. However, critics of organics point out that the current systems of labeling and certification are flawed, and that we now have an overreliance on regulation and inspection, especially given the rapid increase in demand for organic foods, which has resulted in high volume sales through mass outlets and the corporatization of the organic sector. This shift of organics from small scale to big business means that some of the values previously associated with support for organics, such as the fostering of smaller farmers, are no longer valid associations. Some commentators have noted that certain organic products, such as packaged salad mix or mesclun, ironically have now become the ultimate industrialized food product, or "yuppie chow."[42]

Food Products Free of Genetically Modified Organisms

Genetically modified organisms (GMOs) have had their genes altered by laboratory techniques that remove a gene or change its function, or insert a gene from another organism, in order to create desirable attributes. There are a number of GMO plants available on the commercial market, notably soy, canola, and corn. The United States is by far the largest producer of GM food. Genetically modified animals for commercial use and consumption have been slower to be developed for scientific, technical, and commercial reasons.

Foodstuffs that are genetically modified have become of increasing concern to consumers in certain places; in Europe, for instance, there is considerable opposition to GMOs not only because of worries about their potential effects on human health, but also for ethical reasons.[43] Some are aligned with philosophical or religious objections that genetic modification is like "playing God" and should not be supported because it represents an extreme form of human interference with nature.[44] These critics are particularly concerned about genes transferred from one species into another in a manner which goes far beyond what might ever occur naturally. However, even some opponents of GMOs note that this argument is rather limited and Luddite, as it would seem to rule out human interventions in nature more generally and the domestication of plants and animals in particular. The second main ethical argument against genetic modification claims that GM crops and other released GMOs pose unacceptable and unknowable risks of irreversible environmental damage. The most serious concern is that genetically modified plants will cross with non-genetically modified relatives, and could result in an environmental disaster that could not be controlled if the plants were to become invasive.[45]

Some advocates claim that GMOs could result in more sustainable food crops, such as drought-tolerant or saline-tolerant wheat, which could thrive in extreme environments such as Australia. Others have argued that used judiciously and with appropriate cautions, GMOs could represent an important solution to the global food problem. Genetic modification could be used to produce staples that are more nourishing and have higher levels of particular vitamins, which could assist with widespread nutritional deficiencies. "Golden rice" is a prime example of such a GMO; it is engineered to contain beta-carotene, which is a precursor to vitamin A, a deficiency of which is a major cause of blindness in young children in the developing world.[46] Development of strains that are naturally resistant to pests or weeds, for instance, could reduce the use of synthetic pesticides and herbicides, and hence be more ecologically sound than conventional cropping and better for human health of workers and those living in agricultural settings. However, these arguments have somewhat limited impact; given that many of the major manufacturers of GMOs have been multinational corporations driven by profit motives, most GM crops have not been created with the developing world as their target market. Increased research on GMOs may have even led to declines in food aid, as a technological fix is viewed as being within reach.[47]

In addition to broader issues about food policy and GMOs, debates over labeling remain in a number of places, notably the United States.[48] Although the European Union, Australia, New Zealand, and a number of Asian countries have mandatory labeling requirements for knowingly including genetically modified ingredients, the United States does not. The ubiquitous presence of corn, soy, and canola in foodstuffs produced in the United States means that a majority of American processed foods contain GMOs, unless consumers buy organically produced products.

Food Miles and Green Products

The term "food miles" originated in the 1990s, and generally is used to refer to the distance that food is transported from the time of its production until it reaches the consumer. Many people argue that there has been a marked increase in the amount of food miles traveled in recent years due to rapidly increasing global trade, changes in food supply chain patterns (such as consolidation of packaging and supply depots especially in larger supermarket chains), and the increase of processed and packaged foods which often are not produced locally. Food miles are often used as a measure of environmental impact, particularly carbon footprint and contribution to global warming. Major supermarket chains such as Tesco in the United Kingdom have attempted to use stickers on products to indicate food miles traveled or carbon footprint equivalencies, but these schemes have had difficulties due to lack of standardized measurement systems and difficulties in breaking down the components of processed foods.[49]

Criticisms of the concept of food miles are numerous: first, there are many other stages in the food supply chain that also contribute to greenhouse gas emissions, notably the energy used during production of industrial agriculture, including pesticides, fertilizers, and high-carbon processing equipment. For instance, food produced in more temperate or energy-efficient settings and then transported may use less energy on average than food produced in hothouses or livestock raised on feed rather than at pasture.[50] Others argue that the best way to reduce carbon footprint is to eat a vegetarian diet. In short, food miles might be one part of a larger puzzle about appropriate ethical actions for consumers seeking to improve the environment and its sustainability.

Food miles are a subcategory of "green" products more generally, which are associated with buying decisions intended to have a positive impact (or at least to reduce negative impacts) on the environment. Many skeptics note that the "green" category is not well-defined legally and few regulations exist for labeling (as compared for example to organic labeling); hence there is an increasing amount of "greenwashing" products, claims made with little evidence of their environmental impact.[51] As the number of people who identify themselves as "green consumers" continues to grow, some scholars have argued that a shift is needed to viewing green consumers as "green citizens," hence reinforcing a more holistic and broader approach to these issues.[52]

Boycotts and Cause-Related Marketing

Boycotts have been a common way of using consumption decisions to express moral views, or perhaps more skeptically, to use purchasing power to attempt to sway companies or other institutions away from unethical practices. Even some forms of "economic" boycotts might be understood as ethical, because although their main focus is rising prices, they typically target staple foods such as meat, sugar, and milk, and have often been promoted by volunteers, typically housewives, on behalf of others.[53]

An early food boycott campaign occurred in Britain in the late 1700s and early 1800s following the failure to pass the Abolition of the Slave Trade Bill in 1791. Hundreds of thousands of people refused to buy sugar produced by slaves on Caribbean plantations. Some advocated purchasing sugar from East India instead; sugar bowls became available with mottos such as "East India sugar not made by slaves."[54] These campaigns had qualities that often have been seen in subsequent food boycott efforts. First, there was a rhetorical connection made between consumption and moral behavior, focusing on routine consumption decisions as evidence of values and beliefs. Second, women often took a leadership role, as abstention from purchasing and consumption was one way they could assert their moral beliefs, particularly when they were not able to vote.

Among the most visible boycotts of the second half of the twentieth century were two food-related campaigns: the boycotts of grapes in the United States (1960s–1980s) and the targeting of Nestle (1974–1984). The boycotting of grapes began in the mid-1960s when Filipino-American farm workers initiated a strike to protest low wages. Union activist César Chávez of the National Farm Workers' Association (later the United Farm Workers) broadened the strike and encouraged all Americans to boycott table grapes to show support for the workers. The strike lasted five years and brought national attention to working conditions for migrant laborers. In the 1980s, Chávez led a boycott to protest the use of toxic pesticides on grapes, which some believe led to negotiation of new and more favorable contracts for workers, though others question whether the boycott had any lasting impact. Probably the first case of global brand-based activism arose in response to the marketing of infant formula in Africa and Asia despite medical research associating formula use with higher infant morality as compared to breast milk. Although other companies sold formula in these markets, Nestle was a ripe target given its visibility and association with "family values."[55]

Other modern boycotts have focused on rejecting products produced in particular places as a form of political protest, such as the boycotts on South African apples during the Apartheid era or Chilean grapes under the dictatorship of Augusto Pinochet. More recently there has been global attention to palm oil and its connection to environmental damage generated by deforestation, particularly the destruction of habitat for endangered orangutans. Foods made with palm oil, including Cadbury and Nestle chocolate and even Girl Scout cookies, have become targets. Critics of this campaign, including those within the palm oil industry, have noted that palm oil and can be grown using sustainable and high-yield methods and may serve as an important food supplement due to its high Vitamin A content.[56]

The converse of boycotts might be products associated with cause-related marketing, which has grown considerably in popularity since the 1970s. Such campaigns encourage purchase of particular products from which a percentage of the profits goes to a charity. The term "cause-related marketing" generally refers to cooperative efforts of a business with a non-profit organization to promote social or charitable purposes. Some recent cause-related marketing campaigns include pink ribbon campaigns on bottled water and yoghurt in support of breast cancer research, and contributions from water cooler providers to supply clean drinking water to Africa.[57] Another example is the KereKere cafe at the University of Melbourne, Australia, which not only serves a wide range of coffees (organic, Fair Trade, Rainforest-Alliance branded, and sustainable) but also allows each customer to decide how the profits should be distributed. The cafe claims to be fostering "a culture that promotes community wellbeing."[58]

Businesses benefit from increased sales and positive public relations, while non-profit organizations not only raise money but also increase the awareness of their causes. For the consumer, purchasing cause-related products is a fairly simple and inexpensive way to support an ethical cause, usually through a product they were planning to purchase anyway. Criticisms of such schemes note that the percentage of profits redirected to the charities is typically miniscule, and such partnerships allows for-profit companies to look good without making significant social contributions.

Fair Trade

Consumers are becoming increasingly conscious about the human consequences of the ways products they purchase are produced, and the possible injustices promoted by their consumption choices. Exposés including the book *Bitter Chocolate: The Dark Side of the World's Most Seductive Sweet* (2006) and the film *Black Gold* (2006) about the international coffee trade and Ethiopian growers have brought unjust working conditions to popular attention.[59] The "fair trade" movement takes a market-based approach (through providing economic incentives) aiming to help producers in developing countries to achieve better working conditions, sustainable production, and higher profits. Food products including cocoa, chocolate, sugar, coffee, tea, wine, various fruits, and herbs and spices have received formal certification from various labeling schemes implemented since the 1980s.[60]

The history of the fair trade concept goes back at least as far as the mid-1900s, when religious groups and non-governmental organizations promoted handicrafts and other goods from developing countries. The movement became more radical and politicized in the 1960s, when it aimed to empower people in the developing world in a sustainable manner rather than simply through aid. From a small start, this movement has grown rapidly through the adoption of fair trade standards and products by mainstream outlets and large corporations.[61] Larger companies that promote fair trade products include the U.K. supermarket chain the Co-Op (which uses fair trade coffee and chocolate for their home brands) and Cadbury in Australia and New Zealand (whose milk chocolate products have recently become Fairtrade certified).

The ethical imperatives underlying fair trade are fairly clear: it claims that international trade treats producers in developing countries unfairly. Hence buying fair trade products fosters more just conditions for workers and improves everyday life in impoverished areas. Fair trade also is seen as an attempt to address market failures by assuring stable commodity prices, business support, market access, and better trading conditions.

Fair trade has been subject to a range of criticisms: those on the political right see fair trade as marketing ploy that can impede economic growth and glut markets in developing countries, while some on the left see fair trade as overly dependent on a market model and hence not sufficiently revolutionary to achieve its underlying philosophical and economic objectives. Other criticisms parallel those leveled at local food initiatives, pointing to the paradoxes inherent in these attempts to re-connect producers and consumers through the creation of a transnational moral economy.[62]

Waste, Overconsumption, and Freeganism

Though primarily about health and the negative effects of fast food, the now-classic film *Super Size Me* (2004) also helped to raise awareness of globalization and waste.

Most industrial societies waste large amounts of food due to overpurchasing and neglect.[63] Together with the failure to compost or recycle, such habits make a significant contribution to our carbon footprint. However, reducing waste has proven to be extremely difficult to address because of ingrained habits of purchasing and the psychology of consumption. The recognition of increasing waste and its impacts has led to a variety of ethical strategies to attempt to mitigate these effects.

"Downshifting" or "simple living" are general terms used to refer to lifestyles pursued by individuals who wish to have simpler lives and escape from the pernicious influences of modernity and materialism.[64] Such behaviors may not be ethically based inasmuch as they often are primarily motivated by personal desire and not by outwardly focused values. In some cases, however, such lifestyle decisions consciously aim to improve society and the environment. At an extreme, freeganism is a form of simple living derived from "free" and "vegan." Freegans extend the vegan commitment to avoid harming animals or the environment, as well by avoiding purchasing and relying instead on foraging, bartering, and similar non-consumer strategies. "Punk cuisine," an extreme form of freeganism, adds stolen and rotten foods to scavenged products as a means of challenging conventional hierarchies and protesting capitalist environmental destruction.[65]

In all of these types of food philosophies, reduction of waste and pollution is a key goal, particularly given the injustices present between the developed and developing world, as well as the "haves" and "have nots" of the Global North. Freegans are most well-recognized for their strategies for obtaining food through "urban foraging," also known as "dumpster diving" or "skip dipping," rummaging through trash bins for useful goods that are safe and clean. They also promote foraging of wild goods and community gardens to re-connect with the environment and to foster a deeper sense of community.[66] Although the word "freeganism" is new, scavenging has long been a part of urban life. What perhaps is new is the alignment with voluntary political action, environmentalism, and the rejection of materialism, as well as the assertion of identity claims in relation to this type of activity.[67]

Beyond Ethical Food Consumers

Consumerism continues to flourish in the late twentieth century, and skeptics view "ethical consumerism" as simply one form of consumerism without any particularly deep grounding in moral values. According to them, ethical consumers are archetypal consumers making choices based on formal branding such as Fairtrade or organic, or more informal brands such as green, and who are (mistakenly) attempting to construct an interconnected social world through these brands, in part through staking identity claims in relation to these brands. At one extreme, accumulation of property and its consumption (even under the guise of "ethical" consumption) should be viewed as a deeply flawed means of seeking happiness, and we should pursue alternative, less economically driven models of the good life.[68] Ethical consumption has bourgeois connotations, with food choices becoming the newest high-fashion handbag or trendy ingredient, a mere signifier of social status and identity, reinforcing a "brand culture" with all of the associated social problems.[69]

Other critics note that ethical consumption is being promoted as part of a neoliberal agenda in order to transfer responsibilities to individuals as consumers and away from collective action and acknowledgment of governmental responsibility for meeting social needs, especially for fundamentals such as food and water.[70] Doing so may inadvertently promote "food anxieties," particularly because of the lack of clear and regulated labeling, which makes it difficult for consumers to act in an ethical manner. Focusing on individuals as the locus for action allows us to ignore structural inequalities and consumption practices in the modern food system.[71] Allowing consumerism to dominate the discussion may direct attention away from social justice and class inequalities, particularly among workers.[72]

Although historically "marginal" groups such as women and workers were involved in boycotts and movements that we now would recognize as forms of ethical food consumerism, many means of ethical consumption are not open to everyone.[73] As a form of political engagement, it primarily empowers those with the financial or social capital to buy supposedly "ethical" products (freeganism is perhaps an exception, though some would argue that the time to pursue this lifestyle on a voluntary basis is a luxury of the relatively affluent). This situation is arguably exacerbated by the high cost of organic or fair trade products compared to conventional goods. In turn the practices associated with pursuit of these ethical food choices (such as patronizing farmers' markets or stores specializing in green or organic goods) can be seen as contributing to class and geographic divisions, gentrification, and exclusion of minorities and the poor, rather than promoting social unification.[74]

Many people attempting to make ethical food choices rely on labeling, despite the well-recognized limitations of such systems. More generally, focusing on knowledge (e.g., about what is contained in a product or how it was produced) reinforces the dominant consumer culture.[75] In turn the focus on products as equivalent to their contents and their labels reinforces the equation of identity with particular types of consumption decisions (for instance "green" or "local"), rather than promoting the underlying values associated with these goods (such as environmental sustainability or reduction of carbon emissions).

A final line of critique points out that many forms of ethical consumption are produced by multinational corporations for profit, not "ethical" reasons, despite the common rhetoric of "corporate social responsibility." Hence participation in such profit-based endeavors undermines the radical transformations proponents of ethical consumerism envision.[76] Even John Mackey, the CEO of Whole Foods Market, a major U.S. supermarket chain that prides itself on stocking ethical food products, noted that its adoption of a policy in the mid-2000s not to stock eggs from caged hens was a result of "customer demand" rather than ethical motivations.[77]

Co-opting "alternative" discourses about food ethics has become common among mainstream retailers.[78]

In sum, even if it is clear that ethical food consumption can be quite problematic, and perhaps clouds the real goals associated with food ethics (such as assuring food security, including equal access to nourishing, culturally appropriate, sustainable, secure, and safe food), attention to ethical food consumption does allow us to examine the various issues associated with our dominant production and consumption methods.[79] It can allow us to question our choices and to cultivate more popular awareness of alternatives. Perhaps on a deeper level, increasing attention to food ethics forces us to examine our moral relationships with others.[80] It also can allow us to better understand (and potentially transform) our own identities and roles in what is a complex modern world. Being a critical food consumer is an important step in engaging as members of the global community and seeking to improve conditions for all, particularly with regard to basics such as food and water.

NOTES

1. For example, Hub Zwart, "A Short History of Food Ethics," *Journal of Agricultural and Environmental Ethics* 12, no. 2 (2000): 113–26; Peter Singer and Jim Mason, *The Ethics of What We Eat* (Melbourne: Text Publishing, 2006), 3.

2. "The Ethicurian." [Online]. Available: http://www.ethicurean.com/about/philosoph/. [March 30, 2011].

3. Robert Verkaik, "Archbishop Tells Church to Help Save the Planet with Green Policies," *The Independent*, February 3, 2005.

4. On political movements related to food, see Warren Belasco, "Food and Social Movements," in *Oxford Handbook of Food History*, ed. Jeffrey M. Pilcher (New York: Oxford University Press, 2012), 481–98.

5. Tania Lewis and Emily Potter, "Introducing Ethical Consumption," in *Ethical Consumption: A Critical Introduction*, ed. Tania Lewis and Emily Potter (Oxford: Routledge, 2010), 3–23.

6. Jo Littler, "What's Wrong with Ethical Consumption?" in ibid, 27–39.

7. Nick Clarke, et al, "Globalising the Consumer: Doing Politics in an Ethical Register," *Political Geography* 26, no. 3 (2007): 231–49.

8. Kate Soper, "Rethinking the 'Good Life': The Consumer as Citizen," *Capitalism, Nature, Socialism* 15, no. 3 (2004): 111–17.

9. Kate Soper, Martin Ryle, and Lyn Thomas, eds. *The Politics and Pleasures of Consuming Differently: Better Than Shopping* (London: Palgrave Macmillan, 2009); Tim Lang and Yiannis Gabriel, *The Unmanageable Consumer: Contemporary Consumption and Its Fragmentations* (London: Sage, 1995); Yiannis Gabriel and Tim Lang, "A Brief History of Consumer Activism," in *The Ethical Consumer*, ed. Rob Harrison, Terry Newholm and Deirdre Shaw (London: Sage, 2005).

10. Alan Beardsworth and Teresa Keil, "Health-Related Beliefs and Dietary Practices among Vegetarians and Vegans: A Qualitative Study," *Health Education Journal* 50, no. 1 (1991): 38–42; idem, "Vegetarianism, Veganism and Meat Avoidance: Recent Trends and Findings," *British Food Journal* 93, no. 4 (1991): 19–24; idem, "The Vegetarian Option: Varieties, Conversions, Motives and Careers," *The Sociological Review* 40,

no. 2 (1992): 253–93; Jennifer Jabs, Carol M. Devine, and Jeffery Sobal, "Model of the Process of Becoming a Vegetarian: Health Vegetarians and Ethical Vegetarians," *Journal of Nutrition Education* 30, no. 4 (1998): 196–202; Emma Lea and Anthony Worsley, "Influences on Meat Consumption in Australia," *Appetite* 36, no. 2 (2001): 127–136; Annet C. Hoek, et al., "Food-Related Lifestyle and Health Attitudes of Dutch Vegetarians, Non-Vegetarian Consumers of Meat Substitutes, and Meat Consumers," *Appetite* 42, no. 3 (2004): 265–75; Nick Fox and Katie Ward, "You Are What You Eat? Vegetarianism, Health and Identity," *Appetite* 50, no. 2–3 (2008): 2585–95.

11. M.B. Hamilton, "Wholefoods and Healthfoods: Beliefs and Attitudes," *Appetite* 20, no. 3 (1993): 223–8; Jabs, Devine, and Sobal, "Model of Becoming a Vegetarian," 196–202.

12. Paul Rozin, Maureen Markwith, and Caryn Stoess, "Moralization and Becoming a Vegetarian: The Transformation of Preferences into Values and the Recruitment of Disgust," *Psychological Science* 8, no. 2 (1997): 67–73; Marjaana Lindeman and Minna Sirelius, "Food Choice Ideologies: The Modern Manifestations of Normative and Humanist Views of the World," *Appetite* 37, no. 3 (2001): 175–84.

13. Kerry S. Walters and Lisa Portmess, eds., *Ethical Vegetarianism: From Pythagoras to Peter Singer* (Albany: State University of New York Press, 1999); Rod Preece, *Sins of the Flesh: A History of Ethical Vegetarian Thought* (Vancouver: UBC Press, 2008), 13.

14. Colin Spencer, *The Heretic's Feast: A History of Vegetarianism* (London: Fourth Estate, 1993).

15. Greta Gaard, "Vegetarian Eco-Feminism: A Review Essay," *Frontiers* 23, no. 3 (2002): 117–46; Hoek, et al., "Food-Related Lifestyle"; Lindeman and Sirelius, "Food Choice Ideologies," 265–75.

16. Carol Adams. *The Sexual Politics of Meat: A Feminist-Vegetarian Critical Theory* (London: Continuum, 1990).

17. Kathryn Paxton George, *Animal, Vegetable or Woman? A Feminist Critique of Ethical Vegetarianism* (Albany: State University of New York Press, 2000).

18. James Gregory, *Of Victorians and Vegetarians: The Vegetarian Movement in Nineteenth-Century Britain* (London: Tauris Academic Studies, 2007), 11; Spencer, *Sins of the Flesh.*

19. Preece, *The Heretic's Feast*, 298.

20. Spencer, *Sins of the Flesh*, 294.

21. Walters and Portmess, *Ethical Vegetarianism*, 254ff.

22. Roger Scruton, "The Conscientious Carnivore," in *Food for Thought: The Debate over Eating Meat*, ed. Steve F. Sapontzis (Amherst, NY: Prometheus, 2004), 81–91.

23. Leon R. Kass, *The Hungry Soul: Eating and the Perfecting of Our Nature* (Chicago: University of Chicago Press, 1999).

24. Andrew Fiala, "Animal Welfare," in *Society, Culture, and Ethics*, vol. 2 of *Critical Food Issues: Problems and State-of-the-Art Solution Worldwide*, ed. Lynn Walter (Santa Barbara, CA: Praeger, 2009), 227–42.

25. Peter Singer, *Animal Liberation: A New Ethics for our Treatment of Animals* (New York: Random House, 1975).

26. For instance in the U.S., average per capita consumption is around .5 pounds per year, as compared to four pounds per year in the 1950s; see Marion Burros, "Veal to Love, without the Guilt," *New York Times*, April 18, 2007.

27. "European Convention for the Protection of Animals kept for Farming Purposes." [Online]. Available: http://conventions.coe.int/Treaty/en/Treaties/Html/087.htm. [March 30, 2011].

28. Singer and Mason, *The Ethics of What We Eat.*

29. Mara Miele, "The Taste of Happiness: Free-Range Chicken," *Environment and Planning A* 43, no. 9 (2011): 2076–90.

30. For instance on geographical indicators, see Laurence Bérard and Philippe Marchenay, "Local Products and Geographical Indications: Taking Account of Local Knowledge and Biodiversity," *International Social Science Journal* 58, no. 1 (2006): 109–16; see also Moya Kneafsey, et al, *Reconnecting Consumers, Producers and Food: Exploring Alternatives* (Oxford: Berg, 2008).

31. Helen La Trobe, "Farmers' Markets: Consuming Local Rural Produce," *International Journal of Consumer Studies* 25, no. 3 (2001): 181–92; Paul Fieldhouse, "Community Shared Agriculture," *Agriculture and Human Values* 13, no. 3 (1996): 43–47; Sarah Elton, *Locavore: From Farmers' Fields to Rooftop Gardens: How Canadians Are Changing the Way We Eat* (Toronto: HarperCollins Canada, 2010).

32. Barbara Kingsolver, Steven L. Hopp, and Camille Kingsolver, *Animal, Vegetable, Miracle: One Year of Seasonal Eating* (London: Faber, 2007).

33. Dana Frank, *Buy American: The Untold Story of Economic Nationalism* (Boston: Beacon Press, 2000).

34. Matthew Hilton, *Consumerism in Twentieth-Century Britain: The Search for an Historical Movement* (Cambridge: Cambridge University Press, 2003).

35. Exceptions to the lack of nationalism in local eating programs include the long-standing "buy Australian" campaigns and the promotion of local lamb under the banner of nationalism. See Rachel A. Ankeny, "The Moral Economy of Red Meat in Australia," in *Food and Morality: Proceedings of the Oxford Symposium on Food and Cookery 2007*, ed. Susan Friedland (Blackawton, Totnes: Prospect Books, 2008), 20–28. On the 100-mile diet, see Alisa Smith and J. B. MacKinnon, *Plenty: One Man, One Woman, and a Raucous Year of Eating Locally* (New York: Harmony Books, 2007).

36. Carlo Petrini, *Slow Food: The Case for Taste*, trans. William McCuaig (New York: Columbia University Press, 2001); Geoff Andrews, *The Slow Food Story: Politics and Pleasure* (London: Pluto Press, 2008); "Slow Food." [Online]. Available: www.slowfood.com. [March 30, 2011].

37. Wendy Parkins and Geoffrey Craig, *Slow Living* (Oxford: Berg, 2006).

38. Kelly Donati, "The Pleasure of Diversity in Slow Food's Ethics of Taste," *Food, Culture & Society* 8, no. 2 (2005): 227–42; Julie Labelle, "A Recipe for Connectedness: Bridging Production and Consumption with Slow Food," *Food, Culture & Society* 7, no. 2 (2004): 81–96. See also Counihan's discussion of Slow Food in her chapter "Gendering Food" in this volume.

39. Tara Garnett, *Wise Moves: Exploring the Relationship between Food, Transport and* Co_2 (Hoxton, UK: Transport 2000, 2003).

40. For instance, see Gwendolyn Blue, "On the Politics and Possibilities of Locavores: Situating Food Sovereignty in the Turn from Government to Governance," *Politics and Culture*, no. 2 (2009). [Online]. Available: http::/www.politicsandculture.org/2010/10/27/on-the-politics-and-possibilities-of-locavores-situating-food-sovereignty-in-the-turn-from-government-to-governance/. [January 5, 2012].

41. Claire C. Hinrichs, "Embeddedness and Local Food Systems: Notes on Two Types of Direct Agricultural Market," *Journal of Rural Studies* 16, no. 3 (2000): 295–303, 301.

42. Julie Guthman, "Fast Food/Organic Food: Reflexive Tastes and the Making of 'Yuppie Chow,'" *Social & Cultural Geography* 4, no. 1 (2003): 45–58.

43. George Gaskell, et al, "Worlds Apart? The Reception of Genetically Modified Foods in Europe and the U.S.," *Science* 285, no. 5426 (1999): 384–88.

44. Conrad G. Brunk and Harold Coward, eds., *Acceptable Genes?: Religious Traditions and Genetically Modified Foods* (Albany: SUNY Press, 2009).

45. Nuffield Council on Bioethics, "Genetically Modified Crops: The Ethical and Social Issues" (London: Nuffield Council on Bioethics, 2001). [Online]. Available: http://www.nuffieldbioethics.org/gm-crops. [March 30, 2011].

46. For both sides of the Golden Rice debate, see Michael Ruse and David Castle, eds., *Genetically Modified Foods: Debating Biotechnology* (Amherst, NY: Prometheus Books, 2002), 29–64.

47. Jennifer Clapp, "The Political Economy of Food Aid in an Era of Agricultural Biotechnology," in *Food and Culture: A Reader*, ed. Carole Counihan and Penny Van Esterik (New York: Routledge, 2008), 539–53.

48. Paul B. Thompson, "Food Biotechnology's Challenge to Cultural Integrity and Individual Consent," *Hastings Center Report* 27, no. 4 (1997): 34–38.

49. Caitlin Zaino, "Sticky Sticker Situation: Food Miles, Carbon Labelling and Development," *International Centre for Trade and Sustainable Development*, no. 2 (2008). [Online]. Available: http://ictsd.org/i/news/bioresreview/12095/. [March 30, 2011].

50. Caroline Saunders, Andrew Barber, and Greg Taylor, *Food Miles: Comparative Energy/Emissions Performance of New Zealand's Agricultural Industry*, Research Report 285 (Lincoln, NZ: Agribusiness & Economics Research Institute, Lincoln University, 2006). [Online]. Available: http://www.lincoln.ac.nz/Documents/2328_RR285_s13389.pdf. [March 30, 2011].

51. Jo Littler, *Radical Consumption: Shopping for Change in Contemporary Culture* (Buckingham: Open University Press, 2009); idem, "Good Housekeeping: Green Products and Consumer Activism," in *Community Activism*, ed. Sarah Banet-Weiser and Roopali Mukherjee (New York: New York University Press, 2009).

52. Andrea Prothero, Pierre McDonagh, and Susan Dobscha, "Is Green the New Black? Reflections on a Green Commodity Discourse," *Journal of Macromarketing* 30, no. 2 (2010): 147–59.

53. Monroe Friedman, "American Consumer Boycotts in Response to Rising Food Prices: Housewives: Protests at the Grassroots Level," *Journal of Consumer Policy* 18, no. 1 (1995): 55–72.

54. Claire Midgley, "Slave Sugar Boycotts, Female Activism, and the Domestic Base of British Anti-Slavery Culture," *Slavery & Abolition* 17, no. 3 (1996): 137–62.

55. Andrew Chetley, *The Politics of Baby Foods: Successful Challenges to an International Marketing Strategy* (New York: St. Martin's Press, 1986); Penny Van Esterik, "The Politics of Breastfeeding: An Advocacy Update," in Counihan and Van Esterik, *Food and Culture*, 467–81; Naomi Klein, *No Logo: Taking Aim at the Brand Bullies* (New York: Picador, 2000), 336.

56. Noel W. Solomons, "Plant Sources of Vitamin A and Human Nutrition: Red Palm Oil Does the Job," *Nutrition Reviews* 56, no. 10 (1998): 309–11.

57. Samantha King, *Pink Ribbons, Inc: Breast Cancer and the Politics of Philanthropy* (Minneapolis: University of Minnesota Press, 2008).

58. Lewis and Potter, "Introducing Ethical Consumption," 3.

59. Carol Off, *Bitter Chocolate: The Dark Side of the World's Most Seductive Sweet* (New York: New Press, 2006); Sidney Mintz, *Sweetness and Power: The Place of Sugar in Modern History* (New York: Viking, 1985).

60. Alex Nicolls and Charlotte Opal, *Fair Trade: Market-Driven Ethical Consumption* (London: Sage, 2005); Laura T. Raynolds, Douglas Murray, and John Wilkinson, eds., *Fair Trade: The Challenges of Transforming Globalization* (New York: Routledge, 2007).

61. Marie-Christine Renard, "Fair Trade: Quality, Market and Conventions," *Journal of Rural Studies* 19, no. 1 (2003): 87–96.

62. Michael K. Goodman, "Reading Fair Trade: Political Ecological Imaginary and the Moral Economy of Fair Trade Foods," *Political Geography* 23, no. 7 (2004): 891–915.

63. Gay Hawkins, *The Ethics of Waste* (Lanham, MD: Rowman & Littlefield, 2006).

64. Neil Levy, "Downshifting and Meaning in Life," *Ratio* 18, no. 2 (2005): 176–89.

65. Dylan Clark, "The Raw and the Rotten: Punk Cuisine," in Counihan and Van Esterik, *Food and Culture*, 411–22.

66. "Freegan.info." [Online]. Available: http://freegan.info/. [March 30, 2011].

67. For a brief history and a discussion of the legality of freeganism, see Sean Thomas, "Do Freegans Commit Theft?" *Legal Studies* 30, no. 1 (2010): 98–125. For an empirical study, see Emma Rush, "Skip Dipping in Australia," Australia Institute webpaper. [Online] February 2006. Available: https://www.tai.org.au/documents/downloads/WP85.pdf. [March 30, 2011].

68. For example, Zygmunt Bauman, *Does Ethics Have a Chance in a World of Consumers?* (Cambridge, MA: Harvard University Press, 2008).

69. Georges Monbiot, "Environmental Feedback: A Reply to Clive Hamilton," *New Left Review* 45 (May-June 2007): 105–13; Klein, *No Logo*.

70. Clarke et al., "Globalising the Consumer," 231–49; Littler, "What's Wrong with Ethical Consumption?"

71. Julie Guthman, "Neoliberalism and the Making of Food Politics in California," *Geoforum* 39, no. 3 (2008): 1171–83; Elspeth Probyn, "Feeding the World: Towards a Messy Ethics of Eating," in Lewis and Potter, *Ethical Consumption*, 103–13.

72. Deborah Barndt, "Whose 'Choice'? 'Flexible' Women Workers in the Tomato Food Chain," in *Food and Culture*, 452–66; Josée Johnston and Shyon Baumann, *Foodies: Democracy and Distinction in the Gourmet Foodscape* (New York: Routledge, 2010).

73. For instance, the emergence of the cooperative supermarket movement in the United Kingdom, see Littler, "What's Wrong with Ethical Consumption?"; see also Frank, *Buy American*; Michele Micheletti, *Political Virtue and Shopping: Individuals, Consumerism, and Collective Action* (New York: Palgrave Macmillan, 2003).

74. Sharon Zukin, "Consuming Authenticity: From Outposts of Difference to Means of Exclusion," *Cultural Studies* 22, no. 5 (2008): 724–48.

75. Clive Barnett, et al, "Consuming Ethics: Articulating the Subjects and Spaces of Ethical Consumption," *Antipode* 37 (2005): 23–45; Benjamin Coles and Philip Crang, "Placing Alternative Consumption: Commodity Fetishism in Borough Fine Foods Market, London," in Lewis and Potter, *Ethical Consumption*, 87–102.

76. Littler, "What's Wrong with Ethical Consumption?"

77. Singer and Mason, *The Ethics of What We Eat*, 5.

78. Peter Jackson, Polly Russell, and Neil Ward, "The Appropriation of 'Alternative' Discourses by 'Mainstream' Food Retailers," in *Alternative Food Geographies: Representation and Practice*, ed. Damian Maye, Lewis Holloway, and Moya Kneafsey (Oxford: Elsevier, 2007), 309–30.

79. Lisa M. Heldke, "Food Security: Three Conceptions of Access—Charity, Rights, and Coresponsibility," in Walter, *Society, Culture, and Ethics*, 213–25.

80. Lisa M. Heldke, "Food Politics, Political Food," in *Cooking, Eating, Thinking: Transformative Philosophies of Food*, ed. Deane W. Curtin and Lisa M. Heldke (Bloomington: Indiana University Press, 1992), 302–27.

Bibliography

Coveney, John. *Food, Morals and Meaning: The Pleasure and Anxiety of Eating.* London: Routledge, 2006.
Heldke, Lisa M. *Exotic Appetites: Ruminations of a Food Adventurer.* New York: Routledge, 2003.
Kass, Leon R. *The Hungry Soul: Eating and the Perfecting of Our Nature.* Chicago: University of Chicago Press, 1999.
Kjænes, Unni, Mark Harvey, and Alan Warde. *Trust in Food: A Comparative and Institutional Analysis.* Basingstoke: Palgrave Macmillan, 2007.
Korthals, Michiel. *Before Dinner: Philosophy and Ethics of Food.* Dordrecht: Springer, 2004.
Mepham, Ben, ed. *Food Ethics.* London: Routledge, 1996.
Sapontzis, Steve F., ed. *Food for Thought: The Debate over Eating Meat.* Amherst, NY: Prometheus Books, 2004.
Schurman, Rachel, and William A. Munro. *Fighting for the Future of Food: Activists Versus Agribusiness in the Struggle over Biotechnology.* Minneapolis: University of Minnesota Press, 2010.
Singer, Peter, and Jim Mason. *The Ethics of What We Eat.* Melbourne: Text Publishing, 2006.

CHAPTER 27

FOOD AND SOCIAL MOVEMENTS

WARREN BELASCO

REFORMERS attempt to invent a better future by changing the unjust present. The paradox is that in attempting to move forward they are often constrained by views, values, recipes, patterns, and structures inherited from the past. Three time zones thus contend for the attention of social movements—yesterday, today, and tomorrow. No wonder most mortals prefer to focus on matters of moment, especially when it comes to daily meals, whose origins and consequences are far less immediate than the pleasures of the here-and-now.

In a sense food reformers attempt to complicate an already multifaceted process by which people decide what to eat. Daily food choices are determined largely by an intricate negotiation between considerations of taste and convenience. Both of these determinants are complicated enough. Taste is a product of biological, psychological, and cultural conditioning; once embedded at a very early age taste preferences are difficult to change. Food choices are also shaped by convenience, i.e. the availability of particular ingredients, tools, energy, time, and skills, as well as the ability to afford them. To this interaction between taste and convenience, activists seek to impose a third, highly moralized and politicized factor, a sense of responsibility. Responsibility may be defined as a willingness to pay the full costs of one's meal. Such costs extend beyond the immediate market price of a product to what economists call the "externalities," the wider, often unseen, long-range consequences of consuming it. These consequences may include the effects of production on the people who produce it (farmers, food workers), the acute and chronic health costs to consumers (foodborne illness, diabetes, cancer), and the impact on resources available to future generations (e.g., soil, energy, water).

Included in these remote costs, environmental educator David Orr writes, are "1) things of value that cannot be measured in numbers; 2) things that *could* be measured but that we choose to ignore; and 3) the loss of things that we did not know to be important until they were gone." Romantic rebel Henry Thoreau put it succinctly in *Walden* (1854), an account of his own attempts at radical personal reform: "The cost of a thing is the amount of what I will call life which is required to be exchanged for it, immediately or in the long run."[1] Urging conscientious citizens to consider "the long run" effects of their behavior, Thoreau invoked the ethic of intergenerational equity found in many conservation-minded cultures, ranging from the Iroquois' motto, "In our every deliberation we must consider the impact of our decisions on the next seven generations," to the Amish proverb, "We do not inherit land from our fathers. We borrow land from our children." In sum reformers want us to take a multidimensional look at the food chain. Rather than focusing mainly on what's on our plates at the moment, activists want us to consider how the food got here, who got hurt along the way, and whether that meal might do more harm in the future.

For food activists a morally clean plate does no harm. Beyond that rather negative attribute, a clean plate also signals virtue. If "we are what we eat"—and more telling, if we are what we *don't* eat—then food becomes a medium through which to voice social identities and distinctions. Reformers are no more discriminatory than anyone else. All cultures moralize about food, particularly when distinguishing between group members (clean plate) and outsiders (dirty plate). But not all cultures draw such distinctions armed with the economic, sociological, and political tools of modern food reformers, who generally voice two sets of concerns about the modern industrialized food system. The first centers around the seemingly poor quality of the product itself: massified, mediocre, bland, artificial, alienated, adulterated with additives and toxins. The second involves how it is produced: large-scale corporate farming, processing, and distribution that ruins the environment, exploits farmers, animals, and workers, colonizes distant countries, and favors richer consumers while depriving the poor of their rightful share of the bounty. In short, modern food is perceived as uninteresting, unnatural, dangerous, and inequitable. When viewed through the lens of "we are what we eat," modern food becomes a largely negative reflection of modern life itself. Hence the paradox: reformers want to move us forward but they often tend to rhapsodize the pre-modern past.[2]

Not all modern periods have been beset by such nostalgia. Indeed for much of recent history the cornucopian ethic—more food for less money, maximum production by whatever means necessary—has reigned supreme and unchallenged.[3] Cornucopians believe that the tools of modern science and industry are the best weapons against mankind's historic enemy, hunger. In practical terms this has entailed an emphasis on technological innovation, territorial expansion, and business rationalization, all of which have combined to raise agricultural productivity much faster than population growth and have served to head off the global famine and food wars predicted by British economist Thomas Malthus in his classic

Essay on the Principle of Population (1798).[4] Thanks to industrial food production, the pessimistic Malthus lost at least the first few rounds in his debate with cornucopian philosopher the Marquis de Condorcet, who had argued that through technological ingenuity, "a very small amount of ground will be able to produce a great quantity of supplies of greater utility and higher quality." [5] But Malthus also had a third debating partner, socialist anarchist William Godwin, whose followers argued that mankind would be best fed not so much through the technological fixes advocated by Condorcet as by anthropological fixes such as dietary reform (particularly less resource-intensive meat), less greed, and more social justice. For the Godwinians radical redistribution of income and power would produce a healthier, more equitable food system. Demographer Joel Cohen summarizes this three way debate over the future of food: while Malthus advocated "fewer forks" (population reduction) and Condorcet argued for "bigger pies" (more production), Godwin promoted "better manners" (democratic socialism).[6] Most food reformers have followed Godwin's lead in defining a morally clean plate as one that is more ascetic, egalitarian, and "traditional."

While cornucopians occupy the default, hegemonic position in this three-way debate, there are times when dissenting views have come through more loudly. This chapter will focus on three cycles of American reformist activity—the Jacksonian (1830s-40s), Progressive (1890–1920), and Countercultural (1960s–70s) eras. An immediate question for the historian concerns the context for such ferment: what provokes and enables activists to take up food reform as a medium for wider social change? There are five preconditions for the sort of preemptive, pro-active responsible eating we are looking at here.

First, the food supply system has to be large enough that producers and consumers are somewhat unknown to each other. Such "distancing" may be the result of imperial conquest, territorial expansion, urbanization, capitalist development, technological evolution, or all of the above. The food supply chain has been lengthening for a long time, as seen in a 1701 report on the British East India Company, one of the first modern multinational food conglomerates. As a result of this company's entrepreneurial and paramilitary efforts in distant lands, affluent British consumers did not need to give much thought to how their tea was sweetened or how their wine grapes were harvested:

> we taste the Spices of Arabia,yet never feel the scorching Sun which brings themforth; we shine in Silks which our Hands have neverwrought; we drink of Vinyards which we neverplanted; the Treasures of those Mines are ours, inwhich we have never digg'd; we only plough the Deep,and reap the Harvest of every Country in the World.[7]

There are times when such remoteness can seem miraculous and beneficial, for as cornucopians maintain, being able to access the world's bounty is a privilege, and even more so if it can be done without effort on the part of consumers.[8] When it comes to much-prized meat in particular, it can be very convenient to be oblivious to how living creatures are converted into chops and steaks. Historian

William Cronon argues that the meat-packing industry encourages and indeed thrives upon "forgetfulness."[9] The ideal modern consumer, according to farmer-poet Wendell Berry, is the "industrial eater...who does not know that eating is an agricultural act, who no longer knows or imagines the connections between eating and the land, and who is therefore necessarily passive and uncritical."[10] As Ann Vileisis recounts in *Kitchen Literacy* (2007), it took the combined efforts of marketers, scientists, educators, and consumers themselves over two centuries to cultivate and perfect such ignorance.[11]

But there are times when the separation of consumers from producers can seem alienating enough to provoke a moral panic. In each of these three periods the food industry had recently expanded in reach and structure, leading to concerns about greedy, irresponsible marketers taking advantage of their newfound size and anonymity to exploit consumers and workers. In the Jacksonian era, these worries were instigated by the rise of complex urban food markets and commercial services, especially restaurants and bakeries. Steamboats and canals enabled Eastern bakers to purchase wheat from unseen Midwestern suppliers rather than from local millers who had to be more accountable for what they put in the flour. Following the dictates of "we are what we eat" such arrangements symbolized wider social and economic ills. "Commercially baked bread was only a metaphor of the Jacksonian marketplace itself," Stephen Nissenbaum writes, "a place of fevered chaos, laden with products manufactured by invisible men and corrupted with invisible poisons. Anonymity encouraged conspiracy."[12] In the Progressive period transcontinental railroads produced large corporate "trusts," particularly the meat conglomerates made notorious by Upton Sinclair's *The Jungle* (1906).[13] In the 1960s the most striking distancing came through the rise of giant suburban supermarkets and fast food chains; indeed suburbanization itself replaced farms and further separated "eating and the land." The most telling metaphor was "plastic," which was used to describe not just the food, but an empty, alienating suburban middle class culture.[14]

Second, feeding the paranoia wrought by distancing, a lively intellectual infrastructure of published reports, news, and commentary warns anxious consumers about the unseen consequences of their behavior. Each period had highly competitive news industries—the virulent "penny press" of the Jacksonian era, the "yellow press" of Progressive muckrakers, and the insurgent "underground" press of the 1960s. Sensationalistic investigative journalism exposed deceit and also gave voice to radical views and proposals. Not coincidentally each of these periods experienced a boom in utopian experiments, most of them involving collaborative food production that shortened the distance between field and fork. While very few of these communities survived, they did produce a highly influential body of news stories, memoirs, novels, and cookbooks that recruited more interest and encouraged imitators. The 1840s were particularly famous for its Grahamite boardinghouses and Fourieristic Brook Farm and Oneida, the late nineteenth century for its popular utopian novels featuring communal gardens and cooperative housekeeping, and the 1970s for its organic farms, cooperative stores, and natural foods restaurants. The most recent round of countercultural social experimentation also yielded a bumper crop of publicity-savvy celebrity chefs whose mission has been to relocalize food production and thus restore a sense of intimacy and responsibility to the food chain.[15]

Third, paradoxically, while nostalgic activists in each period idealized a seemingly lost food system comprised of neo-traditional foods produced by small, local farmers, artisans, and vendors, in voicing their analysis of modern faults, they often displayed a positivistic mindset that quantified nutritional needs and treated the body as a machine capable of scientific adjustment and improvement. For the larger global picture, many reformers carefully estimated future food supplies, population growth, and likely economic development. As anthropologist Solomon Katz has suggested, "secular morality" is guided by statistics, not theology.[16] And to scare people into action, these statistics usually suggest some rather alarming trends, especially increasing rates of food-related illness and declining food supplies in the face of rising demand. As masters of the worrisome trendline, the Malthusians often play an instigating role here, as their dire predictions fan public anxieties about the future and spark an interest in alternatives that seem more efficient and equitable.[17] In his two-volume magnum opus, *Lectures on the Science of Human Life* (1839), Jacksonian food reformer Sylvester Graham frequently employed "the aids of chemistry and physiology" to detail the ill effects of "bolted" white flour, red meat, and raw alcohol on the poorly nourished city dweller's "lazy colon." At the same time Graham touched a Malthusian nerve by arguing that demand for cheap wheat induced greedy farmers to deplete (or "debauch") fragile soil, thus threatening the ability of future generations to feed themselves.[18]

Progressive journalist Upton Sinclair drew on the latest nutritional knowledge of microbes, protein, and calories to undergird his attack on the meat "trust." His attacks coincided with another round of Malthusian worries about the future of grain and meat supplies. As Donald Worster has shown, these early-twentieth-century "scarcity howlers" encouraged wheat farmers to plow up marginal western drylands.[19] The ensuing ecological disasters of the Dust Bowl far surpassed the agricultural "debauchery" of Graham's period—and led to another round of Malthusian forecasts after World War II. These culminated in the exceptionally gloomy demographic predictions of Paul Ehrlich's *Population Bomb* (1968) and William and Paul Paddock's *Famine—1975!* (1967). In Godwinian response, Frances Moore Lappe's *Diet for a Small Planet* (1971) offered detailed calculations of protein complementarity and feed conversion ratios to make her case that meat consumption was both nutritionally inefficient, socially inequitable, and ecologically catastrophic. More recently environmentally minded food activists have expanded their considerations to include elaborate enumerations of "food miles" and "ecological footprints." Such "carrying capacity" arguments were anticipated early on by Godwin's son-in-law, poet Percy Bysshe Shelley, who in 1813 criticized the meat eater who would "destroy his constitution by devouring an acre at a meal.... The quantity of nutritious vegetable matter, consumed in fattening the carcass of an ox, would afford ten times the sustenance if gathered immediately from the bosom of the earth."[20]

Fourth, to add visceral credibility to activist calculations, basic foods must be threatened in some way, either in quality or quantity. In the West this has traditionally meant concerns about beef and wheat. Such worries often affect stomachs directly in the form of rising food prices, as well as well-publicized cases of contamination. It is no coincidence that Sylvester Graham anchored his rather wide-sweeping indictment of modern morality in his famous critique of commercial bread, the debased staff of life; conversely whole wheat bread symbolized a more coherent and life-affirming social order. Seeking justice for food workers, Sinclair focused on the meat production that symbolically and sometimes physically ground them to bits; similarly Frances Moore Lappe used meat as the focal point for her wider environmental and ecological analysis.[21]

Fifth, reinforcing the threats to staple foods, a host of domestic worries make people receptive to disturbing news and forecasts. These concerns may include domestic political scandals, signs of growing economic inequality, environmental disasters, bad weather, and cultural anxieties about immigrants and alien Others. In Graham's time many of these fears coalesced around the waves of cholera that overwhelmed booming cities. In Sinclair's period it was fear of "germs" associated with immigrants (including the Lithuanian sausage makers of the novel).[22] In the 1960s it was a combination of growing racial violence, environmental pollution, and antiwar protest. These crises add a sense of urgency and missionary zeal to activist claims that *something major* must be done to head off future catastrophe. Small palliatives will not suffice. This apocalyptic tone is reflected incendiary titles like *The Jungle*, *Will the World Starve?*, *Deserts on the March*, *Grapes of Wrath*, *The Population Bomb*, *Mankind at the Crossroads*, *Farmageddon*, *The End of Food*, and "Harvest of Shame," and the frequent use of sensationalistic words like "debauchery," "poison," "peril," "plague," "survival," and indeed, "the future."[23]

Many of these variables first came together in Malthus's own time. For the British middle class, the 1790s was a period of considerable anxiety about the future—as depicted in James Gillray's 1795 cartoon of a huge "political locust . . . nibbling at the remains of poor old England, left destitute by high taxes, military setbacks, food shortages, and an influx of destitute French clergy."[24] The pattern was repeated during the other cycles discussed here. During such periods of intensified worrying the archetypal stories about how to keep a plate clean tend to get dusted off and reissued. Here are eight of these storylines, though there probably are more of them:

The Boycotter is the precision protester, who carefully avoids just the suspect food of the moment. Boycotts are the smart bombs of the food wars. Although the term did not enter the English language until the 1880s, when Irish tenant farmers refused to harvest crops for Charles Boycott, a detested estate agent for absentee British landlords, the practice itself appeared much earlier, as when American revolutionaries shunned British tea, or when abolitionists of the 1790s and 1830s avoided sugar produced by slaves. During the 1830s reformer Sylvester Graham became infamous for his condemnation of white bread, red meat, and alcohol as dietary contaminants that threatened consumers' stomachs, farm lands, and public morality. During the Progressive era some reformers boycotted meat to protest rising prices and, for readers of Upton Sinclair's 1906 expose, *The Jungle*, monopolistic greed and worker exploitation. In the 1960s and 70s civil rights activists targeted segregated or discriminatory public facilities, including restaurants, while grape and lettuce boycotts supported farm worker unionization efforts, and some antiwar protesters viewed red meat as a symbol of patriarchal militarism.[25]

The Accountant or Frugal Parent adopts the language of bookkeeping to convey concern about irresponsible behavior. In line with Thoreau's edict, the Accountant tries to calculate and then pay the "true cost" of the food, including all the externalities. Resisting modern profligacy, the Frugal Parent values sobriety, always settles the bill, dreads being taken for a deadbeat, doesn't want to saddle the kids with debt, and saves for the future. Seeking to balance the books of intergenerational equity, he agrees with environmentalist David Brower that "We're hooked. We're addicted. We're committing grand larceny against our children. Ours is a chain-letter economy, in which we pick up early handsome dividends and our children find their mailboxes empty."[26] The ideal of sustainability—another financial metaphor—underlay geneticist Edward East's 1924 definition of wise stewardship of the land: "The only way to treat the soil is like a bank account; husband it carefully by proper farming and make a deposit once in awhile." Similarly in a 1994 assessment of "Earth's Bottom Line," environmentalist Sandra Postel suggested, "Globally, the ecological books must balance." The rhetoric of accounting leads to a push for banking-style reforms: more "arms length" scrutiny and regulation, more transparency, more prudent investments. At the same time the sober accountant is less enamored of cornucopian technological fixes, which they might dismiss as "wondrous toys," "childish wish-fulfillment fantasies," and "vain and extravagant dreams of fancy."[27] The more "mature" accountant is perhaps the least romantic of activists, a denizen of the white collar world of desks, files, and bureaus. Think Progressive era USDA chemist Harvey Wiley or liberal consumer crusader Ralph Nader. But given the food industry's vehement opposition to even the mildest of accountancy reforms—e.g., soil conservation, public lists of additives, readable food labels, verifiable health claims—an honest broker can make big waves, although these may not add up to the tsunami desired by some revolutionaries.[28]

The Survivalist, dissatisfied with the piecemeal protests of the Boycotter and the wonkish tinkering of the Accountant, the Survivalist shuns not just particular products but all of modern civilization. Hunkering down for Armageddon is a favorite ploy of dystopian fiction, as well as of refugees from more mainstream movements. The Survivalist has roots in apocalyptic literature, starting perhaps with Godwin's daughter Mary Shelley, whose alienated heroes in *Frankenstein* (1818) and *The Last Man* (1826) fled to the wilderness, where they could live in vegetarian peace. In this decision to start over from scratch we also see roots in the Noah story.[29] Recapitulating human evolution the Survivalist learns to hunt, gather, roast, and sow by hand. In 1845 Thoreau retreated in exhaustion from abolitionist agitation to the pastoral peace of Walden Pond. The boom in outdoor camping and hiking during the Progressive period was, in a sense, another form of Survivalist regeneration. And so too in the late 1960s did some hippies flee to the wilds of Mendocino, Vermont, and Appalachia in a desperate attempt to reset their countercultural "revolution." Suitably much of the dietary advice during that apocalyptic period was phrased in terms of "survival," as when *The Last Whole Earth Catalog* recommended *Passport to Survival*, a hip natural foods cookbook: "Emergency procedures and forethoughts stored here will serve you come holocaust, catastrophe, or unemployment." Similarly a 1968 underground news column, "What to Do Until the World Ends," advised, "Learn to eat weeds... [which when] properly prepared are gourmet delights that can keep you alive when other food sources fail."[30]

Once relocated, the Survivalist splits into two variants, the Yeoman Farmer and the Utopian Communist. The Yeoman Farmer is a somewhat more evolved version of the Last Man, as he has shifted from scavenging to more settled subsistence agriculture. A staple of Jeffersonian agrarianism, the grow-your-own ethic was already somewhat outdated when voiced by Jefferson, who was well-integrated into world markets. His paeans to rural self-reliance notwithstanding, Jefferson bought produce from his own slaves while exporting his own grain surpluses and almost bankrupted his family with his lavish imports of European wines and delicacies.[31] By the Jacksonian period the image was even more archaic. Sylvester Graham, scion of a dysfunctional middle-class family, lamented the disappearance the sturdy colonial mother who baked her own bread—a nostalgic notion at a time when many people patronized commercial bakeries.[32] The Progressive Era also produced a back-to-the-land movement that appealed particularly to alienated urban intellectuals Helen and Scott Nearing, who retreated to Maine from radical politics in the 1920s and whose account of their experiment in vegetarian self-sufficiency, *Living the Good Life* (1954) became what Newsweek called "an underground bible for the city-weary" counterculture of the late 1960s.[33] In turn some of those aging hippies stayed on the land long enough to profit from a renewed demand for organic produce and meat in the early 2000s—most famously the evangelical-libertarian peasant, Joel Salatin, lionized in Michael Pollan's *The Omnivore's Dilemma* (2006).[34]

The Utopian Communist is the collective version of the Yeoman Farmer. Groups of like-minded refugees from the modern world attempt to build an alternative community that will survive the coming storm and perhaps serve as a seedbed for new growth once the weather clears. As observed earlier, each of these periods experienced an exceptionally high rate of utopian community formation, as well as the literary reporting that spread their news and popularized their diets. The model had clear precedent in the Puritan "errand into the wilderness" to establish an exemplary "City on a Hill" that would attract "the eyes of all people."[35] Upton Sinclair used the profits from *The Jungle* to fund a rural utopian commune centered around an ascetic, vegetarian diet.[36] Some feminist utopias also drew on the more prosaic model of self-sacrifice found in many poor households, where women routinely denied themselves a full portion of meat, bread, or dessert for the sake of husbands and children. For example, the women of Charlotte Perkins Gilman's novel *Herland* (1915) constructed their ecologically benign vegetarian community around what they called the "instinct" of "Mother Love"—"that limitless felling of sisterhood, that wide unity in service," a deeply seated sense of altruism that drove them to put social needs above personal interest.[37] Seeking liberation from the kitchen, some feminist utopias did welcome the mealpills, nutritive ethers, instant dinners, synthetic chops, and other labor-saving concoctions of modern food engineering. In Mary E. Bradley Lane's astounding *Mizora* (1880) women ate "chemically prepared meat" that was sterile, perfectly "balanced," and easy to cook; housewives never cooked elaborate meals for husbands because men did not even exist.[38] But most utopias were of the neotraditional, whole grain variety. Although men might sometimes be seen baking bread in the kitchen, far too many communes followed the pattern of Fruitlands (1843), where Bronson Alcott's wife and daughters did most of the cooking and gardening while men "tended to spend more time cultivating their conversations than their crops."[39] Such gender disparities were a primary reason for the dissolution of many communal experiments.

Others fell prey to founder syndrome. While these utopias were communal in intent, many utopias were inspired or managed by a single person possessing unusual spiritual magnetism. All too often these leaders outlasted or outshone their communities to serve as Yogis—another reformer archetype with great dietary influence. Hard, righteously thin, the Yogi is above or at least beyond food. The yogi eats just to live, or eats with such responsibility, reverence, and deliberation that food is conserved and cherished. The Yogi is the consummate mindful eater, immune to distancing, gluttony, greed, or waste. Bronson Alcott's utopia, Fruitlands, was strictly vegan, and although the community failed, Alcott's vegetarian Transcendentalism influenced generations of intellectuals and radicals. Numerous progressive activists also followed the ascetic self-discipline preached by Sylvester Graham's charismatic disciples, John Harvey Kellogg and Horace Fletcher. Their work was in turn popularized by Upton Sinclair in the aptly named *Fasting Cure* (1911), written soon after the failure of Sinclair's cooperative colony, Helicon Hall.[40] In the 1960s young radicals found inner peace and fortitude in the "macrobiotic" diet advocated by Japanese philosophers George Ohsawa and Michio Kushi. (From the Transcendentalists forward, American radicals have cherished Asian ideological and dietary imports.) From the countercuisine also came the Slow Food movement, which was dedicated to reenchanting food through unrelenting opposition to anything mass, fast, easy, or mindless. In 1971 Steven Gaskin, leader of one of the more successful hippy communes, The Farm, voiced this meditative philosophy in a short poem, "How to Slow Down:" "Find a little bit of land somewhere and plant a carrot seed. Now sit and watch it grow. When it is fully grown pull it up and eat it."[41] Not coincidentally Gaskin's partner, Ina May Gaskin, applied similar yogic principles in her popular guide to home childbirth, *Spiritual Midwifery* (1977).[42]

Ironically, such mindfulness could also lead reformers toward the more overtly hedonistic strategies of the Pleasure Artist. For every abstemious Sylvester Graham or Upton Sinclair there is a gregarious William Godwin, "prince of spongers," or sensual M. F. K. Fisher, the "poet of the appetites."[43] For this city cousin of the Yogi, eating and drinking well is the best revenge—an act of personal defiance against both obscene courtly excesses as well as against modern tastelessness, particularly the variety embodied in American mass culture. The Pleasure Artist thus stretches the word "survival" from the Yogi's spare "eating to live" to a more self-indulgent "living to eat," albeit not too much, and within budgetary limits. Rebecca Spang has suggested that the French restaurant itself was "invented" as a late-eighteenth-century revolutionary response to aristocratic decadence, a simple, democratic place where people could sample honest, healthy fare, starting with "restorative" bouillons.[44] A product of that democratizing ethos, French writer Jean Anthelme Brillat-Savarin argued for "gastronomy" as a science of balance, discipline, and humanistic pleasure—a formula avidly sought by Thomas Jefferson's well-known attempts to serve haute cuisine in a relatively informal, unpretentious setting worthy of "republican simplicity."[45]

In the bohemian versions first articulated by nineteenth-century romantic poets, Pre-Raphaelites, and gourmands, the preservation of refined taste would wean or at least protect people from the rapidly growing, dishonest factory food system and hopefully return the food system to a sturdier craft ("artisanal") basis. In William Morris's influential *News from Nowhere* (1890), post-apocalyptic socialists enjoyed vibrant peasant foods (including the requisite whole-grained farmhouse loaf) and robust sex in a picturesque neo-medieval setting.[46] The quest for culinary authenticity and populist diversity led urban progressives to the cheap "foreign" restaurants of immigrant slums, particularly the "spaghetti joints" of Little Italy and the "chop suey houses" of Chinatown.[47] The countercuisine combined this affinity for "ethnic" fare with an interest in reviving the "regional." With taste threatened by corporate fast food, traditional European "country cuisine" attracted new interest among hip gourmets. Alice Waters first cooked Elizabeth David's "peasant" recipes for Berkeley hippies and antiwar activists.[48] Espousing a "delicious revolution," Waters would have felt quite at home in the bohemian salons of the early nineteenth century, as would *New York Times* food critic and *Gourmet* editor Ruth Reichl, who launched her gastronomic career in the leftist student ghettoes of Ann Arbor and Berkeley. Similarly, Italian communists like Carlo Petrini translated political resistance into the Slow Food movement, which was dedicated to "taste education" and the preservation of local delicacies.[49] Common to all pleasure artistry was a belief that the better the food, the less one needed to eat. Conversely (and counter-intuitively), "industrial eaters" stuffed themselves precisely they did not appreciate or understand *real* food. Whether at a bouillon-serving restaurant of the early nineteenth century or a nouvelle cuisine bistro of the late twentieth, small but tasty portions seemed to lessen any contradiction between bohemian hedonism and egalitarian, ascetic ideals. And the bottom line was that, like the Yogi, the Pleasure Artist was virtuously lean.

While much of this culinary radicalism was associated with socialist pacifism, it is also important to note yet one more reformer archetype, the Patriot. Generally reserved for wartime, this figure advocates domestic sacrifice for the sake of the troops fighting to protect the homeland, and sometimes also for the sake of victimized civilian allies. Patriots cite wartime scarcity as a rationale for conservation and home production, as well as for research into high-tech military rations that definitely fit the "eat to live" ethic. As Harvey Levenstein and Amy Bentley have shown, both world wars offered opportunities for advocates of ascetic efficiency.[50] "Leave a clean plate," a 1917 New York State Health Department poster urged. "Take only such food as you will eat. Thousands are starving in Europe." On the more positive side, another poster advised Patriots to "Eat more corn, oats, and rye products.... Eat less wheat, meat, sugar and fat to save for the army and our allies."[51] Appeals to conserve and toughen up did work for the duration, but ardor tended to wear out soon after the armistice. First conceived to feed starving Belgians and Armenians during World War I, the "Gospel of the Clean Plate" was somewhat less compelling in the affluent, high-fat 1950s, although remnants lingered whenever news of Asian or African famines filtered into middle-class dining rooms.

In the 1960s and 1970s some hip food reformers revived martial rhetoric on behalf of the revolutionary battle for rights, peace, and justice. "Don't eat white; eat right, and fight!" one underground newspaper food column admonished. [52] Such appeals echoed Upton Sinclair's earlier advocacy of plain food, temperance, and Fletcherism ("the noble science of clean eating") as the best way to shape up for the long socialist "struggle."[53] More recently some local food advocates have taken a national security theme associated with post 9–11 nationalism. For example an ad titled "Homeland Security" depicted a tomato-laden roadside farm stand, with the stark caption, "Buy Local. It Matters." Even more reminiscent of wartime propaganda was a shot of James Montgomery Flagg's original Uncle Sam (1916) pointing straight at the viewer, only this time the caption read "Buy Local," instead of "I Want You." Completing the circle of subliminal wartime allusions were new Clean and Cleaner Plate Clubs dedicated to promoting sustainable, non-industrial meals. [54]

As for the effectiveness of these various activist strategies, the historical record is mixed. Boycotts may be the most successful, but they are sporadic and temporary. Sometimes they are not precise enough, targeting all foods within a particular category, even the virtuously produced ones (Alar, spinach, grapes), and sometimes they are too precise, making invidious distinctions, say, between sugar produced by slaves (bad) and sugar produced by peons (OK), or livers from force-fed geese (bad) and livers from force-fed chickens (OK).[55] Over the long run it is hard to keep track of what is on and what is off the list. Many aging baby boomers still boycott California iceberg lettuce and table grapes in solidarity with field workers, yet those campaigns officially ended years ago. In January 2010 the Ethical Consumer website listed over fifty "progressive" boycotts, most of them food or animal-related.[56] That neither grapes nor lettuce appeared on the lists indicated some successful unionization by the United Farm Workers, although farm workers remained the most exploited segment of the food chain.

The persistence of such injustice and inequality also points to the weaknesses of the Accountant strategy, which pursues incremental, procedural adjustments. All too often regulatory reform winds up favoring the largest enterprises that can best afford the most skillful accountants, lawyers, and advertising copywriters. In the Progressive Era, for example, the consumerist demand for more trust in the marketplace most benefited the national brands that could be marketed as most reliable and "fresh." Upton Sinclair's campaign for accountability and food safety thus accelerated centralization of the food system, which was the very opposite of his intent.[57] Likewise in the 1990s stricter rules for seafood safety favored large scale foreign producers, while federal regulation also fostered consolidation in the organic foods industry.[58]

Consumer capitalism has a remarkable ability to absorb the insurgent innovations of the underground. Bohemians in particular have long served as independent listening posts for larger corporations, who hunger for fresh ideas from the freaky frontiers.[59] General Mills shrewdly converted countercultural granola and yogurt into Nature Valley granola and yogurt bars.[60] Similarly bohemian restaurants spearhead the gentrification of marginal urban areas; once an underground cafe/gallery appears, the conversion of abandoned factories into million-dollar "lofts" is not far behind. For land speculators, "avant garde" foreshadows "real estate boom." This was true long before the first hip coop or commune. Progressive patrons of cheap "spaghetti joints" in the 1890s turned shabby immigrant ghettos into a fashionable liberal districts by the 1920s. Or witness how the wildly profitable Battle Creek, Michigan, breakfast cereal industry mushroomed from the early reformist experiments of the Kellogg brothers. One also wonders how many of the Graham boardinghouses that sprang up in the 1830s to follow his dietary principles now live on as "bed and breakfasts" in refurbished "Victorian" neighborhoods.

Even when not coopted or commercialized, many clean plate strategies face another major difficulty: changing times. As crises end or shift, a sense of urgency abates. Wars eventually end, and so do their moral equivalents. Or the United States invades Iraq, and food riots in Africa are no longer news. The USDA tinkers with some regulations and grain stocks increase. Food prices stabilize, even drop. Malthus would certainly have been shocked that food supplies have outpaced population growth over the past 200 years. Conditions change, wild cards are drawn, we are constantly being surprised. Life changes, too; people get blown off course by what Czech novelist Milan Kundera calls "the unbearable lightness of being." They get tired of being scared, compassionate, or of working too hard, especially for food, whose demands can be so unrelenting and mind-numbing. Subsistence gets boring. Cooks get cooked out. The Survivalist decides to go to back to law school in Chicago. The Yeoman Farmer realizes that life is short and decides to trade the dairy farm for a condo in West Palm Beach. Or conscientious consumers decide that rather than paying the "true cost" of their food at the farmers market, they would rather save for their kids' education by shopping for bargains at Wal-Mart. The founder of the utopian commune sleeps with one too many comrades and the whole thing falls apart. The Yogi opens a high-end fusion bistro in Tribeca. The food business is full of such stories.

Looking beyond these inherent foibles and contradictions of cultural radicalism, we need to recognize that there are very powerful beliefs and institutions that stand in the way of responsible eating, or that make it much more complicated. Modern consumer culture prizes abundance and freedom of choice, particularly the freedom to select foods that are both tasty and convenient. The "we are what we eat" slogan can be used both to attack modern foodways and to defend them. As a Far Side cartoon quipped, "If we are what we eat, then I'm fast, cheap, and easy," which another humorist turned into "If we are what we eat, then I'm pretty damn sweet." Modern culture also prizes statistics and creates huge bureaucracies to calculate and promote hegemonic versions of them. Numbers are a double-edged sword—they can raise fears and they can allay them. In the United States this hegemonic infrastructure has been long centered in the U.S. Department of Agriculture and its affiliated land-grant universities.[61] It is no coincidence that the USDA is the only government department actually located on the Washington Mall, closest to its dead center, the neo-classical Washington Monument, or that its main building, like so many agriculture schools, was designed to resemble an ancient temple. From these holy sites home economists, agronomists, and technocrats preach the gospel of efficiency in which a Clean Plate means a well-balanced set of enumerated nutrients grown in the Clean Fields of industrial monoculture. And if arithmetic does not calm things down, there is always mockery. Those who question these dominant assumptions are reined in by a cultural apparatus of ridicule that casts conscientious consumers as elitists, eccentrics, cultists, Cassandras, effete Francophiles, and Food Police. The *Reductio ad hitlerium* is a particular favorite of those who attack the "food nuts." It is amazing how many elements of the radical critique—whether its Malthusian underpinnings, its public health orientation, or its vegetarian, back-to-nature biases—get tied back to Nazism, particularly the "Hitler was a vegetarian" cliché.[62]

Given the uncertain track record of conscientious consumption, it is appropriate to ask whether the Gospel of the Clean Plate yields substantial political change. Should we try to eat responsibly? No doubt, for once we see the consequences of our actions it is hard to put the blinders back on. But is it the right *strategy*? Will personal transformations yield broader political change? It is easy to deceive ourselves into thinking that voluntary action is sufficient. And yet, despite an extraordinary amount of personal consumer activity, hunger persists, food workers are exploited, and global warming proceeds apace. Engineering social change takes a lot more than the sum of individual acts of grace.[63]

Politics aside, it is hard enough to change a food system. Paul Rozin has argued that the most effective behavioral changes are those that result in active and enduring disgust for the foods that are considered to be risky, whether meat, sugar, or canned soup.[64] When all is said and done, perhaps the most time-tested of clean plate strategies are those that are rooted in orthodox theology and nativism, which are quite effective in embedding disgust for the impure and alien. But neither of these strategies seems all that compatible with liberal humanism, or the scholar's quest for truth. Historians may have trouble watching or approving the blatant invention of tradition by Slow Food and other locavores. Perhaps it is expedient, as Sylvester Graham did, to create foundational myths about righteous breadbaking colonial mothers, but is it ethical to distort the past that way? The same might be asked of the current tendency of food activists to exaggerate the degree to which Grandma's food was healthier, tastier, and more responsibly produced. As even a cursory look at global food history reveals, the past was no picnic.

And despite the efforts of fundamentalists, whether observant Jews or French *terroirists*, to maintain their tastes and taboos, even these cuisines are under considerable pressure from global consumer capitalism. Tackling the Wal-Marts and Tysons of the world may take a lot more than cleaning your own plate. Indeed it may take sitting down for lunch with people who actually *like* bacon cheeseburgers and fries. This issue came up in the early days of the countercuisine, when food coops debated whether to carry sinful white bread or meat; while some members were in favor of carrying such taboo items as a way to make alliances with the working classes, most chose not to—and either went out of business, or became gourmet food boutiques.[65]

Conversely, keeping a clean plate does not guarantee a clean world. President George Bush ate sustainably produced organic/local/seasonal/fusion meals for years, with no apparent impact on his environmental, foreign, or social policies. Similarly during the 2008 U.S. election, the "red-meat" Republican vice presidential acceptance speech by moose-hunting Sarah Palin was written by Matthew Scully, author of an eloquent plea for ethical vegetarianism, *Dominion: The Power of Man, the Suffering of Animals, and the Call to Mercy* (2002).[66] At almost the same time, protesters who were camped outside Bush's Texas ranch dined not on the righteous vegan fare long associated with antiwar events but on a high-fat feast of meaty lasagna, barbecue, and chicken-casserole.[67] Neither George Bush nor his antagonist Cindy Sheehan easily fit the "we are what we eat" model.

Indeed, using food reform as a medium for a wider social agenda might not be the most effective strategy after all. While putting food at the center of political concerns has the advantage of rendering issues more immediate, there is the danger that matters of diet may hijack the wider agenda. Sylvester Graham became more famous for his advocacy of whole wheat than for his abolitionism. Frustrated that consumers may have missed *The Jungle*'s point about the mistreatment of meatworkers, Sinclair famously lamented that he had "aimed for the public's heart and by accident hit it in the stomach." A similar misdirection may have occurred recently with labor reporter Eric Schlosser's *Fast Food Nation*, whose grisly slaughterhouse scenes may be better remembered than those about the problems of food workers unions. And Frances Moore Lappe, caricatured as "the Julia Child of the soybean circuit" after the surprise success of *Diet for a Small Planet* (1971), eventually left her own foundation, Food First, to make political change more clearly the primary focus; tellingly, the word "diet" did not appear in the name of her new organization, "The Small Planet Institute." In each case, food was a handy way of gaining attraction but also proved to be something of a distraction from the wider concerns of the activists.

It may be time to stop trying to change the world by fixing our diets. "We are what we eat" notwithstanding, these case studies show that systemic change does not flow automatically from eating better food. Dietary reform is a worthy goal in itself, but melding it with morality may make it harder to invent either a better food system or a better world.

Notes

1. David Orr, *Earth in Mind: On Education, Environment, and the Human* Prospect (Washington, DC: Island Press, 1994), 172; Henry David Thoreau, *Walden; or, Life in the Woods* (Boston: Ticknor and Fields, 1854).

2. Josée Johnston and Shyon Baumann, *Foodies: Democracy and Distinction in the Gourmet Foodscape* (New York: Routledge, 2010); Rachel Laudan, "Slow Food, the French *Terroir* Strategy, and Culinary Modernism," *Food, Culture and Society* 7, no. 2 (Fall 2004): 133–44.

3. Rachel Laudan, "A Plea for Culinary Modernism: Why We Should Love New, Fast, Processed Food," *Gastronomica* 1 (February 2001): 36–44.

4. Thomas R. Malthus, *An Essay on the Principle of Population* (London: J. Johnson, 1798).

5. Warren Belasco, *Meals to Come: A History of the Future of Food* (Berkeley: University of California Press, 2006), 6.

6. Joel E. Cohen, *How Many People Can the World Support?* (New York: W.W. Norton, 1995), 370.

7. Henry Martin, *Considerations on the East India Trade* (1701) [Online]. Available: http://ideas.repec.org/b/hay/hetboo/martyn1701.html. [February 22, 2010]. On early modern "distancing": Richard R. Wilk, "Anchovy Sauce and Pickled Tripe: Exporting Civilized Food in the Colonial Atlantic World," in *Food Chains: From Farmyard to Shopping Cart*, ed. Warren Belasco and Roger Horowitz (Philadelphia: University of Pennsylvania Press, 2009): 87–107.

8. Belasco, *Meals to Come*, 3–92.

9. William Cronon, *Nature's Metropolis: Chicago and the Great West* (New York: W.W. Norton, 1991), 256.

10. Wendell Berry, "The Pleasures of Eating," *Journal of Gastronomy* 5, no. 2 (1989): 126.

11. Ann Vileisis, *Kitchen Literacy: How We Lost Knowledge of Where Food Comes from and Why We Need to Get It Back* (Washington, DC: Island Press, 2007).

12. Stephen Nissenbaum, *Sex, Diet, and Debility in Jacksonian America* (New York: Oxford University Press, 1988), 19.

13. Upton Sinclair, *The Jungle* (New York: Doubleday, Page, 1906).

14. Warren Belasco, "Food, Morality and Social Reform," in *Morality and Health*, ed. Allan M. Brandt and Paul Rozin (New York: Routledge, 1997), 185–199; idem, *Appetite for Change: How the Counterculture Took on the Food Industry*, 2nd rev. ed. (Ithaca, NY: Cornell University Press, 2006).

15. Belasco, *Meals to Come*, 95–146; Belasco, *Appetite for Change*.

16. Solomon Katz, "Secular Morality," in Brandt and Rozin, *Morality and Health*, 297–330; Jessica J. Mudry, *Measured Meals: Nutrition in America* (Albany: SUNY Press, 2009).

17. Belasco, *Meals to Come*, 88–92.

18. Nissenbaum, *Sex, Diet and Debility*, 3–68; Sylvester Graham, *Lectures on the Science of Human Life*, 2 vols. (Boston: Marsh, Capen, Lyon, and Webb, 1839).

19. Belasco, "Food, Morality and Social Reform," 190–92; Donald Worster, *Dust Bowl: The Southern Plains in the 1930s* (New York: Oxford University Press, 1979), 80–97.

20. Belasco, *Meals to Come*, 5, 38–60; Mathis Wackernagel and William Rees, *Our Ecological Footprint: Reducing Human Impact on the Earth* (Gabriola Island, BC: New Society Publishers, 1996).

21. Belasco, *Meals to Come*, 3–19.

22. Nancy Tomes, "Moralizing the Microbe: The Germ Theory and the Moral Construction of Behavior in the Late Nineteenth Century Antituberculosis Movement," in Brandt and Rozin, *Morality and Health*, 271–94; Alan M. Kraut, *Silent Travelers: Germs, Genes, and the "Immigrant Menace"* (New York: Basic Books, 1994).

23. Belasco, *Meals to Come*, 61–92.

24. Ibid, 21–22.

25. Belasco, "Food, Morality and Social Reform," 185–99; Nick Fiddes, *Meat: A Natural Symbol* (London: Routledge, 1991).

26. Brower quoted by John McPhee, *Encounters with the Archdruid: Narratives about a Conservationist and Three of His Natural Enemies* (New York: Farrar, Straus, & Giroux, 1971), 82.

27. Belasco, *Meals to Come*, 87–88.

28. Marion Nestle, *Food Politics: How the Food Industry Influences Nutrition and Health* (Berkeley: University of California Press, 2002).

29. Belasco, *Meals to Come*, 120–46.

30. Belasco, *Appetite for Change*, 31.

31. Damon Lee Fowler, ed., *Dining at Monticello: In Good Taste and Abundance* (Chapel Hill: University of North Carolina Press, 2005).

32. Nissenbaum, *Sex, Diet and Debility*, 10.

33. Helen and Scott Nearing, *Living the Good Life* (1954; repr.,New York: Schocken Books, 1970).

34. Michael Pollan, *The Omnivore's Dilemma: A Natural History of Four Meals* (New York: Penguin, 2006), 123–33.

35. Perry Miller, *Errand into the Wilderness* (Cambridge, MA: Harvard University Press, 1956).

36. William Bloodworth, "From *The Jungle* to *The Fasting Cure*: Upton Sinclair on American Food," *Journal of American Culture* 2, no. 3 (Fall 1979): 444–53.

37. Charlotte Perkins Gilman, *Herland* (Auckland: Floating Press, 1915).

38. Belasco, *Meals to Come*, 95–188; Carl J. Guarneri, *The Utopian Alternative: Fourierism in Nineteenth-Century America* (Ithaca, NY: Cornell University Press, 1991); Etta M. Madden and Martha L. Finch, eds., *Eating in Eden: Food and American Utopias* (Lincoln: University of Nebraska Press, 2006); Mary E. Bradley Lane, *Mizora* (1880; repr., New York: G. W. Dillinghamn 1890).

39. Belasco, *Appetite for Change*, 82.

40. Bloodworth, "From *The Jungle* to *The Fasting Cure*," 450; Upton Sinclair, *The Fasting Cure* (New York: Kennerley, 1911).

41. Belasco, *Appetite for Change*, 51.

42. Ina May Gaskin, *Spiritual Midwifery* (Summertown, TN: Book Pub. Co., 1977).

43. On Godwin: Graham Wallas, *Life of Francis Place* (New York: Knopf, 1924), 59–62. On Fisher: Joan Riordan, *Poet of the Appetites: The Lives and Loves of M. F. K. Fisher* (New York: North Point Press, 2004).

44. Rebecca Spang, *The Invention of the Restaurant: Paris and Modern Gastronomic Culture* (Cambridge, MA: Harvard University Press, 2000).

45. Fowler, *Dining at Monticello.*

46. Belasco, *Meals to Come*, 95–188; Timothy Morton, ed., *Cultures of Taste/Theories of Appetite: Eating Romanticism* (New York: Palgrave Macmillan, 2004); William Morris, *News from Nowhere* (Boston: Roberts Brothers, 1890).

47. Donna R. Gabaccia, *We Are What We Eat: Ethnic Food and the Making of Americans* (Cambridge, MA: Harvard University Press, 1998), 93–121; Andrew Coe, *Chop Suey: A Cultural History of Chinese Food in the United States* (New York: Oxford University Press, 2009), 180–210.

48. Belasco, *Appetite for Change*; Kamp, *The United States of Arugula* (New York: Broadway Books, 2006); Johnston and Baumann, *Foodies;* Alice Waters, *The Art of Simple Food: Notes, Lessons, and Recipes from a Delicious Revolution* (New York: Clarkson Potter, 2007).

49. Ruth Reichl, *Tender at the Bone: Growing Up at the Table* (New York: Broadway Books, 1998); Carlo Petrini, *Slow Food: The Case for Taste* (New York: Columbia University Press, 2001).

50. Harvey Levenstein, *Revolution at the Table: The Transformation of the American Diet* (New York: Oxford University Press, 1988), 137–60; Amy Bentley, *Eating for Victory: Food Rationing and the Politics of Domesticity* (Urbana: University of Illinois Press, 1998); Helen Zoe Veit, "'We Were a Soft People'. Asceticism, Self-Discipline, and American Food Conservation in the First World War," *Food, Culture and Society* 10, no. 2 (Summer 2007): 167–90.

51. "Teaching With Documents: Sow the Seeds of Victory! Posters from the Food Administration During World War I" [Online]. Available: http://www.archives.gov/education/lessons/sow-seeds/. [February 26, 2010].

52. Belasco, *Appetite for Change*, 48.

53. Bloodworth, "From *The Jungle* to *The Fasting Cure*," 449; Belasco, "Food, Morality and Social Reform," 191.

54. "What is CASA?" [Online]. Available: http:www.greenearthgrowers.net/Homeland_security.jpg. [February 22, 2010]; "Making this Home" [Online]. Available: http://www.makingthishome.com/2008/11/29/your-guide-to-local-holiday-shopping/. [February 22, 2010]. For the environmentalist case for local foods: Amy B. Trubek, *The Taste of Place: A Cultural Journey into Terroir* (Berkeley: University of California Press, 2008); Brian Halweil, *Eat Here: Reclaiming Homegrown Pleasures in a Global Supermarket* (New York: Norton, 2004).

55. Sidney W. Mintz, *Sweetness and Power: The Place of Sugar in Modern History* (New York: Viking Books, 1985), 151–86; Mark Caro, *Foie Gras Wars: How a 5000-Year-Old Delicacy Inspired the World's Fiercest Food Fight* (New York: Simon and Schuster, 2009).

56. "Ethical Consumer" [Online]. Available: http://www.ethicalconsumer.org/. [February 22, 2010].

57. Susan Strasser, *Satisfaction Guaranteed: The Making of the American Mass Market* (New York: Pantheon, 1989).

58. Kelly Feltault, "Trading Quality, Producing Value: Crabmeat, HACCP, and Global Seafood Trade," in *Food Chains*, 62–83; Samuel Fromartz, *Organic Inc.: Natural Foods and How They Grew* (New York: Harcourt, 2006).

59. Thomas Frank, *The Conquest of Cool: Business Culture, Counterculture, and the Rise of Hip Consumerism* (Chicago: University of Chicago Press, 1998).

60. Belasco, *Appetite for Change*, 185–255.

61. Nestle, *Food Politics*; John H. Perkins, *Geopolitics and the Green Revolution: Wheat, Genes, and the Cold War* (New York: Oxford University Press, 1997); Fred Powledge, *Fat of the Land* (New York: Simon and Schuster, 1984); Jim Hightower, *Eat Your Heart Out: How Food Profiteers Victimize the Consumer* (New York: Vintage, 1975).

62. Belasco, *Appetite for Change*, 111–82; Corinna Treitel, "Nature and the Nazi Diet," *Food and Foodways* 17, no. 3 (2009): 139–58; Barry Glassner, *The Gospel of Food: Everything You Think You Know About Food Is Wrong* (New York: Ecco, 2007).

63. Johnston and Baumann, *Foodies*.

64. Paul Rozin, "Moralization," in Brandt and Rozin, *Morality and Health*, 379–401.

65. Belasco, *Appetite for Change*, 87–94.

66. Matthew Scully, *Dominion: The Power of Man, the Suffering of Animals, and the Call of Mercy* (New York: St. Martin's Press, 2002).

67. Ibid, xi.

Bibliography

Belasco, Warren. "Food, Morality and Social Reform." In *Morality and Health*, edited by Allan M. Brandt and Paul Rozin, 185–99. New York: Routledge, 1997.

Belasco, Warren. *Appetite for Change: How the Counterculture Took on the Food Industry*, 2d. rev. ed. Ithaca, NY: Cornell University Press, 2006.

Belasco, Warren. *Meals to Come: A History of the Future of Food*. Berkeley: University of California Press, 2006.

Coveney, John. *Food, Morals and Meaning: The Pleasure and Anxiety of Eating*. 2nd ed. London: Routledge, 2006.

Frank, Thomas. *The Conquest of Cool: Business Culture, Counterculture, and the Rise of Hip Consumerism*. Chicago: University of Chicago Press, 1998.

Johnston, Josée, and Shyon Baumann. *Foodies: Democracy and Distinction in the Gourmet Foodscape*. New York: Routledge, 2010.

Kamp, David. *The United States of Arugula: How We Became a Gourmet Nation*. New York: Broadway Books, 2006.

Lappe, Frances Moore. *Diet for a Small Planet*. New York: Ballantine, 1971.

Levenstein, Harvey. *Revolution at the Table: The Transformation of the American Diet*. New York: Oxford University Press, 1988.

Lien, Marianne Elisabeth, and Brigitte Nerlich, eds. *The Politics of Food*. Oxford: Berg, 2004.

Nestle, Marion. *Food Politics: How the Food Industry Influences Nutrition and Health*. Berkeley: University of California Press, 2002

Nissenbaum, Stephen. *Sex, Diet, and Debility in Jacksonian America*. New York: Oxford University Press, 1988.

Wharton, James C. *Crusaders for Fitness: The History of American Health Reformers*. Princeton, NJ: Princeton University Press, 1982.

INDEX

CPSIA information can be obtained
at www.ICGtesting.com
Printed in the USA
LVOW09*0846231017
553293LV00005B/14/P

9 780199 729937